The L/L Research Channeling Archives

Transcripts of the Meditation Sessions

Volume 12
March 29, 1991 to May 29, 1993

Don Elkins · Jim McCarty · Carla L. Rueckert

Copyright © 2009 L/L Research

All rights reserved. No part of this book may be reproduced or used in any form or by any means—graphic, electronic or mechanical, including photocopying or information storage and retrieval systems—without written permission from the copyright holder.

ISBN: 978-0-945007-86-9

Published by L/L Research
Box 5195
Louisville, Kentucky 40255-0195

E-mail: contact@llresearch.org
www.llresearch.org

About the cover photo: *This photograph of Jim McCarty and Carla L. Rueckert was taken during an L/L Research channeling session on August 4, 2009, in the living room of their Louisville, Kentucky home. Jim always holds hands with Carla when she channels, following the Ra group's advice on how she can avoid any possibility of astral travel.*

Dedication

These archive volumes are dedicated to Hal and Jo Price, who faithfully and lovingly hosted this group's weekly meditation meetings from 1962 to 1975,

to Walt Rogers, whose work with the research group Man, Consciousness and Understanding of Detroit offered the information needed to begin this ongoing channeling experiment,

and to the Confederation of Angels and Planets in the Service of the Infinite Creator, for sharing their love and wisdom with us so generously through the years.

Table of Contents

Introduction 6
Year 1991 8
    March 29, 1991 9
    March 31, 1991 14
    April 7, 1991 18
    April 12, 1991 24
    April 21, 1991 27
    May 26, 1991 35
    June 2, 1991 41
    June 30, 1991 44
    July 7, 1991 51
    July 12, 1991 57
    July 19, 1991 62
    July 21, 1991 64
    September 22, 1991 70
    September 28, 1991 75
    November 17, 1991 82
Year 1992 86
    March 7, 1992 87
    March 29, 1992 94
    April 5, 1992 98
    April 9, 1992 106
    April 10, 1992 113
    April 12, 1992 119
    April 19, 1992 123
    April 26, 1992 128
    May 3, 1992 133
    May 10, 1992 140
    May 17, 1992 144
    May 24, 1992 150
    May 31, 1992 154
    June 7, 1992 159
    June 14, 1992 164
    July 4, 1992 168
    July 5, 1992 171
    July 12, 1992 178
    July 19, 1992 186
    August 16, 1992 191
    August 30, 1992 196

September 6, 1992 203
September 13, 1992 206
September 20, 1992 211
September 27, 1992 215
September 27, 1992 218
October 3, 1992 222
October 4, 1992 225
October 14, 1992 228
October 29, 1992 234
October 30, 1992 241
November 1, 1992 247
November 8, 1992 250
November 15, 1992 254
November 22, 1992 258
November 29, 1992 263
December 13, 1992 264

Year 1993 .... **269**

January 3, 1993 270
January 10, 1993 274
January 17, 1993 278
January 18, 1993 283
January 18, 1993 290
January 19, 1993 297
February 7, 1993 302
February 14, 1993 306
February 28, 1993 311
March 7, 1993 314
March 14, 1993 317
March 21, 1993 322
March 22, 1993 329
March 22, 1993 336
March 23, 1993 344
March 28, 1993 352
April 25, 1993 355
May 2, 1993 361
May 6, 1993 365
May 8, 1993 373
May 9, 1993 380
May 16, 1993 383
May 23, 1993 391
May 29, 1993 396

Introduction

Welcome to this volume of the *L/L Research Channeling Archives*. This series of publications represents the collection of channeling sessions recorded by L/L Research during the period from the early seventies to the present day. The sessions are also available on the L/L Research website, www.llresearch.org.

Starting in the mid-1950s, Don Elkins, a professor of physics and engineering at Speed Scientific School, had begun researching the paranormal in general and UFOs in particular. Elkins was a pilot as well as a professor and he flew his small plane to meet with many of the UFO contactees of the period.

Hal Price had been a part of a UFO-contactee channeling circle in Detroit called "The Detroit Group." When Price was transferred from Detroit's Ford plant to its Louisville truck plant, mutual friends discovered that Price also was a UFO researcher and put the two men together. Hal introduced Elkins to material called *The Brown Notebook* which contained instructions on how to create a group and receive UFO contactee information. In January of 1962 they decided to put the instructions to use and began holding silent meditation meetings on Sunday nights just across the Ohio River in the southern Indiana home of Hal and his wife, Jo. This was the beginning of what was called the "Louisville Group."

I was an original member of that group, along with a dozen of Elkins' physics students. However, I did not learn to channel until 1974. Before that date, almost none of our weekly channeling sessions were recorded or transcribed. After I began improving as a channel, Elkins decided for the first time to record all the sessions and transcribe them.

During the first eighteen months or so of my studying channeling and producing material, we tended to reuse the tapes as soon as the transcriptions were finished. Since those were typewriter days, we had no record of the work that could be reopened and used again, as we do now with computers. And I used up the original and the carbon copy of my transcriptions putting together a manuscript, *Voices of the Gods*, which has not yet been published. It remains as almost the only record of Don Elkins' and my channeling of that period.

We learned from this experience to retain the original tapes of all of our sessions, and during the remainder of the seventies and through the eighties, our "Louisville Group" was prolific. The "Louisville Group" became "L/L Research" after Elkins and I published a book in 1976, *Secrets of the UFO*, using that publishing name. At first we met almost every night. In later years, we met gradually less often, and the number of sessions recorded by our group in a year accordingly went down. Eventually, the group began taking three months off from channeling during the summer. And after 2000, we began having channeling meditations only twice a month. The volume of sessions dropped to its present output of eighteen or so each year.

These sessions feature channeling from sources which call themselves members of the Confederation of Planets in the Service of the Infinite Creator. At first we enjoyed hearing from many different voices: Hatonn, Laitos, Oxal, L/Leema and Yadda being just a few of them. As I improved my tuning techniques, and became the sole senior channel in L/L Research, the number of contacts dwindled. When I began asking for "the highest and best contact which I can receive of Jesus the Christ's vibration of unconditional love in a conscious and stable manner," the entity offering its thoughts through our group was almost always Q'uo. This remains true as our group continues to channel on an ongoing basis.

The channelings are always about love and unity, enunciating "The Law of One" in one aspect or another. Seekers who are working with spiritual principles often find the material a good resource. We hope that you will as well. As time has gone on the questions have shifted somewhat, but in general the content of the channeling is metaphysical and focused on helping seekers find the love in the moment and the Creator in the love.

At first, I transcribed our channeling sessions. I got busier, as our little group became more widely known, and got hopelessly behind on transcribing. Two early transcribers who took that job off my hands were Kim

Howard and Judy Dunn, both of whom masterfully transcribed literally hundreds of sessions through the eighties and early nineties.

Then Ian Jaffray volunteered to create a web site for these transcriptions, and single-handedly unified the many different formats that the transcripts were in at that time and made them available online. This additional exposure prompted more volunteers to join the ranks of our transcribers, and now there are a dozen or so who help with this. Our thanks go out to all of these kind volunteers, early and late, who have made it possible for our webguy to make these archives available.

Around the turn of the millennium, I decided to commit to editing each session after it had been transcribed. So the later transcripts have fewer errata than the earlier ones, which are quite imperfect in places. One day, perhaps, those earlier sessions will be revisited and corrections will be made to the transcripts. It would be a large task, since there are well over 1500 channeling sessions as of this date, and counting. We apologize for the imperfections in those transcripts, and trust that you can ascertain the sense of them regardless of a mistake here and there.

Blessings, dear reader! Enjoy these "humble thoughts" from the Confederation of Planets. May they prove good companions to your spiritual seeking.

For all of us at L/L Research,

Carla L. Rueckert

Louisville, Kentucky

July 16, 2009

Year 1991

March 29, 1991, to November 17, 1991

L/L Research

L/L Research is a subsidiary of Rock Creek Research & Development Laboratories, Inc.

P.O. Box 5195
Louisville, KY 40255-0195

www.llresearch.org

Rock Creek is a non-profit corporation dedicated to discovering and sharing information which may aid in the spiritual evolution of humankind.

ABOUT THE CONTENTS OF THIS TRANSCRIPT: This telepathic channeling has been taken from transcriptions of the weekly study and meditation meetings of the Rock Creek Research & Development Laboratories and L/L Research. It is offered in the hope that it may be useful to you. As the Confederation entities always make a point of saying, please use your discrimination and judgment in assessing this material. If something rings true to you, fine. If something does not resonate, please leave it behind, for neither we nor those of the Confederation would wish to be a stumbling block for any.

CAVEAT: This transcript is being published by L/L Research in a not yet final form. It has, however, been edited and any obvious errors have been corrected. When it is in a final form, this caveat will be removed.

© 2009 L/L Research

Intensive Meditation
March 29, 1991

Group question: Carla would like some information on the spiritual principles that she should keep in mind as she attempts to determine just how much she should do, or can do, realizing that when she does anything, whether it is writing a letter, or feeding the cats, or making a trip in the truck to a doctor, she will pay a price that will come later. She feels that there is a mental anguish, an emotional anguish that comes both to her and to me, and she would like to know what kinds of considerations are well to keep in mind as she attempts to discover the limits of her ability and just how far to take them.

(K channeling)

I greet each of you here this morning in the love and in the love of the infinite Creator. It is, as always, felt by us to be a great privilege to be able to speak with this group, to experience the joy of your presence with you, to share with you a brief time of your own journeys upon the path, the path that we tread with you, though you may not always be aware of our presence. We are, however, available to you in your awareness at any time you request it.

The one known as Carla is requesting information on a portion of the path that she is traversing that is being experienced as particularly difficult at this time. There are many obstacles on this path, and we see her traveling by light of the moon or utter darkness when the moon is obscured by cloud cover, encountering many sharp objects in which to bruise the shins, over which to stumble and fall and injure the body. Yet, each of you, when this happens, picks yourself up once again after whatever period of recuperation is deemed appropriate by you and continue on the path.

This is stated allegorically. As you are aware, however, much the same thing is occurring to the one known as Carla in the third-density illusion that she now experiences, that is, the experience in the physical body of those obstacles encountered on the path. There is no good or bad in these obstacles that are encountered. They are simply there. They are catalysts, as is all else you experience, and the gain that one receives from encountering with these objects is determined by the attitude with which they are approached and the degree of assimilation that occurs following the experience.

We are aware of the difficulties in traversing the path in darkness and of the strong desire many of you have for the illumination of the sun, so that obstacles may be seen, dealt with appropriately, or avoided altogether. The illumination of the sun on the path occurs, however, only when the veil does not exist. You are aware of the necessity of available work done in the illusion. As a result of this, there is rarely perceived any clear direction along the path. It must be taken one stumbling step at a time and that which is encountered will be encountered and dealt with according to the current state of being of the seeker. It is the continuation on the path that is the important thing. The particular manner with which the various obstacles are dealt is of secondary importance. The learning that is acquired as a result of these encounters is an accumulative process and at the end of your incarnation, as you are aware, the various experiences are distilled into further refining of the biases each has encountered and has been developing through many lifetimes.

Each of you in third-density illusion has a tendency to place great importance on the details of your life experiences. This is natural as these details are what your conscious mind must, of necessity, be concerned with as you function in this illusion. They are the stuff of which this illusion is made. However, and we know that you are aware of this also, they are not important in the grand scheme of things, shall we say, but only what is distilled from your experiences with them. This is difficult to keep in mind when the encounters with obstacles are seeming to be overwhelming and especially when they are of a nature perceived as people, the result of which is to draw the attention strongly to the encounter with whatever obstacle is there. The purpose of pain, as you are also aware, is to focus the attention.

Again, at these times, we know the desire is for the glimpse of the sun, the lightening flash of inspiration of clear direction. These may from time to time occur. We would suggest to the one known as Carla that at these times, she focus her concentration and awareness on the deep self that lies beyond the illusion, that she contact that spirit known as the higher self, or the Holy Spirit, that speaks to her most personally and allow whatever awarenesses lie deeply there to seep out to the outer layers of consciousness. And in this way formulate her plans for encountering of further obstacles along the path.

We appreciate the difficulties inherent in such a course of action, and laud the perseverance of the one known as Carla in the traversing of this difficult path she has laid out for herself.

(Pause)

We feel that these words are sufficient for an answer to this question at this time and would now transfer the contact to the one known as Jim in order to close the session of working and answer any further questions that may yet remain with this group. We leave this instrument at this time. In love and light, we are those of Q'uo.

(Jim channeling)

I am Q'uo, and greet each in love and light once again. We would offer ourselves at this time in the attempt to speak to those queries which you may have remaining for us. If there is any way or means by which we may be of service, we are happy to do so. Is there a query at this time?

Carla: Yes, Q'uo. You may not be able to answer this, but one of the complications that a solution *(inaudible)* is how to evaluate this extremely open-hearted and generous attitude as against the humanness of both myself and *(inaudible)* it is hard for me to distinguish where service, in terms of my feelings *(inaudible)* goes into a less-important and unbalanced state with regard to the amount of the stress that I get from my *(Inaudible)*.

I am Q'uo, and am aware of your query, my sister. The means of communication which you have utilized to a great extent throughout your life experience is the greatest means by which you may obtain the information necessary to make your decisions. This you have done. This you have recorded within your memory and as you have stated in your query, know well what [are] the desires of those about you, most especially the one now serving as instrument, in relationship to you.

Thus, when the activities are undertaken or are planned for, and there is any difficulty ensuing, there must again be the communication that attempts to clear the confusions and to once again set the straight course. It must be accepted by each of you that when you are suffering the physical pain and discomfort that accompanies your overall condition, that there will be the momentary shifting from the balanced harmony that is so often present within this household, as the catalyst is confronted and begins to work its way through the mental processes.

Each of you in this situation is possessed of the most refined of sensitivities that serve you well in the appreciation of your environment and of the creation of the One in general. However, these sensitivities will also be able to allow you to feel more intensively difficulties as well as beauties. That you are human enough to experience the difficulties and feel the anguish, not only of your own pain, [and] the of the pain of the other, is the nature of the human condition that wishes to be informed as to the nature of service to others. It must be realized that each entity within this or any situation is entirely human, though it may hold its sight to the highest of ideals.

The fact that one partakes in a situation in which another has difficulty may be seen by either of you as the responsibility for that difficulty in the other entity. However, each would do well to remember that each is responsible for the use of each entity's catalyst. That is to say, you are responsible for yourself and for your own use of catalyst. If the other entity has difficulty, let that entity be a human being with that capability, that responsibility, and make oneself available in that instance in a manner which is as supportive and understanding as is possible without the feeling of guilt or providing catalyst of responsibility for healing, but having only the opportunity to serve in that moment by support and as much understanding as can be found within oneself.

This, in general, is to say that the purpose of your incarnations is to utilize your catalyst together and to move through it as harmoniously as possible, realizing that individual growth is a personal matter. One can only support another. One cannot solve another's problems. This is true for each of you. It is true for all of your kind upon your planetary sphere. As each works with personal catalyst and clears the way towards feeling the love and the light of the one Creator, and being able then, through feeling it, to radiate it to others, then is your illusion lightened and inspirited with that light of the one Creator, which is available to all, utilized by all in the working through of catalyst, yet blocked in some degree, greater or lesser, by all as catalyst is used, reused and eventually harmonized and balanced to the degree that the light is able to pass further up through the energy centers and find its way toward that center within the heart and that center, more especially, within the throat, where there is the beginning of the radiance of this light to others.

However, the path to that point is one which moves through ground that is, as we spoke through the one known as K, littered with the stones, the sharp places, and the opportunity for stumbling. You, my friends, are here, not only to stumble, but to pick yourselves up and to help pick each other up and then continue on this journey, for there is light, both from within and from without, that may shine its clarifying influence upon this journey. As you seek so it, so shall you find it.

Is there a further query, my sister?

Carla: I have been having difficulty with these decisions *(inaudible)*.

I am Q'uo, and am aware of your query, my sister. We look upon your statement and your overall energy pattern in attempting to speak in a manner which avoids infringement and find that you have found for yourself a central portion of this relationship of yourself to any other which would attempt to aid you and, in this aid, provide you with that service for which you may feel or not feel worthy and able to receive. For as one who wishes to serve others, you have learned well how to consider catalyst in the regards of being of service to others and utilizing your catalyst for that purpose.

The receiving of service for one who wishes to give it so whole-heartedly is that which is the more challenging of the opportunities offered within your illusion. For within your illusion, those entities who have been able to activate and to move through the green-ray energy center then do well if they are able to begin the activation of the blue ray, which offers the true radiance of being from Creator to Creator to those that are before one and for whom one may wish to perform a service. The indigo-ray opportunities are those which are explored by those entities who begin more and more to open themselves to the feeling of the indwelling spirit of the one Creator so that the physical vehicle, the mental vehicle, the spiritual and the emotional component of the intellectual vehicle, then are all seen as channels or vessels which are inhabited and utilized by the one Creator. This is a lesson which is advanced significantly beyond that of third-density experience in general. That you have some difficulty in feeling this infinite value and worth and, therefore, feeling as a result no difficulty in receiving the love offerings of others is, as you have ascertained, that upon which you now work.

We encourage your work in this area and note that it has progressed at a significant pace as you continue to see more of yourself as that which is acceptable. This kind of work we spoke of at length with the one known as Aaron[1], as we spoke upon those

---

[1] Aaron is a discarnate entity channeled by Barbara Brodsky. See www.deepspring.org.

concepts that are formed in the thinking as the basic concept of fear is explored. The fear of rejection from one entity or another according to what is thought or done by yourself is the kind of fear that is developed in the early experiences of the incarnation as one is prepared by these early experiences to continue upon that journey which has been set previous to the incarnation.

You now work with what we may call the cleaning-up phase of the indigo-ray work, which works with those attributes which you find less than desirable within yourself. You work to appreciate their nature, to appreciate yourself for having them working within your being, and as you work with accepting those, what you would call shortcomings, then you begin to accept the final portion of yourself that has heretofore remained outside of the sphere of your love and appreciation. As you are able to fully accept all characteristics within your being, and as you are able to see them as those portions that are appropriate as are all other portions within your character, then you will see yourself in a balanced configuration and will see the hand of the Creator moving within each sphere and characteristic of your life pattern.

Is there another query, my sister?

Carla: I have, not everyday, but quite regularly when I see the difficulty for not just me *(inaudible)* wondered if I should pray that the Lord take away *(inaudible)* and I have even sat down to pray that, then found myself *(inaudible)*. I can't sort it out. Do you have anything *(inaudible)*?

I am Q'uo, and am aware of your query, my sister. Indeed, for the greater portion of your life pattern, that quality which you know as "will," yoked with that quality which you know as "faith," has provided you with the means by which you would be able to continue in the incarnation and with the service that you wish to perform in this carnation. Your strength of will has been that which has moved you through great amounts of difficulty and pain, much like the noble warrior's horse would carry it through many, many battles. This quality of will is that which continues to offer you the strength of your beingness. Through the will, the infinite power of your being moves to enliven your physical vehicle. There is also much work done in this regard between you and the one known as Jim as you engage in the sexual energy transfers.

However, the will is the greatest factor which enables your continued existence within this third-density illusion. As you look about yourself, you see that the world of affecting things recedes and becomes small for you as you are able less and less to partake in the doing that most entities of your illusion enjoy. This causes you to wonder if there is purpose for your existence. This wondering is directly related to the query which we previously spoke upon in regards to the seeing of the self as that which is of infinite worth, and which has a value in its beingness without any doing whatsoever. We would encourage you to continue in the work upon the seeing of the self as that which is of infinite value and which may simply exist and be, and have reason enough in your measure to do so.

Is there a further query, my sister?

Carla: It has occurred to me *(inaudible)* pretty sturdily *(inaudible)* that it might be a good teaching technique for all of us to have the question, or to allow the questions to move on *(inaudible)*. You have a far better perspective than I do of how useful a training tool this is to the one who is attempting to discern *(inaudible)*. Do you feel that this particular method has any special aid to offer all of us as students *(inaudible)*?

I am Q'uo, and am aware of your query, my sister. In this regard, we would comment as follows. The one known as K is indeed finding that its channel is opening every more surely and stably to our contact, and that she is able to voice our thoughts with more facility, more complexity, and is able to perceive the finer and finer nuances that may be perceived by the strengthening instrument. In general, for this kind of work, we would recommend that which you have been doing. That is, the longer messages that require the continued concentration, the continued exercise of the instrument, and the continued offering of the opportunity for the expansion of the concepts and the ability to move with one concept to its completion before moving to another.

However, for the continuing nurturing of the interest of any new instrument—or, in this case, the intermediate instrument—there may be added the kind of moving of the contact from instrument to instrument that you mention, so that there is a variety of experience that is offered to the student which has progressed well and far upon the local channeling process. However, over the longer run, shall we say, at this point in the one known as K's work, we would continue to recommend the messages being delivered over a longer portion of the contact.

Is there a further query, my sister?

Carla: Just a comment that you made, Q'uo. I grasp what you are saying, and what you are saying is that K still needs the confidence that can only come from *(inaudible)* had to do with blending her energy, so if it's all right with you, I'll ask the same question *(inaudible)*.

I am Q'uo. We find that there is a sufficient understanding of our point that we need speak no further. Is there another query at this time?

Carla: No, Q'uo. I really thank you for *(inaudible)* I think I have enough material now to think about *(inaudible)*.

I am Q'uo, and we thank you, my sister, as well. Is there any another query at this time?

K: I feel that during this past while you been working with me, complex is perhaps *(inaudible)*. Can you comment on that?

I am Q'uo, and am aware of your query, my sister. We have been blending our vibrations with yours in a manner which utilizes both the indigo-ray energy center and the blue-ray energy center while attempting to stabilize or harmonize the overall green/blue/indigo energies for the purpose of being more able, that is, allowing you to be more able to stably receive the concepts which we impart to you. The work upon the indigo center, again, is more of a stabilizing of the work which you are there accomplishing. We may not work for any other, but may work with an instrument such as yourself, and may utilize the efforts which you have made in each center in order to facilitate the initiating and the continuation of our contact.

Thus, it is most often that you will notice this effect within your meditations, and especially within the intensive meditations in which you are serving as an instrument for our thoughts and words. However, at any time during any meditation or contemplative or prayerful period that you wish this kind of assistance, we are honored to offer it and to help blend our vibrations with yours for the purpose of deepening your meditation and for the purpose of stabilizing and harmonizing this triad of energies.

Is there a further query, my sister?

K: No, I thank you *(inaudible)*.

I am Q'uo, and we thank you, my sister, both for your queries and for your continued desire to serve as an instrument. We are most pleased with your progress and encourage you to take heart, shall we say, and to continue as you have with your dedication and your practice. We thank this group, as well, for its dedication and its persistent practice of the local channeling process. We are able, through your efforts, to offer a service which we give with a whole heart and which is that which allows us to know more of the Creator [and] to know more of ourselves as we see ourselves within your experiences and within your mind/body/spirit complexes.

At this time we shall take our leave of this group in joy, in peace, and in power. We leave each in the love and the light of the one infinite Creator. We are known to you as those of Q'uo. Adonai, my friends. Adonai. ☥

L/L Research

L/L Research is a subsidiary of Rock Creek Research & Development Laboratories, Inc.

P.O. Box 5195
Louisville, KY 40255-0195

www.llresearch.org

Rock Creek is a non-profit corporation dedicated to discovering and sharing information which may aid in the spiritual evolution of humankind.

ABOUT THE CONTENTS OF THIS TRANSCRIPT: This telepathic channeling has been taken from transcriptions of the weekly study and meditation meetings of the Rock Creek Research & Development Laboratories and L/L Research. It is offered in the hope that it may be useful to you. As the Confederation entities always make a point of saying, please use your discrimination and judgment in assessing this material. If something rings true to you, fine. If something does not resonate, please leave it behind, for neither we nor those of the Confederation would wish to be a stumbling block for any.

CAVEAT: This transcript is being published by L/L Research in a not yet final form. It has, however, been edited and any obvious errors have been corrected. When it is in a final form, this caveat will be removed.

© 2009 L/L Research

Sunday Meditation
March 31, 1991

Group question: The question today has to do with the concept related to Easter concerning the phrase that is given in the Apostles Creed and the act which is recognized by most Christians that Jesus, when he was crucified, was then dead, he was buried. He descended into hell and after three days he rose again to sit at the right hand of God the father almighty. I would like to know what it means when it is said that Jesus descended into hell. What has that to do with our own lives and our transformations? What did Jesus do when he descended into hell? What do we do when we do the symbolically similar act?

(Carla channeling)

I am Q'uo. Greetings in the love and in the light of the one infinite Creator. What brightness glows upon your planet this day. We thank each for calling us here and allowing us to share in your meditation and in the offering of our opinions. As always, we remind each that we are fallible and ask each to pursue his own judgment and discrimination.

You ask that we focus on this working upon the three days spent in the tomb [by] an humble, poor man, tired and worn, pierced, crucified and dead, lying in his anointing oil and the wrappings of the grave. We are aware that you do not feel this entity remained lying within that cave and you wish to know what there is about these three days that is so important to the story of the one known as Jesus, that it is at the heart of each Christian profession of faith.

First of all, let us remove the relatively shallow purpose of the number three. There are three points to a triangle. There were three wise men. Three women came to the tomb on Easter morning. The Sanctus is sung three times. And in the story of Christianity that has devolved into a body of dogma the one infinite Creator is divided into three things: the Creator, the savior and the accompaniment or angelic presence that guides each entity in everyday life. The number three is a way of expressing all that there is, not in fullness but by emblematic intentions. Three is the number that expresses an entire class or genre of a particular quality or action, yet universalizes the particular.

Thus, you may see that in the three days this three is intended to mean symbolically the completeness of one kind of activity, that is, death itself. Thus, you may see the one known as Jesus expressing a completion of deadness, a superlative, a universality of that state which those of your density call death.

Let us now move back into more subtle considerations in this matter. In part, this three day journey was that which was required by prophecy before the one known as Jesus. This entity was extremely devout and in the Jewish faith it was written that the temple could be destroyed and rebuilt in three days. Thus, Jesus' death, he being the temple, the holy of holies, remained away from manifestation within this density you call third in simple fulfillment of the prophecy.

Now, let us look a little deeper. Each entity who comes into manifestation in an incarnational experience has a subjective perception of the changes and chances of mundane life. Many things occur which do not alter or disturb the entity and some few things disturb the entity greatly, offering it catalyst for learning and growth. It is no accident that the three-pointed pyramid is the symbol of transformation for those of an ancient culture which is still valued and practiced in varying degrees of faithfulness by those who consider themselves to be illuminated by wisdom.

Each change that occurs that is in any way important to the individual will be experienced only after the pain of changing has been accomplished. In a metaphysically literal sense the process of positive spiritual change may easily be seen to be the tearing down of the previous temple of truth and ethical and moral justice, in order that a greater truth, a greater justice, a greater ethic, may find manifestation.

Some entities call this experience initiation. By whatever name it is called there are certain characteristics which mark it. Firstly, there is the pain of death itself, as the entity strips away the smaller truth and asks for all the tendrils of that truth which have moved into the many, many opinions of the self. Then there is the greeting by those who would contest the goodness of this change, this alteration towards the positive.

When one is in the process of tearing oneself down, in part one is uniquely vulnerable to voices which have power in the spiritual world, both positive and negative. The positive entities do not intrude in any way which is subjectively apparent to one experiencing transformation. However, those who are powerful in the negative path find this an excellent opportunity to challenge and test the faith of the entity that is willing to undergo this pain in order to experience a larger and more spacious life, one more informed in compassion and wisdom. The more profound the alteration of opinion or of bias the longer those three days become when experienced in the everyday world. The three days that are completeness may be for one entity a matter of minutes; for another a matter of many years. They are hidden in earth, in darkness, in heaviness. They are in a prison where they are powerless to do anything but remain spirits of faith.

During this period negatively-oriented experience may taunt, tempt, flatter and terrify the transforming spiritual entity. Insofar as there has been any doubt or any of the old truths held to one so that there is resistance to change, just in such measure shall the challenges and temptations of negatively-oriented spiritual entities have an impact upon the self. This impact is felt without recourse to anything but faith, for when one has removed the program from your biocomputer and has begun going through the process of creating an improved program for the biocomputer, the spiritual entity itself must wait.

How shall that waiting be done? When they offer suggestions waiting is that which needs to be respected to the utmost. It seems within the physical incarnation that the process of change from a small truth to a larger one goes on past all endurance, past all ability of lasting throughout the transformational period. It is often likely that in the deepest part of the night watches, the self going through initiation shall be awakened and shall feel nameless and formless fear. This is the loving greeting of those upon the negative path who would if they could persuade the entity not to transform itself, not even to claim the smaller truth but to become a victim of fear, hiding the soul of the self in layers and layers of armor, becoming numb, bitter, disheartened and lost.

The one tool that an entity going through change has is blind faith. Let us imagine that there is an operation to take place. Doctors tell the patient that it is necessary to become unconscious and to be cut upon, something, perhaps, removed that was not healthy. Certainly something altered. There are dangers in becoming unconscious. A few in ten thousand do not wake up, [ending] their incarnations during that procedure, perhaps leaving the physical body unviable, perhaps leaving it in the suspension of eternal coma. Yet the brave soul who wishes to embrace life to the fullest accepts these dangers and risks and moves through that very physical three days of change knowing only by faith that it will wake up and that the change will be for the better.

Now, you may think of a portion of yourself that is deeper and wiser than your conscious mind as a kind of healer. It may gaze upon you and say, "You must tear down this temple, for there is a greater temple to be built here and you shall tear it down and build it up in three days." To put it in other words, the intention is to move universally and completely past that quality or opinion which was the substance of that small truth which is being removed in order that the larger truth with all its ramifications may be built by the great builder of all things with the free will intentions of the self as the architect and the spirit of the infinite Creator as the miraculous laborer.

Gaze at yourself at this time. What is your situation this day? How many changes have you begun? Are you in the three days in the tomb? All are in some small sense at all times. For the nature of free will is constant movement. It is love that gives a vector to that movement.

Each of you and each to whom we could possibly speak to in third density is also in a far, far deeper way moving through transformations that are like the change from blue to green or the change from a peach to an apple, so profound and fundamental are these changes. Most commonly the changes have to do with that portion of the learning of love which is connected to the self as it relates to the self. For time and again the third-density entity judges itself and rushes to its crucifixion and burial without having an idea of how to rebuild the temple. It is this courage, the facing of the unknown, the facing of annihilation, that marks the act of crucifixion.

Many question whether the infinite Creator can be all good when there is suffering, hunger, lack, pain and death. Yet we say that if one gazes at the resurrection day one must reckon with the death that of necessity must precede that day of feasting and joy. See yourselves now upon the cross in pain, dying, lost and buried. Shall you rise again? This is the example of Jesus' resurrection. This entity expressed in the clearest and most literal way possible the power and the sacrifice of transformation. As each polarizes, these crucifixions, deaths and resurrections shall continue to occur. The spiritually led life is a life best led by those tough and hardy in spirit, strong warriors who can endure all for the love of the infinite One.

In closing, we would ask each to respect that portion of the incarnational experience that expresses itself in the completions of dying daily. If you grieve or sorrow let that sorrow be poignant and pure. Let the losses you feel be passionately felt, intensely experienced, and gratefully respected. Let there be thanks and praise in your dark tomb for within that cocoon of seeming death rises the phoenix of illumination, resurrection and new life.

We would at this time transfer this contact to the one known as Jim that this entity may continue to express that which we have to offer of opinion. With thanks to this instrument, we now leave it in love and light. We are those of Q'uo.

(Side one of tape ends.)

(Jim channeling)

I am Q'uo, and am again with this instrument. We shall continue. Within this kind of attitude regarding the scripture there is the need for stability and certainty so that all questions concerning belief have a certain answer. There is little room for mystery for there is at the subconscious level the recognition of mystery everywhere which is unsettling to the entities who have recently begun the conscious spiritual journey.

Is there further query, my sister?

Carla: I will simply say that I continue to pray for guidance *(inaudible)* in my right use of my body during the portion of my life in which it is always in pain but *(inaudible)* more than pain. There is nothing new to this question but in the name of Jesus *(inaudible)*.

I am Q'uo, and aware of your query, my sister. We recognize the great difficulties through which you travel and through which you have been traveling for a goodly portion of your incarnation. We would take this opportunity upon this particular day to suggest to you that there are some who offer themselves for the service of suffering as a portion of their overall incarnational service so that there might be the offering of every portion of the incarnation including that which you call suffering that might be a glorification of the one Creator, finding within the depth of despair the ability to praise and glorify the gift of life and the opportunity to serve under whatever conditions are present, rejoicing even in the most extreme difficulties and tragic situations.

Is there a further query, my sister?

Carla: I would just note that [Jesus] does not say anything even by inference that the choice of whether to travel the path of devotion or to ethical *(inaudible)* doesn't sit with me very well.

I am Q'uo, and am aware of your query, my sister. It is quite true that we do not speak upon this particular portion of your concern for that indeed rests firmly within the area of your own free will choices and we find that there are opportunities approaching that will aid you in this decision. More than this we cannot say at this time.

Is there a further query, my sister?

Carla: No, Q'uo. That's very well. Thank you very much.

I am Q'uo, and we once again thank you, my sister. Is there another query at this time?

(No further queries.)

I am Q'uo, and we observe the silence within the sound of hearts singing praise to the one Creator and we join in that inner singing with you as we take our leave in the outer sense from this group's devoted seeking of truth and service, thanking each, as always, for the opportunity to speak, to listen, to rejoice, and to walk a few paces upon your journey. We are known to you as those of Q'uo, and we leave each at this time in the love and in the ineffable light of the one infinite Creator. Adonai, my friends. Adonai. ♣

L/L Research

L/L Research is a subsidiary of Rock Creek Research & Development Laboratories, Inc.

P.O. Box 5195
Louisville, KY 40255-0195

www.llresearch.org

Rock Creek is a non-profit corporation dedicated to discovering and sharing information which may aid in the spiritual evolution of humankind.

ABOUT THE CONTENTS OF THIS TRANSCRIPT: This telepathic channeling has been taken from transcriptions of the weekly study and meditation meetings of the Rock Creek Research & Development Laboratories and L/L Research. It is offered in the hope that it may be useful to you. As the Confederation entities always make a point of saying, please use your discrimination and judgment in assessing this material. If something rings true to you, fine. If something does not resonate, please leave it behind, for neither we nor those of the Confederation would wish to be a stumbling block for any.

CAVEAT: This transcript is being published by L/L Research in a not yet final form. It has, however, been edited and any obvious errors have been corrected. When it is in a final form, this caveat will be removed.

© 2009 L/L Research

Sunday Meditation
April 7, 1991

Group question: The question this afternoon has to do with possibility that the Earth energy, the level of vibration in general, seems to have intensified in the last six months to a year. We are wondering if this general level of tension, anxiety, more intense experience of catalyst that many people are reporting, is a result of some cyclical rhythm that the planet itself might be undergoing. Do we move through different levels of vibration as we near the end of this density, and if so could you describe their effect upon us, and in particular this level of energy increase that has been reported of the late six months to a year?

(Carla channeling)

We are those of Q'uo. Greetings to each of you in this circle this evening in the love and in the light of the one infinite Creator. It is a great privilege to be called to your group and to be allowed to share in the oneness of your meditation and in the harmonies of your unique personalities. It is such a privilege for us to be able to hear with your ears and see with your eyes and feel with your skin, to remember so graphically just precisely how persuasive this third-density illusion and how courageous each entity is in attempting to see through all the illusion that which is beyond this illusion.

We are aware that you wish us to speak upon the signs of the times. We would preface this response by two things. Firstly, we ask each to remember that we are not all-wise or all-knowing and are perfectly capable of error. We ask each to listen with discrimination and to allow no authority but the authority of one's own response of recognition to be the way of acceptance of any of our thoughts which we share. Secondly, although we shall speak to some extent upon the specific question which has been brought forward, the particular information which is sought within the strict confines of that query are relatively unimportant, and it is in looking beyond the measurable and noticeable phenomena of the mundane illusion that one may begin to take a more spacious point of view. Thusly, as we answer this question, we shall attempt to be clear. But that which we speak of, which may seem an extrapolation beyond the information required, is given because of our feeling that these extrapolations are in the end more helpful than information having to do with phenomena.

There are several elements which are producing the noticeable changing of consciousness within all of your planetary cultures at this time. The first is that the living entity upon which you enjoy incarnation, that which you call Mother Earth, and which this instrument calls Grandmother, is cycling and circling along with the entire solar system or galaxy of your star and its planets, moving as an whole into previously uninhabited space/time. This is, indeed, that which is at the heart of the so-called New Age. Not the changes within the entities, but the changes in the environment of these entities.

It is precisely time, within your illusion, for this planet to cycle into a portion of space/time which is more densely populated with what we would call illimitable light or the light of the Creator. This cycle has already begun and the planet is, shall we say, most pregnant with its own birth into this new portion of the space/time illusion which supports the incarnational experiences of all sparks or portions of the Creator which have been outflung into illusion in order to gain in experience and learning and make ever more clear to the Creator the vast and yet simple nature of the Creator.

Thusly, each upon this planet is responding without being aware of it to an increasingly variant vibratory rate which is the steady state of the space/time which shall be the appropriate environment of positively oriented fourth-density entities.

A second contributing factor to this perceived intensification of both light and darkness is due to the instinctual awareness of each creature upon this sphere to the changing environment. To many it has been as sparks of hope and light that, because of the changing and intensifying amount of light available, causes those who are preparing for this light to feel energized by the increasing richness of the metaphysical environment, much as the physical vehicle which carries your consciousness about would be gratified to breathe a richer mixture of oxygen in the atmosphere. This, however, has a more or less unpredictable effect upon a large portion of your peoples who have not found it necessary, desirable or interesting to seek for answers outside of the ordinary stream of living, working, resting and seeking contentment and happiness. These entities who have not polarized are, in the main, unpredictably uncomfortable, and at other times unpredictably energized by these vibrations which are not measurable, except in terms of subatomic particular anomalies by instrumentation of your scientists. This is in some cases an unsettling influence; in other cases an inspiring influence. And in this middle group of entities both occur as one experiences the various cycles of body, mind, emotion and spirit.

Thusly, a large number of your peoples are greatly confused. They feel this increased fullness of light as an unpredictable energy, unpredictable because of their own lack of decision to be aimed at a steady increase in polarization one way or another. Thusly, you may see the light of freedom moving through large populations of your nation states because of the focused and prayerful hopes of those who perceive themselves in bondage by a government or ideology.

Those who are upon the path of negative polarization rejoice in this intensification of limitless light just as those who are consciously polarizing positively. However, in their case the expression of the use of this fullness of light shows in more acts of negativity as perceived by your peoples. That is, more self-absorption, more violence, more lust for power. If you may consider with us the inevitable movement of the planetary sphere itself into this fuller density of light, one may see that both positive and negative thought and action, as you may perceive negativity and positivity, are quite predictably more polarized and more active at this time, as you call it.

The third factor in the changing electromagnetic vibratory rate of the planetary sphere as measurable by your scientific instrumentation is work done with the energy of the Earth itself by those in several nation states whose mind is set upon conquest. The planet itself balks at this use of its energy which is intended to make anxious, unsure, paranoid and over-concerned about small things the populations which it wishes to weaken. What those who have worked with the energies first noted by the one known as Tesla are attempting to use for ill are in an instinctual sense not acceptable to the planet itself, which is both alive and aware.

Thusly, as it has been used at the approximate rate of eight hertz to entrain the thoughts of entities and the conditions of the planetary entity, these have in large part come back as an echo more deleterious to the source of these negatively intended actions and have wreaked what may seriously be called havoc within the populations of those nation states which wished to control that which in third density cannot be controlled.

Thusly, you may see an instinctual variation in the energy grid of third density upon your planet and the antithetical result within many nation states of the peoples of those states yearning and hoping with persistence for freedom from precisely the mind control that has been over-used by the governmental structure of these states, thus echoing back to the source of these uses of energy in a way that promotes the yearning for freedom and the dissolution of ties which were unnatural, created as an artifact of hostility and war. Any governmental entity which misuses the instinctual energy of the Earth itself answers not to those cosmic influences of the changing density but to the planetary entity which is instinctually of the Logos, or Love, in an undefiled and pristine sense.

The Earth is solidified by its inspiration to be a nurturing and healing place for the entities of the Creator to learn and to grow. When it becomes aware that these pure energies are being tapped for controlling and debilitating uses there is the simple instinct of a loving grandmother to arrange itself in order to prevent further misuse of its purity.

In years to come all of these factors shall become more and more noticeable and the Earth itself may seem in its birthing to be a giver of negative experience, in that it is not being a particularly easy birthing into the energies of fourth-density service to others. This is regretted by the entity you call Earth, but, just as a mother has the pangs of birthing, so is this planet at this time by instinct cleansing itself continually of the negative emotions and intended actions of those cherished beings which dwell upon this sphere. In the deepest sense it is most helpful to the labor of your planet that the negative emotions be taken from the sphere of activity within the illusion and instead given to the planet in renunciation of these forces within individual consciousness.

The Earth can heal any thing to any degree if it is respectfully asked. Thusly, we urge each not to condemn the self for its inevitable humanity and lack of perspective, but rather to realize that many energies not desired need to be taken to the Earth itself and lain down upon it or within it as one would lay down any heavy burden, for this entity is a pure healer and there is no perceived ugliness that cannot be healed by this beautiful planetary entity which has never strayed from oneness with the Logos, or creative Love.

Beyond these considerations we would like to move at this particular moment. To begin with this second portion of, shall we say, our testimony, we would pause that each within this group may share in our joy and vibrations for just a little while. We do not intend discomfort for any speaking, and would simply ask each to allow gentle contact that we may share in a more personal way the love and the light of the Infinite One. We are those of the principle known to you as Q'uo, and will pause at this time.

(Pause)

I am Q'uo. We must say it was difficult to come back to the strictures of language. It was a great privilege to rest with each seeker within this circle. We are greeting each again in love and light and would speak to some extent of those things which, while connected to considerations of changing electromagnetic properties of the planetary entity, are at the heart those things which are concerned with the actions of those selves who wish to aid themselves and others as this process takes place in the most efficient way.

You each have seen in your experience that often the beautiful entity is an humble entity, one which is obscure. However, there are also many within the public cynosure which, with all of their hearts, also live the life of one who wishes to do the good deed, share the felt love, the subjectively perceived light which is within them. Thusly, we urge each more and more to monitor the self, not simply in behavior or even thought, but in the basic intentions and hopes of the inner self.

The third-density illusion is one created to maximize the impact of pain, suffering and other seemingly negative distortions. This illusion does not grip your planet except insofar as the entities turn away from the intention to polarize towards the beautiful, good and true, which are qualities largely unperceiveable within the illusion. Insofar as entities fail to keep the light of hope alive, the basic vibration of negativity is allowed to vibrate through the planetary entity which then, in order to heal these energies, will express the fever, the symptoms of healing disease, the efflux of, shall we say, the planetary influenza brought into the Earth itself by the unrecognized germs of hopelessness and helplessness which the entity whose hope has failed will place within the Earth.

Your peoples are for the greater part unaware that they have given the planet this fever and ache. Consequently, they cannot aid in the healing which would be desired if they realized the power of thought. Your positively oriented entities focus upon the perceived physical damage done to the planet.

However, it is very slight damage, although it looks considerable to the citizens of its surface, compared to the damage done by those who have lost their hope and therefore their ability to exist as loving creatures aware of their power.

In essence, we urge each who cares for the planet to reckon with their personal power. Far from being powerless, each entity has access to great amounts of power for weal or for woe. All good entities which wring their hands and pass the judgment upon those who do not appreciate their beautiful environment, are damaging the planet in a metaphysical sense by losing hope in the healing of the Earth sphere. What these positive entities do not realize is that the illusion is the illusion is the illusion is the illusion. It will continue to produce possibilities for catalyst. It, itself, is not in difficulty. It mirrors the lack of hope and feeling of powerlessness of positive entities in a more damaging way than all of the environmental obscenities practiced by those who are insensitive to living in harmony with nature.

And we would close this beginning message with the plea to each positive entity to realize that the environmental pollution is not nearly as serious an illness to the planetary entity of Grandmother Earth as the lack, and increasing lack, of certainty among these positive entities that all is well and all shall be well. Not in the illusion, but in the reality, relatively speaking, of the imperishable fields of consciousness that each of you is with relation to the imperishable spirit of unconditional and creative love that is the metaphysical planetary entity. It is good not to pollute the streams and forests of your planet, but this is within the illusion, and you shall come and you shall go. However, outside of illusion both the Logos of the planetary entity and of yourselves lie in potential, mated, loving, faithful and hopeful relationship. And if there is judgment in the attempts to heal the physical Earth, then the judgment harms the metaphysical entity of your planet more than the attempts to teach the love of Earth in a judgmental way could ever help.

At this time and with our apologies for speaking overly long, we would thank and leave this instrument in love and light and continue this working through the instrument of the one known as James Allen. We are those of the principle of Q'uo. We transfer now.

(Jim channeling)

I am Q'uo, and greet each again in the love and in the light of the one infinite Creator. At this time we would take the opportunity to offer ourselves in the attempt to speak to any queries which may yet remain upon the minds of those present. We would again remind each that we offer that which is our opinion. We offer it gladly and we offer it freely but wish no word to serve as a stumbling block. Take each word, therefore, that has value to you and use it as you will, leaving behind all those that do not have value to you. Is there a query at this time?

L: I have a personal question concerning this new healing technique that I've been learning. Should it stay separate from the Reiki that I've learned before, or should I think about synthesizing them, and should I think about using the Earth for healing energy also, using them all together?

I am Q'uo, and am aware of your query, my brother. We scan your recent memory for this information, and we may suggest that the heating—we correct this instrument—the healing modality of which you speak, as you are already aware, is efficacious in your particular case and will be of aid to many who seek its entrance into the untangling process that often moves from the mental to the physical vehicle in what you call the form of disease. As to your path of joining, or blending, the various kinds of healing techniques, we would suggest that this is that process in which you are presently engaged, for you have been drawn by your own desires to those areas which are of most importance to you. This is not by chance but by the design of your own conscious and subconscious minds working in harmony so that there might be a balance brought forth from those distortions that have served as the arrow pointing the way in which your progress lies. Therefore, we do not feel that we infringe upon your own free will as we verify that which you presently suppose. Is there a further query, my brother?

L: No, thank you.

I am Q'uo, and we thank you, my brother. Is there another query?

Carla: *(Portions inaudible.)* I'd like to follow up on L's to ask if there are any techniques or visualizations in which Earth's energy can be used for healing, most appropriately … I know I can feel the energy of the Earth any time I put my feet down on it. Is it as simple as that awareness that one's feet are upon the Earth and the Earth is a healer, or is there a more skillful way to realize that within the healing process …?

I am Q'uo, and am aware of your query, my sister. This is a large field of inquiry, and we shall make but the barest of beginnings, for we are aware that we have spoken overly long and do not wish to overtire those present. The Earth energy is quite helpful to those who wish to serve as healers, for it is an energy that is ever present, an energy with which each is familiar, if not consciously then on the subconscious level, for each entity is a child born of this Mother which you call Earth, and is an energy which is accessible to each entity through the desire that each entity expresses in wishing to utilize this energy for healing.

As to the technique of such utilization, this is the area that is large, for each entity will find a method of utilizing the Earth energy that is most efficacious to the entity. However, there are some generalizations which may be of aid here. It is well to create a form or focus, a channel through which this energy may be tapped as it is used in the healing process. Whether the form is that which is created by hand and may consist of some form of shape or shelter in which the entity may rest as it accumulates the focused Earth energy, or whether the form is smaller and is of a crystalline nature that may be worn about the neck and may rest upon the heart, or whether the form is that which is mentally envisioned as focusing and intensifying the Earth energy, then passing into the area or entity to be healed, matters not for the beginning healer that is using the Earth energy for the first time or is attempting to do so.

The important point is that the desire is used to fashion a focus through which this energy may pass. As the healer becomes more practiced in its art the form or focus may begin to change according to the experience and the findings of the healer. It is well for each entity desiring to utilize Earth energy, or any energy, for the purpose of healing to first begin to purify or heal the self in the more gross or noticeable distortions so that the energy of the Earth or whatever energy is being utilized may flow in a manner which is least distorted and which allows the fullest expression or manifestation of this energy towards any other entity that seeks the healing service.

Is there a further query, my sister?

Carla: No, thank you.

I am Q'uo, and we thank you, my sister. Is there another query?

Questioner: I have a question, Q'uo. To what extent—or is there a limit to the amount of service to another that one would appropriately offer?

I am Q'uo, and am aware of your query, my sister. The extent of any service to another entity is limited by the amount of service that is desired and requested by that other entity, for service is not possible if it is not desired or requested. Thus, it is necessary for the one desiring to be of service to others to operate first upon the basis of a request, then to continue in as clear a communication as is possible with the one being served in order to ascertain whether or not a continuation of service is appropriate.

Is there another in—we correct this instrument once again—is there another query, my sister?

Questioner: When there is a difficulty in communication between the one to be served and the one offering service, there would seem to be a difficulty in determining the service to be desired, even if desired. Can you speak on that?

I am Q'uo. In such an instance we would advise that the first concern is the clarification of the communication in order that those areas which are not distinct or well understood might be understood more clearly. This avoids the confusion of that which is desired by the one who wishes the service and that which is desired by the one who wishes to serve, for many times we find among your peoples those who are of a service to others orientation are so full of the desire to be of service that the offering of service is often done in what might be seen a blind manner, where it is hoped that that which is offered will be seen as service and will function as service, whereas if more time and effort were invested in obtaining the true desires of the one to be de—we correct this instrument—the one to be served, then there would be seen another avenue perhaps would open up.

Is there another query, my sister?

Questioner: No, thank you very much.

I am Q'uo, and we thank you once again, my sister. Is there another query at this time?

Carla: Just a clarification. I am assuming that it is never an infringement on anyone's free will just to love them.

I am Q'uo. This is quite correct, my sister. Is there another query?

Questioner: I have a query. I was wondering as the Earth, this planetary body, changes I sense that other planetary bodies in our system are also changing and perhaps the Sun itself. Can you address this situation, especially with respect to the Sun?

I am Q'uo, and am aware of your query, my brother. Indeed, change is truly said to be the one constant in all of creation, for all of this and all creation is made of the energetic, vibrant and ever-present love of the one Creator seeking and turning in order to know Itself. Each planetary body within this solar system, within this galaxy and within this universe moves in a manner through a process of evolution that is, though quite distinctly different in many ways, is also quite similar to your own as well. Each experiences cycles and rhythms, so that the interaction of each planetary entity with those populations that may be upon it or may be in some fashion in communication with it is affected by these relationships and communications.

The very core of the vibrational nature that is the photon within each portion of each creation vibrates in a manner which expresses a relative harmonic with the planets and Sun bodies that are near and also with those that are what you would call distant. There is what might be seen as a three-dimensional nature to this relationship as regards time so that the revolving and evolving of these planetary and Sun bodies moves into areas of the solar system, of the galaxy and of the universe that offer new opportunities for the perception and the expression of the intelligent energy of the one Creator.

Thus do all planetary and Sun bodies find accelerated means of experiencing and expressing the nature of the one Creator as is uniquely offered to them by their vibratory frequencies and placements within this three dimensional clock face that has a striking upon the hour as cycles change, much as does your clock strike upon the hour.

Is there another query, my brother?

Questioner: *(Inaudible)*.

I am Q'uo, and we would ask if there is a final query before we close this session of working?

(Pause)

I am Q'uo, and we would take this opportunity to thank each entity present for your invitation to us to join your circle of seeking. We especially would thank and greet those who are present for the first time in one of these circles, and would also greet an old friend who has returned again to this circle. We thank you with all of our heart, for through your invitation we have the ability to walk with you in a more conscious fashion upon your journey of seeking and to learn that which is of service, and that which is the Creator speaking through you to us. This is a treasure to us which is beyond any measure.

We shall take our leave at this time, thanking each again, leaving each in the love and in the light of the one infinite Creator. We are known to you as those of Q'uo. Adonai, my friends. Adonai. ❧

L/L Research

L/L Research is a subsidiary of Rock Creek Research & Development Laboratories, Inc.

P.O. Box 5195
Louisville, KY 40255-0195

www.llresearch.org

Rock Creek is a non-profit corporation dedicated to discovering and sharing information which may aid in the spiritual evolution of humankind.

ABOUT THE CONTENTS OF THIS TRANSCRIPT: This telepathic channeling has been taken from transcriptions of the weekly study and meditation meetings of the Rock Creek Research & Development Laboratories and L/L Research. It is offered in the hope that it may be useful to you. As the Confederation entities always make a point of saying, please use your discrimination and judgment in assessing this material. If something rings true to you, fine. If something does not resonate, please leave it behind, for neither we nor those of the Confederation would wish to be a stumbling block for any.

CAVEAT: This transcript is being published by L/L Research in a not yet final form. It has, however, been edited and any obvious errors have been corrected. When it is in a final form, this caveat will be removed.

© 2009 L/L Research

Intensive Meditation
April 12, 1991

Group question: The question is from S, who asks, "Could you tell me the difference between space/time and time/space? This was a question that was covered in the Law of One but I would love to hear Q'uo talk about time/space for I still do not understand it very well even from an abstract point of view. When entities live in time/space, what is their life like? We move freely in space but move slowly in time. Do entities in time/space move freely in time and slowly in space? We do not control our movement in time. Do they not control their movement on space?"

(K channeling)

I greet each of you here this morning in the love and in the light of the one infinite Creator. As always, we are pleased to be called to this group. When you seek that which we also seek you chose to know more and ever more of the mystery which surrounds us and expands infinitely in which direction we choose to go.

We have spoken many times of the path of seeking, of the mystery we see before us along this path. But the path of seeking is not a straight line, my children. If you wander off any line that is not straight you are still on your path of seeking. For to the one who seeks the mystery the entire life is a path. It contains many seemingly circuitous roads. But when it is realized that each present moment contains infinity, that each point in space/time or time/space contains all that there is, the concept of a straight line being the way the path is is recognized to be only an analogy.

You wish information this morning on the concept and the nature of time/space. Time/space is that which surrounds you at all times and in all spaces, shall we say. In your present illusion you are consciously aware of space/time and it is that in which you conduct your daily activities. It is that with which you are most familiar. Time/space permeates all of space/time and you move within this as well, although you do not have as great a degree of awareness of this.

You are aware that space/time is the home, shall we say, of the illusion of incarnation and that when an entity is not conscious of being within the incarnational illusion, whether between incarnations beyond the process of physical incarnation or in some other way aware of the dimensions of space/time—whether in the dreaming state or other means of alterations of consciousness—then the field of time/space is that of which the entity has primary awareness.

Time/space is that realm within which we are able to be with you at all times, that we may inhabit space/time as well. The movements which are possible to make in time/space are variable as are those in space/time and perhaps more widely variable because of the greater divergence of types of entities that inhabit time/space. There are entities of more differing densities that inhabit these realms and their abilities to move vary according to their individual development. [This] is also true of space/time which in your current illusion is inhabited by the first, second, third and beginning of fourth-density entities. And you may see the divergence of the abilities to move in, for example, the rock entity which moves very slowly in space as compared to the third-density entity which moves about in space seemingly at will, limited only by such physical laws as the entity is aware of.

There are similar laws governing the fields of time/space and similar divergences in the abilities of varying entities to move therein. We ourselves have developed abilities to move much more freely, shall we say, than the time/space counterpart of the walking entities of which you are familiar. Each entity that has the appearance of solidity in your illusion also has the time/space counterpart which exists in a superimposed, shall we say, manner. This time/space counterpart is discernible to some of your entities who have developed the capacity for this type of perception.

The time/space counterpart is that which is worked with very often by those with healing abilities. Each here is aware of such instances. Thus, the separation between time/space and space/time is not such a clear-cut distinction as you may have thought, although it is possible to move purely in the realms of time/space without being a part of space/time. It is not possible to be in space/time without also being part of time/space or the time/space realm containing, shall we say, those of space/time.

We notice this instrument's struggle with the various terms used and apologize for the limitations of language and speech for we are attempting to communicate complex concepts with a very limited amount of words that may be applied to them and thus of necessity reuse words in slightly different applications when the meaning would be clearer were there different words available. However, this being the illusion we must all do the best we can, shall we say.

I am Q'uo, and we feel that these words are a sufficient beginning upon this topic and would be happy to respond to further questions should they arise among those here or others that participate in seeking with this group. At this time we transfer to the one known as Jim and will close the session of workings with this instrument. I am known to you as those of Q'uo, and leave this instrument at this time.

(Jim channeling)

I am Q'uo, and greet each again in love and in light. It is our privilege to offer ourselves at this time for any queries that you may have for us. May we speak to any query?

Carla: I have a question *(inaudible)*.

I am Q'uo, and am aware of your query, my sister. The question of praying in a manner which is helpful and efficient, as you may say, is a question which could be answered briefly if one were willing to accept a synopsis, or a question which could be answered at great length for it is one that, as do most questions concerning the spiritual journey, could be answered infinitely, for it is one which also touches upon and reflects the entire spiritually oriented life. For as one learns to live in a conscious fashion one is learning to pray. And as one learns to pray, as you call it, one learns to live in a consciously oriented fashion. For to pray and to live the conscious life is to become aware of the central feature of all life and that is love. To live consciously in love is to see the Creator in all and this includes, of course, the self. To learn to pray is to learn to address the love within oneself and to speak to that love which resides in other individualized portions of the one Creator. And to ask that love [to] move and use its forming abilities to aid another self or system of selves or situation.

As one becomes aware of the relationship between the Creator and the creation one sees that the power of love is that which moves all things and all entities in patterns or in rhythms, cycles and in seasons, that this enabling function of love may be hindered or blocked by thoughts and attitudes that express themselves in behaviors that stop up or block the free flow of love. This alteration of the power of love in any life pattern allows for a more varied experience, for it would not be thought of by any entity who lived in perfect harmony with love to stop its movement.

However, as each entity within the creation desires to serve the Creator by providing experience that allows the Creator to know Itself so then does each entity alter to some degree this basic motivational power of love. Altering or distorting the flow of love causes the necessity for a balancing action that will once again allow the love to move freely. This process of blocking and unblocking the flow of love is that process which you call experience or evolution. This is a simplistic description but [one] which we feel is basically accurate for each portion of the Creation. Thus, as you pray and seek to intercede or call for another's intercession on behalf of one you feel is in need you ask that the power of love to move freely be restored in an area where it has been blocked.

As you are more in touch or in tune with this power of love within your own life pattern you are able to appreciate and manifest this power in your own life pattern and to offer a catalyst or way by which love may be offered to others. Engaging in the process which you call prayer is one way which you may open a door or gateway for another entity by calling upon individualized portions of love to share their love with the one for whom you intercede or seek intercession. Your own awareness of this process and your own desire to be of service to another are those qualities which enhance the prayerful attitude.

As you call upon entities such as Jesus the Christ, various saints or archangels, the mother of Jesus known as Mary, or any angelic presence to intercede for another you are providing the purity and intensity of your own love as a request, a call which is heard because of the purity and intensity by the presence whom you seek and this presence hears the call no matter how weak and responds according to its strength, purity and sincerity. The response is in a form which the one whom you wish to aid can accept, whether it be an immediate healing, as you would call it, which occurs in some few cases, or the sending of the general quality of healing, love and light energy that the entity may utilize in a less immediate or more diffused manner according to the entity's own ability to contact those qualities of will and of faith that may open the door to the healing power of love for it.

Is there another query, my sister?

(No further queries.)

I am Q'uo, and we are pleased to have been able to utilize both the one known as K and the one known as Jim. In this session of working we feel that each entity has been able to open itself to a wider range of concept and we are pleased that each has continued to improve the desire to serve others in this manner. We applaud the perseverance that is necessary within your illusion to penetrate the great wall of mystery that surrounds all third-density entities. Your perseverance and your desire are likened to small but brilliant lights that illumine a portion of your way so that you may continue your movement in seeking and in service.

At this time we shall take our leave of this group, thanking each for once again inviting us to join you in your journeys in a way that is immediate and effective in expanding the limits of perception. We are known to you as those of Q'uo. We leave you in the love and in the light of the one infinite Creator. Adonai, my friends. Adonai.

L/L Research

L/L Research is a subsidiary of Rock Creek Research & Development Laboratories, Inc.

P.O. Box 5195
Louisville, KY 40255-0195

www.llresearch.org

Rock Creek is a non-profit corporation dedicated to discovering and sharing information which may aid in the spiritual evolution of humankind.

ABOUT THE CONTENTS OF THIS TRANSCRIPT: This telepathic channeling has been taken from transcriptions of the weekly study and meditation meetings of the Rock Creek Research & Development Laboratories and L/L Research. It is offered in the hope that it may be useful to you. As the Confederation entities always make a point of saying, please use your discrimination and judgment in assessing this material. If something rings true to you, fine. If something does not resonate, please leave it behind, for neither we nor those of the Confederation would wish to be a stumbling block for any.

CAVEAT: This transcript is being published by L/L Research in a not yet final form. It has, however, been edited and any obvious errors have been corrected. When it is in a final form, this caveat will be removed.

© 2009 L/L Research

Sunday Meditation
April 21, 1991

Group question: The question this afternoon has to do with the general qualities as a light center that the area occupied by N would have as a center for individuals and for individuals that are seeking to work out their own ways of learning and of being of service to others by what they learn. What kinds of energies are necessary for such a center? How are these energies being expressed there now with the opposition that has occurred in this area and how can people who wish to partake in the center help as individuals in producing the light that might be of service to others? And how can the center, as a grouping of individuals, be of the most service to those whom they would wish to serve?

(Carla channeling)

I am Q'uo. Greetings to each of you in the love and in the light of the one infinite Creator. We are very grateful to be able to share our thoughts with you and to share in the beauty of your meditation. And we thank you for calling our particular energy to your circle at this time. There is a peace, a quality and nature of peace, that is seldom grasped or understood by those who have not suffered from its seeming loss, and it is that peace that we share with you and which we thank each of you for sharing with us.

To begin to answer the questions that you have asked about spiritually helpful places to be—in the body, in the mind, and in the spirit—we would begin by gazing at the question of energy points or grids, places of power, as they are sometimes called among your peoples. The third density places of power are not particularly close together. The energy web does not have as many nexi of concentrated energy. With each level of vibration, each sub-octave of awareness, the energy grids become more tightened and numerous. Thus, if one were to superimpose over a chart of third-density energy centers, the selfsame chart of fourth-density energy centers of the planet would fit into it but would also greatly elaborate and expand the number and kind of places of power.

This potential web of power or energy is available not only in third density, but a third-density entity may, by its own spiritual work in consciousness, become able to discern more and more the multiplicity of places of power if one is seeing from the standpoint of the love of fourth density, the ever-multiplying wisdom of fifth, and the immensely bright and universal pattern of energy grids of sixth density. Consequently, we would answer the question about the placement of any spiritual center by saying that it is as light-filled as is the awareness and crystallization of the entities upon whose soil these entities wish to grow, to learn and to manifest whatever fruits come from the journey of the pilgrim.

Thusly, we would simply remove from the question the idea that we could in some way judge energy or power in any one place, for it is quite subjective in terms of how the power of any one place will aid an entity. This information must be learned in a subjective way, in a way of experiencing and feeling the tug of heart which in its wisdom knows a great deal more than the mind can ever find words to express. There is no place that is closed off from the love of the one infinite Creator. There is no place which is not holy ground.

Now, let us look at the situation in other terms. The journey of the seeker is from its Source to its Source. It is a circular journey—or, rather, a spiral journey—of learning, awakening, manifesting and gaining the strength within each part of the field of consciousness that is your true self that in time, as you would call it, enables an entity to have the spiritual mass to be affected by spiritual gravity, which becomes more and more nearly irresistible until, ultimately, there is no interest whatsoever in manifestation, but only in becoming the unthinking, unsolidified, infinite and unself-conscious Logos or Love, that is, the nature of the one infinite Creator.

As you begin your experience as a being, you find yourself first in a very simplistic kind of environment where the Creator's hand visibly moves, as this instrument would say from her holy work, "upon the face of the waters." Earth, air, wind and fire form many, many places where there is more and more the possibility of solidification from spirit to a very simple manifestation of some kind. This manifestation is a process that continues, and, as each entity grasps the conditions and the learnings of one particular school room, it moves to another.

The bodies that you carry about with you are good examples of the work of second density. It is always an error to assume that that which is your physical vehicle is in any way yourself. The physical vehicle which you enjoy is a creature, valued and valuable to the Creator. It has come from the unsolidified ethers before manifestation to the point where, were we talking in terms of normal circles, the nadir or lowest point in the cycle of spirit and manifestation occurs.

This is your position at this time. You shall never see this particular kind of manifestation, this excellence and thoroughness of illusion, when lessons within this density have been learned. This is the density of confusion, suffering, loss, risk and choice, for the spirit that is you is now able to manifest through its physical vehicle the most of which each is capable in terms of the fruits of the spirit, in terms of the silent witness to spirit that may be seen within the eyes and the auras of those who have taken up their choice. This particular state has been called "maya," illusion.

The irony of the Creator's humor is never more present than in calling the third density one in which one is able to do great things, for, indeed, at the point at which you are within the conceptual framework of maya, you are least able to do spiritual work. It is in this environment that you must do the foundational spiritual work upon which platform, builded by you, you shall stand as you refine, and refine again, and refine again the concepts which you have of the Creator, of the nature of the creation, and of your responses to the Creator and the creation. Thus, as each of you believes in the illusion that this is the place to express and manifest and do work that can be seen by others, it is joyfully and humorously true that you are at your least sharp, your least keen, with respect to spiritual journeying, for this illusion is extremely good. And that which you learn within this illusion is learned through a surrender you shall never have to make once you have made it now.

The surrender of which we speak is the surrender of the life, the perceptions, the gifts and the talents, the troubles, the woes, the beauties, all of these things surrendered to the energetic and infinite one Creator. As you sit in your seemingly very solid supports, as your ears, your skin, your eyes, all of your senses, feel and hear and see so many things, it would seem as though this was the realest of all possible environments or experience. However, the illusion is intended to be seductive; that is, it is intended to move the attention away from invisible and infinite things. It is an illusion in which it is a feat of great difficulty to experience the deepest truth about oneself, which is that each self is not solid, is not permanent, does not have an ego, does not have a form, does not have blue eyes or brown, golden hair or dark. How can one refute such a seemingly silly point of view about third density, for there it all is in front of your eyes, in front of your ears, in front of your heart? Things which seem good; things which seem not good; things about yourself which you would judge; things about others that you would judge. All of these ephemeral and useless activities being made possible by the excellence of the illusion of this density.

In meditation, in sitting with the self and allowing the self to be, just to be, there is a process which goes on within each, below the level of conscious awareness for the most part, where the spirit is preparing itself for the surrender of all that it thinks it is in order that it may do the will of the one infinite Creator in all situations.

You seen so solid to yourself. Yet, if we were to suggest to you that there was a microscopic animal which dwelt in the vicinity of your bed clothing and lived off of the flakes of skin dropped by the sleeping entity, you would dismiss the importance of knowing about such a small being. Yet, could you not also be one of the molecules of such a creature, being fed by one which would seem to you to be so gigantic that it would create a universe? It is well to remember that size and all manifestations are illusory. You could be that small entity which lives in the mattress, and you can allow yourself to feel that smallness at this time.

Be aware of the smallness of your solidified self. Look at that self in relation to this gigantic being which, of itself, offers you food. It is no mistake or coincidence that the universe that is seen by the greatest telescopes and the universe that is seen by the greatest microscopes in cyclotrons seem identical. Relax that solidified self at this time. Allow the spirit within you to feel the consciousness which you truly are, to release itself from the judgments and condemnations of humankind. Feel yourself as the servant that you are, as the prodigal who wished to move forward, to climb that great arc which is the second part of the circle of being, finally to come to the house of the infinite One, to be greeted and fed and rejoiced over as prodigal sons and daughters.

Now, what we have been attempting to do is to give you some idea of the actual environment in which you live because that which each wishes to do to praise the Creator's name is within each, has been placed within each by the self before the incarnation—not the solidified self, but the field of consciousness that you truly are. Consequently, this incarnational experience is all about making choices. You may call them choices between darkness and light, hate and love, discord and unity, or any of the numberless theses and antitheses that bark your shins as you walk through the waters of experience.

So, what can you do in one place and yet, not in another? You can do that which you allow yourself to do. Do you feel weak? Examine this. Do you feel strong? Examine this. For what are you feeling—the illusory environment or the love and the light of the one infinite Creator? We ask you to see that all things, from your environment at its farthest distance to the intimate environment of your conscious mind, all things are illusion. This is the worst possible environment for you to make sincere, heartfelt and loyally kept choices having to do with the path of service which each wishes. It would not be an effective environment for the maturing spirit were it not completely believable.

You are working in the darkest of nights and there is a sliver of moon which is your only illumination, besides that star of hope, to guide you as you seek to become spirit again, in no way displeased with the entity, the creature, that carries you around so sacrificially, but that you begin to see that the spaces you wish to explore are other than the commonly understood spaces of time and space. Because this is the worst possible condition for you to make your choice of service, this is where all entities must make their choice. We do not say that it is an easy school room in which to learn, but, rather, that you were put in the most difficult situation in order that you could begin to distinguish between the things that occur, that happen to you and around you, and the response which you give to these things. Any number of things, positive and negative, occur to entities. Yet, it is within each entity, and each entity for itself alone, that each choice is made.

We ask each, as you sit upon this illusory furniture within this illusory house upon this illusory earth, to allow yourself to release the illusion and to feel the strength of your field of consciousness, to surrender this incarnation to that field of consciousness that you are, that, in surrendering the illusion—that which can be measured—you open yourself to eternity and that which cannot ever be measured. For, within the spiritual seeking, it is those things that are immeasurable and infinite which draw one onward and ever onward to the greater and vaster beauties of the immeasurable that are to come. It is in this seeming battlefield of negative emotional states that the pure spirit within you must allow itself to be born.

How frightened each of you is during this birthing process. How often you wish to move back into the measurable, into that which can be handled and controlled. But the choice that you are making as a spiritual infinite being of light is the choice to express, first of all, a recognition of the infinite love of the one infinite Creator, that Creator which loves you personally, intimately and infinitely. The choice then seems to become easier: to give back that love, to allow oneself qualities and not quantities of love.

And when one has realized itself as the servant of the Divine One, as the channel through which infinity, light and love may be channeled, one prepares oneself for the basic choice. Having experienced the immeasurable beauty of the Creator, having experienced those things that cannot be measured by any instrumentation, you prepare yourself for this choice: to love the Creator by serving other entities in the Creator's name, or by serving the Creator by controlling others in order that they will be able to move along the path which you have found to be helpful. The difference upon the surface between these two choices seems not so wide. In actuality, it is the greatest abyss imaginable, for those entities whose paths and service are positive and those who are negative have within themselves, first, the way they gaze at the self and at what occurs day by day and minute by minute.

There is every possibility in the beginning that it may not seem that you have made much of a choice, for the first job of those who seek to serve is to fall in love with themselves, not as creatures who are perfect, not as creatures who are elite or in any way better than anyone else, but as creatures who have, quite reliably, a dark side. All of this you must fall in love with, for it is written within this instrument's holy work that the one known as Jesus said, in eradicating the Ten Commandments, that there was a new covenant, a new agreement, that each entity was to love the Creator with every possible part of the self and to love others as one loves the self. So you see, when you have become aware of the Creator, you must then become aware of the beauty of the self, for only insofar as you love the self can you have true compassion for other selves.

And while you are learning to love yourself with all of your imperfections, it seems somehow as though there were a selfishness to this process. This is incorrect; it is the learning process. In the Creator all things are perfect and all things are one. In manifestation, all things are imperfect and all things are several. You stand at the crossroads upon the greatest illusion that you shall ever experience, and you must allow yourself to love yourself, to forgive yourself, to accept yourself, so that you may go forth rejoicing and then gaze at the illusion with new eyes.

If you have fallen so completely in love with the self that the self becomes the universe, then the path upon which you tread will be more and more negative as you attempt to show other entities just how wonderful it is to experience the Creator and the self as do you. This is a path of that which is not; this is a path which celebrates that separation that the world of maya offers to the discerning observer.

The other choice, once one has learned to love the self, is to move beyond the self, not in judgment but in compassion, loving this way or that way, whichever way one can, accepting inevitable, seeming barriers as well as seeming successes because of the realization that you shall never know within this illusion how well you have done, how close you have come to the mark which you set for yourself before this incarnation. You have no control, no power over circumstances such as which occur within the illusion. You do, however, have enormous power to choose that which you shall pay attention to, that which you will assimilate deeply, and that which you will allow to be shed from the back as if you had on the raincoat.

So, your situation is that you are, as far as possible, in the great realm of eternity from spirit and more full of illusion than you have ever been or will ever be. This is a bright, flashing moment—a parenthesis in eternity—during which you make the choice of how you will proceed upon the great road which wends its way at last to the Source and Ending of all things.

We would ask you to be aware in all things of what the choice truly is, how deeply it begins. You don't simply choose your actions; you choose your perceptions. If you are a stewardship of the love of the one infinite Creator, you will gaze upon all circumstances without fear and simply plumb that situation as deeply as possible in search of options which are loving both to the self and to other selves.

So, all places are places of power if that place is your geographical, topological home in this illusion. We would not have entities dashing off to the "Mt. Shastas" so prevalent within your literature. With all those well-meaning entities in one spot, surely the Earth itself would tip and be unbalanced! Your home is where you are; your place of power is where you stand; and that which you receive is as pure and complete as you may allow it be.

We ask you to keep this joyous story of heartbreak and larger life gain nearby to the self and not in any way to brag or boast about the exciting process of nurturing that small spirit within you and protecting it from the illusion. For, as one speaks of those things …

(Side one of tape ends.)

(Carla channeling)

… for all are going to the same home; all are submerged in illusion. And the loving heart that will open to the infinite love and light of the one Creator is that entity which shall witness to a quality indescribable within your illusion: absolute and unconditional love.

There is more material upon this subject. However, this instrument requests that at this time we move to a question and answer period, for the energies of this particular instrument are somewhat depleted. And so, with thanks to this instrument and to each of you, we leave this instrument in love and light and would continue this session of working through the one known as Jim. We are those known to you as the principle of Q'uo.

(Jim channeling)

I am Q'uo, and greet each again in love and in light through this instrument. At this time it is our privilege to offer ourselves to any queries which you may have. Is there a query with which we may begin?

Questioner: *(Question is difficult to hear. It has something to do with meditation with one's focus being the sun.)*

I am Q'uo, and am aware of your query, my brother. For many, many ages have peoples of your planet, and others as well, worshipped that entity that you know as your sun body, for it has been known by many peoples in a variety of your cultures that there is great energy that is life-giving embodied within this spiritual being that manifests as your sun. This entity is that which you may conveniently call Love or Logos, for it is with the one Creator a co-Creator of this portion of the one creation and, as a being of completeness, offers itself wholly, that life in all forms might be nurtured in the area of its care.

Thus, you may offer yourself in meditation to this being in any manner which expresses your connection to, and appreciation of, the creation or any portion of it in which you move and have your being. There is great depth of awareness that may be awakened as you continue to offer your honestation or devotion to those principles of unity, of love and of light which are perfectly embodied within this sun body. Thus, you may with benefit contemplate, before your meditation, those qualities which you wish to nourish within yourself and to radiate in an outward fashion to others as a result of your communion in meditation with the sun body.

Is there a further query, my brother?

Questioner: *(Question is difficult to hear. It concerns planetary information contained in the Vedas and whether this information is accurate, particularly with respect to descriptions of "hellish" planets where punishment is given.)*

I am Q'uo, and believe that we have a grasp of your query. We would refer your thinking to the underlying symbolic nature of all inspired writings that seek to impart those truths that lie beyond the boundary of words by using the vehicle of words in a fashion which describes relationships and the various levels of relationships of one portion of the creation to another, in order that the student of the evolutionary process may begin—and we stress begin—to appreciate the vastness of the creation of the one infinite Creator.

We would speak to the particulars of your query by suggesting that there are many, many inhabited planets that are at a level of evolution that is not as accelerated, shall we say, as is your own at this time, that have experiences which are of a more gross or unrefined nature that would appear to many of your own people to be of what you describe as a "hellish" quality. However, it must be kept firmly within the mind that each environment or planet has its own perfectly revolving system of entities, relationships, experiences and possibilities. Each fits perfectly within its own evolutionary scheme so that there is no punishment or reward, in the absolute sense, other than that which is contained within the mind of any seeker, for as you are well aware, that which many would see as the greatest of difficulties or punishments may be seen by one who has a broader perspective as the greatest of opportunities for advancement, just as it can be said that what would seem to another entity to be the most fertile grounds for advancement would seem to another to be narrow and restricted in possibility. The breadth and depth of the perspective is that which allows an entity to see greater or lesser opportunity.

Thus, it is well said that the area that you call Heaven could easily be destroyed if occupied by a fool and the area that you call hell could be enlightened if occupied by a saint.

Is there another query, my brother?

Questioner: Is it important to accept our sensuality and sexuality in this density or illusion in order to develop a sense of wholeness? In other words, is there a danger in denying that aspect of this illusion and thereby missing the lessons that the sensuality and sexuality of this density have to offer?

I am Q'uo, and am aware of your query, my brother. It cannot be said to be a, as you would call it, "hard and fast rule" for all entities, for each entity is unique, and a pattern of incarnations previously completed may require of an entity certain particular lessons within the current incarnation. But there is the path of the kundalini that, traveling through the energy centers or chakras, is a necessity for all entities at some point or within an accumulation of incarnations, so that the red-ray energy center, which deals with the reproductive and sexual energies of the entity, may be seen as that which is the foundation stone upon which the rest of the building of the personality shall be placed.

Just so, this energy must also move in a balanced fashion from the red ray and proceed upwards to the orange ray, where the individual power of expression is manifested in the incarnation in a fashion which allows the uniqueness of the individual to express itself, using that same energy which has moved through the red ray and which continues, if unblocked, to the yellow, the green, and so forth, so that when an entity has been able to activate and balance each energy center the intelligent energy or prana of the one Creator moves through each center to be met at the indigo ray center or brow chakra, allowing the union with the indwelling love and light of the one Creator and the opening of the entity to the fully experienced presence of the one infinite Creator.

Thus, it is necessary at some point within each incarnative pattern that all energies and their manifestations shall be experienced and balanced so that the prana will have free access to, and movement through, each center of energy.

Is there a further query, my brother?

Questioner: Are there teachings—are there stones, in the center of this planetary sphere that have information for each individual entity on the surface of this sphere? And is there benefit to contacting these stones for information that can help us understand the lessons that we are learning?

I am Q'uo, and am aware of your query, my brother. There are many resources, including the stones of which you speak, that await the exploration of the seeker of truth so that as each seeker progresses upon its chosen journey there may be the opportunity to accumulate knowledge and experience at all levels of its being. There are enough resources of this nature that there is, what you might call, a redundancy factor inbuilt into not only the third-density planetary sphere which you now inhabit, but also inbuilt into its inner planes, as you call them, so that as a seeker calls for assistance in attempting to understand and balance those lessons that are before it, it might receive information and inspiration from those resources or areas which its previous experience and current desire have prepared it to be able to hear with that inner hearing that is necessary for the discrimination of those messages which are received in many, many different ways.

Is there another query, my brother?

Questioner: No, not right now. Thank you very much for your response.

I am Q'uo, and we thank you, my brother, for your queries and your devotion. Is there another query at this time?

Questioner: I have one that follows up on what's just been discussed. It's been my personal experience in this life that lovemaking is a magical ritual, like Holy Communion in the Christian church. And that has been supported by more and more feeling through the years until the point now where I realize not just the pleasure of myself or the sensuality of myself but that it is offered as a prayer to the infinite One. I know a lot of people don't see it that way. I was just wondering, could you comment on that?

I am Q'uo, and am aware of your query, my sister. As you are aware from previous study, there is a path to the one Creator that may be traveled by utilizing that which you may call the high sexual magic or ritual magic where the energy that enters through the root chakra is built and stored until it is allowed to move upwards through the centers of energy and is released through the brow and crown chakra at that culmination which you call the orgasm. And, at this point the energy then moves into the energy web of the planetary sphere to be harmonized with by the realization of the unity of the small self with the great Self which is the one Creator.

As the small self reaches, then, with this experience of ecstasy, the one Creator begins to reach in return in a fashion which allows the harmonic expression of the creative power of the universe to reverberate in the sine wave fashion within the small self which has offered itself and its experience as a means by which the one Creator might be known and glorified.

Is there a further query, my sister?

Questioner: No, thank you.

I am Q'uo, and we thank you, my sister. Is there another query?

Questioner: The energy that rises in the base chakra—is that Earth energy? And how much of that is unlimited and can be stored? Are there unlimited vast amounts of this energy that can be stored?

I am Q'uo, and am aware of your query, my brother. If we understand correctly the definition of your Earth energy, this is not the energy which moves through the system of chakras or centers of energy during any experience of energy exchanges of your third-density population. Rather, the energy which is moving through the system of chakras is that which may be called intelligent energy, or the prana which gives life to all creation, and which may be opened in the ability to receive by any seeker as the seeker balances those distortions that exist within each center of energy, and in this balancing crystallizes or regularizes the centers of energy so that they may traduce the prana of the one Creator in a clear and lucid fashion, losing not one iota of energy to distortion, but allowing this energy to be stepped up in each center until it joins with the indwelling intelligent infinity that resides in each entity as the identity of the one Creator expressing itself as the small self.

Is there another query, my brother?

Questioner: When the energy rises up through all the chakra centers, and if lost—or the centers have any distortions—does that cause blockages to that energy flow?

I am Q'uo, and am aware of your query, my brother. This is correct, and this is the reason that the work upon one's distortions is the path of the seeker, for the path is quite literal within each system of energy centers or chakras, and as one studies the nature of these chakras one may place one's distortions within the proper center of energy and gain an overall perspective as to the nature of the lessons, and the blockages that represent these lessons, that awaits the attention of the seeker.

Is there another query, my brother?

Questioner: Do these blockages usually manifest in pain in the physical?

I am Q'uo, and am aware of your query, my brother. The blockages of energy within any energy center may manifest in a variety of ways, depending upon the amount of awareness that the seeker has gained regarding the blockages. When there is an increased awareness of a blockage and there has been work offered upon removing the blockage, the tendency of catalyst in this area is to repeat until there has been a balancing of the energy, or a removal of the blockage, as is another way of describing this process.

If there is relatively little awareness of a blockage, the blockage then has the likelihood of being given to the physical vehicle by the mental vehicle so that it may be symbolically represented as a form of what you would call disease or malady within the physical vehicle that then has the purpose of catching the attention of the mental vehicle which previously did not notice it. Pain may or may not be a part of this learning process, depending upon the needs of the seeker at a particular time. Pain is a very effective way of gaining the attention that has long been lacking.

Is there another query, my brother?

Questioner: The instreamings of energy that come in from, what we may say, is the sky or the heavens and through the crown chakra, is that intelligent energy, and is its function to raise the consciousness to a higher state of unity and nourishing the body? In other words, what is the function of these instreamings of energy and what would you call it?

I am Q'uo, and am aware of your query, my brother. The intelligent energy of which we have been speaking is also known as that called prana, is also known as love/light, for it is the enabler—that which has created all that is and that which gives life to all the creation. It is the Creator in Its active mode, and enters each third-density physical vehicle through the feet and the base or root chakra, and attempts to move upward through the system of chakras to its mating point with the indwelling intelligent infinity, or whole Creator, which resides within.

Thus, you may see the intelligent energy as a feminine aspect of the one Creator seeking Its mating point with the masculine aspect of the one Creator that is indwelling within each entity as the intelligent infinity that waits in the brow and crown chakras.

The point of meeting or mating of these two energies is determined by the level of awareness of the entity that seeks the one Creator, and the success, shall we say, that the seeker has experienced in learning those lessons or removing those blockages in balancing those distortions that it has placed, itself, within each center of energy before the incarnation began in order that there might be experience gained from the discovering, the balancing and the harmonizing of each center of energy.

Is there another query, my brother?

Questioner: Not at this time. Thank you.

I am Q'uo, and again we thank you, my brother. We feel that there is energy remaining for a final query. Is there a final query at this time?

(Pause)

I am Q'uo, and as the only remaining query is one for food from the second-density creature *(the cat meowed)*, we shall with great gratitude thank each entity present for inviting us to join your circle of seeking this afternoon. We are overjoyed at this opportunity, and cannot express our gratitude to you in terms that are sufficient. We have no beingness within your experience without your call and without your sincere queries, and we are blessed, indeed, this afternoon with your presence and your queries.

We shall take our leave at this time of this instrument and this group, leaving each, as always, in the love and in the light of the one infinite Creator. We are known to you as those of Q'uo. Adonai, my friends. Adonai. ✺

L/L Research

L/L Research is a subsidiary of Rock Creek Research & Development Laboratories, Inc.

P.O. Box 5195
Louisville, KY 40255-0195

www.llresearch.org

Rock Creek is a non-profit corporation dedicated to discovering and sharing information which may aid in the spiritual evolution of humankind.

ABOUT THE CONTENTS OF THIS TRANSCRIPT: This telepathic channeling has been taken from transcriptions of the weekly study and meditation meetings of the Rock Creek Research & Development Laboratories and L/L Research. It is offered in the hope that it may be useful to you. As the Confederation entities always make a point of saying, please use your discrimination and judgment in assessing this material. If something rings true to you, fine. If something does not resonate, please leave it behind, for neither we nor those of the Confederation would wish to be a stumbling block for any.

CAVEAT: This transcript is being published by L/L Research in a not yet final form. It has, however, been edited and any obvious errors have been corrected. When it is in a final form, this caveat will be removed.

© 2009 L/L Research

Sunday Meditation
May 26, 1991

Group question: The question today has to do with how one can use the heart chakra, the opening of the heart chakra, as a springboard to the acceptance of self that is a process usually found or engaged in the indigo-ray center. How can one, by learning more compassion and understanding, begin to accept the self in a way in which the self has previously not been accepted?

(Carla channeling)

I am Hatonn. Greetings to each of you in the love and light of the infinite Creator. We are extremely pleased to be able to be called to this group today to be able to share our opinions with you, and at the same time to learn so much from each of you as you receive our opinions and work with them in that way of choices which is the purpose of your density. The drama of your work and the choices at this time is quite apparent to us, as the vibration in which we work has far less drama and far more precise work in refining those dramatic choices which face each of you. We would like to thank this instrument for allowing the one known as Hannibal to rest in this group during this experience. It was quite suitable that this instrument announced this entity which otherwise would be unknown. This is an entity which does not speak and does not teach but has it's own place in the Confederation, and we are pleased to find this group open to these who come in the name of the Christ.

You wish us to speak about the opportunities offered to the seeker by the open heart with regard to developing an inner strength of consciousness which is equal to the task you set before yourselves. Perhaps our best approach to this question is to discuss the way of the unopened heart, for it is that way which most among your peoples have used and continue to use in your density, in order to do work in consciousness.

We must pause while this instrument gets a drink of water.

(Pause)

I am Hatonn, and I am again with this instrument greeting you in love and light. In speaking of the subject, we wish you to be aware that we are using the system of the energy centers, the root energy center of survival, the orange ray of dealing with the self and dealing with individuals other than the self, the yellow ray of social or group dealings, the green ray of the heart, the blue ray of communication, the indigo ray of inner work, or work in consciousness, and the violet ray which is, shall we say, the readout of the balance of all those dynamics that are in an integrated individual entity within the life experience.

In the case of most seekers and the case of most entities whatsoever upon the planet, whom you may not call seekers, and who may not call themselves seekers, but who do indeed seek to make more skillful choices, the heart is not allowed to open, because there is judgment of the self. Consequently, no matter how extremely good the intention and how determined the attitude, there is the entire life which is filled with the process of failing, and holding that in the heart. It is thought by these who do this that they are quite correct in assessing their faults as well as their virtues. Perhaps it would be expressed that it is the feeling that it is not humble to ignore one's failures, although each entity identifies a slightly different field as that of failure. Almost without exception those upon your plane judge themselves, and this judgment is remembered in the heart.

One of your poets has called the heart "a rag and bone shop." This is precisely the nature of the unopened heart. It is far less common to see people hating others or disliking them than to find the self holding in the heart judgment against the self. Consequently, the learning over a period of most of an incarnation is the repeated experience of failing in a way important to an entity, until finally the mind becomes weary of thinking, puzzling, musing and analyzing in relation to the various failures. This process is excellent. It is safe to say that in most if not in all incarnations which entities have chosen upon this planet which you enjoy, there will be life enough, which you would call time enough, for you to work as a seeker through the unopened heart and by the end of the incarnation to be able to forgive the self rationally and to allow compassion to flow to the self.

The difficulty in doing this remains not just equally in these who follow an orthodox religious practice. It is even more marked among those with a specifically orthodox religious practice. Even though these practices teach that the Creator forgives and redeems, there is also the fear of judgment. There is the sense that there will be an unfair test which the seeker will not be able to pass because he has failed, and that imagined voice of the Creator becomes the voice of the self, judging and condemning without mercy. That is the way of justice among your peoples.

It is not the way of balance or truth. Now, you may see each in your own life patterns that you do indeed have enough time to experience failing to the point where you shall become tired of judging, of thinking, of reasoning about the imperfect self. You may see it in your older entities who become mellow and tolerant and charitable, for they have seen that not only they, but all seem to themselves to be extraordinarily imperfect and much in need of fixing. Were you to be able to live the lifetime your physical vehicle was originally created for, this process would be nearly fail-safe. Indeed, you leave your incarnations while the spiritual search which you have begun within this incarnation is only just underway.

Yet, still you may harvest in this manner an increase in compassion, as you become old enough and experience enough to see that there is nothing unusual or fatal about failure, and that all failures eventually become part of a healing. We say all this to preface speaking about the open heart and work in consciousness, or indigo-ray work. As each in this group is already aware, the process of opening the heart is a process of letting go of those things in the lower chakras which are clouding, blocking or overstimulating those centers. Therefore we will not go into this in detail, but simply say that keeping the heart open is simply a matter of noticing and paying respect and attention to these times in which a blockage, an overstimulation or a distortion is noticed in a particular area of life corresponding to a particular energy center.

If there is a failure of direct communication, for instance, between yourself and another entity, opening the heart involves not only speaking with that person to the full extent of one's capacity to communicate, but also forgiving the other self, yourself and the situation which arose betwixt the two which did not partake of the open heart. The blockages of each lower chakra are fairly easy to pinpoint, since as the energy is blocked there is also a feeling tone within one, an uneasiness, which speaks as loudly as any words, and certainly far better than any rationalization of behavior or thinking.

The work of opening the heart is the work of letting go, of surrendering, of realizing the true importance of the details of any blockage, that is to say, of realizing that what is important about a situation which has caused a blockage is the forgiveness and the healing which may now be evoked by the learned skill of paying attention and respect to the incarnational experience that is going on.

When one first attempts to open the heart one may feel that it is impossible to forgive the self enough times to keep that heart open. That is not the heart speaking, that is still the mind. And the mind complex suffers from the either/or of your illusion. There is no "either/or" in an open heart. The open heart is "an/and," an "a/a" unity. To the open heart all things deserve compassion, all things deserve food, physical and spiritual, all things deserve love. And to refrain from opening the heart to the self is not something that occurs to the heart's wisdom. However it makes no sense, it is important to realize that the way of the open heart may begin in clearing the way to the open heart, but it ends in accepting that the open heart is all-compassionate, all-loving, all-giving. There are no second thoughts to an open heart. There are no true thoughts in the open heart, but only the endless and impersonal compassion, but one who stands not on sense, not on things known, but on the thin and unpredictable air of the abyss of the unknown.

As we said, most among your people attempt to preserve a balance in that abyss of the unknown, *(inaudible)* attempt to think their way through this blockage. This is slow work but it is a perfectly good path. The way of the open heart is simply a shortcut, a more direct route to the ability to do work in consciousness.

How is the heart kept open in such a way that the experience of the open heart will be the steady state? We would, in looking at this aspect of this question, remind each again that the offering of praise to the Creator, and the offering of thanksgiving for blessings received, constitute a continual touching into divinity, a constant song heard by all that there is. The steady state of open heart is a state in which each flower, each blade of grass, each thing that is beautiful that is seen says to you, not only, "This is pretty, this is lovely, this is beautiful," but also "I praise the Creator for this beauty." It is a way of claiming that mystery which is the Creator, a way of relating to the Creator which is unseen, invisible, unheard, unknown, for we are aware that the Creator is not obvious to all, nor is His will seen to be very beneficent in many cases. Yet, if there is the faith to continue to praise the Creator and to bless the Creator when your experience blesses you, the relationship with that which is holy becomes more and more real by habit and replication of sincere praise and thanksgiving.

Now let us look at the advantage of working with an open heart when doing work in consciousness. In the previous way of working, energy is constricted in the heart and the work is slow and hard, for not only is the heart short of power, but it further reduces the power which moves into the communication energy which an entity needs to speak with itself, just as much as it needs it to speak with others. Often, if the green ray is constricted the blue ray would also be constricted, and each entity must judge for itself whether or not it has things said in the heart that have not been said to those who should hear them, so by the time the energy is received by the indigo ray, it is not only much reduced, but it is hampered by a lack of skill and energy in communication with itself.

Communication moves higher and higher into the surface mind, becomes bogged down in speculations, rationalizations and considerations of details that do more to obscure than to illumine a particular thing about the self that one is doing inner work upon. Contrariwise, if the heart chakra be open, then it is likely that there will be more honest communication, because absolute love is something which fear cannot touch or bias. So that the fear that entities have in communicating, either with themselves or with others, is reduced to the extent that the heart is truly opened.

The truly opened heart often appears childlike because it is blindingly honest, speaking that which it thinks without judgment in an attempt to understand the self as well as other selves. In this configuration, the communication is at its most effective, given that there are those which can accept and communicate in return while hearing those blunt truths that may not be as pleasant as the euphemisms, rationalizations and clichés that surround most timid and tentative communication.

An entity with an open heart is likely to speak the truth in a desire to express the compassion of one who does not care whether or not this speaking will gain any advantage, but cares only to offer the entity with which the difficulty is experienced the chance for the healing that is possible only through sincere honesty and fearless communication. The open heart is the ultimate optimist. That is the wisdom of the heart. The heart does not lose hope, even if the end is not in sight and not known. The open heart gives every entity in every situation the benefit of all possible ways of gazing in compassion at that entity, be it the self or the other self. The open heart is not a compromiser, for it does not try to get anything for itself. It is ready to move into adaptation, it is ready to change if that seems wise. It is ready for anything, and since anything often happens, it is the skillful heart that is the open heart.

When the heart is open, it is well first for the seeker to work upon communication. This is the primary and strong means by which your people may offer the most love, the most inspiration, the most clarity. Those who communicate well, those who communicate in love and without fear may find themselves often told that they are wrong in some way, but this will in no way disturb one with an open heart, for the compassion of the open heart is as much for the other self as it is for the self, and there is no fear that one is right, or not right, or definitely wrong, for whether one is right, or not right, or definitely wrong, the heart has compassion and all is well.

As one becomes able to communicate honestly and skillfully it becomes less important to communicate skillfully because it has become natural. There is no fear of reprisal, for the reprisal is coming from an entity that is loved with compassion of the open heart. Consequently, there are no entities to be feared; there are no failures to be feared. Part of the blue-ray opening is the development of a sense of humor, so one finds ways to say things in a light way, in a gentle way, in a way which shows a spaciousness of prospect, and for the purpose of this discussion, most importantly in ways in which the entity is enabled in its inner work, for if full living light is able to move into the indigo chakra, that chakra will have the maximum opportunity to do work in consciousness. The open heart regards the personality. It enables the blue-ray chakra to communicate from the level of the heart, that is the place of wisdom, to the self that is attempting to effect changes in consciousness by faith and will.

When the tongue of judgment is quieted, the tongue of joy and peace is loosened, and one may speak to the self while working on the personality, attempting to understand it and see the balances that are desired. In words of comfort and support from the self to the self, the open heart creates the opportunity for the entity to fall in love with itself, to love it dearly, not simply as a perfect expression of the perfect Creator. That is relatively irrelevant to the experiences of choices made. It falls in love with itself with all self-perceived imperfections thriving gloriously. It sees the self in all its rambunctious childishness, and nods happily, saying, "Yes, that is humanness, I recognize it and I embrace it."

The heart is no longer, then, the "rag and bone shop," the place where sad memories are wrapped in tissues only to be opened again, that the scent of failure may be relished. The open heart has itself a yard sale, and sells off all of its rags and bones to the universe, to the Mother that is your Earth, to the deep healing essence of your planetary caretaker, the Earth itself. It is often well when one is attempting to achieve the open heart to take all the judgments and name them, and take a stone for each one and name the stone and name the judgment, and bury these stones and the judgments that they carry in the breast of the Mother, the earth of your planet. And then hold the hands on high, and say, "Mother, take this for I know not how to heal it, and I know you do."

Let these failures become impersonal, let compassion roll in, experimentally, put aside your disbelief in your own lowliness for a little while each day and feel the love rolling in. Feel the freedom, the space, the joy of simply suspending your disbelief in your own failures and imperfections. As you offer praise and thanksgiving, as you communicate, often in difficult ways at first, to open up that great primary communication chakra, the inner work begins to do itself, for, dear entities, you are entities of habit, the habits you begin eventually become automatic.

If you have the habit of praising each beauty that you see, there is no effort to continuing to praise those things which you see. If you have the habit of gazing at a challenge which you might also call a difficulty or a trouble with an eye to the most positive action or thought which is an available choice, then when difficulty overtakes you unawares, that habit will move as instinct or muscles do in reflex, and some of your work will be done before your mind can make sense.

The eventual priority of compassion over intellectual acceptance is a key process, for many choices are made instinctively. When you open the heart, when you clear the communication energies and when you can rest in the work in consciousness which simply requires one to gaze without judgment at the self, you have achieved a configuration which will greatly accelerate both your process of spiritual evolution, and your effectiveness as a being of light and an agent of the Creator to those whose lives you touch.

Most of what entities see of the Creator is seen in your faces and in your outstretched hands and in the compassion with which you listen and communicate with entities about those things which trouble them. The simple listening with an open heart is in …

(Side one of tape ends.)

(Carla channeling)

I am Hatonn. You act, then, as the Creator, not as your imperfect self, for as you forgive completely the imperfection of your self and toss those considerations aside in order to have more time for praise and thanksgiving, so you cleanse yourself of the need to deal intellectually with these difficulties of others which do not make sense but which are causing difficulty, whereas you listen and allow the love to flow through you to the other person in an accepting and loving way. The work is being done through you. It does not tire or weary you. And this is true whether the work is upon the behalf of another or upon the behalf of the self.

We realize that we have spoken overlong. We are sorry. This instrument seems unaware of time, and we usually depend on the instrument to let us know when the time is sufficient. However, it does now tell us that it is time for us to leave. There is more upon this topic, however, we are satisfied that we have done a good deal of what those of the density of love and compassion may do in regards to this question, which is, in many ways, a question answerable only by those of fourth density, yet in other ways, far better answerable by those of fifth density, for there is a balance in true love which is achieved when compassion is balanced with wisdom. However, both portions—that is, love and compassion and wisdom and compassion—need to be addressed separately, and that is why we were called to your group.

We very much enjoy being here with you. We thank this instrument both for accepting one who comes in good faith, and for being fastidious about the challenging process. We would close by saying that because of the work each of you does in consciousness, each of you is far more prone to the influence of psychic reading or enhanced registering of any negative thought or emotion than those who are moving more slowly along the path of evolution.

Remember always to respect what this instrument calls loyal opposition, and when one is greeted in some way, we ask each to remember to take time to dwell in love, to take the hand of the one who comes in psychic greeting to create fear, or dislike or despair, take that tortured entity's hand and sit with it in love, and when it has received all the love that it can—and that is not overmuch—it will have to depart. But meanwhile there is a service in acknowledging the presence of what is called evil, and acknowledging the agents of that path with respect and love and compassion. You cannot get rid of negative entities by loving them so that you can be rid of them. You must love them truly and have compassion upon their pain and their misunderstanding. Realize that these entities are taking the long and slow road, and that they must pass through much more than you who are on the positive path.

Never be afraid. These entities may seem large and bullying as they enter your thoughts and your dreams, but, my friends, they are sad souls and fully worthy of compassion. Can you cleanse the lepers sores, can you nurse the afflicted of your generations' leprosy which is AIDS? Can you gaze upon a dying child and gently sweep the flies from the sickened and closing eyes? There is passive evil, and there is the Christ. When you gaze upon the rude address of negativity, think of the sick child and reach out your hand in compassion and take cool water, and comfort that negativity with compassion and great feeling of brotherhood. You are that negativity just as you are positive, and to heal negativity is to take it into the open heart and love it. All that is not love will fall away.

In terms of negative greetings, the entity will indeed run away quickly, for this type of love is as fire to them, painful and deadly. So, my friend, stop making sense; allow the heart to open to the self. And when each impropriety occurs, judged by the self, take it not into the mind but into the heart first, that the wound may be healed quickly and the scar may be small. Only after compassion is achieved is it at all sensible or effective for the seeker to analyze the imperfection. Let your heart speak first.

As always, we remind each that we come as brothers and sisters, not to preach but to share our opinions with you, for we are seekers on your same path, and though we may have more experience, we have no more authority than any other seeker. We ask you to discriminate among those things which we have said, choosing those truths which are yours, and neglecting the rest. We are humbly grateful for allowing us to share our opinions. We would close through another instrument. We are those of Hatonn, and we transfer now.

(Jim channeling)

I am Hatonn, and greet each again in love and light through this instrument. We would ask if we could address any queries at this time which would add to your understanding. Is there a query upon any mind that we may speak to at this time?

Questioner: Is Hannibal the traveler a single entity, such as the one we have *(inaudible)*?

I am Hatonn. The entity Hannibal which greeted this group at the beginning of your session, is indeed an individualized single entity which has found its way to your group because of the nature of your seeking. The identity of the entity is not one which is known in your history but is an identity which has found its full flowering in the concept of compassion, and moves to those areas where compassion is helpful in healing wounds which have long been untended, shall we say, by the conscious mind of those suffering the wounds.

Is there a further query?

Questioner: Yes. Does this entity wish to be of service by being with those who are attempting to *(inaudible)*?

I am Hatonn. The one known as Hannibal is desirous of sharing the compassion that it possesses and sharing the compassion that this group possesses, much the same way that the traveler shares company with those that it finds in faraway places around the friendly campfire.

Is there a further query, my sister?

Questioner: No. I would just like to thank Hannibal for *(inaudible)*.

I am Hatonn. And this entity is grateful for this opportunity and accepts your good wishes with joy, and returns them as well. Is there another query?

(Pause)

I am Hatonn. We again thank each for the great opportunity that you have afforded us by seeking information which is within our provenance. We are always glad to speak to this group, for we have long cherished this group. We are with each upon request to aid in the deepening of your meditations. We shall take our leave of this group at this time. I am Hatonn. We leave you in the love and in the light of the one infinite Creator. Adonai, my friends. ✸

L/L Research

Sunday Meditation
June 2, 1991

Group question: The question this afternoon has to do with the concept of "Not my will but Thy will be done." When a seeker wishes to know what the will of the Creator is for him or her, how does a seeker prepare for receiving that information? How do you know when you are doing the will of the Creator? How do you meditate upon that concept? How do you get from "Not my will but Thy will" to actually discovering what the will of the Creator is?

(Carla channeling)

I am Q'uo. I greet you in the love and in the light of the one infinite Creator. We are most pleased to be called to you. We are strictured by the circumstances of this particular session of working to allow the instrument to more deeply rest in what you would call sleep, so that we may speak upon the question of how to recognize the will of the One Creator when wrapped about with the physical vehicle. Were we to have worked with this instrument in the waking state, we would have been unable to express our humble thoughts without significant distortion.

The question of finding the Creator's will is in a way self-defeating, and for most who wish to follow that will the skill lies in that which this instrument has always done, that is, to surrender the personal will, and then express the gift of faith, love and unconditional support when and in such manner as the opportunity appears to the lucid inner eye. To ask what the will of the Father may be is in its own way predisposed to looking at the creation as a place where the Creator's will is manifest, largely or wholly in physically observable ways—the speaking, the manifestation of right action.

Therefore, when a seeker wishes information from the infinite subjective consciousness that is the Creator, many times the seeker will receive directions which it cannot process, for its biases are those which see inaction as slacking of one's desire to serve. This is due to a lack of ability to gauge in an accurate manner, or to skillfully value, those messages in which the only instruction from the Father is to abide.

In the state in which this particular instrument exists in the physical vehicle at this nexus, for instance, the will of the Creator has been fulfilled, this instrument having called again and again upon the deep reservoir of its spiritual will. It, like many doughty and powerful spiritual warriors upon your plane, is using more than the strictly safe amount of vital energies than it would be wise to use. It, as many such, is biased towards the sacrifice of the incarnated physical complex in order to use its gifts to the fullest. As in many cases, the instrument is less interested in the continuation of the physical vehicle than in the amount of service it may offer. This is a quantifying of spiritual stewardship. Spiritual stewardship is more lucidly approached by regarding the quality of that of its gifts which it can offer. This is to say, that the work ethic of your peoples is misaligned to respect things that can be seen and counted, at the expense of those infinite qualities of consciousness which cannot be seen or counted.

There is a line beyond which we choose not to venture in this particular offering of opinion. Already we have moved well over the line of free will in attempting to address this query. We have removed ourselves from this unacceptable invasion by encouraging this instrument to sleep. Thusly, were we able to speak at all—for although it is ever service to share our opinions—nevertheless, the strong will of this instrument could not hear the bell of rest and compline which its physical vehicle sounds within, whether it were mentioned or not. The spirit of love speaks as the instantaneous, emotional, attention-getting fire. That instantaneous light offered itself to the instrument as the rather precise readout of available physical energy. This reading was rejected by the instrument, serving as a perfect example of the situation in which the spirit speaks, but the message is rejected because of bias and the desire to use up all incarnational energy because of love of the One Creator.

This is more common than it would seem to the observatory powers of an observer of your environment who sees most entities in somewhat profound degrees of unawareness of the Creator, Its love, their nature, or their opportunities to worship in service to others and to the Creator. Most who discover the love they have for the Creator, no matter what the individual experiences of the palpable presence of that Creator, choose again and again to give all possible energy and intensity to serving more and more, without judgment concerning its own state of vital energy. Consequently, in the midst of the darkness of ignorance and unawareness among your peoples, there burn the torches of many who have chosen the path of sacrifice in order to burn as brightly and accountably as possible.

We do not have a clear resource for aiding an entity in the evaluation of its level of vital energy. When the path of service is consistently sacrificial, the entity who serves becomes unable to evaluate with any precision the state of its own energy. The usual suggestion offered by service-to-others entities is to ask those familiar with the instrument to aid the instrument in the decision to work as this group does now. It may be seen that it is not the instrument, but the harmonies of the working group which are the unity, both calling for the contact most beneficial and the degree of purity and intensity of the information offered. We have no choice, if we are to honor the energy dedicated to a session, but to communicate according to our best opinion on any question asked. Therefore, we cannot say we shall not communicate, for the energy of the instrument and of the group would be wasted.

In general, this response should be considered personal material. Although there are points of information acceptable for general use, this answer is highly anomalistic, as is the actual state of dedication which this group shows, is, although blind and suffering in darkness, still a towering faith and will. We chose to deepen the instrument's link with the consciousness of sleep and address the level of dedication which we here find.

The general run of seekers contains little enough acceptance of servanthood that the usual encouragement is towards surrender. The will of the Father—if we may call a co-created will of self and the All Self that—is instantly manifest, not when the query is asked, but when the time and place of service is matured. The greatest portion of the Creator's will is so interpenetrated by that which is unattached to space or time that it is in the present moment that the opportunity for service arises and is placed upon the heart of the Hierophant.

We ask such entities as you who together seek and who seek in harmony, to aid each other in encouragement of all kinds, including the encouragement of discretion. We may say that in the case of the questioner, there is no judgment, but there is the desire to give all. Each of you has this desire, but with the questioner it is also a lack of ability to estimate a state of energy, as there has been the stress of pain for a substantial portion of your time. Therefore, if the questioner is conscious, it estimates its energy as satisfactory. We do not criticize this degree of purity in any, but suggest that those with competent discernment aid the entity which wishes to bankrupt its vital reservoir.

We may conclude this query in considering that which we have described as fire. It does not come to one and not to another. It is explicit in the unfolding of circumstance. If an entity wishes to hear the voice of the Creator, to hear aloud the appropriate service described, it must wait for the rhythms of destiny to unfold in their spontaneous way. Nothing, including a surety of service, is intended for those within your plane of existence to hear and mark. Rather, the opportunity is instantaneous, and it is the entity who has surrendered all private desires to respond to the situation, not questioning whether it be one's service, but moving from a position of spiritual abundance and rest to trust in the spontaneous opportunity for service at the level of instinct. The appropriate meditation, then, upon the will of the one infinite Creator, is the trustful relaxation into apparent ignorance.

Those who feel that they have the experience of the presence of the one Creator, and those who have the experience of lack of perceptible union with the infinite One, appear to be in different situations as regards the choosing of how to manifest the love and the light of the Creator. However, the openness of both kinds of entities to being of service are identical. Some have the experience of aloneness, of loving the Creator but feeling isolated; others feel the consolation of the spirit always. These apparent differences are an artifact of the incarnational lessons to be learned. There is no true distinction between those who love the Creator. As the strength of faith and will is, so is the entity's true association with that great Self of which any atom of consciousness [is a part]. Each of you is the same, though your experiences vary. The dedication which is not apparent moves as the true measure of service.

Rest in knowing that many who are distressed in the search for the infinite One are beyond the illusions of the consciousness mind quite directly where they wish they were, that is, in communion with the loved infinite original Thought. Likewise, many of those who more vociferously state the closeness of the self and the Infinite are lacking true unity with any Creator except ambition and the creatures of ambition.

We find this instrument to be moving into awareness of muscle spasms, and would at this time cease to communicate, as the level needed for this session of working of sleep is soon to be finished. We again ask that this be considered personal material. We thank this group for its fidelity, and name you our friends.

We leave you in the love and in the light of the one infinite Creator. Go forth, therefore, rejoicing in the power and in the peace of the one infinite Creator. We are those of Q'uo. Adonai. We leave you in love and in light. ☙

L/L Research

L/L Research is a subsidiary of Rock Creek Research & Development Laboratories, Inc.

P.O. Box 5195
Louisville, KY 40255-0195

www.llresearch.org

Rock Creek is a non-profit corporation dedicated to discovering and sharing information which may aid in the spiritual evolution of humankind.

ABOUT THE CONTENTS OF THIS TRANSCRIPT: This telepathic channeling has been taken from transcriptions of the weekly study and meditation meetings of the Rock Creek Research & Development Laboratories and L/L Research. It is offered in the hope that it may be useful to you. As the Confederation entities always make a point of saying, please use your discrimination and judgment in assessing this material. If something rings true to you, fine. If something does not resonate, please leave it behind, for neither we nor those of the Confederation would wish to be a stumbling block for any.

CAVEAT: This transcript is being published by L/L Research in a not yet final form. It has, however, been edited and any obvious errors have been corrected. When it is in a final form, this caveat will be removed.

© 2009 L/L Research

Sunday Meditation
June 30, 1991

Group question: The question today has to do with the concept of how we deal with our emotions such as fear and anger, jealousy, feeling unworthy, feeling inept, any negative feeling that we have that has been with us for quite awhile and we've been working with. We're wondering if, according to what Q'uo and Aaron had to say to us, that the most appropriate way of dealing with these negative emotions is to be able to accept the self and the emotion that we have when we have them so that there is no longer any feeding into the emotion by holding on to it longer, hoping that eventually, by being able to accept ourselves and the emotions when we have them, that there will be a falling away of these negative emotions. Is this the most skillful or appropriate way of dealing with negative emotions so that we are able to be more harmonious and more productive and feel more whole and complete in our small selves in this illusion?

(K channeling)

I am of the principle of Q'uo. Greetings, blessings, love and peace to each of you in the love and in the light of the one infinite Creator. We are most pleased to be speaking with your selves this sultry, beautiful, greening day which you allow us to enjoy as we temporarily use the senses of your own physical capabilities. Yet there is no beauty outside of each of you that can even be compared to the beauty that lies within each questing soul. As each gazes at the challenges of the present moment it is well to lift that gaze as if one were upon horseback, lifting up to get a different perspective, a bit of an overview, and the means of locomotion through the processes of loss, change and transformation.

You ask us about the living in an apparently imperfect, entirely flawed crystallized [state of] being without yourself, becoming vulgar, splintered and uncrystalline. Many there are among your peoples who feel that they have been broken by circumstance. The one known as K refers to these as the walking wounded.

Let us begin with this concept then. Have you personal knowledge of any entity whatsoever that is perfectly sure, with no spiritual arrogance of the meanings and the lessons to be learned from each challenge? You could not expect this skill of anyone. Cast about in your mind, in your heart, in the experiences that you have read and seen and heard and ask yourself, "Did this person live in the heaven of bliss and peace and joy which shines effulgently from the great heart of the creation, that great Sun which lies deeply within each of you?" To answer our own question, it is not to be hoped for or to be desired in a non-relative way for one who wishes to proceed along this beloved and dusty path, not with slowness nor with haste but with utter respect for the processes we know, each of us, that are taking place. For just as the fish must move at all times to breathe, so too the mind, having been fed its physical manna must then yearn for that divine touch of that heavenly food.

The attitude expressed in the question, that is, that one simply sits and accept the imperfect self in its apparent manifestation, is a good suggestion. Like many good suggestions from entities who know a great deal more that most third-density entities, it is, idealistically speaking, quite without error to say that the process of maturing is a process not of becoming better, not of becoming wiser, not of becoming more of any quality which you may judge within yourself or others but only of one thing: the patient persistence of faith.

So we describe each of us and you as being continually at the crossroads. To one who travels without imagination and without soul, streets, byways, lanes and highways are simply places for which to travel. However, to the spiritual seeker the ride is the experience not the destination. Each spiritual seeker has chosen to walk its own path with its own topography and terrain, its own blessings, challenges and seeming nuisances. Its own thanksgivings and its own pain.

To say that this is the human condition is vastly to overstate that generality. Yet it is true that if an entity is able to recognize more and more inwardly that the situation in this illusion will apparently be imperfection in memory, in the present and in the future, this creates a good start upon dealing with the pain and seeming destructive and negative characteristics of an ongoing spiritually based life. Each of you who is on this trail finds the dust beloved, finds the hard rocks and the wood splinters a cause for joy, for that person has found that which is worth the various inconveniences and seeming muddled confusion of the third-density illusion.

So firstly, my dear ones, each place yourself in this basic attitude of watching, observing and accepting everything about the self. Yet this is only a bare beginning from the first step outward into the abyss of mystery. There is often sometimes dramatically a shift in perception. To some entities this shift is extremely painful, for there is rigidity in character, and there are solidified opinions from feelings in the taking upon oneself of all the transient personality as if it were the character of the self.

So you see as you attempt consciously to live with emotions which do not seem appropriate to you there is only a small amount of spiritual work in consciousness that may be done upon the level of logic, analysis and hopes for doing better. Of these things alone is the mind and brain of your beautiful analyst equipped. Consequently, the hope of achieving comfort within, peace and self-assurance is a lost cause if it is pursued by the intention of attitude alone. For attitude is, until it has become you yourself, a piece of clothing to place between the vulnerable and naked self and the world which impinges so harshly many times upon the wounded seeker. Yes, all seekers are wounded.

The need to examine mystery goes not well with an attitude of complacency, comfort and mundane peace. Even as you ask yourself why so many seem to slip through life as if they were greased lightning while you the seeker, each of you, must again and again and again find oneself stuck, stopped completely by overwhelming catalyst. Catalyst which, because the world knows it not for the most part, is catalyst unique to you in a far more precise way than some superlatives. For each of you is unique in his or her way. Each of you, though aiming for the same destination, have plotted carefully to ensure, no matter how many detours are mistakenly taken, that within this incarnational experience the seeker will have ample opportunity to learn each lesson of love.

Thusly, as we move into the second part of our thoughts we simply suggest that each of you take away the cutting board upon which you slice yourself. Place the knife, cleansed and oiled, back in its sheath, for you are not now working with the tools, the power or the values of the mundane society in which you have chosen to experience this illusion of humanhood. Gaze as we leave the conscious minds dealing with spiritual progress as one would gaze upon the last days of a summer in childhood. These days are precious, yet they cannot be stopped or controlled. There would be the school the student must go back to. The job that the entity on holiday must take up again upon return from that holiday. There is, as far as we know it, no way past the ego, or perhaps more accurately, a self perceived as self without ego.

So in our quest to gaze at the most appropriate way to aid ourselves in our seeking for an attitude not skin deep but within the very marrow of each bone, within each pore that opens to the sunlight and the rain, within each sense that tells you of beauty, destruction, peace and confusion, consequently, the seeker must gaze beyond, beneath and around the negative emotions such as anger or fear. Gaze at them unblinkingly. Gaze at them lovingly. Yet how can an entity, no matter how much meditation, study, desire and training, really have a certainty and a surety that there will more and more be the feelings of wholeness and harmony of which you have spoken?

In this entity's mind there is a quote from a poet named Yeats: "It just is that there is"—an almost bottomless and infinite self which each seeker is attempting carefully to build the roads that may take the feet to that place of rest amongst the discomforts, sorrows and losses of a life lived in faith.

Again and again the Creator calls you. Again and again you call for the Creator. And again and again you are distracted by the pains of living intensely. Because each is already a poem, a chosen path within this circle, we may be general and say that this is itself sufficient preparation for further work in consciousness.

The distinctions we are making are subtle and we ask for your patience. Indeed it is true that it is extremely helpful and informative to each seeker that he look carefully, humorously and undauntedly at each apparent lapse in faith, loss of hope, or disappointment within the life experience, be it with relationships with the society or as is most common, with the self. Your conscious mind simply cannot tell your subconscious mind that you are worthwhile and of the mistakes that you make are as much a virtue as the apparently unmistaken ways of acting which are part of your being and ours.

There is a life independent of the conscious mind, that part of the self that is a hologram of all of infinity. That self is as a sun and the experience of living the imperfect and wounded life is the experience, if we may use one of your myths, of Icarus flying too close to the sun. The feathers drop off, the structure melts, and the sun has been not benevolent but unwittingly destructive.

After one has properly devalued the information given by the analytical and curious mind of your physical vehicle, you may then place that attitude which governs behavior just where it should be: upon the behavior shelf to be brought out and used carefully and sincerely in gazing at various concepts which endear themselves to each of you. Then in order to grasp the means of coming to forgiveness of the self must needs be seen to be so far below the [level] of consciousness that there are no mental or emotional stairs which one may use to move from the house of illusion to the house of the infinite Creator.

Between this great central Sun and the experience of mundane living lies a great river of blessing, healing and pain. The structure of the subconscious mind, as you would call this portion of your field of consciousness, needs to be evoked layer by layer, layers as thin as the skin of an onion and sometimes layers that have a markedly saddening effect upon the seeker who is living through the inevitable changes and feelings of perceived failure which constitute the conscious perception of catalyst.

What are these intermediate subconscious levels? We chose to borrow the words of the one known as Aaron. There is much that occurs before a consciously generated mental formation may occur. The one known as Aaron simplifies this in a way which we feel is helpful so let us look at this process. Become aware now of your attitude posture, that is your true physical, mental and emotional states. Gaze at them. This is your unique beingness at this time, at this very moment. If this is who you are and if you are of the Father that is love, then you as a seeker know in some deep way that the apparent challenges of the incarnation are much like the scenery of the play for which you are the star.

As an actor expresses its lines again and again in front of your theater audiences the actor begins to become more and more aware of the true nature of that character or person which the actor wishes to portray. So that after repeating the same two hours or three of lines said, movements made, and emotions expressed, the wholeness of this mentally and emotionally crafted persona becomes more and more nearly complete. Cast yourself therefore as an actor. You do not need to change the play, to alter the script. You need simply to be as faithful to the character you perceive as yourself as possible. This acceptance of the self, although it may begin intellectually, begins to open the doors into that portion of the subconscious mind that may aid you in dealing in a joyful and peaceful manner with the many things which within your illusion seem to be challenging, difficult or even despairing.

Sit now and feel your body, your head, your gently resting eyes, your lassitude as you wait alertly but patiently for the hope of some germ of truth that we may offer to you that may be of help. This is your play. We have a far subordinate position in this play. It is yours. Each occasion upon which the self sees itself as angry or in fear, one—we correct this instrument—each then moves back into the reading of the script so far, into the nuances that have been found so far within the message of the play in between the lines and the emotions generated by the drama which is neatly tied up in a play in five acts or less.

Upon your own stage it is far better to see that the play will run indefinitely and that you will have every chance every day to create an openness and spaciousness of spirit and glee that allows the Creator to play in the summer sunlight of your open mind and heart.

Let us move back to perception. Again we thank the one known as Aaron for creating a simple way to express ourselves in terms of dealing with disappointments. Imagine that you are seated in the midst of a busy public place, perhaps awaiting one of your modes of transportation in its scheduled departure. You have brought with you something that is absorbing and as you sit amongst the hubbub and turmoil of the many, many unsettled entities and the many, many emotions, these do not confine you. In you there is no turmoil, no hubbub. You have the correct time. You have your ticket. You are ready to climb aboard for your journey. And so you read your book or do something else which is equally absorbing and the hubbub and turmoil is not there.

Were you to be regressed, as you call it, by hypnotism to that scene, you would be able, in a deep enough state of trance, to remember precisely all that has occurred while you were reading the book. However, as far as the conscious mind is concerned, there has been no stimulus but the book. So the first flaw in hoping that by taking thought one may become more skillful, one may see that there is no hope of beginning from the outside in, in a truly objective way.

Now let us say that the book has been absorbed and you have the consciousness of reading that book. Do you yet have an attitude? We suggest to you that you do not yet have an attitude. For you have been impressed with certain thoughts and certain feelings, certain resonances and rhythms which are at one level or as many as you wish to embrace. But firstly, there is the choosing amongst all sense impressions of that which will come at highest priority into the consciousness of your heart and soul. The perception itself is a narrowing of the infinite Creation.

(Side one of tape ends.)

(K channeling)

With the experience of polarization what opinions and biases have each brought to the naked perception already clothed somewhat? It can only add further clothing, further coverings, further defenses, and further distortions. For each entity is intended to be biased. These biases, though they cause a great amount of pain, are spiritually desirable. Not that one would seek out difficulties or challenges, but that in a challenging situation one may see clearly that one's own previous biases, one's own prioritizing of consciousness and one's own sense impressions do a tremendous amount of distorting to what each would hope to be a life lived in full consciousness of love.

The last thing which occurs in this process as it moves up through the subconscious mind is the formation within the mind of a response to this heavily flawed perception. At that point you are again dealing with the conscious mental formations familiar in the mundane world. However, if you have been careful to see the processes which precede actual mental impressions you may gauge them lightly without rancor or judgment. Not because you wish to advance, not because it is wise but because it is a kind of habit, a way of stepping just a bit back, of getting just a bit of height. And seeing not only that mental formation that feels so painful but seeing also with utmost compassion, the weary, weary walker who must heave himself up in the saddle from time to time and say to itself, "I am grateful for this horse and grateful for this body and grateful for these pains and joys and I wish to look at each of them as a good part of myself."

We have focused today on the details of perception, for your query has to do with the process of perception. Entities realize, for the most part, that they cannot anticipate or understand other entities' every action and word. However, in terms of you within this physical incarnation, you are in the position of attempting to understand and accept an entity that is noticeably distanced from your true self. This standpoint or point of view is not helpful in terms of its being used as a tool to create the desisting and the ceasing of painful emotions so that one may somehow come out upon the pleasant valley of enlightenment. Can you see now what folly it is to expect or even consider the possibility of, by taking any thought whatsoever, releasing the self from the fears and the anger with which it has fueled its very seeking?

Thus we may say yet consciously observe the anger, the temper, the emotional dyspepsia. But at the same time open the door of the threshold of the deep mind by whatever means creates in you the sense of approaching and going through a door that is holy, a door wherein you are protected, bathed in light. And whether you can feel it or not, be healed little by little of each and every perceived pain. Keep that door open. De-emphasize to the extent appropriate for the individual personality all consciously received data and move beyond words, beyond judgment, and beyond the self into the point of view that sees all things as acceptable and not only acceptable but glorious. Each of you is an epic. Each within third density chooses some form of drama. Some are stuck with charades for they know not how to be but only to behave.

And so some move through the incarnation creating behaviors, speeches and attitudes designed to manipulate the environment for comfort and security. This is not your path. In your path you have truly broken yourself and offered that sacrifice of heart and soul and mind to the one infinite Creator. As you rest back in that relationship know that the "I Am," "that is all that there is," is you.

Know that you are not simply a pawn moving about on some cosmic checkerboard—we correct this instrument—chessboard, this instrument is not good at games. Take the mind off of the moving pieces, the stratagems, and the ploys. Gaze at your situation more and more without judgment, indeed, embracing the seemingly difficult, negative or challenging situation. This positive action of love is as a healing balm as the true nard[2], the true salve, the true healing ointment of [Gilead]. This is not a gift you can give yourself. You can only open yourself to the opportunity.

---

[2] Nard is an ointment prepared in part from *Nardostachys Jatamansi*, an East Indian plant of the Valerian family.

Each of you, each entity within the third-density physical being, will experience a vast and constant irritation if that entity is a seeker and a sensitive one. Yet you have, day upon day, week upon week, and year upon year, a rising to the play. Each day the performance is unique; the audience sometimes cold and sometimes sympathetic; the lines felt not from the heart or felt completely from the heart. How various experience seems, my friends. Yet you are simply doing the day's work in consciousness by giving this seemingly hypocritical persona the very best work that you can do as an actor, learning the motivations, gazing at the patterns, reading between the lines of your lifetime.

Let a time fall upon you as twilight falls upon the grass at the end of a golden summer day. Let your selves be as lush meadows, welcoming and drinking in the feeling of love, loving and being loved, for in love we are without judgment.

We realize that this has been a bare beginning but this instrument is requesting that we close this session before too much longer. We are afraid this will be an ongoing difficulty with this contact, that is that this entity is in a state where it does not have an awareness of a time flow but is rather in a place of utterness which does not have the characteristics of time and space. If this is acceptable to you we shall simply continue until we hear through this instrument's ears the recording equipment stating in its unthinking way that forty-five of your minutes have passed.

Perhaps we may learn to be shorter in our seeking. But for the most part we ask your patience in allowing us to, in order to leave this instrument on its stead in its sincere work free from the necessity of attempting to keep part of the consciousness upon the level upon which time holds sway.

You stand, each of you, upon a play stage—we correct this instrument—upon a stage. What is the nature of your play? How long has this been running? Has it been a success on Broadway? Did it die in Boston? Are you on the road with it? Over the hill touring the provinces? Appearing in Saskatchewan? It is still your play and you have every reason to attempt always to move through that play so authentically that the play becomes a poem and the poem becomes a life, and the life becomes a presence of love to love. May you encourage, exhort, support and cherish each other. For you have chosen the high road. The road that is the wisest. The road that is the most seemingly barren.

May you make peace with your decision to join the confederation of all consciousness. May you find yourself, even when most weary, ready to lay down that particular load and rest. Not to a place where you may be consoled and healed and have your work finished, but so that you can get a restful kind of consciousness unrivened by the carings and strivings of mundane difficulty.

These things are among your choices in each moment. To some we would say it is well to use the intellect to attempt to spot and work with mental formations before they become toxic. But remember also that each of you is already toxic. For there is in earth not sterility but a growing living soil for both the good and the bad vine. What is your choice? Which part of that vine of self that begins in the Creator and moves only up to you as the fruit of the vine will be for you at that moment the way in which to ventilate the pain, difficulty or the darkness with the spacious light of a faithful life?

We would now close this session and would offer the communication to the one known as Jim and if that entity does not wish to work this day we are most grateful if the one known as K would wish to use more discussion time. We shall attempt at this time therefore, with many thanks to this instrument, to transfer the contact to the one known as Jim. We leave this instrument in great joy. We will transfer now. We are of the principle of Q'uo.

(Jim channeling)

I am Q'uo, and we greet each again through this instrument. We realize that your patience, your ability to rest comfortably in your positions have been tested by the length of our *(inaudible)*. We would ask if there may be any queries to which we may speak before we take leave of this group?

Questioner: *(Inaudible).*

I am Q'uo, and am aware of your query, my sister. Each, both consciously and subconsciously, already does this but the sending of such energy to the most efficacious would be done in a carefully conscious fashion where the energy does seem to be entering through the crown chakra and moving through all centers of energy for the instrument. This done as a visualization will aid the contact in that we also move through the crown chakra and activate primarily the blue-ray center. The balanced configuration of the entity seen in the visualization and seen to be receiving the energy entering through the crown and moving to all portions of its physical vehicle would be a means whereby the instrument could be aided not only in its physical comfort but the contact could be aided as it moves through the instrument.

Is there a further query, my sister?

Questioner: *(Inaudible).*

I am Q'uo, and am aware of your query, my sister. We would recommend that this energy be seen as that which is universal, is drawn from the ethers or the cosmos as you may term it, but that would be seen to be flowing from infinity into the crown chakra, moving through the physical vehicle in a downward fashion so that each center of energy was bathed in light and the energy was also seen to be exiting as it travels through the arms and legs to exit the hands and the feet. And this seen as a washing of the instrument's physical vehicle in general and, in particular, a washing and energizing of the energy centers or chakras.

Is there a further query, my sister?

Questioner: *(Inaudible).*

I am Q'uo, and we are most grateful to you as well, my sister. Not only your patience and your persistence but also your querying in this area for it is an area that is not unique to you but is shared by all seekers who travel this journey long enough to find that there is the necessity of facing the self and accepting the self with all of the characteristics that have been added to the experience for the purpose of enhancing the learning, the tempering, and the serving.

Is there a further query at this time?

Questioner: *(Inaudible).*

I am Q'uo, and am aware of your query, my sister. If you feel with urgency that this is a portion of the workings then we would recommend that you follow that feeling and undertake to create such a circumstance. However, it is our observation that if these sessions are to be offered to any entity which walks through your door, that you not undertake such efforts. For this could easily be misperceived as that activity which sets you apart from those who join you for these sessions. If it is your desire to work only as a triad of working, this would be well.

Is there a further query?

Questioner: No, thank you very much.

I am Q'uo, and we thank you as well, my sister, for offering yourself with such ample heart. For these workings we are honored and greatly overjoyed at the opportunity of speaking through this group and for the ability to utilize your instrument. We shall take our leave at this time thanking each again and leaving each in love and in light. We are those of Q'uo. Adonai, my friends. Adonai. ♣

L/L Research

L/L Research is a subsidiary of Rock Creek Research & Development Laboratories, Inc.

P.O. Box 5195
Louisville, KY 40255-0195

www.llresearch.org

Rock Creek is a non-profit corporation dedicated to discovering and sharing information which may aid in the spiritual evolution of humankind.

ABOUT THE CONTENTS OF THIS TRANSCRIPT: This telepathic channeling has been taken from transcriptions of the weekly study and meditation meetings of the Rock Creek Research & Development Laboratories and L/L Research. It is offered in the hope that it may be useful to you. As the Confederation entities always make a point of saying, please use your discrimination and judgment in assessing this material. If something rings true to you, fine. If something does not resonate, please leave it behind, for neither we nor those of the Confederation would wish to be a stumbling block for any.

CAVEAT: This transcript is being published by L/L Research in a not yet final form. It has, however, been edited and any obvious errors have been corrected. When it is in a final form, this caveat will be removed.

© 2009 L/L Research

Sunday Meditation
July 7, 1991

Group question: This is a continuation of the session from last week in which we were discussing the query of how to proceed on the path of, shall we say, perfecting the self: working to the point where we're able to accept the self and the distortion—whatever feeling one has—whether it be anger, jealousy, depression, covetousness, greediness, laziness, overachieving … We'll stop there, and proceed into the area of a certain attitude or perception that Q'uo talked about last week, where we see the world around us as a blessing, as a means by which we learn what we need to learn. How do we now proceed when we've begun to accept ourselves and the distortions that we feel? What is the next step in order that we can more easily and fully achieve the balancing of all of these distortions, so that the light moves through us in a way that allows us to radiate it to others, rather than hold it in the distorted form in one particular energy center?

(Carla channeling)

I am of the principle known to you as Q'uo. Greetings, love, light and blessings to each of you. We have gently aided this instrument's physical vehicle into a far more relaxed configuration than it was able to achieve consciously, and so we shall be somewhat measured in our speaking; however, we are pleased to be aware that this does not create any difficulty for this blessed group of seekers after the truth.

The central question of consciousness is its definition, and the central concern of those who wish to work in consciousness is to be enough aware of that definition that the quest becomes centered and focused. When we spoke last concerning the spiritual path, and moved seemingly backwards into underlying material concerning the processes of perception, our intention was to begin a dialogue in which each [seeker] may gaze at the mechanical, as well as metaphysical, means of prosecuting a plan of development as a seeker in the most lucid way possible. Consequently, we felt that we needed to stress to each seeker the enormous subtlety of the process by which each gathers the information which is then put to use in grasping where this consciousness moves, where it lives, where it is exultant and alive beneath, above and beyond all perceived limitations.

It is common for those who are seeking to assume that their role in the seeking has some intended emotional bias that would appear as noticeably metaphysical or spiritual. However, we pin you to the spot where you may gaze at the mechanical process of perception; for, if consciousness is, but is not perceived, this consciousness is infinite and intelligent, but without any form.

Each seeker senses an enormous framework of form and substance, not only about each organ and bone and muscle of your physical vehicles, but also of each tender sprout of new thought, each seemingly larger truth. It is well for serious seekers to begin squarely gazing at the impossibility of, in any final way, becoming able to control perception. If spiritual seekers or any who experience third density, put within their intelligence the estimate that intelligence will deliver correct answers, this entity has made a fundamental error. Each seeker perceives poorly. Each seeker planned to perceive poorly.

Thusly, as we begin this day, we ask that you see yourself in compassion. For every truth that you may feel you know, there are a thousand biases that have moved into the web of your energies and become solidified, in some way that only dimly reflects the actual consciousness that each seeker is. You are not shoddy materials. The improvement of the spiritual quest is not particularly dependent upon the accuracy of the perceptions noted, since all perceptions will be, to a very linear and mechanically seen extent, biased and imperfect. Thusly, as one works consciously to form an ever more authentic and true life experience, one must move into an authentic humility concerning the nature of this particular classroom which you now enjoy.

Let us rest in peace and in self-compassion, in the truth that is most nearly true; that being, that there is no intention or necessity for becoming wiser, more mature, more special, as your harvest and bounty of lessons learned is brought in. You do, indeed, have harvest each day in your experience. You do, indeed, store it and work with it. But start from this point: that you are aware that the work that you can do will be done as well as each can do it, and it will be imperfect perception.

A choice fundamental to the third-density experience is the decision to become individual in an apparent and gross fashion. When two hands meet, they do not join organically to form a being with four hands and two bodies. No individual touches another in the deepest sense; yet, all individuals are you, so that as you perceive others' paths you are then at your most skillful in ascertaining your own spiritual sensibility. The third-density entity cannot perceive, because it is imperceptible that there is only one being and that each of you is the "I AM." So you gaze at the dark mirror of yourself, and find the need to refresh the self as one sees one's self in the endless series of distorted and flawed mirrors which one may find in a carnival. You may see yourself tall or short, fat or thin, strange or lovely; but all the mirrors of the self are flawed. That flaw continues as the entity gazes at others. However, as the seeker gazes at pilgrims upon the same road, the artificial separation creates a spurious but helpful clarity, in seeing in another a far less distorted mirror. Consequently, a tool that can be used at any time to center and focus the self upon learning is to gaze at that seemingly separate self with your more impersonal viewpoint, and thusly, see yourself.

What have you said about others today? What have you thought about your companions? Whatever it may be, it was only apparently a consideration of an other self. It was, far more deeply, an examination of the self in the mirror which another self has offered you. This leads us to suggest that, although persistence and determination are absolutely fundamental to working within spiritual consciousness, there is far, far more that moves into the equations of learning. Take the self, then, off of the barb, away from the hook of one's own judgment. You did not come here to memorize lessons. You came to this arena of choice to be a choice, not simply to espouse a point of view. The espousal of a point of view is cerebral. The beingness or essence or vitality of the self is without words. It simply is.

It, of course, is a difficult task to learn anything, and doubly difficult when all the books are open but there is no illumination by which one may read the simple, generous and lovely answers from the textbook. You can only hold that Book of Truth that is your heart's wisdom in a trusting awareness, and so give up yourself to yourself by your self-compassion, that this beloved wisdom begins to soften that which is you, not that which you think or that which you feel or that which you do, but that which is. You are a verb, not a noun. You are not a thing. You are. The simplicity of this beingness eludes the mind, and refuses to obey any particular form of behavior. As the seeker moves along this self-perceived path, it acts and thinks and talks and believes that it is those activities, there being no evidence to the contrary; but, as you turn and face the inevitable distortions involved in the process of perception itself, it is easier to see that the path of the seeker is not going to fall along any planned or consciously desired outcome, unless that happens to be a natural fruit of your particular being.

We ask all seekers to remove from themselves the request to have more or less comfort, more or less perceived awareness, or more or less of any valued quality, for each of you is now infinite, and in this moment is all things.

Imagine this all-ness of you. Your consciousness is attempting to pack the baggage that you may carry along this path of seeking. Can it put in the sky, the moon, the stars, the universe, the question, the mystery? Can any suitcase of selfhood hold the burden of imperishability? No, my friends. This classroom will continue, while each is willing to put one's self to the task to offer falsehood after falsehood and trouble upon woe, in addition to all joyful things; for, the suitcase you carry is a suitcase full of your masks, but you are not in the suitcase. You simply carry about in this classroom a collection of personas, of masks, of behaviors that have seemed helpful and hopeful in past choices.

When one enters the first grade, one expects to have some difficulty learning the alphabet, the handwriting, the simple mathematics of your childhood days. It is, within the scholastic system of your peoples, recognized that as each entity moves towards the study leading to the getting of a diploma indicating a skill in study—more and more complex, difficult, challenging and interesting lessons—perhaps the graduate student cavils at the increasing difficulty at producing what seems to be excellence; yet, the graduate student does not feel betrayed because higher learning is harder than memorizing sums or the spelling of words. The incarnation, as it moves forward, sideways, in a circle or whatever model your truth tells you you're moving, will be constantly offering puzzlement, difficulties and many, many unanswered questions. The hope of one who hopes to know the truth is simply that.

Within your third-density illusion, it seems that if one becomes wise, in just such measure will one become more comfortable; yet, true learning has as its hallmark, discomfort. Look gently at the body that bears you. Feel the points of pressure as you sit. Feel the breathing, the musculature, the saliva in the mouth, the noise in the ears, all the many, myriad sensations of this particular environment. Feel the weight of the thoughts that do not go away, even in the most interesting discussion. Feel the self wishing to delimit itself, to make boundaries, to define differences, to express uniqueness. See the uneasiness that this will cause consciousness, for, insofar as each perceives itself as unique, so does it perceive itself with distortion.

We wish to give you tools that you may use in order, more nearly, to love the Love that is you—that is all other things whatsoever that, indeed, **is**. You are as a small vase, perhaps beautifully made, perhaps made with some clumsiness, but a good watertight vase. You see the vase. You are the flower. You will never see yourself in flower. You will see the vase, the tending of the vase, the watering, the cleaning, the movement towards the light …

Thus, the first tool we would offer when an entity perceives discomfort and agony, is to suggest that the entity drop all known facts about the self, that the entity allow that structure, that vase, to be just that: that which holds an ineffable, singular consciousness, and holds it in common with all the creation.

You may, without spiritually defaming yourself, be critical of the vase. You may choose in this non-physical vase of which we speak, to beautify in your own unique way that vase. You may hallow and honor the privilege of being the container of self-perceived consciousness. But to know the flower that is your consciousness is not part of your choice-making experience; for, if you knew beyond any doubt that you were the flower, why would you need the vase? Why would you ever have cut this flower away from the root of all that there is? Why, but to regard not your flower—for you are blind, "inly"—but the flower that is all other entities, that is **you**.

Look again at all you have seen this day. Do you see the vase? Do you judge the vase? Do you notice the bloom, the flower, that which is in each face that you see? This choice-making density is intended to move as quickly as the seeker wishes through the various lessons of learning to love the flower of consciousness, and to embrace consciousness …

(Side one of tape ends.)

(Carla channeling)

You are the beholder and you are beheld. When emotions run high and spiritual exhaustion is deep, you may wish that you were not this vase and you do not have to be the vase that you are. The flower is unchangeable, immutable and everlasting; and you are learning how to value that flower, not because it is you, not because it is something that you have called the Creator, not because of anything, but because that is all that there is. And in these choice-making lifetimes, you are shaping that gift to yourself that is the most beautiful receptacle for love that you may create.

Each hardship, each disappointment, each perceived difficulty is, in its own way, true. Vases crack, break, must be made again, must be scrapped and started over, must be retouched; but you are not working on love, you are working on how to honor love. Let this be your first tool when your emotional vase seems crazed and twisted and altogether out of round: know that you can throw that pot back into the wet, soft clay, take the slip cut, and re-cut and re-cut your pot anew. Line it as you will, paint it, enamel it, fire it, stud it with jewels, or be unassuming, knowing that love needs no decoration. But you are safe; these things are occurring to the vase, to the vehicle that carries the blossom of ineffable and perfect consciousness. Vases may bump together, and clang and crash and nestle in so many, many configurations. The blossom is always the blossom.

Do not fear loss, for you have only clay to lose. You are the blossom. Rest, beautiful, beautiful blossom; rest.

We are glad to continue as you wish, at a later time of working, and we are honored, as always, to be called to you for such discussion. As always, we ask that you remain within yourself, feeling the thoughts we give you, to know if they may be for you or not for you. Retain your powers of discrimination, but remember that you can only discriminate about the vessel of infinite consciousness.

We would now leave this instrument and conclude through another channel. We are those of Q'uo, and we transfer now.

(Jim channeling)

I am Q'uo, and greet each again in love and in light through this instrument. At this time, we would ask if we may aid any entity present by attempting to speak to those remaining queries that may have value to each. Is there a query at this time?

Carla: *(Difficult to hear.)* I would like to express a situation, if you could comment about … not without saying that I truly do wish to preserve free will. I have had a puzzle lately. My body doesn't seem to want to work, and it's painful. My spirit seems to be fairly heavy, and I don't know, frankly, why I'm having all of this difficulty, unless it happens to be dealing with my life. I feel that a dream that I had recently expressed for me the reality that I've experienced for about seven years, of basically becoming a person again after the death of Don Elkins; and I am very interested in knowing any way in which I can use the realization that I did, indeed, die in a very literal sense, as far as my personality goes … and have been building it since … how I can use this knowledge to aid myself in being more centered and less crazy with the pain of … I would like very much to use this as a tool, and I don't know precisely how to go about it. If there are any comments which you could make, I would greatly appreciate it.

I am Q'uo. We look upon this query with an eye that is set toward the preservation of that free will, which we see you also hold in great esteem, for the query is one which explores fundamental qualities of your incarnation, which are most valuable to the seeker when they have been discovered as a result of the personal efforts upon a continued basis. We shall speak upon some points of your query and your observations.

Your difficulty within your digestive system is one which has been echoing through your incarnation, dating from the time of the psychic greeting. Some of your years ago that was possible due to your creating an opening that, though quickly and effectively healed, provided a target of opportunity for your friend of the negative polarity. This situation is one which has continued to present you with great difficulties of the physical vehicle, and the attending concern of the mental and emotional complexes. It is a situation which we find you are attending to with all due care and respect—one which we find has continued to provide you with catalyst that suggests to you the need to place accomplishment upon a physical level above the appreciation of your beingness. For, this is a central theme, shall we say, not only of your incarnation, but of almost all entities who inhabit this illusion; for, within this illusion, it is seemingly the case that one's mastery of manifestation and accomplishment of details is most important for the gaining of value and the storing of the wealth of this value.

The dream, as you have remembered it and utilized your understanding of it, is indeed an experience that has summarized your healing process in relation to the one known as Don, so that there is, upon that level of your experience, a completion that will free further energies for your use in whatever manner you choose to utilize these energies. The application of that message from your subconscious mind to your current abdominal distress is an area where we find that we may not tread, due to the joint desire to maintain free will.

Carla: Is that … *(inaudible)*?

I am Q'uo, and we slipped that one past this instrument for your pleasure. To conclude our remarks upon this query, we would suggest that your straightest and strongest course at this time is that course which you have followed faithfully, and that is the attempt to see and experience the love of each moment no matter what the challenge before you, to pursue the understanding of your beingness with faith, with will exercised by, as you call it, an happy heart. No entity may know the end of the story, for the future is indeed mazed to all eyes, including our own. We recommend to you that you continue this journey with the joy of the seeker who walks with the Creator in the garden of the creation, experiencing the delights of the moment and keeping the eye inwardly ever upon eternity, for all within your illusion live a life that is but fleeting no matter how the measure of your years may quantify it, and yet, live a life that is eternal in its choice of what we find you have called "the attitude"—the attitude that sees the illusion before one and feels the Creator within one. And though there may be little of understanding the illusion before one or the Creator within one, yet, there is the sure faith that the Creator may be known in all illusion, and that one is never alone or without purpose and guidance. Always are you cradled within the hands of the infinite One.

Is there another query, my sister?

Carla: I would like to thank you for the beauty of that answer. Yes, I have another question on another thing. I had an experience this week which I did not know precisely how to deal with. It was a situation in which I was put in a position by students who needed to have somebody to admire. Not being an admirable person or guru or teacher, people sat at my feet and I was afraid they smelled … no, they just were worshipping my feet; and nothing that I could do or say could sway these people. Now, this isn't the problem—I know that's their problem, not mine. My problem is, they take something from me that I don't know how to give so that I am still comfortable. When these people leave, I am always feeling as if I have been sucked on by a vampire, and I know they don't want to do this to me. I know they have no intention of doing it to me. I know that there is something about myself that is giving too much, and giving heedlessly, which is not at all what I intended as a teacher. If you could comment on that in any way, I would appreciate it.

I am Q'uo, and we may comment by confirming your conclusion that you are of a nature which gives without stint, in many cases giving to the point of bankrupting your own energies, for at this time and for some time as we have previously spoken, you have been in deficit. As an entity which seeks the fullest expression of love, you have little of the what we find have been called "boundaries of the self," which are utilized by most third-density entities in an automatic holding or confining of the personal energies that may flow to another at the request of the other for assistance. You perceive requests for assistance that are both spoken and unspoken, conscious and unconscious, on the part of the entities that join you.

In the fashion in which those of whom you speak joined you in the previous week, we are not aware of a strong possibility that this central feature of your personality can be altered significantly without altering your concept of service, and are further unsure as to whether or not this would be the most efficacious choice—we correct this instrument—even if it were possible. However, leaving this choice to you, we can suggest that before you are joined by such a grouping of entities again, or before you join such a grouping of entities again, that you construct about you a sheathing of light that allows the energies of your mind/body/spirit complex to circulate freely within this field created by the sheathing, and that there is a transparency to the sheathing that allows radiance of light to be emitted, but that retains the energies for your complex as necessary to maintain mind, body and spirit at a basic or fundamental level of functioning.

This sheathing of light is created mentally, much as you create that circle about you across which no thoughtform may move, as you bring your hands from the touching position in front of your body in an arc so that they complete a circle, touching behind your body. This may be done mentally, and may be reinforced at any time that you feel that there is a significant draining of energies from you by those who call both consciously and unconsciously for that which you have to give.

Is there a further query, my sister?

Carla: I know precisely the prayer and the practice that you speak of, and I thank you for that. My only other question is of curiosity. There is a similarity in a part of the gospel, an alleged story about Jesus the Christ, where a woman who has had a hemorrhage for twelve years—crawling along the way—finally manages to grab Jesus' robe, and he says, "Who is getting healed, because I perceive virtue is going out of me?" Obviously, he didn't have his shields up either, and I just wondered if there was a similarity. It seems like there is quite a bit of similarity, and also a similar weakness, in that he wasn't very much on limits either.

I am Q'uo, and this description of the one known as Jesus is a central feature of your personality structure, and is the feature to which we referred in our previous query, as a feature which we feel is unlikely to be altered to a great extent upon your part, due to your feeling that this is of great importance, that is, the serving without stint.

Carla: Thank you so much, Q'uo. I have no more questions.

I am Q'uo, and we thank you, my sister. Is there another query at this time?

Carla: *(Inaudible).*

I am Q'uo, and we are most grateful to those who sit within this circle of seeking, once again, for inviting our presence which we share as fully as is possible for us, and through this sharing do we take great joy, for it is the means by which we may be allowed to know and serve another facet of the one Creator, and thereby enrich the experience of ourselves, of the Creator, and we do hope, of those we serve as well. We shall take our leave of this group at this time, leaving each, as always, in the love and in the light of the one infinite Creator. We are known to you as those of Q'uo. Adonai, my friends. Adonai. ✣

L/L Research

L/L Research is a subsidiary of Rock Creek Research & Development Laboratories, Inc.

P.O. Box 5195
Louisville, KY 40255-0195

www.llresearch.org

Rock Creek is a non-profit corporation dedicated to discovering and sharing information which may aid in the spiritual evolution of humankind.

ABOUT THE CONTENTS OF THIS TRANSCRIPT: This telepathic channeling has been taken from transcriptions of the weekly study and meditation meetings of the Rock Creek Research & Development Laboratories and L/L Research. It is offered in the hope that it may be useful to you. As the Confederation entities always make a point of saying, please use your discrimination and judgment in assessing this material. If something rings true to you, fine. If something does not resonate, please leave it behind, for neither we nor those of the Confederation would wish to be a stumbling block for any.

CAVEAT: This transcript is being published by L/L Research in a not yet final form. It has, however, been edited and any obvious errors have been corrected. When it is in a final form, this caveat will be removed.

© 2009 L/L Research

Intensive Meditation
July 12, 1991

Group question: The question we will deal with this morning has to do with anger. Where does anger come from? How can we use it and how can we heal from it? There is a feeling of being out of control that people who are sensitive to other people's feelings fear. There's the fear of the injury that would be caused by the anger. There's the fear of the actual feeling of the anger, the feeling of not being able to control it, that there would be some damage done. There's the great unknown of where does it come from within ourselves. Is there a value to anger? Can we use it constructively after the anger has passed? How can we use it to heal up whatever wounds were caused before or during the anger?

(K channeling)

I greet each of you this day in the love and in the light of the infinite Creator. We bring greetings to this group also from our brothers and sisters of Hatonn who are called to be with this group this morning and yet prefer not to speak, but simply to aid in the meditation process of those present.

You request information this morning about anger. Each in this group has given much thought to this subject and has done work in this area and there have been queries upon this subject both directed to ourselves and to the one known as Aaron who has also worked with this group in this area.

We are pleased to see that this working continues, that the interest of those present in such matters is not simply a shallow and passing interest but that answers to questions upon such subjects provoke further thought and introspection and further experience which again generates more material for thought and reflection. This is the nature of the process of knowing the self and it is this process upon which all seekers are embarked.

There may be consternation experienced by the seeker when a subject such as anger is studied in that depth of the self hitherto unknown well plumbed. The resultant knowledge is not always experienced as either pleasant or comfortable to the one who seeks, either because the information thus uncovered is judged to be of an unacceptable quality to the seeker or simply because it is unfamiliar to the seeker as being part of the self and thus the immediate response is one of rejection and judging it unacceptable.

This process of discovery of the self and of accepting the unacceptable is known to each in this group as part of the seeker's lot. However, it is always disconcerting to discover these things close to home, shall we say, rather than dealing with perhaps the same subject in what you perceive of as an other self at what may seem to be a safer distance. The reality is that there is no distance and whether anger or any other uncomfortable or undesirable emotion is discovered in an other self or in the depths of the self is no different. It is always the self that is being explored and experienced.

We know you are [aware] of this and that it is a function of the nature of the illusion to foster such differences and indeed to aid in the learning process. For it is for the beginning seeker often far easier to deal with these matters in a manner that is perceived as being more distant and somewhat less contiguous with the self. As the seeker continues in the journey the awareness of the unity of all becomes more apparent and more felt and experienced within the life. Therefore, more and more frequently the seeker will discover directly in the self what is needed to be learned, rather than needing mirrors of other selves for this process.

Each seeker is also unique as to the biases that have been accumulated over the distillation of many lifetimes and the processes which are most helpful to each will differ. Therefore the experience of each will differ accordingly.

You wish to know about the source of anger. The source of anger or any other emotion which the service-to-others seeker may be tempted to judge as negative or unacceptable lies in the misperception of the separateness of entities. For in order to feel the emotion of anger there must needs be an object of the anger and this object is necessarily seen as being separate from the self. Therefore a very simplistic answer would be that if all things were realized in their true unified form there would be no anger for there would be no separate objects.

This is a gross oversimplification of metaphor. It would also serve to disintegrate the entire illusion in which you dwell and other emotions which are judged as positive or helpful would also be dissolved for they too require an object in order to be elicited.

However, if anger or other such disquieting emotions is the subject of discomfort at the time then we may suggest that meditations on the true nature of each, that is, the unity beyond the illusion, may be helpful in both the understanding and the dissolving of the same. The dissolving not being a process of elimination or eradication but of absorption and acceptance of the existence within the self and the other self and the acknowledgement that there is a place for this within the self that does not of necessity bring harm. It is the concentration of such matter that may be used in what is perceived to be a harmful manner.

In a similar way that a concentration of what you may view as a harmful chemical that may exist harmoniously in nature is brought into a concentrated form and as such is considered to be what your peoples would call a toxin and may then be used to bring harm to different types of entities, this is a same type of process that operates with emotions such as anger.

The uses of purposes of anger and of other such emotions may be varied according to the desire of the one experiencing them. Their primary use to the seeker is of course to foster further investigation of a knowledge of the self. The uses of the outward expression of such anger may be used also variously. So the expression of such usually takes place in a concentrated form as we spoke of. They are most often utilized by those on the negative path for they are very useful in affecting a greater separation in situations of manipulation and control. So [anger is] that which the negative path uses.

For the positive entity we would suggest that the deliberate and intentional use of such anger would be most probably realized by the positive entity to be not of a helpful nature and therefore would not be likely to be chosen as a manner of expression but more likely would occur as a spontaneous expression of that which is felt within the self in an overwhelming manner. We would suggest that the most likely cause of such a concentration and eruption of this substance, shall we say, would be the lack of awareness of its existence within the self in its more quiet and nontoxic form, shall we say, and that a greater awareness and acceptance of the existence of this emotion in its more natural and absorbed, shall we say, state would be most helpful in the work of the seeker that has concern about the possibility of the uncontrolled expression of such.

The question of control is another issue altogether and quite separate from the process of anger or other emotions. We are aware that control is one of the primary tools of the negative path. Yet to the positive seeker chaos is surely not the desired state. Therefore this is an issue also that will certainly be investigated by any who delve deep enough into the self. We would suggest that the issue for the positive seeker is not so much one of control but one of choice. That choice is only possible when there is awareness and that therefore the path to the availability of choices lies once again through the ever-deepening knowledge of the self and the subsequent awareness and acceptance of what is found in the self.

When the seeker has reached a point of awareness of, to use the current example, the anger that exists within the self and has accepted that as being a part of the self even as the various chemical components run through your various strata of rock then the seeker will have also a greater awareness of the process of concentration of these substances. These processes then may be observed and the choice will be available as to the continuation of the process and the various means of expressing the same.

You ask also about a process of cooling what damage may be caused when such an eruption may occur. The healing of each entity is again another subject which may be plumbed in depth and we shall comment but briefly at this time. Each entity serves as catalyst for the other and the process of knowing itself. When entities, especially those such as are in this group which are embarked upon the conscious efforts of knowing the self, act as catalyst upon each other the results are never, shall we say, completely unasked for. That is to say, the entity receiving the catalyst is aware of the need for such although this may not be a conscious awareness and is thus given the opportunity for greater knowledge of and acceptance of the self. This is not to attempt to foster any sense of irresponsibility but we feel no danger with that with those of this group for each here is most conscientious about such matters.

The healing process, in essence, lies with each individual. The one who feels they have caused harm have need of healing and the one who feels they have received harm have need of healing also. Ultimately each entity must do the work of healing the self. It may be possible for entities who work together in harmony to extend to the other the open heart, the understanding mind, the statement of loving intent that may facilitate such self-work in healing. But ultimately the responsibility is with the self.

The popular, shall we say, concept of healing seems to imply a reversal of whatever action has taken place so that the effect is as if it never happened. We would suggest to you that the true nature of healing is rather the process of absorption, acceptance and ingestion, shall we say, into the self of whatever concept is being offered. This dissolution and acceptance into the self then is the nature of the process of healing rather than the eradication of the perceived harm. We realize this concept is somewhat at variance with those concepts commonly held within your society and would suggest that each look within the self for the verification of such, as always.

We urge each to take from our words only that which rings true to the self and to set aside all else, perhaps for another time, perhaps never. We would at this time transfer the contact to the one known as Jim and will be happy to continue with any further questions upon this subject or any other. We thank this instrument and this group and leave this instrument now in love and light. We are those of Q'uo.

(Jim channeling)

I am Q'uo, and greet each again in love and in light. At this time we would ask if we may further speak upon any topic if there is a query yet remaining upon the mind.

Questioner: First of all, thank you. There is an aspect that especially interests me because I'm used to being very honest, even to the point of bluntness and I discovered that when the anger hit me that I had two choices, either to sulk and pout and be silent and repress it. I mean I couldn't keep it in check. There was no way I could do that *(inaudible)* but I wanted to say things because I wanted to express my opinion on it. I wanted to hurt somebody else. It's a real foreign feeling for me. And there was nothing true that I could say that would do this for me so the only thing that I could do was to think things that I virtually knew at the time were untrue and I played the victim but it was a means of taking this thing that felt like a real poison and getting it out of my system. When the communication is definitely not going to be true in terms of the *(inaudible)* it seems like it's better to say false things than to say nothing and let it go on longer. What is the best way not to tell the truth if you don't have any choices but to tell a falsehood if you're angry because whatever your trying *(inaudible)* true. Is that still better? It seems to be still better than being silent and sulking and not being able to *(inaudible)*. But why is there a need to say lying hurtful things when the anger is there? Why doesn't the truth, which is just that a person's upset, why doesn't that satisfy the *(inaudible)*?

I am Q'uo, and are aware of your query, my sister. The emotions that culminated in the expression of anger for you yesterday are emotions that have taken some time to find their fullest flower, shall we say. It was not just the experience of just a moment but the experience of a lifetime of feeling that you had been abandoned and that there was no other entity that could give you the comfort that you sought.

When one feels emotions that are of such a deep nature and which have been worked upon in a conscious fashion for a significant portion of the incarnation and when there is a trigger that is seemingly unrelated it is well to go, shall we say, with the flow of the emotions and to speak in a spontaneous fashion so that whether what is said makes sense or not, it is said with the true feelings that generate the words. This allows a beginning, an entry, into the deeper emotions which are more to the point or the heart of the experience.

It is well of course in such situations that one have at one's disposal or at one's service an other self which is willing to work with the self in this matter. The great fear of each of your experiences of anger is that there will be a further enraging of the experience, not only for the self but for the other self, and a further confusing of the catalyst that has brought the both of you together in this culmination of emotion. It is very, very helpful to be able to express freely to another self that which is upon the mind or of one's heart, shall we say, and to explore the ramifications. For in almost every instance your conversation and thought processes proceed upon a symbolic or surface level so that what is really the genesis of the feelings may be hidden both to the one who speaks and to the one who listens. This is the great value of communication and dedication: perseverance of communication.

This will allow you to uncover other areas of your experience that are more fundamental that have been sown with a certain seed that has not been fully exposed to the light of the sun that it might grow in a natural way and produce a fruit that is obvious and easy to appreciate. The emotions that are deeper and which are often the true cause of an outburst of anger are those seeds which have not received the full light of the sun, the full light of one's conscious attention and recognition of the kind of seed that has been planted. Who has planted the seed and who has tended the seed as the gardener? Thus, we do not recommend the repressing any emotional experience, even that of anger unless the entity with whom one is expressing these energies is, because of being a stranger or being too young to understand, unable to partake in the experience without suffering on its part great confusion or misapprehension of a gross nature.

We find that the experience of the anger is fortunately in this case that which is experienced with those that are more closely known to and aligned with the self as the self and other selves seek to relate in a manner which is intimate and compassionate and is so on a stable basis. Thus, we would recommend that the spontaneous expression of all emotions is that which is most helpful in what you call the long run so that these expressions of emotion become the point at which you begin to delve more deeply into the experience with an other self that is compassionate and understanding concerning your needs and your fears.

Is there a further query my sister?

Questioner: *(Inaudible)*. Would doing something like saying, "I know these are all lies," *(inaudible)*.

I am Q'uo, and am aware of your query, my sister. We find that in your illusion it is difficult in the great coloration of emotion called anger to operate at such a rational level as to be able to discern that which is true and that which is not true in the moment that the anger is experienced. Or if one were able to do this, the great energy of the anger would be blunted insofar as the realization of what was being said was untrue. Whether what is felt and said is true or not is relatively unimportant in the moment of the expression of the anger. It is well to express that which is, shall we say, on the tip of the tongue and that which wishes to rush from the mouth and from the heart. Then the process of sorting and evaluation may begin by looking at all that was said, even those areas of expression which one later determines to be untrue. For that moment of anger in that particular experience may yet hold some value for the self as one relates these speakings to earlier experiences or other experiences within the incarnation, so that there may be a kind of following of a trail of that which was spoken so that there might be a possibility of gaining greater understanding as this trail is followed and discussed and shared in open fashion with the other self.

Is there another query, my sister?

Questioner: No, I really thank you *(inaudible)*.

I am Q'uo, and we also thank you, my sister, for your query and for your dedication. Is there another query at this time?

(No further queries.)

I am Q'uo, and we are once again most grateful for your invitation to us to join your group and to work with the instruments that are present. We find that the one known as K is becoming more flexible in her ability to receive and to transmit our thoughts, doing so in a manner which suggests that the confidence in this process is building even upon the subconscious levels in spite of any conscious doubts. This is due to the basic trust in …

(Tape ends.) ✤

Sunday Meditation
July 19, 1991

Group question: We'll be looking at the question today of how does one look at and interact with people, especially friends and family that you are closely associated with, that you have disagreements with and perhaps even a dislike with and for. I would hate to leave all those prepositions at the end of a phrase, but I don't know where else to put them, so, I guess that'll do it.

(Carla channeling)

I greet each of you this morning in love and light. We thank you once again for the opportunity to be called to this group and to work with you, for we feel a great sense of harmony and comradeship with those of this group who, as we, are focused in the will and the desire to search for whatever truth may be discovered out of the mystery. Each is aware that this is a progressive process. That truth is not static. That as each portion of the mystery is seemingly discovered other vast unknown regions are disclosed, apparently beyond the nature of those seeking.

So that the process, or the goal, is not one of attaining the truth or discovering the mystery, but rather becoming aware of the harmonies and balances that exist within the self at each moment. These vary from moment to moment. The apparent nature of the self, in terms of perceived awareness, varies from moment to moment. Thusly, there is much flexibility required of the seeker, for when a particular truth or belief system or particular awareness is grasped tightly and applied to each situation that is encountered, then it becomes dogma and force is required in its application over a much wider area than was intended. This has been experienced and encountered in various ways by each here. Therefore we request, as always, that those hearing our words sift them as a grain that is harvested, taking to the self those truths that resonate with your harmonies and balances at the present moment, and allowing the rest to sift through the fingers as the chaff, as that which simply does not apply.

You ask for information this morning about how to deal with those other selves which are encountered in a close fashion in life. In any relationship with an other self there is even more room for variance in truth than in dealing with just the perceived self proceeding from moment to moment, for not only are one's own ever shifting balances to be contended with, but there are also the equally shifting and much less known balances of the other self. Therefore, we may only offer information of a very general nature in this regard, for the specific dealings with other selves will always be unique to the self and the other self involved and the very moment of interaction.

There is information which we do feel may be of help in this regard. First of all is the knowledge of the true nature of unity that is beyond the illusion within which you now work. There is no separation between self and other self. Secondly, each self and other self is within the illusion a manifestation of a portion or facet of the One. This portion or facet also contains within itself various portions or facets or blendings of energies, so that while the manifestation of the self may be perceived to be changing at various times, it is still reflecting different aspects of all that there is. Each other self is doing precisely the same thing though the appearance may seem to be completely different as the other self is like the self, reflecting aspects of the one, so the other self is also reflecting aspects of the self.

Each here is aware of the function of self and other self as mirrors for the other in the process of the seeker of knowing, accepting and balancing itself. Thus, when one encounters an other self with which one has difficulty, the ultimate cause of the difficulty will always be the difficulty in perceiving the absolute unity of all and, more on the level of the illusion, the lack of ability to accept the self fully, as manifested currently by the other self.

When one encounters another self with whom one is having difficulty we would suggest, on a more long term basis, shall we say, meditations on the concept of unity, and specific concentrated periods of contemplation on the aspects of the self called up by the other self that are experienced as unacceptable, and the specific exercises in balancing and accepting that each has found most appropriate for one's own use, for these differ with each entity.

In the case where one experiences an other self as draining the energy or continually presenting those types of negatively perceived energies that are difficult to deal with, we may also suggest that it is helpful to protect the self, and again there are varying ways of performing this task.

At this time we will transfer this contact to the one know as Jim as this instrument is having some increasing difficulty maintaining this contact. We are known to you as those of Q'uo, and leave this instrument in love and light.

(Tape ends.)

Sunday Meditation
July 21, 1991

Group question: Questions were asked about how any seeker of truth might use various ways or techniques to know the Creator. So what we would like to know is what techniques to use, what any being may use to mirror the supreme presence of the Creator within his or her consciousness and how does this mirroring of the Creator within the individual consciousness aid us in our service to others, or how is it a part of that service to others that is really the determining factor for the harvest? Elaborate upon the techniques that beings may use to connect with or to mirror the supreme presence.

Carla: OK, the chant that I will teach you is … you can use all different words with it; and I'll say a few and if anybody has a few we will just go on for a while. I like to chant for enough time that it does change the vibration, maybe nine, ten, something like that. The words to it are:

Love is flowing like a river
Flowing out through you and me
Spreading out into the desert
Setting all the cactus free.

And you can say "Peace is flowing a river," etc. Bliss, faith, hope, light and so forth. Anybody that wants to sing one is welcome to stick one in at the beginning, otherwise I may just keep hitting back on "love" from time to time.

(Group chanting.)

(Lord's prayer.)

(Carla channeling)

We are the principle known to you as Q'uo, and we greet you in the love and in the light of the one infinite Creator. It is a great blessing for us to be called to your group at this time and we bless and thank each whose desire for the truth cannot be denied when we come together in one bright circle of light to seek that truth. We, too, are pilgrims on the path of truth, and we, as you, make many errors; we are not infallible. We ask you not to think of us as authorities but as fellow travelers. Perhaps our feet have moved through more dust, perhaps we have experienced more, but still the Creator is a mystery. So how can we ask you to trust us as an authority? Nay, my friends, trust your own hearts, for if it is your truth, you will not learn it; you will recognize it. If you do not recognize it, release it, for we would not be a stumbling block before you.

You ask this evening how we may better know the Creator, we being those of several densities. Let us go back to the assumption implicit in this question, that is, that the Creator can be known. What is it to know? What things do you know? If you gaze at what you know, you find yourself dealing in quantities and measures, things that can be touched and counted. Thus, you can say, "I know I have three apples," "I have a piece of paper." Yet, this knowing does not satisfy the consciousness within the grasp of each of you. Each of you knows that that which is called knowledge is not knowledge; it is observation, and it can be used to create many, many gadgets, to fuel a technology, yet what does that technology know?

The basis upon which technology is built is observation. That which lies behind the observation is unknown. Mass has never been seen under the microscope. There is absolutely no way to explore absolute objectivity, for without an observer there is no knowledge of any experiment. No one has yet been able to explain or know gravity. No one understands or knows the so-called speed of light, why it is apparently a constant. Magnetism and electricity are also fields which are in some ways inexplicable.

What do you know? Let us look a bit deeper. Move, each of you, from the mind that is in your brain. Relinquish it and think courteously, gently, and with the skill of a suitor, to pay court to your heart, for it is the unconscious and silent wisdom of the heart that gives to an entity its closest experience to that of knowing. Within the illusion in which you enjoy yourselves at this time, nothing can be known. The sooner the seeker becomes aware that the truth will beckon ever onward, the sooner the seeker can set to rest the hunger for proof which so often leads to a debasing of the pure love of the truth. Relinquish your hold upon the need for proof, for that which is proof is proof within an illusion. Would you wish to know something in the illusion, for all that you know in the illusion is an illusion. Or would you wish, rather, to gaze straightway at the mystery that is not known and know that you are tabernacling with that mystery; that you live in that mystery and in a very central sense you are that mystery which is Creator and creation.

Listen with your ears to all that you hear at this moment in time: the subtle inhalations and exhalations of your brothers and your sisters in light, the songs of the small animals, the gentle whir of the cooling fans; for some who are sensitive, even the hint of a heartbeat heard in the ear, a pulse felt, the energies of this circle. How many things there are to apprehend in this one moment! It is normally thought that one knows what one knows by the process of observation. But let us look carefully at this, for we would ask you above all things to be stewards of your attention. How do you pay attention to your incarnation? All of these things that we described to you were probably not part of what you were aware of knowing at the moment at which we described all the sounds. They were not in any way important to your survival; they were only incidental to your purpose for conversing so kindly with us. Yet, all of those things lie in the matrix of your mind, not only now but eternally. All that has happened to you, all that you have taken in, and all that you shall experience are in a small part of the infinite being that you are, forever you. So is each of you a knower, is that the activity you would describe as yourself? Perhaps you would see why we would ask you to pull back from being one who knows, and ask of yourself if it is better to investigate being one who asks, for the answers have very little meaning compared to the questions.

What questions move you, my children? Can you not see that you spend your attention like money, yet, unlike money you are not often thrifty; you are not often listening with your spiritual ears open. Why is that? In this western culture we may suggest that one reason is the great emphasis upon accomplishing the visible tasks. This entity would call this distortion the "work ethic," and this entity itself is less and less a slave to the work ethic, but certainly still highly distorted towards valuing actions above essence—the essence of intention and desire, of passion, for there is a quest for truth. It is not the truth to be proven, it is not the truth to be trotted out, elegant and set before all, tidy and finished forever. Truths come and they go, and they are useful for one person only. Each of you will find some truths to last for years, incarnations; other truths to last a week or a month or a year.

So, let us move back to beyond the need to know and prove, and investigate the processes of perception. When you have heard, felt, seen, smelled, tasted, touched your environment, a moment has occurred, the present moment. You have chosen that which you will notice and examine. Day upon day, and moment by moment, you will notice what has moved you. This you will discover for yourself the kind of mind that you have to this point created. For you see, as fields of consciousness you are stewards of this bio-computer; you are stewards of what you perceive and stewards of your actions, whether they are creative or reactionary.

So what happens after you have heard all the things that you do not pay attention to? Perhaps someone has entered the door; this, then, is the next perception, this is your choice. You have chosen to observe this one thing. Before you can form a mental thought about it, you will, willy-nilly, be informed by all your biases concerning that which you have noticed. What is your attitude toward the entity who has entered? How has that entity been a catalyst for you? In what way have you distorted an emotionally neutral occurrence? There is a palpable pause between the first sense consciousness, and your consciousness' willingness to take on a mental formation in relation to the present moment. Has it occurred to you that you can be stewards to the extent that you may choose more wisely the sense perceptions to which you wish to pay attention? Have you thought, perhaps, to investigate those things which cause you to generate biased observations rather than emotionally neutral ones or balanced ones?

This is indeed possible and is part of the discipline of the personality that will deliver to you a more lucidly working partnership betwixt consciousness and the mental and bodily complexes which carry that consciousness about within your incarnation.

Perceive, then, that you are both less powerful than you think—in that you will not perceive all that you can perceive—but see also that you are more powerful than you may think you are, for you can be creators of those thoughts, attitudes and actions which you choose when you see the catalyst and sense perceptions and biases within yourself which resonate in the present moment.

Now, all of this has been discussion of activities. The portions of these exercises all take a great deal of practice, persistence and devotion. Yet, it is beyond them that the heart of your question lies. You are perhaps familiar with the words which the Master known as Jesus has been said to have said: "I am the way, the truth and the life." Let us look at the entity who said this. This entity spoke always in parables, never plainly. This entity taught by telling stories, by suggesting mental formations and biases that went beyond the words which were used. Moreover, this entity often said "When you hear me, it is not I who speak, but the Father within me." Would this entity then have said "I am the way," or would this entity have made a small pun, perhaps a slightly irreverent one, upon the name of the Deity as this entity knew that name? For the name of the unnamable Deity to the one known as Jesus was a word formation which translates, roughly, "I AM." In fact, it says it twice: "I am that I am."

Now, gaze back at this famous quote and see in a more spacious way the I AM that is the truth, the I AM that is your road and your path, the I AM that is your service and your life and perfect freedom. We of Q'uo are. We are an I AM, for we have come together, yet each of us also is an unique I AM, and each of you listening to this instrument is the only one of you in the infinite creation. You are utterly necessary, precious and perfect, for you are part of all that there is, part of an infinity which is from everlasting to everlasting.

How can you know? You cease asking to know, and ask to learn to ask who you are. As you move deeper and deeper in this quest, you become more and more authentic essences. You see, within your heavy, chemical, third-density illusion, what you see as your physical vehicle is seen by us basically as large quantities of water with some few chemicals in them—an ingenious design, indeed, but a second-density one. Yet, this second-density entity knows in every cell of its vehicle, "I AM," for it blooms just as a flower does. You, in your second-density body, are so beautiful! The Creator has made all things well and this includes you.

Thus, your relationship with this physical vehicle need not be one of scorn but one of thankfulness and praise, for this second-density entity could have had a perfectly good instinctual life of its own. The brain, the personality, all of those things which seem to you mundane are things which this animal which carries you about could sociably and naturally do, with grace and even elegance as is the way of things created by the infinite One which do not have the self-consciousness to be awkward, but move with the infinitely appropriate rhythms of growth, blooming, evensong and death. Treasure this entity that carries you about. Nurture it; love it; pamper it. Be a good boss to it, and know that there is a wisdom in every cell of that second-density body that your consciousness, infinite though it may be, is blocked from seeing because of the veil of forgetting between the conscious and the subconscious mind, that veil dropped specifically so you cannot know, and gaze at this creature who asks questions it cannot answer.

How is that logically possible? Here is the beginning of the mystery. You cannot help but know that you are other than you think you are, for you ask questions that you simply cannot possibly answer. You sense truths that you cannot possibly ever touch.

The genius of living consciously in an illusion that is heavily biased toward sleep is in paying attention, for you are an I AM, you are a creator experiencing itself. Do you strive to be virtuous? Thusly does the Creator know of hope and virtue. Do you strive to be aught else whatsoever? Thusly does the Creator know of aught else whatsoever. Have you served in your own opinion as a bad example? How valuable that I AM is you have probably learned by your self-perceived failures.

Knowing is a shallow thing. Asking in the heart is the beginning of wisdom. As you move deeply, deeply into your heart breathe, breathe full into your belly, into your abdomen. Feel the light, the energy that is infinite. Feel the love that expresses itself as your consciousness. Ask your heart, "What is this love? All these people, why are they so dear? Why are we so pointed toward the light we cannot ever know? Let yourself be overwhelmed, for this is the knowing that you seek—I AM, I AM, I AM. Every iota of the infinite universe, of the One Infinite Thought of Love which creates all that there is …

(Side one of tape ends.)

(Carla channeling)

… with you always 'til the end of the age. Move deeper in your heart. I AM. Breath again and again softly, deeply—I AM—and feel in the womb that is within any entity that bourning present, that birthing moment that is a brand new I AM. This is your essence. This holds your passion. This is you—I AM. As you tabernacle, know that the I AM that is at your heart is much closer to you than your breath, far nearer to you than hands or feet or face or stomach, or any portion of the physical vehicle. You are essence, you are all that there is, you are a quality that is infinite, a flavor not quantifiable, not measurable, but infinite. It will take you all the life that you are and that you will live in your subjective stream of consciousness to learn to focus upon your essence and not upon your activities, for activities may be done with or without love, with or without that great sense of I AM.

Let your intuitions, your intentions, and especially those intentions about which you are persistent form within you an ever more tangible I AM. How can we know the Creator? I AM. I AM. You are. We know the Creator partially in our essence and to a great extent in the essences of the I AMs that we perceive as other than ourselves due to our continuing distortions of understanding. How can you know the Creator? Precisely that way, my children. Learn yourself, love yourself, for you are love. What other appropriate response is there to love but love? As circumstances befall you, see them as love, for all things are the I AM, that one great idea, Love. It may be very distorted, the branches may have gotten twisted, seared, burned, ruined. Then you must look to the roots, for I AM is the root system. You have a good deal to do with the branches, but gaze at your roots.

Others will look at the fruits of your incarnational experience and say that you were such and such a person," but the I AM gazes at the I AM in you, and is one with it, and fullness of love is added to fullness of love in a mystery that has no answer that is known to us.

We shall at this time, with apologies for our length of speaking, open the meeting to any questions each might have. We realize that the hour is late and if it is decided that there is a need to end this meeting you have only to say so or to cease asking questions. We would at this time thank the instrument known as Carla for offering itself in the service, and would at this time transfer in love and in light and in such delight in your company to the one known as Jim. We are those of the principle of Q'uo.

(Jim channeling)

I am Quo, and greetings again in love and in light. Through this instrument we would ask at this time if there are any queries of a shorter nature to which we may speak briefly?

Questioner: I have a question of Q'uo. I channel, and oftimes the next day I get an imbalance of potassium, and I was wondering how that might be corrected afterwards or prepared for ahead of time?

I am Q'uo, and am aware of the query. We find that this deficiency is one which is easily rectified by the ingestion of your banana fruit, the ingestion of your potassium pill prior to the working.

Is there another query, my sister?

Questioner: Thank you.

I am Quo, and we thank you. Is there another query?

Questioner: Once we understand that we are the I AM, how may we bring this understanding into manifestation in this density to help others?

I am Q'uo, and am aware of your query, my sister. As each devoted and diligent seeker has for so many, many incarnations attempted within the heavy, chemical, third-density illusion that you inhabit, you seek that I AM where the heart leads. In the silence of your meditation you reach as fully and firmly as you can to grasp the essence of that quality that you experience and bring it forth into your life as the attitude of your beingness, and attempt to see and feel and be and touch and smell and experience and share the one Creator that you find within, in whatever way is open to you. However well or poorly you may proceed at each moment that you experience in a conscious fashion, you try, you give, you offer in every instance of opportunity, and although you shall not fully succeed at all times or even in a majority of your attempts, it is the perseverance, the dedication, the continual reminders that you see about you and that you give to yourself, then, that are the refining qualities of the fire of experience that is yours within your evolution. Seeing but glimpses of the one wishing to know more purely, sharing but partially, becoming weary with effort, pulling together the desire again and again and again, it is this desire that is your most honored ally upon this journey.

Is there another query, my sister?

Questioner: I have one. I don't know why it happens, and I have no control over it when it happens, but sometimes for a moment, sometimes for an hour, sometimes for several days, I will be the light. I won't have any real awareness of myself as a being … I will just be the light … ecstatic. But it has about as much to do with language or telling people about it as a pumpkin. So I realize that this is part of being, what interests me is how does it translate into helping other people, because it's absolutely indescribable, nor can I produce it in other people.

I am Quo, and am aware of your query. Again, we remind you that the great desire to know the one Creator, and to serve that one Creator in all about one is that quality which works its wonders in silence and mystery at the heart of your being, so that as you continue upon this journey there is a tempering of the soul that manifests in various ways within the entity. You experience that which is appropriate at your time upon your journey, whether it be light or passion or devotion or any of those qualities that point one toward the unity of the one Creator, and you shine forth that quality as a natural portion of your being in any encounter with others without needing to form a way by which such may be done or understood mentally beforehand. Thus, it is your nature that shines forth from you without effort.

Is there a further query, my sister?

Questioner: Yes. Just to make sure I understand it. So, basically our knowingness is mostly achieved through seeing the essences in other people, in their unselfconscious spontaneous essence unknowing. Is that right?

I am Q'uo, and shall repeat for clarity that you have produced a fruit, each of you, according to your seeking and your desire to know the truth. This fruit is a quality of your being that shines forth without effort as you spontaneously engage in your daily round of activities and touch that quality in some form in each other entity and call it forth by that touch.

Is there another query, my sister?

Questioner: Well, no, I think that's really beautiful. What you are basically saying is we know by loving each other and supporting each other. Thank you.

I am Q'uo, and we thank you once again, my sister. Is there another query at this time?

Questioner: I have a query. First I greet you in love and light, and thank you for your presence. In these accelerated times in this density of space/time that we are now in, how essential and vital is it that we rely on another person for our guidance, let's say in the form of a spiritual master? That is my question.

I am Quo, and am aware of your query, my brother. We do not mean to sound facetious with our reply, but the importance of such catalyst or any catalyst for any seeker at a particular time within the incarnation is determined by that seeker. Thus, the importance that you give to that which you call holy is importance that you have placed there, and have desired to use as an avenue to a fuller apprehension of the one Creator. Each entity must needs find a path of what we will call faith, a structure for the next step upon the journey that will expand for the entity the opportunity to know and experience the one Creator, the I AM within in a fashion that is more filled with opportunity, shall we say, to more fully apprehend the one Creator. An entity may find that this faith moves into foreign lands, and that there will at some point need to be the refining of that faith or the structure through which the faith is focused in order that the entity may go higher, shall we say.

Thus, it is the function of the mind and your bio-computer's channeling of the greater line of the one Creator to form for the self the idea or possibility of the idea of the one Creator and a more complete apprehension. So that this journey does indeed continue for a great portion of what you call time.

Is there another query, my brother?

Questioner: No. Thank you.

I am Quo, and we thank you, my brother, and, with apologies, must bring this session of working to its completion for there is fatigue within the circle. We cannot thank you enough for the opportunity to blend our vibrations with yours, and to walk with you upon your journey at this time. We are humbled by the intensity of your seeking and are thrilled at the joy of your being. At this time we shall take our leave of this instrument and this group, leaving each, as always, in the love and in the light of the one infinite Creator. We are known to you as those of Q'uo. Adonai, my friends. Adonai.

L/L Research

L/L Research is a subsidiary of Rock Creek Research & Development Laboratories, Inc.

P.O. Box 5195
Louisville, KY 40255-0195

www.llresearch.org

Rock Creek is a non-profit corporation dedicated to discovering and sharing information which may aid in the spiritual evolution of humankind.

ABOUT THE CONTENTS OF THIS TRANSCRIPT: This telepathic channeling has been taken from transcriptions of the weekly study and meditation meetings of the Rock Creek Research & Development Laboratories and L/L Research. It is offered in the hope that it may be useful to you. As the Confederation entities always make a point of saying, please use your discrimination and judgment in assessing this material. If something rings true to you, fine. If something does not resonate, please leave it behind, for neither we nor those of the Confederation would wish to be a stumbling block for any.

CAVEAT: This transcript is being published by L/L Research in a not yet final form. It has, however, been edited and any obvious errors have been corrected. When it is in a final form, this caveat will be removed.

© 2009 L/L Research

Sunday Meditation
September 22, 1991

Group question: The day before fall, a season ends, a new one begins. Our question is the same. We had a season of a threesome together here for a time. It seems, if we look in subjective terms, that there might have been a failure in the effort that the three of us put forth in this forming of a group to be of service for the life pattern. But, we would like to know from you at this time how you would look at a situation such as ours where three people come together with the desire to be of service to others and may have certain goals in mind of a specific nature that would allow them to consciously define for themselves the effort as being a success. First of all could you comment upon that type of a definition of a success, and could you also comment upon how we can move from this point where we are working more individually, with K moving on her own to study those things of herself that are necessary for her to continue on her journey, and how we remaining here, Carla and I, work on our own to do that which is ours to do.

(Carla channeling)

We are those of the principle of Q'uo. We greet you through this instrument in the love and the light of the one infinite Creator. We see you as you call to us with a sorrow of life upon your hearts, with the heavy burdens of living upon your back, with the stress and the confusion and the turmoil and the great inner travail of growth to which you have committed yourselves spiritually, causing you ever to feel uncomfortable. We see within this group those who would prefer to be uncomfortable and seek the truth, and we can only share with you our blessings to you as you search for that truth as you share with us the blessing of allowing us to speak with you in an attempt to be of some service, always knowing that our opinions are but as nothing compared to the overarching mystery and truth which we in poor, tattered *(inaudible)*, dance and strut upon our stages, miming and acting and singing and dancing and telling pretty stories, and doing anything we can think of to alert people who are ready to awaken to a new search for truth, that faculty of awareness of the mystery that lies between, around, above, beneath and beyond all things, the mystery that is in fact you, each of you and each of us.

We are aware that you wish to know at this time what some of the dynamics are which cause completely sincere seekers of the truth who wish to band together to be of service sometimes [to] work and sometimes not, in the critical subjective evaluations of each of you. We can begin by asking each of you to gaze at the moment of commitment to this task. Much emphasis has been placed upon promises given and commitments made. But we ask each of you, in all earnestness, when each of you first said, "I commit myself to a life of service in this particular way called L and L," was there some special, permanent, unusual commitment, a commitment that took you from your humanity and made you into some entity with no capacity to do anything but keep that commitment? We ask you to look at this question very carefully. Can you not see, my friends, the absolute dedication of yourselves at that moment to the task of a lifetime, but the absolute ignorance, in that moment of dedication, of what sacrifices would have to be made to create a common path of service.

We of the Confederation in the Service of the One Infinite Creator, make such commitments and are able to keep them, because we are able to see, in a way that you are not, the harmonics of interpersonal relationships. We are able to see if there are tone clusters that can never be resolved. We are able to see if there is that within a twosome, a threesome, a foursome or a social memory complex that will hold, that will keep its centre, that will not fly apart. My friends, each of you is a third-density student, regardless of what you were before you incarnated upon this planet. As you came into this world you accepted darkness, spiritual blindness, and an unknowing so deep that it beggars the imagination. The only tools that you have, and the only tools that you do have now or will ever have within this incarnation, are the spiritual biases with which you came into this incarnation, and which have been worked upon within this incarnation. You do have comrades along the way, but that service that you wish so much to give is being given. It is simply that there are some harmonious threesomes or foursomes in a third density and there are many who are not harmonious, as this instrument would say, to the bone, and so must deal with each other and find it very educational, shall we say, to learn to deal with each other, trusting entirely in the good wishes of each other, having no fears that any will be rejected and simply continuing to do that which feels appropriate, knowing that as the work did not begin because of an event which you have called contact with the one known as Ra, so it did not end with the ending of that contact. Your service did not begin with your birth and it shall not cease with your death.

What you have achieved is something we wish you to gaze upon now. There are many levels of achievement in learning to live together in peace. Each of you has been learning lessons of respect, of charity when one cannot understand yet one must accept, of the strengthening power of being firm in friendship against adversity and in being loyal against discomfort. Please see these beauties. For these blossoms, though painfully born and raised in some season of drought, are beautiful to the Creator. This threesome has accomplished much. It has brought into physical expression words which each intended would be of service not necessarily to them alone but to any who might read them. But the main service we ask you to look at is that which you have felt less than excellent about, and that is functioning as a trinity in this world of darkness and moonlight that you call life.

See yourselves in compassion at this moment. See with compassion the pain within you. All the pain about these relationships, see it and bless it for it has taught each of you much. Gaze at the unquenchable spirit of hope that's shown when all else was dark at so many times within these relationships. Gaze at the courage that in blind faith you exhibited each, and working towards an ever higher goal of harmony together. Look at the adaptations and the flexibilities which troubled each of you in that you could not be flexible enough. Gaze and see what each entity is, who he is, and to deny that would be a far greater harm to you than to attempt to behave in such a way that there was apparent harmony. See this not as failure but as an honest effort, cheerfully and wholeheartedly given, with but a single mind between the three. And see that there are three pilgrims upon this path that shall always be safe places for each other. Within this incarnation, within this experience, within this illusion, the harmonics of the three gathered here today were extremely powerful, yet there was not the complete loosening of fear. There was always the feeling of some separation and this was because it was necessary. These feelings of separation among those who seek to be one cannot be seen in terms of failure. It must be seen simply that it takes an enormous spiritual courage to attempt to offer a life to the Creator, especially one in the context of other entities. Always each has his own ways to be of service to the infinite One, and for many that path of service suffices and more than suffices for it is a sacrifice of a life in love. So that it matters not that which you do, but the spirit in which you do that which you do.

We ask you to take these heavy loads of things you feel left undone away from your shoulders. You do not need to carry them. Those were constructions you placed upon yourself. You planned to go backpacking and you chose a high mountain. And though the flowers of the meadows were beautiful in their alpine bloom, the air grew thinner, the temperature colder and the rocks, crevasses and cliffs ever more difficult to climb. There was not, within this threesome, that harmony which is a gift and which comes from before incarnation, that enabled each of the three to carry the other two. No, my friends, there were different lessons for each of you to learn. For becoming a social memory complex is not becoming an entire society made up of mates who are able to pull well together. In fourth density the situation which you observe at this moment continues to be observable, but the archetypical mind and the realizations of your mind and other minds are open to you in a far greater way than they are in the third density. Within fourth density, my friends, you still would be the one known as K, the one known as Jim and the one known as Carla. You still would have the same harmonics. The same ways of expressing and of not expressing. The same choices and the same disagreements as well as agreements. The difference is that these things would not distress you because you would see them as perfect, and you would see yourself as being able to harmonize in this way and in that, if not in all the other ways. You would see those opportunities that now, in third density, you have a tendency to lump in with all of those things which you feel you have not done correctly. Yet indeed, my friends, there has been great learning between the three that sit here.

Each has been trustworthy, each has given, and each has suffered. Feel this, respect this and honor this. Things that you do not see are always at work in you, and if you wish to glorify that mystery that is within you then as these things work within you they work in such a way as to open the heart, to clear the eyes and the voice and the ears, to sensitize the heart to the wisdom it may feel but not explain. We ask you not to see any portion of this experience as beginning, middle or end. You did not begin, you are not ending. You have worked together before, you shall work together again. You have given the best of yourselves, you have done so before and you will in the future. You are comrades along the way.

Now I ask you to look in a slightly different way at the concept of being of service. The way entities feel that they are of service is the ways in which the counting may be done. The number of words offered as spiritual inspiration, the number of jobs completed so that others may see the published works that have been created. The gazing at the past and the gazing at the future for what can be done better to serve the Creator. What new things can be added to the pile and the quantity of things offered. My friends, we do not say to you that this is not only illusionary, but fruitless; that is not so. When one attempts to be of service to the infinite Creator, one is of service to the infinite Creator. That is in the eternal now. What we would ask each of you, and especially this instrument to consider, is where the service begins and where the service resides when something of quantity is not upon the centre stage in the limelight. Are these words of service or is it the personality and the determination of an entity to open itself to contact in the right manner for service? If these words were not here, would that careful tuning and intensity of seeking still be helpful? Yes my friends, it would indeed. It would not be something that could be shown to the world, but many, many things have been shown to your world, and many, many complexities have arisen as entities attempt and strive more and more to study the truth, so that the truth becomes more and more detailed, more and more complex, more and more studied. Do you truly see the greatest service that you offer adding to that pile of words, no matter how well intentioned or inspired?

Perhaps we can move to a slightly less quantitative kind of evaluation of service when we say to you what have you given of yourself? You have given the stewardship of time. You have spent time in seeking. You have spent that precious coin which can never be got again. Of the moments of service, of upliftment, of inspiration and above all in offering, in hoping, in begging in all of one's heart to be of service in any way which the infinite Creator intends for you. Yes, you are still working with thoughts of quantity. You are still saying, "I gave this much time," and so you know in a way that this too is hollow. Yet is it not closer to an honest evaluation of the self to say, "I gave of my being, I was not doing something else, I was doing this," and as you say that of yourself, to yourself, the Creator within smiles. And in that joyful smile the universe is suddenly infinite and you have transformed time into eternity.

But to move to the true value that you have been to each other, as well as the Creator and others for whom you intended the service, we ask you to look at who you are, what you have sacrificed to be with each other, what you have attempted with the best heart possible to you to offer. Soft words that have been spoken when harsh words filled the mouth and the mind. Trust that came from the heart while the mind was holding back saying, "I am afraid." You have been courageous with each other. You have trusted. You have gone beyond that which you thought you could do. My friends, each has grown. Each a teacher to each. Let the benediction of your love for each other, that you have had such difficulty in expressing, fill your heart. Pause in this moment and feel this great love that you share.

(Pause)

I am Q'uo. Remember this feeling, and this love, and this moment. You have been good and kind and caring, and you have struggled. But beneath it all you have been three wounded soldiers in arms, soldiers for peace, soldiers for love. Soldiers become wounded and sometimes die, whether they fight in hate or whether they fight by refusing the hate. Each of you has had wounds and the group has had its casualties [as] the war of love that is endemic to this illusion carries on. Look and see and rejoice that you have never stopped attempting to love and support and care, each for the other, and in the name of the Creator for service to others.

Was this wagon that you hitched yourself to a bit bulky? Sometimes, in a desire to do so much, entities move faster than their deepest selves can walk. So unhitch yourselves from this yoke. Let the wagon go, you have pulled it long enough. And come always together as new entities, new souls, newly dedicated as if at the very first of meetings. For each of you is new this day and will be new tomorrow, and the service that each of you does will be different yesterday, today and tomorrow. Do not write long sentences with periods as you describe this portion of your life that you have walked together in a certain way. But rejoice that you have had companionship and as you walk into your future, let the knowledge of a companionship that has been tried in the fire and has remained lovely be your strength and your armament. You have been soldiers. You shall continue to be so. Let those deep feelings within guide you to each new day and each new field of battle in which love and fear strive. And as you are unafraid, know with certainty that you are old soldiers, and that you can and will persevere. Not as

you think the Creator has in mind for you, but as you receive from the Creator those opportunities which spring up day by day. You are in no way diminished by this time that you have had together, though you may have, as this instrument has, called [yourself] a failure. You have not failed. You have begun to attempt to become a social memory complex and you will continue in each relationship, and in the relationship within yourself, to be more and more harmonious as a comrade in arms. But remember always the great and sturdy team that you were and are in your honest and single-hearted desire for the truth, the desire to know the love of the infinite One, and to offer all that you are and all that you ever will be to that service.

Go forward from this meeting saying not farewell, for you are only moving into the part of the path in which you may not see each other so often You are all still working together.

We would ask you lastly to think about the implications of becoming a social memory complex. We have said one does not learn to become a social memory complex by the mating of individuals alone. Just as important is the relationship that you have with all others. Whether you experience that relationship as positive or negative, successful or failing, you are attempting to learn the mind that is yourself but not yourself, that mind that is hidden from you by the illusion of separation. And rest back in the knowledge that in addition to all guidance that is unseen, each of you has learned that there is a—we correct this instrument—totally trustworthy entity in each other. Someone with whom it is safe to speak of things that are painful. Someone who you know will not harm you in any way that is intended. Someone that you know will not be petty or mean. Someone whom you can trust to give its best not only on your behalf but in any concern that you might have.

These things do not take place simply in what you call marriage. That which you have attempted is almost completely impossible within the third density. That you have attempted this forming of the family of spiritual entities stands in its intentions golden and perfect, and we ask you never to doubt that that which you have done was truly beautiful and without blemish. Let all else fall away, and remember only this, that three entities loved the Creator and worked and prayed and gave of time and energy and will to the absolute limit of possibility in the attempt to serve. Know that that intention and that perseverance of attempt are the truths that will remain, are the truths which you have chosen to work on in this incarnation. And as you each have moved closer to some idea of what love is to you, for it is to each entity a different lesson, know that no work that you have done has been in vain. For you have under adverse circumstances loved and been loved, and that is the lesson of this density.

We shall meet again. The illusion which you call time will speed very quickly and we shall be with you. We bless each of you with our love and our admiration. We are aware that there is sorrow, but we ask you not to hold that to yourself, but to release it little by little, until all things between each are positive and free. For each has done nobly. So in the end we shall not say farewell to you but we shall say hello. Hello to each, you are new this moment, and we look forward to experiencing that new self that you are becoming in what you call the future. Our joy in meeting that which is becoming you is very, very great. And our deepest respect to that which you carry from the old self to the new is also very great, for you have chosen wisely. You have not released your faith into despair. You have not given up. You have not condemned yourself as being without the ability to serve.

(Side one of tape ends.)

(Carla channeling)

Hello, my friends. We shall meet again and we greatly look—we correct this instrument—and we greatly look forward to this delightful prospect. Meanwhile, we are with you and if you wish us to be with you in a way that comforts and quiets you, you have only to ask. We will of course not speak with you, for we would not interfere with your free will. But you may feel our love and our blessing and our support, just as you know the blessing and love and support of your friends in this room. You may have this at any time, you may have this at all times, you have only to ask.

We are those of the principle of Q'uo. Go always with the Creator. Be always the Creator to your friends and allow your friends to be Creator to you. This is the meaning of "adonai vasu borragus."

We leave you drifting from your ear's hearing, but never from your consciousness, in that one great original Thought—love. And in all the areas of manifestation—life. And in these two things we leave you with the sum and the substance of the one infinite Creator. As you feel yourselves move towards eternity, as time has less and less grasp upon you, we ask always, simply, that you meet your experiences, unafraid and with love. With love and with light. We are those of the principle of Q'uo, and with love of the morning when the sun shall shine upon all of our souls again. And that sun that is the kingdom of love and understanding. Adonai. Adonai vasu borragus. ✦

L/L Research

L/L Research is a subsidiary of Rock Creek Research & Development Laboratories, Inc.

P.O. Box 5195
Louisville, KY 40255-0195

www.llresearch.org

Rock Creek is a non-profit corporation dedicated to discovering and sharing information which may aid in the spiritual evolution of humankind.

ABOUT THE CONTENTS OF THIS TRANSCRIPT: This telepathic channeling has been taken from transcriptions of the weekly study and meditation meetings of the Rock Creek Research & Development Laboratories and L/L Research. It is offered in the hope that it may be useful to you. As the Confederation entities always make a point of saying, please use your discrimination and judgment in assessing this material. If something rings true to you, fine. If something does not resonate, please leave it behind, for neither we nor those of the Confederation would wish to be a stumbling block for any.

CAVEAT: This transcript is being published by L/L Research in a not yet final form. It has, however, been edited and any obvious errors have been corrected. When it is in a final form, this caveat will be removed.

© 2009 L/L Research

Special Meditation
September 28, 1991

Group question: M has a couple of questions. One concerns an experience she had for about nine months of 1990 where she felt that her spiritual body was separate or apart from her physical body. She could see as the observer in her spiritual body that it was observing the things that were happening to her physical body, was like a 3-year-old child having a lot of people's negative emotions and difficulties thrown upon it, visited upon it, and she felt like the spiritual body was more an observer and was not in close contact. She would like to know if this is something that could be commented upon and what kind of comments you would make upon that, and then if perhaps there might be any relationship between what is happening to light workers, such as M, and what is happening in the world as far as the metaphysical evolution of our planet is concerned. Is there a comment you could make upon how our planet is evolving, and are there particular times that we experience certain changes in our vibratory rates that can be pinpointed, say, next January 11, is there some kind of time framework that has meaning for us. Can you comment at all upon the changes occurring on the planet and how they are occurring and when they occur?

(Carla channeling)

I Yadda. I greet in love and light of infinite Creator. We stop in only to greet the one known as M, to wish her laughter and light upon the pilgrimage. Shed all that is other people's clothing of the mind and the heart and the spirit and there shall be new clothing of light in your spirit, but only if you ask. We encourage you to call to us, that all be made anew each day, to feel the fullness of joy which is the joy of the servant who serves well. We thank this instrument for allowing us to speak, for this instrument also has the longer message that [she] wish to express. Our joy and blessings upon each. We are Yadda. Adonai.

(Carla channeling)

I am Q'uo, and I greet you in the love and the light of the one infinite Creator. We thank you for this blessing of calling to us for this wisdom which is not at all infallible, but seems wise only to those who have not yet come to where we are. But we assure you that we have very much further to go in our own development, and would not wish any word of ours to be a stumbling block for any who may listen. Therefore, discriminate in our source as in all sources, that your personal truth be remembered and recognized by you so that you may live the life that you hoped to live.

Let us speak about the visualizations of the child and the adult and the observer in the dreamlike state of being out of one's own body, and seeing this child also, not only out of its mental body, but its physical one as well. Gaze at this child's eyes, for this child is your spiritual self. Gaze in compassion on the hardships and the difficulties of being a young entity, for no matter how very hard one tries as a newborn soul, one cannot exert its will in order to make itself comfortable or warm.

Now, as you gaze at the observer, look at the observer and ask what relationship this observer has to the self. We would be going beyond our boundaries of free will were we to solve this riddle for you, but can only say to you that, indeed, you saw a symbol of that which was occurring in heaven, occurring, the making of hardship for the spiritual self because of the feelings and emotions of the physical self.

Each entity has many roles: the observer, the audience, the critic, the players, those who paint the scenery, those who work the lights. And all these parts of you are still all of you, so that all that any secret does is inevitably seen at last in the mirror of the self. When the physical third-density animal which carries an entity's consciousness is not loved by the self or others, is not shown to be beautiful by the self or by others, there is a slowing down of the energies of the self. Consequently, the observer may note the entity upon the floor, very weak, very weary, very saddened, and completely at a loss as to what may be done better when one's best has already been done. And as you gaze at that situation, and as each gazes at such situations, we ask each to ask forgiveness from the self, for within you there is that critic that will not give the self its rightful place as a wonderful instrument through which each is learning the laws and the ways of love.

If this spirit child casts itself in vision in an inner plane to some distance from its own physical selfhood, its own womb, it is expressing a hunger and a thirst for love. And is there not in each of us not only the spiritual child but the human third-density child—(or for us, various densities, but still children—that yearn for attention and love and respect and care.

It is most common that one who is seeking with utmost might, in the main, moves quickly to the heart to begin doing work in consciousness when this occurs and [for] an entity [who] has not yet balanced the energies that move below the heart chakra into it, there will be some blockage of energy and a mismatch between the energy of the spiritual self and the energies that are coming in because of the request of that spiritual self, because one needs to live that which one has learned. It is most often the case that the one who too quickly undertakes the higher spiritual, almost discarnate skills, of devotion, may well have been leaving behind a neglected body, an unloved body, and without the knowledge to do any other, the neglect of the spirit child within which was born in each entity when each entity first chose to seek the truth with all of his heart.

The experience of being outside of one's own physical body is, in the strict sense of the available data on your plane, common. However, this vision was not given simply that you may see that there is a spiritual child and, indeed, a child, a simple human child, that was not given what it needed, that was hurt when it should not have been hurt, that was helpless to fight against or to balance the pain of living. And as long as this child remains within, the spiritual child has a great deal of difficulty growing because it is the child within that chooses not to love the self, not to love others, and not to love this that you call Earth.

So, in dealing with this clear memory we would encourage the swelling of compassion. Allow the upsurge of compassion for this child. No harm was meant, no evil or sin was committed, but only a simple unknowing, a simple ignorance of how very special, and how very helpless, the child within is.

We do not mean to suggest that those who have not become aware that there is an unhappy and grasping child within who constantly wishes reassurance should drop all that they do and pay attention to this child. The childhood of the body is now past. That child that was abused is no longer, for that which is occurring occurs now and for the first time.

Now, when a baby is born it is most important to nurture it, to feed it, to hold and jiggle it on the lap, so gently cradling it in the arms, sending it love, letting it feel the beat of your heart. So, without saying a word do you love that little child, and in general we would, in our opinion, advise each to see and recognize first that the human child must be balanced before spiritual work can be done safely. And secondly that the spiritual child that is, in Christian terminology, born anew through love of the Creator equally deserves nurturing, this protection. For when an entity is young even the smallest tree blown over upon it can hurt it, even the tiniest tripping, so many things can harm and hinder the spirit within from its growth.

So, in terms of those who realize the infancy of themselves as spiritual beings, to take that infant and cradle it in the heart, to protect it, to nurture it, to honor and respect and support it. For this child is more truly who you are than the entity which you see in the mirror, and it is in this density that this spiritual child makes its most important and its first choice, a choice for love or a choice for fear. Let the environment of your spiritual child be such that there is no fear, but only love and you shall have done your utmost to nurture your own spiritual evolution, not simply in this density but in the infinity of destinies that await the seeker.

As we leave this image it is well to thank the observer for the observer has seen what the eye could not see but what the heart can understand, and by [this] vision has given a picture, an image of the beauty of the perfect child within. Be maternal and fierce in your protectiveness. Do not offer these beautiful gifts that you have to those who do not ask. But simply move through your days honoring Christ consciousness, honoring love, and honoring that child within you which is the metaphysical being which is truly yourself.

We turn now to the question of psychic greeting and the movement from our first topic to the topic of psychic greeting is organic, in that the difficulties posed in the first question are some of the causes of a lack of protection in doing spiritual work. That is, that the lower energies, the energies of sexuality and survival, the energies of relationships with yourself, with other people one at a time, and your relationships with all the groups in your society, all of these things have been in many cases pushed aside, perhaps placed in boxes and tucked away in the attic of yourself. But these do not stay in the attic. These rags and bones climb back down the stairs and back down into the lower energies and recreate the blockage. These blockages are not to be overcome, they are not wrong, they are simply unbalanced, as if instead of standing on the fulcrum of a seesaw you were to stand to one side or to another and the whole side would go down.

Each energy expresses itself uniquely through each unique entity, so the balance in each ray for one is not necessarily the balance for another. The job of the seeker is constantly to attempt to keep those energy *(inaudible)* clear in whatever way the entity has learned. It is especially so in orange-ray difficulties, where not only does the entity have things about himself which he sincerely dislikes, but is being bombarded by others who also have a sincere dislike, distrust or fear of the entity.

The difficulty of doing profound and high reaching work in consciousness is always going to be apparent. For when there is true light generated, attention is drawn to that light, and there are those forces who wish to …

(Telephone rings. Pause.)

(Carla channeling)

I am Q'uo, and greet you again in love and light. Pardon us for the interruption.

When one has a great desire to be of service and wishes to work with powerful energies, [one] well may not know that it is not in balance. It may well feel that it is in balance, but that is the human cerebral, intellectual judgment, not the wisdom of the heart. So it is always well to ask the heart, "What is the work I must do upon myself this day to be in line with the will of the one infinite Creator?" And insofar as this question is not asked and higher energies are brought forth while the heart itself is constricted somewhat in its energy flow, there will be illness or nightmares or hallucinations or a conviction that a contact has been made that is indeed a negative one which is passing itself off as a positive one.

So, instead of moving quickly past those lower charkas, those who aspire to being holy among men must look first to the most common, mundane and everyday things for that is where holiness begins, that is where transcendence and courage begin. As you arise in the morning and when you look at yourself you think, "Oh, what a pretty face," instead of, "Oh dear, I don't want to look in the mirror." It is that simple. It is a matter of opening your heart to yourself, to others, and to the society. It is easier to do each time that you fail, because each time that you perceive within yourself that you have failed and make the subjective judgment that may not at all be true, it nevertheless teaches you the way in which you [are] to go, the way in which you wish to live a righteous life. So there can be no mistakes. You cannot feel guilty. You cannot feel truly a failure in anything because all things whatsoever in the mundane world are also holy.

So, the first requirement of one who wishes to do higher work is to fall in love with the self. Not in a selfish way but in a way of recognizing that within that strange body that the consciousness carries about lives a wonderful, everlasting and perfect spark of infinite light. If you denigrate yourself to some extent you also repulse the light that is within you and tell it to back away from you because you cannot see it. So we stress to those who wish to do positive work in consciousness the valuing and the hallowing of mundane and earthly tasks, for all things are of service and nothing is to be thought better than another way of service.

It very often does happen that when an entity skips through the lower chakra work and moves directly into the invocation of names and the evocation of power, that one may contain far more wisdom than it can possibly express. Consequently, the entity will in some way express the discomfort that it has put upon itself because it asks of itself those things for which it does not have the power. It is always well then in all work to ask to give the highest and best of which you are capable in a stable manner. In a manner which can be held steady for an indefinite length of time.

In other words, it is not necessary to make a brand new self to breathe the Creator. The Creator is already with you and loves you already and does not need you to be more beautiful, but needs only the beauty which you now are at this moment. And most of the beauty is seen in terms of intention and desire. The intention to help, the desire to help, the desire to be closer to the one infinite Creator, and to know true love. These desires are precious and are treasures to be held close to you, for these are the desires of the young physical child within. When you open carelessly—by ignorance, usually, not by design—the energies overwhelm the self as it is, energies which cannot be held stably in the daily life, that cannot be brought back into the work, the ordeal and the joy of living. Then that entity is simply opening itself more and more to the possibility of difficulties occurring, whatever they may be. And in each case where this happens we ask each first to forgive the self for doing this, for the self did not know and was not aware, but was only attempting its very, very best. And that attempt is what is noted, not the degree of success or failure, but that the intention was pure and persistent and as full of joy and laughter as possible.

We will leave any further questions to the question and answer period. As to the date "1-11-1992," it is to be noted simply that there is the master number of 11 which cannot be broken down, and which in its way indicates that it is a powerful time when everyone sees that one one. It is also to be noted that the eleventh day of each month in this coming year will be a master number. The reason for this is that if one adds together in the way of numerology the 11 and the 1992—we correct this instrument. It is to be noted that with the 1-11-19-92 there is a master number also, and one which is to be hallowed, not necessarily on this plane. As a matter of fact, probably not at all upon this plane, in terms of visual sensation or manifestation. But that there are many planes which interact within third density with your own.

See this master number, the 30 degree which this date represents, as a time of completion of certain things upon the spiritual level. Yes, of course, entities may help to rejoice in this energy, but it is an energy which falls like rain from heaven that shall fall whether one appreciates it or not. Whether one finds it good or unfortunate, it is simply that which vibrates in a certain way.

This day, then, may be seen to be a day for powerful or spiritual work and paradoxically for those who wish to relax the spirit, to regain the rest and the comfort that being with people who live spiritually can give you. Much is coming to an end in this particular portion of your race's history. Much is beginning. The mood need never be one of grief, but always one of celebration. We ask each always to remember to respect what other people see, what other people believe, and what other people hold true, not attempting to correct them but simply supporting them in whatever they do, for each has an unique path. It would be well upon this particular day to be more mindful, perhaps, than usual and more aware of the power of choices made and gestures of love extended and broken nets mended upon that day.

We would, at this time, wish to transfer this contact to the one know as Jim, if this entity desires contact at this time. We thank this instrument and leave it in love and light. We are of the principle of Q'uo.

(Jim channeling)

I am Q'uo, and greet each again in love and light. We would take this opportunity in speaking through this instrument to offer ourselves to further queries at this time. Is there a query to which we may speak?

Carla: I have a question *(inaudible)* from Susan *(inaudible)* her situation. First of all I would *(inaudible)*.

(Side one of tape ends.)

Carla: *(Inaudible)*.

(Jim channeling)

I am Q'uo, and am aware of your query, my sister. We cannot answer this query for it is that which infringes upon the free will. We are, as always, sorry that we cannot speak in a way which seems to be of the immediate comfort for we know that you and many like you upon your planet are suffering from distortions of mind and body which cause pain and discomfort. And there is much desire to be able, if not to be free from such, then to treat such so that there is at least a modicum of comfort. The comfort that we have to offer is a comfort that is not of the mundane world, but that undergirding reality which supports all creation, that Thought of love of the one Creator that expresses itself in your illusion in a manner which is mysterious and elusive.

We are aware of the confusions and the frustrations that attend attempting to penetrate the mystery of your illusion and we can only commend your continued efforts in this regard. For by persisting in your seeking in the face of all the difficulties which you encounter, you bring yourself to the peak of the Creator, humbled in worship of the might and the majesty that can create a universe that contains the stars, the planets, all the galaxies revolving in their time and in their turn, along with all of the energies of your life pattern that move about you as do the planets move about the stars.

There are those experiences of difficulty which you face which seem at times overwhelming and which seem to be beyond any comprehension according to purpose or plan. We can only assure you that there is much purpose in the suffering within your illusion. For suffering done in service to others and in the name of the one Creator is a kind of tempering of the spirit that strengthens and crystallizes this means by which the Creator may be known and may shine through your being.

Is there another query to which we may attempt a response?

Carla: Yes, a couple more *(inaudible)*. I have observed in my eating, not preferences, but in what is easiest for me to eat in that I am not able to eat very much solid food. If I can make this choice for myself of what to eat it would be all liquid or partially liquid or whatever. I realize you can't give me a diet, but, in general, gazing at someone with longstanding difficulties, could you confirm that the intelligent thing to do would be to eat even more sparingly, and even more sparingly until an equilibrium is reached?

I am Q'uo, and am aware of your query, my sister. We are aware that your intuitive capabilities allow you to discern those foodstuffs that are available to you that would be most easily assimilated by your body. And we would recommend that you utilize this intuitive capacity in the greatest degree during this time of difficulty for your digestive tract. We would recommend that there be a variety of foodstuffs, as great as possible, in whatever form, be it solid or liquid, that you ingest, in order that your body be given as much opportunity to take from those foodstuffs that which was offered and that which it needs.

The human body has a great deal of ability to utilize foods in the most appropriate manner, however, there is a certain variety that is necessary in order to allow the body to find those ingredients which are most helpful to it in whatever its given condition. Thus, we do not recommend one kind of diet that is liquid or solid, over the other. Rather, the blending of these in a fashion which feels to you to be appropriate according to the time and condition of your body.

Is there another query my sister?

Carla: Yes. I realize that I'm not the only channel who's ever been told that my body is weak *(inaudible)* and that if I continue channeling it will shorten my life. I'm also aware that in each of the cases of which we've heard both channels chose to continue the work. I realize that there is much to be said for the wisdom of being, and not attempting to add to the productivity. But I find it impossible to grapple with intellectually, and consequently to move into my heart, with a feeling of real worth in just being, instead of doing.

I was thinking, for instance, this evening and tomorrow of going to do more exercise and yet I have heard Ra say before, "You do not need the pain, you only need the limitation," which would suggest that I accept the limitation of being on my bed all the time. Yet it has only been since I have been on my bed all the time that my stomach troubles have become more threatening and I feel that there is a delicate balance there between the desire to live longer and the very way of living longer being an instrument which will lead to a shorter length anyway.

So, basically if you have an observations on that, in other words, exercise seems to be a fighting against my limitations. And, indeed, it does usually, if I am successful, enlarge my arena of possibility of action. If I do not attempt to go beyond my limitations at this point, I will be bedfast except for my walks, which may or may not shorten my life, simply because of the diseases or illnesses or whatever is, I think, the result of not exercising. Mainly the difficulty with the digestive tract. I can't think my way through this. If you have any comments whatsoever I'd appreciate them.

I am Q'uo, and am aware of your query, my sister. Again we find ourselves in the position of not being able to give a specific response for the confusion which you express is that particular condition which is a product, or shall we say the precursor of the exercise of free will. We are aware of your confusion, we are aware of your concern, and we can only recommend that you follow that which you feel is most important to you at this time, whether or not it is that which has been recommended previously. Follow that which wells up within you as the greatest desire amongst all your desires. Follow it to its completion, observe again, choose again. Whatever wisdom has been shared with you previously will prove itself or not by your own experience.

Is there another query, my sister?

Carla: Only how could I better serve the Creator?

I am Q'uo. We do not find a better possible, for each here in this dwelling place attempts to serve in every way possible. We instead would recommend the compassion that is given to the self by the self in order that that vehicle that you offer to the Creator as your means of glorification of the Creator, namely your very self, might be nurtured in a manner that would allow it to bloom to its fullest extent as a flower in a field, providing the beauty and aroma to the Creator according to the nature of its beingness.

For all the work that you do in your life pattern is that which adds to the beauty and the fragrance that is yours as a flower in this field. The work itself is not that which is of importance, though you are aware that many have expressed gratitude at the work which you have accomplished. However, it is not the work that is important, it is the enhancing of your own beingness as you seek to serve that is important. Your work in this illusion is a means toward that end and we commend each for the great dedication and sincerity with which service to other selves and to the Creator is attempted. We suggest that you appreciate yourself. The acceptance of self by self is that which builds the firmest foundation for any other service that may be offered.

Is there another query my sister?

Carla: No. As I search my mind I see that any questions I would ask you would have to say that *(inaudible)* unable to answer because of free will so I just thank you for coming to *(inaudible)*.

I am Q'uo, and we thank you, my sister, for the dedication to service that your queries indicate. Is there another query at this time?

Carla: I do have one last query which I'd almost forgotten. I repeatedly get mail from people who explain to me that I am very unhealthy and that something within me, by my own decision, has caused me to remain unwell, and I'm holding onto it and if I let go of it I will become well. I don't defend myself against people like this, there's nothing to defend. On the other hand I don't precisely know how to thank someone who has spent large amounts of time attempting to change me around so that I will be well, when in my own perception of myself, given my birth defects, my very, very bad sickness at the age of two, rheumatic fever when I was thirteen, all the things that have gone wrong with me since, I see myself as one of the most healthy, tough human beings in the world. I've survived all that. So my vision of myself is a very well, whole person. I do not know how to say this to people without causing them to feel that somehow they haven't gotten across to me my own wrongness and the error of my ways. And I have no wish to quarrel with anyone. Is there a more skilful way to deal with this sort of attitude towards wellness than I have so far discovered?

I am Q'uo, and am aware of your query, my sister. You may respond to each such entity as you have responded to us if you wish to go into the same amount of detail with each entity as you have at this time expressed. There is no need for the defense for each is as he or she is and each entity will in time discover that there are situations which confound and perplex each entity. That the old ways of approaching a problem with solution fail. That there is mystery all about and that there will be suffering, bringing forth the questions, "For what end?" and "How best to respond?"

Each shall face these challenges again and again, for your illusion is one of challenge. You are here to be challenged. It is challenging to live in a manner which does not directly partake of the immediacy of unity and seems to be cut off, each entity separate from the other. You may assure each that you are aware of the value of their suggestion, that you have valued that concept enough to have considered it carefully a number of times in your experience, and that you find that there is mystery and that you feel you share this mystery with all. And that sometimes there is the confusion that surpasses all efforts, and that this also is that which is to be treasured, accepted and worked with in the most loving and harmonious way possible.

Is there a further query, my sister?

Carla: No, I truly am through now. Thank you so much, Q'uo.

I am Q'uo, and we thank you once again, my sister. Is there another query at this time?

Carla: I'd like to ask on M's behalf that if physical people looked at her in a *(inaudible)* way, in a scary way, were in any way different from the metaphysical or dream type psychic greetings which come to many in the process of initiation, was there something special about these being actual physical people, or was it simply a matter of one person's character or personality being such that that was the best *(inaudible)* of teaching *(inaudible)*.

I am Q'uo, and am aware of your query, my sister. To those who work for the spreading of the light upon the surface of your planet, there shall be attracted those entities and energies which are desirous of controlling that light or, if necessary, to put that light out. Most of these entities are of what you would call the discarnate or unseen nature. However, they are able to work their efforts through a variety of means so that they might utilize incarnate entities with certain mental and emotional distortions that fit their purposes for a specific working. Thus, all is seen by such a negatively-orientated discarnate entity as a tool or target of opportunity that may be pursued at a specific time and in a certain way according to the desires of the negatively-orientated entity.

Thus, such entities may utilize other incarnate entities, the circumstances of a certain pattern of activities, the various distortions of the mind/body/spirit complex of the entity that is being greeted, and so forth. Thus, there is much interweaving of effort of such negatively-orientated entities, as there is the same kind of interweaving of effort by those entities of a positively nature which also seek to aid, as they are called, and to guide as is possible.

Is there another query, my sister?

Carla: *(Inaudible).*

I am Q'uo, and we thank you yet again, my sister. Is there another query at this time?

(No further queries.)

I am Q'uo, and as it appears that we have completed the queries for this session of working we would take this opportunity to thank each present for inviting our presence in this circle of seeking this afternoon, as you term it. We are most grateful to be able to blend our vibrations with yours and to walk with you yet a few steps further upon your journey of seeking. Your journey and our journey is one journey that does not partake, strictly speaking, of time or space, yet is that which always continues, for always does the One seek Itself through the many, and always do the many seek the One through every breath, word and step that is taken.

We are known to you as those of Q'uo. We leave you at this time in the love and in the light of the one infinite Creator. Adonai, my friends. Adonai vasu borragus. ❧

Sunday Meditation
November 17, 1991

Group question: This Sunday's meditation has to do with the practice of astrology. And we're wondering if it is a helpful thing to look more deeply into the practice of astrology, to get more of an idea of the patterns and the rhythms, the opportunities and the lack of opportunities that present themselves on our path, or if it's just as well to content ourselves with a passing knowledge of astrology. In other words, do you think astrology can be used in the seeker's daily life and, if so, how?

(Carla channeling)

We are those of Q'uo. Greetings in the love and in the light of the one infinite Creator. It is a privilege and a blessing to be joining in your circle of seeking this day. And we wish to thank each who has called us for the purpose of transmitting information, for by so doing, each has enabled us to perform that service which we seek at this time to do. We are most happy to share our thoughts on astrology with the disclaimer that our thoughts are to be heard as the thoughts of a friend rather than those of an all-wise teacher, for we make errors. The request we have of you is that you simply leave behind any thought which does not seem worthwhile to you.

We give this instrument the picture of the world that lies in a darkness, a kind of waiting or anticipatory darkness such as the eve of a great holiday. The present period among those upon your sphere's surface at this time is an increasingly exciting one as there has been more and more of that consciousness among all of your world's peoples that some great event seems to be in the offing, so that the coming of the night is more acceptable. It is into such a frame of consciousness, if you will, that we bring the discussion of astrology. This instrument wonders what we do, but we ask it to relax and go with us on this.

There have been centuries in which it would not have aided most to look more closely into the archetypical mind. These centuries have passed. For this third-density experience which you enjoy at this time, the end truly is near, if you will. Not physically, but more and more mentally and spiritually. There is that subconscious or unconscious amongst your peoples that there are special reasons to look more deeply into natural phenomena and their possible effect upon the self, be it body, mind or spirit that is affected.

Astrology offers one way of learning more about the deeper mind, or what we have called the archetypical mind. It is a complex and detail-driven technology, if you will, the system of ephemeral, mathematical constructs having to do with configurations of heavenly bodies. To the student who wishes to probe more deeply within the self, to become more and more familiar with those uncharted regions of the self represented by the marker in consciousness which you could call sub-awareness, there is this sub-awareness that the deeper studies at this crux may be those which have fruitful results. On this level, let us say, the awareness of specific and personal detail is not that which we speak of at this time, but rather the archetypical mind finds explication by the relationships of heavenly bodies to each other and to this planetary sphere upon which you presently enjoy incarnation. At this level much deep awareness can be encouraged by immersion in that complex set of relationships of star to star, and star to the system of star and planets which you call home.

On another level, the personal level, the yield of useful information from continued study of, and awareness of, the progression of one's own—this instrument would use the word "chart"—is, shall we say, a good way to develop both an instinct for inference and a relatively authentic feeling of control over the continuing life experience which is so precious to you.

To one entity, such a study would be work—a difficult chore done in order for the learning. To such an one, we would suggest investigating other avenues for becoming more attuned to the environment and for aiding in the feeling of control over the life experience. Astrology, then, is that for which some entities are well suited, others not.

To the entity which feels positively or affirmatively concerning keeping up with the chart's progression for the self, astrology can become that aid in consciousness which creates for the seeker a vantage point in consciousness which can act as a collecting area for the amassing of one's psychic self. The gift of being psychic or aware in non-physical ways is within all persons. The means of developing this gift are tremendously large. Infinite, we would think. However, to a fairly large percentage now seeking to increase the rate of learning, spiritually speaking, a substantial number would indeed find in astrology that place from which to continue to learn how to gather more and different information from the environment. For the environment is illusory. And more than that, is an illusion with many, many sub-illusions which further color the catalyst which is retained for use by your minds.

Now let us speak more in general, for there is a point to be made as regards the use of systems created by the mind and observations of mankind. Insofar as the system is internally valid in its logic, that system may be to the entity which plumbs its depths that crutch or aid which acts as the collector for the abilities and gifts of the seeker. In general, it is well to choose a system, whether it be astrology or numerology, the study of the eye, or head, or hand—and we could list systems for a substantial length of your time. What avails them to the seeker as efficient tools is that very systematic nature, for the mind within incarnation has the instinct for the pattern. Each entity in each experience is, in part, working internally to place the present moment into a context which will yield the maximum amount of information. This information is usually heavily biased toward comfort and well-being. However, the mind can be increasingly trained to retain catalyst which is presented to the mind, which perhaps has little, if any, survival use, but which does indeed aid in spiritual learning.

And the way to become more able to do this work in consciousness is to persist in experiencing and studying one system, be it of myth, science, philosophy or ethics, or any system whatsoever, which—we correct this instrument—to which the seeker is personally and individually drawn.

For you are, indeed, living on the eve of that which shall come to be. It is almost impossible to describe the nature of the shift of consciousness from basic third density to basic fourth density. This shift shall take you with it, if you dwell now on the planet Earth. Therefore we encourage the twin awarenesses that it is a good time to be watchful and that it is a good time to celebrate. That which astrology or any "ology" might do is aid in development of that sharply tuned hunger for the truth revealed within the present moment.

How we do encourage each to more and more dwell and marinate the complete entity in that present moment? It may seem odd that the mind's structure is such that the entrance to the present moment is often round about, moving not through the invisible door into the fully accepted present, but rather going completely around the entire structure of living to surprise the present moment only after the long walk has sharpened the appetite. Astrology is, shall we say, the *hors d'oeuvre* which encourages an entity to more aptly fit the intellect to accept an increasing number of inferences.

This ability to loosen the self from the physical, and move into an abstract system of gazing at the self, is key. What you do in gazing at astrology is to sharpen the intellect's ability to let go enough so that the gifts which are called psychic may express themselves intelligibly to that mind which has been softened to accept increasing numbers of inferences. For that which you seek cannot be deduced or reasoned. Discuss what you will, you cannot bring instrumentation, as you now know that, to bear on the nature, the power and the position of that Word or Logos which is the original Thought of the one infinite Creator.

We would at this time declare with regret that this is the substance of our discussion at this time, unless there is a query which would take this line of reasoning further. Might any have the desire to proceed further at this time with this particular query?

(Pause)

In that case, we would close this particular session through the one known as Jim. We leave this instrument in love and light. We are known to you as Q'uo.

(Jim channeling)

I am Q'uo, and greet each again in love and in light through this instrument. It is our privilege at this time to ask if there be any queries upon any other topic that we may attempt response to?

Questioner: I have a question, Q'uo. Prior to the session, a situation was discussed about helping ourselves to *(inaudible)* the disadvantaged within our particular society, and my observation was that the feelings that came to me during that *(inaudible)* were unexpected. I wonder if there is any use for logical reasoning in trying to observe one's own reaction in giving aid or helping another, or if it is more useful for a seeker just to accept it as it is and sort of try to do the best every time with the situation that comes up? I wonder if you could comment on it?

I am Q'uo, and am aware of your query, my brother. The situation of which you speak is one in which you were offered the opportunity to be of service to another in a very direct and immediate fashion. This quality of immediacy is that which catches the seeker, shall we say, in an off-guard position, as you may put it. The spontaneous response of any entity to any stimulus is to act in this off-guarded moment in a pure and unpretentious fashion. To look at this experience as it has been completed, and to review one's reactions, thoughts and emotions is the archetypical path of the seeker, for the examination of the life pattern is the seeking of truth.

The illusion exists for your seeking and your learning. Thus, we applaud the care taken in investigating one's responses to significant stimuli. The significance is chosen by each of you according to that which moves your inner rhythms, those patterns programmed previous to the incarnation. Thus, is it well to spend time daily reflecting upon the day as it has passed, to note those experiences of significance where there was movement in your own consciousness that felt and left behind a strength and a mark upon your memory.

May we speak in any other fashion, my brother?

Questioner: I will take it further by saying that when I agree to help, I have some expectation of the way it would feel, and it did not feel that way. So I would ask you, what kind of experience does a seeker set himself up for when the approach is giving aid with some frequency of idea of what it might be like, or what it should be like? If you could comment on that in any way you feel you can.

I am Q'uo, and am aware of your query, my brother. To have a preconceived idea as to the outcome of any event is to confuse the perception of that event when it occurs. This provides additional catalyst to the seeker, and it is not inappropriate to have these preconceptions; however, it may be noted to be inconvenient. It may also be noted by the seeker that there are a great many responses possible as a result of the giving of service, and each response may be carefully noted and investigated so that the connection with giving without condition can be made.

Is there any further query, my brother?

Questioner: No, Q'uo, thank you.

I am Q'uo, and we thank you once again, my brother. Is there another query at this time?

Carla: Well, this is personal, but I was talking with Jim the other day and we were wondering what had changed since the readings that I was given by Ra that had enabled me to do things that at that time I simply could not do. If this is not a subject you can speak upon, that's fine. If you can comment, great.

I am Q'uo. We first ask if we spoke too soon?

Carla: Well, Q'uo, only because I always have something else to say. I was just going to say I'm just asking in general.

I am Q'uo—still. And we give this instrument the image of the steel door locked carefully, and apologize for the lack of information. Is there another query, my sister?

Carla: Would it aid my understanding of the energies at work in my life for me to mediate on this door?

I am Q'uo. And we would suggest that the query itself be the focus of meditation.

Carla: Very well.

I am Q'uo, and again we thank you, my sister. Is there another query at this time?

Carla: No, thank you.

I am Q'uo, and we thank each for your patience, and most especially for your invitation to us, for we are always filled with joy to receive it and to have the opportunity to blend our vibrations with yours. We are most grateful to walk with you during this portion of your journey and assure each of you that there are many such as we who walk with you always, and there are those who rejoice at your every step. We shall take this opportunity to leave this instrument and this circle of working, leaving each, as always, in the love and in the light of the one infinite Creator. We are known to you as those of Q'uo. Adonai, my friends. Adonai.

Year 1992

March 7, 1992 to December 13, 1992

Sunday Meditation
March 7, 1992

(Unknown channeling)

I am Hatonn, and I greet you, my brothers and sisters, in the love and the light of the infinite Creator. My friends, it is our great pleasure to perform this small service of addressing you this evening. And it is our desire that it be known that if our service be desired at any time by any member or members of this group, you need only ask, mentally request our presence, and we shall be with you.

My friends, tonight we would share with you a few thoughts on the subject of purity. It is difficult to conceive of purity within the realm of your illusion, for, as your illusion is permeated with indecision, as your illusion is the point at which the individual must select—correction—elect to polarize in one direction or the other, there is a strong tendency to accept a proximity to purity as the totality itself.

At this point, my brothers and sisters, the question occurs to a number of you, "What type of purity is being discussed?" My friends, in using the word purity, we refer to the non-resistance to the outward reflectance of light from the individual. As you well know, every molecule, every atom, every portion of substance within your universe, being a facet of the Creator, is imbued with the light of the Creator and is capable of projecting that light in all directions. However, the influence of the individual—correction—individualized consciousness which organizes the various molecules into a physical vehicle for the purpose of experiencing this density exerts a controlling influence over the amount of light emitted from the total vehicle.

More briefly, my friends, you have the ability to restrict the amount of light which you are capable of emitting. The ramification of this act is that the energy level of your planetary sphere is being controlled by those entities upon that sphere—yourselves. And [in] restricting the amount of spiritual light and energy which you are capable of exuding, you reduce the amount of energy and therefore the vibratory level of your surroundings. When taken in terms of your race, the effect is to reduce the vibratory level of your planet which results in the physical and emotional traumas that your planet and its populace continually experience.

My friends, the statements in your holy text which decry the attempt to hide one's light beneath a basket refer to this type of choice. It is within the realm of your abilities to restrict the light energy that you would choose to return to the Creator. It is also within the realms of your ability to restrict your own growth and that of your brothers and sisters. My friends, we are aware that on your planet there is pressure from those about you to conform to avoid standing out in a crowd. But we would request that you consider whether [there is] a greater service to be performed in willing to be brave enough to allow your light to shine forth fully.

[This] service that you would perform for your brothers and sisters in attempting this in your day to day actions [is immense,] for there is no being in existence who is capable of resisting the beneficial effects of this action. We would suggest, dear friends, that this be an object of consideration as you live within the confines of your illusion.

At this time it is our desire to transfer this contact to another instrument that we may accomplish the exercising of those who have made themselves for this purpose. I am Hatonn.

(Unknown channeling)

I am Hatonn, and I am now with this instrument. I greet you once again in the love and in the light. Within your illusion one who stands out from the crowd is often isolated, scorned, ignored, but each is unique, each has their own rate of growth, each has the choice. As you progress you will find that times you will be alone in the crowd for as you grow and gain knowledge, become more aware that which you've learned *(inaudible)*, you shall find that you will be more intent with your particular place upon the planet. Each works upon oneself, each self between. As you become more aware, you begin to see that though they are experiencing difficulties in relating to others on the planet that they also become closer for they will begin to see that which makes them, and others, one in the love and the light of the infinite Creator. Though you will experience difficulties, they will be but lessons in the acceptance of others, but mainly, acceptance of self. The light is ever within, without, it is all things and it will shine, it will glow. As one becomes more aware of its presence, the knowledge that you gain, increasingly guided *(inaudible)* feels more and more comfortable within your being.

My friends, as you grow, as you sit within meditations, allow yourself to feel, experience, the light; allow love. Be that which is you. Allow yourselves to be. My friends, we are with you and shall be whenever asked. But we wish whatever of the way we can to aid you as you search to seek to experience, to become aware and grow. We are one with you as all are one with you. We are known to you as Hatonn. We will now leave this group so that another of the Confederation may be with you. I am Hatonn.

(Carla channeling)

I am Latwii. I greet you, my friends, in the love and in the light of the Creator. We speak briefly through this instrument in order to thank each of you [for] the privilege of being allowed to share our humble thoughts with you, and with our brothers and sisters of Laitos and Hatonn to offer as wide a variety of the types of the Confederation energizing which we can at this time. We are aware that there are those who would wish to use this vibration for aiding and deepening the meditative state; others who simply wish to feel the sensation of our presence; others who are working to become vocal channels. Please take from this band of vibrations that which you personally would find most helpful.

We shall pause at this time and *(inaudible)* on you that you may become aware of our presence and may be aided insofar as we may aid you with our vibrations. I am Latwii.

(Pause)

(Carla channeling)

I am Latwii, and am again with this instrument. We are sorry that we are heating some of you up. We will attempt to adjust for your comfort and close the message through this instrument that we may transfer to another. We would like for you to notice that we are not shouting through this instrument. We are very proud because we have finally figured out how to do that.

My friends, we would offer only a few foolish thoughts which we ask you not to take any more seriously than necessary. We would like for you to think of what has been said by the brothers and sisters of Hatonn. The concept of purity is one which pertains not to all of those foolish things that your peoples find so interesting but rather to a quality as simple as light. If you will gaze out of your window, my friends, in the early morning hours, you will find the tiny crocuses moving upwards towards the still cool spring sun. They are few. You will find these squirrels chasing the birds from the seed you have put out, their bright eyes darting back and forth, their tails moving quickly and cleverly as they maintain their balance. You hear the song of the birds and all these things, my friends, are pure. They are pure because they are not conscious of themselves. They are creatures of the creation of the Father and they are what they are without question.

(Inaudible), my friends, have you not been given a complicated task? To find again that beingness, that feeling of being a part of the creation with no effort while you are conscious of yourself. The greatest task, my friends, is to stay out of your own way, for that which you are will shine. And all that might obstruct it is that which you might do. Some obstruct the light on purpose, but, my friends, many, many others in their efforts to increase their helpfulness actually confuse the quality of that vibration of beingness which we have so often described to you as the original Thought of the one infinite Creator.

You are already a being of perfect love and light. So staying out of your way is a tremendous service to yourself and to others. [With] all of the intelligence and analysis that you can produce through the time of your incarnation, you cannot yield up one more iota of light. That is the totality of your being to begin with. So, my friends, go within and trust that that which you are to be [or do] is least of all a function of that mind which analyzes and far more [truly] the function of your ability to feel comfortable being one who is loved totally by the Creator. If you are loved, you can then love, no matter what other function you may have in this illusion. Love, my friends, is the heart of your gift to those about you and to yourself.

We are very happy to have used this instrument. We do not often receive the requisite amount of call to offer a little sermon but are most grateful to you for allowing us to share these thoughts with you. We would now transfer the contact to another instrument in order that we might attempt to field any questions that you might have at this time. I leave this instrument in the love and the light of the infinite Creator. I am Latwii.

(Jim channeling)

I am Latwii, and am with this instrument and greet you all once again in love and light. May we at this time attempt to answer any questions which those present might have for us.

Questioner: Latwii, I have a question. If you are willing to *(inaudible)* for you to get me some feedback on the effectiveness of the channeling on the Friday night sessions? Specifically, the accuracy of the channeling?

I am Latwii, and am aware of your question, my brother. May we say in this regard that your attempts to be of service during your meditations on the evenings have been quite successful. We have been very pleased with the quality of thoughts transmitted and received by your group. We have found an unusually receptive audience at your Friday evening gatherings and for this reason have been able to provide information which has been called for and which has been transmitted with accuracy.

May we answer you further, my brother?

Questioner: Yes, is there any advice you can offer as to the manner in which we could improve?

I am Latwii, and am aware of your question, my brother. In this regard, may we say that the seeking, the desire of each entity within your group, is that quality which, when taken as an unit, is responsible for the quality of both your meditation and information which is received. The desire which has caused this group to be formed is of a high quality. Therefore, to suggest the improvement of tuning, shall we say, this desire might be at this time too much to ask, for we feel each does present to the group the fullest amount of desire and will to seek the one Creator which is possible at this time, though it is always the nature of the pilgrim to continue the journey in ever a greater degree of depth and purity. [And this refining of your purity shall we are searching also continue.]

May we answer you further, my brother?

Questioner: You answered me fully, thank you.

I am Latwii. We are most grateful to you.

Questioner: Are you the same entity that has been contacting us in Nova Scotia by a *(inaudible)* group leader.

I am Latwii, and am aware of your question, my sister. We of Latwii have had the privilege of making contact with your group on some few occasions. We of Latwii have not been able to make a contact with many groups upon your planet for the information which we have to offer is not often sought by such groups as this. We have been honored to join you on these occasions of which you are familiar and do offer our thanks and our appreciation for this opportunity.

May we answer you further, my sister?

Questioner: No, we offer our thanks to you for joining us.

I am Latwii. We see that there is …

(Side one of tape ends.)

Carla: … is not actual purity or that it is not conducive to the development of actual purity or it is just not relevant or what?

(Jim channeling)

I am Latwii, and am aware of your question, my sister. May we say that, in general, you have expressed some degree of our perception of purity. Those of your people who have considered the concept of purity have quite frequently chosen to whittle away at their being in order to find the purity which they sense must be achieved by the removing of, shall we say, the catalysts of your illusion. By this we mean to say that the world which surrounds the self is too often seen as being of no value and is too often removed from the experience of the entity so that the entity seeking purity does isolate the self in what might be described as rigid and strict guidelines and frameworks and perceptions of the way purity must be expressed. This, of course, is the free will of each entity and does have the lessons to teach.

The concept of purity which we have perceived as being, shall we say, more natural in its beingness is that concept which recognizes that you are pure and perfect as you are without removing any ingredient from your experience. That, indeed, each experience about you has a value to you for it can teach you. And you, a pure and perfect expression of the one Creator, are quite capable of learning each lesson that is made available to you by the world in which you find yourself immersed.

We do not, in our perception, see a need for living what might be called the monkish existence of the aesthetic. For this type of perception quite frequently does further confuse the seeker, for if the world about one is seen to have no value, then part of the Creator is seen to have no value. If the entity is aware of the self as part of the Creator, the feeling of worthlessness then does intrude upon the consciousness and the perception of the entity seeking union with the Creator which has part of its being that is of no value.

We instead would suggest the seeing of the Creator within all creation, within each other self that one encounters in the daily round of activities, and within the self as well. And we further suggest the attempt to discover the value of each experience, the lesson which does wait within each experience which will point ever more accurately to the heart of your being which you seek; the heart of your being which is perfect, which is pure, and which, when allowed to express itself to its fullest, will purely reflect the one infinite Creator.

May we answer you further, my sister?

Carla: I think I understand pretty much exactly what you're saying, Latwii. What you're saying is, for instance, instead of removing sex from one's life as do monks, you would instead request of yourself the most careful search for the Creator and the truest of love within this experience. And instead of removing money from the experience you would instead accept whatever amount of supply that you had in your station of life and see what you could do with that money to be of service as a part of the creation. Is this what you're saying?

I am Latwii. My sister, we have indeed attempted to express thoughts similar to these. We would also add that we cannot speak specifically for any entity, for each must make these choices as a result of the free will and, in this regard, we can only speak in general and express these thoughts which you have accurately reflected.

May we answer you further, my sister?

Carla: No, thank you, Latwii.

I am Latwii. We are most grateful to you as well. Is there another question at this time?

Questioner: I am curious about angels. Are there angels or beings who would help the choice that we've requested, that can help take care of us, or guard us, be with us to lend support and love if we request it? I've always felt there were, I'm just curious.

I am Latwii, and am aware of your question, my sister. There are beings within the inner planes, shall we say, of this planetary influence which many of your peoples have described as being of an angelic nature, for their nature has been perceived of great and intense love and light. These beings do serve, shall we say, as guardians for entities upon this planetary sphere. Each entity upon this planet has a number of such angelic presences which have as their honor and duty the guidance of individuals who have incarnated within this third-density illusion. Each entity may therefore call upon a variety of beings which reside within the inner planes.

Each entity may determine the means by which the call is made and the light and the being is evoked. It may be a simple ritual of prayer, of meditation, a simple sentence mentally asking assistance. It is helpful for each entity desiring this assistance to meditate upon the guides and beings which are in charge, shall we say, of the protection of the entity. Attempt then, in your meditation, to discern some aspects of the entity whose assistance you seek. Whatever aspect you are able to perceive, be it their form, their face, their color, shall we say, their tone, their quality, or their purpose—use this aspect as a part of your calling for their assistance. When this technique of seeking their nature is refined to a great enough extent, you may receive additional descriptions, shall we say, of such beings and may eventually come to know their name and their form and be able to call them by the visualization of either.

May we answer you further, my sister?

Questioner: Are they allowed to work with us unless we request it? What form of aid are they allowed to give?

I am Latwii, and am aware of your question, my sister. The assistance which such beings render is that assistance which is called for by the entity, either consciously or subconsciously. Each entity upon this planet does call for some type of assistance, whether it is consciously recognized and verbalized, or whether it be subconsciously expressed; each calling is answered. The degree of desire, the conscious seeking and strengthening of this desire is that key which shall determine how the call is answered.

Many calls, shall we say, are answered in sleep and dreams, providing inspiration and answers to problems. Many calls are answered by intuitive hunches or inspirations of the moment which seem to occur and appear out of the blue, shall we say. Other answers are of what might be called the coincidental, or synchronistic nature where you may wish to proceed along a certain path, to undertake a certain activity, and do not know exactly how it shall be done, and within a short period of time an answer appears in the form of another self with a proposal, or with a part of your solution, or a situation which fulfills your needs. Many are the ways in which calls are answered. Each entity which calls does take part in the answering of the call by making the call, by desiring the answer, and by arranging the, shall we say, landscape of the inner being so that the proper sequence or scene of events might be painted upon that landscape.

May we answer you further, my sister?

Questioner: So the more in harmony you are with the creation and with the Creator, the more of a better landscape we provide for working with these entities?

I am Latwii. We perceive this statement to be basically correct with the addition that at all times is each entity in harmony with the Creator. That variable which does change is the conscious awareness of this harmony and the ability to learn those lessons which have been provided in each opportunity.

May we answer you further, my sister?

Questioner: One more question. Do you ever work with these entities in your service here on this planet to us?

I am Latwii, and am quite happy to answer that. At this time, we do so.

Questioner: Thank you.

We are most grateful to you as well. Is there another question at this time?

Questioner: Yes, I've read a lot in the last few months, and, in fact, sometimes it's given me a sense of real joy and bliss and my question is, should I try to share this? At this point I don't really know anybody whose got a very listening ear and I don't know whether I have any responsibility in this respect.

I am Latwii, and am aware of your question, my sister. In this regard may we say that the experiences which each entity such as yourself encounters are those experiences which have been programmed by the self so that certain lessons might be learned for the evolution of the mind, the body, and the spirit of the entity. Part of this process of learning includes not only the evolution of the self but at some point within that the radiating of this information, this inspiration and this feeling of oneness to others. The sharing of such inspiration with other selves is that experience which then allows additional learning to become part of the experience of growth which each seeks.

The sharing of this information does require a careful balancing, shall we say, for few are the entities you shall meet that will request which you have to share that is of a spiritual nature. To share such information when it is not requested is not the most efficient type of service to provide. Therefore, as, shall we say, a simple guide we might suggest the full experience of this illusion in the way which is most beneficial to your own growth and the natural flowing of this exuberance for life through your being when you feel the proper moment has presented itself to you.

May we answer you further, my sister?

Questioner: In other words, unless there is a request or a fairly obvious opportunity, then I don't make any real outward attempt at sharing what I experience?

I am Latwii, and am aware of your query, my sister. To refine our previous statement, may we say that each moment in your existence is part of the one Creator, as is each entity. Each seeks the union with the Creator. Each moment then does present an opportunity to make the self available for the sharing of that which is most dear to the self with an other self, [and] is that which is most helpful to the growth of both. To become the evangelist which requests and requires the open ear and mind is that activity which shall prove to provide more results. To make the self available at each opportunity is most helpful, whether the opportunity be a simple smile, the granting of the right of way at one of your intersections, the listening to the sorrows of a friend or stranger, the sharing of your deepest insights, or the offering of a simple piece of advice when asked for. Each is an opportunity to share that which is the love and compassion for the self and each that the self will meet.

May we answer you further, my sister?

Questioner: No, that's an excellent answer, thank you very much.

I am Latwii, [and] we thank you. Is there another question at this time?

Questioner: I have a quick one. What causes and what are actually déjà vu experiences?

I am Latwii, and am aware of your question, my sister. Each entity upon your planet, as we have said many times, is a part of the fabric of the one creation and the one Creator. And by their very nature, therefore, have the ability to become aware of other parts of the creation. Within your third-density illusion, the forgetting is in sway and this unity with the creation is, shall we say, a more foggy part of your being. There are times, however, as the rhythms of your being change frequency that you may become aware of a possibility which does exist for what you would describe as a future occurrence. This is one of many possibilities.

Each entity does have such insights, shall we say, whether they be the dreams during sleep, daydreams during waking consciousness, or random thoughts floating through the mind. Most do not occur for they are possibilities which were not taken, roads which were not traveled. There are, however, times when the thought, the daydream, the dream during sleep, does coincide with that road which was taken in what is perceived to be the future. It is at such times that the entity then becomes aware that the previous conscious knowing has transpired. This you have called the déjà vu experience.

May we answer you further, my sister?

Questioner: Yeah, but on another subject. This is a pretty much personal question. I spoke of a *(inaudible)* of dreams and I didn't ask this question. In such a dream I spent time with an individual that I did not know but it was a one-to-one contact and it would teach me lessons. I was wondering if you could enlighten on me on who that was?

I am Latwii, and am aware of your question, my sister. To speak specifically to your query would be, in our humble opinion, infringement upon your free will, for the seeking of the solution to this riddle is, of necessity, for you at this time to accomplish through your own efforts. You have been quite successful in remembering these experiences. Your dreaming experience can be quite valuable if you wish it to be so. If you wish to return to this place and this entity it is quite possible for you to do so, for the dream experience is one which offers a wider latitude, shall we say, for the entity which seeks to learn certain lessons. These lessons might be more difficult to experience within this third-density illusion and are more easily expressed and perceived in the state of consciousness which you have called the dreaming state.

May we answer you further, my sister?

Questioner: Another question. When dealing with people in school I'm trying hard to be myself around them and in doing so am getting rejected by many. I am at the point of quitting and not trying to work with them anymore. I'm having a hard time figuring out what's right.

I am Latwii. We have listened to your description and assume that your question is whether you should proceed in one direction or another, and find that we can not give this advice, for to travel your path for you is to remove the opportunities for growth that wait upon it for you, and this we do not feel to be a service at this time.

May we answer you further, my sister?

Questioner: No, thank you.

I am Latwii. We are most grateful to you as well. Is there another question at this time?

Questioner: When we see people that we know in dreams and deal with in working out problems, are we actually speaking to that entity on a different plane or is it just working out problems in our minds?

I am Latwii. My sister, may we say that each possibility which you have mentioned is indeed possible. The state of consciousness which you call the dream state, as we have mentioned before, does lend to the entity a greater scope of experience. Most often the experience of the dream state does include realms beyond that which you might consider the normal range of being. These realms do include the conscious awareness of other selves which you are in contact with during your daily existence. In such dreams the work of experiencing the catalysts of this illusion might be more easily accomplished and the conscious mind might therefore be apprised of those lessons which are most in need of concentrated effort.

In many such dream experiences the conscious mind is seated with the necessary information which will allow the waking entity to experience those lessons which are, shall we say, pregnant within the being. The conscious mind, then so fertilized, shall we say, does provide the focus of attention in these areas by its very consideration of the dream and its possible meaning. The dream state is far more varied, and, shall we say, multi-dimensioned than it has been imagined by most of your peoples. To give an accurate description of what is possible within this dream state is, in our humble opinion, not possible, for the possibilities are infinite since the conscious mind does not have its limiting perceptions to reduce the effectiveness of the learning, shall we say, during this dream state.

May we answer you further, my sister?

Questioner: No, thank you.

I am Latwii. We are most grateful to you as well. Is there another question at this time?

Questioner: I read a book written by a psychic who talked about walk-ins: people who wanted to leave this Earth—this is nothing personal, it doesn't apply to me—but people who wanted to leave this Earth and beings who had something to accomplish who did not want to go through childhood would take their place and fill out their [life] and then grow into doing things that they could accomplish in this particular body. Have you heard of walk-ins?

I am Latwii, and am aware of your question, my sister. This phenomenon which you have described as the walk-in is indeed that situation which has occurred upon your planet but which is not usual, shall we say. The integration of the mind and the body and the spirit in the evolutionary process of union with the Creator is that process which is most necessary for each entity to accomplish upon this planet at this time. This process is most carefully watched over by those entities we have previously described as being the guides, the guardians, the angelic presences. There are rare occurrences in which an entity incarnates with many lessons to learn. The lessons are of such a nature that the integration of the mind, the body, and the spirit is not harmoniously achieved. Such an entity quite frequently upon your planet will then engage in that activity of which …

(Tape ends.) ☙

L/L Research

Sunday Meditation
March 29, 1992

Group question: The question this afternoon has to do with relationships in general, and in particular, when we find ourselves in a relationship that isn't exactly to our needs or specifications, how we can accept that portion of the relationship that is other than we would have it be, if it is to be the spouse, or ourselves, or the situations that we find ourselves in, whether they are financial or social or any situation that we would like to change and seems to be unchanging, or perhaps changing too quickly? How can we find within ourselves the acceptance and the support that will help us to help our spouse and to strengthen the relationship so that the relationship and the ideals for which it stands will endure?

(Carla channeling)

We are those of Q'uo, and we greet you in the love and in the light of the one infinite Creator. It is an enormous privilege and blessing to us to be called to your group this day, to be able to share our humble service with you, to offer our opinion in sure knowledge that you shall not take us as authorities, but as companions upon the way of seeking the truth, for we have no authority that you do not also have—just do we have a few steps more along a very dusty path that, as far as we know, has no ending.

It is a joy to speak with companions upon this path, a beauty to us to feel the companionship of your seeking, and to share in your beings as you meditate in one circle of seeking. You ask us this day about that which you know not, that you ask, for you believe you are asking an active social question, a question concerning a relationship. You wish to know how to be better at relationships, at the important central relationship of mates, of dearest friends and companions, of lovers and those who hope together and despair together, and share the deep places of life together. Yet without knowing it, you have asked about yourselves, and how you may achieve that which is yours by nature, but has slipped your mind. That is the balance of a quiet and sure peace, a gently quiet mind that is staid upon faith and confidence in the balance and appropriateness of each occurrence in each present moment of the incarnational experience which you now enjoy at this point in which you call your time and your space.

This little experience of life, my friends, is set about like a gaudy gem, full of brilliance, but quite without the purity of true crystallization. The lives you experience consciously are rhinestones—false and beautiful, part of a complex series of illusions of dreams within dreams. Is the Creator, therefore, the carnival master who delights in fooling His sons and daughters? We do not believe this to be so. We believe that every puzzlement, every confusion, every distortion that is part of the house of mirrors that is a perceived life, is given to you that you may have pain and pleasure in great intensity, so that you may look at the distortions and say to yourself, "What lies behind this distorted mirror? If I had a true mirror, what would this experience be?"

Yet all about you, whether it be sought by science, or mind or feeling, is perceived with significant and persistent distortion. This is not a life experience in which you may depend upon knowing anything at any time with any provable or objective surety. That which you think should be, and that which you think should not be, whether it seems to be about the self, or about the self as seen in other selves, is in actuality misperceived to some degree and in several ordered and hierarchical ways.

This being a large subject, we merely indicate these directions and move back to the heart of the query, for this query about manipulating relationships so that one may be more metaphysically or ethically correct and skillful and free of fear in giving all one can to a relationship, is in actuality a question about the inner balance of an individual with no relationship whatsoever to contact, communication or manipulation with or of another entity.

Let us step back at this time and view one relationship more mysterious than any other, that which has been spoken of by the master known to you as Jesus the Christ, as the relationship of a metaphysical father and son. In the holy work known among your people as the Holy Bible, a question was asked this rabbi or teacher having to do with prayer. "Teach us how to pray, Teacher," asked those who truly cared to know. And after this teacher gave to those who questioned that which you know—with some distortion—as The Lord's Prayer, he asked the simple question about the relationship of father and child. If a child asked for something good to eat, would his father give him a poisonous snake to bite in? You see, this teacher had a sense of humor, and asks people to look at things with a light touch. After all, is a father's relationship to his child so complex? Does a father not simply wish to keep the child alive, to keep it fed, to keep it comfortable if possible and to preserve its life until it can take hold of things for itself?

You have this relationship metaphysically, each of you, with an indwelling and eternal father, if you wish to think of this, shall we say, in [local?] or archaic relationship in terms of that which you know, that which you have experienced within this incarnational time and space. You have been supported, you have survived into mature years physically, yet spiritually you are but children, and spiritually your father wishes also to feed you. Yet, when does a father feed his children? Yes, he does the work, he has the groceries, and is the same father as mother metaphysically is, in the terms of your people's culture, prepared with a meal, with a feast, with all the food and drink needed for nourishment. But does a father and a mother prepare the table when there is no hunger and no request? And do children always know when they are hungry, if they do not have habits of regular times to ask for food and drink, to expect it, to look for it, to find it and consume it with blessing and thanksgiving and happiness of heart?

We speak to you about prayer, for this is at the heart of any query that has to do with dealing with the mirrors that other selves offer to you. Any—shall we generalize—any question concerning the lower energies—and by this we mean dealing with the self, dealing with any other self, or dealing with groups of other selves—has reference either to being energies that are blocked within the self, energies that are distorted by over-action within the self, or energies that in some way do not find it possible to move into the open and loving heart, that great energy center which is the first energy center capable of unconditional love.

Moving from this center, the first communication is, "Lord, teach me how to pray." Everyone's Creator is different. Everyone's mode and method of prayer and hope and desire is different, often radically different, yet each path is utterly appropriate for the person to whom it is natural and the part that is appropriate to an entity must needs be respected by that entity with an authority that is above all teaching, all outer authority and all discrimination that is not one's own, for the truth that is yours is not heard, but heard and recognized, somehow remembered. If it is not recognized, if it remains in the head and does not move to the heart with a feeling of recovered memory, it is not your truth, and no matter who says it to you, it is to be laid aside gently and with respect, but with a firmness that allows no stumbling block to enter your path.

So when we say to you that questions about relationships are actually questions about how to seek and to pray, we offer this as opinion, and we ask you to subject this and all opinions to your discrimination. Let us look briefly now, as briefly as we can look—this instrument has just said, with some irony—at the nature of prayer, at the nature of asking.

As it is also said in your holy works, "Seek and you shall find, ask and you shall be answered, knock and it shall be opened to you." My friends, there is so much more truth in these words that we ask you to be careful what you seek, what you ask and what doors upon which you would knock, for you will learn the answer that fits this particular moment in your seeking, that opens to you the understanding—if we may use that word—that may be available and useful to you at this moment, and this is a heavy responsibility for that which you have become aware of, that seeking that has ended in a desired response, becomes for you a ribbon to wave in a very courtly battle against the dragon that caused you to ask this question. It is something to take up and work with and live with and sit with in silence, not asking, but only listening, allowing the ground about you to become holy ground, allowing these answers of the moment to become part of a metaphysical muscle memory, if you will. Fundamentally, you are asking for a change in consciousness, and this is uncomfortable in the progression which brings about the seating of the change desired, the seating of the information desired, so it becomes part of who you are.

How can you pray? How can you seek? You simply put aside the time—thirty seconds, a minute, five, twenty, there is no time in metaphysical seeking. There is only intent. You seek with the attitude that you are aware that everything in this illusion is mirroring to you, with more or less accuracy, the processes of your own balancing and centering and seeking. You sit and you spend time as you would spend precious, precious money, for you have so little time, my friends. And all that occurs after you sit, after you learn, and as you are undergoing the discomfort of spiritual change, you become aware that all that occurs to you is a reflection of the processes that are occurring as the spiritual child that you are grows, sometimes jerkily and awkwardly and sometimes with unexpected grace and freedom.

Love one another, my friends, for it is the outward expression of being in love with yourself. All that you wish to know, and, indeed, the Creator in all of It's infinite intelligence, lies in mystery within you, and you shall not know anything. But you shall seek and you shall learn more and more about loving and allowing the being loved to occur as a reflection of an unjustified and utterly appropriate spiritual oneness with the Creator.

Relax into unknowing. Find the faith to seek without ever hoping to know and prove it, and in mid-air you shall find the relationships that are so central to your comfort and peace becoming more and more full of the love that is the special and exquisite freedom of a quiet and faithful mind and heart.

My friends, it has been a great joy to speak with you. We cannot express how much we have enjoyed meeting the one known as M, greeting again the ones known as C and Jim and Carla, and using this instrument. We thank this instrument for making itself available to us and we would close this meeting if the one known as Jim will make itself available at this time through that entity. We leave this instrument in the love and in light and in unity. We are those known to you as Q'uo.

(Jim channeling)

I am Q'uo, and greet each again in love and in light through this instrument. It is our privilege at this time to offer ourselves in the attempt to speak to any further queries which may remain upon the minds of those present. Is there a query with which we may begin?

Carla: I have one to start this off. When two people are talking together and both feeling confused and maybe frustrated, what active thing besides going into the silence—which feels passive and like going away from each other—what thing in the moment can two people do to clear and sort of clean the air?

I am Q'uo, and am aware of your query, my sister. It may be that such centering and clarification could be aided by selecting a passage from whatever source of inspirational information is pertinent and has meaning for you that would become a focus for your attention at those times when you seek to bring yourself and your mate to a point of receptivity. Choosing such a passage, whether it be written prose, poetry or perhaps even the song that is played upon your recording device, would be a symbol for the centering that you wish to achieve and could be a triggering device, shall we say, that would give each of you the opportunity to allow your confusion to recede as the waves upon the ocean, and to focus upon the inspirational passage that you would make together at a time when you feel centered and whole and without confusion that causes misdirection and miscommunication at the moments of crisis.

Is there a further query, my sister?

Carla: Just one follow-up. I've always noticed, as a person sensitive to poetry and to music, that if you think something or if you read something, it has a certain amount of power, but if you, well, I would say vibrate it, if you say it out loud or if you sing it, it has not just more power, but it has a different order of power. Would you say that something that is not just listened to or read together, but is said together or sung together, in addition say, to being heard or looked at, would have that kind of difference in getting into the real heart of both people?

I am Q'uo, and am aware of your query, my sister. This is, of course, possible in just the manner in which you have described it, but is also possible that the confusion of the moment could be of such a degree that participation would be difficult. If this is so, then the listening or more passive participation would provide the easier entry into the reading or the musical passage. If it is possible to actively participate and to read or speak together that which has been chosen for the centering or the focus, then this is also recommended.

Is there another query, my sister?

Carla: Just to confirm. Probably, if two people are confused together, they can get a whole lot more out of listening, in general.

I am Q'uo, and this could well be the case. Each situation has unique characteristics, and must be dealt with uniquely. Follow that which feels most appropriate in the moment, my sister.

Carla: Golly, Q'uo, you mean I can't make another rule? Thank you very much.

I am Q'uo, and we thank you, my sister. Is there another query?

Carla: What about if just one person is willing to do the work? Can it still work with that one person, can it still help?

I am Q'uo. We believe that this is so, my sister. As one entity finds the center of love and acceptance, then this energy of love and acceptance is radiated to the other entity and the possibility of calming the storm is increased.

Is there another query, my sister?

Carla: One, and then I promise I'm done. Do you feel that if we listen to this or read this and have more questions that this is fertile ground for further examination and questioning?

I am Q'uo, and we believe that if there are further queries upon your part upon this topic, there is fertile ground always. Is there another query, my sister?

Carla: No, thank you, Q'uo. Thank you very much. I really appreciate your time and your effort.

I am Q'uo, and again we thank you, my sister. Is there another query at this time?

(Pause)

I am Q'uo, and we would like to take this opportunity to thank each present for inviting our presence in your circle of seeking this day. We are honored to have been invited to join you in seeking clarification for your journeys as you travel together that great road that leads into the mystery of unity and into the experience of the love and the light of the one infinite Creator.

At this time, we shall take our leave of this instrument and this group, leaving each, as always, in that same love and light. We are known to you as those of Q'uo. Adonai, my friends. Adonai. ✣

L/L Research

Sunday Meditation
April 5, 1992

Group question: The topic this afternoon has to do with communication, especially communication between partners or people who are very close in their relationships, where we would expect that such a situation would lend itself to clearer and easier communication than one with perhaps a stranger. What occurs frequently is that there is a difficulty or a baffling in the communication, where even though both people try to their best abilities to communicate clearly, there is something that injects itself in the communication that causes a difficulty or a muddying of the communication. What would be the advice in such a situation? Would it be better if we attempted to stick it out and work as hard as we can with the person and to finally achieve a mutually agreed-upon clear communication? Or, when you find such difficulties and they recur, perhaps as a pattern, is it better to look at yourself in the contemplative or the meditative state to see if there might be some kind of an internal blockage or problem that you are working with in that particular area where the communication is unclear? Would that be an avenue that might provide clarification, not only to that particular communication, but in your ability to communicate in general? What would be the advice in such a situation as a way by which we could clear our communication?

(Carla channeling)

We are those known to you as the principle Q'uo. Greetings to each of you in the love and in the Light of the one infinite Creator. What a privilege it is to be called to your group this day and to rest in the beauty of your vibrations as you sit in meditation. We would offer to you our opinions this day upon the subject of communication, more especially, the problems of communication with those with whom an entity communicates most frequently, those best known, those most familiar other selves within an entity's environment.

As we speak of communication in this light, it is well we begin by pointing out that the difficulties of communication with strangers are far more easily addressed by linear linguistic analysis than those difficulties in clear communication harbored by those whose interactions are numerous and have taken place over a substantial period of what you call your time. If there is a misunderstood word betwixt oneself and another self which is a stranger, there is either the prejudice which is generic—the one not knowing the word feeling the other is a snob, the one knowing the word feeling that the other is ignorant—or there is a querying as to the meaning of the not-understood word, and communication resumes quickly. If there is a point of view that does not make sense to another's point of view, strangers may well say they do not understand. Again, communication breakdown is not at all probable, for it is more obvious that there needs to be a question for information.

There are many cases where, because of deeply ingrained distortions in concept about the nature of certain kinds of entities, whether the prejudice be racial, or economic, or social, or intellectual, breakdowns in communication will follow more closely the pattern of breakdowns in communication amongst intimates. The more heavy the bias or distortion, the more frequent the breakdowns and the more characteristic is the underlying cause being a distortion of mind which refuses to admit certain information from certain types of people as judged by the communicator. Now, let us move into the area of your query this day.

Moving back beyond the beginning of a relationship, moving to a time before there was a relationship, each entity within the relationship was an entity unto itself, yet beneath that truth lay substrata of influences carried into the incarnation and further distorted by early experiences with other selves in the intimate family circle. When two entities meet, they are seemingly to each other fresh out of the bandbox:[3] sparkling, virginal and new. Yet in each case, the surface appearance deceives, for each carries a tremendous baggage of previously held biases, some of which might be contradictory to the self, yet equally strongly held, many of which may well be self-destructive. These biases and distortions of opinion are as much a part of what is to be called good about an entity as those things which seemingly would be more apparently good, clear and positive traits such as honesty, judgment and fairness. For each eccentricity, each distortion creates a catalyst with regard to the reflections given to the other self in an intimate relationship, a catalyst that the entity would not have if there were no distortion whatsoever within the intimate mate or companion.

So, as the one known as Jim was thinking and feeling earlier it is indeed true that miscommunication, as well as communication, is good and proper and to be appreciated. Even with clear communication and no bias, errors in transfer of opinions, concepts, processes of learning and ideation will occur. There is not such a thing within your density as perfect communication, certainly not while words are being used. So we do not suggest devaluing the self because of biases that seem to thwart easy communication. Before any relationships have importance enough that they constitute that to which attention must be given, lies the attention to the self, to the grasping of the generalities about the self, while respecting always the infinite mystery of the self.

The life experiences need to be examined, not simply analyzed, but felt and considered, somewhat out of focus, in their relaxed and reflective manner so that patterns will appear, so that dream material can be correlated to events of the day, so that all of the parts of the mind and the deep mind may, in that relaxed state of mind, merge together to form new possibility, new avenues of thought, and a grasp of situations, so that new ways and tools may be found to forge simpler and more lasting bonds of word in body motion, making communication lighter and clearer and more lucid. So, as always, the work with another begins within the self and communicating with the self. When your feet are on solid ground in regard to the self, there is then the placement of the pivot, the point of balance, the fulcrum, the place from which one may move without losing the balance, without toppling too heavy a load, and without toppling as a life experience as one falls completely away from balance in a traumatic situation.

So we assume as we go on that it is understood that always the work by the self, for the enlightenment of the self, be undertaken in a humble but daily method or manner. Emphasis being given not to the length of the experience, or the perceived depth of the experience, but rather to the purity of intention to seek, to desire to know the infinite One, to feel one's ground as holy ground, and to discover the will of the infinite One for the self in service to all other selves. If this be daily, it need not be elaborate, and the elaboration may come as each entity finds its own path and its own most efficient way of processing information, insight and depth of worship.

Now let us see two selves: A and B, shall we say. As they meet each other and begin to build a bridge of communication, the first efforts at communication may well be very unsuccessful, but may also be quite undervalued if A and B are extremely fond of each other. It may not seem to matter so much what is said as the fact that there is the sound of the voice

---

[3] bandbox: a usually cylindrical box of paperboard or thin wood for holding light articles of attire.

wishing to speak, and that feeling of one who wishes to hear what you have to save. This communication level is so satisfying that there is very little editing of information, and all kinds of information are allowed into the mind's memory without editing or rejecting. This is a very efficient way to communicate, for a large base of data is gained.

The secret to this type of communication is the refusal to interrupt that which another is saying, upon both A and B's parts. This joyful type of communication bubbles forth when each experiences the other for the first time, when history must be learned, and it is particularly exhilarating. More than entities realize is communicated during this period in which the subjective evaluation of information transfer is that much has been lost because of the bedazzlement of infatuation, love or friendship. However, insofar as this has been the first and imprinting information, it does remain the very most important and deepest of the information base and is the basis for communication with the other entity until such time as any misperceptions in the original communication base have been discovered and work has been done to reprogram that misperception so that it reflects more accurately the true nature of the other self.

We may look at the base of information, then, as a kind of bottom of a pyramid. For as the time moves by in its perceived stream in your illusion, fewer and fewer bits of information transferred seem new to the self about the other self. A knows more and more of B, and begins to predict more and more of those things which B will tell. B does the same with A. A and B discover they have swapped their history to the point that there is less and less new to be learned. The base that was once so broad has been built on and built on until all of those things which are central and predictable within the terms of that special relationship begin to overshadow the entirety of the information base, and the useful bits of information are now perceived to be fewer and simpler and larger.

A and B begin to predict that which the other will think, begin to assume that they will have a certain reaction to a certain question, each from the other. We are not talking here about those times when A may be upset or angry with B, or B depressed or upset in some way. We are speaking of two entities of good will who have begun to assume that he or she knows the other entity.

This is the central difficulty in communication between intimate companions. Each entity has very riveting experiences, certainly, and much behavior is predictable, certainly, but the possibility of depth, eccentricity and nuance is prominent in any exchange of information which deals with deeply felt things, especially. And it is skillful not to assume that anything is known. It is skillful to listen precisely to what is said, and not to what is assumed to be true if that is said. This is a subtle point, simply because entities do not realize how many assumptions they make about their intimate companions. Such assumptions may be in general true, but all spiritual truths contain paradox. And no paradox is plainer than that every rule has its exception. Every generality that you use to predict your companion's way of thinking and behavior will have substantial exception, and this exception is most important and needs to be given pride of place, needs to be given that blank space where there are no assumptions yet, in order that a difference may be explained.

How then does one move into an awareness of the assumptions one is making? And perhaps should not make? We may suggest, not the walking away from the conversation, nor the working harder at the conversation, but a shift in the direction of the conversation. For in conversation entities normally tell each other things. In the midst of perceived breakdown of communication, we would suggest for those who are in deep distress, that perhaps a brief song, wise word, or some brief seconds-long ritual of centering, even in silence with held hands, provide a new base, a new place for two spirits to begin a different kind of communication. When this has been achieved, then we would suggest this general approach: Let either one begin by saying, "This is my reality. I know I have created it myself. And I am aware that there are things in it that are misperceptions. Otherwise, we would not have trouble communicating. Let me tell you the world that I, at this moment, create, and how in my world I am seeing myself in perceiving you." This is done without interruption. Then the other takes the responsibility for the self, too, and says, "This is my universe. I am aware I have created it and I allowed and am alone responsible for it. In my universe, I have created my feeling this way, and feeling that you feel this way."

These are not declarative statements alone; these are statements that are also requests, requests that the other not only state its reality that it has created, but also that it speak quite directly to those things about the creation of that entity, which is the self, that the other entity feels have biases that are not justified by that which the other entity's creation contains. It is a feeling of the way, a moving back from an addiction to fact. One moves away from knowing what one knows when the blockages of communication between two intimates are to be cleared away. For it is not only the words themselves, it is the assumptions that have been created through years of repetitive actions that can destroy communication so effectively.

If there is the expectation, and it is not owned, if there is the prejudice and it is not owned, if it is not brought out into the open, how can the other entity do anything but respond to the feeling that lies behind the statement, which is seemingly innocent and harmless. So when there is a blockage that is inexplicable, it does not have to do with vocabulary or amount of information given. Then it is that one begins anew at another level of communication: a telling of the story of the self, a speaking of the legend of the moment. "This is what I have created. Respect this, but tell me what you have created, and I shall respect that." And from this exchange, all differences in perception may be communicated back and forth, back and froth, until the two creations have a consensus reality, special to those two entities at that moment in the combined myth of two entities upon a journey of seeking together, thus unifying what was broken, and healing that which was sore and painful.

This does not mean that agreements can be reached in which each party feels the same, for each entity is unique and each path is different. Yet, if free will is respected, we feel that it is always possible to come, if one is humble enough, to express one's perceptions and misperceptions as one who is responsible for them, to come to some mutually acceptable pleasantness and unity, wherein each respects the other's points and sees what preferences caused the other person, who is quite honorable, to continue to hold a varying opinion.

Agreements do sometimes occur, but this is not the goal of communication. The goal of communication is the exchange, in freedom and peace, of information. To have an addiction to agreement is the same with the answer as having an addiction to fact in posing the question. Fact is to be released, for there are always exceptions. Agreements are to be released, for there are always possibilities of two unique points of view, both of which are correct in the personal truth of each. Thus, free will is preserved, mutual respect is given, and respect to the self is also given.

Now we would only touch less centrally upon what would seem to be clear, that is, that other disturbances in the life pattern, changes in work, in geography, in circumstance, the loss of friends or family, these and many other things can cause one to be quite erratic in communication skills. There are two ways to deal with this truth. One is less efficient but more merciful. The other is more efficient, but does not partake much of tenderness.

It is the nature of each entity to move as he will between these two types of coping with special problems at special times. The merciful way to cope with an entity which is under tremendous strain is to move away from speaking of serious things, to attempt to give support, and to attempt to share the laughter, and to attempt to find ways, always to make merry and to, in the deepest sense, distract the entity from gazing at the situation which is so difficult and so puzzling because of its newness, and because of the grief and pain of loss. A far more efficient way to deal with this type of situation, which is special, is to continue to communicate as if both entities were not under stress. To continue to take responsibility for creating the universe in which each is living. This will lead to a large volume of communication. It is, however, a very efficient means of assimilating and aiding each other in assimilating the processes of change, wherein much old information is found no longer to be useful and must be, as this instrument would say in computer language, "dumped," and that energy of the dumped program used then to create a new program, if you will, a new software program that will work in the new reality, which is perceived as true by the self.

Neither way is more correct than the other. How one deals with special circumstances, how one deals with self-pity, with sorrow, with all of the tragic sentimental and enfeebling emotions connected with the reactions of loss, pain, and limitation are equally acceptable. The less self-destructive that they are, may we say, the more efficient. Consequently, if one perceives oneself to need to cry, to feel self-pity, to feel weak, and to feel helpless, then by all means we suggest feeling this way; but feeling this way when it does not infringe on communication with others. And if one must feel this way in the company of another, it is well to communicate simply that one is incapable of clear thinking, thus again taking responsibility for the inability to communicate clearly before difficulties have arisen because of these special circumstances. Some entities need very badly to act out all of the anger, pain and frustration of loss, whatever it may be. Others find themselves more invigorated by distracting the self, and moving positively in any direction while allowing the work of change to be done more or less subconsciously.

This information is known only to the self. And it is the skillful spirit which knows the self well enough to allow it the tenderness it may need or to give it the action in all directions that it might need, but in each case being responsible enough to say to the companion with whom one must communicate, "I am being unhappy now." Or, "I am behaving in a manic way now, because this is how I need to deal with this trouble and sorrow. Consequently, I will not communicate well, and if I become troubled, I ask you please, to [for some] hug me, [for some] reassure me, [for some] leave me alone." Each entity may fill in the blank.

However, my friends, most communication problems between those who are intimate are those of assumption and the lack of knowledge of the programs that the self is running. As you sit in meditation each day, if you find yourself coming to the end of your meditation and you see that there may be time for prayerful quiet thought, and something is puzzling you, set your mind upon it gently, lightly. Don't worry about it or attempt to untangle it, but gaze at it. There it is, this thing that seems rather fearsome; this place where one cannot communicate with another. There it is. Look at it. Do you fear this? What do you fear in this? Do you fear abandonment? Do you fear a loss of love? Do you fear being completely understood? Do you fear being right? Do you fear being wrong? Where there is a blockage, somewhere there is fear. Rest and gaze and sit with this companion of yours that you call a blockage, and when you again come to that state of mind, move to that again and rest and sit and admire it. And one day, it will burst into a candle flame and lucidly, clearly show you the untangled, the clear situation. For you ask, and so you receive, not in the time of humankind, but in the time of knowing, when you are completely ready to accept responsibility for the knowing. Be patient in these searches of the self, with the self, for your time of knowing may be now, or it may be some time from now, but once you ask, you may be sure that you shall know.

May you have the faith and the grace to have that patience and to seek in that steady persistent manner, regardless of circumstance. It is to the humble persistent seeker that doors are opened, questions are answered, and desires are given. Often not as you would expect it, but in the end in ways that always seem to contain so much more than you ever thought possible. May glory be with you in the harmony of the process of pilgrimage. In darkness and in light, in pain and in joy, love one another, my friends, and realize that you are never alone, that you always have the help of those friends who are unseen, those energies which are those of grace and clarity, beyond all human understanding.

At this time, we would transfer this contact to the one known as Jim, if this entity would accept it. And we would leave this instrument in love and in light and in thanks for this instrument's willingness to serve in this way. We are those of Q'uo.

(Jim channeling)

I am Q'uo, and greet each again in love and in light. At this time we would offer ourselves to the speaking to further queries, if there be further queries upon the minds of any present. Is there a query to which we may speak?

Carla: Well, I guess the thing that puzzles me the most is that you are into a communication blockage before you know it. The kind of work that you were speaking about seems like you are like two blocks ahead of the place you are supposed to turn off before you figure out that you should have made a turn. How do you get back to where you can say, "Wait a minute, this is the way it looks to me. Is this the way it looks to you?" You have already gotten stuck. There are emotions, not just words, but there are emotions.

(Side one of tape ends.)

(Jim channeling)

I am Q'uo, and am again with this instrument. We are aware of your query, my sister, and would suggest that when you become aware of the turn that was made at some point previous to its realization, that you state that fact as soon as you can, so that there might be a reevaluation of the conversation. All of your interaction with others is that which is of the moment, that which is inspired by the thoughts that spring both from your own mind and from the mind of your fellow creatures as you attempt to communicate and act together in a certain fashion. As there is a movement away from the desired objective, the noting of this movement is that which is most helpful in bringing both entities once again into the alignment that each has desired, whether the desire is spoken or consciously recognized, or not. For you are more than you think you are as you interact each with the other. You have your histories with you, both that which is known and that which has become unavailable, shall we say, to the conscious mind, and these histories are a kind of momentum that are colored by experience so that there is an unknown factor in all intercourse, the factor of the creative expression inspired by that which is within the experience of one or both entities. As you find your interchange of energies, of ideas, of directions, of feelings, moving in a fashion which becomes uncomfortable or unfamiliar to you, then it is your responsibility to note this deviation and to move again toward the desired objective that you have set before you.

May we speak in any other fashion, my sister, to this query?

Carla: I have one more question. It may not be worth anything, but I was thinking about the model of the triangle shape that you showed, or the pyramid, and I was thinking about our actual situations, which is that, although we do get a broad base fairly early in life, still, if we don't limit ourselves to that base, we use that broad base and we get even broader if we don't insist that we are this kind of person or that kind of person and hold on to those early things, then we do what the model was in the renaissance of man, and that was just to have more and more options of ways of thinking and ways of processing information and so forth. And that's true of other people, too, so that instead of the model being a pyramid, it would be more like a trapezoid, I guess you'd call it, with the top side broader than the base, but not an upside-down pyramid because you don't really start with just one thing as a very young child. You get everything at once, but always with that kind of pulsar center of the essential self, so that it is not that we are getting more scattered. Do you see what I am saying, and does that make any sense as the kind of model that we might be trying to keep in mind for ourselves and other people to open up the possibilities? They might be different this time than they were yesterday, or last year.

I am Q'uo, and am aware of your query, my sister. Indeed, the triangle shape is one of the simpler models that can be used to describe an entity and its base of experience and information upon which it shall draw and build further experience in the life pattern. It would more nearly be correct to look at each entity as a faceted gem with many sides and many angles or perceptions on a number of topics, for each entity has within it the ability to pursue interests in a wide variety of fields of endeavor that will enrich and influence the further learning and growth of the entity. So that when entities gather together to share that which is theirs to share and to learn that which they desire to learn, one may see the shining of the light of this desire through the facets of the gems which each entity is, and as the desire is moving through the different points or angles of perceptions, there will be a light that is bent in a certain way as your white light is bent and separated into the colors of the spectrum as it moves through the prism. Just so is the desire to learn and to share, in its movement through the faceted gem of each entity, bent and colored by the experiences, the information, the desires and potentials that are within the entity and which make it a multi-layered being. Thus is intercourse or interchange between your entities enhanced and enriched.

May we speak in any other fashion, my sister, to your query?

Carla: First, let me thank you for that answer. I'm going to have to read it to get it all, but that really sounded rich, meaty.

I had one other question that just came to me as an image. The triangles again. I was thinking about how we do have an essential self and if it was a triangle, then it would start at the point and not get very far out before it began the line through the very essential middle of the shape of the triangle. And if you took the triangle of one person with the point upward and the triangle of the other person with the point downward, and you moved them together until they sort of clipped into place with that central essential point in alignment and agreement, then you would have a six-pointed star which is the symbol of the white, Western, Christian magical tradition. I was wondering if there was truth there of the magical way that people can interact if they are linked together, because if you can follow the image, when the six-pointed star is made of the two triangles that move together with one point up and one point down, the essential selves would look like a pencil that is sharpened at both ends within the triangle, and it would also then look like a common crystal, a quartz crystal, which is known to be magical, but only when it is charged by a magically oriented entity who holds it in the hand and is itself crystallized. Are we crystals to and for and with each other? And does our communication, our coming together, have that kind of absolute magical nature, if we can find it?

I am Q'uo, and am aware of your query, my sister. There is much within your query that is fertile ground for communication and we shall chose only the most basic portions to comment on at this time. Returning to your original image of the two triangles coming together in a manner which creates the six-pointed star, one may look upon each entity as having the mind, the body, and the spirit sides of the triangle, both in the conscious and in the subconscious realms, shall we say. So that each entity is both that which you may call male or conscious, that which you may call female or subconscious, in that the functions of each of these portions are somewhat different but complementary. Blending the two together in a balanced fashion creates that which you have called the six-pointed star that makes available to the entities all of the experiences during the life-pattern so that there is very little that remains in the shadows, shall we say, or in the distant memory, yet affecting the present experience. The entity that has been able to gain a knowledge of itself to this degree is the entity that has increased its crystallization, shall we say, its regularization so that when it desires to move in a certain direction, it has at its disposal all of the energies of its incarnation, both those that are normally conscious and those that for many remain subconscious. Thus, its resources are greatly enhanced and it may move with more certainty along any line of desire that it constructs for itself due to the regularization of its mind, body and spirit complexes on both the conscious and subconscious levels. Thus, each of you is truly a crystallized being, becoming more and more crystalline as you discover those facets of yourself that have heretofore been unavailable to you as resources upon which to draw for further problem-solving, shall we say.

Is there a further query, my sister?

Carla: No, thank you. That's more than enough. I take it that the question about that general line thinking might be a group question at sometime.

I am Q'uo. And this is correct, my sister.

Carla: Very well. Thank you so much, Q'uo.

We thank you, my sister, once again. Is there another query at this time?

Questioner: Yes, what suggestions would you have for stubborn pride that keeps people from taking responsibility for themselves and communication?

I am Q'uo, and am aware of your query, my sister. If that, as you have called it "stubborn pride," which blocks one's ability to assume the appropriate responsibility in communication and relationship, resides within one's own being, it is well to take that concept as an image into your meditative and contemplative or prayerful states and look therein the silence within at that quality, observing how, as the pebble thrown into the pond, it ripples outward in all its affects and effects within the life pattern; to see a trail of its experience within one's being and to trace that trail to its source so that whatever impulses or experiences were the genesis of this trait may be looked at and reexperience in a safe environment, perhaps within this same meditative state, so that the entity which experienced this need to behave in this manner might have a chance once again to re-respond to this situation and fashion a more helpful means of response to others.

If this trait is within one that is close to you and not within the self, there is far less that can be done, for the desire the work upon those qualities which are seen to be hindrances to affect teaching and learning need to have an inner motivation in order for any actions to be effective in removing or balancing such traits. One can make the suggestion that such a trait exists, and can be worked with in a helpful manner. Various suggestions can be given, as we have suggested to you in the working with such in a quiet place and quiet moment within. One may suggest that such work may be accomplished together if the other entity is in relationship to the self in a close enough fashion to allow such work, and for it to be appropriate. In most instances, the general run of the day, shall we say, the interaction of entities in a normal way, as the daily round of activities moves in its pattern and each entity within that pattern will provide the periodic mirroring effect where this trait of pridefulness will show itself, and at those time there may be a gentle reminder made that will allow the entity with this trait to note its presence and also note its effect upon the interaction that is being mutually experienced.

Is there a further query, my sister?

Questioner: No, thank you.

I am Q'uo, and we thank you, my sister. Is there another query at this time?

Carla: No, I don't think so, not from me. Thank you, Q'uo.

I am Q'uo, and again we thank each for allowing us to speak to those topics which are of importance to you. And we would take this opportunity to remind all present that we do not wish our words to provide stumbling blocks upon your own journey of seeking. We suggest that you take those that have meaning to you, and leave behind those that do not. We are those of Q'uo, and at this time we shall take our leave of this instrument and this group, leaving each, as always, in the love and in the light of the one infinite Creator. We are known to you as those of Q'uo. Adonai, my friends. Adonai.

L/L Research

L/L Research is a subsidiary of Rock Creek Research & Development Laboratories, Inc.

P.O. Box 5195
Louisville, KY 40255-0195

www.llresearch.org

Rock Creek is a non-profit corporation dedicated to discovering and sharing information which may aid in the spiritual evolution of humankind.

ABOUT THE CONTENTS OF THIS TRANSCRIPT: This telepathic channeling has been taken from transcriptions of the weekly study and meditation meetings of the Rock Creek Research & Development Laboratories and L/L Research. It is offered in the hope that it may be useful to you. As the Confederation entities always make a point of saying, please use your discrimination and judgment in assessing this material. If something rings true to you, fine. If something does not resonate, please leave it behind, for neither we nor those of the Confederation would wish to be a stumbling block for any.

CAVEAT: This transcript is being published by L/L Research in a not yet final form. It has, however, been edited and any obvious errors have been corrected. When it is in a final form, this caveat will be removed.

© 2009 L/L Research

The Aaron/Q'uo Dialogues, Session 6
April 9, 1992

(This session was preceded by a period of tuning and meditation.)

Q'uo: We are those known to you as Q'uo. We greet and bless each in the love and light of the one infinite Creator.

If the one known as Barbara and the one known as Aaron are sufficiently prepared, we should enjoy commencing this session of working. We would wish to express our deep enjoyment of the opportunity to share our thoughts with each of you and to work with the entities which may express through the instrument known as Barbara. As we would prefer to allow the one known as Aaron to begin the working, we would at this time content ourselves with the expression of our joy at the beauty of this circle of seeking, and for the moment leave this instrument in love and in light. We are Q'uo.

Aaron My greetings and love to you all. I am Aaron. The energy of spirit, not just disincarnate spirit but of all spirit in this room, is very lovely to behold. Barbara is bursting with joy inside at the heightened frequency vibration she is experiencing; and experienced secondhand through her, that energy is still very brilliant. It is a great joy to speak in this way and share a conversation with my brother/sister Q'uo.

The last time we did this we were making an attempt to move back and forth with more frequency, rather than for one of us to talk at length and then the other to speak at length. And if Q'uo and Carla are willing, I would like to suggest that we do it that way—no long monologues, but a more flowing conversation between us. There will be no difficulty in this. I will know when Q'uo wishes to speak and will simply pause, and Q'uo will know when I wish to speak.

No decision has been made as to the nature of the questions or the direction of the channeling tonight, and it is not my place to direct this; but I would like to offer a suggestion that it feels relevant to me that we speak, at least to some extent, about the nature of service and the misconceptions that the incarnate being may move into about the nature of service, which create a distortion in that service and give rise to fear. I would pause here for your responses to this suggestion. That is all.

(Pause while Aaron's suggestion is considered.)

It is not necessary that you hold to this idea of service at all. It feels to me to be something relevant to all of you, but I do not wish to impose my concept on each of you. Is there a totally different area that you would prefer to explore?

Carla: Why don't we take this opportunity to form a group question on service? What is it that we wonder most about service? The thing I notice most frequently that people ask me is how to be of service to other people when they have not yet learned how to love themselves as human beings with faults, so that they can have compassion on themselves and therefore have compassion on other people. So, my first question about service would be, "How can people be encouraged to see themselves as people worthy to offer service to others?"

Barbara: I understand Carla's question. I feel a different discomfort with service. I think it's a question partly of being versus doing, but it seems more a question of the arising of fear; that as soon as I get into wanting to serve, I separate myself from that part of me which is already serving. I can't really explain it. I wonder if you can explain it. I don't know how to get past that. I know my question is rather vague, but there's a sense, not of aspiring to serve but at grasping at service that gets in the way of actual service. Can you speak to that distortion and how I can move past it, how any of us can?

Q'uo: I am of Q'uo, and greet each again in love and light.

Ah, to be upon the road and
To forget that the feet are walking,
To become numb to the dust,
To smell not the heat of the damp
Of the dew upon the dust as you trudge
In the morning light of young and unskillful pilgrimage;
To carry your brother and your sister in your heart
And think that they are upon your back;
To be numb in the feet, in the heart, and
To feel burdens that are not there.

This is one way to describe one who serves with every heartbeat, yet believes that one must carry a load, one must show weight and effort in order to serve. Is not every step an effort? Are those feet not dusty and sore? Is the heart not full to bursting with compassion and love and will? What is this fetish about the showing of burdens? About the suffering that is visible? Is this carrying of burdens what each thinks that service is?

Let us move back from this scene and think of the heart of each entity who desires to serve. Is this heart active, defined by action? Is it completely passive, asleep, and incapable of action? Or are both sleeping and waking, dreaming and acting, informed by an unsleeping and ever-living consciousness that merely and utterly is?

Any determination to be of service begins not with dreaming and not with acting, but with consciousness itself. And that consciousness is that which is purified by a fire of desire which tempers consciousness, cleanses it of the confusing, self-deprecating, or arrogant emotion so that one is neither consumed with unworthiness nor battened by pride, but merely is, as is the Father of all things; merely is, as is the Nurturer of all things; merely and utterly is, as is the spirit of love that is the nature of all that there is.

One serves because one is of a certain nature. If that nature be impure, the service shall be impure. If that nature is undisciplined and unguided, the service will be undisciplined and unguided. If this consciousness chooses negative ways of distorting itself, its service will express itself in manipulation and control of others. And if the purified consciousness has been purified towards love without any hindrance, let, or stint, then the service of such a one will be beyond description. Whatever the action, the essence of the service will remain within the beingness that informs the service.

No one can keep from serving, no entity whatsoever. Thinking upon this may begin to take the emphasis off wanting to serve, for that desire is after the fact. We would transfer this energy to the one known as Aaron at this time. We are known to you as Q'uo.

Aaron This is Aaron. Q'uo spoke about unworthiness and pride. These are both manifestations of ego. I would suggest the usefulness of beginning to regard service in a different way, not as a strained giving or even as an eager giving but as a gift. There is no joy that I know so deep as that of serving, and a part of the joy inherent in service is the emptiness of self that one comes to when one truly moves out of oneself in order to serve.

So much of your pain comes from the illusion of a solid self. Without that illusion, neither ego nor pride can exist. There is no unworthiness. There is no grasping. Service is truly your path beyond ego, because as you walk that path of service you see constantly how that illusory self arises, see the seeming solidity of ego as you become bound in fear.

What you see is a magnification of what exists. We have talked about this at length, and I believe we spoke about it a bit last year when we were here. If you offer something 99% percent purely and 1% percent with the impurity of ego, you are aware not of the 99% percent but of the 1%, and you condemn yourself for that. You forget so quickly that this service is offered by a human. The spirit is unlimited, but the human does have its limits. Thus, you tend to become lost in that small percentage of the service that is guided by ego, rather than the much greater percentage that is guided by true aspiration to serve God and the deep love for all that to which the servant feels itself connected.

As you move into that minute distortion of fear, you start to feel yourself unworthy; or in an effort to override the fear, you move to pride—the latter more rare than the former for those of you who serve in the ways that you in this room do. You are more prone to unworthiness than pride. When you can remind yourself that the path of service is a gift wherein a reflective mirror shows where ego still exists, it gives you a very different perspective on that ego.

At that point you may turn with compassion to this human being that is doing its best to serve despite the occasional arisings of fear, and use the path of service as a constant reflection of the arising of ego so that you may allow that illusion to dissolve. If you were not given this catalyst of service in the way that those in this room ask themselves to serve, you would not have the strong promptings that you each have to purify yourselves. Yes, you are here to serve others; but the wonderful gift of that service is that in the course of it, this aspect of the one that you identify as self must be allowed continually to dissolve and dissolve more fully until all illusion of separation is eradicated.

I would like to relate this thought to Barbara's question. Barbara spoke of the arising of fear and the distortion created by the desire to serve, by grasping at service. Can you see that the grasping is a manifestation of unworthiness? When you know that you serve simply by being, there is no longer need for grasping.

Last month K shared a very beautiful poem with us, a poem she was taught as a child by her grandmother. I do not know if I have it completely accurate, but as I recall it, the words were:

I am the place that God shines through
For God and I are one, not two.
God wants me where and as I am.
I need not fret, nor will, nor plan.
If I'll just be relaxed and free,
He'll carry out his will through me.

This is truly the essence of it: relaxed and free, not willing, not planning, just being and trusting that you will be placed where you need to be to serve as you are asked to serve. You do not need to set up such situations of service so much as to allow them to happen. You allow them to happen by purifying your own energy, by constant work on yourselves, by prayer, by your constant offer to be of service without grasping at that service, and by deep awareness that when you say, "I *need* to serve," that is a manifestation of unworthiness and of ego—"I need to serve so I can feel better about myself." Well, fine, but first feel better about yourself and then all the service you want will pour through you. It really is as simple as that.

I believe the important thing here is to become aware each time that "I need to" arises, that there is a sense of unworthiness behind it, a sense of fear. The first step, then, is mindfulness, deep awareness, each time that sense of fear arises. The second step is acceptance of this human who sometimes feels fear; just a smile and a, "Here is fear again. Come in fear, I have been expecting you." Give yourself a hug and return to the act of loving, of worship of God, of extending your loving energy in whatever ways you can, not just to others but to yourself. With the acceptance of that small arising of fear, it will not grow into distortion.

You do not have to get rid of fear. You only have to recognize that it is there. The fear does not interfere with your being a clear channel, for example, but your relationship with fear interferes with it. If you wish to serve others in any way—serving food in a soup kitchen, working in a homeless shelter, counseling others or whatever ways you may choose to serve—you need not eradicate fear but recognize it and find mercy for this human who sometimes feels fear, and in that way change your relationship to fear.

Until you change your own relationship to the fear that sometimes moves through you, you cannot clearly serve another because you will always be in some amount of judgment of his or her fear and the distortions that fear creates in another. There will also always be "he who serves" and "he who is served" as long as you are not friends with the fear in you. But when you can make friends with that and thereby befriend fear and all its distorted manifestations in another, you remove the separation of self and other. And then there is no longer "servant" and "served." Both are servant and both are served.

Do you think that when you serve another by offering them food, that does not serve you? Here is the distortion of pride: "I am the servant." And again it creates separation, and such separation cannot serve anyone. When I offer you food and you offer me the opportunity to offer you food, I thank you for that. You give me a gift, truly.

I offer you my thoughts right now, and I cannot express the deep gratitude in my heart for the opportunity to speak to you all and the ways that you serve me by giving me your listening and your open-hearted attention to my thoughts, because when you listen to me, it makes me be more responsible for the purity of those thoughts and thus stretches me and aids me to grow.

So, I ask you to remove the duality in your mind between served and serve and to look closely at your discomfort with the arising of fear and see it more clearly for what it is. Truly begin to understand that the fear does not create the distortion in your service, but your relationship with the fear creates that distortion.

I feel that Q'uo would like to speak at this point. There is more I would like to say but I would prefer to turn this over to my brother/sister for comment, and allow us to move back and forth. That is all.

Q'uo: We are those of Q'uo. We greet each again in love and light and apologize for the brief pause, but we were conferring with our friend, Aaron.

We hope that each has listened to these words concerning desire, for desire purified does not partake of fear, is not separate and does not create separation. Remember two things which this wise entity has said: The path of service is a gift. The path of service is a reflection.

Let us look from a slightly different perspective; from a slightly different set of opinions, at these statements. These statements can be pondered over and over.

The path of service is a gift. What is the path? Is it something you walk, or is it you? Are you the path and the gift? And are you by your very nature serving and served? For if you are of love, and if you have consciousness aware of itself, is this not the only undistorted transaction of which you are capable: the giving and the receiving of that great service which is loving?

Can you conceive of yourself as a gift; perfect, immutable, whole and complete, yet transitive—the self as a verb? Only those selves who see that they are not only *on* holy ground, but they *are* holy ground, can move from being a "he"; a "she"; an "it"; a noun, into being a verb—a transitive, acting verb that connects love with love; that acts as catalyst between subject and object, because it knows that subject and object are one. Subject is love/object is love if the subject is self and the object, other self.

One who is the path and one who knows itself as holy knows that self and other self and all that there is exist in a ground of love; and love speaks to love, serving and served, loving and loved. And as distortions are released; as fear becomes less necessary; as this process gradually takes place, the self becomes the path, the gift and that servant which is finally transparent to love flowing through it, never from it, flowing to it but never remaining, for love flows as endlessly as the sea.

The path of service is a reflection. This is simply the same statement turned backwards so that one may see that one is served as one serves. We would not belabor this point but only wish each to ponder it. You are a reflection to others, just as others reflect you to yourself. What, my friends, shall you reflect to others? Is your mirror transparent? Are you love? Can you allow love to flow through you and allow the images that you show to others by reflection to be clear and lucid and shining with the light of a truth that is beyond you but can only flow through you?

We ask you to ponder this second statement as a corollary of the first, for it does deepen and aid understanding and grasping of the nature of the self as a servant of love; and thus, in serving, served; and thus, when served, serving.

We would at this time again move to the one known as Aaron and the one known as Barbara that we may have the pleasure of listening and learning and enjoying Aaron's opinions.

As always, we ask each to know that these are opinions that we offer. We have no authority over you. Know that we are your friends and perhaps your teachers, but not those who ask any to refrain from discrimination. For you know that which is the truth. And if you hear it not through these instruments, we ask you to put it down and walk on without a second thought, for we would not be a stumbling block before you.

We leave this instrument. We are those of Q'uo.

Aaron I find it a great joy to share in this way with my brother/sister of Q'uo. I would like to look at a distortion of service that was inherent in both Barbara's and Carla's questions. In your human form it is so easy to lose track of what you are doing. This is natural to the human, which is not perfect and is not expected to be perfect. I am not condoning unskillful choices here, but only asking you to have mercy for this being that is sometimes unwise in its choices.

At times many of you have a fixed idea of what it means to serve, an ego attachment to one type of service or another, and you forget so quickly that, as Q'uo just explained, service is a type of *being* not a *doing*. When you fully allow yourself to be transparent, and allow light and pure energy to move through you—both into you and out of you, giving and receiving—then you *are* service. You are not serving, you are service.

When Barbara phrased her question, she had in mind a kind of distortion. Let me give you an example. On Wednesday evenings she has a channeling session. Her family comes home at 5:30. They are hungry. They have things to tell her and to share with her. She feels a need to get them fed and to get the kitchen cleaned up and to sit and meditate and prepare herself for the channeling session.

She is almost never short-tempered with them in actuality, but she sometimes feels impatience although she does not manifest that impatience. She feels a sense of wanting to hurry them through their dinner, wanting them to get their dishes washed, and so on. If she goes in to meditate and her youngest son comes in and shares his homework with her, she looks at her watch and is aware that "A houseful of people are going to appear here in half an hour and I need to meditate. Get out of here with your homework!"

Now, she does not say that. She sits him down on her lap and she looks at it, but she is feeling that impatience. And then she feels anger at herself and says, "Who am I serving here? Am I ignoring my family to serve others?"

She has learned that when she can let go of her fear; when she can feel compassion for this human who is feeling fear so as to allow that fear not to solidify, then it does not matter whether she is sitting in meditation or washing dishes or holding her son on her lap and admiring his homework. It is *all* meditation because at that point, as she washes the dishes or holds her son, she *is* service; she *is* love. What could be better preparation for channeling than holding a child on your lap and giving him love? But the voice of fear distorts that and says, "I must have silence to prepare," and then self-criticism arises because she knows that to follow up on that impulse would be to hurt the child.

It would be well worth your while to look at the ways you manifest this in yourselves. No being of third density is immune to this. No matter how aware you are, it catches you sometimes.

What does it mean to serve? A friend shared a story in which he was leading a large workshop, and a woman who had kept talking about her family of eight or nine children all weekend and the demands they placed on her spoke up toward the end of the weekend and said, "Oh, I want to serve! How can I serve?"

Many in that group had been talking about working with the homeless or those with AIDS or another disease, and so on. And this man, S, turned to the woman and said, "You want to serve? Get up in the morning and serve your family bacon and eggs."

What is service? It is not a doing, but a being, an attitude, a way of approaching the world and yourself with love.

Now, I know those are inspiring words, but the reality is that it is much harder to do it than to speak of it. Each time that you fall into that trap of mistaking service for a specific kind of doing and see yourselves attached to that doing, might I suggest that instead of looking critically at this human who has made that unskillful choice, you find acceptance for that human. What is behind that grasping at service in this specific way or that specific way? Can you begin to see the layer of fear under there? And as you allow loving self-acceptance to replace that fear, then you become love again and you become service, service to all beings.

We have spoken at length about negative and positive polarity as service to self and service to others. When there is not distinction between self and other, then service no longer takes on that direction. You become aware that when you serve others, you inevitably serve yourself because there is no self or other. And truly, even that entity which you think of as a negatively-polarized being in service to self, without having the intention of doing so, does serve others because there is no difference between self and other.

Thus, the difference is not in the direction of the service so much as the intention. When there is intention of service to self, it is because fear is present; and greed, needing, and grasping. The distinction, then, becomes intention to serve fear and the solidified self that grows out of fear versus intention to serve love and the deep connection that grows out of love.

Perhaps this distinction can help you clarify the direction you move your energy. When you think of it in terms of service to self and service to others, the whole direction becomes distorted, because those of you with strong positive polarity who think in terms of service to others find yourselves uncomfortable when you feel yourselves receiving from that service.

I would like to ask Q'uo to speak at this time as I hear very delightful thoughts coming from my brother/sister. That is all.

Q'uo: I am Q'uo, and we greet you again through this instrument in love and in light.

In this working we have grappled long with the concepts of being of service. This, obviously, in our opinion, is one of the more misleading phrases concerning itself with serving the one infinite Creator. Therefore, let us look at what we say to ourselves and let us look at what we feel that the Creator may say to Itself.

Does the Creator say, "I should; I need; I must; I desire?" Or does the Creator say, "I create and it is good?" What is the name by which the Creator in the Judaic system of myth and culture is known in its highest form? Is it not "I Am" or "I Am that I Am"?[4] Or perhaps, "I Am always becoming"?[5]

We speak individually to each within this unified circle, for each of you has a universe peculiar and unique to yourself. It is your universe, your creation, and you are co-Creator. No one creates this universe but you. It is your creation and the creation of the Father. All that is created and realized and sensed within your creation is yours, either by being or by reflection of being. Your creation is unlike any other, and all that you feel is outside of you is actually occurring within you.

We speak of mirrors. Yet do you realize that in actuality your eyes, your ears and all those things which you use to garner information are illusions also? Do you realize that the sense impressions which are filtered through to your conscious thinking have been through so many judgmental screens that they are in fact already myth and legend before you are aware of thinking, perceiving or realizing each sense impression? The depth of the illusion which you experience is infinite. You will not know anything within this illusion. You may have our permission to stop trying.[6]

You are becoming. You are creating. There is no "must."
There is no "should."
There is no "want."
There is no "desire."

What is your true nature? If you are a creature of the one infinite Creator, then the answer to that for those who feel that the Creator is love is that you are a creature made of love. Here you are. We speak to you in a limelight all your own even though you are one with all in this group. You are love and you are becoming and you are creating. Rest in this bright light, the surest sign of beingness.

This is your incarnation. This is your experience of being; of consciousness. This is your chance to examine the nature of yourself. And as you examine that nature and you say, "I need; I should; I want," stop and say to yourself rather, "I create." And then look to see if you think that the creation is good! For that which is of the Creator within you will say, "It is good." And if you create and can say, regardless of

---

[4] *Holy Bible*, Exodus 3:14.

[5] JHVH, Jahweh or Jehovah is a name of mystery supposedly given to Moses on Mt. Sinai. The definitions Q'uo suggests for this unpronounceable name are some of those translations of JHVH given by theologians.

[6] Q'uo uses the expression "our permission" figuratively and light-heartedly.

all imperfections which are apparent in this immensely deep illusion, "It is good," then you are upon the holy path of seeking and of service.

Are there any brief questions at this time?

(No further queries.)

Q'uo: I am Q'uo, and as we see there are no questions which those present wish to verbalize at this time, we would ask the one known as Aaron to close this session of working with our expression of profound gratitude for the delightful opportunity to share in this teaching, in this service, and, my friends, most, most deeply, in this being served by being able to blend with the vibrations of each of you the hope, the prayers and the faith of each of you. How beautiful you are and how inspiring is your steady and persistent gaze upon truth, beauty and love.

We leave this instrument now in the Creator's love and light, and transfer this energy to the one known as Barbara and the one known as Aaron. We bid you adieu at this time. We are those of Q'uo. Adonai.

Aaron This is Aaron. For those of you who are interested in pursuing this, I offer a bit of homework. In the coming evening and morning, watch yourself very carefully. Service is not just the big things, but the little: smiling to another, washing a plate or glass, petting a cat who is seeking affection, being love.

Watch yourselves very carefully. Watch for any arising of "I should." Begin to distinguish the movement of "I should" through the third chakra of will and determination and the "I Am" of love expressed through the open heart.[7] The more deeply you can move into awareness of these patterns in yourselves, the less control habitual pattern has over you.

You are so used simply to reacting, so deeply patterned in your responses, that it takes very careful attention to break those responses. It is like a habit of biting the nails, perhaps, or scratching, pulling at the hair, or whatever one may do when one is nervous. In order to change that pattern, one must begin to observe the nervousness. To change the pattern of moving from a place of "I should" into a place of the open heart, one needs to observe the arising of separation which moves one back from the open heart center to the third chakra and pushes one in the direction of "I should."

So, just watch it, holding no judgment about it. There is nothing bad in making that move. As you bring increasing awareness to it, you find freedom from reactivity to it—simply noticing, moving back to "I should," moving back to separation and coming back to allow the heart to open again through loving acceptance and compassion for this being who moved momentarily into fear.

I love you all and am filled with joy at the opportunity for this sharing. I thank Carla and those which is known as those of Q'uo for allowing me to participate with them in this teaching, sharing, and learning. May I suggest that we close with a moment or two of silent expression of our joy and gratitude to each other and to God for bringing us together in this way. That is all. ❧

---

[7] Aaron is referring to the chakras or rays of the energy body. This body interpenetrates the physical body during our lifetime. The Chinese call this body the electrical body. Acupuncture is based on working with this body. The chakras are points of energy focus that run from the base of the spine to the top of the head. There are seven rays, the colors of the rainbow, red through violet. Red is the first ray and has to do with survival and sexuality. Orange ray has to do with personal relationships. Yellow ray has to do with one's relationship to groups such as your family and work environment. Green ray is the heart chakra and has to do with loving unconditionally. Blue ray is the chakra of communication and acceptance. Indigo ray is the chakra of work in consciousness. Violet ray is a report on the whole of the energy body; a kind of read-out. Aaron is suggesting that one move from the use of the will and "should" in yellow ray to the use of love in green ray.

THE AARON/Q'UO DIALOGUES, SESSION 7
APRIL 10, 1992

(This session was preceded by a period of tuning and meditation.)

Aaron: My greetings and love to you all. I am Aaron. I would like to continue where we left off last night, to ask you to consider service in still newer ways. Service is a manifestation of love. We spoke last night about being service rather than doing service and of the ways that doing creates a distortion of self and other, of server and served. Being service is simply opening yourself and moving away from any duality.

Something I find very interesting is that those of you who aspire to serve, grasp so hard at something that is innate to you. It is not that you must work in order to serve. That is natural to you. When you are not "being service" there is a distortion. Your energy is being distorted into some misconception of separation. Therefore, the ideal is not to aspire to serve but simply to pay attention to where that pure "being service" is blocked by fear.

I spoke last night of intention, of moving away from the limiting concept of service to self and service to others—which is quite disorienting because service to others is service to self and vice versa—and to begin to see with clarity the ways that service to others springs from a ground of love and service to self springs from a ground of fear.[8]

When you begin to see the intention to offer love or to react to fear, to allow fear to direct your choices, then you can move away from the concept of service to self or other-self and towards the pure experience of "being service" or the pure experience of reactivity to fear.

Once you move away from the concept and into the experience, those of you with strong positive polarity will find the experience of "being fear" is an ample check in itself. As soon as you allow the reality of that experience to arise in you, something within you stops and pays attention and says, "No, this is not the way I choose to express my energy." You then allow yourself both to be aware of the fear and non-reactive to it, so that the aspect of "being love" and expressing service through the being of love can manifest itself.

---

[8] Reference to these two orientations, service to self and service to others, may be less confusing and more easy to understand when viewed from the perspective of their essential oneness; however, the two orientations are validly distinguished from each other in any objective discussion of the choices available to the seeker. The Confederations channels such as the Q'uo group, as well as Aaron, are oriented towards service to others, and that is what their teaching discusses.

The most important point to remember here is that expressing service through being service in love is natural to you. And when you do that, you are not doing anything; you are not creating anything. You are simply expressing your own true nature. When that nature is in full harmony with the external positive energy which may move through you, your energy to serve is magnified. At that point, you do not need to ask, "How can I best serve?" You simply choose the paths that lie right at your feet, whatever they are.

I shared a story at Christmastime of the one whose name was known to you as Jesus. I told how, at that time, I was part of a group that was with this being. This is a being known for his service. I want to use this story as an example of what service may really mean.

We came to a place where there were followers of his who welcomed him and prepared a meal—an elaborate meal by their standards; simple by yours. They gave the best of what they had.

It was a poor village. There were those who despised and feared him and they also were part of this village, but not within the group that sat to eat. He was served first; offered a bowl of food. As he sat there with that bowl in his hands, ready to begin, he saw children on the edge of our circle. An elder of the village got up to shoo the children away. He said, "This child is the son of one who disdains your teachings," and went on to say, "Get out of here! Go!"

That one child hung back. He was a young boy of nine or ten years; emaciated and with sores on his body. This being that was known as Jesus simply got up and walked toward the boy. The boy was frightened because he had been told to leave and here was this stranger walking toward him. And Jesus said gently to him, "Do not be afraid, I will not hurt you. Do you want food?" And he offered him that bowl. And while the boy ate, he asked for cloth and water and washed his sores. And then he came back very simply to his seat and took another bowl.

There was no lecture about service. There were no words, like "You should love your enemy." There was no verbal teaching. He simply served. He was service. He was love. He took, not the universe, but one child that needed to be fed at that moment, and fed him and washed his sores. Just that. There is no teaching in my many, many lives that I have received on service that has touched me as deeply as that one.

Think, then, about what service, being service versus serving another, really means. When you move into that distortion of seeking to serve another, begin to recognize it as a distortion. See that your serving makes them the one who is served; makes you separate and unequal. See that this is a violence to another.

Is that the course you really choose? How can you learn to express being service in ways that do not create separation? We will speak further on this. I wish to pass the microphone, as it were, to Q'uo. That is all.

Q'uo: We are those of Q'uo. We greet you in the love and in the light of the one infinite Creator.

The one known as Aaron asks, "Do you wish this dichotomy betwixt self and other-self, betwixt servant and served?" Each would, as a beginning servant, say, "Yes, I must have someone who needs my service so I may be a servant." Outwardly there seems no falsity in this reasoning. We, ourselves, have often thanked you for the opportunity to serve you, merely noting that your allowing us to serve is your service to us. Service by this chain of reasoning seems an endless loop. Yet how does the one desiring to serve enter this loop and become part of the infinite, upward, spiraling light and love of all serving all in love and for love's sake?

Many are the seekers who feel guilty because they must take time to work within their own consciousnesses. Many also are those seekers who pridefully state that mate, family, and all the mundane aspects of life must take second place to the self's work in inner enlightenment. Whether one feels guilty for taking this time for one's own purification, or arrogant and elite for taking time for this purification in an impure world, so they assume, still the concept of taking time to work within the self always is suggested and encouraged by any spiritual teacher.

Now, is this time taken for the self, by the self, in doing work in consciousness service to self or service to others? You may perhaps see by this question itself that the tendency towards dichotomy when thinking of service arises here, at the beginning of a student's preparing to start the journey of seeking to know how to serve. The immediate thought is, "I must do this work. Am I selfish? Should I take this time? What good am I to others?" And of course, the prideful will become absorbed in this inner process and neglect outward-gazing compassion.

The story of the one known as Jesus, told by the teacher, Aaron, shows an entity who has awakened to his own inner love. This entity has done his work in consciousness. The personality is disciplined. The emotions are purified and the response lacks either prideful humility or prideful arrogance and seems natural. We suggest that in our opinion it is part of a life lived in service to others to spend time as if it were the most precious coin or money, always budgeting a portion of this exchequer of finite time for work within one's own consciousness.

At this moment, do you love yourself without reservation? How can you know this? Examine your thoughts for the last hour. Were you nervous? Were you irritated? Were you impatient? Did you have any negative emotions? We speak not only within one's inner dialogue but also of mental responses to the actions of others, for those responses are your material, reflected to you by the mirrors provided by the presence of other selves.

That which you think of another, you think also of the self. If there is judgment, turn it upon yourself and analyze the root cause within the self. Here is material for this day's budget of work in inner consciousness: nervousness, irritation, impatience, anger, resentment, disappointment.

Make an appointment. Let all of them see the doctor within. Analyze and examine these responses. Let them sink into the self and find their root and their home. Then touch that home with your compassion, your love and your redeeming forgiveness of self by self.

Do you feel that the infinite One keeps a score, has tidy books and forgives not? We do not believe you think so, else you would not try to serve. Therefore, we ask you to do this work with the same fervor, intensity and respect as with the work you do for others, those whom you call other-selves, for work upon the self and work upon the other-self is all work on behalf of the infinite One whose name is Love.

To serve the raising of one's own consciousness is to worship the infinite Creator. To extend the beingness and consciousness of love to perceived other-selves is to be the clear and transparent extensions through which the Creator's hands may actually touch another human spirit in manifestation. Simply do not separate these two activities within the mind, but do both as two sides of one coin. That coin is serving.

We would at this time return this circle's energy to the one known as Aaron. We leave this instrument in love and in light. We are known to you as those of Q'uo.

Aaron: I am Aaron. There is another area of duality and misunderstanding of which I would like to speak. You identify those who bring love to others as those who serve others. The attributes of those who "are service" are gentleness, patience and generosity. And you identify those who cause others pain in some way; those who affront others and are greedy or arrogant, as those who do not serve others. I would like to explore this a bit further.

Most of you have heard me say that we are all beings of light, even those who manifest very little of that light; even those who are very negatively polarized and in the conscious levels of self would affirm their desire to serve negativity. Even those who feed off the fear and pain of others, at some level, are servants of the light. It is well to move past the duality of seeing them in such sharp contrast as good and evil; servants of love or ones against love.

Some of you have heard me tell a brief story about the spiritual teacher Gurdjieff, that in his community there was a man who was very unpleasant to others. He did not do his share of the work. He spoke in a harsh way to others. He was arrogant and prideful. He even smelled foul and did not take care of his physical body. Nobody wanted his presence. The others in the community were in great accord with each other and everything ran smoothly except for this one unpleasant being.

He got tired of the way people were treating him and one day he packed up and left. Gurdjieff went after him and asked him to come back. The man, of course, refused. Gurdjieff then offered to pay him to come back. Those of the community were aghast at this: "How could you pay him to come back? We were well rid of him."

Gurdjieff said, "He is the yeast for the bread. How would you learn compassion without a catalyst for that compassion? How would you learn non-judgment without a catalyst for that non-judgment?"

Granted, there are negatively-polarized entities. There are those who thrive on the fear and pain of others. There are beings that are mired in deep misunderstanding, and yet, even their negative polarity and misunderstanding is a service. How would you learn without such catalysts?

When you can begin to view such misunderstanding and negativity as another way of service to the light, you begin to view such individuals differently. For most of them, it is not their intention to serve the light, although for some that may be true. No being whose intention is to serve the light will willingly do so through causing harm and pain to others. So it is not their intention; but nevertheless, they do serve the light by offering you the catalyst that you need for your own learning.

When you can begin to find welcome for such beings, to move beyond your judgment of them and open your heart to them, to the very real pain that their misunderstanding causes for them, and to thank them for the ways in which they offer you the catalyst that you need, then you can begin to do the same for yourself in those moments when fear and other negative emotions arise in you. I have spoken often of the reverse of this, of coming to a place of non-judgment of yourself as a way of learning non-judgment of others. I am just offering the opposite side of the coin.

When you see yourself in a position of possible service to others and fear or any type of negativity arises, if you can remind yourself of something such as the story I just shared and allow that this fear in you is also a catalyst which may be transformed from darkness to light by your clear observation of it, by your awareness and acceptance, then you find that even the so-called negative emotions in you can give rise to purity of action, speech and thought. Fear becomes a catalyst for compassion. Hatred and the fear behind hatred can be clearly seen for what they are: not as an intrinsic part of you, but as a reaction due to certain conditions that have arisen and led to that fear. And the knowing that there is fear within you, in itself, becomes a path to clarify your energy so that your response to this being that is feeling fear, to this aspect of yourself, becomes even more loving, more clear and pure than it was before.

To do this takes deep awareness, a constant awareness of the ways that patterns of connection and separation, love and fear, move through you; noticing the conditions that give rise to each; beginning to break it down into small parts to see that you do not just suddenly become afraid; you do not just suddenly become jealous; it is a process that you have moved through, conditioned by old mind-patterns. You can break into that process at any time you choose with awareness and love and make the choice to move into a new pattern.

This is the crux of it: choice, responsibility. The being who acts in reactivity to fear, and thus acts in what we have called service to self and with the intention of harm of others, has either denied his responsibility and his ability to make a choice or is frightened of that responsibility and choice.

The being experiencing deep fear who watches the patterns of the arising of that fear and then makes a choice for love is acting with freedom from conditioned patterns and thus is able to make skillful choices. The more you see this in yourself without judgment, the deeper awareness you are able to have of that moment of choice: "Here I can act with conditioned mind and the old patterns of fear," or, "Here I can act with awareness of the patterns in which conditioned mind pushes me and choose to say no to that, to trust and move in a new direction."

I would like to take this thought around now to a very real, practical application. You are all beings who aspire to serve. You are all beings who aspire to offer love and non-harm to all else, and yet you constantly find arising within you old patterns of conditioned mind leading to fear, self-hatred, negativity, greed, jealousy and anger.

Each arising of such discomfiting emotions that have the possibility to harm another is a gift; a chance to observe the old patterns in yourself and a chance to practice. It is practice that you need over and over and over again. That is why you are offered it over and over and over again. As you work with these patterns in yourself and are aware that some of the response has been prompted by the negative energy of others, it gives you a chance to transcend the duality of negativity and positivity, and to begin to see the gift even of that negative energy in others and the gift of negative energy in yourself as a catalyst to learning; to moving deeper into non-judgment, compassion and love.

This is the wonder of being human. You are here with this emotional body for a reason. Even those emotions that you deem negative are not to be gotten rid of, but to be used as part of a transmutation process by which hatred and fear become the catalysts for love, greed becomes the catalyst for generosity and so on. When you really begin to know that, in a deep way within yourself, you will not have so much fear of the negativity in yourself. When you make peace with that, then you really can give an answer to Q'uo's question: "Yes, in the past hour I have not found anything I disliked in myself. I truly have loved myself, as my friend Carla is fond of saying, warts and all."

I would like to pass the microphone to Q'uo if my brother/sister wishes to add anything here. If not, we wonder if there are specific questions we may answer. That is all.

Q'uo: I am Q'uo, and greet each again in love and in light.

Our one addition to this examination of the service-to-others efforts and lessons of third density is a simple suggestion which may be summarized in two words, first heard by this instrument from the entity known as R: Go higher! Go higher!

Aaron and we have long discussed the painstaking, careful and subtle work of removing the perceptions of duality and thereby balancing negative and positive impressions and opinions. As a balance for this careful, analytical approach, we would suggest the concept of experience as a game sphere, a ball. This instrument has called such earthly balls "trouble bubbles." When a trouble bubble flies at you, to lose the game is to catch it and fall under its weight. To win the game is to leap towards it in joy, praise and thanksgiving. And as the bubble meets this sea of joy, praise and thanksgiving, it simply pops.

There will always be another trouble bubble, another conundrum to solve, another bump in the road. Leap towards them with affection and joy. If it be another self which is a decided irritant, instantaneously be that entity, and as that entity, experience all its sorrows. Then, as that entity, leap for joy in praise and thanksgiving. You are not infringing upon free will, for you are playing a game; but in this game you allow your mind to become that which you fear, and then give thanksgiving and praise for the joy of it.

Go higher! This is work best done when one is, as this instrument would say and as we trust you soon shall be, "full of beans," and not for those days when, like the cloudy, pearly skies, you feel muted and reflective. However, this technique makes a welcome and energizing change to the endless repetitions of analysis, understanding and acceptance of experience. It is a leap of blind, pure faith from immediate experience to immediate acceptance. Only choose this option when it is honestly within your abilities.

We feel the energy waning, and therefore would take our leave of all of you. May we say with the one known as Aaron how utterly delightful your company is and how very, very much we have been thrilled to blend our energies with yours as we all move from moment to moment in ceaseless and abiding love.

We thank you for allowing us to share our opinions and, as always, remind each that we are not final authorities. We leave each of you in the blessing and peace of the love and the light of the one infinite Creator. Adonai. We are those known to you as the principle of Q'uo.

Aaron: I would like to make only one brief remark, as I asked if there were questions, and as the principle Q'uo made its last statement there was a bit of a wrenching cry from somewhere inside Barbara saying, "Yes, all of these thoughts are fine, but how do I do this?" A moment of deep pain—this is the gift of being human. It is not going to go away. It is the catalyst which challenges you constantly to purify that energy that you are, knowing that it will never become perfect; that while in human incarnation you will never become pure service, constantly and without error.

And yet, each moment given with mindful attention and love brings you closer to that beautiful ideal of "being service."

And each moment of attention to the arising of fear in you brings you closer to the purity of non-judgmental acceptance of everything within the experience of mind and body, not mine or yours, but all of ours. It is this unconditional love that you are here to learn and practice and express in whatever ways you are able.

I do thank you for the opportunity to share with you today. My love to you all. That is all. ☙

L/L Research

L/L Research is a subsidiary of Rock Creek Research & Development Laboratories, Inc.

P.O. Box 5195
Louisville, KY 40255-0195

www.llresearch.org

Rock Creek is a non-profit corporation dedicated to discovering and sharing information which may aid in the spiritual evolution of humankind.

ABOUT THE CONTENTS OF THIS TRANSCRIPT: This telepathic channeling has been taken from transcriptions of the weekly study and meditation meetings of the Rock Creek Research & Development Laboratories and L/L Research. It is offered in the hope that it may be useful to you. As the Confederation entities always make a point of saying, please use your discrimination and judgment in assessing this material. If something rings true to you, fine. If something does not resonate, please leave it behind, for neither we nor those of the Confederation would wish to be a stumbling block for any.

CAVEAT: This transcript is being published by L/L Research in a not yet final form. It has, however, been edited and any obvious errors have been corrected. When it is in a final form, this caveat will be removed.

© 2009 L/L Research

Sunday Meditation
April 12, 1992

Group question: … or any transformation occur in both the metaphysical and physical sense. What steps can we go through to bring about change in our lives, particularly in respect to slowing down and enjoying each experience more fully?

(Carla channeling)

I am of the principle known to you as Q'uo. We greet you in the love and in the light of the one infinite Creator. We find it to be a great blessing to be called to your group at this time to share our humble opinions with you. And we bless you in return, and share the love of the infinite One with you from all our hearts. We are bathed in a sea of love and light, walking forever supported in a net made of love, a metaphysical net that caresses one in all directions and supports one in whatever modality and vector each desires.

You have asked us about moving quickly through life, rushing through experiences during an incarnational period so quickly that the details of that experience begin to blur and some of that experience is, therefore, lost. As we listen to your chimes that sway and sing in the wind, we are minded to suggest to you that these wind chimes do not have a previous agenda. The wind moves them; they readily yield to the extent of their mass. And when mayhap two pieces of this metal touch, the pleasing sound is emitted for which this instrument was created.

So it is with a human instrument. There are, metaphysically speaking, winds that come sometimes and sometimes are still, that may move from one direction or another, at one speed or another. An incarnational experience is marked by its variety. The wind, whereby experience goes by, is not measured as your clocks measure time, but, metaphysical weather plays about the sea of experience as do ocean winds upon the liner. Certainly, the ship is big enough to withstand gale winds as well as calm and pleasant breezes. But the captain of that ship adjusts his methods of navigation according to the wind, the conditions of the ocean, and the weather in general.

Each of you exists in a frail barque, that physical vehicle which you call your body, and it does move through a physical sea and a metaphysical sea of experience. In sheerly physical terms, the winds of stimulation and the potential for experience are so numerous that they can best be described as infinite. No entity can process the information that comes through the physical senses. There is a thousand, nay, ten thousand times too much information to be processed. And so, a ruthless making of choices ensues. Those bits of information that come in that seem to apply most directly to survival and comfort are recognized and processed first. And the hierarchy of those things which are noticed is individualized and put into place in what you may call your bio-computer very, very early in your incarnational experience.

Metaphysically, each entity also is buffeted about with the mystical winds of metaphysical chance and destiny. There are the strong trade winds of destiny, those that blow from forever; and there are the delightful, seasonal, unpredictable whims of spirit that offer the chance and change that marks the unique experience of being a conscious individual given the gift of free will. Metaphysically speaking, the dance between destiny and free will provides a way of thinking about those whims which affect the spontaneous, expressive self, that meaningful, substantive self to which that question about "hurrying up" has reference, for the blurring of experience through rushing too much is not simply a physical phenomenon, but also a spiritual one.

Let us attempt to gaze at why this may be so. We speak many times of the dynamic between service to others—or the radiation of light in a free and spontaneous manner—and service to self, which consists in control of the self and control over others for the benefit of the self in a magnetic, attractive kind of energy which pulls those things which are needed to it and orders them carefully for the self's best advantage. We see the way of love expressing radiantly without stint, often foolishly in the eyes of the world, as opposed to that which may seem to be very logical and civil in the same eyes of this same world, the ordering, the controlling of the self for the benefit of the self, and of circumstances and individuals, also for the benefit or convenience of the self.

It is not usual that entities who are rushing through life have any conscious intention of behaving or providing catalyst in a service-to-self or negatively-oriented manner. Indeed, the rationale for moving without rhythm, but simply as quickly as possible, is that of service to others, that the utmost be done, and all of the things that are done are intended to be of service to others.

My friends, the work of disciplining the personality and purifying the emotions is subtle work. The entity which is yourself is not all good, nor is it all negative. The more positively-oriented an entity is, the more quickly it will jump to the conclusion that it is behaving in a negatively-oriented manner, and the more judgmental it will be with the self. Therefore, as we show to you the basic negative polarity of rushing without rhythm, without consciousness of the winds, physically and metaphysically, we also say to you, refrain from any judgment. Do not assume that because you see the negative cast of this attitude you are indeed a negatively-oriented or polarized person.

Under no circumstances should a spiritual student who is seeking the truth attempt to monitor its rate of success or its place within its journey or pilgrimage. What value could such self-judgments have? One looks into and pulls out of the same informational system the question and the answer, for the Creator will not inform any entity of its spiritual score. We may say, as this instrument would put it, that the Creator grades on a curve. It is not yours to know or to be concerned with the relative positivity or negativity of actions or intents. It is yours to desire and to make choices based upon the deepest and truest emotions, biases and opinions which one is capable of finding within the self. And, at this point, we are observing the amount of awareness of the rhythms of life mundane and life eternal which each entity might have.

Now, those who rush through an agenda, crossing things off the list of the day, may well not be very aware of the mundane or metaphysical wind. Thus, they may well cut themselves off from the dance that enlivens the rhythm that blesses and makes spontaneous and joyful the thoughts and the actions of each moment. If one stands ignorant of the wind, gazing only at the compass and saying doggedly, "This I shall do now, then this, one step then another; I shall go north, I shall always go north, I have my compass and I shall go north," one shall not go long before one runs into a tree, a bus, a child or some wind of destiny that, if caught, if heard, if felt, could indeed transform the experience—not from the level of the bio-program, but from the level of the meta-program, that deep program within each entity which has to do with the unique patterns of one individual who has a spark of the infinite Creator within, and thus is set upon a lodestar that cannot be seen by the self or any other, but must indeed exist awaiting that moment when the wind of destiny does indeed cross the path.

Perhaps the most characteristic feeling of one who is dogged and determined and unrhythmical is the feeling that one is deadening one's own experience, numbing one's own enjoyment, killing one's own gift of spontaneity. How can one lift one's feet from the ground and not throw away the compass, but place it amongst other instruments which will read the mundane and metaphysical weather?

Perhaps what we may suggest in this amount of time, as you call this measurement, is that one ponder at odd moments how one feels about the rhythms of life, how one feels about missing the dances, how one might feel about the possibility that one is unwittingly behaving in a way that is apparently along the negative polarity and gives others catalyst that is along those lines? For you see, the greatest hindrance to changing oneself is the honest and genuine belief that one is actually fine just as one is, and that there are things about the way one is that are more worthwhile than what would be gained by change.

The consensus reality and cultural values among your people are those dealing with a deep and endless illusion. All judgments made of the effectiveness of action using the rules of the culture—and of the self that has been taught by the culture—shall reflect the values of that culture and shall deal exclusively with illusion. Now, each of you is here because you feel that there is something deeper than this illusory experience, something of another order of being, something which does not fade, which does not die, which has not been born, but which simply is. Stubbornly, as you gaze at the bone-white graves of the centuries of people before you, the ideas that have gone down to dust before yours, oh so stubbornly, you stand in that dust and you ask, what is truth? What is real? What is beautiful? What endures? And praise and thanksgiving well up within you because you know that this question is a question that has more substance than all of life as you know it, regardless of the answer.

So, as you ponder the rushing and imagine the joy of the rhythmic dancing, of the chiming with the wind's blessing and motion, think of that field of beingness that you know enough about to seek. Think of the mystery of that deeper reality, and of the inadequacy of cultural wisdom to rightly value such things as getting things done. This will not eliminate your ability to perform tasks or to perform them well. But, if such thoughts are mused upon over a period of time, you may discover within yourself a burgeoning attitude which allows, while keeping to the polestar of existence, for the metaphysical and physical windage and weather of the body and of the soul.

What can you *do* to change that program of rushing? We would not suggest that you *do* anything; you are already *doing* too much. What would you *not* do? We would not suggest that you *not* do anything either; this is more subtle work. The biases within your consciousness are available to you for self-knowledge. Analyze them. Accept them. And if you feel that they can be better informed, ask yourself to open a little to the possibilities of further work in consciousness, of the self by the self for the self, in order that one may become more and more an instrument that chimes in the wind and less and less a heavy metal object screwed down to consensus reality and dead to the chiming of eternity.

At this time we would transfer this contact to the one know as Jim. We thank this instrument, and especially thank this instrument for the care with which it challenged at the beginning of this contact. Some energy was required to purify the portals of contact from our end and we greatly appreciated the effort taken by this careful and cautious instrument. Such care is that which makes communications such as this possible. We leave this instrument in love and light and would now transfer. We are those of Q'uo.

(Jim channeling)

I am Q'uo, and greet each again in love and in light. At this time it is our privilege to offer ourselves for any remaining queries. Is there a query with which we may begin?

Questioner: In all that was said I didn't hear anything about how one may aid a companion or a loved one in this quest for feeling the rhythms of life. Am I to assume that it is not the place of another to do this sort of work?

I am Q'uo, and am aware of your query, my sister. It is appropriate to provide the atmosphere of support for a mate or a friend who is working, as is each seeker, upon some aspect of the self which is seen as less than balanced. Each entity must make the decision that work is necessary and then must set about to accomplish that work. One cannot work for another or change another, for that is neither appropriate nor possible. Each entity lives a life which is generated from those patterns of perception and experience that have been gained over the entire period of that life and, indeed, which have been set in motion by choices made prior to the incarnative experience. The free will of each entity is paramount in the pursuing of the life pattern and in the attempt to alter or transform that pattern in the desired fashion.

When one sees another that is close to one's experience, and, indeed, may be an integral part of the life pattern, and one wishes to offer the greatest assistance to that entity, we would suggest that one begin from a point of view that is as filled with compassion as is possible, so that understanding and support for the entity and the experience in all of its ramifications may be given without qualification. To give this kind of unconditional support provides the free and open reach for the entity seeking change and transformation and does not provide any other obstacle for this transformation, other than those that the entity may find within itself.

If one attempts to tinker, shall we say, with this process that is internal for the other entity, it is more likely that there will be the interference that becomes as the stumbling block where the desire to aid the other may become distorted into becoming a desire to change the entity in a fashion which meets your needs rather than the other entity's needs.

Thus, to provide the atmosphere and the freedom for the other entity's free will to operate is the greatest aid one can be in this situation.

Is there another query, my sister?

Questioner: No, but I would like to thank you for the clarity of that answer. I think that was really helpful to me. Thank you very much.

I am Q'uo, and we thank you, my sister. Is there another query?

(Pause)

I am Q'uo, and we would take this opportunity to thank each present for once again inviting our presence in your circle of seeking. We are most grateful for this opportunity, for it allows us to see how valiantly each of you struggle within this heavy chemical illusion in which the mystery of life is ever present and the rays of light and illumination are treasured as they shine in response to your desire to seek that which you call truth. We walk with you upon your journeys, and we value you as companions. We shall at this time take our leave of this instrument and this group, leaving each, as always, in the love and in the light of the one infinite Creator. We are known to you as those of Q'uo. Adonai, my friends. Adonai. ✻

Sunday Meditation
April 19, 1992

Group question: The question this afternoon has to do with truth, personal truth in particular, when we are speaking to ourselves or to any other person and relying on what we feel is a personal truth or a general truth. Is there some way in which we can present this information so that the person to whom we are speaking can get the feel for what we see as a truth, and yet realize that the information may not be as particularly applicable to them as it is to us?

And, as another part of that question, how can we know just what our personal truth is when we dig down past habits, defense mechanisms, fears and other habitual ways of behaving that may be covering what really is the truth that we hold and the truth by which we act; how can we know what our truth is, and how can we share it with others in service to them?

(Carla channeling)

We are those of the principle known to you as Q'uo. Greetings and blessings to each of you in the love and the light of the one infinite Creator. It is our privilege to be able to be called to this group and to have the pleasure of working with each of you, with energy, with your desire to know and with this instrument. We would say a preliminary word or two concerning the event mentioned previously by this channel. The perception of contacts during the process of challenging by a fastidious instrument is affected by subtle alterations in consciousness. One which affected the challenging this particular day of working was the song of tuning, as there was the focus upon the suffering servant. The tuning of the group was satisfactory, however, the tuning of the more sensitive, inner sensibilities of this instrument were gently affected towards perception of suffering. Consequently, that shining consciousness called Christ had taken upon it for this instrument the shadow of dark suffering.

When a challenge is made in the name of the consciousness of Christ the focus is upon the consciousness itself and not upon events to which this consciousness reacted. Therefore, the refocusing of the instrument's tuning was necessary in order to avoid what could be called a "voice of doom," in actuality not as negative as misled. We are grateful, as always, to this instrument's sensitivity to the process of accepting contact, for we would not have been able to speak through this instrument at this working had the instrument not accepted the contact as being less than that which it had tuned itself to discover, that being the highest contact it could stably carry.

We mention this at this length because you ask us to speak concerning the question "What is truth?" In something as central to this instrument as the truth of its most basic and life-giving faith, it had the ability to be swayed towards a perception of the savior of this instrument's choosing that celebrated a behavior at the expense of the truth of the one known as Jesus the Christ that informed the behavior. That is, the one known as Jesus is not a man upon a cross, suffering unselfishly, but rather an entity willing to do the will of the one infinite Creator at whatever cost to itself. This is the essential Christ consciousness.

Let us examine this consciousness. Gaze upon a consciousness whose personality consists of one query—"What is Your will for me, beloved Creator, Father and teacher?" Immerse yourselves in the feeling of this consciousness. It lacks salt, it lacks personality, it lacks any persona or mask. It is infinitely vulnerable, infinitely willing, and infinitely desirous of serving the infinite One. Does this consciousness not feel full of light, almost a quality of floating, of being lighter than the air which you breathe? Yet to bring the circle back to what you call so well your Earth, let us point out that the circle is not levitating, the circle remains glued by gravity and humanity to the illusion in which there is personality, in which there must be the persona, the mask. Each of you desires to know the truth in an illusion which will forever deny knowledge of that truth. In your incarnation you shall not know a factual, provable, repeatable truth. All your truths shall be subjectively perceived, subjectively proven, and subjectively held. They are not transferable.

Why would the Logos, that Original Thought which created all that there is, that thought of Love, create an illusion in which people make serious choices, and create it in such a way that the choices must be made without sure and certain knowledge of any provable truth? Let us attack this question from a completely different vantage point. Each of you walks alone, and if there were no ground, if there were no bodies, if you were spirits, yet still you would walk alone, perhaps without legs but certainly as spirits unto yourselves, each unique. Not precisely the "Monet" of philosophy, but certainly in any apparent way, solitary.

What is the situation of millions and millions of spirits who move in patterns and out of them again, intertwining with one another and moving back out of a pattern, moving into other patterns with other entities, perhaps back to the first, perhaps real while alone, the combinations freely chosen, freely left? If each of you is a light then it could be said that each of you is a version of truth, a wandering, questioning mystery in which the truth is, yet cannot be reached consciously.

As each light is light and has the quality of unchanging reality, so are all spirits one, yet each is unique. Each is the product of one line of experience, one set of choices made that lead to other choices that lead to others. Where, then, is the common ground, where is the truth? We have said already that the only truth that can be held in common is the common mystery of the sure and common knowledge that there is a truth worth seeking, that truth shrouded in mystery in this illusion.

Each experiences the impulse to know the truth, that certainty that there is one somewhere that makes humans moral beings. That stubborn impulse is the hallmark of your species and the glory of your kind, and it opens to you the possibility of maturing into the light of a reality that you seek and will not find within this incarnation, within this illusion. You seek that which you will not know until you leave this illusion, yet you seek it all and all of you shall experience it.

What is the ground of that which you seek? Where within this illusion of yours can the truth be said to be hidden? We would use this instrument's knowledge of its Christian holy work and recount to you the parable of the vine. The one known as Jesus said "And I am the vine, you are the branches." There is something called the consciousness of Christ—which is personified for those who choose to follow the myth called Christianity by the name of Jesus the Christ—that lies deep within each. It is rooted in that one great creative Original Thought, that Logos, and it makes all one. From these roots grow a vine and as the roots are made of love, so the vine is love, and entities discover within themselves that root and nurture it until it springs forth into the conscious light of consciously lived, philosophical, ethical, moral or religious life.

We ask you to call it that which is most comfortable to you. Like a young and wondering child, that spiritual self that is born within this incarnation, within this illusion, within this density, wakes up in the crib of experience and looks around, and its first thought is "What is truth? What is happening? I see between the bars of my crib but it all is so loud, so stunning, and so much, where is the sense, where is the truth?" And as that spiritual self begins to grow it begins to make choices. It may choose one way or another, and that which is now above the ground of conscious living begins to make a bend in that branch of vine that is rooted and grown in love, and still is love, but now is love veiled and unknown.

How many twists and turns to the branches of that vine make each of you consider the twists and turns of your life, the spiritually, morally, ethically based choices that you made. The ways that you have turned your leaves to the sun or felt that you must shelter them from the sun that burns, that is too intense. Think of those pesticides that you have sprayed on yourselves because you felt a threat, other vines that do not seem to be lovely, other branches of that vine that threatened. Yet, do not all the branches of the vine have the same root? Are there male branches and female, you ask. We say to you, in your culture, in your learning—yes; in any spiritually based sense—no.

Yes, we have talked about the archetypical mind, but the archetypical mind is that which is held in the root, not in the branches. It is used as a blueprint for that which is the deepest treasure of the mind, its deepest and most primal distortions as it looks at itself against the vast background of passing experience. It is not the truth, it is a categorization of attitudes which may aid in influencing behavior. Is the truth about behavior? Each of you says inwardly, "Nay, in no way can the truth be behaved." But we say to you that there are shining moments when each branch of the vine finds the grace that illuminates the self and makes the truth visible to others for one bright moment. That often is enough to change the course of a relationship or of a personal understanding on a very deep level within the illusion, so that one comes closer and closer to accepting that there is a basis for seeking the truth, and that it can be glimpsed in the behavior of the self and others at gifted, illumined moments.

Now, how may one seek to dwell within the incarnation in such a way as to make these moments more accessible? We ask you, as always, to move to the inner closet of meditation, opening the self to the silence, sometimes, yes, to speak. You call this prayer, but, oh so importantly to listen, to listen to that silence, to accept it, to allow it to wash over the self until the self is full and more than full, until the self begins, indeed, to feel that light, heady effect of fuller light, fuller life, what we have called the consciousness of Christ. Open inwardly if you would

wish to open outwardly, for the straightest road to the roots of being is bathed in silence and in the listening in a focused and caring manner, full of desire, to that silence, that silence in which the creative principle of love ever speaks without sound and without words.

The more grounded that a spirit becomes in this root system of love the more this grounding may inform the persona and the more transparent that persona may become to the love itself. This does not make an entity, now matter how spiritually aware, able to speak the truth on command, for, indeed, there is no such thing precisely, although one may live the truth of a straight branch, lifting itself to the sun of love and light that is eternal. That is essence, and there are no words and no behaviors that speak the truth which are essential. Yet, can you come ever closer to being the truth through the discipline of the daily turning within to being washed in silence. There the work is done.

As you treat with each other, may we say it is our opinion that the greatest truth that each may offer each is the truth of fearlessness, for when one abandons fear and speaks from as close to the heart as one may find the grace to speak, and this does vary, one is as open as possible to that which cannot thrive in fear—honest and open communication. Shall you communicate that which is subtly wrong, that which is inaccurate, that which is less than perfectly understood within the self? Very well, what is to fear in that? What is to fear in any communication? One must always tell some onion skin of mistruth if one is speaking at all. But if one speaks that mistruth as carefully and lovingly and honestly as possible, then somehow every distortion is lit with the obvious good intentions.

There is one last secret we would share with you. There is great truth in laughter. One who takes himself seriously and goes solemnly about the business of telling the truth will find himself with his leaves turned away from the sun, unfed by light and love. Take a light touch, each of you with yourselves. Love and care passionately, and burn for your highest ideals, but not for your own performances and behaviors. At these you may laugh, for to be human and to be foolish is to say one thing twice. You will be foolish. Enjoy the folly that allows you to care so much, too much, that you risk everything and leap into midair knowing nothing because of your love of mystery that you know only by faith and hope.

How glorious you are in your folly, oh humans! How glorious is your search for the truth and how telling are your choices. We commend each of you as you courageously seek to know the nature of love, to know the mystery of faith and to find the gifts that you have that may serve the one infinite Creator and each other. To others you are the hands and the voice of the one Creator. Treat yourselves and each other gently, humorously and tenderly and you shall not be so afraid to let the branches that each of you are become close, almost as close in consciousness as is implicit within the root of the vine.

What is truth? Each of you is the truth, yet to be born. Nurture yourselves, and smile as you wait in care and intentions the days of understanding that are yours in what you would call "a life yet to be experienced." We do not believe there is any final truth, yet at each juncture of your path, at each death and entrance to a new life, you shall discover a larger version of the ground of being that informs the branch that you are, of the nature of your essence, and this mystery is the truth.

May you love each other, may you love yourselves. We thank you once again for allowing us to speak upon this—we search the instrument for the word we wish—Jesuitical subject. Words to discuss that which has no words—that is, the truth—must of necessity be roundabout, intertwined and complex. We hope that out of this knot of reasoning and unreasoning you may have found the flavor of that legacy which we would hope to leave you with our opinion, that although the truth is not reachable it can be experienced and it can be your gift to each other when truth, that being love, chooses to give the gift of grace and illumine the self with sudden, essential meaning.

We would at this time transfer from this instrument, thanking it for its service, and as always asking each to value our words only insofar as they have meaning for each of you, for we are not authorities. We are those of Q'uo, and leave this instrument in love and in light.

(Jim channeling)

I am Q'uo, and greet each again in love and light through this instrument. At this time it is our privilege to offer ourselves in the capacity of speaking to further queries, if there are any at this time. Is there a query to which we may speak?

M: Yes, I have some confusion about truth not being possible in this incarnation yet possible in another incarnation, but then the statement later that there is no truth. Can you help clear the confusion for me?

I am Q'uo, and I am aware of your query, my sister. Within this illusion, the life that each of you leads, there is almost complete covering over of those basic qualities or truths which are the foundation stone of your being. That is, those answers to questions such as who each of you is, how you are related to the one Creator in a very fundamental sense, and how the power of love moves through each life to shape and form it in a way which is perfect, and yet which to each of you may seem confusing and out of kilter, shall we say, from time to time. There is the possibility of approaching these truths in ways which words cannot begin to assume, through a kind of experience which many of those of your religious orders have called the transformative or unitive experience, where the light of truth fills one's being, and one for the extent and duration of the experience is able to become those truths.

There are these opportunities presented to each entity, perhaps not in the current experience but in one which shall follow it in another of what you may call incarnations. This illusion which you inhabit is one which is by its very fabric one which causes you to ask these questions and to begin to make tentative assumptions concerning the quality of truth, yet the very fabric of illusion is one which only permits the beginning, for here you are as the student who first enters school at an early age and you begin this process which shall take you …

(Side one of tape ends.)

(Jim channeling)

I am Q'uo, and I am again with this instrument, as it was necessary for it to accomplish the tending of the recording device. The one known as Carla is asked to speak that which it desires.

Carla: Thank you, Q'uo. I'd just like to restate M's question. There were statements that in reality there is no truth, also that there is a truth that will be experienced later in our evolution, and a third statement that no truth is final. Could you clarify?

I am Q'uo, and I am aware of your query, my sister. We can say that the means of transferring information which we use at this time—that is, words and concepts—are incapable of transferring that which is truth, and we can suggest that there will be opportunities offered to each as your journey proceeds for you to experience the truth of unity with the one Creator and All That Is, and we can say that as you continue upon this journey in that fashion that the creative power that is the one Creator shall learn from Itself those lessons that shall increase Its knowledge and experience so that that which was true shall be added to, shall we say, so that experience grows for all of creation as each portion of creation learns and seeks this one creative force, so that which has been true and which has become the foundation stone for one experience shall be built upon for further experience, further truth, and shall enhance that truth, so that in the ultimate sense, though all is one, all learns, all grows, all teaches and evolves in a fashion which causes truth to be enhanced, and in the sense of apprehending such a truth, there is no truth that can be apprehended and kept in a static and understandable fashion, for it is a dynamic universe and Creator in which we all live and move and have our being.

Is there a further query, my sister?

M: No, that's clear *(inaudible)* and involving God *(inaudible)*.

This is so, my sister, as far as we are able to ascertain, and we are but the humblest of messengers for such a dynamic Creator.

M: Thank you.

We thank you, my sister. Is there another query?

Carla: One last one. So that is the reason why, as the possibilities of one creation end and all coalesces back to the one infinite Creator, there is always another creation, and the branches are sent out again from the roots of the vine. That's why it never stops, because the Creator Itself is infinitely learning, infinitely *(inaudible)* is that so?

I am Q'uo, and I am aware of your query, my sister. Again, to the best of our knowledge and the knowledge of those who serve as teachers to us, this is so, for all entities gain from experience and produce a seed, shall we say, of knowledge, and when all such seeds have reached the final ground of being in reunifying with the one Creator, there they are planted to grow again into another creation that stands, shall we say, upon the shoulders of preceding creation and the one Creator harvests in a cyclical fashion those experiences from all of its portions and utilizes them in a learning fashion so that each succeeding creation becomes enhanced by all that which has gone before.

Is there a further query, my sister?

Carla: Not for me Q'uo. That's just a wide and wonderful picture, thank you very much.

M: And from me, thank you.

I am Q'uo, and we are also thankful and grateful to each of you for inviting our presence and presenting us with the queries which illuminate the journeys of all of us, for we also learn from you that which is of importance to you, and especially do you learn that great desire which you have for seeking that which you call truth. This desire also is felt, may we say, by all of creation, for each portion seeks to return to its source and that source of all creation seeks the knowledge and experience of each of its portions. Thus, this dynamic desire to seek, this yearning between Creator and created, is that force which propels all creation forward that the one Creator may be glorified by each of Its portions, and each of Its portions may know the Creator through each experience.

We are known to you as those of Q'uo, and we again thank you for this blessing and opportunity to speak with you. We shall join you again in your future upon your request. We shall take our leave of each at this time, leaving each as always in the love and in the light of the one infinite Creator. We are those of Q'uo. Adonai, my friends. Adonai.

Sunday Meditation
April 26, 1992

Group question: The question this afternoon deals with behavior that is intended to be of service to others but which seems, in the eyes of the one offering the service, to fall short because the one that one is attempting to serve is somehow impaired, either perhaps by old age and difficulty in remembering conversations and visits, or by alcoholism so that the memory there is also faulty, or perhaps just a pattern of behavior that has been set up through the life that makes it difficult to really feel like one is making a solid contact, that there is clear communication, and that there has been a recognition of the visit, of the service, of words, of conversations.

What kind of consolation can one take in attempting to offer such a service to another person, knowing that the person, for one reason or another, probably won't remember it, won't appreciate it, and may not be affected by it in any observable degree? Is there some value in continuing to attempt to serve in this manner?

(Carla channeling)

We are known to you as those of Q'uo. Greetings and blessings to each in the love and in the light of the one infinite Creator whose intelligence is the intelligence of infinite love. We would preface this discussion of service by informing this instrument as to the reason for the gathering of other discarnate entities at this working. This instrument usually prays for all those unseen friends symbolized by the archangels to attend in strength in the purification of the place of working. On this particular occasion, this instrument asked for all of its unseen friends and did not ask for the archangels as symbols but as those among others who would be present. Consequently, this is a very crowded meeting. Each and all thank the instrument and the group for the privilege of being able to share in this meditation. And we thank this instrument that we may through it offer our service, that of humble opinion.

When the question is asked, "What service is not such a good service?" there are two general ways of approaching the query. One is from the viewpoint of that entity who desires to be of service; one is from the viewpoint of the actual needs of the entity which is being apparently served. Because the query is more centrally that of the one serving, we would like to address the confusion generated by gazing from the viewpoint of the one who is apparently being served.

The needs of an individual entity are never completely apparent unless the entity is transparent to all that is beautiful and true. Entities seldom know their own needs or how to judge them. So, it is not surprising that the third-density servant becomes confused and loses sanguinity when faced with the task of attempting to determine what service is appropriate, what service meets the real needs of the entity being served.

From the most general standpoint, we might opine that true service involves working with spiritual principles that will in some way aid in teaching the one who is being served about what spiritual evolution consists in and what the process of spiritual maturation might involve. This teaching does not necessarily have to be a teaching of words. Silence and actions speak loudly also. However, if one who is a servant is ruled by the calm logic of spiritual principles in the abstract, one is moving from a place of impersonal compassion, and this attitude is conveniently and comfortably separated from a deep involvement with, and fellow feeling for, the entity one is attempting to serve.

Thusly, we would not recommend that one approach each and every opportunity of service by using the calm and detached logic of the analysis of events in terms of spiritual principles. It is perfectly acceptable to inform oneself of one's opinion from this point of view, but it is the wisdom of the heart which moves the servant into open and full giving of the self without reservation, not the temperate demands of logic. This information may be helpful to ponder when one truly does feel that one is not of service. In this case, an analysis of the entity's situation in terms of the opportunities for spiritual maturation may yield telling results and we recommend it for this use.

The weight of the query at this working revolves about the consolation one might find when performing a service which one feels is a portion of one's duty, one's responsibility, indeed, as the one known as Ra would say, "one's honor." It is an honor, a responsibility and a duty to treat with perfect love those companions of family, and the informal family of deep friendships, with the dedication to being the mouth, the hands, and the lifting and carrying shoulders in manifestation of the one infinite Creator which is forever unmanifest. The very heart of service is the request of the one know as Jesus to love others as one loves the self.

If the self gives the self a bath or tidies its habitat or offers itself food, the need for thanks of self to self seems small. When one serves another self one does not interiorize the service, but rather perceives the service as moving from one field of energy, that being the self, to another field of energy, that being another separate self. This reach seems long to the servant and it is no longer of the relaxed mind of one who is hungry and so prepares itself food, or one who needs society and so calls a friend or goes to the amusement. Now it is one entity reaching out through space and time to a separate entity. It seems there is a transaction. The servant gives a service like a gift or a present to another self. Perhaps the reason is a desire to express love, to express loyalty, or to express some one or other of the many strands and kinds of emotion one feels concerning those things which one's personal character structure inform one's conscience that it is just, rightful, dutiful and honorable for the self to do.

In actuality, whether one who is served is a parent, a child, a member of the family or of the extended family of friendship, or of the nature of complete strangers, service is always service if it is given purely. The challenge is to love others as one loves the self.

When one is becoming spiritually mature, one loves the self without reservation, seeing in full the iniquity, the foibles, the insecurities and fears which it as a third-density illusory entity carries. Each self in third density does walk carrying a burden. That burden is its humanity, and that is a work which describes those things which the illusory self experiences as successful distortions of the truer, deeper nature of the mind, body and spirit as a unified being. The humanity contains all those energies concerning the self, the relationships with others and with groups of others, be they churches, nations or athletic teams, which affect the true entity—or may we say—more deeply true entity, by baffling, distorting, blocking or causing to be over-active the energies which must be penetrated by the energy of the Creator which is breathed into the being from the base of the energies and comes up into the heart to be used for spiritual work such as service.

Insofar as these energies of what we would call the red ray of survival and relationships with the self, of orange and yellow ray which concern relationships with self, other entities, and other groups of entities, all can be most confused. And insofar as these energies are allowed to remain murky, the power that moves into the heart will be less. It is only when one is able to release the so-called lower energies so that no grudges are held, no sorrows clutched close, and no fears ruling the nature, that the energy centers become clear and are able to pass on the full strength of the infinite energy which many call prana.

When this prana moves into the heart and then moves out upon the wings of service in full strength, there is no need for any concern on the part of the servant as to the relative success of the service. It is then that one may experience the treating of another as one treats the self. That which seems appropriate is done. If it is good food and is eaten and appreciated, very well. If the food is not that which can be taken and the plate must be refused, that is too bad, but not a reflection upon the service offered.

Now see where each is caught. It is at the point where one wishes for one's service to be successful that one finds oneself suddenly separated from the flow and the process of the Self serving the Self by serving the other self. That is, the flow of the Creator, the capital "S" Self serving the capital "S" Self. This is true service to capital "S" Self, service to the infinite Self.

Linguistics can become confusing, but it is a point trenchantly to be considered that the left hand path is service to small "s" self, and the right hand or positive path is service to capital "S" Self. The difference is in the definition of the self, and as a small self serves another small self and does not remember that one is serving the capital "S" Creator Self by serving another Self, that service will seem incomplete without the thank you, without the good feeling of success. But if service is offered with the firm memory that one is serving the infinite Creator, one intends by the greatest desire to serve the infinite Creator, and one is simply serving other selves as a means to this noble end, then one can free oneself of the misery of feeling unappreciated and unnoticed. Perhaps the service is appreciated, perhaps it is not, by the self which is apparently being served. But in the generation of positive intentions in the great and ever more purified desire to serve the one infinite Creator in all of Its infinite parts, one may more and more feel falling away from the self the need for recognition, the need for the thank you, for the justification of the service.

That extreme good judgment of offering only the excellent service is a butterfly too elusive to catch. Better it is to gaze at one's duties, one's responsibilities, one's honors, and the ever present strangers in one's midst as perfect opportunities for service to the Creator Self so that service is not scattered among people and places and categories but, rather, service is a way of life expressing the spiritual principle of offering love to one's Creator and Preserver, offering the self to the Creator Self, and in return feeling the Creator Self pouring through the self in infinite energy so that there is always energy for more service, until this way of life becomes, may we say, self-perpetuating and the life glows with love reflected in love.

Now, this we realize is cold consolation for us to say, "Do not expect any outcome when you serve, for your desire to serve is that which is relevant." This is not emotionally satisfying. We may, however, remind each to think in memory of all the unexpected gifts of service which have moved into manifestation in each of your lives: the bread returning upon the waters again and again tenfold, a hundredfold, until you cannot count all the blessings which come into the life. The energy for these blessings is begun in the self's desire to give of the self. As it gives, it creates an energy which is forever spherical, and returns and returns and lifts one higher and higher each time it returns. The way of service is a way of spiritual evolution. To figure out how to be unselfish in an illusion—and a deep illusion, for it is ours also—where service to others is the most efficient of service to the self if one desires to evolve spiritually, is somewhat marvelous, is it not?

May this bread returning upon the waters be a sign to you. When you see the manifestation of love given to you, hear that consolation, hear those energies being registered in the heart of the Creator Self, for all is one and as you serve one, those tender and merciful feelings, those gentle hands and soft, kind words, those strong supportive silences move out through whatever bafflement may seem to stop the service into the memory of your entire planetary sphere and become a part of that which is positive about your planet. No good intention, no desire to help is ever lost. Do not let the illusion's disconsolate, apparent nature cause you or any to stumble upon the path of service to others. But let it redouble your desire as you know that all your love has flown to the heart of the Creator Self of this planet and is immediately a portion of the light of the world.

We would continue through the one known as Jim with thanks to this instrument. We leave it in love and in light. For the vast company here assembled, we leave this instrument, saying greetings from all and blessings. We are known to you as those of Q'uo.

(Jim channeling

I am Q'uo, and greet each of you again in love and in light. At this time we would offer ourselves to those present for the purpose of speaking to any queries which may remain upon the minds or which have arisen as we spoke. Is there a query at this time?

M: Yes. I'm having a hard time posing my question. My thoughts are from my work, when I see a person who is an over-functioner in a relationship or in relationships, usually this comes from their need to either please and be acceptable or to avoid conflict and cross words or rejection. The relationship gets out of balance, because one gives too much and the other takes, and it's crippling for both. So, what I hear from Q'uo is if we can only find love, possibly through the red-orange ray—that being the chakra—so that our heart feels love, we can discern the difference. However, many people don't know how to do that and don't stop the behavior of acting out of the need to please, to find something else. Again, I'm not sure what I'm asking, but if you can clarify this, I'd be grateful for the answer.

I am Q'uo, and am aware of your query, my sister. Within the illusion that is your life pattern that each of you share, there is a tangle of mental and emotional relationships that has as its purpose the untangling and balancing of all relationships so that love without condition may move freely between entities. Thus, the tangle has value, and we suggest to each seeker of truth which wishes to balance relationships and release this power of love that the effort to do so be continued in the fashion which is most accessible to the entity, realizing that your life pattern is much like your ladder, where each succeeding step moves one upward to another point of viewing that is more comprehensive than the one previous.

When entities are confused as to how to proceed, then it is that we suggest that there be meditation without action so that the heart of each may be allowed to speak in the silence. The speaking may or may not take a verbal or conceptual form, but may express itself in a feeling …

(Side one of tape ends.)

(Jim channeling)

I am Q'uo, and greet each again in love and in light. We shall continue.

The feeling that develops from the silence of the meditation and which proceeds from those levels of one's being that are accessible only when the conscious mind has been quieted may serve as a direction so that the entity may begin a step that may be new or may be taken with a new attitude. As one becomes confused in the daily round of activities, the confusion is usually of the mental or emotional nature, and then it is that the silence and the meditation is recommended so that some small part of the tangle may be worked upon by those levels of those beings which are aware of the path that is being traveled and the appropriateness of the next step.

Is there a further query, my sister?

M: Thank you. The archangels that were spoken of, I'd like to know more about what that was about.

I am Q'uo, and am aware of your query, my sister. Many there are of an unseen nature who cherish and watch over the activities of those of your peoples as each day's activities are accomplished. Each entity has those guides and guardians, friends and teachers in whose care the entity has been placed, in a metaphysical sense, so that there is for each entity a significant number of unseen hands and hearts that join in your journey. In addition, there are those whose honor and duty is more of a light-bringing nature so that your experiences are blessed from time to time according to the invitations, shall we say, that you make with your seeking, with your desire, and with your observance of certain rituals, such as the attending to the church service, and, most especially, the attending to the ritual of the Easter season which has just passed.

There are entities who are evoked and invoked at this time by this particular group in its gathering and seeking for information and inspiration. This group has many friends that rejoice at each gathering and which send wishes of love, light and healing as a normal part of their relationship with each in this group.

Is there another query, my sister?

M: Thank you, no.

I am Q'uo, and we thank you, my sister. Is there another query at this time?

Carla: I just wanted to clarify something that M was asking before. If you're doing something to please someone, but you think you're doing something to serve someone, is there a desire to serve, and is that part of it still pristine, and still part of the good of the planet?

I am Q'uo, and am aware of your query, my sister. Indeed, this is so, for it is the intention to serve that is the heart of all service. It is said that the uninformed desire to serve is, at its heart, foolish in nature, for it is not informed by what you would call wisdom, for wisdom is a lesson that is learned in a higher density after the lesson of compassion and love has been accomplished. It is necessary that the foundation of service be placed upon love, with wisdom refining it at a later time, in order that that quality which is strongest and most important in the seeking and serving of the Creator be emphasized and placed in its proper place.

As you become aware or informed by wisdom, it may be that your service becomes more effective, but until one has the pure heartfelt desire to serve and to offer oneself in service at each opportunity available, wisdom is useless. The desire to serve is that which begins the process in a manner which is, in the overall sense, most effective. That your service may or may not be effective according to your estimation from what you call "hindsight" is relatively unimportant. The important factor is that the desire is generated to serve. This desire is that which you have incarnated to find and to nourish as the seedling which later becomes the great oak.

Is there another query, my sister?

Carla: Kind of a half query and a half confirmation. So the pathology of trying to please or trying to avoid conflict and therefore doing things meets its own reward of exactly what you fear happening. In other words, you don't please and you do have conflict because you never can predict what is going to please somebody or what is going to avoid causing conflict. But still, beneath it all, there is that germ of desire to serve, which is healthy no matter what pathology is there. I think that's very comforting. Is that true?

I am Q'uo, and am aware of your query, my sister, and we would agree that this is the summation of our previous statement, though there is still a long journey to be accomplished. To begin with the desire to travel is of utmost importance. There will be times of testing that desire. The discovery that one may not be able to please another, even with a strong desire to do so, is such a test. But, each entity has carefully laid the groundwork for these testings and opportunities to demonstrate the desire to serve, so that in the larger sense there is always a progression of possibility so that the entity will have the opportunity to learn from its own experience, and to discover that the desire to serve is the primary quality that it wishes to harvest from the life pattern.

There is time enough in all entities' experience for the refining of service. The generation of the desire is the most important portion of this illusion's experience.

Is there a further query, my sister?

Carla: No, Q'uo. I think I would prefer to let the session end with that gem. Thank you very, very much for being here, and thank all the guys.

I am Q'uo, and thank you once again, my sister. We would also take this opportunity to express, not only our gratitude for the invitation to join this circle of seeking, but to extend the great and joyous gratitude of those entities present who have offered their vibrations of love and light to this group as well. We all shall take our leave of this group at this time, leaving each, as always, in the love and the ineffable light of the one infinite Creator. We are known to you as those of Q'uo. Adonai, my friends. Adonai.

L/L Research

Sunday Meditation
May 3, 1992

Group question: The question this week has to do with "why." Why, if there is a benevolent, higher force that we might call God or the Creator, is there so much sorrow, suffering, sickness, violence, disease and general disharmony in the world, in individual and in group experiences? Why do people have to go through so much difficulty in order to just survive in many cases? Why is there not a more active participation, either on the part of the Creator or the forces of light, the angelic beings, to intervene and to provide sustenance, relief, healing and so forth on all the levels—mind, body, spirit and emotions?

And, as an adjunct to that question, how does this interaction of the Creator and the forces of light in our personal, mundane lives relate to the New Age, so called, now dawning where we are supposedly ending one cycle and about to begin another experience. Is there a relationship in the sorrow and the suffering that is going on now on the planet in its intensity and its widespread nature to this supposed ending of one age and beginning of another?

(Carla channeling)

We are known to you as those of the principle of Q'uo, and we greet each of you in the love and in the light of the one infinite Creator. It is a blessing and a privilege to speak to this circle of seeking concerning the great "why?" of personal and planetary suffering, and the possible connection with the end of the age. We are the brothers and sisters of sorrow, and are part not of your answer, but of your query. We would ask each of you to weigh our words as those without authority; friends, but not divine friends, merely those of somewhat more experience than you have conscious memory of at this, your present moment.

Let us begin with our name for ourselves. We have called ourselves "the brothers and sisters of sorrow," for we are social entities whose members have decided to move far from our planetary home to speak to those who sorrow, who stumble, who are faced with deeply central choices, when the surrounding atmosphere is one which is profoundly lacking in accurate, trustworthy information upon which to base choice. We speak to one entity at a time. "We are not those who will save the planet." You may put that phrase in quotations.

We witness the suffering, and, although we shall proceed to speak upon some portions of the answer or answers to, "Why is there suffering?" more important is it to us to verify and underline the centrality of this question, for it is not the starving, the freezing, the sickening unto death alone who are suffering. Each entity who is born into your third-density illusion begins immediately a process of loss, suffering, increasing limitation and ordeal, followed by physical death. Each of you recapitulates in a leisurely manner the misery of the starving infant. It simply takes many entities, born into healthier climes and circumstances, longer to complete the menu of suffering. And, oh, my friends, there are so many interesting entrees on this menu!

Why are you in the place of suffering? We ask this to bring each who listens into the same environment as those for whom one feels the compassion, to focus upon an instance of suffering close to this instrument's mind: each is the beaten, each is the one which wields the instrument of beating, each is the jury member forced to evaluate the incident, each is the rioter, each is the shopkeeper. Each of you lives a life that is seemingly personal, truly unique, but deeply planetary. Each entity's uniqueness lies not in the specific experiences alone or in the specific reactions in thought, word and deed to these experiences. But, rather, each is also part of a sea of consciousness shared by all who dwell within, upon and around your planetary sphere. You are beginning to become more and more aware of the connection betwixt the personal inner self and all consciousness upon your sphere.

The query, "Why is there suffering?" then can perhaps be brought back home [for consideration] to each of your personal journeys, as well as remaining cognizant of the [world's] intense and acute examples of suffering. The conversation earlier touched upon the term karma. Karma, in our opinion, is a kind of residual energy or momentum. An action which produces an imbalance betwixt the giver and the receiver creates a bond of imbalance. This is called a karmic bond. The momentum is often visualized as circular, and thus the term "wheel of karma" is used to describe the way that a balance is offered repeatedly to those who are imbalanced. Again and again, a situation will occur in which an entity may forgive the self and the other self involved in this karmic tie. When forgiveness is complete—that is, there is forgiveness of the other self and of the self in full and unstopped measure—the wheel of karma stops.

There is a planetary karma also, for nation states and large economic, social and, what you term, religious groups of entities have offered unbalanced action to other groups of entities. Thusly, the individual karma and the societal karma mount to the level of the heavens. The planet as a whole does not at this time have one karma. Thusly, there is the opportunity for entities which wish to aid in the societal karma to do so, and many among your peoples are those which have incarnated to do personal work in consciousness, to make choices which further refine choices, to work for the one infinite Creator, and to serve in a healing capacity upon the level of the consciousness which is deep enough in the roots of mind to be that consciousness shared by all upon all levels of native being within, upon, and around your planetary sphere.

Why is there suffering by those starving in foreign lands? We may suggest that there are many who have chosen to incarnate for the purpose of suffering as intensely and as long as possible before the inevitable death by starvation or illness, not only in less technologically oriented cultures, but also within each culture, for within the culture which is your own there are those with short, hungry and brutal lives. These, may we say, Christ-like entities are pursuing a beautiful, poignant and terrible service, absorbing the deadening, merciless, pitiless and ruthless service-to-self distortions which have caused motives of greed, revenge and slaughter to erupt into actions against groups of other selves through, what you call, your history.

Others there are among you who do a great deal of work within, calling it prayer or meditation or worrying or concern, sending love and healing to those who watch and suffer and wait and perish. There is a lovely orison sounding, with millions of souls blending at all times; your planet prays without ceasing. Always, in every night watch, there are those millions unknown to you who keep the watch for humankind. When others sleep, you may well be raising your internal voice in praise of the infinite One in thanksgiving and in intercession for all who suffer. And so, by lives lived in some part sacrificially, the societal karma is being, to some extent, alleviated through the heartfelt caring of very many of your peoples.

We know this query is far-ranging, but we would attempt a focus upon the heart of the query before we leave this instrument. Gaze with us at the pattern of the incarnation you now enjoy. There is the pain of the learning, the growing, the changing to fit new heights and weights and emotions. Then, seamlessly, there begins the long decline of the physical vehicle which carries your consciousness about from the first health of youth to the last breath before the physical vehicle is no longer viable. In the space between, one experience after another challenges, baffles and confuses the mind, the spirit and the emotions. Each may dream of utopia, of the Garden of Eden, yet each is soundly thrown out of it. This is your circumstance at this time.

Why does the infinite Creator place you so firmly and decisively in a milieu of loss, ordeal, limitation and eventual dying? We ask you, what gets your attention: the perfect halcyon day or the moment of toxin, the alarm, the adrenaline and the sudden movement to cope, to save, to defend? Each of you has two minds: one will keep you in this density forever; the other will evolve. Your two minds sometimes have very different ways of dealing with circumstances. The first mind is the intellectual mind. Its soul purpose is to manipulate the environment in order that you may survive, find shelter, be fed and have comfort. The other mind is that mind best described as the "wise heart." This heart's wisdom is that portion of the mind whose roots move into racial, societal, planetary and Creator mind. It is this mind that is always and forever.

The suffering, the ordeal of living, is specifically designed to grab the attention of the intellectual mind and then proceed to baffle it so thoroughly and completely that the intellectual mind gives up, and the thrust of inquiry moves to the heart. In the heart lies that beingness which gazes at this experience of third-density illusion and chooses, in faith alone, to be a part of the love—the good, if you will—of the personal, societal, planetary mind.

There is no "why?" in the heart's wisdom, nor is there any answer. The heart sees suffering and embraces it, for, to the heart, any entity who is thirsty is the Christ waiting for a drink. Any entity who needs clothing is the Christ waiting to be covered. Thusly, the ordeals become opportunities for service and are seen as challenges worthy of attracting one's attention.

We glory in the beauty of your sunny day and of the peace each has found within the heart. But more, my friends, we glory at the suffering that each encloses. We ask each of you to touch yourselves with loving and forgiving hearts, to be healers of the self, and to allow that healing which is from eternity to eternity to move into the ever-wounded conscious self so that each may become a healing expression and manifestation to those about each, not by word, but merely by the point of view. Let your hearts be those open channels of love, and may you love each other, for the suffering is part of learning how, truly, to love and, eventually, how to be love.

We are pilgrims with you in this quest. We thank each and this instrument for calling us to you in this matter. We are at this time happy to speak to your further questions, but find that this instrument grows weary. Thusly, we would transfer this contact to the one known as Jim. We are those of Q'uo, and leave this instrument with thanks in love and in light.

(Jim channeling)

I am Q'uo, and greet each again in love and in light through this instrument. At this time, we would offer ourselves in the attempt to speak to those queries which may yet remain upon the minds of those present. Is there a query at this time?

Questioner: I'd like to ask about the changes that will be taking place in this area around the year 2000.

I am Q'uo, and am aware of your query, my sister. We are not those who have the desire or ability to describe in detail those changes which are as the weather at your graduation. These changes have begun many of your years ago as the planetary entity itself is also making the graduation, shall we say. There has long been upon the surface of your planet populations of entities who have engaged in disharmonious relationships even unto the war, and have, through the heat of the emotions, transferred this heat into the crust, as you call it, of the planet itself, so that as the planetary entity attempts to make its own movement from this density of light into the succeeding density of light there is the necessity for the reharmonizing of the planetary garment that will allow for the release of the excessive heat in a variety of means in order that the planetary entity shall remain and retain in its whole nature; that is, shall proceed into the next density of light intact.

Thus, the release in a controlled fashion of heat energy is achieved as those natural, shall we say, catastrophes, as you call them, are experienced in the form of eruptions of volcanoes, the earthquakes, the heating and cooling effects of your geothermal forces, and other forms of the release of energy that will allow for the continual harmonization of this planetary influence as it moves through this period of transition.

Thus, there is much of choice on that part of the populations of this planet that will determine the precise location, duration, intensity and nature of heat release. As entities and groupings of entities are able to resolve difficulties and achieve a more harmonious perception of relationship, there will be less need for the drastic, in your terms, release of this heat of emotion energy. Thus, it can be said that these releases of energies shall continue. As to their location, etc., this is, as you would say, in the process of being determined by the movement of thought …

(Side one of tape ends.)

(Jim channeling)

I am Q'uo, and am again with this instrument. Is there another query, my sister?

Questioner: What visions do you have for the New Age which is approaching?

I am Q'uo, and, though the query is most general in its point, we would suggest that the nature of that which you have called the New Age is one that is quite different from the experience which is now enjoyed by the population of this planetary influence. We shall attempt to give only very general descriptions, for this is a large field of inquiry.

There is the graduation into and use of a physical vehicle which is more densely packed with light than the one which you now utilize in your current experience. This vehicle is that which is associated with the fourth energy center or chakra, that having to do with the heart, so that the primary influence of this body and its experience is that of learning the lessons of love, compassion, mercy, understanding, forgiveness and acceptance so that entities will have a greater opportunity to see the Creator in the creation about them, and to see and express that Creator within the self as well.

This perception and expression shall take the form of the communication that is more of the, as you call it, telepathic nature where the transmission of concepts is accomplished much as you would transmit the contents of your field of vision in a moment and this picture would include the feelings and responses that you would have to that in your field of vision. There is in such a form of communication no ability or desire to hide those feelings and thoughts which an entity may entertain. Rather, there is the great desire to blend the individual energies and abilities with others so that there is created what might be called a society of memory-complexes or social memory complex that allows each entity within the grouping access to the memories, talents, experiences and abilities of all others within this grouping.

The grouping of entities itself has chosen the means of further seeking the Creator in that there is the great desire of such groupings to serve others by utilizing the expanded knowledge and abilities that are experienced at this level of being. Further knowledge of and learning of the creation and the Creator is gained primarily by seeking to be of assistance to other entities who may not yet have reached this level of understanding. Thus, there is the waiting for the call from such entities, be they individuals or civilizations, upon planetary influences such as this one.

We feel that this is a good general description of that which awaits this planetary population, and would ask if there is a further query, my sister?

Questioner: If you talk on the subject of going home, returning home, and explain that, I would appreciate it.

I am Q'uo, and am aware of your query, my sister. We are aware of the feeling that many entities within this planetary influence experience of being away from home, and may suggest that there are many, many entities upon this planet that have journeyed here from elsewhere, that is, from another planetary influence. In the majority of cases, this journeying has been as a part of a grouping of entities that has sought to complete the cycle of learning that this third-density planet offers, and these entities have sought to complete that cycle upon this planetary influence as it was beginning its third-density cycle at the time of their joining it. This is true for the great majority of entities upon this planet, for you see you are not all of one source or origination as far as progression from a second-density influence into the third density, and this accounts for much of the difficulty in relationships between societies, nationalities, races, religions and so forth upon your planetary influence.

There is also another grouping of entities that has come from elsewhere, either within this solar system or outside of this particular solar system, that has chosen to return to a third-density planet in order to be of service to the entities upon this planet, even though those who return have progressed beyond this third-density experience. As we spoke to the previous query in suggesting that those who proceed into the next density of light seek to learn by serving others, there are many of these kinds of entities within this planetary influence at this time who have come from elsewhere to be of service in a certain manner as they join this planetary influence. These entities offer their light and love just as a portion of their very being glows more brightly with the honor of standing closer to the light of the one Creator. This service is offered, as we said, as a general kind of lightening of the vibrations of this planetary influence.

Each such entity also has a specific talent or service to offer that is accomplished in a unique way for each entity, whether this be by teaching, by healing, by communication, or by any of a number of means of being service-to-other entities. These entities also pass through that which you call the "forgetting process," so that as they enter this planetary influence they are completely the citizens, shall we say, of this third-density planet, and do not retain those abilities that would seem to this planet's population as being that of a paranormal nature in general, so that there is an equality of status, and no entity's service would be accepted without question simply because it came from one with abilities that were obviously in excess of what is the norm on this third-density planet.

These entities, however, have within them the distant and dimly lit memory of their origin as being from elsewhere, and in many cases this feeling is in the form of what you may call a kind of homesickness or alienation from the planetary influences and vibrations that are of a more disharmonious nature within this third-density influence. However, each entity in the heart of its being is aware that, though there is a home that may be located elsewhere, that the true home of all seekers of light and servants of the one Creator is within that service and within that light that comes from only one source, the one Creator, and each may take solace in knowing that the Creator resides within each entity and shines the light of love and service to all equally.

Is there another query, my sister?

Questioner: So, you were just saying that, basically, home is within us, is that right?

I am Q'uo, and am aware of your query, my sister, and this is correct, that the home is truly, as your peoples say, located where the heart is able to love.

Is there another query?

Questioner: When I was referring to home I was referring to returning to the First Cause … passing through Christ consciousness and returning to the First Cause.

I am Q'uo, and am aware of your query, my sister. This journey, that of returning to the First Cause, is more closely aligned to the latter portion of our response where each entity becomes aware that there is a Source from which each comes and towards which each moves after the great cycle of learning and experience has been achieved. For each portion of the Creator that becomes an individualized portion of consciousness moves out from this Source with the desire to seek and to serve the one Creator, for it is felt within the tiniest portion of each entity's being that it is the great desire of the Creator to know Itself, and that each entity is a means by which this Creator shall know Itself.

As each entity moves through the various densities or dimensions of light, learning each lesson that is possible there, much experience of a various nature in intensity and in type, all having to do with the qualities of love and light, are gained. Aand as these experiences are gathered, the individualized portion of consciousness that is each entity then takes on these qualities and widens the perspective or the "eye-shot," the point of view, shall we say, so that each entity, then, is able to see more of the other entities and experiences about it as the Creator knowing Itself.

As the final lessons are learned in the last of the densities of light, the entities begin to take upon themselves that which you may call a spiritual mass so that there is the great desire to move into complete union once again with the one Creator, and this union is achieved so that each entity brings each experience with it as an offering or glorification to the one Creator. Each such offering, then, taken cumulatively, becomes the seeding of another great octave of experience and cycle of beingness, as the one Creator once again sends out portions of Itself to gain in experience, to learn that which can only be learned by the giving of free will choice to those portions of Itself that venture out as pilgrims into what is to each the great unknown and mystery of being.

Is there another query, my sister?

Questioner: No.

I am Q'uo. Is there another query at this time?

Questioner: I'd like to ask a question. I'm trying to focus back down into what you were saying and trying to apply it to Rodney King and the events in L.A. and around the country. If I'm applying this correctly, please tell me, and if I'm not, just briefly tell how I'm not. The victim, Rodney King, and the victims—all the shopkeepers, the people whose places were burned—the people who, at some level, were accepting acting as a safety vent for energies that otherwise would have been worse, resulting in, say, a revolution within the entire nation … The ones who were doing the negative—the shooting and the beating and the burning and the looting—where those who had the impulse to do that but, also, at some level, who were accepting the karmic results of that, perhaps as part of the same equation …

I'm really fuzzy on this. And all of the people around the planet—and I know that they are all around the planet—who are praying for peace and for justice and to save the Earth, these energies were aiding in keeping the venting points open so that the energy, the heat, could be vented safely and not trouble the entire nation or the entire planet, in this case, the entire nation. Is that a fair application of what you were saying to current events? That's why the suffering—it's kind of like a safety vent?

I am Q'uo, and am aware of your query, my sister. We find that there is indeed some confusion in the interpretation in that which we have spoken, and would attempt to speak briefly to alleviate the confusion. The experiences of sorrow and suffering of whatever nature by any individual or groupings of individuals upon your planet is the result of those learnings and services that have gone before and which have been improperly integrated or incompletely assimilated within the individual or grouping.

All experience within your third-density illusion has the purpose of teaching some facet of love and acceptance. As entities move through various experiences there are those challenges or testings that further teach those areas that have previously been lacking in their balance or refinement. The more difficult the challenge or test, the greater the possibility for learning love and acceptance. The traumatic conditions, such as that of your warfare, offer great immediate opportunity for entities to see the possibilities of love and service to others, such as when a soldier would jump upon that which you call the grenade to save the life of a friend. This is the greatest service.

There is a variety of response available at all times to each entity in any experience. Each experience shall offer the opportunity for the entity to demonstrate his or her level of understanding, and this shall be demonstrated by the spontaneous response to each situation. Thus, the difficulties that may be experienced within your illusion are as the catalyst for a process of learning that occurs, in the larger sense, to the metaphysical or spiritual entity that each of you is. The experiences in your daily round of activities are those physical or mundane means by which metaphysical lessons are distilled.

The venting process, of which we spoke previously, is the process by which the Earth itself as an entity has absorbed the heated vibrations of disharmony and difficulty over many, many generations of many, many civilizations. This absorbing of disharmonious vibrations has created a difficulty for the planetary entity in its transition from third to fourth density, as those populations that have inhabited it for many, many millennia have had their own difficulties in reaching harmonious resolutions to differences between entities, races, religions, nations and so forth. Those difficulties are of an extreme nature at this time and require the periodic venting of this heat energy so that the planet may remain intact, shall we say, as an entity as it passes into that experience that you have called the fourth density of light, the transition into a new age.

Is there another query, my sister?

Questioner: So, people don't have the possibility of becoming part of a venting, a safety valve, to relieve pressure on the birthing process? Just the planet itself?

I am Q'uo, and am aware of your query, my sister. These processes are interrelated, and as entities are able to find, what you may call, a higher or more harmonious choice to each of the testings or difficulties that face them, each entity then adds to the harmonious vibrations of those who pray for peace and send light and healing thoughts to entities in distress. Each time an entity is able to increase the level of spontaneous, harmonious response to a difficult situation, there is a lightening of the vibrations of this planetary influence that aids the entity that is the planet itself as it also makes its transition into that density of love which now beckons.

Is there another query, my sister?

Questioner: Just one last one, because I noted something that you said and I didn't quite understand it. I believe that you said that we as a people had personal karma, societal karma, national karma, racial karma, but didn't have planetary karma. Is that just because we haven't blown the Earth to a cinder or actually blown it apart? Is that what it would take to have planetary karma?

I am Q'uo, and am aware of your query, my sister. All entities that will remain with this planet in its transition are a portion of the planetary population or personality, shall we say, that does indeed gather about it a certain quality or nature as a result of those experiences, those lessons and those services which have been learned and accomplished. This quality of personality may also be seen as a kind of karma, for as all karma is that which moves one in a certain direction, there is also the direction that is determined for the population of this planet by its own choices and experiences that are taken in a cumulative manner, shall we say. Thus, in a more general sense, there is indeed a karma or quality of being that adheres to this planetary influence.

Is there a further query, my sister?

Questioner: No, Q'uo. Thank you.

I am Q'uo, and we thank you once again, my sister. Is there another query at this time?

(Pause)

I am Q'uo, and we shall take this opportunity to thank each for inviting our presence to your circle of seeking, and we thank each with a glad and joyous heart, for we are greatly honored at your invitation, and especially at the queries that reflect the deepest desires of your heart to know that which is the nature of your journey, your beings, the Creator and the creation. We shall take our leave of this instrument and this group at this time, leaving each, as always, in the great love and ineffable light of the one infinite Creator. We are known to you as those of Q'uo. Adonai, my friends. Adonai. ☥

Sunday Meditation
May 10, 1992

Group question: The question this afternoon has to do with the general topic of how do we cooperate with our destiny? How do we use our free will in making choices that when they are made will perhaps change us in very significant ways as we are all seeking, as portions of the Creator, to return to the Creator—each choice becomes a part of our path, a step that may be unlike any other step we've taken, but becomes as integral as any step we have taken? How can we make enlightened choices? How can we cooperate with that which is our highest and brightest path in learning and serving others?

(Carla channeling)

I am Q'uo, and I greet you in the love and in the light of the one infinite Creator, the one Intelligence, the one original Thought which is love creative. We greet you in all that there is, seen and unseen forever.

How blessed we feel to be with you, to feel the blending of your meditative vibrations, to experience amidst the complexities of each of your conscious minds the single-minded desire for truth. We thank you, for this is the call which brings us to you and enables us to offer our humble service—that of our opinions. We only ask of each one thing, and that is that our words be taken as opinion and not fact, for there is no authority in outer words, but if our words meet with your feeling of remembrance of truth, then you may trust your own authority. Otherwise, we ask that our words be left behind.

People of passion and courage sit in this circle, each desiring and hoping for the most lucid life of service and the most beautiful and rich life of conscious learning and spiritual evolution. Passion and courage should not be confused, and we shall speak to this.

The experience of moments which have added up to years constantly informs the mentality of a seeming continuity of direction, or a seeming discontinuity. When a possibility of discontinuity becomes attractive and provocative, then the mentality says, "Let us by all means cast ourselves into the new effort with all our hearts." However, passion has one central lack. Although passion seems to come from deep within the heart, the conscious mind untutored by certain practices is not capable of discriminating between the passion of the emotion, the passion of the spirit, the passion of the mind and the passion of persuasive circumstance.

Therefore, as any approaches a personal or services oriented cusp of decision, it is well to know that one has the requisite passion to accomplish what shall be and the courage to see it through. But then one may step back and ask the self to pause so that the spirit may go into the inner room and take all adornments off—all things of the world, all the trappings of circumstance, all of the aura of success renown, of reputation and of desire itself. Lay it to one side and become of a quiet mind and a quiet heart, and say, "Here am I, what would you have me do? What is that highest and best that I may achieve and remain a stable person? What would you have me do?"

A few moments spent in this tabernacle asking this simple query aids one enormously in fitting into the regalia of life's circumstances, girded within with a promise to do that which has been desired in the highest way. One may then don the garments of reputation and success and be unswayed and unimpressed by the patter and the tap dancing that all of us are capable of achieving in one way or another.

When one faces that choice which seems to be the fork in the road, it is especially worth considering to move into this place of asking and dedication of self both individually and as a group, for you see, the attempt to desire well is that which is done by faith alone. The attempt as a group is also done by faith alone, and entities which converse consciously may not be aware of the power and utility of conversation in the silence of the tabernacle of asking and dedication, for no words are spoken, only "What is your will?" and "I am your servant, send me." Yet, as you sit together physically in the silence of this shared imaging, there is set up betwixt the group lines of communication that will not stop humming when the conscious minds leave that tabernacle of asking, for after the choice is made and destiny is being followed, yet still, there are choices every moment that work towards harmonizing energies or do not. And every shared moment in this holy silence together is productive of deepening and ever clearer channels of communication which are blessed with a more informed viewpoint, that of your higher selves, and aids in information, and that higher self that is you as a group. This may well be respected and time and attention paid to it.

We are aware that the personal portion of this query is just as important to each and so would turn to the query of service long enough to speak of the personal choices, the coming to them in the most appropriate spiritual manner.

In each personal spiritual evolution there is a repetition of information, a pattern to the individual lesson. If the seeker always got the message the first time, there would not be the repetition. However, your incarnational circumstance is a deeply illusory one designed specifically to addle the brain and confuse the mind totally, so it is not remarkable that almost no entity in your density understands the main thrust of incarnational work the first time the lesson is presented.

As an example, we would give the lesson which your culture feels certain entities should learn. Still within your peoples' cultural minds there is an opinion that males learn love by learning to provide physical safety and comfort for those whom they love. Females learn the lesson of love which involves sacrifice of the self to the life path of the provider. We use this specific example not only to express our direction of thought, but to express why one cannot generalize concerning personal lessons.

In your density, lessons all have to do with learning to love in society. The society begins with self. You are your main company. Are you a good friend to yourself? Do you treat yourself well? Do you care deeply about yourself? As you are able to fall in love with your, shall we say, human self, that is the persona or shell of personality through which your spirit expresses itself in this experience, just so will you be able to treat other selves.

When one is in pain, be it physical or spiritual, the instinct is to avoid it. However, compassion and love do not grow from avoidance or neglect, and trouble avoided is the unlearned lesson of love which shall even more surely and more clearly be presented to you again. The more times a certain pattern is avoided, the more marked will be the characteristics of that lesson presented the next time around. Consequently, it is well, we feel, to take situations where compassion is lacking into the meditation time of the inner room. Not only speaking and conversing with infinite intelligence concerning this situation which you dearly hope and desire to find a way to manifest love in, but also to bring it into the silence, for words unheard have deep, deep effects upon the conscious ability to manifest as you desire. The key is silence. The door that is opened is that door which you desire. You may not recognize the room on the other side of that door at first, but answers to prayers are various, though always to the point.

Thusly, the personal pain and trouble in relationship—be it with the self, with one other self or with a group self—is that in which the self is …

We must pause. We are known to you as Q'uo.

(Pause)

I am again with this instrument. I am Q'uo, and greet you again in love and in light. We wished to allow this instrument to move to a deeper state. It is well.

Whatever the level of self you are dealing with, it is a self to which you wish to connect with love. Therefore, the pain and the trouble are those things which attract the attention and let the self know that here is an opportunity to learn and hopefully to manifest the results of that learning. Much has been learned by an entity, even a young entity, for much is brought into incarnation—biases towards certain choices and away from others. Yet here sits this intractable, irritating seemingly negative outer other self or aspect of self—a stone in the shoe, an aggravation. One wishes to take the walking staff and stomp away and say, "I go around this, I am not here to climb rocks." But each is here to walk a stony path, to experience the loss of much, the various limitations that occur, the ordeal of the pilgrim on the pilgrimage, and this entity is there not to please, but to be welcomed as an opportunity, no matter how challenging.

As you consider how to make a compassionate response, let the mind dwell on images of compassion; the wise old man in the desert who sits patiently aware that there is no escape from the merciless heat, and therefore composes himself in blissful meditation to await the change of consciousness from the life in the physical body to life in another body; the tears falling upon the body of the wounded as the nurse and medic attempt to save the life, tears of deep love, of frustration and of gratitude when a life is preserved, yet those tears bless those whose lives are not preserved.

Now gaze at yourself. You are an object of compassion. Does the sun not shine upon you whether you are happy or sad, feeling virtuous or distinctly unvirtuous? Does the breeze not lift the tendrils of your hair from your neck? Do the trees not give you oxygen no matter what your condition? You are objects of love and mercy and infinite compassion because you are part of love—part of a Creator. If you move from your humanity, from your shell of personality, you shall quickly run out of compassion, for you have it in small supply within your ratiocinative mind. But if you can open your heart and sweep aside the pretensions and blockages of self, of relationships, of all those things which would seem so important, and move to yourself as the object of love unlimited, free flowing and infinite, then you are merely that through which compassion moves, and you shine infinitely.

Now, this, this is the answer to both queries, for if you shine with that which moves through you, you are doing your utmost to manifest compassion in your personal evolution and learning, and you are also in the mental, emotional and spiritual situation, from which standpoint you are directly adjacent to the inner room of asking. How can you give more than infinite light? How can any choice made in this frame of heart and mind be incorrect?

We do not recommend sitting and waiting as one among you said before the meeting. We grasp the point of the working on one's behalf to ask to move forward towards the desire. Yet we ask each to consider the natural compliment to this energy, which is the utter receptiveness of the request to do the will of the one infinite Creator, whatever that may be.

As you open your eyes and greet the world again and move into your daily round of activities, the first challenge to your manifesting compassion may be an obstreperous child, a difficult co-worker, or a pile of dishes, none of which seem particularly central or worthy of all of the machinery of dedication of self to the loving way. Yet all services are equal. To love the dirty dishes is worthy, just as to offer instruction for healing to many is worthy. There is no quantity to right action or just service, but only the quality of unrestrained compassion.

We would at this time transfer this contact to the one known as Jim, thanking this instrument and this group and leaving this instrument in love and light. We are of the principle of Q'uo.

(Jim channeling)

I am Q'uo, and greet each again in the love and in the light of the one infinite Creator. We would offer ourselves once again at this time to any who may have further queries upon this topic or other topics that are of interest. Is there a query at this time?

Carla: I have an obvious one to start off with. In J's case, before she said the word, there is somebody who simply doesn't like her. I know you can show compassion just by feeling compassion. Is there any way that you can address an already, you know, in place feeling from somebody else—that he just flat doesn't like you, other simply than forgiving him that and loving him anyway? Is that the extent of it?

Let me ask the question more specifically. Could you write the person a love letter and then drop it down a well and expect it to do any good? Is there anything active you can do on the personal?

I am Q'uo, and am again with this instrument. We are aware of your query, my sister. The writing of the love letter, as you have put it, can be effective if that letter is written in the heart's true compassion, for, indeed, all are one, and as you search your heart for the foundation of your feelings, you open a pathway to the entity that is the focus of concern, and offer to that entity upon the metaphysical levels the gift of your love, which will, in what you call time, so move both that entity and your own entity in the daily round of activities in a manner that will allow that love which has been found at the center of one's being to move to the more mundane and daily round of activities. There is the need, however, to be certain that the seeds are sown in true and honest compassion, thus, the need to explore one's own heart first.

Is there another query, my sister?

Carla: No, Q'uo, thank you.

I am Q'uo, and we thank you, my sister. Is there another query?

Questioner: I have a query. I feel that I am on a … I am at a turning point, not only with my spiritual life, but I feel even in my everyday work I have, I am close to a turning point there also. I very much want to be aware and keep in touch, and perhaps I've come here today for some words of wisdom about this.

I am Q'uo, and we feel the concern and the dedication for your journey that you have expressed, and would comment by suggesting that when it is felt within one's being that there is the opportunity to progress upon the path and to become a new being in seeking and in service, that one be especially vigilant for the opportunities to serve and to see the Creator about one in those areas in which one may not commonly look or expect to see the Creator. This is to say, that in all transformations—or as they are often called amongst your peoples, in all initiations—there is the testing, the opportunity to express the quality of love and acceptance that are yours to express. These opportunities oftentimes present themselves in situations which are commonly viewed as difficult, confusing and disharmonious.

In such situations, it is easiest to respond in a manner which is, shall we say, of the world, in that there is the expression of hostility for hostility, anger for anger. When you become aware of any situation which is not as you would have it be, look carefully for the place that your love may be put so that that which is the highest and best of your offering may be that which you give freely. Look at those who seem separate from you, and see not only the Creator there, but see yourself there as well, and feel the compassion for that entity that you would feel for any honest and sincere seeker of truth that has for the moment closed its eyes to the heart of love.

In such a way, may you aid your own transformation, for as you are able to see yourself and to see yourself as the Creator in all that surrounds you, thus you aid the shedding of the old ways which were an useful step upon your journey, and thus do you aid yourself in taking a new step and in donning new garments of light.

Is there a further query, my sister?

Questioner: No, thank you.

I am Q'uo, and we thank you, my sister. Is there another query?

(Pause)

I am Q'uo, and we thank each for inviting our presence once again to your circle of seeking. It is an honor most great to be so invited, and we cannot thank each enough for this opportunity. We again remind each that our words are but our opinions, and though we offer them freely and joyously, we wish each to take only those words which have meaning and to leave behind those which do not. We are those of Q'uo and at this time shall take our leave of this instrument and this group, leaving each, as always, in the love and in the light of the one infinite Creator. Adonai, my friends. Adonai. ✾

L/L Research

L/L Research is a subsidiary of Rock Creek Research & Development Laboratories, Inc.

P.O. Box 5195
Louisville, KY 40255-0195

www.llresearch.org

Rock Creek is a non-profit corporation dedicated to discovering and sharing information which may aid in the spiritual evolution of humankind.

ABOUT THE CONTENTS OF THIS TRANSCRIPT: This telepathic channeling has been taken from transcriptions of the weekly study and meditation meetings of the Rock Creek Research & Development Laboratories and L/L Research. It is offered in the hope that it may be useful to you. As the Confederation entities always make a point of saying, please use your discrimination and judgment in assessing this material. If something rings true to you, fine. If something does not resonate, please leave it behind, for neither we nor those of the Confederation would wish to be a stumbling block for any.

CAVEAT: This transcript is being published by L/L Research in a not yet final form. It has, however, been edited and any obvious errors have been corrected. When it is in a final form, this caveat will be removed.

© 2009 L/L Research

Sunday Meditation
May 17, 1992

Group question: The question this afternoon has to do with coordination between the feminine portion of our minds, the subconscious, and the male portion of our minds, the conscious mind. How this interaction can produce a symbiotic relationship and create a wholeness of experience, a wholeness of being, so that we are inspired to move in the direction that is most appropriate by the subconscious, and inspired to accomplish the work that is before us. How can we gain a clearer, more stable access to that subconscious, feminine portion of our minds; how can we learn to appreciate this process? What exactly occurs in this process when the inspiration is given from the subconscious to the conscious, where does it come from, how is the subconscious aligned with our overall pattern of learning and serving that allows this process to occur? How can we, as we appreciate our own subconscious mind and ability to transform ourselves, how can we become examples or teachers or facilitators to others who may come to us seeking this kind of assistance?

(Carla channeling)

I am Q'uo. Greetings in the love and in the light of the one infinite Creator. How blessed it is to be with you at this circle of seeking. We offer each of you blessing and thanks, for by calling us to respond to your query you offer us employment in the service of the one infinite Creator. This is our dearest desire and our chosen mode of learning, for as we teach, we learn, as we serve, we are given service by your beautiful hopes, ideals and single-hearted desires. You cannot imagine how manyfold are the blessings we receive, the learning we receive as we do what is called teaching. We share opinion, not truth, and would not do any the disservice of asking for the status of authority. Please discriminate among our opinions, choosing those thoughts which seem useful and discarding the remainder. This we would appreciate.

As we look for an entry into the wide question asked this day we find that we first would wish to examine the terms male and female as sexual terms, for these terms create a kind of stumbling block to grasping more thoroughly the actual goal of the seeking for the wisdom within. Each, as you sit in this circle, is biologically male or female. The self-consciousness concerning this is at a minimum, yet there is within each some distortion concerning the relative excellence of the body which carries sexuality, and the mind, emotions and spirit which are given masculine and feminine characteristics, seemingly somewhat separated from the consideration of biological sexuality. To lift the stigma of physicality from sexuality would be a well-conceived effort. The sexuality of the physical vehicle expresses very well, very beautifully, and sacramentally the dynamics which are seen in the mental, emotional and spiritual journey. Yet, because of the vulgar use of bodies by their owners and by those who would possess bodies, the body is seen as beautiful in its sexuality or innocent of sin, if you would use such a word, yet this sexuality has much to study in its possibilities in this incarnational pattern.

To many cultures, the eroticism of hidden genitalia and physical forms in general is considered a positive beauty, a pure truth, and were each biological male and female to value the body sacramentally it would become clear that human physical sexuality is an information resource which like any other speaks of the love and the light of the one infinite Creator. Therefore, as one turns to face the mystery of the deep mind there is a close resource, that being the seeker's own sexuality. As each seeker moves along the highway of the Father's mystery seeking love and truth it is well to encourage the self to love and accept the self, beginning with the physical body, its sexuality, its every curve, dimple and seeming marred place or imperfect place. Loving the self within the skin is far more readily attempted when one has loved and accepted the skin, the shell of physicality which carries about the consciousness which you truly are and which manifests within this illusion your field of consciousness, desires, questions and often cryptic answers.

To this end, let us pause and let each feel the heavy, familiar physical vehicle. This is that which has given itself that you may think and feel and express your free will and your choices in this life experience. Feel the breathing, the limbs resting, the muscles as they are supported. You may perhaps feel as if you are driving a car all of a sudden. This is a feeling we would like for you to experience. You are not your body, but your body is a second-density form. Every cell of this body vibrates with the love and the light of the infinite One. Take this moment to thank this beautiful animal form for the sacrifice of its instinctually lived life. That life you have tipped upon the ear, and that life is not possible. This body of yours is living your life and dying your death.

Very well, if we have been able to encourage feelings of acceptance and respect and love for the gallant body, then it is time to move on to the seeking of that within which seems archetypically female. Within each culture the male and female dance a somewhat different courting dance, play somewhat differing roles. It is not well to generalize, and we hope to be accurate, but insofar as one can be general, the male feels that it has chosen a female. The female waits for the choosing. When one applies this to the seeking of the intuitive wisdom of the subconscious one may focus upon the male portion which chooses to reach for the chosen one, the pearl among all other and less entities, the very most nearly perfect of all possible choices. It is with this lover's delight in the right choice that the conscious mind reaches for the lovely, gentle and very powerful subconscious.

The subconscious is coy, hidden and not always immediately responsive. The first feminine characteristic, therefore, of the conscious mind's learning is patience. There is the reaching, but not the immediate grasping, not the rapid, obvious success, but the long, patient, tender courtship of these qualities within which are lighter, freer and more wise than conscious plodding thought. How difficult it is to be patient, how weary one is of the waiting. At this point the second feminine quality is evoked by need, that is, the faith that patience is deserved and appropriate. Faith is a fruit of the wisdom within the spiritual self of the deep mind, yet it cannot be reached except by faith.

Thusly, as the male portion of the self—and we are generalizing—as the conscious mind reaches for the unconscious, intuitive heart's wisdom it uses faith, that which it believes it does not yet have, yet the very reaching for this perfect bride of wisdom evokes that principle and faith is found and persistence is able to be sustained. In the journey of the seeker there are times or periods when the spirit within seems to burst into bloom and flowers appear in the conscious mind, the blossoms that are daughters of the patience, the faith, and the waiting. The farmer cannot say how the seed germinates and grows, nor can the seeker say how inspiration has come, yet the farmer knows to collect seeds of the appropriate type when it is planting season, and so the intelligence of the conscious mind chooses its seeds in the fastidiousness of its courtly, loving and patient approach to the fertile subconscious.

Let us use a sexual image to further focus upon the fertile aspect of the spirit of truth. The desire of the conscious mind for truth, for information about how to love the Creator, how to know the Creator, how to serve the Creator, may be further and further purified as seeking proceeds. The questions do not change but the process of seeking the answers can be more and more refined so that the lover of truth has ever more abilities to penetrate in a gentle yet fruitful way the recesses of the unconscious. The reaching becomes very single-pointed, very courtly and very passionate, and the fruitful wisdom within is made into a living being of new concept. Something is born, something that as a unit may rise through dreams, through daydreams, or for those whose thresholds of consciousness are permeable, simply through the limen of the conscious mind. The desire truly impregnates intuition.

There may perhaps be a figure which may explicate this feeling. The guide or teacher has been seen in your spiritual studies often as angelic, wise, without a body or with a light body, but certainly that which comes down from the higher planes to touch the hearts of seekers. See that consciousness within which is the spirit of truth, the unconscious as that which is touched by fire, that which becomes the fire so that as the seeker seeks within itself it is aware that that which it seeks within is a miniature, holographic representation of that highest truth which is the infinite Creator, the intelligent infinity which moving through ethers and ethers, dimensions and dimensions, stays true to its spirit as octaves stay true to their tone so that the subconscious or unconscious is in a fruitfully thought of way the Creator, the Highest Self, and this Creator may create, and you as co-creator may co-create and invent and manifest so that as you seek within, the unconscious organizes itself according to the gentle, loving courtliness it has received from the conscious mind, and becomes attuned towards wishing to give the outer or conscious portion of itself more information so that the way in which you approach wisdom creates the precise kind of information you shall receive. You are creating your own information because you are the spirit you seek.

Now, the other portion of this figure is that when information has been reached for lovingly and received with respect and molded to the self's person, or spirit, or character it may then have a strength which is not simply your own but which contains higher octaves of spiritual wisdom, so that as you are able to manifest the blossoms and fruits of the subconscious these retain a quality of infinity and are able to refresh and renew not simply the self but other selves as well, and this without tiring in any way the conscious self.

The more the conscious mind becomes impatient for knowledge, the more knowledge will recede from the spiritual seeker. The instructions are to desire greatly the wisdom of the heart, yet one is not rewarded for translating great desire into eager and impatient great desire. In this kind of desiring we ask each to consider the value of feeling the beauty and purity of this desire, appreciating it in and of itself, seeing its virtue and knowing that no matter how long it may seem that the search goes on before results occur, this desire, this stance, this way of being is in itself a witness to a life lived in the heart, for is it not a value of the heart to wait patiently upon wisdom, knowing that it cannot come at an appointed time but must always surprise the seeker? Dwell peacefully with the desire without taking away the intensity, so peacefully and intently await the impregnation of the heart by your desire. Seek and ye shall find. These words of your holy book are true. The time factor is not mentioned.

A portion of your query looked into how to aid others concerning the seeking and learning of and from the unconscious portion or deeper portion of the mind. In this regard it is well to reflect upon the entities which have aided the self. Perhaps within there was the need for reassurance, but insofar as the teacher took responsibility for your learning, just so did the teacher vitiate the progress made by creating a false dependency, so when one gives counsel and is able to act as an effective catalyst for deep learning, the overwhelming response of the client or patient is gratitude and the giving of credit away from the self to the catalyst.

The way in which this dynamic is handled by the teacher is potentially quite helpful and potentially quite disempowering. To empower the student, the client, the patient, one may do one of two things. Firstly, one may smile and say nothing. The lack of feedback will be catalyst for the student to work through the realization that a blank wall cannot be given credit. The other, and perhaps more seemingly humane method of dealing with this situation, is to explain the action of the self with the self when it strikes a catalyst. The catalyst remains unchanged, the work and the reward are both those of the reagent, in this case the mind and portions thereof of the student.

In either case, only so much can be affected by any means of communication. Entities which wish to be dependent will simply choose to be dependent. In those situations it is well to know the self well and to protect the self as if from the biting insect. The repellent is thought, a simple thought that catalysts are only that, that responsibility cannot be taken, that much as one would like sometimes to have effects upon others, one's work is always with the self. Dwelling in this realization, giving thanks for it, and praising the infinite One for the harmony and resonance of this aspect of the Creator's universe seats one in this fluid thought, marinates one in the precious well of self-knowledge. The limits are here and here, this is peacefully affirmed and known, and like balm upon the skin which insects will not choose to taste, so do the hungry dependencies of students find themselves unable to fasten upon you.

In the world of metaphysics, thoughts are your tools. We began with the sexuality of the third-density physical body because the process of spiritual evolution is sexual without the stigma attached to that word among your peoples. The wisdom of the heart is not touched but absorbed, and it does not move in a linear fashion to inform, it is born and its DNA is coded by the purity, patience and lovingness of your desire.

We realize we have barely scratched the surface of this interesting query, yet the instrument requests that we move on. We would leave some portion of this working for queries, however, this instrument is somewhat fatigued, and we would prefer to transfer the contact to the one known as Jim. We thank this instrument and leave it in love and light. We are known to you as the principle Q'uo.

(Jim channeling)

I am Q'uo, and greet each again in love and in light through this instrument. At this time we would ask if there might be any other queries to which we may speak. Is there a query at this time?

J: I have a query. I am curious as to the nature of restlessness, restlessness and always constantly needing to *(inaudible)*, boredom in things and this *(inaudible)* different work that I do, I do it for a while and become bored and must move on to something else, and I do that for a while and there never seems to be anything that I am settled in for very long *(inaudible)* is there something that I can do to become more rested and settled?

I am Q'uo, and I am aware of your query, my sister. As we look upon the characteristics of any seeker's life pattern we see that there are those which are understood in some degree and not understood in yet other ways. Each entity, as it journeys upon the path of seeking the truth, will find that there is a pattern that develops that will inevitably create the web of information and service opportunities that was desired before the incarnation began. Thus, we are cautious in attempting to give information that would infringe upon this process, in that there would be the loss of opportunity if certain characteristics were altered. However, as we look upon the query which you have offered to us, we may comment by suggesting that within the personality structure that you have adopted for this incarnation there is the need to gather a great deal of information in a variety of fields so that there is a resource available to you upon a very deep level of your own being that will allow you to create a mythology, shall we say, that is various, that is full, and that is of a balanced nature so that you are able to express feeling tones and emotions and desires in a way that is satisfying.

We can suggest that if you feel that this quality that you have described as restiveness is playing a detrimental part in your overall process of growth that you examine your desires to move from one endeavor to another very carefully within the meditative state, and that you picture that which is your current experience as fully as is possible and see this experience from a point of view that looks at relationships of self to others, self to concepts, self to the environment about you, and begin to see this experience as one portion or piece of a larger puzzle. Look at those areas that have been enriched by it, look at the possibilities that depend from it, and then look at that feeling that has grown within yourself that you describe as boredom and follow that feeling as it were a trail, exploring each turn and tangent that is touched as you explore it so that you come to a more complete understanding of its origin, its process, and its consequences.

Thus, as you accomplish this meditative examination you may inform yourself as to the step that you are taking and become aware of its significance upon a level which is more fully informed than would be possible if you merely moved upon the impulse with a more cursory kind of examination.

Is there a further query, my sister?

J: No, thank you very much.

I am Q'uo, and we thank you, my sister. Is there another query?

Carla: Is there a principle here to look at? Is it probable that each time we think we have a fault or that something is inconvenient to us, if we follow it through we see that it's one side of the coin, the other side of which is our greatest opportunity?

I am Q'uo and we are aware of your query, my sister. In general, this is correct. It is easy within your illusion to see feelings and experiences as separate from the overall journey that is being made so that there is the possibility that one portion of value may be discarded as irrelevant when, in fact, it has a close connection to the primary program for the incarnation if more carefully examined. Thus, each portion of the experience presents the opportunity for discovery of the self and of the great Self from which we all come and to which we all return.

Is there a further query, my sister?

Carla: No, thank you very much.

I am Q'uo, and we thank you once again, my sister. Is there another query?

R: How does one find lessons for the self in frustrations encountered during the seeking?

I am Q'uo, and I am aware of your query, my brother. The lessons that are before one, oftentimes as they are becoming apparent, are in large part hidden so that what is necessary is the continued application of attention and effort by the seeker upon that which is the source of frustration, for there is within each frustration a trigger point or place of beginning which is the key to unraveling more of the nature of the experience that is before you. If you can look—and again we suggest the meditative state for this looking—at the experience which provides the frustration and look at that experience objectively so that it is but experience and see the frustration that comes to you as that which you have created and which is not inherently contained within the experience, then it is more likely that you will see the point at which frustration becomes the experience for you.

This examination will provide you the means, once again, of following a trail. The trail begins at the point at which frustration is noted. Look at the series of events, the relationships, the entities involved at each of the portions of the experience before you. Look at them not only in their practical and mundane senses of everyday activities but look at them also as symbols of higher principles that are at work within your incarnational pattern. The more carefully you have observed patterns of all kinds within your incarnation the more easily will you be able to connect the relationships of these patterns to the nature of the lessons that are yours to learn and the services that are yours to offer within your incarnation.

The point of frustration is as a sticking point, shall we say, at which time there is more that is not understood than there is that which is understood. If you can explore what qualities within yourself have brought about the response of frustration in relationship to the experience before you, you will have informed yourself of the basic relationship that can yield more understanding of not only the experience but of yourself as well. If you can, shall we say, cross-reference the various causes of this frustration you may begin to see themes repeating in your pattern of experience, and as these themes repeat you may discover that there is a certain quality within your character or personality that you are developing and that the feeling of frustration is a kind of friction that wears away those lesser qualities, those which are no longer useful to you and which provides you a more polished surface so that you may see yourself more clearly. Thus, frustration can be an indicator that there is an opportunity to expand one's concept of self, of service, and of learning within any particular experience.

Is there a further query, my brother?

R: No, thank you very much.

I am Q'uo, and we thank you, my brother. Is there another query at this time?

(Pause)

I am Q'uo, and as we have exhausted the queries, we would take this opportunity to thank each of those offering queries and each present for inviting us to join your circle of seeking on this afternoon. We are most honored to do so, and feel a great joy of walking with you upon your journeys. We feel a great affinity for seekers such as are gathered here this afternoon, for the desire that is evident to know the nature of your paths and the desire to be of service as you travel them are most inspiring for us to observe, for we know that the paths that each of you travels during an incarnation in this illusion is a path that is filled with mystery, is a path that is filled with difficulty, and is a path that has much confusion, for most of the qualities of the one Creator that we all seek have been covered quite carefully by the nature of your illusion so that those lessons and services that you are able to discern are far, far more valuable than would be lessons and services within an illusion that were less heavy, less dense, and less filled with mystery. Your challenges are great, yet we see that your desire is greater, and we commend each of you for your stout-heartedness, your good will and your cheer upon this difficult journey.

At this time we shall take our leave of this instrument and this group. We are known to you as those of Q'uo, and we leave each of you, as always, in the love and in the light of the one infinite Creator. Adonai, my friends. Adonai.

Sunday Meditation
May 24, 1992

Group question: Our questions today have to do with how we tend to look at a new challenge before us with some fear, foreboding, dread, wondering if it's going to work out. No matter what the situation is, there is in many people the tendency to feel that the worse case scenario is staring them in the face and that there's a good chance that it will come about.

Is there a value to what we might call this fearful or fear-filled approach? To some apprehension? To anxiety? Is there some way that this might be used in a positive fashion by people who are preparing to set out on a new adventure, to undertake a new challenge or opportunity? Or is it better if the person completely relies upon what we might call blind faith and just has the optimistic point of view that everything's going to be all right no matter what it might look like to begin with, and that if we just believe that things are going to be all right that this is the proper attitude with which to meet any challenge? Or is there a dynamic tension between blind faith and anxiety that brings out the best in us? Is there a balance that can be achieved to increase our efficiency in problem-solving and in meeting new challenges?

(Carla channeling)

I am Q'uo. Greetings in the love and in the light of the one infinite Creator. We are grateful this day to be called to your circle and to be able to speak upon the subject of the usefulness of fear and pessimism as regards entities looking at situations and needing to make decisions. As always, we ask each to be aware of the paucity of our wisdom and the fallibility of our statements. We offer the best opinion of which we are capable, but this opinion is flawed by our own distortions, which do in some measure continue. We thank each for allowing us this luxury, else we could not in good conscience speak.

Our statement to you that we are fallible is an example of our use of pessimism. We find there to be occasion to use what seems to be pessimistic thought at times when we are dealing with ourselves or other selves in a way which may cause a difference to be made in the decision-making processes of spiritual evolution. It is not likely that any would consider our words infallible, but, as this instrument would put it, the worst case scenario is that an entity would take our words out of context and literally, and, using them rather than the entity's own discrimination, make a choice which would have an impact upon that entity's spiritual evolution. We hope to have the impact upon your people's spiritual evolution which your people choose to take from us, thinking for themselves. We do not at all wish to ask any to take our words on blind faith. Thus, you may see that we cannot give an easy answer to your question.

Let us consider the aspect, nearness of decision. Many are the times when one creates mentally a possible future situation. It may not be probable, and, if probable, it may not occur. And if it is most probably to occur, it will be long enough in coming that consideration of a decisive kind is premature. In this case, the use of consideration which could be called pessimistic of many possible scenarios is not recommended, as it is not utile. When there is simply a concern or worry on the horizon, it may be seen as weather—the storm cloud which is over someone else's land, some other farmer's crops, some other person's hapless head. It will not impinge upon you.

This concern or cloud is real. Far more real in the thought world—or, as some perceive it, the world of spirit—than it is within your continuum. However, only damage can be done by the application of rational intelligence to a situation which has not yet become susceptible to rational thought. In this circumstance, the appropriate frame of mind or attitude would be prayerful and affirmative. That is to say, that any storm cloud of difficulty not directly impinging upon one can, with good results, be placed in the heart, be taken into meditation, and be contemplated with affirmative visualizations concerning its eventual process of outcome. In the example we used, it would be appropriate to know that the cloud brought rain to the farmer and watered his crop well, but that lightning did not strike the farmer while crops were being so fed.

When a worry, anxiety or concern enters the mind, therefore, the first question to put to the self is, "Is this a concern which has come to the proximity wherein I must needs consider and choose a plan of action?" If the answer is "No, this situation is not proximal, but is further from the entrance into imminent illusion than that," then the persistent and gentle effort may well be made to downgrade concern until it becomes that which is the concern of one who prays in faith, holding all things up to the light and asking for light so that the possible situation dwells in thought in light, and the self possibly overly-concerned about this question dwells also in light in the beneficial rays of faith's connection with the spiritual riches of an inexhaustible Source of love.

There is another category of considerations which we shall mention, for those considerations are important; yet, they have but a slender portion of the percentage of room in an entity's usual considerations. These are general questions which one may have concerning keeping one's word, being a certain way, dwelling with a certain point of view, and then noticing that one has emotionally or mentally slipped away from this standpoint or point of view. We may use the example from your holy works of the ones who awaited the bridegroom, each supposedly a bride to be. Each had, in this story, a lamp which used oil. Yet, some who hoped to marry did not carry the fuel to light the lamp. Others were prudent and had both light and fuel.

In this case, it is always well to look most pessimistically and firmly upon one's perceived lack of forethought in fuel-carrying. One's principles are the result of choices already made. They are your lamp. They are what you hold up before you as you await marriage with the present moment. However, without the fuel to light this lamp, the bridegroom of the present moment cannot find you in the darkness. Your forethought, your energetic concern in backing up previous ethical and metaphysical choices with the fuel to keep them fresh and lighted, are your way of being prepared for the usually unexpected arrival of a present moment, the bridegroom of which has need of your light, your face, your ethical positivity, your polarity in consciousness.

One who seeks the truth cannot rest upon the previously found truths or previously made ethical choices of one's pilgrimage, but must continuously be prepared to meet that present circumstance which uses all past choices and demands then a living witness of your own polarity. Your choices without the energy of your will are like lamps without fuel and are not useful. Thusly, in your theoretical, abstract, metaphysical being, be very conscious that the entity who seeks shall be tested and the seeking shall go forward when the test has been passed, the passing of the test being the responsible and reliable remembrance and embracing of past choices which have increased positive polarity.

The third consideration in wondering about the wisdom of pessimism is the largest of the three considerations, for it is the one which needs balancing and which has an impact upon the decision-making process. As in many things, there is the balancing act. Let us divide this third kind of pessimism into two parts: firstly, the situation where a possible difficulty is intuited clearly as being present; the second, a situation which is proximate and has come to what may be called a "turning point."

Firstly, there are those things about which one may have lucid intuition. A well known example within your culture is also found in your holy work, the Bible. It is the situation in which Joseph of the Many-Colored Robe is asked to interpret the dreams of a ruler. The young Joseph does interpret the dreams of the ruler in such a way that the dreams seem to have an internal order and consistency and to point to right action. Therefore, the ruler and Joseph move upon this dream's suggestions concerning an unknown future. Seven bumper crops are first to be harvested and plenty is to rain. Then there are predicted in the dreams a like period of drought and consequent hunger and even starvation. The response to this clear dreaming is the preservation of enough food to buffer successfully a drought, should it indeed occur. This is a right use of what you might call fear or pessimism.

If there is a lucid and clear dream or process resembling clear dreaming wherein a precaution seems wise in the taking, and if this precaution is able to be done without destructive impact upon the integrated life of the self or family or society as a whole, then such a precaution is well made, as long as the effort is made not to dwell upon such a possibility being inevitable. The example in this instrument's mind closest to its surface is the placing of the matches and the lighting instruments such as candles and lamps in case your electrical power fails. It is not foolish to prepare for this possibility, and shows prudence rather than random fear.

In the case of being faced with the necessity for making a decision, we hope you may see that much of the concern evinced in this query is irrelevant. When a decision must be made, there is no fault either in blind faith or in worst case scenario spinning. The movement of a personality through third density provides each entity with various lessons concerning loving. What love is, how it may manifest through one, how it may come to one, how it can be discerned, are all questions which the pilgrim of the king's highway must needs ask. In some cases, an entity's lessons are those in which an entity must learn to be less wise and more faithful.

Let us give the example told by Jesus in your holy work where a master gives several servants money. One servant buries the money. The others create, through enterprise, interest compounded to the money. When the master receives again the money, those who acted in faith that their judgment in investing for their master was adequate were rewarded with thanks and more duties, more services to perform for the master. The one who buries the coin, the pessimist, has what it has had, that and no more. And then the master takes even that coin away. This seems, in your logical terms, to be a harsh penalty. However, within the parable, the point is being made that one who acts without faith will not progress in polarity. The use of faith as a portion of each decision is a central requirement. The faith may show itself simply as a compassionate way of expressing wisdom, but it is centrally important that this impulse be respected and nurtured in each and every situation.

Upon the other hand, many are the lessons of love wherein an entity moves foolishly and quickly, in blind and unreasoned faith, thereby abandoning tools and resources which have been given within the illusion in which each lives by the infinite Creator. These faculties of reason were not given in order to create excess. These abilities of reasoning and questioning are valuable tools. Thusly, when one must needs make one's personal choice, one first ascertains that the time has come to make the choice. If the time is not yet, the mind should remain out of gear and the concern given to the heart, to the inner room of prayer, and to the affirmative workings of an over-reaching faith in the rightness and goodness of all that there is behind and beyond the visible illusion.

The second consideration is that of one's principles, one's spiritual or metaphysical facets of one's gem of spiritual or magical personality. Are these principles upheld with the enthusiasm of one with the fire to light the lamp of builded, metaphysical structure? If such principles are in place and are not being subverted or denied, then this consideration may be closed. If one sees oneself slipping away from a truth which one has responsibly perceived, then efforts must needs be made to restore the firm potential of builded polarity for further evolutionary choices.

If a concern still rests within the mind, then there is a decision to be made. We can only suggest to each that when that self which is uniquely you sets out to choose, both the faculty of faith and the faculty of wisdom may usefully be invoked. If a balance can be achieved quickly, very well. If there is a continuing disquiet, then there are two ways in which one may learn more about one's true desires. Firstly, one may refuse any thought concerning this choice for a limited period. This neglect allows the deep unconscious roots of mind to express deeper wisdom. The other technique is to choose on one diurnal period to spend every free second espousing a positive choice. In the next diurnal period, one must then take every free moment espousing the wisdom of a negative choice. This over-stimulation of the mind's duality—yes, no, yes, no—achieves the same inner quiet within, and, again, a way is made for the wisdom deep within one to rise to the surface either through dreaming, a sudden feeling, or, as is more nearly the general case, a growing awareness which soon amounts to certainty that one particular choice is the appropriate one for the self at this crux.

We do not disparage the intellectual mind. We do not disparage the uses of fear. We do not disparage the uses of faith. We point out to one who wishes to be an ever more radiant person in the citizenry of the universe that both faith and doubt are necessary in the discovery of the true self and the truth of that self by the becoming, birthing being that is the universal citizen known locally as the self.

Each of you builds for eternity. Make haste, therefore, slowly, knowing that the safety of corrected error is absolute. Any self may feel, after the fact, that a choice has been wrong. Another choice shall come. The same procedure is available and the self-perceived previous error is that for which one may give thanks. It is the homework problem solved wrongly, explained to some extent by the teacher within or without, granting the self better tools and resources for making the choice again.

You gaze upon our perception of the entire point of the third-density experience which you now enjoy. Each present moment brings its burgeoning harvest of possibility. Some moments are over-burdened with the need to choose. Let your faith keep you as unflustered as possible. Let your skills at using reason keep you aware of mundane concerns. But, above all, realize that both are but tools. The decision, the choice, is best made when it is made not only by you, but by such a deep portion of the self that one is one who knows, one who has a quiet mind because there is an inner sureness, "Yes, I have opened the heart to faith, the mind to rational consideration. Decision is not mathematical. Beyond a certain point, I cannot defend my choice. However, I know and feel sure that it is the one I need to make."

If this luxury may be yours in times of hard choices, then truly have you done all that one in your life experience can do, for you have used your resources and then opened the self to the greater compassion and wisdom which lies within in that portion of the self which is a portion of the one infinite Creator's love reflected in love, as this instrument would say. You are all entities of love reflecting the Creator to each other. Be aware as often as possible of the nature of the self and other selves. This is one of the greatest resources for spiritual evolution which exists.

We would close this working through the one known as Jim. We thank this instrument and would transfer at this time, leaving this instrument in love and in light. We are known to you as those of Q'uo.

(Jim channeling)

I am Q'uo, and greet each again in love and in light through this instrument. We realize that we have spoken overly long and wish to ask if there might be any queries with which we may complete our presentation this afternoon?

(No questions. All thank Q'uo.)

I am Q'uo, and again we shall take this opportunity to thank you, each one of you, for your patience, your dedication, and your desire to know more of that which you call truth. That which we have shared we share with great joy, and also share with the admonition that you take only those words which have meaning to you, leaving behind those that do not. At this time, we shall take our leave of this group and this instrument, leaving each, as always, in the love and in the light of the one infinite Creator. We are known to you as those of Q'uo. Adonai, my friends. Adonai. ✦

L/L Research

Sunday Meditation
May 31, 1992

Group question: The question is about our apparent separate realities and the delusory nature of reality itself, where we think we exist in the world and a universe which is quite solid, which operates according to laws we believe we understand; and yet when those who understand them the best, our scientists, look carefully they see fields of energy but no actual mass. We look in our individual lives and we attempt to discover the principles by which we live, and those which we would carry out in our daily lives, and we see metaphysical and spiritual qualities that we appreciate. We join with others and attempt to aid each other in groups, and yet we find that many times the groups have differences among themselves, within the group and from group to group. There is separation and division, and the unifying factors that we believed in don't seem to hold us together.

So, we would like some information today about the qualities within us and within the creation around us that are dependable, that are real, that are sustained, that we can look to in times of difficulty to support each other and support ourselves on the journey of seeking the truth.

(Carla channeling)

I am Q'uo. Greetings in the love and in the light of the one infinite Creator. It is a privilege and a blessing to be with each of you, and we greet old friends and new in the name of the infinite One.

We speak to you this day upon a subject difficult to deal with by means of words, for any discussion of what unity is must needs be undertaken in the fragmentary sense created by your various ways of speaking. The letters of an alphabet are several, but the words of a language very many; yet each word tends to separate thought rather than unify thought. The language itself, then, tends towards divisive understandings. However we shall offer our opinions with the request that all that we offer be taken as opinion and not as authoritative fact. We do not have that sort of authority and are prone to error. However, insofar as our thoughts may be of use to you we offer them with gratitude and a feeling of honor that we are called to offer our service to you.

The pebble drops into the pond; the ripples flow out from it. So is each monad of personality, which you experience as a self, a pebble with its own ripples impinging upon the ripples of other pebbles dropping into the pond. This is the experience each has of interactions upon the social scene. The mate, the friend, the group does not know how to move in synchronized perfection, but rather each self and its energies ripple into the energies put out by others.

The way these energies meet has a great deal to do with how the two entities view each other, and what information of themselves or of their opinions the two are liable to share. One is one person to self A, and seemingly quite another description to self B, and so forth; each entity receiving a somewhat different facet of the projected energies of the self and connecting with those energies in a way comfortable to the energies projecting from that other self. So no two of your friends know the same person in you.

Nor do you know yourself as the same person, even though you seem to be a pebble, a solidity which impinges upon the societal world. Yet, also within your self there are many pebbles being dropped at various levels of consciousness into that admixture of personae which make up the mask of personality which defines, refines and confines one within the illusion you now enjoy. Therefore, you define and redefine the self again and again and again, yet never do you even know the self in its entirety.

The crux of this point is duple: firstly, it can be seen that the same perceiver sees all of these differing selves within the self. Here lies the first unity. We shall return to this thought. The second corollary of this process of statement is that as each entity sees many differing views of other entities, and even in a simple small societal complex there are misunderstandings, confusions and disagreements as to events very commonly, it is not difficult to see the same tendency repeated in larger and larger groups of entities.

Why does a group form? Supposedly, a group forms because there is a vision, an ideal, or a set of principles which the group all wishes to express honor for and respect for. However, entities which place great emphasis upon things that can be known will have the chronic tendency to define the precise nature of those ideals, principles and so forth that they wish to honor.

That which begins in the generous outburst of honor, respect and devotion, soon becomes that which has been defined, and ceases its growth. It then has a hard carapace, a builded structure which will not accept expansion or the movement into different shapes.

Consequently, faith of all kinds periodically eschews and sheds the exoskeleton of dogma and doctrine, and begins retelling the great story or myth which is used to focus upon the great set of spiritual or metaphysical principles which each wished to honor.

And so the faith, free in the individual urge, and free in the first communal urge and the moving together under the banner of a great principle such as love, soon becomes prey to the desire to nail down and put structure to a system of believing which can be built as a model airplane, and admired, painted, viewed and discussed.

In the moving from the first rapturous experience of love for this principle to the desire to codify it, the entity or group has moved from the open heart to what must always in the end be the closed mind. The trip is typical of your peoples, who are not encouraged by your culture to dwell, abide and trust in the wisdom and compassion of the heart, but have learned through many dealings with other entities to put up the structures which are ways of communicating belief systems easily, and are therefore capable of being discussed more easily. The intellectual discussions concerning belief systems is circuitous and tautological; however this only makes the pursuit more appealing to many who simply do not wish to change, but rather to consider endlessly the various delightful aspects of a certain and known truth.

Consider, as each sits in this circle, what each thinks of the nature of the self; of the nature of the environment about the self; of the path upon which the self is journeying; of the purpose of this path. Although there would be many points of agreement, there would also be radical points of departure as each entity has its own way of perceptions, its own way of weighting and valuing perceptions, and its own way of creating, recreating, or reacting to these perceptions.

It would seem thusly that for factions to occur divisively is inevitable in any group situation. The inevitability of this pulling apart is, in service-to-others organizations which remember their polarity, a dynamic which is matched by the adherence to, and overriding respect for, the free will decisions of each, and an underlying respect for the power of the metaphysical principle which has brought these souls together. Thusly, in a spiritual family there will always be the disharmony which can be tempered by daily, constant remembrances of the power of that great original Thought which brought the group together.

Though this thought is called by many names, and has many faces, may we simply call it love. The

Logos, the creative principle, is in our opinion, love. Not the dead love of fixed romance, nor the friendship, or any definition which lies within the parameters of your experience, but love as a fiery creative principle which has dynamically created and set free the universe, which moves endlessly from its source back to that same source, dwelling always in what has been called a cloud of unknowing.

We gaze at what may be helpfully said about the eternal divisiveness of spiritual and all other groups, and can only refer each again to the inner divisiveness of the self. When the self has so far learned its own nature, and accepted that nature unconditionally that it can love the self, that self is then ready to become part of an unity of selves which shall remain unified; not in the deadened sense of agreement to a dry, creaking structure of words and creeds, but because of adherence to love. That love is diverse; each self which loves itself unconditionally is unique, yet each is love.

When entities can rest comfortably within their own skins, shall we say, then shall the peoples come together; not to become clones, all reciting the same credo, but gloriously various, with all the colored strands of ribbon imaginable, to fly together as the rainbow, strengthened by love and blessed by a lack of judgment.

Entities who fear the divisiveness within the self will also fear the divisiveness within societies, and will choose to adhere to one group within a society to which it can belong and with which it can be sure of acceptance. Then when another way of believing is offered this self, it rejects that other way for fear that it might lose its safety, its haven, its structure of faith. The faith that becomes one is the faith without structure, without an initial cause or reason which can logically be explained.

Entities may come together in faith in the mid-air of absolute faith. Not the faith that says, "I believe this and this and this," but the faith that trusts and believes that all is as it should be, all is truly well. This quality of faith survives war, disease, loss, limitation, death and the myriad other ills facing one in physical body form.

A faith which describes limits unto itself will not comfort the sick, the lost, the hurting, the pained; for there is, in any prescribed set of virtuous ways of behavior, the implication that other ways of behavior will be punished.

You see there is a marvelous richness of reasons for the divisiveness nature of your density's societal structures. That which is true for the self will reflect upon the society. As the self is divided over against itself, even so shall this be reflected in the dynamics of the social structure created by such entities.

Those who wish to be peacemakers may work upon the self, gazing patiently and without judgment at the activities of the emotions, the mind, the stirrings of conscience, and the desires of the physical complex. Over a portion of your time, such an entity shall learn that it is by its own set of standards quite iniquitous. This is a helpful realization, as it opens the way for true humility. Not that humility which abases itself, but the humility of one which knows itself, and without judging the self for being imperfect, acknowledges that being within incarnation, and being veiled from knowledge of the true nature of things, the self will necessarily be somewhat confused, and full of unknowing and doubts.

The first act of the peacemaker is to have faith in this dubious seeming self. When faith has been found in the self, then the entity has no more point to prove; no more battles to win; no preferences which reach the point of necessity to receive or promulgate. Such an entity then is a likely peacemaker, for with a humble heart such a self listens to divisive speech and by its nature finds the point of balance wherein each party departed from the unifying principle. The means of making peace then lie in an accurate observation of the spiritual principle from which two seemingly warring entities have departed. The path back to unity from discord lies in the calling to remembrance of this unifying principle.

We feel this is sufficient for the first general statement, and at this time would leave this instrument and move to the one known as Jim, that queries may be asked, if indeed any would wish to do so. We are known to you as those of Q'uo, and we thank this instrument and leave this instrument in love and light. We transfer now.

(Jim channeling)

I am Q'uo, and greet each again in love and in light through this instrument. May we ask if there are any queries to which we may speak at this time?

Questioner: Yes. From what I understood of what you said before, it sounds like all systems, philosophies, religions and principles that we in our density follow arise out of the present moment and are presentations of that present moment. In order for us to be able to continually relate to these, in a certain sense we need to come back to the present moment and revive them from that present moment. As soon as we try to codify them, put them into words, and then study the words, we are no longer in the present moment and they loose some of their validity. Is that a correct understanding?

I am Q'uo, and am aware of your query, my brother. We would agree that you have well stated that which we have spoken in regards to this afternoon, for it is the great strength of your intellectual mind that it may analyze and observe many phenomena and relate them in an infinite fashion. Yet, in all this complexity, there is the tendency to move one's experience from the moment in which all occurs to a distant and objective reality that is created by this work of conceptualization and relation. Thus, we have suggested that it is well to leave that kind of mentation for a time in each diurnal experience for the practice of that which you call meditation, in order that the mind might be quieted, be brought back to its source and experienced in its new and untouched fashion, thus opening to the meditator the doors of perception of the present moment.

Is there a further query, my brother?

Questioner: Yes, but this is a question on something I have observed in the two sessions that I have attended. I noticed that in my first session it was very difficult for me to stay present with this experience, that my attention and consciousness would tend to wander, and that in some respects I felt that I fell asleep. I have felt that today I have had to make a conscious effort to keep bringing myself back to this experience, because in a certain sense I felt a loss of focus when I was present in this experience. In looking at the people with me today I felt that a similar process—although from the outside it is hard to know—seemed to be happening with them. I wondered if you could tell me what is going on that creates this kind of an environment that makes it hard to keep one's attention focused?

I am Q'uo, and am aware of your query, my brother. We must assume a good deal of the responsibility for this phenomenon, for our manner of speaking is that of giving information at a set and uniform rate, shall we say, which has the effect of causing some of that which you call sleep or the attaining of a hypnotic state, for the conscious mind that you possess is oftentimes easily led into a more relaxed state by such regularized input of stimuli, thus there is that portion of the experience for which we are of necessity responsible.

There is also the quality of what you may call a kind of spiritual fatigue that many bring with them to sessions such as these, for those seekers of truth which are attracted to these gatherings have long sought that truth, both within themselves and in the world about them in their daily round of activities, and are much worn, shall we say, by the persistence that …

(Side one of tape ends.)

(Jim channeling)

I am Q'uo, and am once again with this instrument. We would also suggest that there is the physical fatigue that also works upon the mental processes, and tends to lead one so fatigued to the state of sleep or drowsiness. And we have observed that the kind of personality that pursues the metaphysical quest with persistence, also in many cases pursues the physical experience with an equal amount of energy expenditure, thus wearying the physical vehicle, so that the sense of communion, peace and companionship that is offered in the group meditation is also a quality which allows the physical vehicle to relax to the point of drowsiness.

We commend those present for exercising the focus of the attention and the intention that is necessary in order to remain aware of the information and its direction. We are grateful to be able to speak to groups such as this, and willingly accept the, shall we say, drawbacks, that are necessary by the nature of your reality and ours blending at these times. We assure you that though you may find difficulty in consciously following the train of thought at these times, that your subconscious mind is absorbing many of these concepts in a more fundamental structure than the speaking of words allows. Thus, there is an understanding that is gained upon that more subtle level that can enhance the conscious apprehension of the information which we share.

Is there another query, my brother?

Questioner: No, thank you.

I am Q'uo and we thank you, my brother.

(Tape ends.) ❧

L/L Research

L/L Research is a subsidiary of Rock Creek Research & Development Laboratories, Inc.

P.O. Box 5195
Louisville, KY 40255-0195

www.llresearch.org

Rock Creek is a non-profit corporation dedicated to discovering and sharing information which may aid in the spiritual evolution of humankind.

ABOUT THE CONTENTS OF THIS TRANSCRIPT: This telepathic channeling has been taken from transcriptions of the weekly study and meditation meetings of the Rock Creek Research & Development Laboratories and L/L Research. It is offered in the hope that it may be useful to you. As the Confederation entities always make a point of saying, please use your discrimination and judgment in assessing this material. If something rings true to you, fine. If something does not resonate, please leave it behind, for neither we nor those of the Confederation would wish to be a stumbling block for any.

CAVEAT: This transcript is being published by L/L Research in a not yet final form. It has, however, been edited and any obvious errors have been corrected. When it is in a final form, this caveat will be removed.

© 2009 L/L Research

Sunday Meditation
June 7, 1992

Group question: The question today has to do with the concept of the ethics of control. When we are in relationship with friends or family, especially children, we often find ourselves in the situation of exerting some sort of influence over the person, oftentimes for his or her own good. We do this to friends, family and even to ourselves, controlling our behavior, our thoughts, our responses, in order to make them align with what we think is more appropriate or "higher" or better. And we are wondering today what the ethics are of attempting to affect our own, and especially other peoples', behavior because we think that the effect we desire is better or more appropriate or will be more helpful to the person in the long run. What are the ethics or results, metaphysically and spiritually, of attempting to affect other peoples' behavior in this fashion?

(Carla channeling)

I am Q'uo. Greetings in the love and in the light of the one infinite Creator. We are transformed with joy that you have called us to offer our opinions at this time. We do ask each to be aware that we are imperfect, sentient beings such as yourselves. Our store of memories and experiences is consciously greater than your own, but our opportunities for error precisely the same. Therefore, we ask that all of our thoughts be understood to be opinion and not fact. We ask that each discriminate within the self to take up those ideas which seem welcome and useful and to leave the rest behind. This would be doing us a great service.

You ask of the ethics of control. The foundations for such a question must move back to the larger view so that we may begin from a sturdy foundation of thought. It has often and often been noted in scientific, nonscientific, brilliant and foolish ways that the universe is in one way or another in balance: the stars in their courses, the galaxies in their huge orbits, the seas within their limits. All speak of the immeasurable amount of control with which the universe is created. The tiny fertilized egg has the life and the death of the body it shall become written in miniature within its tiny self, just as the seed knows precisely what form of plant it shall grow into, the manner of its blooming, and the nature of its fruit. Thusly, the universe is set upon its course with an intricacy the finest watchmaker could hardly conceive.

Against this fundamental dynamic is its echo and that which offers the opportunity for balance; that is, the freedom which all sentient beings have within the Creator's universe to choose that which they shall pursue, that which they shall think and choose. Were the universe to relax its discipline, there would be no universe. Yet, the fixed quality of stellar events and cycles is the backdrop against which is played out the choices of humans for themselves, for their families, for their communities, for their nation states, and for the sphere, the world, at large. Therefore, each entity has both more power and less power than it may think it has.

No entity may stop the sun in its course. No entity may control the stars or the tides. Yet, the cosmic influences of star and planet and moon move the tides of the blood within each entity's veins. The various energies within an entity create cross-tides, cross-currents, the flooding of emotion, the desert of blocked emotion. These things are offered not simply by fate, not by predetermined laws, but by the series of free will choices which has been made by the seeking individual as the individual walks upon the path of spiritual evolution. That each free will choice is one's own means to each seeker that it is powerful in its choice-making. This power is underestimated.

The effect that entities have when controlling or attempting to control other entities is far from fixed, for the relationship betwixt the two entities shifts constantly as your experience and your time seem to pass; and the relationship, the connection, between two entities shifts and grows as constantly and restlessly as wind or tide. Therefore, the ethics of choosing to control another, or choosing to attempt to control another, are ethics of a corollary nature, the primary ethic being the control of the self.

The ethics of the control of the self may be seen to be a careful and subtle process of learning and making choices. The advent of consciousness into the physical vehicle, which is the body of those in third density such as you, creates a situation where a self-conscious, sentient being lies helplessly within a nearly completely useless physical vehicle. Thusly, from babyhood to adulthood there is a continuing spiral of the attempt to order and control one's universe: the small universe of the infant with needs for comfort and food; the larger world of the toddler, the world of parents and personal ability to say "no"; the larger still world of the young, learning, growing child with friends and teachers, and a growing sense of the self; until finally, one day, the culture in which an entity lives says to that entity, now you are legally and officially an adult.

At this point, the adult is the product of many, many choices which have been played out against the dramatic interplay of the child needing and grasping enough control of the self to be comfortable, and those who are concerned for that entity attempting to describe boundaries within which choices may effectively or safely be made. Suddenly, the shoe, as this instrument would say, is upon the other foot. This young adult moves into environments of work, of bearing and raising children, of mated relationships, of far more group participation, in that adults are more often asked to help make decisions for church or community or charity, or in some way take part in making social choices.

The, what you call, political system is an example of theoretical free choice-making. It is to be noted that the concept may become overburdened when too small at one end and too large at the other. Your societies tend to spin like tops because the balance point of power is small, those over whom power is held, many. In this regard, we may say that for the ethics of control to be more nearly applicable to yellow ray social decision-making, the communities in which decisions are made must needs be small, small enough that each entity choosing has some small idea of who and what sort of entity each person is.

We move back to our image of the young adult discovering that now, instead of being the radical or rebellious youngster attempting to be free from constraints, the situation now is that there are times when it is ethically correct to attempt to control others to some extent. This is a shock, indeed, to many a young parent in particular.

As an entity gazes at the choice between allowing another entity to make what seems an unwise choice, questions may helpfully rise to the mind in this process of ethically controlling or ethically refusing to control. The first question is, "Will my inaction prevent this entity from surviving?" There is no case where there is any negative karma, shall we say, which is accrued from the attempt to keep another from becoming unviable. To save another, indeed, is a hero's or heroine's service. But, usually, the questions are more subtle.

Ethics is a system of thought which describes those actions which are appropriate. So, one may ask, is this a situation in which I should attempt to control because of an appropriate end? Appropriate ends are suggestions that may aid someone in achieving spiritual maturity, suggestions that may aid another in a savings of time or other valued commodity. Perhaps you see the general tendency of this word "appropriate." If control is used when it is appropriate, then, regardless of whether the entity controlled is in fact able to be controlled or not, the choice has been well made. If, on the other hand, an entity desires to control another from fear—that is, the fear that another is not doing the correct thing spiritually, politically, socially or economically—then this choice of control may be seen to be inappropriate.

The term "war" may be seen as the largest written, broadest spanning, example of inappropriate attempts to control others. The choices for spiritual, economic political, and social movements that have only rhetoric and ideas behind them are those things which one need not attempt to control. Look at how much control is attempted to be exerted by those who would that others do as they do, believe as they believe, dress as they dress, behave and so forth.

When teaching the child what is appropriate, many are the choices made for the child. When gazing at an adult, it may be seen that these choices have passed from the need for outer control. When an entity has the discipline of the self and the personality is touched and quieted by the surrender to that great original Thought of love which is the nature of the infinite Creator then questions of control become far less necessary, for the more centered, self-knowing, and quiet-hearted an entity, the less fear this entity will have that entities seemingly different from him will in some way harm or hurt him or his sensibilities.

Intolerance, prejudice and the cant of religious rhetoric are based upon fear. The ways in which individuals with fear may see themselves controlling may well be that of love and concern for the other self. Yet, no entity can learn for another, be safe for another, or do another's work. Suggestions can be made. There is no harm in suggestions. If the expectation is that they will be taken, then the matter must be referred to ethics: is this desired result appropriate? Is this desire appropriate?

Leaning upon one word, love, one may learn a great deal about ethics. In your own way, you aid the infinite creation in its path. Each individual's consciousness, if it rest in love, is more and more a part of that infinite, eternal, constant creation of the Father. As the whirlwind within the mind and emotions of living calms itself, and spiritual maturity advances, that part of each self that is of the infinite Creator and is an holograph of the infinite creation begins to manifest itself without words. Yet, this manifestation of love, flowing through one in infinite measure, gives to those entities whose discipline has been towards maturity an authority that makes it unnecessary to attempt to control, in most cases. For, as one is more and more the authority over the vagaries of the human self, just so does the heart within that self find itself peaceful and open and, therefore, a shuttle through which the love of the infinite One may flow freely.

We began with the image of the planets in their courses. We would end with a view of the constellation of the self. Gaze within. See the starry heavens of your own fixed universe as an electron microscope would see it. Your physical vehicle, all that is massive about you, is as the infinite creation: tiny, tiny apparent specks of matter in a vast, vast area of space. Each cell of your body is unimaginably vast compared to the particles which give it, through their motion, a field of electromagnetic unity. Within each of you there are subsystems or galaxies: the heart, the stomach, the liver, the musculature, and so forth. Each has its instinctually given work to do for the good of the whole. The liver does not sit down and say, "I will not work today." Barring accidents of ill health, the liver will do what livers do, the stomach what stomachs do, the muscle what muscles do, all directed involuntarily by the primal mind, much directed by the conscious mind. All this space within, all these fixed orbits within, and you as controller over all.

You are a co-creator. Step back from the constellation of the self. See the constellation of your own mind. See the unimaginable number of choices that have brought you to this moment. And see that you will treat others as a corollary of the way you treat yourself. As you venture forth within this incarnational experience you are enjoying, see and feel the dance of interstellar space, of the constellations of the body and the marvelous structure of the mind, and realize that you enter the present moment powerful within yourself. As each fear is noticed, addressed, blessed, accepted and eventually dropped away, for it is unneeded, there will be fewer times that the constellation that unifies as yourself finds, through fear, that it wishes to control an inappropriate way. Look always first to the discipline of the self and the acceptance, blessing and forgiveness of the self, as the self is imperfect, so it seems. Then when you gaze upon a fellow being there will not be the blinders of fear to distract the thinking or blind the eyes of judgment. As this instrument often says, free will is paramount. Let this and love be your guides.

There is more material upon this subject if subsequent questions have a meaning to the group. At this time we shall depart from this instrument, thanking it for its service, and leaving each through it in love and in light, and would transfer to the one known as Jim. We are known to you as those of the principle of Q'uo.

(Jim channeling)

I am Q'uo, and greet each again in love and in light through this instrument. At this time, it is our privilege to offer ourselves for any further queries that may be upon the minds of those present. Is there a query at this time with which we may begin?

Questioner: I'd like to ask how does one let go of one's self-control, to learn to contact personal guides like you are or just get in touch with your own feelings?

I am Q'uo, and am aware of your query, my sister. We would suggest that one possible technique would be for the entity wishing to release that which it sees as control that it does not wish to retain within its behavior patterns to enter into the meditative state and to look at the patterns that the entity has developed throughout its life pattern, and to see these patterns of behavior as a web of rituals or habits which have given comfort to the entity for a large portion of its experience. Look at this pattern and the barrier that it presents to further experience, in that there is the holding of the thought and action of the entity within the pattern. Imagine the experience that would ensue should the pattern be altered. Look to those areas where there is the desire for inspiration, for innovation, for the breaking of the patterns and the introducing of new experience. Feel how this breaking of old patterns and the introducing of new behavior would affect the life, the feelings, the concept of self. Imagine this process mentally.

Then, when you feel that you would like to experiment with such innovation, allow yourself a period of time that is unstructured so that whatever feelings or intuitive inclinations might wish to surface may do so. Move with these feelings as you wish, as feels appropriate. Explore in this safe arena of unstructured activity and thought all the attendant feelings and activities that move into the mind as you are experimenting. Repeat this process a number of times so that you begin to get the feel of releasing comfortable patterns and the feeling of accepting that which is new and unknown within one's self. Become aware of the intensity of feelings that result. Explore the feelings and their ramifications within your life experience and within your being.

Then, again, in the meditative state, look for other areas where there is the possibility of introducing new behavior or of releasing old behavior without knowing that which shall follow. As you become more familiar with the feeling of letting go of control, you will find that there is a kind of skill developing, much as you developed the ability to ride a bicycle as a young child.

The ability to release that which is structured and safe and accept that which is new and unstructured can be learned by any entity that has the sincere desire to release that which it has held onto for a great portion of its life experience. The meditative reflection before and after entering into this process prepares the deeper self for this experience, and, once the experience has occurred, seats the new learning at that deeper level of the self so that it can become a portion of the patterns of behavior that are your tools for processing catalysts, for learning, and for being of service to others by utilizing that which you have learned.

Is there a further query, my sister?

Questioner: No, thank you.

I am Q'uo, and we thank you, my sister. Is there another query at this time?

Carla: *(Carla talks about how she has helped many people with such concerns as that of the previous questioner, and has noticed in her work that others give her more authority in their lives than she feels she should have. She asks Q'uo if there is something that she is unconsciously doing that she could learn more about so that she would not have inappropriate, unwanted control or authority in others' lives.)*

I am Q'uo, and am aware of your query, my sister. We would suggest that a large portion of your fear of assuming too much authority in the eyes of others can be quelled by simply reminding each entity that

that which you share is but your opinion, and, though joyfully and freely shared, is but opinion. Once this is stated and understood, both by yourself and by the other self, then we would recommend the free sharing of that which is yours to share without further concern, for over-concern in this area may simply become a stumbling block for yourself.

Is there another query, my sister?

Carla: *(Carla follows up with the statement that with some people, the more one says that one does not have all the answers, the more respect one is given and the more people will take what one is saying with weight, and she doesn't know a way around that. She notes that Q'uo may share this problem as well.)*

I am Q'uo, and am aware once again of your query, my sister. This difficulty we find is that which resides not in the one seeking to offer assistance but in those to whom the assistance is offered. Not all learning or all experience of any kind shall be free of difficulties. Thus, we suggest the going forth bravely without over-concern for this feature of many student/teacher relationships, but continuing in the open-hearted giving without this concern. For, as one shares in a free and open manner the, as they have been called, "clay feet" will make themselves apparent time and again so that there will no longer be the necessity for the reminder to any that the feet are made of clay and the opinion is prone to error.

Is there a further query, my sister?

Carla: No. Thank you very much.

I am Q'uo, and we thank you once again, my sister. Is there another query at this time?

(Pause)

I am Q'uo, and as we appear to have exhausted the queries for this session of working, we would take this opportunity to thank each entity for inviting our presence in your meditation this day. We are most grateful for the opportunity to walk with you upon your journeys of seeking. We are always filled with great joy at such opportunities, for in this manner we are privileged to experience the depth of your seeking for truth and the intensity of your desire to be of service to others.

At this time we shall take our leave of this instrument and this group, leaving each, as always, in the love and in the light of the one infinite Creator. We are known to you as those of Q'uo. Adonai, my friends. Adonai. ☙

Sunday Meditation
June 14, 1992

Group question: The question this afternoon has to deal with the phenomenon of the visitation of a third-density human being by a negatively-oriented entity or energy that is sent from another third-density human being practicing what is usually called the black magical arts.

We are wondering how the person receiving this energy or another wishing to help this person receiving this negative energy would deal with it. What is the best attitude, the best actions and the principles that need to be considered when dealing with negatively oriented visitations, whether of an entity or an energy?

(Carla channeling)

I am Q'uo. Greetings in the love and in the light of the one infinite Creator. We are most blessed to greet each of you this day, especially welcoming one new to our circle, the one known as K. Those of Oxal greet the one known as H, and are with this entity in silent enjoyment during this period. We are honored to have the privilege of being called to your group to speak of negative entities among your own people, and to speak also of those non-physical principles and entities which may be called upon by those within your density who are polarizing upon the path of service to self or negativity.

Let us first define the term black arts or black magical art. The metaphysical—both of the service-to-others path and the service-to-self path—is that which takes place upon a field which appears to be dark. The background of metaphysical work for both polarities is a metaphysical environment of darkness, for the metaphysical consciousness of the living spirit within third-density illusion is hidden within the deep and unlit roots of mind. Consequently, both those who seek the darkness and those who seek the light begin in a common ground of darkness, the darkness of that which is not known.

Upon this level of seeking for energy or power the search for truth is conducted in night conditions. The moon's dimmest light is the brightest illumination as one seeks spiritually. It is extremely subtle and difficult work to distinguish truth from *(inaudible)* or outright falsity, to distinguish the positive leaning towards the love of the infinite One in service to others from the same activity which may seek service to self. Many are those metaphysical seekers who expect that the seeking towards the positive truth will be done in noonday sun metaphysically speaking; this is untrue. The metaphysical search is not clear, obvious or simple. Each of you here who listens to this voice speaking our thoughts knows of the case of mistaking apparent truth for truth, and can recall instances in which that which one thought one had discovered to be a shining light was instead relatively valueless and not filled with light or power.

In the dim moonlight, shadows can be deceiving. The metaphysical search, then, is one in which faith is the great illuminator, that faith which cannot be given by one to another, that faith which each gestates within the spiritual part of the mind and body so that there becomes a faith which is personal, founded by the self.

Now we return to a view of how to deal with negative entities. As a positively polarized person living a life in faith, one is prone to feel safe in the arms of the good, the true and the beautiful. However, the entity upon the negative path feels that there is no safety, feels that there is no haven, feels that it and only it shall be the one to be counted upon, relied upon. Therefore, this entity wishes to build personal power with a greater initial reason and impetus for building a magical personality. Furthermore, this magical personality is simpler to build than the positively oriented magical personality. The negative entity need only attempt to *(inaudible)* to the self all possible power of any kind whatsoever without the need for discrimination or judgment.

The positively polarized entity instead is moving through processes of balancing the seemingly opposite of all things to ascertain the most careful balance of truth, of beauty, of goodness, for to the positively oriented entity it is clear that the illusion has the appearance of a bias toward negative events and circumstances. In order to clarify right action and the positive use of power, careful balancing of all stimulus needs must be done. Thus, each of you has the seemingly more difficult task in living a chosen life of faith, for both paths are given by the one infinite Creator. Although the Creator offers suggestions implicit in experience that the positive path of serving others is preferable and more to be desired, the negative path beckons and it too is *(inaudible)*, as this instrument would say, godly in that there is no energy [but] that of the one infinite Creator.

Further, the *(inaudible)* of your experience in third density offers simpler beginnings to a metaphysical base of power for those which choose negativity. What is not obvious is that the negative path becomes more and more difficult, until at last it is a road impossible to be walked, whereas the positive path is eternal.

Therefore, one who is assaulted by word, dream, feeling or other action by a negatively polarized entity of third density is dealing with not only a godly person but his own self, for all are one in the creation of the Father. In each mind, body and spirit which together make up the person there is all that there is. Each person is an holograph of the creation, the created and the Creator.

Thusly, when negative greeting is known or suspected the positively oriented person of power sits down and prepares itself to reckon with its own universal nature. It is fully capable and fully supplied with negativity. The perceived negativity from the outside in is successful when the positively oriented intended victim knows not that it is being greeted by its very self. If a ravening beast comes at one's body, one attempts to slay that beast to save the self. If a metaphysical ravening beast attacks one in the manner of magical arts, one reckons with this attack by visualizing this creature, welcoming it into the self, and accepting fully that this horrible monster is a part of the self.

When one chooses a path one has the full spectrum from which to choose precisely because one contains all that there is. The first defense, therefore, is to visualize this negative power and fearlessly to invite it to take up a loving absorption within the very heart, for positive power is power balanced by knowledge of the self. The decision not to attempt power over another is made when the entity grasps that there is no need to have power over others, for all of creation expresses its power in the self. All magical work, therefore, is done upon the self. There is no need to manipulate, teach, control, move or advise other entities. The need is only to do these things within the self, disciplining the self to a more and more balanced and clear acceptance of the universal nature of selfhood, and therefore choosing lucidly and clearly to serve others, to withhold judgment of or control over others, and to practice loving the self, accepting the self and allowing the errors perceived within the self to be self-forgiven.

As one forgives one's self, one then is able to forgive all. As the negative greeting is seen, then it is visualized and made materially real within the metaphysical world of thought as a creature of the night, a mythical creature which then is lovingly absorbed, accepted and forgiven. The forgiven selfishness becomes harmless. This alone is enough to dissuade most negative third density entities who are wishing to control others, for most are not particularly skillful. Being accepted is *(inaudible)* to a negatively oriented entity, who gains power by causing fear, anger, hatred, disgust and other negative reactions of emotion.

When this entity's selfhood is seen for its blackness, yet lovingly, compassionately accepted, absorbed into a strong goodness of self and forgiven, the negative entity experiences loss of all *(inaudible)* power and chooses to attempt to control others who will be satisfactorily afraid and terrorized by such. In the case of the very few who have the energy and endurance to pursue the path of control over others to the point where they are able directly to contact metaphysical sources of negativity, the situation, while no less solvable, is not as easy and simple to deal with from the standpoint of the one greeted. Again, in the unthinking person of third density, the response to perceived attack is counter-attack.

It takes a good deal of wisdom to be able to calmly and objectively gaze upon the face of metaphysical malevolence, for those who have contacted those metaphysical sources which are of fourth density have garnered to themselves two things. One is a third-density personality within incarnation of sureness and confidence. There is in such entity a true blackness of spirit, a honed hatred which sees no shadows. The positive path is full of shadows, of questions and doubts, of continual learning and balance. The choice for positivity is not the choice for simplicity of early lessons. The choice for negativity is a choice for simplicity of early lessons. Thusly, an entity which is negative has an apparent advantage once it has progressed to a certain point of being absolutely sure of the self without the need for faith, whereas the positively polarized entity is still dealing with the endless and confusing shadows of the spiritual landscape, which is lit by the dim star of hope and the thin, delicate moonlight of faith.

In this situation where there is not only the living incarnate negative entity who greets one but also the spirit of higher density cooperating in its peculiar manner in this negatively oriented entity, the positive path must be seen to be a place of hope and faith which are accepted without proof. The positive pilgrim takes into the heart a strong desire to leap foolishly into the abyss of the unknown, unprotected by certainty, facing in mid-air the seeming destruction of personal safety, clinging to nothing but a faith that all is well and that there is nothing to fear. Many are the loving and positively oriented souls who yet are not able to do this. When such entities are greeted by these relatively powerful negative sources the most—we search this instrument's mind for the appropriate word—practical solution is to find one among your people which is positive in nature and is steeped in rituals of positivity, which include in their language the seeking of the greeting of fourth-density or higher positive metaphysical entities. Such people are the so-called priests of various of your religious belief systems which believes in the war betwixt good and evil. This war is fought by fourth-density negative entities and fourth-density positive entities which still believe that a battle is appropriate.

Before we leave this topic we would focus once more upon the *(inaudible)* and fertile land of spiritual choice, the dark world within. Each of you gaze within. Do you feel magical? Do you feel powerful? If the answer comes too easily it is likely that there is that within you which would choose the easy way towards power, that is, the path of negativity, for each step upon the negative path seems from within to be positive: one wishes power so that one may help people; the way to help people is to give advice, give teaching; make sure that all is well by controlling various people and circumstances. All these things feel natural and good. Most beginning negative entities have no idea that they are embarking upon the path of negativity.

Contrasting with this is the positive path, where power is accrued by being the weakest, *(inaudible)* greatness is achieved by being the servant of others, where advice and teaching are given only when offered. How many among your religious systems, caught up in the fervor of rightness and righteousness, judge, condemn and control many for their own good? How few there are in your belief systems of religion who *(inaudible)* doctrine and dogma and seek to serve each entity according to its requests when it can, and offering only benediction, forgiveness and acceptance when it cannot. Yet to those few who know themselves well enough not to judge, not to control others, but to work on the self, to these few come strength, magical power and illumination of incandescent light which shoots through that darkness of metaphysical field like lightning. The world, as this instrument would say, cannot see that lightning. Only each individual pilgrim upon the positive path who moves into a life in faith, a life without fear, may be illumined. It moves through one, it does not stay with one. And such entities are channels of joy and peace.

Whether the greeting of negative entities seems, or seems, or seems not to succeed, such entities are forever safe in spirit. We are those of the positive path. We are also dusty pilgrims who have searched long in the shadows of hope and faith. We do not expect third-density entities to be without fear. We simply ask entities who wish to live in faith not to be afraid of their fear, not to be ruled by their fear, but to accept this fear, to love this fear, as part of the universal self, and to move on, leaping foolishly into the next step in blindness and in faith. May each of you find each step to be one which is offered to the infinite One as a gift, a testimony of love, for if the Creator is love, then the choice of fearlessness is always correct.

We encourage each to be patient, [forgiving], accepting and slow with each fear that keeps it from progressing. Take time to work through the balancing of that fear, overcome it never, but take it within the self, love it, accept it, and gently, strand by strand, part the curtain that keeps the self from progressing fearlessly. This is slow work but it moves one ever towards the truth, the good, and the beautiful.

We would at this time transfer this contact to the one known as Jim. We thank this instrument and the *(inaudible)* and in light. We are known to you as Q'uo.

(Jim channeling)

I am Q'uo, and greet each again in love and in light through this instrument. We are aware that we have spoken long and apologize for the length of our delivery. We are aware that we have fatigue in the circle *(inaudible)*. We are, however, privileged to offer ourselves at this time for any further queries that you may have for us. Is there a query at this time?

(Pause)

I am Q'uo, and we shall take this opportunity to thank each once again for inviting our presence into your circle of seeking this day. We are most filled with joy to be able to walk with you upon your journey at this time. We shall now leave this instrument and this group, leaving each, as always, in the love and in the light of the one infinite Creator. We are known to you as those of Q'uo. Adonai, my friends. Adonai. ✾

L/L Research

Intensive Meditation
July 4, 1992

Group question: The question this evening has to do with the concept of gurus. In many of the eastern traditions a guru is seen as an indispensable part of the seeker's journey, that no true enlightenment can occur unless the seeker follows the footsteps of the guru, and puts him or herself under the guru's guidance and instruction. In the west we have various religious traditions, the protestant and the catholic focusing around the entity Jesus Christ and this is a kind of guruship where there is a model or there are footsteps left, patterns and rituals, the use of faith and will to live a life as described by Jesus. How important to a seeker is the concept of the guru, the dispeller of darkness, the one who makes the model or lives the life that is patterned in a fashion that can aid a seeker along the journey of evolution? How much of that quality of the guru can we find within ourselves and how much of that finding is made possible or only possible with the assistance of a guru?

This evening we have Jim and Carla supporting the work of S's intensive meditation channeling …

(S channeling)

[I am Laitos.] We greet you in the love and in the light of the infinite One. We are most happy to have been given this opportunity to speak through an instrument which was not prepared for our presence but had anticipated instead the presence of another with whom it is more familiar. It is the mark of the maturing instrument that it shall recognize the nature of the call it is offered, and it is the—we correct this instrument—it is the mark of an instrument that is willing truly to serve that it place itself in the arms that are proffered.

We have come to offer a kind of comfort that [we] feel we are able to uniquely to offer to this group at this time. We wish to offer this comfort in a preliminary way and then to make room for those of Oxal who are also prepared to speak. We wish to give encouragement to a group which has known much ordeal in the past brief measure of your time and which has nevertheless courageously persisted in its seeking and its intent to serve. This kind of dedication offers opportunity upon opportunity for those of us which are, as you would say, discarnate, to serve in the small ways which are given us to serve through the instrumentalities not only of highly concentrated efforts like that which you undertake today, but in the myriad ways of everyday life dedicated wholly to service. We ourselves are comforted by your dedication and would offer this our blessing to you in love and in light, a brief silent offering. We pause.

(Pause)

I am Oxal. We feel now the instrument has profited by the steadying influence of our friends of Laitos.

We greet you in the all embracing love and in the purest light of the infinite Creator. It is our privilege this evening to be called forth in response to a query that weighs upon your minds, this being the question of the nature of the role of the spiritual teacher. We most happily would address this question, but first we would ask that all present be aware that we ourselves are spiritual teachers only in a very, very limited sense, for all too well we know our own feet to be of clay, and we ask that you too be aware of this and use discrimination in taking in and weighing each of our words, for our words can have no greater effect than to resonate with what each here already knows and is willing in some measure to examine more closely.

The function of the spiritual teacher cannot be separated from the more general process of spiritual seeking. In the density that you enjoy this process of seeking spiritually has certain features that are unique to it, for in the third density seeking occurs from a position that is unknown to the seeker. The seeker gropes blindly and has but what is, at first, the faintest of inner lights to guide it. The process of seeking is one of allowing this inner light progressively to illumine more and more of the path, until the path, though it is never fully mapped out, seems sure and certain to the footfall as you walk ever more in faith, ever more in a dedication to service.

We find, however, that this experience can be a very lonely one and that the temptation arises again and again to seek in the reassuring words of one who would lead one to find more than comfort, more than solace, but also direction. Now, it is the best of our understanding that, in truth, direction can never be gathered from another. There is, indeed, the wonderful mystery of paths of seeking that cross and intertwine and run together in a mutual love and compassion which gives great comfort. We find, however, that all too often it is the case when one doubts one's own way one relies rather too heavily upon another, which one puts before one as the teacher.

Thus, one has arising amongst your peoples traditions of religious worship which set the teacher so far above the seeker that the seeker has effectively abandoned all native power and given it over to the teacher. When this occurs, it is but a short step to hardening the words of the teacher into rock solid doctrine, which may then be slavishly followed and used as a basis for judging self and other. This leads inevitably to a loss of seeking. Like a stream bed no longer fed by the flow of water, dry and barren the seeking becomes.

Having said this, we wish to add, however, that in the relation of pupil to teacher, disciple to guru, there can be something of value and of spiritual importance. We address this point in light of the concept of sacrifice, for if the student/teacher relation is maintained with the most delicate of balances, the teacher being scrupulous to keep in perspective the fact the teacher, at best, is a gateway or a channel for that which lies beyond the teacher and which is as—we correct this instrument—which is as accessible to the student as it is to the teacher, and, in addition, the student must keep in perspective the point that the teacher is but a mutual seeker which has perhaps a certain steadying influence upon the student that contributes to a more stable pattern of seeking, within the context where these cautions are scrupulously observed, the student may look to the teacher in such a way that the teacher inspires within the student a certain highly potentiated kind of humility which the student expresses by deliberately setting aside those known personality features which may tend to distort or disrupt the seeking process.

When this process is being consciously directed and intensely perused in a sheltered environment, the teacher or the guru in this respect may accept the sacrifice or the laying aside of the Earthly personality in a symbolic way, understanding that what there is to be offered coming through the teacher is further empowered by this act. Now, this process can be successful only when the teacher has similarly laid aside the Earthly personality and is willing to join hands with the student in a fashion which allows each to participate in a sense of a greater reality to appreciate the unity that is all embracing. The strength of the teacher flows back to the student even as the student's gift of its devotion to the teacher further empowers their function of the teaching.

We find then that this group was quite correct in its surmise that the greatest gift that the teacher has to give is the beingness of the teacher. As soon, however, as this beingness is contracted into [mere] personality which the teacher may claim as its own, it has been lost and lost as a source of inspiration to the student even though the student may continue to take it as such. There are connections of energy that connect student to teacher, though we find in principle that these connections are not different than those connections of energy which prevail from one loved one to another, and just as the lover must be prepared also and equally to be the beloved, so must the teacher be prepared also and equally to be the student. All are fellow seekers in the spiritual world. All of the distinctions which can in the veiled experience seem so important vanish into utter nothingness, leaving but a full democracy of spirit. One seeks, then, with all of creation, and the seeking of all creation is within one.

We ourselves seek with you as we attempt in reaching out to you and in reaching within ourselves to touch this center of seeking, and to allow it beingness that it may be the more our beingness, which we most happily share with you as you have most happily shared your beingness upon this occasion with us.

We find that there is so very much more that could be said upon the topic of the guru, but what we have said serves as a sufficient beginning, and we would ask if there are more specific queries to which we may address ourselves in response. Are there queries at this time?

Questioner: *(Inaudible).*

I am Oxal. It has been our very great pleasure to be given the opportunity once again to speak through this instrument which desires to serve, but finds itself frustrated in this capacity. May we offer the encouragement that what has happened, is happening, and will happen, is but part of a much larger process, and the entire process can be viewed as a mode and a moment of the same service. We thank this group for its dedication and its persistence. At this time we take our leave, leaving you in the love and in the light and in the all embracing glory of the one infinite Creator. Adonai, my friends. Adonai.

L/L Research

L/L Research is a subsidiary of Rock Creek Research & Development Laboratories, Inc.

P.O. Box 5195
Louisville, KY 40255-0195

www.llresearch.org

Rock Creek is a non-profit corporation dedicated to discovering and sharing information which may aid in the spiritual evolution of humankind.

ABOUT THE CONTENTS OF THIS TRANSCRIPT: This telepathic channeling has been taken from transcriptions of the weekly study and meditation meetings of the Rock Creek Research & Development Laboratories and L/L Research. It is offered in the hope that it may be useful to you. As the Confederation entities always make a point of saying, please use your discrimination and judgment in assessing this material. If something rings true to you, fine. If something does not resonate, please leave it behind, for neither we nor those of the Confederation would wish to be a stumbling block for any.

CAVEAT: This transcript is being published by L/L Research in a not yet final form. It has, however, been edited and any obvious errors have been corrected. When it is in a final form, this caveat will be removed.

© 2009 L/L Research

Sunday Meditation
July 5, 1992

Group question: The question today has to do with the concept of nurturing self-love. How do people who are naturally oriented towards being of service to others, and perhaps even serving beyond the ability to fully care for the self, take the time and energy and effort to nurture themselves? What is a way in which people can look at the nurturing of the self as a natural part of service to others? What kind of suggestions can you make as to how we can become aware of our needs for nurturing, and fulfill those needs as we go about the process of serving others and learning and growing in our daily activities?

(Carla channeling)

I am Q'uo. Greetings in the love and in the light of the one infinite Creator. We find great joy in joining in your circle, blending our vibrations with your own, and experiencing the unity of your seeking and the beauty of your meditation. You ask this day if we have some thoughts upon how to nurture the self, as well as nurturing other entities. The service-to-others path through the fourth density of love asks the question in this manner, and by this way of asking, points directly to the core of confusion. For the question, when wisdom is applied, becomes "How do we nurture other selves, if we are those who nurture the self?" Yet, we do not encourage you to feel foolish by putting others before self in thought or action.

We wish to note for your benefit the stance which you rightly and justly, as developing spirits, take. The lesson of compassion is learned first, then the larger lesson of wisdom. You are those seeking in the school of love, therefore this query is central. The beginning of grasping the way of nurturing the self is, however, implicit in the question. We have said to this group before that the one known as Jesus taught that there was a new covenant, a new set of commandments, which superseded the commandments given to the one called Moses. The commandments were two: to love the Creator with all one's heart, all one's soul, all one's mind, and all one's strength; and to love the other selves within your environments as you love yourself. The second of the commandments was not to love yourself as you love others, but to love others as you love yourself! Thusly, this master of compassion suggested the turning of mercy inward upon the self, prior to asking the self to expand the manifestations of mercy outward.

The way of those within the illusion wherein one cannot usually hear the thoughts of others is to take others at their word in trust, and to take the self not at one's own word, but with each and every thought which is unexpressed held like a load upon the back. Thusly, it seems appropriate to serve others, but there is a chip upon your shoulders in your attitude toward yourself.

One set of suggestions concerning the nurturing of the self is nurturing systematically each chakra by vivid visualization, and not only by meditation, but by contemplation also. Let us demonstrate using this instrument to avoid infringement upon free will of others. Each needs must make assessments of chakra strength and clarity for each. The first chakra is always the root or red-ray energy center. Gaze at this center which loves life, which breathes the air and has appetite for preservation and procreation. This root energy is anything but base. It, as this instrument is fond of saying, contains the first sacrament, as all energies are potentially sacramental. This energy gazes—we correct this instrument—this instrument gazes at this energy and finds it very strong and clear.

There being no visualization to do, this instrument proceeds to the orange-ray energy center or chakra. Here there can be seen those muddied energies which, though small, yet block some energy from moving into the open heart. How can one gaze at the shadows that dog one's path? If one turns about to look at them, they shift. They cannot be directly confronted, for they are shadows, yet the more firmly excellence is striven for, the darker will seem every small imperfection. This instrument then must contemplate indirectly the cause for shadows. This is the area of relationships person-to-person. Whom is this instrument not in good relationship with? The answer comes by reflex. The instrument is not in good relationship with the self. There ensues a forgiving process. Why should this instrument forgive? Intellectually, the instrument can say, "I am forgiven because I am a child of the Creator." To the heart, no reasoning is necessary. One evaluates the self. First, may we suggest that the self be visualized as being held in the arms of the infinite One, lovingly, firmly and comfortably, rocked in eternal rhythms and loved with infinite love. When one can see oneself as the child of eternity, one can see oneself at the correct distance.

How important the instrument finds the environment of the present illusion, and how typical this is, indeed, how necessary to the growth of each spirit. Yet, in the nurturing process the reestablishment of the point of view of infinity, eternity and mystery is central, and can bring order and simplicity out of chaos.

We linger at this energy center because in your particular nation state, the outer forces which compromise free will are comparatively lesser, so that the most common blockages and over-activations of energy which confound the open heart are those of orange ray.

Now, this instrument is willing to forgive the self, and we know that each is willing to do so for the self. However, this willingness is time limited because within the experience which has become memory of your peoples, it is almost without exception that this state of self-forgiveness is lost. The attention shifts, the polarity is lessened and forgotten for the moment.

The instrument moves to the yellow-ray energy center, and gazes at the energies which deal with the societal groups which affect it. This energy in this case seems fairly under-energized, but quite clear. This is normal in general for entities to have certain energies which are not the *forte*, not the strong point of an entity's service. Yet, they do need to be visualized to be sure that, though relatively small in influence upon the learning process, the energies are clear.

Moving into the heart chakra, the green-ray energy center, the instrument visualizes a nearly fully open, very strong heart energy which is normal for this instrument. The entity finds it sparkling at this time, and realizes the effect of those in a group which love one another, causing the heart energy to dance and shine. This is the portion of the nurturing of the self wherein others move in help from whatever other energy center is being used, the blue ray of communication, the orange ray of interaction in addition to communication, and so forth. All then comes through the heart chakra to others and from others.

It is to be suggested by us that when one sees the heart fully open, one then may do well to suggest to the self the beauty of giving and receiving of love. The reception of love, it has been noted this day, is often very difficult. When the orange-ray center is blocked by self-judgment, then the shining love of others is blocked from entering the heart. Loving gestures, thoughts and words may batter against the heart closed to itself in vain. Until the entity is willing to open the door to comfort by ceasing to judge the self as unworthy of comfort, no comfort can move into effective service.

Thusly, service to others directly denotes the allowing of others to love the self. This is often the most difficult relationship lesson of all, for if one is not in love with the self, how can one believe or have trust and faith in the illuminating light and love pouring into one's heart from another? There is no basis for trust, for the self is not willing to trust the self. It is an irony of the third and fourth-density illusions that more and more energy is consumed in the desire to love, to open the self to more and more complete service to others, while there remains the grudge against the self. It is as though each were running away from the self, throwing the self into as many seemingly good actions as possible, in an attempt to even the terribly lopsided score of unworthiness of the self.

However, worthiness is not a quantitative matter, and is not available to the point grading system. There is no amount of service one can be to others to offset one's own self-judged lack of worth. Until one forgives and accepts the self, one's service will be stunted; one's heart will be darkened, even in the fullness of the most loving service. Perhaps this points to the centrality of the learning of self-nurturing ways.

Moving into the blue-ray energy center, this instrument sees its strongest center working well, and not in need of further balancing or energizing. This is the center of communication. It is most often blocked by those who would communicate that which has not been requested. It is well to have opinions and thoughts on every conceivable matter; this is the fruit of an active mind. It is not loving, however, to answer questions or address seen problems which have not been asked about or advice sought upon by the one to whom the entity is attempting to communicate. Service to others is very much a matter of waiting and having the patience of being the quietness of mind to feel and respect other entities' freedom to make choices.

If there is a great desire to communicate without there being a request, it is possible to enter into conversation about whether the entity you wish to serve would be glad to hear an opinion. If the other self agrees, then an appropriate channel has been opened. If the other self does not agree, then woe betide the spirit which plunges ahead regardless, for this is specific infringement upon free will. Remember that other selves and the self come into the valley of the shadow of death that is third-density life, not to be comfortable or correct, but to make mistakes and thereby learn the lessons of how not to express love and how to express love; how not to accept love and how to accept love; and most of all, how not to conceive oneself that is as unloving, unlovely or unloved, or how to picture that same self loving, lived and love itself.

The violet ray is fixed, and can simply be assessed as a good indicator of the balance which is present in the energy of your own self as a whole. If it seems weak, then meditation upon power, that is, the aspect of the self which expresses power, is recommended. Although, as in the material this instrument has recently read, it is recommended that meditations about the power aspect of the self not be accomplished more than once in a row, rather, if the power aspect needs work, then one works upon the love aspect and the wisdom aspect in two subsequent meditations before returning to the power aspect. This is recommended, as in the work of the one known as Butler, to avoid the distortion of the personality which is the spirit's own attempting to find itself on what this instrument would call the King's Highway.

Now, this is one way in which the nurturing of the self can be done. This way is important in that it is completely inner in the nature of its work. Just doing this work, that is, taking the time and the energy to do this series of visualizations, is a way that moves deeply into the self's perception web of saying that the self is indeed considered worthy of attention. Often the service-to-others path is strewn with those who have paid attention to every opportunity to aid others' needs, but have not given the self the same gift—the gift of time, the gift of energy. Outer ways of nurturing the self—the new dress, the new car or computer game or trip—is a very kind and good gift to the self. But nothing moves more deeply into the area of the self which deals with self-judgment than the self sitting down and taking time to pay attention to the self's spiritual health. This is subtle work.

Now, you may note that we moved from blue to violet. That is because that of which we are speaking, the time to work with the self, is the function and the only function of the indigo ray! This ray works completely within the self, and only upon the self. To find the discipline to spend time upon the self's spiritual welfare is more of a challenge than finding the time to attend to another's spiritual or bodily or emotional or mental welfare. We cannot stress enough the importance of this point. Think you that one of the highest of energies possible within the self, in terms of subtlety and strength, is somehow to take the very back seat, nay, even the trunk of the automobile of life? Please see and honor the instrument that you are, no matter what outward way you treat yourself, you love yourself, you give to yourself.

The first gift of the spiritual wayfarer is the time and the energy to move within, to work upon the discipline of the personality, that more and more of the personality may be imbued with the indigo ray of joyful accepting love of self. Consider the usual indigo ray of the underdeveloped student as a pool. The polarity of service to others fills this pool, but it is simply rain falling into a conserving receptacle, a still pool within one, until it has been enlivened by the acceptance of love that is beyond the possible love when judgment remains. Until this block is removed, this pool of polarity remains still and lacking in appropriate propinquity to the …

(Side one of tape ends.)

(Carla channeling)

… There's a moment when the pool of polarity within is opened to what lies beyond acceptance of the self. Then it becomes a truly potent force within the life, as though a fountain or spring came forth from that still pool, and sprayed and dropped like rain into each present moment; so that no key must be turned to start up the engine of self-acceptance which opens the door to unconditional channeling of infinite love through one. The key is already inserted. The work is being done within in such a way to genetically affect the energies of polarized beingness.

Thus, if you now feel that you are accepting yourself over and over and over, the secret may be that the gifts you give yourself do not include the appropriate concern for inner loving work. Not so that discrimination becomes judgment, but so that the powers of discrimination within you may help you to become that which you are, but have not realized or allowed yourself to be. And why? Because you fear to look too closely. You have heard those thoughts. So, all becomes fearful at a deep level.

We ask you to free yourself from this fearing of thoughts deemed unworthy. We assume in general that entities in service to others have largely mastered the techniques of avoiding manifesting of unacceptable actions, and so we concentrate on what is considered by the self to be unacceptable thoughts or intentions. Let us gaze for the last of these thoughts at this fear. The one known as Aaron, as spoken through the one known as Barbara, has said in this group that fear is not a bad or wrong thing; it is therefore a reason, it is a good protection until the self is ready to deal with it. Then and only then, may one sit down with the fear, gaze at it, picture the self within the cave with the—we correct this instrument—opening to the cave blocked by many bands that hide the light from one.

This is the fear, and no fear is greater to the good, gentle and kind of heart than the fear of finding the canker within. It need not be thrown away from the mouth of the cave all at once, for this might do damage to the fearful self. Take one band away, and see if that much freedom from fear is comfortable. When it is, move to take another, and another, but have the patience with the self to accept less than perfect deliverance from that fear of unworthiness at any one sitting. You have infinite time to do this work, but in each present moment, you have only that moment to do this work. Therefore, be importuning for the present moment, yet patient in the long view. If the self cannot or is fearful to do this work now, return to the image of being held in the arms of the infinite One, and rocked and lullabied and loved, for this is your true state at a deep, deep level. How you are loved! How you are loved! Feel that. Know that. Spend time with that. When you feel how much you are already loved by the infinite One, how treasured you are, then you can gain courage to go ahead and walk the King's Highway, and do the work of falling in love with the self, even in its illusory rampant imperfection.

What an illusion you have, my dear, dear ones. What a magnificent bubble of utter confusion. You are brave souls to sail forth in this chaotic illusion. May you be to each other the beacons that bespeak love for and to each other. We send our love and light to you through this instrument, and would at this time transfer this contact to the one known as Jim, that it may conclude this working. We are those of Q'uo.

(Jim channeling)

I am Q'uo, and greet each again in love and in light through this instrument. At this time, it is our privilege to offer ourselves in the attempt to speak to any further queries which those present might have to offer to us. Is there a query at this time?

Questioner: I would like to know more about the polarization *(inaudible)*.

I am Q'uo, and believe that we have a grasp of your query, my sister. The polarization of the mind, in brief, is the process whereby the desire to be of service is set forth as that which is foremost of all desires that one may have and exercise during the incarnation. The means of clearing the centers or chakras of energy by the use of the polarization of the mind is that process whereby you take that desire and move through each chakra in turn, utilizing this desire to find those distortions or imperfections of manifestation within each center of energy, and seek for that moment to visualize or imagine the balanced expression of energy that is appropriate for you at that time in that center, assigning to each center those properties that are appropriate for each center, beginning as we said, with the first, or root center, and looking at this center as that which is the love of life, the expression of the desire to be, to move, to breathe, to do.

Moving to that center of interpersonal relationship next, that of the orange ray, where you put yourself in balanced relationship with one other being at a time, so that there is the one-to-one exchange of energies.

Moving therefrom to the yellow-ray center where you are in relationship with many others, with groups of beings with whom you share interest, energy and activity.

Moving from this center to that of the heart, the green ray where your love of others extends beyond any group that you may have association with to all entities simply because they exist.

Moving from this center to that of the throat and the blue ray of communication, where the love that you feel for all creation is expressed in a means of communication that is freely given, and which speaks in inspirational tones to those about you as a result of your feeling of the love of the green-ray center.

The indigo-ray center being that of the brow, where there is the work in consciousness that each seeker achieves when it begins to use the force of its will and faith to move its attitudes and perceptions into alignment with the ideals that are its guiding star.

Therefrom moving to the violet-ray center where the totality of the being is expressed as a measure, a mark, or a register of the entity. By utilizing this desire to serve others in balancing and harmonizing each center of energy, you have cleared this path for the flow of the love and light, or the prana of the one Creator to move cleanly through your centers of energy, in order that you may be a smoothly functioning reflector and creator of the love and light of the one Creator.

Is there a further query?

Questioner: *(Inaudible)*.

I am Q'uo, and we thank you, my sister. Is there another query?

Questioner: I have one, but it might be a question that needs its own time, and that is that the times that I get maddest at myself, the times that I get the most aggravated and judge myself the most harshly, are times when I'm repeating errors. Not only do I see the error that I've made, but I think to myself, "Again? You know that you're not supposed to be doing this, you know that that's self-destructive and self-defeating and you're doing it again." I see the pattern, yet I don't change the pattern. We have this phrase "Forgive and forget." Does the Creator forgive and forget both? Is there some way we can not only forgive ourselves, but forget the pattern? Could you comment at all?

I am Q'uo, and am aware of your query, my sister. This is a query to which a great deal of information could be given as a subject of its own, or a query to which a brief response may be given as food for further thought. As we are aware that you have exercised a great deal of patience as a group this afternoon as you listen to that which is a significantly lengthy discourse, we shall give that briefer query to suffice for the nonce.

As you see yourself repeating those patterns of behavior which you have designated as non-desirable, or as those which you wish to change into a more harmonious configuration within your being, you may take note within that portion of yourself that sees and observes all your behaviors that there is once again an opportunity to refine that which you feel you have learned. For as the dancer moves through each part of the choreography attempting to reproduce each step as it has been designed, there is the need to repeat this dance a great number of times, so that there is no need for thought when the time to perform the dance arrives. There is the need to put these steps into the, as you may call it, body memory, so that there is the automatic moving through each portion of the dance without thought. When you see yourself repeating behavior patterns that you wish to change, notice that there is the chance now to express the pattern in a new fashion, beginning at the moment of notice, so that you have in effect a biofeedback device before you, noticed by your observer, commented upon and altered accordingly.

There is a great deal of work in the metaphysical sense that is necessary in the changing or transforming of any perception or behavior so that it becomes automatic within your being, so that it becomes seated at the deepest portion of your being, and available for future reference. Do not be discouraged when you see the need for further repetition, for this repetition makes the groove, shall we say, somewhat more deeply etched and engraved in a manner whereby you shall have it as a resource to call upon.

Is there a further query, my sister?

Questioner: No, thank you very much, it was wonderful to hear.

I am Q'uo, and we thank you, my sister. Is there another query at this time?

Questioner: Yes, if I may follow up on that just a little bit. Sometimes one finds within oneself, in addition to a weakness, perhaps, that causes one to repeat a behavior that is not desired, something amounting even to a resistance or defiance almost. When one finds this within oneself, is the same course of action recommended, or is there another possibility in dealing with this kind of *(inaudible)*?

I am Q'uo, and am aware of your query, my brother. Each of you has a number of aspects to your being. Perhaps it could be described as portions of personality that have been gathered about you from different times, during this incarnation especially, and perhaps previous ones as well. You look at these facets of your being if you look with the broad view, as the parent looks at the child or the children that are in its care. At some portion of your life experience there has been that imprinting of experience which has caused whatever kind of resistance you feel, whether it be the stubbornness to accomplish the task, the anger at being forced, the sadness at the not understanding, or whatever the resistance might be, there is that imprint which carries a charge, a power, shall we say, within your being.

When you find it, it is well to look at that portion of yourself that is as the child that has been somewhat damaged by an experience and needs a certain understanding from the parent at this time. It is well, then, to look at this child in the meditative state so that you may see where this child was born, shall we say, and how the birth occurred, looking at those events that formed this response in this child. Perhaps there will be the need to look into the subconscious through dreams, through hypnosis, or through your deeper meditations to discover these experiences.

It is well, however, to follow whatever memory you have of these experiences as fully as possible in order to achieve the understanding of how this resistance and this child came to be. When this understanding has been achieved, then you may look with a clearer and more compassionate eye at this portion of yourself as you seek to learn, relearn, balance or harmonize certain behaviors or thoughts that you are working upon as a portion of your journey of seeking.

Is there a further query, my brother?

Questioner: No, thank you very much, that's very helpful.

I am Q'uo, and we thank you, my brother. Is there another query at this time?

(Pause)

I am Q'uo, and we feel that we have exhausted both the queries and this group's attention for this circle of seeking this afternoon. We are most grateful to each for the invitation to join your circle, and we thank each for this great opportunity to walk with you upon your journeys and to speak that which is our opinion, hoping that in some fashion we might be able to serve you by sharing that which is our opinion. Since we do share opinion, we wish to reiterate that we do not wish to place a stumbling block before any seeker. If any word we have spoken does not ring of truth to you, leave that word behind quickly, saving only those that ring of your truth. We are known to you as those of Q'uo, and we shall take our leave of this instrument and this group at this time, leaving each, as always, in the love and in the ineffable light of the one infinite Creator. Adonai, my friends. Adonai. ✻

L/L Research

L/L Research is a subsidiary of Rock Creek Research & Development Laboratories, Inc.

P.O. Box 5195
Louisville, KY 40255-0195

www.llresearch.org

Rock Creek is a non-profit corporation dedicated to discovering and sharing information which may aid in the spiritual evolution of humankind.

ABOUT THE CONTENTS OF THIS TRANSCRIPT: This telepathic channeling has been taken from transcriptions of the weekly study and meditation meetings of the Rock Creek Research & Development Laboratories and L/L Research. It is offered in the hope that it may be useful to you. As the Confederation entities always make a point of saying, please use your discrimination and judgment in assessing this material. If something rings true to you, fine. If something does not resonate, please leave it behind, for neither we nor those of the Confederation would wish to be a stumbling block for any.

CAVEAT: This transcript is being published by L/L Research in a not yet final form. It has, however, been edited and any obvious errors have been corrected. When it is in a final form, this caveat will be removed.

© 2009 L/L Research

Sunday Meditation
July 12, 1992

Group question: The question this afternoon deals with the concept of change and transformation, and the confusion, the anger, the frustration that comes when we don't feel that we're changing in the way that we wish to change. Most students of their own evolution look at their lives, and, at some time, attempt to match the life with the ideals that they hold, and feel that there are certain things that they can do. But most of us look at our attempts to change and feel that we are inadequate in our change and that we are perhaps not even moving in the right direction. And as we begin to change and have this confusion and anger, we become further befuddled when we don't move as we wish.

It seems to be a self-perpetuating cycle, and we're wondering if there's a way that we can make the process of change one more easily accomplished; or is there some necessity for change, in order for it to be seated in our being, to become a tumultuous sort of experience? Are we supposed to be in turmoil? Is there some benefit that we can gain from being in turmoil? Is there some way to deal with the turmoil that is erroneous? Can we communicate with our higher selves through dreams? Can we do exercises? Can we watch our diet? Can we meditate more? What can we do that will make our perception of our change more balanced and harmonious? How can we accomplish change in the most efficient manner as seekers of truth?

(Carla channeling)

We are those of Q'uo. Greetings and blessings to each in the love and in the light of the one infinite Creator. We wish you the peace of heart and mind that seekers have, yet often know not that they have, and would offer our thoughts in reaction to your query upon the ways of dealing with confusion when the changes in life feel as though they were coming too quickly to understand or guide. As we offer our thoughts, we remind each that our opinions are fallible, and, if any thought disturbs any of you or feels misplaced, simply to omit it from your memory, as we would not offer even more confusion of an unhelpful kind.

We imply that change can be helpful, confusion can be helpful, and do so on purpose. There is a difference between discomfort and injury. The confusion of incarnate life, in general, is massive, and was meant to be so in order to challenge and successfully baffle the intellectual mind, which thinks in black and white, yes and no. The point of this baffling effect is to coax the seeker into opening the heart to the processes of thinking, evaluating and decision-making. Those with unawakened hearts may reason perfectly, yet come to inappropriate or inefficient decisions and conclusions relative to their own deeper desires. The spiritual journey is many things, but is not linear or logical.

Earlier this day, this instrument was thinking of a story within its holy work. It is an apt tale to share at this time. It concerns a traveler who was robbed, beaten and left upon the road. He was passed by a very well-placed gentleman who had an appointment. The man left the traveler on the road, as did another wealthy man. But there was a stranger who found the man, and although he was not from this particular region, the stranger took up the robbed and beaten man, carried him to a place of safety and succor, and made sure the beaten traveler had what he needed to recover.

In the context of the Holy Bible's story, this was an answer to a question concerning who one's neighbor is. The answer indicated that all were neighbors, not simply those clustered geographically around one. In the context of the query concerning confusion in a time of change, the story may be seen to be an inward representation of a frequent circumstance which occurs when the seeker attempts to monitor, review, analyze and interrupt the process of change in order to make it more like the picture the seeker has in the mind.

When a seeker becomes an actor—not only of desire, but of grasping the life as it is being lived, and attempting to help the process of change along—the seeker is standing athwart what may loosely be called "desire-driven destiny." The resulting cross tides of confusion are a mechanically-created artifact of this stance. Yet, each seeker wishes to so live the life and so cleanly make each choice that it is in charge of the life experience and gives it up to the infinite One as a beautiful gift.

Of course, seekers wish to help along the process of transformation. But if the seeker can pull the point of view back far enough to gaze upon the conscious self living through the confusion of change, which has been put in motion because of purified desire, this seeker may see that once the desire is honed and tempered then there comes the time of faithful patience. The intellectual mind may rush ahead and seem to predict accurately outcomes which are not actual outcomes, thus creating confusion on top of the necessary initial confusion which accompanies any change.

How much better to respect the work in consciousness which has been done, and then to see the self as the first neighbor, the nearest one to the observing portion of the self. The conscious seeker moving through the frustration, pain and anger of not yet understood changes is a weary, broken, tired and needy traveler. Yet, there is a portion of the self which may remember to forget the rush towards the next appointment, to let go of the control of happenstance, because there is a neighbor, a self—which happens to be the self, rather than an other—which needs aid and comfort in his travail.

The seeker is so eager to go through the process of transformation, yet, it is a long, subtle process. The implications of any one decision seem, on the surface, limited; but, when one is transforming the being, the seemingly limited ripples of effect give way to a much more complex field of interwoven options or varieties of tone and color in the, may we call it, "sub-programs" within the mind, which are in fact effected by seemingly simple changes in the way of being.

To change an action is relatively simple in its effect upon the essential core meta-program of beingness. It often does not touch any deep programming to change a behavior. But you are asking about changing a beingness, changing the way of perceiving and experiencing one's own essence and this is endlessly subtle work.

You can, and may well, take the uncomfortable self and visualize the giving of healing and love to this self. You would do just such for another. You also may do this for the self. When the self is somewhat comforted, the gaze again may be turned to the observation and watching of the working out of the destiny requested by the purified desire already spent. Faithfully and trustingly place the deeper observational self, with eyes clear and alert, at the right hand of all that occurs; but ask for the patience and the faith to remain an observer while a process seems to be working itself out.

All your work as an entity of spirit is groundwork laid in before confusion overtakes one. Once the cloud of confusion is there, the realization simply may be maintained and remembered that this was asked for, this is occurring, and this is a time-bound phenomenon. In this way, you are able to affirm your own desires, to comfort your own discomfort, and to position the heart open and lovingly addressing the confusion in tones of faith in the process and trust in the kindly nature of the Creator, which allowed you as co-creator to create this vortex of transformation and to go through it, powered by desire.

You ask, "What can be done to aid the process of change, to ameliorate the discomfort of the confusion?" Firstly, we do not recommend attempts to become comfortable. If change is comfortable, it is likely not to be effectual. One wishing change is dealing with power which is moving in one direction. This power and all its ramifications are being asked to alter their vectors. In any study of movement of things with weight, one can see clearly the mechanics of turning to be those of the braking, the balancing, the changes in the steering, and so forth. A good deal of dynamic work is done when there is momentum to overcome and a new direction to be taken and then to be accelerated in the new direction.

So, too, when doing work in consciousness, you have a certain amount of spiritual mass which has a certain amount of momentum. When change is desired, prayed and asked for, visualized and preparations made, then there is a very graceful moment available when the realization may come that the spiritual visualization preceding change has been completed, and now the spirit, along with the conscious self in incarnation, must hang on for a bumpy ride, for there will be the braking to overcome momentum, the proper shift in direction which takes several adjustments, and then the process of gradual addition of power to the direction so that the pace is accelerated once again. The one who attempts to wrest change too quickly is doing work against the self and subverting his own spiritual, purified desires.

The various helps mentioned as possibilities—such as working with dreams, changes in diet, and so forth—are valuable individually insofar as they offer to a seeker a comfort. What is most uncomfortable about confusion? It is the disorder. It is the feeling that one is out of control. Those who seek tend to see this feeling, which is natural, and say "I should not be feeling off-balanced; I should be clear." But "should" is not an helpful word. The way one should be is the way one is. We do not mean to split hairs, but to take one word out of the language would be perhaps rewarding to those moving through change, and this word is "should." The heart has a wisdom concerning time which the mind lacks. Thusly, it is well to let the heart choose what form of comfort it may appropriately and skillfully take to bolster the endurance while going through transformation.

Such things as the cleansing of the diet may well give one a feeling of more control. The keeping of the dream notebook is a way of glimpsing the material which the deeper mind is discovering, recovering and restructuring, and this may give one a deeper sense of some control in understanding the process. But, intrinsic to the process are two things: the willingness to endure through discomfort, and the faith that invokes unlimited patience, for the time of change is, in spiritual terms, timeless. Yet, that instant which in time/space exists for so long, being fully potentiated to come into manifestation in space/time, occupies a variable amount of space/time in the experience of one in incarnation. Thusly, there is not a standard waiting period, and patience needs to be given without limit.

One thing we do recommend for all who experience confusion is a very well-encouraged sense of humor. The most helpful point of view for a changing spiritual seeker is light-hearted irreverence. Play with that which is occurring. Be playful. Allow the vision to relax, the eyesight to become less than entirely single-mindedly keen when the pressure mounts and the anxiety builds, when frustration and anger begin to accumulate. Lighten your own load with laughter. And if you can laugh with another, the strength of this joy is doubled. Part of the service spiritual seekers may be to each other is to exhort and encourage each other to take it easier with the situation and the self.

Many are the times when a serious seeker feels very inadequate to that which he wishes to accomplish. The earnestness begins to become more tight and urgent. The seriousness is taken further and further until this *beau geste* consumes one. To a point, this intensity is helpful. Beyond that point, it always needs to be remembered that the most serious things in a life experience are made more clear and understandable by the enhancement of turning the spotlight off the seriousness of the situation and onto the beauty, the praiseworthy beauty, of the overall plan.

When one may praise the plan and give thanks for going through the necessary confusion, one is then taking very seriously and single-mindedly the transformation itself, but has let up the pressure on the self to do "such and such" or not do "such and such" in conjunction with this transformation. To take the principles, the ideals, seriously is excellent; to take the self seriously is folly. Let the self be human. Laugh at this humanity. Love it and see that it is perfectly normal to fear that which is painful.

In this group there is not the holding of the fear to the self, for which we would need to request correction; there is only the judgment of the self by the self as the self sees that it has fear. May we say that, in our opinion, fear is a normal and healthy reaction to pain. When you were small you recoiled from the touch to the oven. This was wise. Now you put yourself to more subtle testing of the boundaries and nature of your journey. You will frequently touch something very "hot" and have the healthy fear which allows you to recoil and remove the self from spiritual or mental pain. Allow yourself to move naturally and vulnerably through the unknown. Accept and love the fear, the frustration, the anger. Note them. Honor them. Comfort the self experiencing them, but do not deny them their appropriateness.

Why should you not feel the difficult process happening? Why should the changes not cause many bumps, stops and starts, and discomforts, which express themselves in manifestations of fear, anger and frustration? When the unknown has been penetrated by desire, the new country cannot even be seen. A transforming individual is mapping for the first of many times the new and changing territory of its road. The way is mazed and muddled, and, in many ways, the sensing self is blinded by so much incoming data concerning a novel situation. The computer mind of the physical body gives many, many alarms when receiving this kind of data from the meta-program. The resulting fear, anger or frustration is completely understandable and acceptable, at least to us.

We hope we have enabled you to have compassion upon yourselves. You have asked a question which can only be asked by those who are consciously working within themselves and who have accomplished to have purified the desire and begun to co-create a life in faith. We speak to experienced wayfarers and we say to you: When did you expect to be perfect, comfortable or settled if you wish to be a pilgrim on this particular road to infinity? You know well you expected none of those things. Comfort yourself, therefore, through the frustration. Love yourself through the anger. And cherish yourself through the depression and the grieving at the loss of the old, familiar ways. Above all, release the spirit pilgrim from the strictures of perceived time and know with every fiber of the being that the Creator's time will become your time at the absolute moment of manifestation of transformation. Watch, wait, pray, praise and give thanks. Always give thanks. And this thanks and praise will inform to a great degree the attitude that must lighten up the load of negative emotion.

We cheer you on in your desires and we are sympathetic with the painfulness of transformation, but we realize you wish to know not only comfortable words, but uncomfortable ones, if we feel them to be true. We do feel that it is just to experience negative emotions in an illusion which seems chaotic. We exhort you to lean on praise and thanksgiving, and then, filled with this buoyancy of spirit, gaze again and again with compassion on the weary, weary traveler that is your outer conscious self.

We apologize for taking this much time with this query, but we felt that there was no quicker way to express what are a fairly complex and subtle series of points which attempt to ground you in a new way of perceiving the spirit self in transformation. We would, at this time, thank this instrument and transfer from it that the one known as Jim may conclude the session. We leave this instrument in love and in light. We are those of Q'uo.

(Jim channeling)

I am Q'uo, and greet each again in love and in light through this instrument. It is our privilege at this time to offer ourselves in the capacity of attempting to speak to any further queries. Is there a query at this time with which we may begin?

Questioner: When one is cycling in the negativity, understanding that there may be a judgment of self occurring, a lot of times that manifests in the physical. One can feel it through tension headaches or through difficulty with stomach or intestines. It will affect you in the body in some manner. There's concern as to whether that negativity that is festering … obviously it's turning into internal damage in the physical body.

How do you define the difference between healthy negativism and negativism that actually goes deeper, and, in effect, ends up being destructive to that self who, in essence, is only trying to heal the self? It seems to be a paradox. Are there ways in which you can either attempt, through that period of negativity when you don't seem to be able to get to your higher self and understand the higher concepts … is there some other way or other methods that you can work towards healing the physical aspect of what you're feeling and what you're doing to yourself in terms of being able to block that from happening so that you don't further self-destruct with the negative patterns while you are attempting to heal yourself of being negative?

I am Q'uo, and am aware of your query, my sister. The overriding concept, in our opinion, as regards this query is the feeling that is at the heart of the entity as it is attempting to move itself into a new pattern of being, perceiving and doing. There is that fear of not living up to the ideals that is a kind of angst, which we have suggested may be utilized by the seeker in a manner which will have the overall effect of enhancing the transformation. This is that small, quivering fear that remains at the corner of the mind reminding one that there is the need to give the best effort at each moment. This kind of fear we find to be not deleterious in the usual sense, but that which spurs the entity on to its best effort.

The kind of negativity that takes center place upon the inner stage of being and thinking, and tends to cause a gathering about it of further fear, is the fear which begins to rot, shall we say, various connective points within the mind/body/spirit complex, and eventually causes physical degeneration of those organs connected to the emotional bodies, as you have been studying them. This kind of fear is that which is indulged in by those who have either little reign upon their inner doubt or who have a tendency from time to time to indulge in self-destructive, as you would call them, behaviors and thoughts, tempting the good intentions of the entity itself, so that the entity becomes divided within itself as to how it shall expend its energies, attempting for a good portion of time to affect those positive changes in which it has invested its ideals and its concept of self, and, at the same time, seeking to undermine those ideals and the effort to match the life pattern with them.

This darker side of fear is that kind of fear which has given a certain sort of pleasure to the entity in its previous experiences, a kind of punishment of the self which the entity has seen as necessary according to those experiences with the parental and other authority figures within the early life experience, so that the entity does, then, when there is the challenge that presents itself in the form of transformation and change, is to behave in a split fashion, so that one portion of the self exhorts the self to move to those high ideals, and the other portion of the self, for a variety of potential reasons, assumes the punishing parental figure and punishes the self with the kind of fear that not only undermines the desire and effect of the change, but also can cause the physical disease as well.

For this kind of fear, and any other behavior or thought that moves one into the areas of disharmony and imbalance, we recommend the daily meditation and use of the balancing exercises which each in this group has utilized for some portion of time in the past. This looking at the inventory of mental and emotional experiences for each day can find the roots of such fear and remove them by balancing them with their polar opposite in the manner which those of Ra gave as the balancing exercises. We recommend the daily review in the meditative state of all thoughts and behaviors that have passed through one's being, as the water moves through the river channel, so that disharmonies may be detected as early as possible and balanced in a manner which makes more whole the entire range of experience of the seeker.

Is there a further query, my sister?

Questioner: I think I understand what you're saying, and the split I well understand. The only other question I have, I guess, are fears that I seem to have and confusion in reference to being able to identify them. I will certainly attempt to do so during my meditations. The only other concern I have is, are some of these fears so deep-rooted that I may not be able to consciously find them in my day-to-day experience? Are they things that will come up in the future as I do these practices? Or are there certain fears that are innate and part of the incarnational experience that will eventually cause this continued split? Is there a way to mend the split in this particular incarnation or is this going to be part of the learning lesson that I must experience? And are some of the negatives that I seem to be experiencing—are they "old" negatives that I seem to be harboring or are they just a continued perpetuation of a lot of little things that seem to add up and turn into a pattern, that seem to coagulate into this big huge pattern that then seems to self-perpetuate itself?

I am Q'uo, and am aware of you query, my sister. Within each entity there are fears, not because there is the necessity for fear to be a fundamental portion of this illusion or any incarnation, but because that which is mysterious, hidden within the depths of the self, unknown and which has obvious effects upon the conscious seeker, is that which poses the potential threat.

The seeker which moves upon the journey of illumination and which moves into the depths of the self is well advised to look at the overall perspective of each incarnation, and the creation as a whole, as that which is made of love. Any deviation from that love is, in some form, a distortion of love which may be discovered by the persistent application of daily meditation and the review of the experiences of each day's round of activities. There is no fear buried so deeply that the love-inspired seeker of truth cannot uncover and balance this fear with love.

We do not mean to seem to be naive in this regard, for our recommendation in many instances where seekers feel confusion and fear is to focus upon the fundamental quality of love. We continue to recommend this focusing upon love as the foundation stone of all creation and all incarnation, not only because this is so as we have experienced it, but because it is well for each seeker to look for that love within the life pattern in order that the desire to see and to seek this love may perform its part in attracting this love to the seeker. For it is a metaphysical principle that you shall find that which you seek. We recommend, therefore, that as you plumb those depths of mystery within that you remind yourself that you move within a creation of love, a creation which is in harmony with itself and with you.

These fears that motivate from the depths of one's being have power only because they are distortions of the power of love. When you are able to untangle the distortion of love, then you shall see how this distortion was first caused. The cause is almost always within the early portion of this life experience in accordance with choices that were made before this life experience regarding that which one wished to learn.

Is there a further query, my sister?

Questioner: Not at this time. Thanks.

I am Q'uo, and we thank you, my sister. Is there another query at this time?

Carla: I have an observation and a query. Being the channel, I couldn't really catch everything, but it seems to me that in describing the way you go about getting through transformation it's a lot like the way you go about channeling, in that all of the work that a channel does is done before the channeling ever begins, and it has to do with cleansing the self of human opinion and world opinion and just the junk of everyday thinking, and trying to tune oneself to the highest and best in one, but then also to ask for the highest and best that one can carry in a stable manner. And when you were talking about change it seemed to me you were saying that the work that you do is done before the change really begins—it's when you desire to change something about yourself and that desire is purified to the point where it actually starts a change occurring. And, at that point, your work is over and what you need to do is, in the midst of your desire, to say that you want to approximate your ideals—the highest and best that you're capable of—and the change that you're capable of in a stable manner. Is this a just observation and is this a valid point?

I am Q'uo, and am aware of your query, my sister, and we can agree wholeheartedly that you have made a point that is quite valid. For each seeker of truth is a channel for the life experience, and when one finds oneself in the midst of change or transformation, this experience is the result of much desire previous to the beginning of the change, for first must come the recognition of oneself as one is at a particular moment. Then there comes, or perhaps does not come, the desire for change in a certain area of the life experience. Only after these recognitions have been achieved is the seeker able to undertake any portion of the change, which then may be manifested to the eye, the ear, or the emotions of the seeker undergoing the change.

By the time the changing and the frustration that comes with change is noticed, most of the work of the seeker has been accomplished as regards setting the change in motion. The work that remains for such a seeker, noticing the change within its being and experience, is the work of moving in harmony with the change. For this reason, we recommended the lighthearted approach which tends to see that all is well, that discomforts can be humorous and certainly can be survived, and can be survived most efficiently when there is this lighthearted approach.

Is there a further query, my sister?

Carla: No, Q'uo. Thank you very much.

I am Q'uo, and again we thank you, my sister. And, as we appear to have exhausted the queries for this session of working, we shall take this opportunity to thank each seeker present for inviting our presence into your meditation and circle of working this day. We are very happy to be invited and privileged to partake in your seeking. We offer our words and opinions freely, with the only admonition being that you take those which ring of truth to you and leave behind those that do not. Again, our great gratitude for your desire to seek and for your invitation to us that we might seek with you.

D: Wait! Before you go, can I ask another question?

I am Q'uo, and we are happy to entertain another query from the one known as D.

D: Okay, great. We were discussing earlier about tones and things that we receive here, and I guess as we become more aware, at least in my own experience, I've become more aware of certain things that would not seem to be the norm to most people. The discordant tones that I heard in one particular instance—which were all very loud and buzzing in my ears—I wanted to know why that occurred? What was happening when that did occur? What happens on other occasions when just one single tone occurs? Does this have something to do with discord always, or are there various reasons for these particular things?

And the other thing that I've been lately experiencing which was the freeze-frames of patterns which I see, which have only happened in the last couple of months. Is that just another awareness happening? They're interesting when they happen. They seem to crop up more and more as I become more aware, and I was wondering if you could define these? And, if there are reasons for the discordant tones, is there any way that I could work with them when they do occur so that I can either rebalance myself when it occurs, or is there another reason that it occurs?

I am Q'uo, and am aware of your query, my sister. To begin, we must speak carefully in these queries, for we do not wish to infringe upon your own free will discovery of the symbols which your subconscious mind provides to your conscious mind as a means of focusing the attention. Those tones which sound disharmony are often utilized to signify just this. Look at that experience which was most important and which preceded such tones in your previous experience and correlate those experiences with these tones. As the number of tones of disharmony increase, look at this symbol of increased disharmony.

The query concerning the freeze-frames is one which we must be most careful with, for this means of communication from the subconscious mind is one which is more specific in its indication of the need for attention. Look at the frames. Meditate upon the images. Make the correlations which appear within your inner view as you meditate upon the images.

Was there a further query, my sister?

D: Just in reference to the freeze-frames. Right now, at this time, they appear to be so fast I can't grasp them, perhaps because it is just meant to be an attention-getter, seeing as my attention is not always there in meditation. Should I focus on attempting to draw them out so I can recognize those as patterns, or is it just occurring because my attention span is not where it should be when I am meditating? It's not just when I'm meditating though, it happens all the time now. So, when I close my eyes, and whether I eat or go into prayer or just attempt to close my eyes for a few minutes, they occur. And they occur quite frequently, so I take it as some kind of signal that I should be doing something, but I can't seem to grasp it. And I can't seem to grasp the patterns because they are so instantaneous. They're almost quicker than a second. I'm just not sure as to how I can do as you said and take those frames and meditate upon them, when I can't even seem to catch them.

I am Q'uo, and am aware of your query, my sister. To meditate upon that which moves quickly before the inner eye is perhaps to move into a different kind of meditation. That is to say, that as the images move quickly, rather than attempting to stop the movement and capture an image, it would be helpful to feel the feeling tone that such rapid moving images leave as their residue. Perhaps an image will remain with a feeling tone. Perhaps just a feeling. Perhaps just an image. Perhaps a series of images.

Whatever is the residue, the charge, the power of the experience, then, take that residue and meditate upon it and make whatever correlations present themselves.

In this way, we feel that you may begin to follow a trail, shall we say, which is being left for you by your subconscious mind which has been alerted by the conscious mind, through your intensity and desire of seeking, that information is desired in regards to a certain kind of level of seeking. This trail is that which is of importance. Follow the trail to the best of your abilities, realizing that the methods used are those to which you are the most susceptible or most able to glean information from.

Is there a further query, my sister?

D: The only other query I had was in reference to the dreams. You had mentioned earlier that we were a series of complex illusions of dreams within dreams. In reference to the [framework] of information between my self and my higher self, how can I go about deciphering what seems nonsensical dreams? I find patterns that I begin to recognize. Carla has been a great help in reference to helping me to decipher some of these. But is there a better way, is there some kind of thing, seeing as I have a tendency to work in the dream field … It's very natural to concentrate on something before I go to sleep so that I may be able to attain the highest clarity of connection between myself and my higher self, so that I can begin to also work in conjunction with meditation and prayer. When I do this, is there a method of visualization or something that I can do just prior to sleeping—while just on the verge of going to sleep—so that I can mentally attune myself to receiving the highest or the best work, for either that particular day or for the particular situation that I'm in where I need help?

I am Q'uo, and am aware of you query, my sister. We feel that you have well prepared yourself for the work with dreams, and can only suggest that you provide yourself with the tools for recording your dreams as soon as you have experienced the dreams as is possible. The repeating and reminding to the self that you wish to remember the dreams is most important. And the preparation for the dreaming by mental contemplation upon the topic of most concern is also recommended so that the brain will have access to as much information as is possible to feed into the dreaming process. This is helpful as a preparation at all times.

Is there another query, my sister?

D: Yes. I've experienced, in the past, hearing telepathic messages through my dreams from what seems to be various different entities when I've asked certain questions. One of the reasons I've refrained from doing this for the last year was the caution involved. But there were times when I telepathically received things. Was that coming from my higher self? Was that coming from guides? And should I continue to attempt to work with those who have obviously worked with me in the past through dreams, or should I really within the next year continue as I have been doing, working directly with the higher self and from the higher self into God?

I am Q'uo, and am aware of your query, my sister. We must apologize for being unwilling to give advice in this regard, for it is in the area that is of most importance in the exercise of your own choice-making ability to determine those practices which are more helpful than are others in your seeking. Thus, we leave these choices to you, reminding you that you are aware that your higher self portion does indeed communicate with you in your dream state.

Is there another query, my sister?

D: No, but thank you very much for all the information.

I am Q'uo, and we would ask if there are any final queries at this time.

(Pause)

I am Q'uo, and once again we shall thank each entity for the honor of spending time and opinion and inspiration with you. We are inspired by you as much as we hope that you are inspired by us, for you seek within the illusion of the third density, where so much of the Creator must be sought in darkness and in mystery. Brave and courageous souls are you who so seek …

(Tape ends.)

Sunday Meditation
July 19, 1992

Group question: The question this afternoon has to do with how we accept those retrograde moments when the world around us does not seem to respond in a way in which we would either want it to or expect it to—whether it is a desire we have to control a situation and make it come out the way we think would be favorable; or relate to another person in a way we think is most harmonious, and yet the person or the situation does not seem to allow us to do that; or when we wish to live according to our highest ideals but find ourselves falling short, and we tend to make ourselves feel guilty because we have not done that which we feel is within our capability to do. How do we deal with our own feelings of falling short, how do we accept the moments when we are in the midst of anguish, and what is the most effective way of handling these moments where we find disharmony within ourselves or another and we feel that we have been responsible for that.

(Carla channeling)

I am Q'uo. Greetings to each of you in the love and in the light of the one infinite Creator. We are gratified to be called to this session of working and especially greet the one known as C and the one known as J, who have not been with this group for some of your time. We are honored to offer our humble opinions on the topic of some of the balancing of relationships appropriate to those seeking polarity in service to others, and ask only that you be aware that our opinions are prone to distortions, as are all opinions. We therefore ask each to use the inner discrimination in evaluating our suggestions and thoughts; we would prefer you to forget that which we said rather than attempt to accept an opinion of ours that did not feel right for you personally, for you and you alone recognize your own truth and we would not put a stumbling block before any.

We shall begin the consideration of the balanced and non-controlling handling or treatment of seemingly disharmonious situations with some suggestions for consideration. We suggest that you retreat in mode of thought from the conscious self that sits in this circle, retreat until you have gained a stance outside of your circumstances, outside of your personal conditions in life, and gaze at the phenomenal illusion which you incarnated to enjoy and are enjoying. See that distance between that which phenomenally occurs and the way you construe in thought formations those many things which have risen in the phenomenal world. There is, shall we say, a world of difference between the two. We suggest that in your considerations and from this stance of increased objectivity you look at the long process that is long in description though seemingly very, very quick in your time, that proceeds from the original sensations by the physical body and its senses of the phenomena that are arising and the thought formation.

Many, many things arise in each moment. Feel with your senses now the sense of touch responding to the slight breeze of the fan, the pressure of gravity upon you as you sit in meditation, the comfort and discomfort of the position held. Listen, there are vehicles moving at a distance from this dwelling, there is the drone of the fan, the calling of a bird and so many other small sounds, even those within your own body. Follow this thought through the senses not covered by sight, through the sense of smell, the sense of taste. All of these sense impressions are thrown at you moment by moment, millions and millions of bits of information, ninety-nine percent of which you automatically tune out because they do not impinge upon your needs for survival, for comfort, for courtesy, or for those other qualities that you have prioritized in your own programs of what you will pay attention to.

We suggest that each thought that is formed within you is in actuality the result of many, many calculations based upon sense impressions largely ignored, the one percent of sense impressions remaining being distorted by the somewhat biased attitude of each seeker, including yourself, towards the issues of survival, personal comfort, and so forth. When put in this way it may not seem outrageous for us to say that in a very substantial way your thought formations are not experience but recent memory, not that which is occurring but the carefully worked out summary and recapitulation of that which has occurred.

As each knows, when four people witness a traumatic event there will be four different versions of what occurred. They will agree on some points and disagree on others. Those instances wherein there is disharmony between people, part of the disharmony lies in the basic distance between the arising and dissolving of phenomena and the arising and dissolving of thought formation. That which you sense is not that which you live. In some we are suggesting the consideration that life and the experience of living is a story which you tell to yourself. Even in the most clear minded, quiet and objective individual this will hold true to some extent, therefore, that feeling of absolute surety that is the basis of righteous indignation and certainty of various kinds is, though useful and sometimes needed, also less than completely accurate, for if life is a story told to the self then there is the haunting knowledge that all thought formations coming into your mind are already biased.

When two biased entities interact, a portion of any seeming harmony or disharmony will be what you might call real, and what we would call less of an illusion. Then the portion that is already distorted, which we might call an illusion within an illusion—or less real, thusly—if there is the need to deal with disharmony it softens the heart and makes more fertile the ground for harmony to move in realization that in the simplest illusion things are simply arising and dissolving and that you have got a portion of what is arising and are dealing with it as it dissolves. But you are not getting the whole picture, you are not responsible for getting a whole picture; you are not getting it entirely accurate, nor are you responsible for such.

In this way you may already take a short moment to smile at your predicament, for you don't have all the facts, you are not hearing anyone else's sum total of all his facts. There is no possibility of perfect communication because there is no possibility of perfect realization within the illusion. There are those who seek perfect realization, but within the illusion we have the opinion that the purpose of the illusion is to present you with difficulties and frustrations in order that you may test the wings of your love and desire to serve, and test also the structure of your belief system of ethics, how you put into action the tools and resources you have gathered about you as ideals, ethical points of view, and tenets of faith.

Now, when one is asked to accept the self or another self there is fundamentally, precisely the same difficulty, but because of the self-consciousness so important to your learning experiences within third density the work done in regard to the self and in regard to the other self will differ somewhat. When working with acceptance of the self there is the push towards a complete self-honesty. This is not so difficult for the spiritual seeker to accomplish. Then there is the desire for acceptance of and desire for the self. This is very difficult for all entities in third density to achieve. The ability to accept the self is hindered by the feeling that since the thoughts of the self are ever imperfect it seems reasonable not to accept the self totally but to continue to judge the self.

In your density you are not privy to the private thoughts of other selves. You may think that other selves have more pristine thought processes. This assumption is likely to be false, yet you are able to forgive and accept other selves a hundred times more easily that you are able to accept the self. We say to you that you do not need to accept the self all at once. Since you are home to yourself at all times you have a long relationship with your own student persona. Trust in that relationship, and be to yourself as the excellent teacher, one who encourages the student, one who accepts the student's errors, pointing them out and then giving another quiz or test which the student now may pass with honors, having learned the facts as opposed to erroneous and mistaken facts of a given situation.

Lean into the persona of the nurturing teacher to the self, the nurturing parent, the nurturing authority, and in the end, the nurturing Creator, and realize that you have no need to consign yourself to some perdition because of errors. The moment for an error comes and dissipates, and the process of healing may begin as soon as you allow yourself the charity that must needs accompany the beginning of such healing. This is important to your polarity in service to others for you have been told by the master known as Jesus to love others as you love yourself.

Learning to love the self in the midst of perceived imperfection then is, we suggest, a key to going about the steady work of one who is of service-to-others polarity.

Now, gaze at another self which has assaulted the senses with unexpected hostility or simply has presented some situation which is awkward or in which there is a high degree of possibility for miscommunication. If the life is a story, then it is well to tell the story to each other when there is the possibility for missed signals and confusing conversation. If there is an accepting ear and a willing communicator on the other side of the equation of the self and other self we suggest taking the time, and time is most valuable, to communicate in vulnerability and honesty with the other self, allowing yourself to be shiningly clear. This means not defending the position that you find yourself in but simply stating it and asking for clarification from the other self. When there is such a one there is formed at that moment a true bond. Two entities have entered into a heart-felt transaction, and that which was difficult has become clear, for there is open communication, there is an open heart, and where there are two open hearts there is always exchange of energy and the healing of breaches which were experienced.

If the entity which is the other self is not at this moment ready to communicate openly and clearly but rather continues to be accusatory or frustrating or simply puzzled in some deleterious way then the matter is imperfect yet concluded, and the rest of the work is done within the self, forgiving the self for being unable to create apparent harmony, forgiving the other self for the same, and accepting in the self the desire to control the harmony of the situation even though this control is positively intended and ends up seeming to be a negative value since control exercised without resolve is more apparent in its manipulatory aspects.

Gaze at that seeming manipulation and realize that with self-consciousness comes the manipulation of objects and of thoughts to understand, to accomplish. The manipulations are not all of the same kind nor are they to be judged the same way. Negative manipulations are carefully to be recognized, but the attempts towards harmony, if not carried beyond the first attempt, are certainly not negative, except that each entity has the responsibility to manipulate the world of illusion, to mold it in love and in light. Mistakes may seem to be made—simply keep the intention high and the efforts to understand the other self intensive and persistent.

As for the recalcitrant-seeming other self, we suggest the use of prayer; realize that one which runs from love and compassion is a sorrowing and hard-pressed entity. The root causes of this sorrow or misery are not necessarily known even to the other self, yet you may pray that light may bless this self, that love may touch the heart of this self that you have no way of understanding unless that self speaks clearly to you, yet always is there the strength of praise and thanksgiving for the opportunity to hold another in the heart and offer that held other self up to the love and the light that streams infinitely from the infinite One.

Energies in a confrontation feel like jagged lines. What one wishes to do as a positive entity is to attempt through clear communication and the right use of compassion and compassionate manipulation to cause a mutual feeling of dancing in one spiraling circle, upwards in the light. When this is not possible you simply continue this dance by yourself, swirling and dipping in the rhythms of the eternal with a keen and loving ear to the music of love and light. This way of speaking of prayer is hardly literal but this is the sort of feeling we encourage in the prayers. One does not always know for what to pray for another's needs, yet one may, when in the flow of the eternal, pray those abiding prayers of love, praise and thanks for each and every experience which has been experienced with this entity, thereby offering this entity to the Creator in order that the Creator's love and light may be felt more and more in that other self's life to the end known best by the other self and its Creator.

At this time we would transfer this contact to the one known as Jim that it may conclude this session of working. We thank this instrument and this group again, and would at this time leave this instrument in love and in light. We would transfer now. We are those of Q'uo.

(Jim channeling)

I am Q'uo, and greet each again in love and in light through this instrument. At this time it is our privilege to offer ourselves in the capacity of attempting to speak to any further queries which those present may have to offer us. Is there a query with which we may begin?

Questioner: Yes, I have a query. Is channeling—the way Carla and Jim do that here—is this something for everyone, is this the way of the future, or is this something that derives out of the desire upon the entity *(inaudible)* to do?

I am Q'uo, and we are aware of your query, my sister. Each seeker upon the path of truth seeks that which is most helpful upon the journey, and by far the great number of seekers is that kind of seeker which you would call unaware that there is a journey, and these entities utilize the daily round of activities in a sense which is less efficient, shall we say, but more filled with the mystery of the journey, and these entities utilize that which circumstance provides as they attempt to find a sense and a center to the life pattern.

Those seekers who are conscious of the journey and who place themselves there in faith and in love utilize tools, methods and teachers which are drawn to them according to the manner in which they seek, some finding great comfort in the process which you have called the channeling and which we at this time partake in. This kind of catalyst is of an unusual nature in relation to the great number of alternate …

(Side one of tape ends.)

(Jim channeling)

We are again with this instrument. We shall continue.

The unusual nature of the channeling process makes this kind of method of seeking difficult for some to utilize and makes it more attractive for others, for there is much notoriety which has been associated with this phenomenon through much of your recent past. We find as we observe those not only within this circle of seeking but the great number of conscious seekers upon your planetary sphere that the movement into the utilization of channeled information has as its natural continuation the opening of each seeker's channel for finding the personal and internal sources of information so that each seeker is more nearly an instrument of a purified and rarefied nature, which is to say that all catalyst—such as channeling, astrology, tarot, numerology and so forth—serves as an intermediary for a certain portion of time for the seeker. Thence there is the movement towards refining that channel which is ever and always available to all seekers, for each entity upon your planet channels the life, channels the responses, the activities, the words, the thoughts, and so forth. This channeling of the life then provides the basis by which each entity may refine this movement of energy and inspiration through the life pattern.

Thus, we would respond in short to your query by suggesting that channeling as a life endeavor and as a personal process is far more important than is the channeling in which we now engage, for we wish to serve as catalyst, and as each seeker channels his or her own journey there is where the treasures are truly found.

Is there a further query, my sister?

Questioner: No, thank you.

I am Q'uo, and we thank you, my sister. Is there another query?

Carla: I have one. I was surprised a little bit, even though I was the one channeling—when we talked about the question beforehand, I had thought to myself that there is probably going to be some channeling on, oh, just surrender to that which was required of one or desired of one by the infinite Creator, just a faith in that, and I was sort of surrendering to faith instead of trying to work with things, and I noticed that in talking about how to deal with this particular question there wasn't any talk of surrender. It was really pretty well focused on the ways and means that we can work within our own minds and our own parts. I wonder if you can speak to that.

I am Q'uo, and I am aware of your query, my sister. As we spoke on the query for this session of working we observed that each entity present was well aware of the value of the surrendering to the undeniable circumstance, for each has journeyed long upon the path and has felt the force and momentum of the daily round of activities, so that the need to surrender to that which seems inevitable and right is obvious to each. We wish, therefore, to build upon the concepts of action considered in the light of surrender, for all activities that you accomplish within your life pattern are of a nature where there is a necessity for interaction of some kind. The conscious seeker of truth will wish to give the effort that is of the highest quality, reflecting the essence of its deepest being and wishes, to know how to form the response that is loving, intelligent and flexible in any situation.

Thus, we spoke to activity and response as those means whereby entities may gather their resources, shall we say, and utilize them to the fullest within the boundaries of the illusion in which you move, and with the recognition that the surrendering heart and mind are the attitudinal components, shall we say, by which all such activity may be accomplished. Thus we thought to provide the paradox how one may act with the attitude of surrender.

Is there a further query, my sister?

Carla: Let me just sum up and have you say "Yes, you have an understanding" or "No, you don't." You say that it is the living of a life in faith or the attempt to live a life in faith which is continuous surrender that enables one to raise the question "How can I best find honesty and acceptance in my personal interrelationships?" Would that be a fair summary of what you just said?

I am Q'uo. Not only would we suggest that is a fair summary, but an eloquent one.

Is there a further query at this time?

Carla: No, you old charmer, thank you very much. Q'uo, it's a pleasure to talk to you.

I am Q'uo, and I thank you, my sister. Is there another query?

(Pause)

I am Q'uo, and as we assess the energies and lack of queries at this moment we feel that we have spoken for the appropriate length of your time, and we thank each entity for providing us with the desire to know that which we have to offer and with the patience to listen to what we are aware has been a somewhat lengthy discourse. We are always grateful for the opportunity to speak to this group and to any group which seeks so wholeheartedly for the love and light that will illuminate the journey yet one step further. We cannot express our gratitude enough to each present. We thank you, my brothers and sisters, and we shall take our leave of this group at this time, leaving each, as always, in love and in the light of the one infinite Creator. We are known to you as those of Q'uo. Adonai, my friends. Adonai. ❦

L/L Research

Sunday Meditation
August 16, 1992

Group question: The question this afternoon has to do with the concept of releasing our mental plans and control enough in our lives in order to either in general channel alive and be in the moment and experience the moment as fully as we can, for what it has to offer us, or in some cases to specifically be able to verbally channel from other sources, our higher selves or perhaps guides or other entities that would wish to communicate information of spiritual evolutionary value to us. What would be your recommendation as to how we can be enough in the moment to be able to do any kind of channeling that we wish whether that would be to channel alive, a relationship, a job or a message from another entity?

(Carla channeling)

Greetings, my friends. We are known to you as those of Q'uo. We greet each of you in the love and in the light of the one infinite Creator whose property is to be infinite, invisible, everlasting and intelligent. We greet you in the love and in the light of this everlasting intelligence because that is all that there is, love and manifestation. Love in a manifestation built with light. We ask you to pause momentarily as we wish to take this instrument to a deeper level, so that we may speak more clearly through this instrument. We shall pause for a moment. We are those of the principle of Q'uo.

(Pause)

I am Q'uo, and we are again with this instrument. Again, we greet you in love and in light. It is our great privilege to be called to this circle of seeking to speak upon the question you have posed. Indeed we are with your peoples for this purpose alone, and you give us the precious gift of an opportunity for us to serve and to learn. For we in our density also have lessons to learn. Ours are those of wisdom, whereas yours are those of the student learning to love and be loved. We ask you to realize firmly that we are prone to error, not great or exalted, but pilgrims upon the dusty road of spiritual seeking. You seek an accelerated pace of spiritual evolution. All beings evolve; that is their destiny. It is within each seeker's control to choose the rate of learning and the rate of changing or transforming. We happily share our thoughts with you; but use your discrimination. Any thought that you find not to be useful, we ask you to discard it. For you will not learn from us. We are only the catalyst for you to remember your personal truth. Thus, take only those thoughts of ours which you recognize and feel "Yes, I knew that, I only forgot!"

All in third density begin with a vast forgetting, then see only those things which are visible, hear only those sounds which the ear may transmit to the brain—and so forth through the senses. Your physical vehicle was designed to deal with this illusion, this grand illusion, this carnival which passes in third density for reality. However, at the very heart of all that is visible is both metaphysical and physical awareness that nothing can be truly understood on its larger terms. That is, telescopes show to the eye that which the eye cannot see, yet those scientists which use those telescopes always stress how much more there is beyond the limits of their measuring devices. Similarly, as the microscope becomes more and more powerful, it begins to see smaller and smaller particles.

The cyclotron throws the atom, seeking the sight of the first particle which has mass. Yet, we hear from these scientists that only the path of energy of these electrons can be documented. Mass itself can not. This is because all things are created by light, by the revolutions and buildings of revolutions of the unit of light, called the photon, which has never yielded any suggestion of mass—only the wave of energy. Your illusion is perfect. It offers you that which you need to act out the learning which you came to this lifetime to receive.

You are old, old souls and you have given yourself your own choices of those relationships and environments which you feel will give you the most opportunity for learning. This is done by the friction of difficulty and trouble, frustration and other seemingly negative reactions, those things which trip up the attention and move your consciousness off the balance upon which you walk, balancing the various positive and negative catalyst which you receive, so that you may work with this catalyst and at your own pace continue the evolution of spirit. The evolution of third-density physical vehicles is at its end. Further evolution is all spiritual.

It is written by one who was close to the master known as Christ through vision that you should look not at those things that are seen but at those things that are unseen. For those things which are seen are temporal, while those things which are not seen are eternal. Let us look at this thought, spoken by the one known as Paul, the Apostle. When you wish to work with spiritual evolution, you take that which is before you, say a mismatched relationship apparently or a great chasm betwixt boss and employee. There is a tendency to focus upon the physical, chronologically arranged events which have caused the disharmonious feeling of being swept off of balance, of being tumbled by [lies].

It is much more difficult to look for the heart of the dilemma. To gaze not at the topology and chronology of the disharmony but rather to penetrate the illusion to move by faith alone through the veil of forgetting. And to by faith ask for help from the world of the spiritual on the level of those things which are not seen. The workings of the heart are not seen. The self-acceptance or lack of it is not seen. The love or hunger for love in relationships is not seen. Circumstances only are seen. There is, my friends, a reason for this. The design is to so baffle, frustrate and confuse the intellect with all the data of the senses that the student will be forced to move the center of investigatory energy from the intellectual mind, which is a creature of this illusion only, to the wisdom of the deep mind, which is vastly more informed and which resides in what you would call the heart energy center. This center is the gateway center wherein, when the lower energies have been cleared, the gate becomes opened so that you can effectively focus the heart's wisdom upon the situation you wish balanced within you.

Each of you is aware that it is well to keep the mind's eye upon the moment which is now. And many are those who feel guilty that they do not spend more of your time in the meditation, contemplation, prayer and simple reading of inspirational material that has been valued by you. The world, you say, is so much with me I cannot do these things which take too much time. We ask each to release the self from this judgmental frame of mind and firstly to realize that there is no physical time to seeking but only the energy of intention and desire. Secondly, that this can be called upon at any moment during which you are aware enough of how to judge and discriminate to choose what to look at. This meditation of the moment is not a will-o'-the-wisp. It is the dipping into the deep pool of peace in a moment, so that you may turn again and face the illusion without being drowned and overwhelmed by the information pouring in from your senses. Your body's mind would, if it could, speak only of the illusion. Thusly, it is only by conscious choice of the point of view that you may have the option of looking at what forces shaped the situation at the present moment.

This, my friends, is not a theoretical training ground for soul! This, your third-density illusion, is boot camp for souls! You see, in third density you have one choice to make. It is the choice between service to the self and service to others. Upon this choice depends millions, of what you think of as years, of future evolution. For both the service-to-self path and the service-to-others path are viable ways to become one with the one Creator which is the source of all that there is, and indeed is all that there is.

Again, we shall pause as we find this instrument going to sleep. We shall bring the level up a bit. Please allow our apologies for another pause. We are Q'uo.

(Pause)

We are again with this instrument. We cannot wake this instrument up. Therefore, we feel it best to speak only a bit longer. For while this instrument is perfectly safe, we wish not to intrude upon this instrument's free will. And as we are in trance with this instrument, she has no free will. This constitutes an unacceptable contact, for we believe above all things in the free will of each individual and would not speak our thoughts to any which did not ask. Nor would we enter into the trance state with an instrument without the prior agreement. Therefore, we simply will sum what we have said and then transfer.

Whether in channeling or in living, the focus upon the principles governing that which occurs rather than [on] that which seems to be occurring will yield to you the more accurate point of view from which to use your personal powers of discrimination and choices of action, so that you stop reacting to the illusion and begin the freer and more transforming activity of acting as you believe in the present moment to be your deepest understanding. This process is guarded by the one who loves you very, very much. The protection of the seeker is grounded in love. You are loved infinitely, and you are channels for infinite love. We thank this group for allowing us to speak, and we thank this instrument and would now transfer to the one known as Jim. We leave this instrument in love and in light. We are Q'uo.

(Jim channeling)

I am Q'uo, and greet each again in the love and in the light of the one infinite Creator. At this time we would offer ourselves in the responding to any further queries which those present would have for us. Is there a query at this time?

Carla: I have a question. Could you tell me what happened? I was channeling and then suddenly Jim pulled the microphone away from me and so I assumed I came to a dead stop. What happened?

I am Q'uo. I am aware of your query and your confusion, my sister. We were unable to bring your level of consciousness up to a sufficient degree away from that level you call sleep, so that we were of necessity bound to complete that portion of our message through your instrument. We can assure you that you did not stop and could have continued if we had wished to infringe upon your free will by utilizing the trance state. Since we had no prior agreement with you to utilize the trance level of communication, we found it necessary to give a summary of that information which we had been transmitting through your instrument and then transferred our contact to this instrument in order that questions and answers could be entertained, as is the practice of this group in its relationship to us.

Is there a further query, my sister?

Carla: Yes, Q'uo, could you please speak to me what I did incorrectly, to bring about this situation. This has not happened before.

I am Q'uo, and I am aware of your query, my sister. We find no error upon your part. Only the body's response to the opportunity for rest as it is suffering of that which you call the infection, which has weakened it significantly, and we applaud your desire to serve under these conditions, and that which occurred is not unusual in this instance. Therefore, we do not suggest any corrective action or further concern upon your part.

Is there another query, my sister?

Carla: Yes, a last one. Is there a desire, is there a need in your opinion for any, let's say, series of special sessions in trance, such as we have done before, or is conscious channeling that which the Confederation prefers at this time, through me?

I am Q'uo, and I am aware of your query, my sister. We do not recommend the utilization of the trance level of contact for your instrument at this time but would continue with the conscious channeling as you have called it.

Is there another query, my sister?

Carla: No, Q'uo, thank you very much. I appreciate it.

I am Q'uo, and we thank you again, my sister. Is there another query at this time?

Carla: I do have one more before you stop. Do you wish to speak upon this subject again, to finish what you had to say?

I am Q'uo, and we find that as with all topics *(laughter from Carla)* there is an infinite amount of information available. At your request we feel that we have given a good beginning upon this topic, one which offers each food for thought shall we say and we shall be happy to speak further if it is requested of us.

Is there another query, my sister?

Carla: No, Q'uo. And I thank you and am glad to talk with you as usual.

I am Q'uo, and we thank you, my sister. Is there another query at this time?

Questioner: I have a query. First of all, are you familiar with my … inquiry or … ah, earlier what I was speaking of as an experience which I had in California in which I …

(Side one of tape ends.)

(Jim channeling)

I am Q'uo, and am again with this instrument. We are aware of the information which you shared with this group, my sister, but do not choose to read further before you have given information, for we do not wish to infringe upon any entity's free will and therefore will respond only to this information which you have spoken and to which you wish further response. How may we speak, my sister?

Questioner: My query has to do with … getting in touch with … whether this is something with which I might continue or should continue?

I am Q'uo, and I am aware of your query, my sister. Our response, in order to assure your free will in its action, is of necessity general. We may suggest that, if there is an interest in this kind of information and its method of transfer that indeed you may pursue this type of seeking. We would suggest that if there is a question or doubt upon your part that this is a topic upon which meditation would be helpful. For those areas of inquiry, which are of value to the seeker, will cause a feeling of rightness to rise from the subconscious to the conscious mind where it will become apparent that the next step upon the path is the one in question.

Is there a further query, my sister?

Questioner: I feel the doubt is only in my own ability, because there is definitely a desire and an interest in pursuing this.

I am Q'uo, and we would respond by suggesting that it is appropriate that each seeker feel a certain amount of doubt as it approaches a new experience upon the spiritual path. For this kind of doubt or questioning is that which prepares the seeker in an inner sense to take the step from the cliff not knowing whether the foot that steps shall rest upon firm fundament or not. Thus, if there is interest upon your heart and doubt in your ability, we recommend that you rely upon that desire which you feel and that you put aside for the moment the doubt in order that your journey may continue along that path which is designated by the passion and desire within you. Is there a further query, my sister?

Questioner: No further query, and I thank you.

I am Q'uo and we thank you, my sister. Is there another query at this time?

(Pause)

I am Q'uo, and as it appears that we have completed those queries which have formed in the minds of those that are present, we shall take this opportunity to thank each entity for inviting our presence in this session of working. We are most grateful to be able to join you and to walk briefly with you upon your journeys of seeking. We applaud each entity's efforts at moving through this illusion which is filled with mystery and confusion, for it is a valiant effort which you make within such a heavy chemical illusion.

Each has friends, guides and teachers that walk with each, whether seen or unseen. And we can assure each of you that you are never alone upon this path though each will feel a loneliness many times during the journey.

Each time you are calling inwardly or outwardly for assistance, your calls are heard and if you will listen carefully with your inner ear, you will hear the response, for the one Creator cares for each of its children and hears each call. We shall take our leave of this group at this time, leaving each as always in the love and in the light of the infinite Creator. We are known to you as those of Q'uo. Adonai, my friends. Adonai. ☙

L/L Research

L/L Research is a subsidiary of Rock Creek Research & Development Laboratories, Inc.

P.O. Box 5195
Louisville, KY 40255-0195

www.llresearch.org

Rock Creek is a non-profit corporation dedicated to discovering and sharing information which may aid in the spiritual evolution of humankind.

ABOUT THE CONTENTS OF THIS TRANSCRIPT: This telepathic channeling has been taken from transcriptions of the weekly study and meditation meetings of the Rock Creek Research & Development Laboratories and L/L Research. It is offered in the hope that it may be useful to you. As the Confederation entities always make a point of saying, please use your discrimination and judgment in assessing this material. If something rings true to you, fine. If something does not resonate, please leave it behind, for neither we nor those of the Confederation would wish to be a stumbling block for any.

CAVEAT: This transcript is being published by L/L Research in a not yet final form. It has, however, been edited and any obvious errors have been corrected. When it is in a final form, this caveat will be removed.

© 2009 L/L Research

Sunday Meditation
August 30, 1992

Group question: The question this afternoon has to do with voices and emotions that we hear as we go through our daily round of activities, that might speak to us of fear, of memories of the past, of feelings of abandonment, of feelings of joy and peace, of anxiety, of wondering exactly how we fit our lives into the larger picture of the world scene. When we hear these voices, is there the need or any benefit to bringing the voices under any kind of supervision or control? Is it well to allow each voice to speak its own message and then determine what value the message has for us?

What value do these voices have as we go through our daily round of activities, and how can we make reliable decisions concerning our service and our growth as we listen to the variety of voices in our heads and in our lives?

(Carla channeling)

I am Q'uo. Greetings to each of you in the love and in the light of the one infinite Creator. How precious each of you is and how grateful we are that you would wish to call us to share in your meditation and to offer our service of speaking upon the topic of the inner dialogue and its reason for being, its way of working, and its relevance to your spiritual journey. To say that we are offering a service is true; yet, we also wish to say that we are fallible. Therefore, if any opinion of ours does not seem right to you, it would be very gratifying to us if you would leave it behind and keep for thought only those things which seem helpful and right to you, for each has a personal discrimination which is far wiser in its instincts than any outer authority.

As foundation for this collection of thoughts, we would ask you to visualize the seeker that you are in meditation with the entire universe of meaning, both without and within you. You are perhaps more used to thinking of an inner and an outer experience. Yet, the outer experience is, at a deep level, formed sometimes decisively by the inner self. Thusly, the visualization of the self in meditation, bringing the outer world within by allowing, accepting and forgiving outer experience, becomes half of the self's realization that all of the infinite creation is within each seeker, each self-conscious entity. The outer struggles seem light except when those outer influences come too close, and resemble too much, the difficulties of the self within. The outer experience is most usefully thought of as a mirror reflecting to you your inner situation and the joys and challenges of it.

Within you lie all qualities: those that you think of as contradictory, those you think of as good and as bad. All imagined possibilities of self lie fallow within each person. Each is completely universal. You are all that there is. Within your consciousness lies this knowledge. Yet, as you come to your work of spiritual seeking, it is not usually one's desire to begin with the broad and untamed bewilderment of self-contradictory forces. Far more natural to one seeking is the urge to move into a positive service and love-filled environment.

This is a good instinct, and for the student who is beginning to be aware of the choices that can be made, it is a functional and practical point of view. The decisions are normally fairly simple in an ethical or philosophical sense. Faced with a choice between loving behavior and self-serving, lying or other negative behavior, the student will either choose, usually, to do the positive thing or to fail to do the positive thing but to remember the preference in 20/20 hindsight, as this instrument would say, looking at the undone thing that would have been positive or the error that was not positive and saying, "I will remember to affect future decisions because this decision did not satisfy me."

However, the query that you have asked is about those times when there is no obvious positive choice. That control of choosing the positive thing is a kind of artifact of one doing work while attempting to open the heart. The choices at that level bloom like flowers and are often irresistible. The virtue of service, the joy of giving, the desire to make those you contact feel better—these are the choices made easily, lovingly and freely by those moving to open the center of heart energy.

Yet, the spiritual path of evolution becomes like the planet that you rest upon—creatures of night as well as day—and after the heart is first opened on a reliable basis there yet remains the traversing of the twilight and evening and midnight of the spiritual journey. As you advance in your choices, they become less than obvious. The deepest, most profound darkness lies upon the advancement of the spiritual path. Within this darkness there is one light: the reflecting light as of your moon to this planet of yours. This spiritual reflective essence may be called your higher self, the larger self, the all-mind. It may be called the Christ within or simply guidance. Whatever it is called, it does not cast a clear and bright light, but casts an often deceiving, very subtle moonlight of the spirit. And in this light, with only your guidance to have faith in, you make the more subtle, more difficult, and very important choices having to do with the energies of communication and inner work. Most of the inner work is done in this spiritual, deep-shadowed twilight.

Why is this so? The gates to learning the truth open only to those who are able to use the keys. The first key is the silence of meditation. And after the resources of meditation, contemplation and prayer have aided the seeker enough to open the heart, then the choices become those focusing into the universal nature of the self and an archetypical understanding that allows the seeker to have more keys minted and placed in the spiritual grasp.

Each period of learning at this level is called initiation by your people, and it is, indeed, the beginning of a new subtle pattern which you shall choose. Yet, this choice is not simple, for it is a choice of an entire pattern, a pattern of thought, of intuition, certainly not a clear-cut process. Rather than working upon opening the heart to all that there is in service, the initiatory lessons have to do with solidifying the nature of the self, of envisioning and seeing the more desirable pattern or way of being the self, and, overarching all, the pattern by which the seeker chooses personally and only for the self to discipline itself.

The personality is a magical thing at this spiritual level. It is not the personality of your culture, the right word, the ready joke or laugh. We speak rather of focusing into the true unique nature of you, this one seeker. For you, the joy that awaits at the end of each choice is an enlarged vision, not only of the self, but of the nature of service. You know in your open hearts that you love very, very deeply, to the core of your being, the one Source of all that there is, the one great Thought that initiated and continues creation. You wish all good things. This is always so.

Yet, the later lessons are often tedious to the impatient spirit who wishes to get on with being of service. Yet, as you gaze backwards and see a completed initiation and testing and feel the enlarged strength and stability of your compassion, you feel that all the subtle inner discussion was, indeed, not pointless and not irritating and certainly not a sign of laziness or personal weakness, and you are encouraged by a feeling of inner strength. You see yourself not only open-hearted, but free, for the open-hearted one has not yet dealt with the murderer, the thief, the traitor, all of the negative possibilities that lie within, except by closing the door upon them.

The last artifact of negativity in the open heart is the unforgiven universal self. You think you are serving all those you meet, and you are; but, in more advanced learning, you discover that you serve and are served with no breath between the two, that service is another way of saying praise or thanksgiving or intercession for forgiveness, and you begin working on the universal self within.

Now that we have described the basic path as we feel it to be, we can zero in a bit upon the so-called "voices within." Let us place them in three categories. Firstly, there are those voices within which are memories from very early times within this incarnation and sometimes having the feeling of experiences not limited to this incarnation. These voices of parents and those in the early world of incarnational time come plangently and persuasively across any number of years to tell you the first things that you heard regularly again and again. These voices may have been wise or unwise, or, as in most cases, a confusing mixture of acceptance and non-acceptance, of forgiveness and of punishment, of stability and abandonment, of security and insecurity. The tangle of emotions wells up within those who are parents and the child remembers so well.

In this first category of voices within, the voices are often fairly easy to pick out, for you hear almost the voice of that early authority speaking. It is fairly clearly not your voice, although you allow it to be so. In this first category of voices, it is well to examine the thought welling up within you for any possible aid. And if there is no real justice, fairness, or help in this voice, it is well to remove it regularly and for a period of time by saying, "You are my mother; you are not me," or whatever the entity and its relation to you is. These voices may be respected, but need to be taken very lightly, for now you are making these choices and that voice speaks to a young child no longer in need of harsh measures of protection.

To allow these voices full sway is the equivalent of failing ever to pick up the matchbook when you are cold and could start a good bonfire on a forest journey because the father or mother said, "Do not use matches." You are now in charge of your equipment for life. The use of any fire to warm body, soul or spirit can be both helpful and destructive, so you must be careful in your choice. Yet, to fear to pick up the tool by which you create the light and warmth is to refuse to move further upon your path.

The second category of voices within is the category of, shall we say, the stray negativity which surrounds and envelops the third-density illusory experience which you call life. Within your density you are specifically guaranteed to be kept off-balance, continuously to encounter situations that baffle and confuse your mind and make it necessary to abandon the intellectual logic and move into the feelings of the heart wherein lies wisdom. There is always the illusion of more negativity by far than positivity, for in the illusion it is often so that loss and limitation cause the spiritual seeker in its pain to do more good work in consciousness than it does during easier times. The easy times, so-called, are seldom well used. May we say that many of those issues which have been brought up this day at this working are of this type.

When the time is fairly joyful, the spirits and will to serve are high. Within this period of experience many entities slack off in their spiritual work. Each of you is expressing an extremely good aspect of spiritual seeking by focusing in, for the purpose of learning, on those motifs that keep reappearing in the inner life that are exceptions to your basic joy. That you not stress these difficulties is good. That you realize them and respect their value enough to do work in the indigo ray or brow-level area is that which will bring you more sharply into the position of initiation where a new key, an enlarged realization of the clarity of the pattern of the self, may begin its process of transforming you by enlarging your stable point of view. We hope that each values these voices that are not parental but are those inner portions which observe the self and speak to the self of patterns not yet fully realized, not yet fully conceived.

You see the pattern by the incompleteness which moves into manifestation in conscious life as the "fly in the ointment," the inner ambivalence, the something not quite comfortable. There need be none of this process, but, if there seems to be the need for some fear, then allow and accept that you have a concern, that there is something that makes you feel the negative rather than the positive. Allow this, for it is a part of the process. Only end always with the realization that the process is positive, and the resulting seeker—that is, you—will learn from this quiet, constant testing, not any large detail of spirit, but, rather, the undergirding patterns that support continued spiritual evolution.

As you evolve, the race which you are a part of evolves. You are all entities within your planetary sphere in that, as you evolve and are able reliably to be more of a clear, transparent channel for the infinite waters of love, so you shall be both less yourself and more yourself. You are attempting to move from the personal self to the magical or impersonal self, and these small voices within tell you of the pattern that you are just missing.

This is subtle work. Do not be discouraged, but move forward, and in forgiveness of self—not the forgiveness of one who may confer from the outside, but forgiveness of the universal self by the universal self. To serve love is truly freedom; yet, to perfect that freedom, you move into and through the large choices involved in opening the heart in non-judgmental compassion to the realization that beyond all these choices there is a universal nature which includes all things, and as all-self there is forgiveness of the forever incomplete all-self being perceived as becoming. The more you become, the more freely and gladly you will take on this subtle and essential task.

The third category of voices within is peopled by those presences to which you become sensitized. These are not, in your way of speaking, parts of the self. They seem to be people, entities, energies which are apart from you, which have their own lives, their own bodies and their own thinking. It may be useful for you to think always of your inner guides or the Holy Spirit, or whatever you find to be your guidance. If that be so, then stop right there, for that is an excellent way to relate to these essences, these energies, these people. They truly are here to serve you as a seeker, to aid you in attaining that perfect clarity which lets the Creator shine through undiminished and undistorted.

There are, however, many who find it useful also to feel kinship with or to find themselves to be part of these presences. The way to consider them then might well be that there are energies, essences and traits within yourself which draw and attract these entities, energies and so forth to you. It is well always if a new voice is heard—and all voices are new until challenged—to be clear about being in charge of either accepting these voices or requesting that they leave in no uncertain terms. If you find a portion of guidance—one of the guiding voices—to be destructive, then you must do that which is natural for you to do to remove that voice from the opportunity to speak further. To do this is a matter of knowing where your essence lies so that you can stand solidly upon the spiritual rock upon which you have placed your journey and say, "By this imperishable ideal which I take most seriously, I command you to go and stay gone."

You are not without power. Your thoughts have power. But for them to be full of your true power you truly need to become clear within your heart about your choice of path, for there are many, many paths to the one infinite Creator. For instance, we are such a voice through this instrument. This instrument spent some of your time in moving carefully over its basic faith, its basic way of relating faith theoretical to life specific. This instrument challenges us in the name of Jesus the Christ, and because, to this instrument, Jesus the Christ is the way, the truth and the life, we may then say to this instrument, "We come in the name of Jesus the Christ; Jesus is Lord." We can say this because this is this instrument's true heart. There is no equivocation. This instrument has chosen.

If you were to form your spiritual life upon conversations with your bedpost, we would have to come into harmony with what you and your bedpost conceived to be the way, the truth and the life, and we would see that this bedpost had given you the energy to move into serious consideration of the infinite nature of your spirit. And for you and you alone, we would, silly as it may seem, need to come to you in the name you had given your bedpost. This is very simplistic. However, we are attempting to crash through the barriers of words to express that when you speak to guidance, you must test it.

And do not think that, because you know the energy of your guides, that they are necessarily your guides. There are negatively oriented, spiritually advanced entities who are excellent mimics, shall we say, who work with as much light as do your guides, and their guidance moves in to those who do not take care, first fooling the instrument with positive information, then gradually de-tuning the instrument, asking it to turn from imperishable ideals to specific dogmas and doctrines, be they obviously spiritual or tangentially so, as in thoughts about the diet and the ways of being healthy or unhealthy. Eventually, an untested voice may well become quite negative. This occurs only to those who are already listening to the silent wisdom of guidance. This protects those who have not moved to a magical point, a powerful point, in terms of the infinite spirit, the journeying seeker within; ignorance is truly bliss.

To each of you, more knowledge has meant more care, for as you become powerful, you attract attention. As you serve and create light and radiate love of the infinite One, you also cast an ever sharper shadow. You become harder upon yourself, setting yourself up for the forgiveness of the universal self. My beloved ones, know that this query is one asked by those who already love and are already upon the path. Know that you now are working with the discipline of your universal personality. You are beginning to set archetypical habits for yourself and building, ever more polarized, a channel for compassion.

As you do this work, we hope you have the light touch, the sense of humor, the ability to take yourself lightly, for attaining the keys to learning the correct and appropriate use of personal power is a long, long process. You have moved into an area that will be continued in your development for many, many incarnations, and through at least one more density. This situation of loving, serving and trying to become the forgiving universal self, and, therefore, the forgiven universal self, is a sacred and a monumental task, and you are working in the all too dim light of inner work.

You now plumb the depths and wait for the flashes, rare though they are, of perfect realization. May you have faith in this process. May you help each other to bear the burdens and to meet the testings of this process. And may you see always before you the love that surrounds you, the support of that infinite love, and the utter clarity that is possible to achieve when once you have freely forgiven, forgiven and forgiven.

We know that we have spoken overlong, and this instrument has been very formidable in her disapproval; however, this was a subtle query and we could not leave it until we had said at least our outline. We thank you for allowing us to keep you in this circle, and at this time, if there are any queries that you wish to raise, we would answer them. However, we find that this instrument is very willing to transfer this contact to the one known as Jim, and, therefore, we shall take this opportunity to thank this instrument and transfer. We are known to you as the principle of Q'uo.

(Jim channeling)

I am Q'uo, and greet each again in love and in light through this instrument. At this time, it is our privilege to offer ourselves in the attempt to speak to any further queries which those present may have for us. Is there a query with which we may begin?

Carla: Can you give us some kind of insight on how to hold onto the humor and to not get so intense that we can't see where we are?

I am Q'uo, and am aware of your query, my sister. The sense of humor that is so valuable an ally upon the spiritual path may be described as a sense of proportion which allows you to see beyond the moment in which you are experiencing one motion, event, experience or another. This perspective allows you to place each individual experience within the larger continuum that moves ever onward as the river flowing.

Look then at any moment in which your humor has seemingly evaporated, at the entire situation in which you find yourself. Look at the world about you, seeing those entities and events which are momentous and powerful. See yourself placed within the context of a Creator which has made an infinite variety of entities of Itself which seek their identity and the nature of the Creator through myriads of interactions that may or may not make what you call sense, and which may reveal to you the humorous nature of the human creature.

This creature is one full of desire to know the truth, full of the energy of inspiration, full of the confusion of the illusion, and yet which moves valiantly forward, sideways, up, down and around in order that it might progress yet one step further. See the anguish, the confusion, the joys, the determination, all of the emotions that comprise the resources upon which you draw. See them moving with you as colors of the rainbow. Look at yourself upon this rainbow journey and remember that that which is of value is the love which you create in each moment and all else shall fall away, having little of impact in your future. As time progresses, only the love remains.

Is there a further query, my sister?

Carla: No, thank you, Q'uo.

I am Q'uo, and we thank you, my sister. Is there another query?

Carla: To follow that one up, I would like to ask if there is a way that we can trigger remembrance of all that you have said in the middle of having a fit of some kind, being intensely, overly involved, the way we all do get sometimes, and not seeing anything funny about anything? What kind of trigger can we use to get out of that intense and ever-inwardly spiraling kind of way of concentrating and frustrating ourselves?

I am Q'uo, am aware of your query, my sister. We are of the opinion that it is well for each seeker to experience fully the emotions of the moment without contrivance or control, for it is in these spontaneous responses to life's "slings and arrows," shall we say, that the truer nature of your inner self is revealed. And, as this nature is revealed, then you see those areas of strength and those areas of weakness and may work more successfully upon your weaknesses having them thusly revealed.

Thus, we would not suggest that one attempt to impose a sense of humor, or of any other kind of control, upon the moment in which the experience is "hot," shall we say, and the emotions are turbulent.

However, to remain with such turbulence overly long provides the difficulty, much as the electrical circuit that has had too much voltage in the weakest point [and overloads]. Thus, it is at this time that we would suggest that the humor be invoked by any means which has value or shows efficacy. These possibilities would include the making of a taped reminder to yourself while you are feeling the inspiration of the overview and have with you the ally of humor. This tape could then be played back to yourself as a reminder that that which you have experienced has value. And when the value has been determined, then the humor may be invoked.

It may be that you find there are others in the field of consciousness expansion which have written upon the subject of humor and which give an overview that is felt by you to be valuable and which could be referred to at the appropriate moment. It may be that there are certain moving pictures that bring you this sense of humor and relief from the difficulty of the moment that might also be utilized. Find that procedure or method which has value to you and use it when you feel that the time is appropriate.

Is there a further query, my sister?

Carla: Just a clarification. I take it that you mean not to attempt to move into that which is going on in your thoughts, not your actions. You're not talking about the world of manifestation here, you're talking about the world of internal thought, right? Because you obviously wouldn't want to allow yourself to give into your impulse to kill your employer or something like that.

I am Q'uo, and am aware of your query, my sister. You are in the large part correct, for we do not advise the losing of the self-control to the point of infringing upon the free will of another, but were suggesting that the internal experience which moves you so mightily is that which must needs be expressed in order to be examined at a later time for the fruits of such experience.

Is there another query, my sister?

Carla: Not at this time. Thank you very much, Q'uo.

I am Q'uo, and again we thank you, my sister. Is there another query at this time?

Carla: Yeah, one more. No prejudice intended—could your answers not possibly be more direct and to the point, being as we here on the Earth plane think that way? Do you understand?

I am Q'uo, and we are not certain that we grasp your query. Could you find another means of stating it?

Carla: No. Thank you anyway.

I am Q'uo, and we shall speak to that which we feel we grasp. Our responses are tempered by two features of this illusion, the first being the limitations of the instrument and the language with which it is familiar; the second, being more important, and that is the free will of each entity, so that as we speak in response to any query, we give that which will inspire thought, rather than that which will completely sate the hunger, wishing not to do another's work for that entity, for it is the work that is the value of the decision-making and the choosing.

May we speak in any further way to any other query, my sister?

Carla: No. Thank you.

I am Q'uo, and we thank you. Is there another query?

Carla: I have one more. You're talking about having already opened the heart and working in communication and inner work, but I don't feel like my heart's open all the time at all. I feel like I'm frequently screwing up and blocking energies or over-spiking them so that they're overly active and so forth, and that my heart isn't always just great. I don't really feel that I could really say, "Well, yeah, I'm doing lots of inner work now because I'm all done with that open heart stuff." I'm not. Could you comment on that, because I don't feel like I'm "here" and not "there." Maybe I'm "there," but I'm also back down in blocked personal relationships and stuff, too.

I am Q'uo, and am aware of your query, my sister. As you learn any skill, whether it be how to open the heart in unconditional love, how to juggle, or how to cook a certain meal, there will be those expressions of the skill which are better done, shall we say, than others. There will be the dropping of the ball for the juggler. Yet, if the juggler can accomplish a certain skill or procedure, the ability is present. And it is to the entity that has moved into the opening of the heart that we speak in relation to the seeking of truth and the serving as an instrument or vocal channel. If an entity has the ability to do this, called "loving without condition," it is not important that the entity is not always able to express this loving without conditions, but it is important that the entity has the desire to do so and will examine its experience with that desire foremost in the mind.

Is there another query, my sister?

Carla: Just sort of a left turn into the question about why can't you speak more simply? Let's see how to put this. I realize that you want to teach and not do our learning for us. There are often teachers around that give you a very simple—and something you can hold onto—type of answer, and they seem to have real success in being able to deal with spiritual questions a lot of times. Does the infringement of free will sort of "catch up" to you after awhile, is that what you're saying, when the spiritual student goes over these own issues himself, looking basically at what you have said just for principles that he can use as resources … that the student has then done a better job than if the student just heard somebody that was absolutely brilliant just telling him everything, and said, "Okay, I'll believe that"? There is a difference between those two? If you both have the same belief in the end?

I am Q'uo, and am aware of your query, my sister. In a large part, you are correct. However, we are as we are and we must, in order to remain true to that which we are, speak in the way in which we speak when given the constraints of the language, the ability of the instrument, and the free will of those to whom we speak. There are many teachers. There are as many teachers as there are entities and experiences, and each will teach with a certain voice, a style that will be unique to that teacher. Those words which have value to the student will find their way to the student's heart. This is why we always recommend that each student discriminate those words and concepts which we offer, and forget those that have no meaning, saving only those which ring of truth for that entity. We recommend that each student find those teachers with which the student is comfortable, for all teach and all learn.

Is there a further query, my sister?

Questioner: No. I thought that that was a really helpful answer. Thank you very much.

I am Q'uo, and again we thank you, my sister. Is there another query at this time?

(Pause)

I am Q'uo, and we feel that the queries have been exhausted for this session of working, and we would take this opportunity to thank each for inviting our presence in your meditation this day. We are greatly honored to be so invited and we cannot express to you the joy that we feel at the opportunity of walking with you upon your journey, even but a step, for as we walk with you, we walk with the Creator, and are overjoyed at the opportunity to learn from you as we share with you of that which is ours to share.

At this time we shall take our leave of this instrument and this group, leaving each as always in the love and in the light of the one infinite Creator. We are known to you as those of Q'uo. Adonai, my friends. Adonai. ☙

L/L Research

Sunday Meditation
September 6, 1992

Group question: The question this afternoon has to do with changes and transitions and the use of faith in making these transitions. The issues or lessons of our lives seem to be the lens through which we look at our lives, and we're wondering if, as we continue to walk on our path and go through the various changes and learning of lessons, if we are able to provide our own inspiration for this journey by simply making the journey—a kind of perpetual motion machine—so that we gain the confidence of being able to make transitions and to solve problems by doing it. And yet, we find that these issues or problems are with us at deeper levels, showing other aspects and requiring the continued application of faith and will in order to continue on the journey.

So, what we would like to know is how this process actually works. Is it true that we can provide our own inspiration for this journey? And do we continue to work with the same kinds of issues as we make transitions in our lives, simply making them on different levels or with different applications?

(Carla channeling)

We are those of Q'uo. Greetings to each in the love and in the light of the one infinite Creator. It is a great privilege to be called to your group for this session of working by seekers such as you. We so enjoy sharing in the meditation of your circle. We would greet those from places distant upon your sphere to this domicile, and wish each love, peace and many blessings. You offer us a wonderful opportunity for service by asking for our opinion. We make mistakes; consequently, we would stress that these words must pass the authority of each seeker's own inner discrimination. If any thought we share is not your personal truth, we ask you please to lay it aside.

There are two truths concerning the inspiration to will and faith. We shall offer them both. They contradict each other, which we have found to be a sure mark of true spiritual territory, for that which is mystery is self-contradictory and illogical, as all enigmas are. Yet, there is a resolution, if not solution.

The first truth is that you inspire others; others inspire you. In your holy work called the Bible, the master known as Jesus spoke of sowing where one did not reap. There is no possible way to avoid taking others' fruit from them. This is a central lesson of love. When love is given, it is given away. It seems quite often not to be returned. That is due to the illusions of time, space and personal identity.

The love coming to you can be thought of as the light of stars. The light of the nearby star which is your sun burns hotly from such a relatively close distance, and, perhaps, within the wisdom of this light, there seems also a danger. But the light from the distant stars is cool and moves through your time to shine upon your upturned face years after that star has disappeared.

The gift of love and light radiates to you from elsewhere and from other selves. You, in turn, radiate in essential being and in your thoughts and actions to serve as a channel for that light and love that inspires, comforts and soothes others. There is no way to keep an account ledger to be sure that what is given out is again received—not because there is not balance, but because love and light do not contain in themselves quantity but only quality. They are essences, not things to be measured: infinite qualities, rather than finite forces of a certain magnitude.

Each is personally aware of the many inspirations received from others. We would reassure each that as each attempts to be of service, the attempt fosters and encourages the essence of each self so that even when efforts to serve and love seem to fail, yet that desire, that will, that love is effectual. It not only moves others' hearts in ways you do not ever know, but adds to the planetary transparency, to the limitless light of the one infinite Creator.

Thusly, we encourage each to offer thanksgiving continually for blessings received, for inspiration received, for all blessings are that which comes to one. By no amount of exerted control can one control one's infinite source of all good.

This instrument has, at this point, asked us to move on as this instrument feels the energy would be better spent in a shorter transmission. Therefore, we shall move on to the second truth concerning inspiration, towards loving and serving in new and expanding, changing ways. The door to the deep self is fairly carefully closed when a spirit enters into manifested third-density incarnation. Vision fails, awareness recedes, finely tuned senses within are muffled with flesh, and the incarnation grows darker as the child grows to be the adult. Yet, the small being survives in the growing complexity of the personal universal awareness that is the self's awareness of a subjective universe.

In that first look at one's universe, the outcome is dim. Things look dark, difficult and dreary. There is work in all directions to support the physical self, to corral the emotions, to find the truest heart of self amidst all the vicissitudes of change. Yet, there is within a universe of suns, of, shall we say, energies that represent, and in a holographic sense are, the vibrations of wisdoms represented by the outward sun and stars.

This door to the deep mind where this universe revolves and can gradually be seen is opened by the self and the self only. That is, it cannot be opened by another person in incarnation. Yet, in the inner room of meditation, when silence is truly reigning and the spirit somewhat freed, the desire to find inspiration taken into silent meditation yields an inner guidance. Inner resources come into more and more developed usefulness.

This occurs over a long period of time, and though one may sometimes feel one has made a breakthrough, yet always the most effectual ally is persistence. Patience, dogged persistence in practicing one's way of approaching infinite values and truth, becomes more and more clear with time, for the effort necessary to put aside that time says to the outward being that this being values the resources of the deep mind. Thusly, inspiration is felt by the self's efforts as the asset of the deep mind. It begins to be used constructively through looking at dreams, through ways of listening to one's own hunches and intuitions. Faith, then, does breed faith. The use of will aids greatly in the next use of will.

We spoke of a resolution to this seeming paradox, and there is truly the most lucid resolution; however, it is not logical in the usual sense. Those other selves that inspire and teach you are also allowing to move through them the same energy that is the energy of the deep mind's wisdom. In your illusion, you may look at all other selves not only as teachers, but as mirrors also, reflecting yourself to you. Thusly, those things that inspire you in someone else equal those things that would inspire you from within if you were able to have access to the appropriate depth and location within the deeper mind. When inspiration comes from another, you are listening to that which you have already thought but were not able to bring close enough to surface awareness to deliver to yourself.

The desirable way to look at this is perhaps to be thankful and grateful and full of praise for those you feel teach and mirror to you well, while allowing these teachings that enter your awareness to stand not as the teachings of another given to you only, but also as the goad, the encouragement, or exhortation which coaxes you into a more persistent and regular attempt to work within the self to find deeper and deeper stability of awareness within the self. For the more work done within the self by allowing the infinite guidance to speak to you, the more you have your incarnational time free so that you may spend more time gathering new information and offering this awareness of yours, so long sought after, to be shared with others.

The query ended by asking whether there was a recurring cycle of circular nature or a spiral of cyclical nature. We agree with each in this group that the lessons of a particular incarnation are largely of the spiraling variety. When a lesson has truly been learned in an incarnation, then it may not appear in that same form. However, the undertones and overtones or connotations of a lesson concerning how to love unreservedly are such that the layers of meaning are always capable of being added unto, and that original lesson seemingly learned moves into a challenging stance regarding the next seeming lesson. Look carefully, ask lovingly, for guidance. Listen to teachers and see yourself in the faces of others, and you will find that the learned lesson has become the jumping-off place for the present challenge.

We feel that all is one. That is so simple that most cannot understand it. The faces, voices and all sensed impressions from the outer world and you are one. The guidance from those sources which aid you—whether they be called the spirit, the inner guide, or any other name—are you. Your nature seems limited; your life, abbreviated, begun and ended in the wink of an eye, cosmically speaking. Yet, you did not begin and will not end, and the learning goes on infinitely, with the truth always receding before one.

So, we encourage each to rejoice in the faith gained. Some has been due first to the inspiration of others; some has been the product of patient courting of the resources within one's own heart. All are of the one infinite Creator and partake in Its nature, which is love. May you love one another and love the self just as much, for inspiration comes from both places and is still of one piece.

We would leave this query and this piece at this time, and open the meeting to any questions that you might have. Are there any queries at this time?

(Pause)

We find that we have no "takers" for our wise answers, so we had better get on our horses and ride back to our own identity. How we have loved being with you, dear ones to us. We thank you for your courage, and encourage you to see changes as parts of an ever-rising spiral into the light. We leave you in that love and in that light. We are known to you as the principle of Q'uo. We leave you in the Creator's peace and bid you adonai. Adonai. ☙

L/L Research

L/L Research is a subsidiary of Rock Creek Research & Development Laboratories, Inc.

P.O. Box 5195
Louisville, KY 40255-0195

www.llresearch.org

Rock Creek is a non-profit corporation dedicated to discovering and sharing information which may aid in the spiritual evolution of humankind.

ABOUT THE CONTENTS OF THIS TRANSCRIPT: This telepathic channeling has been taken from transcriptions of the weekly study and meditation meetings of the Rock Creek Research & Development Laboratories and L/L Research. It is offered in the hope that it may be useful to you. As the Confederation entities always make a point of saying, please use your discrimination and judgment in assessing this material. If something rings true to you, fine. If something does not resonate, please leave it behind, for neither we nor those of the Confederation would wish to be a stumbling block for any.

CAVEAT: This transcript is being published by L/L Research in a not yet final form. It has, however, been edited and any obvious errors have been corrected. When it is in a final form, this caveat will be removed.

© 2009 L/L Research

Sunday Meditation
September 13, 1992

Group question: The question today has to do with accepting the limitations that are put on us by our own point of view, by physical illness, and by physical limitations. And we're wondering if there is a value to feeling the frustration of limitation, or if there is instead a need to separate oneself from the illusion, not be so affected by it—to be more, shall we say, at a distance? Or is it better for us to be immersed in the illusion, to be moved by it, to be emotionally swayed, and then to look at what results and do our balancing according to how the illusion has moved us?

(Carla channeling)

We are those of the principle known as Q'uo. Greetings in the love and in the light of the one infinite Creator. How blessed it is that we are invited to your circle this afternoon. Our enjoyment of your vibrations is surpassed only by our humble delight in accepting your invitation to share with you our opinions. Please remember to use your personal discrimination as you hear these fallible thoughts, and together we shall serve and we shall learn.

We would ask you to come with us in your imagination as we take a mental journey. Begin in the seated consciousness that sits in your circle. Absorb the experience of feeling the energy, moving around the group, the sounds spilling into the ear, the many details that would meet the eye, were it open. Now move with us in thought away from the seated physical vehicle. Remain in the dwelling, but gaze at the seated figures below. See the postures, the way the hands fall in unconscious emotion and desire. See the quiet, waiting figures that house your consciousness.

Move again now with us to an imaginary place somewhat above the dwelling in which you now are seated. Gaze down upon the abode in its nest of trees. Is the dwelling as large to the eye seen from this perspective, as large as it felt when your consciousness looked through your physical vehicle's eyes? Move again, far enough into the ethers to observe the village as a whole. And again, move until the topography of the terrain becomes clearly visible. No longer can one find the small village, much less the abode, much less the physical vehicle's awareness. And continue now, moving faster, until you can see the sphere upon which you dwell as it moves like a spinning ship through the ocean of what you call space.

Now move still farther away from this planet of your nativity until it disappears but the sun is still visible. Stop and reflect upon the particular essence of light and love that is the gift of your sun being. And now move, once again, away until the surrounding stars eclipse any one small star and the galaxy gradually becomes visibly conjoined; and further back, until you have no reference point. Stay there. You have no reference point. This your mind can give you, this degree of removal from detail. This process is helpful to remember to use when reference points seem to be confusing. For fast, fast relief from the agony of unacceptable confusion, we may suggest this alternative to counting to ten, for it not only allows time to elapse, but also space.

We would bring you now back into the manifested universe through myriads of stars, galaxy upon galaxy, until the sun system of your Earth is entered and the speed of travel is slowed to allow a gentle reentry into the planetary energies, those energies so colored by the unique beingness of your sun. Move into the atmosphere, and as the planet rotates upon its axis, gently enter into the arena of your particular life stream once again. There is your nation state, there your village. Slowly now into the energy vortices of home, friends and kindred. And, so gently, rolling, rolling softly, move into the physical vehicle and again take up the experience of sensation. You are now again aware, to a greater degree, of stimuli and of your individuality.

What have you learned? What has the distance taught you? Perhaps you may see that although distance is that which offers relief from confusion and frustration, it is not the teacher that speaks loudly. Indeed, that which teaches was simply quiescent during this expansion of the viewpoint—merely observing, merely recording, not coming to a cusp where a decision should be made. A great many things are to be honored about having a very wide point of view, but the clearing and crystallizing of desires and the schooling for choices perhaps may be seen not to reside in the distant, observing consciousness which gazes in safety at the tiny time-bound confusions of a living entity. However, there is likewise little of immediate value to confusion deep enough that it stops the mind and the heart from thinking and feeling in a coherent manner.

Now come again with us to the imaginary ability to stop the process of time. Imagine that this instant is captured in a photograph, or, shall we say, a frame of your film. The instant is, and is no more. Look at the picture. What is there in this picture to cause all this confusion? Let us again choose this instant, take a picture, look at this picture. What in this picture is causing the confusion?

You may profitably consider time and space to be illusions, for it is our opinion that confusion lies in the illusion of motion. In this motion, you learn and choose and learn again. But to value the process is one thing, to use it maximally as a resource is another.

When you allow the self to move on, choosing and feeling very intensely and continuing not to resist the seeming flow of catalyst, the spirit is often weary and battered. However, when the catalyst is resisted, the resulting confusion and pain is far worse and less helpful. So, we do not advise the moving back from the situation as a kind of "doppleganger" that is wiser than the actor in the midst of the catalyst simply because neither point of view is more revealing of deeper wisdom than the other.

In the close point of view, you often must act and make intuitive guesses far beyond any logical ability to reason correctly. Yet, the process of transformation occurs better and in a way more attuned to your heart's desires. The pulling back from experience to control or affect the chosen actions taken, though sometimes necessary to solve ethical questions, removes from experience the richness of observed catalyst that can be retained in what you would call the matrix of your mind.

However, the deepest reality that we ourselves see is that there is no motion, but the present, rather, is. The still picture of each moment is as close to manifested reality as that moment can manifest. This means that if you perceive something happening, the truer statement is that this something is. And, rather than observing a process, you are, in the deeper sense, observing the essence. Nothing is occurring, nothing is happening. This is the standpoint from which you may most helpfully work with your own understanding of the self as it reacts to and creates more catalyst.

The truth is that all that is, is all that there is. Nothing comes into consciousness; nothing leaves consciousness; nothing is happening. You are experiencing an illusion. When you can see, in the moment, that a complex stack or series of levels of feelings and actions is at this moment adding up to a very rich tapestry which is being observed and recorded, and, at the same time, can sit and simply allow this tapestry to be as it is, you have within you what we would suggest to be a useful asset to use in moving, as one who is graceful, in the motion within the manifested illusion of time and space.

All the intensity of desire and emotion may be honored. You are here to honor as well as observe and experience the incarnation. That which occurs so often seems cantankerous, wrong-headed, deliberately cruel, or simply confusing beyond words. Can you allow this richness to abide? Can you allow the illusion and also allow that it is illusion? It is this dynamic that enables you to choose which of the avenues of action is appropriate to this particular moment. Perhaps this moment is one where distance is needed for relief from too high a level of stimulation. If you allow the fullness of this moment to enter deeply into you and engage you, you shall perhaps know when you need the protection of distance.

We suggest it is better to stay distant until you are not overcoming any resistance as you walk into close, intimate experience of catalyst. As long as there is fear, the fear that produces all of the confusion, you may do wisely to honor that feeling—to allow protection, the protection of mental distance. Perhaps at another moment, you find you can move closer in mind to the present moment, for you are no longer threatened and off of your center, your balance. Then move closer.

The closer, the richer the experience; but the need is there to be able to experience and not to close the mind and say, "No, no, it is too much." Find your own balance, moment by moment—the balance between being too distant to feel the wealth and infinity of the moment, and being too close to experience this wealth as any quality but injury. You do not wish to be without experience, nor do you wish injury. You then use this technique of remembering to poise the self at the threshold between fear and its precincts, and chaos and its wilderness.

It has often been said that contemplation, meditation, the listening to the still, small voice within, is the greatest asset to one who wishes to accelerate the process of spiritual evolution. Why is this force within—which one finds access to in meditation or prayer—called "still," but that it is a descriptive term which applies to the source of aid and comfort which you find in the love and light of the one infinite Creator to which you have access through this technique. It is from infinite intelligence that the still, small voice broadcasts its silent message of harmony and peace.

We encourage each to refrain from judging the self as it moves off balance into fear or into unwise haste. These are illusory movements within an illusion, dreams within a dream. Allow this dream to remain fluid. Allow as much motion as you find optimal for comfort and desire. See the ideal of the balance, always. And take comfort, not in your judgments of your own progress, but in your focus upon observing and paying the infinite gift of loving attention to that which seems to be occurring with you.

In reality, nothing is occurring, but this fact gives the Creator no information. The Creator infinitely loves you and feels enlarged in Its infinity by the burden of information that comes to It through the receptor of your unique consciousness. From the close point of view, lean into the wind of catalyst when you can freely and lovingly. When you cannot, remove yourself to the place where you can receive the most information, however distant that needs to be. But remember always that the gift you offer the infinite Creator is the still photograph of each moment.

How well do you observe? How deeply are you moved to praise, to thanksgiving, to new awarenesses? Or to pain, to horror? If the former, then we have no more advice on this topic. If negative emotions, so-called, continue to be part of the rich photograph that is this moment your complete sum of awareness, then perhaps you might wish to examine more closely each negative emotion to find the source of the discomfort. See that discomfort as an area which dependably exists because there is a fear …

(Side one of tape ends.)

(Carla channeling)

… only to observe it. Allow this observation to remain nonjudgmental. Allow yourself this fear that is. See it. Rest in it. Gather and collect your consciousness. And when you are moved by positive feelings to explore once again the unprotected consciousness beyond the cave of fear, allow that impact upon the senses to be felt. Is there fear now? If so, again honor it by paying attention to it, loving it in you. As you allow love to flow, you may find the need for fear to be less. Thus, you can observe and note more of your moment, and your tapestry of experience is thereby enriched. Little by little, you may lead yourself into the heart of right action, even as you become more and more aware that nothing is occurring, but all is.

You and we, my brothers, are alike: those who move and experience only by accepting illusion. This illusion is a brilliant and kindly way for that which is infinite to be reflected to Itself in some finite, dream-like form. Welcome to a dream so beautiful, so brilliant, and so crystalline that we could sing praises forever and never express our awareness of the wonder, the excellence, and the beauty of the illusion. But we share this joy with you insofar as we can and welcome you to the tenuous, lovely dream of becoming.

At this time, we would open the session of working to questions.

Questioner: Sometimes cancer is said to be caused by holding anger. I wonder if there is some cause, in general, for colds?

I am Q'uo. The energy that is in motion, shall we say, when the cold is experienced is, more often than not, the manifestation of intense requests upon the energy of the self, which in some way seems uncharitable to the body complex or to the spiritual complex. The body—or in some few cases, the spirit complex—then reacts by lowering the immune response to bacteria, for it is experiencing reluctance to move at that intensity. Thusly, it physically slows down the mental processes and requests a less intense configuration of all energies.

It may be seen that in any illness and its treatment, care may profitably be taken gazing at the energies in motion with regard to one's own movements. Evaluate each request made of the self. From what point of origin comes this request for action? What honing mechanism sharpens the desire to intensity with this particular energy? If this analysis is assayed when the body complex is expressing imbalance, insights often may occur.

May we answer further, my brother?

Questioner: No. Thank you, Q'uo.

We thank you also, and may we say how much fun it is to answer a query from the one who usually has all the answers.

Is there another question at this time?

Questioner: My query concerns feelings of fear and emotion coming over the physical body. Do they manifest as feelings of tightness in certain parts of the body that are where the energy centers are? Could that be used as an indication of where the work needs to be done? And is the disappearance of such a feeling an indication that progress has been made?

I am Q'uo. Rather than these two being always together, it is truer that sometimes the blockages of a certain chakra may affect the physical vehicle in the same general location. To diagnose and treat the self, judging the illness by its position in the body and working on the difficulties within the emotional and mental complex which apply to that center, is to oversimplify the nature of the physical vehicle. Secondary energy centers create many subtleties. Furthermore, when any of the centers is going through a certain kind of process—for instance, the desire for control of a process—then that which is affected, whether it is work in red ray or in indigo ray, will be of a control position in the yellow ray of the mental emotional vehicle and will often show as difficulties with the stomach. We mean here to show that a stomach problem may be caused by any of the chakras that can be worked upon, being in the midst of a functional process.

May we answer you further, my brother?

Questioner: No, thank you. I'll have to think about that. But I want to also thank Q'uo for answering the original question in such a way which seems to reply so exquisitely to that which is in my mind at this time. I express my appreciation.

We are those of Q'uo, and we find ourselves simply wishing to close the circle of love. Please know that as you find our opinions excellent, so we find your desire exquisite. We thank you for your single-mindedness, for your passion, and for your persistence. Merrily together, we move within stillness, we go forth within a circle, we exalt in illogical and infinite love of the fictional, yet all-important, road onward in our joint pilgrimage to light and love, and, ultimately, to the Source and Beginning of all that there is. Thank you for your companionship. May each of you be good, loving companions as you are at this moment. No more could be asked.

We leave you in the infinite love and light of the Logos. May you gird yourself in that love and light and go forth rejoicing. We are known to you as those of the principle, Q'uo. Adonai. Adonai, my friends. ✤

L/L Research

L/L Research is a subsidiary of Rock Creek Research & Development Laboratories, Inc.

P.O. Box 5195
Louisville, KY 40255-0195

www.llresearch.org

Rock Creek is a non-profit corporation dedicated to discovering and sharing information which may aid in the spiritual evolution of humankind.

ABOUT THE CONTENTS OF THIS TRANSCRIPT: This telepathic channeling has been taken from transcriptions of the weekly study and meditation meetings of the Rock Creek Research & Development Laboratories and L/L Research. It is offered in the hope that it may be useful to you. As the Confederation entities always make a point of saying, please use your discrimination and judgment in assessing this material. If something rings true to you, fine. If something does not resonate, please leave it behind, for neither we nor those of the Confederation would wish to be a stumbling block for any.

CAVEAT: This transcript is being published by L/L Research in a not yet final form. It has, however, been edited and any obvious errors have been corrected. When it is in a final form, this caveat will be removed.

© 2009 L/L Research

Sunday Meditation
September 20, 1992

Group question: With today's question we are asking what kinds of service that the Confederation of Planets in the Service of the Infinite Creator has to offer the population of our planet. We are aware, of course, of the channeling service we offer here, we are also aware that there are inspirational dreams where people are helped with the direction in their lives and the services they are to offer, and the lessons they are to learn, with coincidental meetings, with people, books, ideas that are important for the person to be concentrating on … and we are wondering if there are other services? In what ways does the Confederation offer itself to the people of our planet, and are there cycles or seasons of certain services so that it is felt that some are more helpful at a certain point in a person's or population's evolution and other services are more helpful at another time? For example, with so much channeling going on today all over the planet, and there being so much that is of questionable value, does channeling or any other service after a while tend to lose effectiveness so that there is the need to move on to other kinds of services?

(Carla channeling)

We are Q'uo. Greetings to you in the love and in the light of the one infinite Creator. We greatly thank you for requesting the presence of the Confederation at your meditation, and are honored to share in your vibrations at this space/time. As we answer your question we, as always, request your appreciation of our fallibility and our hope that discrimination will be used in assessing the worth of our opinions in your own seeking for the truth.

As we begin the consideration of what our service to humankind consists in, we feel it wise to express that we and you who listen alike have the same service, that is to do the will of the infinite Creator, to live in such a way as to be continuously focused upon that will, surrendered to that will, and willing to either act or wait as the spirit makes itself known to you to do. That being said, we may turn to details of our particular service to humankind at this space/time.

We have chosen for a season to attempt communications with your peoples. The communication is of several levels, and these begin with the level of introductory material having to do with the infinite love and light of the one Creator being all that there is and the author of all that there is, concluding with the need for daily, regular and persistent meditation, contemplation or prayer. This is perhaps to be considered as the kind of instrument such as this instrument's so-called telephone answering machine. When there is a request for this information which is below a certain vibratory quality, the automatic information begins flowing. This is, shall we say, in place about your sphere and has been for some of your years. It is only when entities begin attempting to realize their universal self aspect that we begin to be able to communicate more advanced material, whether it be in thoughts or images.

By universal we mean that there is a distinction between personal sources of information and inspiration and universal sources, such as we. The inner planes of your sphere have many greatly wise inhabitants—and many not so wise—all of whom are moved to at times become involved with a living—that is, incarnationally lying—entity. These inner plane beings and energies have a right as those of a native land to be very frank and personally helpful to the extent of their knowledge with those to whom they may speak. We may speak to those whose vibratory level and ability to receive information is of a certain quality. Let us then look at this quality.

The path of seeking moves each seeker through the trials of regularizing, crystallizing and clearing out the basic and central energies of self, self-love, love in relationships with others, and relationship with the society in groups and as a whole. The clearing of the heart and its opening is exceedingly important and usually much of a seeker's time is continually spent in keeping this heart energy flowing and radiant. The work turns, then, from the obviously radiant to a more tightly focused radiance in the development of communication skills which are based upon a certain depth of personality or depth of a point of view, that is in the blue-ray center.

We do not say that an entity has blue-ray energy simply because the entity speaks a great deal. The communication of one working in spiritually vibrant blue ray is of a certain quality or order. This in turn is based more upon work done in the brow or indigo-ray energy center than simply upon the open heart. Thusly, we are able to address this instrument in its highest tuning because we worked with our energies to find a harmony which was euphoniously interactive with this instrument's ability to receive in-depth information. This energy is one which will not endure beyond this particular channel's use of us as we formed this union in order specifically to work with this particular channel.

We see the concept of the universal self as one which may bear some interest to you. When you receive a certain level of, shall we say, initiation or transformation a peculiar thing begins to occur. The self that has many, many details to concern the self with begins a little at a time to receive from the deeper mind—that part of the deeper mind which speaks consciously. You may have noticed the growing tendency of your own mind to have a kind of knee-jerk response in terms of how one looks at events and occurrences. Spontaneously, there begins to be a larger part of the self which sees each thing occurring as being part of an universal experience, that is, one common to all beings.

It is to this energy that we communicate. We have no right to interfere with your free will. For those who wish personal advice we have only spiritual principles to share, and often this is not satisfactory. However, we can only offer that which is rightfully ours to offer. It may be said that we who have been among your people have the right to be in your inner planes and speak from that standpoint. However, we see one kind of information as being, shall we say, horizontal and the other as vertical. The inner planes attitude is level with the mundane experience but has, in addition to the mundane, further mundane-oriented information which applies and somewhat crystallizes thinking about situations. We chose as each of two planetary groups to refrain from inner planes' work for our, shall we say, gifts lay more in the vertical or the transformative, universal information. The worth of this information, as all sorts of information, remains at the level at which it was delivered. Truth seen through various biases of contact and channel does not go out of fashion. It is a matter of entities choosing to continue to improve their abilities as channel which limits the excellence of the channeled material, not the cosmic rhythms which have to do with the perusal or use of such material. There are more entities attempting to create teaching tools and resources at your space/time present than at other earlier or later times. However, the material is timeless insofar as the channel has held to the universal viewpoint while preparing to make contact.

If, for instance, this instrument asked us if we came in the name of Christ but did not love the universal Christ as well as the specific entity Jesus the Christ, we could not use this instrument. An inner source could, however, use this instrument very well. For us to accept a call the necessity is for the instrument to be aware of the omnipresent, omnipotent Creator, ever invisible and ever mysterious. This instrument has this point of view at a strongly fundamental level, thusly the contact is stable and we have enjoyed the privilege of communicating through this instrument for some time.

Do you then wish to be universal entities? This question is valuable to consider at this time, we feel. Are you able to look calmly upon the gradual decrease of a strongly personal service and judgment of service in favor of a nonjudgmental and nonpersonal attempt to be, in a spontaneous enough way that experience will be tempered in their formation by inner gifts of universal awareness?

In this regard we remind each of the request of the one known as Jesus the Christ, that if a man were to follow this entity it must hate its mother and father. This is what we speak of. The spirit of universal love and service speaks in silence, yet its urgings are strong and the time inevitably comes when the seeker must choose between personal preference and doing the will of the infinite One. This decision does not have exceptions for family, friends or convenience. It merely is offered without any tangible reward for turning one's back upon sources of financial plenty, emotional comfort or other excellent mundane benefits. It offers only the impersonal satisfaction of being totally willing to do the will of the infinite Creator.

Not all entities aspire to this type or quality of service. It is especially frustrating to those who seek a feeling of truly being of service that there is no one service more beneficial or high than any other service; the service is completely within in the total loving dedication of heart, mind, soul and strength to carrying into manifestation the Creator.

Consider that which this instrument does to prepare to channel. It always asks that it be completely transparent, so that all that flows from its mouth may be the words given by the spirit of the infinite Creator and not the instrument's own opinion. This seems an act of self abnegation, yet it is the key to this instrument's ability to receive fairly advanced material. Were the instrument to be requesting very wise-sounding material, wishing to be thought of well, inner planes energies would then be attempting contact with this instrument. We do not deal with those whose personal—or what you would call egoic—nature is the primary mover causing the entity to seek contact. We are able to make good communication establishments only with those who have surrendered to the will of the infinite One, to the point if nothing occurs the entity will simply carry on without any feeling of being less of a channel.

For those who are living in continuous prayer or meditation or are truly attempting to do so our help is ever present as a kind of keel underlying and strengthening the ability to be stable which each entity has in its seeking. This is perhaps the most used of our ways of communication, and we are not identified as a source other then the self. That is because selves who can receive us in this enspiriting manner think of themselves in a universal way.

At this point we would ask if there are questions which may help to clarify this material. Is there a query at this time?

Questioner: Not from me, thank you.

I am Q'uo, and am again with this instrument in love and light. Perhaps the heart of this session's query is a consideration of the nature of service to others. It is obvious that this instrument serves as it channels. It is not obvious that this instrument serves as it observes and reacts to sense impressions by creating mental formations which bless charitably those events observed and reacted to. In each entity's life pattern there is the inevitable assumption that dramatic services are more important than non-dramatic services, that those who are healers or teachers are somehow more advanced than those whose service is to tend machines or to aid other entities in menial and mundane tasks. The truth is that what is most of service is the attitude of the heart. Each entity must work within its own self to create the holy of holies within, to become aware of that occasion within the self and to move gradually, a little at a time, the heart and the seat of the mundane self into the holy of holies that is being prepared within so that the life experience is mundane experience seen from a standpoint which is stably spiritual in its structures of perception.

As we have said, this is subtle work. We feel it is an appropriate direction, and encourage each to contemplate what true service is. Is there truly a necessity in order to be one's very best? To be obviously a leader among humankind? Or does it feel more likely to you that true service is involved in the surrender of the self, moment by moment, to the inspiring energies of the universal self. The universal self is all of you, yet you are the universal self alone. You are holy and profane, you are as much a mystery as is the Creator. Your mystery and your service may be contained, convenient and finite, or you may choose the high road of attempting to universalize modes of perception so that you move more and more into an acceptance of that which the mind brings. Full and loving action in the face of circumstance is your path of service. Each is on that path. Sudden changes take place in such paths and the scenery changes. As long as the attention is kept upon the will of the infinite One whatever service lies before you will feel most blessed. It may also feel inconvenient, uncomfortable and not at all fun. The persistence and even stubbornness of entities as they move through paths of service which have encountered difficult terrain …

(Tape ends.) ❧

Special Meditation
September 27, 1992

Group question: My name is K, and I will give a preamble to the basic question by giving some details on why I am interested in this question. My interest is in the Law of One, especially as it pertains to the manifested world. Current science states that many manifested variations are caused by multiple forces and laws, and is the outcome of compartmentalization brought about by specialization and the many scientific disciplines. There is but one law and one cause. Walter Russel produced the most comprehensive study of the Law of One and some of his writings are in this room now. Nicola Tesla, or Tesla's inventions, gave most practical demonstration of this law. Tesla's work was performed when the electrical applications were in their infancy, hence were somewhat crude and cumbersome, yet functional. Russel suggested the use of vortical coils to generate heat, and the details of that are also in the documents that are available in this room. The current need to find alternative power generation methods due to environmental pollution and … crystal technology is not appropriate at present, although it is the preferred solution, therefore there is the need to investigate Russel's suggestions to determine the viability of vortical coils. Three possible solutions from vortical coils are as follows: the first is the one suggested by Russel which is to produce steam from water cooled centering units which are placed in the center of the vortical coils. One could also use the increased electrical energy at the vortical coils centers. The third possibility is to use vortical coils to generate torque to drive alternator shafts. Please discuss the viability of these options.

(Carla channeling)

I am Yom. Greetings to each present in this circle in the love and the light of the one infinite Creator. We thank you for the privilege of this invitation to share our opinions with each of you. It is a service to us that we cannot overestimate, and we are grateful for the opportunity to attempt to be of service. We ask that it be accepted that our opinions are fallible and that each use his own discriminatory faculties.

We are limited in what we can verbalize using this instrument, however the contact is stable and we shall proceed.

The concern for methods of healing the effects of the indulgence of naturally destructive actions of humankind is certainly understandable. We find that what you might call destiny has rather overtaken the energies of those entities who have heard the sorrowing cry of the Creator's second density creation manifest before you. Further, it is greatly to be appreciated that there be visionary entities whose education and patterns of thought are scientific, focusing into issues concerning the removal of manyness from what is called scientific research. We shall come back to this thought but would like now to address the specific query insofar as we are able through this instrument.

It may be understood in our opinion that the key to the use of vortices for [weal or woe] depends in part upon that which overarches and overshadows the illusion which you now enjoy. The nature of light is such that within this density we have called third a relatively sparse degree or amount of radiant light is received into the gridwork of natural vortices within and upon your sphere. A portion of the information that is necessary to use the quanta of energy from vortices is unavailable to entities whose intelligences, shall we say, accept, recognize, appreciate and thrive under light that is denser than the light available within this density.

Given that this crystallized channel were to be found to speak to the essences which are full of life energy at each vortex, the crystallized entity must bid farewell to much, however, given that such a facilitator were present, some considerations might be interesting. The concept of the vortex, though not congruent in many minds with what is called pyramid energy, is indeed the same quality of manifestation. It may be helpful to visualize the shape of the triangle balanced upon triangle, both having the same base, then at the perpendicular to other triangles of the same base. When these four triangles are moved together, the outside of the figure is the square, indicative of the manifested illusion of third density, or, in many cases, of types of manifestation in other densities. The inner shapes are interesting, but the inner-most bears consideration.

The use of water connected with what you have called vortical energy, given the transducer of denser light, is benign, and it is probable that consideration of the crystalline properties of water and its interaction with qualities of light might prove helpful. The use of torque, while certainly practical in some ways, may be found to be not the dead end but the least desirable avenue of inquiry. We find considerations which cause us to refrain from speaking further at this moment.

However, we shall accept queries when we have finished our consideration of two things. Firstly, we ask each to consider the depth of the illusion. To a non-scientist it seems that the world which is inhabited is secure and permanent. To the careful scientist this picture alters due to considerations of the ultimate total lack of knowledge of first principles. The unlimited and infinite beings that each entity is contribute to the waking consciousness the urge or impulse to question that unknown area left by authority. This is a consideration to be pondered.

Our second concern is to speak of the preparation necessary to be a what may be considered a crystallized channel. We speak as those of the Confederation of Planets in the Service of the Infinite Creator when we say—not without regard or sympathy—that the key to the Law of One in its manifested form is, to our knowledge, not, nor will it ever be, any thing. Things may be created by a crystallized entity which would in history's memory overshadow that servant's identity or renown. However, the greatest single manifestation of the Law of One remains each of you. If you cannot master the universal self which you are, then other secondary manifestations will accordingly suffer.

To become crystallized is the work of an infinite number of incarnational experiences, no one number being correct. Even though the disciplines of personality are nearer to hand than the breath, yet such is most difficult to discover within one's self. Nothing that one may learn from another is sufficient to ignite the ultimate realization that places an entity in a state of purity of discipline within which allows all things to occur as the forces and tides of happy circumstance unfold. Much of what feels as though it were one's personal identity is stripped, not from the exterior of the worker in consciousness, but rather from the interior structure of self-perception.

The releasing of effort is difficult for humankind, for it seems as though the harder one worked, the more one would prosper. In our understanding, the deep bio-programming alterations necessary to enkindle and engage the pure love within are those things which are sensed as deeply threatening to the outer consciousness. The time, as you realize this illusion, needed to move in one's inner life into a choiceless, compassionate position which transparently radiates a fullness of available light is long in coming. When it arrives, it is a probability that the crystallized seeker will then find laid before it the manner of its service, which in great probability will be unexpected.

We would enlarge upon that spoken, or entertain other queries at this time. Is there a further query?

K: I thank you for your deliberations, and I fully appreciate that in order to fully understand the Law of One, one must become the Law of One, and only then will one not need to ask these questions.

I am Yom. My brother, we do not perceive a question. If there be one, please restate.

K: There are no further questions at this time.

I am Yom. As we leave this circle we pause to thank each for the intensity of seeking which brings you to this domicile to offer this call to us at this time. Knowledge seems to be that which contains truth, yet that which is known is not truth. To move this seemingly endless paradox is the rightful work and learning process of the children of paradox, those within the creation you now dance through. To each of you fan out the paradoxes which create the dynamics for causing each in his own way to hunger for the truth. Hold to that divine hunger.

One last clue, as the one known as K would say, is this: light is the first manifested thing, moreover, light is all manifested things. However, the energy that creates the whim of manifestation is inadequately but best described as love. We regret the nearly useless term, but feel each grasps that the one original Thought, the Logos, is unmanifest and remains the sole receptor of truth. You may embody that truth and then, through the quality of reflected love within the self, may open doors in service to one or a few or many entities. When light is considered, consider also that it is [not an] artifact of time and space nor does it transcend the illusion in the way logically or intuitively available to the educated mind. We encourage the consideration of … We must pause.

We are those of Yom. We are again with this instrument, and find it has become uncomfortable enough to be less than adequate for good contact. Therefore, we thank and bless each with great affection. Thank you each for seeking with persistence and passion. May your journey be one which is irresistible. In the Creator's infinite love and light we leave this instrument. We are known to you as those of Yom. Adonai.

L/L Research

Sunday Meditation
September 27, 1992

Group question: This afternoon we have talked about topics ranging from the feeling of the loss of control over the environment around us to the fear within ourselves that we might not be able to survive economically. Rapid change, frustration, learning how to balance various positive and negative aspects of our lives yet remain within an equilibrium that we feel is the quality that is most helpful in dealing with most of these various forms of catalyst and stimulus and also is the fruit, shall we say, of successfully balancing the opposites in our experience. We are aware that this centeredness and this feeling of equilibrium is important to incorporate into our lives. We are wondering if there are suggestions that you would have as to how we could more easily incorporate or find ourselves with that feeling of centeredness, equilibrium and balance. Are there certain attitudes that would help? Humor, meditation, or anything else?

(Carla channeling)

We are known to you as those of Q'uo. Greetings to each in the love and in the light of the one infinite Creator. It is on wings of joy that we obey your call at this session of working. We so appreciate the blending of your meditative spirits and feel privileged to mingle our vibrations with your own. As we speak, kindly remember that we are not without error. Use your own discrimination and accept nothing that is not your own personal truth.

We shall speak a story taken from one of yours religious systems. There was once a seeker who found a guru in a small village in the mountains. This guru recognized the student and without much discussion took the student to a cave, and bid her to sit until she had learned all she needed to know. Each day he came to the cave and asked her if she had learned all that she needed to know. She replied in the negative, she had not learned all yet. At this the guru's hands raised high, holding a stout stick and the teacher firmly rapped the stick against the student's hapless head and went away.

One day he came into the cavern and asked again, for perhaps the thirtieth time, "Now, have you learned all you need to know?" "Yes," said the student, and ran from the cave. "Ah," said the guru, "that is all I have to teach."

My dear ones, the energies of the biochemical mind are not all of your consciousness. The mind which lives and dies with your body complex is one geared towards knowledge which enables one to control its environment, to maintain survival and comfort, and to pursue goals within the reach of the horizon. It is your consciousness which neither lives nor dies but is infinite and eternal which asks the questions it cannot answer, which aims the incarnate self at goals which the self cannot encompass in total.

And the role within incarnation of this consciousness which is infinite is quite often reduced in efficacy because the intellectual mind complex is fairly [sure] that it may know and be sure of anything which it sets out to know. How confident you are in the efficiency of the intellect. Yet the experience of incarnation as it passes shows again and again the error made by any which assumes that because it knows truths it will be able skillfully to propagate those truths in a life pattern.

We ask you to gaze inwardly at the physical vehicle. Is the head, the neck, relaxed or do you strain for truth? Is the abdomen, the breathing, relaxed or is there tension? We ask you to breathe deeply and feel how the tension goes to a lower level with each breath. Allow the belly to become soft, allow the neck, the shoulders that carry so much thought to be relaxed and know in a completely non-mental way that you are receptive.

Feel that emptiness that few of our words have created within each, that delicious, restful feeling of the empty cup. No leaves in the bottom of some forgotten, previous drink but all clean and ready. Ready for what? Ah, you are ready to accept and allow the fullness of love. Feel that sweet wine filling your cup as the many workers in the spiritual realm that are concerned passionately with you bend to you lovingly, faithfully, continuously, freshening that living vine of love within. Now, allow this visualized self to be held up to the light and feel the energy, the creative power of quickening, enlivening, space-giving light.

You have friends you are not using, dear ones. You have covered your half-empty cups because of the fear engendered by the realizations that you shall not manifest the vision or ideal that lies within your faithful, open hearts. Why do you have this darkening, closing fear? You have it because it is needed. Your mind, the mind of the body, has said "This and this must be if I am to be as I wish," and then the mind judges because of a perceived error or a falling short of the ideal exists. Could it be that the self takes the self too seriously, and the irreplaceable, infinite ideal too lightly? To love the highest truth is very, very well. To love the self as the perpetrator and controller of this unlimited truth is a judgment error. Thusly, hold to the ideal but not to the extent that there are forces of judgment within which take the self into the cave of fear and thereby stop further catalyst from occurring.

Now, let us return to the student coming from the cave. Into the sunlight comes the student, not perceiving any truth except the desire to avoid being beaten about the head. This is your situation. Into this situation come a great company of those who would aid, not far from you or unavailable during activity but as near as memory. You are required to ask for help. When help is requested, mentally, that help flows and the open heart receives it and feels its healing touch in every cell. As each knows, so to speak, it is not the vision that fails, not the love, the compassion, the ideals, but that self which cannot empty itself of the dregs of used up experience. Trust the plangent cords of memory to sustain the learning implicit in each and every perceived error and block. Then allow the self to open slowly, slowly, until the feeling of relaxation is such that you are not threatened by the act of will of uncovering the self within and allowing these dregs to be poured out. Visualize even if this helps that you are giving this distillation of disappointment, frustration, and other seemingly negative emotions into the all-healing Earth energy which is all about you.

Now, thirdly, empty and cleansed, having released the fears of failures, accept the love and compassion of those mystical beings, essences and energies of spirit that wish to support you to aid in filling the pot with new, living compassion, its liquid crystalline, sparkling beauty, soothing, invigorating and enlivening the small human self so that this self may take its place in the full identity that you are, for you are all of these manifestations, concerns, and thought patterns, and you are pure consciousness as well. This help from guidance moves into the portions of the deeper mind, not the conscious mind, so that help from without, in your way of discernment, finds the appropriate nodal [resonance] point which is the receptacle for that particular guidance form.

All that comes to you, those blessings that touch the spirit with healing, touch not a human as you know yourself, but that portion deeper than the conscious human mind which profoundly resonates with the conscious mind if this is allowed, and enables you to see through moments of intense activity, as well as peaceful times, that all things truly are well. Allow your sources of help the invitation needed for you to be touched innerly and you will feel at the moment you ask the aid that is given. Gradually, the path winds as it will, difficulties and tests mount as the capacity to learn increases, but in those who have learned to pour out and leave behind now useless, inanimate dregs of exhausted experience, the marvelous, sparkling joy of one who is accepting of the gifts and blessings of and infinitely transforming energy of love.

This love created, this love destroys. All that is is within that which we must for lack of other words call love. This awesome and terrible love shall test and stretch each of you. That it does so with sure purpose is very hard to see. When you are emptied and the filling of your cup has begun, rest in the hollowness within, and allow the open heart to feel the peace of this one moment without fear. May you be sustained. As you are you shall be; transform the face of the Earth.

We would at this time transfer this contact to the one known as Jim, if the one known as Jim would wish to receive this contact. We shall attempt to transfer at this time. We are those of Q'uo.

(Jim channeling)

I am Q'uo, and greet each again in love and light through this instrument. It is our privilege at this time to ask if there are any further queries of a briefer nature to which we may speak. Is there a query at this time?

Questioner: How would you go about asking for guidance *(inaudible)* at the spur of the moment?

I am Q'uo, and I am aware of your query, my sister. For those who have little or no experience in requesting guidance from those whose honor it is to provide such, we would recommend that there be those times of meditations reserved for opening the heart in this seeking to the inner guidance, and during this time we would recommend that the seeker begin to familiarize the self with those sensations and feelings that rise up from within as this request is made. Thus, the seeker will come to feel the response to this request, and will come to recognize the feeling tone, shall we say, of those who respond.

During these meditations it is helpful if the seeker is able to begin the meditations by centering the self upon those qualities of the self which are, shall we say, more securely set and which can be used as the building block. By centering upon the qualities that are stable the seeker offers its call and is in a position to remain open to the response according to the stability of centering qualities, be they humor, balance, care, devotion, intensity of desire or whatever the seeker feels are the most stable and available characteristics. Then, when the seeker has become familiar with the feeling of the response, it is then possible to ask for such in the normal round of activities, outside of meditations.

Is there another query, my sister?

Questioner: Not at this time, thank you.

I am Q'uo, and we thank you, my sister. Is there another query?

Carla: I have one final one if no one has anything. I would like to have your opinion, if there is any opinion that you can offer, as to whether the longer group question is a better teaching tool at this time for this group, or questions that are answered in a shorter manner and then each question being answered leading to another question. Are you able at all to give some indication as to … how you feel about the efficacy of these two ways?

I am Q'uo, and I am aware of your query, my sister. We are, as always, happy to serve in whatever manner is requested if it be within our abilities. As we look at the changing faces within your group we can see that there may be instances in which the shorter query would be more efficacious, other instances in which the group question of the longer nature would be more helpful.

We must leave this determination to your group, as its personality is formed from session to session, according to those entities that join your seeking and the concerns that each brings with him or her. However, as a general practice it is well to offer this segment of questioning at the end of your session so that those queries that arise in the mind may be offered for our opinion.

Is there a further query, my sister?

Carla: No, that was helpful. Thank you very much for being here today.

I am Q'uo. Again we thank you, my sister. Is there another query at this time?

(Pause)

I am Q'uo, and as we are aware of no further queries we shall take this opportunity to thank each, once again, for inviting our presence and our opinions to your circle of seeking this day. We are most honored to have been able to join your group and walk with you always upon your journey of seeking as do many others, unseen to your physical eyes, but who wait for your inner call to lend their assistance and support on this arduous journey that you find yourself upon.

At this time we shall take our leave of this group, leaving each as always in the love and in the light of the one infinite Creator. We are known to you Q'uo. Adonai, my friends. Adonai. ☙

Special Meditation
October 3, 1992

Group question: My name is K, and my first question is as follows. In our previous session the advice to the entity known as K was terminated due to the discomfort of the instrument. Would you kindly continue from the point as follows: "… you may embody that truth and then, through the quality of reflected love within the self, may open doors in service to one or a few or many entities. When light is considered, consider also that it is [not an] artifact of time and space nor does it transcend the illusion in the way logically or intuitively available to the educated mind. We encourage the consideration of …" *(Contact was terminated at this point in the last session.)*

(Carla channeling)

I am Yom. Greetings in the love and in the light of the one infinite Creator. We are most happy and pleased to have the privilege of meditating with this circle at this working, and thank you for calling us to your session to offer our humble opinions in response to your call. As always, please use your powers of discrimination, as we are fallible. The clue which we had intended to offer was this: consider whether manifestation is a creature of the powers of manifested physical energies or a creature of what you know as mind.

May we respond further?

K: I have a further question, which is as follows: Is the vortical electrical coil suggested by Walter Russel worthy of research, or can similar effects be obtained using the triangular or pyramid forms?

We are those of Yom, and appreciate your query. In our opinion it is equally fortuitous to experiment with the vortical coil as the one known as Walter has discussed and to consider the pyramid energies if it be seen that the pyramid shape is the replicated shape of the downward portion of the gathering force of the pyramid. The physical, shall we say, pyramid then would be that which received the windings of both clockwise and anti-clockwise spirals as the unmanifest reflection or gathering or blessing portion of the coil then be able to use the reflected grid to complete the same double-phased energy as expressed by the windings of the vortical coil.

May we say that it is, in our humble opinion, the work of the inner discipline whose moment in your space/time and time/space has arrived and that these energies shall meet with representational mind capable of ethical usage of power, not at this juncture but in the fourth density or density of the love or compassion vibrations more harmoniously and predictably being in balance.

Is there a further query?

K: Yes. I appreciate the need to become a transparent radiator of available light. Am I correct in believing that a closeness to nature will in my case aid this process?

I am Yom. We answer in two portions. Firstly, the creation of the Father, as this instrument calls the second-density sphere and biota upon which you enjoy incarnation, is full and replete in undistorted love, therefore the Earth and its creatures are helpful whether or not the individual entity is aware of this aid. Secondly, to one whose spirit rejoices in the creation and the energies of this harmonious and beautiful creation these positive effects are many times magnified. We may note in this regard that the impulse to seek nature can be somewhat wayward when one finds oneself in a position athwart the forces of this natural, harmonious and sometimes inconvenient world of nature. Therefore, it is well consciously to pause in good weather and evil days alike, sun and rain, to give praise to the infinite One for this perfected manifestation, and to offer thanks for beholding Its face.

May we answer further, my brother?

K: I have no further specific questions at this time.

I am Yom. My brother, we are limited in that which we may relate to you. This we realize you understand and accept, further, we feel that your intentions are pure. Consequently, we encourage your heart to remain pure, your goal to become more pure, and your manifestation shall indeed surprise you and delight as well.

With our farewell we clear the way for our brothers and sisters of the principle known as Q'uo, as this entity is waiting to speak also. We leave this instrument and group in the love and in the light of the one infinite Creator. Adonai.

(Carla channeling)

I am Q'uo. We greet each in the love and in the light of the one infinite Creator. As our brothers and sisters of Yom have said before us, the honor of sharing this discussion with this group is keenly felt and your service to us in calling us to you is greatly appreciated and hopefully deserved, however, we request that our error-prone nature be considered in evaluating our thoughts.

We are called to this question not because of specifically physical work, physically oriented information which we have to share. We have nothing of that nature to offer; however, the structure of the empowering intention or desire of the one known as K inadvertently to this entity calls for a type of inquiry and way of viewing which we might share with some efficacy.

The manifested world may be viewed in a terseness and plangent depth by study of that portion of the deep mind which you and we have termed the archetypical mind. The myths of the Titans, of Lucifer, and many other mythical examples of light bringers show the bringing into manifestation of this light which allows the consciousness within incarnation to expand. As the gaze turns to the archetypes of the mind and the archetypes of the body it may be suggested that the powers progress through the vortical coil, for example, might be seen to involve the archetypes of the Matrix and the Potentiator of the mind or of the body.

Let us gaze at the archetypes of the mind. Firstly, the Matrix of the mind. This essence or energy is the untaught seeker, the beginner's mind, reaching, reaching and again reaching. For what? The Potentiator of the Mind is that which receives the desire and enables it by a process of reflection and blessing. The Significator of the Mind is then the result of the Matrix entity or archetypical figure reaching or intending that which can only be potentiated by the seemingly passive Potentiator, that seated figure which has within the bosom great wisdom.

Thusly, the Matrix of the Mind is able to record incoming data, and through the Potentiator once again is able to deliver to the archetype of the Catalyst of the Mind the catalyst which shall become experience.

In the archetypes of the body the process is reversed, the matrix of the Body being even-functioning or balanced. This equilibrium is moved one way or another by the interaction with the Potentiator of the Body which may be called informed judgment or wisdom. The Matrix then is the blessing, is, indeed, manifested perfection which moves it away from balance and the pattern repeats in reversal until we see in the Significator of the Body the entity which is completely suspended upside down, thus showering the manifested body energy with its treasure as it falls from the clothing of this archetypical figure.

This has a relevance due to the triple—we correct this instrument—the three-fold cycle which is the pattern within the thought of the one known as Walter, that is, the first cycle which is not until it is manifest by the second cycle and recorded in the third cycle.

We are having difficulty speaking upon this topic through this instrument and would ask this instrument to move a bit deeper that we may have a firmer contact. We shall pause. We are those of Q'uo.

(Pause)

We are again with this instrument. Within the context of the questioner's concerns we would suggest the consideration of a fourth cycle, which may be called the cycle of blessing or enabling. The Matrix, then, of the Mind would equal, archetypically speaking, the voided first stroke; the Potentiator of the Mind, the second stroke which makes manifest; the matrix of the Mind is then again the third stroke, as it has become enlivened by the Potentiator. However, until this is moving through the Potentiator's blessing or enabling it cannot become catalyst, or, in terms of physics, it cannot work. The fourth cycle, then, is that area which may be profitably considered, not for windings of coils manifested, but for the personality of the facilitator of such designs. For in order for these to work the potentiating position must begin within the mind of the observer or facilitator of the process. This intangible set of mind, body and spirit, but for beginning study the mind, is necessary in order that the device that effectively works might be conceived and manifest.

These words are as slippery as the stem of a water lily, and we grasp them as one would who believes that where there are lily stems there are also water lilies in bloom. Before, during and after all attempts to manifest truth lies a shining, loving, powerful and wise mind which is in each of you. We ask that more and more you learn to rejoice not because of any one thing but because the true nature of creative love is more nearly truly expressed in joy than in most other states of emotional mind.

Let the point of view remain as closely [attuned] as comfortable to the nascent spirit to remain with this joy, for it abides within and is not simply a response to that which is without or beyond the five external senses. Seek always this steady state of balanced joy and the mind that is the higher mind will more and more find itself at home and more and more shall the small one that each apparently is become graced with the overshadowing unity of a larger oneness.

We, as always, emphasize the patient, persistent practice of inner silent listening which is generically called meditation. And, further, encourage the use of those who guide, not for outer information but for the homing towards unity which the disciplined personality seeks to become.

Are there any queries at this time?

K: No, there are no specific queries.

Does any have a query?

R: I don't have a query.

Jim: Not I. Thank you very much, Q'uo.

R: Thanks for the elaboration.

We are those of the principle known to you as Q'uo. It has been like riding the tiger to get this transmission through, and we ask that care be taken to keep this instrument quiet until the next diurnal cycle. As usual, this instrument would not quit when it became discomfited, therefore we needed to use the proper energy. However, though we thank this instrument, we would encourage it to be careful when it is uncomfortable with an acute difficulty in your future. We smile at this instrument's desire to continue, for it is charming. May wisdom more frequently accompany such charm.

Each of you, how blessed we feel by you, and in return offer our love and like blessing. Truly you and we are loved and all that we do in return is only that which has rippled through from you to return. This is your love, our love, your, our, your, our … until there is one. In this oneness greet each other, always.

We leave you and this instrument in the love and the light of the one infinite Creator. Adonai. Adonai. ✥

L/L Research

L/L Research is a subsidiary of Rock Creek Research & Development Laboratories, Inc.

P.O. Box 5195
Louisville, KY 40255-0195

www.llresearch.org

Rock Creek is a non-profit corporation dedicated to discovering and sharing information which may aid in the spiritual evolution of humankind.

ABOUT THE CONTENTS OF THIS TRANSCRIPT: This telepathic channeling has been taken from transcriptions of the weekly study and meditation meetings of the Rock Creek Research & Development Laboratories and L/L Research. It is offered in the hope that it may be useful to you. As the Confederation entities always make a point of saying, please use your discrimination and judgment in assessing this material. If something rings true to you, fine. If something does not resonate, please leave it behind, for neither we nor those of the Confederation would wish to be a stumbling block for any.

CAVEAT: This transcript is being published by L/L Research in a not yet final form. It has, however, been edited and any obvious errors have been corrected. When it is in a final form, this caveat will be removed.

© 2009 L/L Research

Sunday Meditation
October 4, 1992

Group question: In an out-of-body experience—which is the question this afternoon—when the exit is via the crown of the head there is impression of movement, at great speed, as if one were drawn up through a tunnel or a funnel. Please describe this process and account for this impression. We would like to know, in this area of out-of-body experience, if this feeling of movement is actual. Does it take place in time/space? Is it a movement in consciousness or is it simply a feeling of movement that accompanies a more profound experience or process?

Also, what would you recommend that the seeker of truth take as the attitude or position regarding out-of-body experience. Of what value, in another words, is it to a person to experience out-of-body experience, and what would one think of such?

(Carla channeling)

I am Q'uo. Greetings, my friends, in the light and the love of the one infinite Creator. Thank you for asking for our participation in your session of working at this time. We are honored to be called to your circle and bless each with a whole heart. As always, we ask that our words carry no authority except that of opinion.

The out-of-body experience about which you ask is a subject which many are focused upon because of an underlying desire to be shed of the heavy chemical machinery of the third-density physical vehicle, or body. The spirit or consciousness of an entity is bound by choice to its physical vehicle in order to persevere throughout an incarnative experience. It is no wonder that the consciousness often may yearn to be free of the seeming tyranny of flesh. However, there is much to be said for the consideration of that which is uncomfortable and inconvenient being also far more useful in the production of catalyst.

Let us look briefly at the experience itself, of moving from within the physical vehicle to observing the physical vehicle through the eyes of the finer bodies which are within incarnative stricture, however are not necessarily tied within the physical vehicle permanently. The consciousness, as it were, in the most natural or easy way of egress from the physical vehicle may visualize the tucking and rolling motion of certain practiced falls or yogic postures. When the physical vehicle is exited and entered with this visualized method the trauma is minimal.

The experiences spoken of in the query, of the squeezing feeling and the tunnel, are those feelings associated with a less skillful method of exiting the physical vehicle. The imagination, if we may use that term, is helpful to those who would wish not to experience the less than optimal symptoms of exit and entry, by visualizing the tucking and gently rolling, both leaving and entering the physical vehicle.

In most cases of unintended exit of the physical vehicle, the finer bodies carrying the consciousness are within the same illusion, or, depending on the vibratory patterns of the individual, there may be the precise location which one enjoys in the third density but the out-of-body experience may be in fourth density. This still appears to the consciousness senses as a normal, solid, seemingly third-density illusion, and though the electrical nature of energies between people is far more apparent, nonetheless the work which might be done in this out-of-body environment is no more or less effectual in creating new polarity than experiences within the third-density physical vehicle.

There is a very old tradition amongst your people of spiritual quest involving work done without the physical vehicle. For this type of moving out of the body a very precise and lengthy tradition or school of training has been followed by the aspirant to, shall we say, holy or magical orders. Within these orders the discipline of the personality is labored upon by visualization and austere practices which begin to reclaim the linkage between the physical mind and the mind of consciousness.

Perhaps we could use the term "brain" to indicate the natural thinking capacity of a second-density animal which your physical vehicle is, to differentiate it from the term "mind," the mind being that of infinite consciousness. The linkage betwixt brain and mind is normally set within incarnation in a matrix which allows free communication from brain to mind and limited communication from mind to brain. The magical training—which may be called cabalistic or white magical traditional—attempts often quite successfully to restructure the matrices—we correct this instrument—the matrix so that the points of connection are denser between the mind and the brain so that subconscious material is made more available to the brain or that which controls the day-to-day living.

This application of out-of-body experiences is a form of information gathering. In and of itself we do not find it to be useful, however, when a desire is formed to examine the surrounding inner planes and the consciousness which is sent forth is carefully laden with instructions which move it into inner planes, then such a spiritual scientist may make notes and learn more of the subtle inner environments which in total make up the inner structure of the deep mind or deeper aspects of the self. We do not encourage entities to move out of the body without there being a spiritual goal involved, for as many have said before us, it is a crowded universe and many of the citizens of it are particularly interested in those whose life force of spirit and will dims before the life force of the physical vehicle.

The danger here is that those who do not yet value or respect the incarnation may yearn so to be spirits that the emphasis upon finding holiness and worship within the physically bounded experience is lost or tossed away, and instead the entity simply wishes to escape the bounds of the physical body. We encourage each to contemplate the manifold opportunities within the confines of the physical vehicle to be a spirit, that the house of flesh involved does not limit the desire to experience as a spiritual entity, a magical entity, but rather offers to such spiritual questing the sharpness and substance of experience which cannot be had outside of the physical body. This incarnation which each now enjoys is a rare gift. We encourage each to respect and love this gift of intense time, of intensive actions, of deeply difficult choices made perforce in the darkness of illusion. To escape the bounds of body is also to deeply blunt the efficacy of precious incarnational time, space and time where the questing spirit may make blind choices. This blindness, this darkness is precious, for choices made herein strike deeply into the infinite self.

I am Q'uo. Is there a further query?

(Pause)

I am Q'uo. We find many questions in this group, but none of them spoken aloud, so we are not allowed to answer them. We own the terrible pun. What can we then do, having exhausted the queries, but bid you every possible blessing of love and light in your journey towards the One. We leave this instrument with thanks and this group ditto, in the love and in the wondrous light of the one infinite Creator. Adonai, adonai.

(Carla channeling)

I Yadda. I greet you also in the love and in the light of one infinite Creator. Greetings and salutations to so many solemn minds today. We ask you who are here why are you so serious? Be less serious. The importance of your work is like clothing; you have on too many clothes. Take off some solemnity! Yes?

A vest of serious, a tie of responsibility. Away with these things! And when you are naked and no longer so solerm … solmn … solenn … so solemn—haha! We got it!—when you are not so solemn anymore then bounce and jiggle and jump for joy and feel the waters of love that you so solemnly seek now.

You know you keep yourselves from your own bliss by holding too tightly to the clothing of righteousness. We thank you for allowing us to share our thoughts with you, and would say good-bye with much blessing … blessing … ha! We are Yadda. Adonai. ✺

L/L Research

L/L Research is a subsidiary of Rock Creek Research & Development Laboratories, Inc.

P.O. Box 5195
Louisville, KY 40255-0195

www.llresearch.org

Rock Creek is a non-profit corporation dedicated to discovering and sharing information which may aid in the spiritual evolution of humankind.

ABOUT THE CONTENTS OF THIS TRANSCRIPT: This telepathic channeling has been taken from transcriptions of the weekly study and meditation meetings of the Rock Creek Research & Development Laboratories and L/L Research. It is offered in the hope that it may be useful to you. As the Confederation entities always make a point of saying, please use your discrimination and judgment in assessing this material. If something rings true to you, fine. If something does not resonate, please leave it behind, for neither we nor those of the Confederation would wish to be a stumbling block for any.

CAVEAT: This transcript is being published by L/L Research in a not yet final form. It has, however, been edited and any obvious errors have been corrected. When it is in a final form, this caveat will be removed.

© 2009 L/L Research

Special Meditation
October 14, 1992

Question for S: The question we're considering this afternoon for S is why things seem to have gone so far astray from the path that allowed her to provide the most service to others, and that was when her husband R was alive she had the opportunity of being in a mated relationship and of helping a family to communicate and to live together and to grow together and she felt that in that role she was able to provide services that were hers to provide. Now that R is dead she is faced with possibilities that just don't feel like they are right—going to school and taking classes that she has no interest in and pursuing a career working outside the home, which also seems to be a dead end as far as interest and opportunity to be of service. The picture of her life seems to have a number of dead ends and we are wondering this afternoon what kinds of considerations should be foremost in her mind, what opportunities are presented by the seeming dead ends, is there something that she's missing, is there something wrong with this picture, and if so what is it?

(Carla channeling)

I am Q'uo. Greetings to you, my special friends. We thank you for calling us to this circle of seeking and are most privileged to offer our opinions, with the understanding that we are not imbued with perfect knowledge. These thoughts are our opinions. Please choose those thoughts which aid and leave the residue behind.

Once, as the saying goes, upon a time all of those things in heaven and Earth, as this instrument would say, were one, and yet all existed in chaos. Into this chaos came one great creative Thought: love or the logos. At this timeless time each of you and we were already created, the manifested universe no less than your manifested selves is the intimate abode created to house and offer an environment to the spirit that each of you is. For millennia your peoples have sought and sought to discover by what means they might find a comfortable, pleasant and productive existence, they have sought help from inspirational words and from the myths of their cultures, yet none who has awakened to a realization of the nature of evolution are very comfortable in this house of Earth created so carefully for spirits to dwell in and learn.

How could this extreme discomfort be a part of the plan whereby love itself created an abode for those infinite parts of itself which it wished to offer experience to? How could such an unimaginably pure love create such pain and suffering? Once upon a time there was a point in your planetary sphere's development when it became able to support third-density beings such as yourselves. The gift of self-consciousness was offered and accepted and the human animal form based upon instinct was sacrificed to the third-density consciousness. This consciousness is your infinite self. It does not work logically or sequentially but rather by deep feelings and the persistently held desires of a seeker. However, there are no outward signs which may tell you when your second-density instinctual brain is thinking and when your infinite consciousness is running the show, only by hindsight can a guess be made as to from what part of the complex being that you are this thought or action came from. The experience of loss, of overwhelming confusion may be received either by the brain which thinks in black and white and is forever subject to duality.

We pause to move this instrument somewhat deeper.

When the brain copes with pain and difficult suffering, it wishes either to attack or to flee or both. In contrast, the consciousness which carries with it eternity looks at the same catalyst, it functions as all self-conscious things do, to observe, to analyze, to figure out what is occurring. Once this has been done, the way consciousness works is to take all of this ideated material and let it sift down through the roots of the deeper mind so that at some point dreams, visions or certainties will be clear, clarifying in lucidity beyond words, not the particulars of transformation, but the feeling of surrender and acceptance of the catalyst which occurs.

As we blend with your vibrations we find that we need not spend long portions of our precious time with you in speaking of meditation and other spiritual disciplines. Indeed, we must turn about and encourage the consideration that short, even momentary times spent asking for the Creator and It's silent messages are extremely effective. The time spent in company with the infinite One is timeless. The purified desire that leaves the seeker to the momentary thought of the Creator is the powerful portion of the meditation. The long sitting meditations are far more for the purpose of becoming a fairer observer, not becoming one with the infinite One. It is desire that moves each to that close relationship and continuing conversation with the Creator.

It is often assumed by those who are not on a spiritual pilgrimage that the greatest boon of living a spiritually oriented life is the peace of having made such a deep choice and, indeed, there is that peace of commitment to a life in faith. However, what those not on the path often forget or do not know is that the pilgrimage towards eternity, while greatly speeding up the pace of spiritual evolution, is terribly uncomfortable and inconvenient.

Each in this circle is already aware that he does not come from around here; that is, each is aware of being a wanderer. Into this particular experience come entities who must plunge into the darkness of illusion and live through an incarnation to be of service by the quality of consciousness. Each of you volunteered to be here. From the point of view beyond the third-density environment the suffering which each has gone through or now goes through seems to be a very small thing. Within the illusion it swells and seems to become overwhelming and as deadly as any disease of the body. We can only encourage each to turn from the questions of "why" long enough each day to spend a few moments or minutes with the infinite Creator. The answers are within and there is far more help than each here can imagine which is available to those who call upon loving positive discarnate energies.

We encourage this leaning upon the invisible company of those who would support you. As you ask within you will feel that sympathy in the depths of your heart and so will know that truly no one suffering suffers alone. The invisible company of those who love is there just as close as the breathing or the thinking.

Once upon a time two entities lived happily ever after. We know that few in the third density ever experience this fairytale, yet it is beyond all joy when such occurs. When one seeks hardest, on the other hand, for the fairytale romance then it comes that this is denied. This then places each, whether having loved truly or knowing no true love, in the position of wondering "Why?" May we remind each that it is well to seek the Creator's will and in that seeking there is guidance available. This guidance may be found in any of your planet's holy works. We would use this instrument's Christian bias to state that it is said that those whom the Creator loves best are those who are tested.

As wanderers, you came for two reasons: to serve and to be tested. If there is comfort in knowing that the path that is in front of each now is the appropriate destined path designed by yourself then please take comfort in that. There is always in the illusion the feeling that to be without the heavy body and heavy experiences of third density would be greatly desired, yet as soon as the incarnation is naturally over the seeking spirit gazes backwards and thinks, "Why did I not learn more? What a great opportunity!"

Once upon a time, there was to each seeking soul a moment. For each here this moment has come, the great incarnational decision has been made, the positive path will be striven for. Now that each is committed to love the source of all and to love the self and all other selves there now remains only acknowledgement of any emotional feelings, recognition and respect for the unique suffering of your own lives and the true peace which is not a comfortable peace, that peace which is the knowledge that the path of your destiny is true and its aim is straight towards infinity.

When this path is through desert wastes and bleak wilderness there seems no hope. We urge each to encourage each other in the faith that this seemingly disharmonious and painful situation is the correct and worthwhile path. The grass, shall we say, is in truth not greener elsewhere.

We will come back to this instrument. However, we would wish to yield our speaking position in this instrument's energy web to an inner planes entity. Please accept the pause necessary to open this particular channel. We leave you briefly in love and light. We are those of Q'uo.

I am Michael. In love and light I come to you to speak those words of comfort which we may offer. We would wish to share the acceptable to free will information that we can concerning the one known as R. This entity may now speak to some extent through this instrument …

I am so glad to talk to you, sweetie. Hi, I am with you. I am so pissed that I had to go and you had to stay. I wanted so much to stay if one of us had to stay. Why couldn't it be me? I want you to know that there is never a single, single minute that I am not inside you, where I always wanted to be anyway. I am in your heart and I will never leave you. I just wish that Carla could make some cigar smoke and you could see me but this girl does not have that ability so I will just say, honey, you hold on and just flow because things are going to turn out. We did everything OK, and I know you will keep on doing that. I have to go but you know I am with you. Can I ask a favor?

S: Yes.

Will you talk to me sometimes and say the special things? I would really like that, just tell me what you feel and stuff. Good-bye for now.

I am Michael. We could not use this instrument further this day for inner planes work. We are sorry we had to cut the one known as R short of expressing the immense love and unity he feels. Yet he is well and the waiting will be only as a few minutes, so he is happily awaiting the one known as S when her learning is done in this incarnation and together there will be a new experience, new lessons, and new suffering so that the Creator may learn and learn and learn.

We would leave this instrument at this time that the one known as Q'uo may receive queries. If the one known as Jim wishes to channel, we shall transfer to this instrument at this time. We are those of Q'uo, and leave this instrument in love and in light …

(Jim channeling)

I am Q'uo, and greet each again in love and in light. At this time we would ask if there are any further queries to which we may speak?

S: Yes, I do talk to Ron a lot, I'm bothered by the fact that I feel so cut off from him, when he was here I was able to feel his presence, whether I knew he was there or not. When I kissed Ron for the last time in hospital he was still alive, I knew he was not in that body, he was gone. I no longer felt what I knew [as] Ron to be in that body, he was not there. And now I'm expecting, I think, to feel something when he's with me and I don't and that scares me, and I know on some level that he's with me most of …

(Side one of tape ends.)

(Jim channeling)

… to approach you in the dream state and to communicate there his love and unity with you. There are many such dreams which are not in your memory but in which you and he have moved as one. If it is possible for you to again open a channel in your heart of the love of this life and experience there will be an easier means by which the one known as R may make himself known to you.

Is there a further query my sister?

S: That's a tall order. Yeah I have another question. I'm really confused as to where … I feel unable to go on, and basically that sums it up in a nutshell. I lack the ability to go forward, I lack the desire, I feel a real strong sense of wanting to die, I don't know where, I've tried to … oh god, this is going nowhere. I feel like I'm lacking the ability to continue, it almost seems as if life has come to a point where the test is am I or am I not going to kill myself, which I really don't believe I will because I know there's a big price to pay for that one, so I find myself praying and hoping … you know, it's really strange that I watch a show on breast cancer, I'm thinking, gee, I hope I get that soon, you know, and I've just, I don't know where to go from here, I don't know where to get what I need to go on. I'm so confused and no direction seems right, but at the same time in practical manners, I don't feel like I can sit back and wait for something to be shown to me, you know. I don't want to wait to the point where I'm a bag lady, to hopefully get an answer, if it gets that bad, I won't be around for the answer. If you could make any sense out of that?

I am Q'uo, and am aware of your query, my sister, and aware of the great pain and sorrow which are yours to bear at this time. We feel great sympathy for you, for the experience of love which you enjoyed with the one known as R seems at this time to have been cut short, when in the larger view of the lives which continue before and after this Earthly illusion there is but a moment's experience to complete within this life, though it may take what you call years to do so.

We may suggest that you re-examine those basic beliefs which you shared with the one known as R. We are aware that you have brought many of them into question as a result of the death of your beloved, but we would recommend that you look to that faith most especially that each of you shared, that lives do continue, that there is a purpose, however seemingly absurd in this life for this life, and that you, in general, begin to build again the foundation of attitude and ideals that were your foundation with the one known as R.

There will be suffering and confusion throughout this illusion, for it is by such testing that these basic principles are forged in the fire of experience within each entity's heart. Be gentle with yourself, not expecting too much, yet placing before yourself the goal each day of renewing faith in the fact that there are truly no mistakes within this illusion. There are great puzzles and riddles and experiences of confusion and doubt which each seeker of truth will find placed upon the path and with which each seeker must grapple.

We encourage you in your struggle and would hope to give comfort with the suggestion that as this experience of sorrow and grief continues, that there will be born within you the ability to withstand it and even to overcome that which seems to overcome you at this time. There is a great plan within each entity's life which is the pattern, the dance within the illusion. Each entity has before the incarnation chosen this pattern in order that it might balance and intensify and refine those qualities gathered before this illusion that are felt to be of primary importance in learning of the mystery of creation and in the honor of service. Each entity must trust the destiny that has been chosen and fuel that trust with the will to persevere, knowing that even if confusion and sorrow and suffering have their day, there is the resolution at some point within this illusion so that each seeker will find the indication that it is truly upon the right path.

We know that a great deal of anguish has been your lot for this past year in your time measure and we cannot express enough our sympathy, for few within your illusion have had the harmonious, loving, honest relationship which you have been privileged to experience and to lose such is to lose a great, great deal. But we encourage you, my sister, to persevere beyond confusion, beyond doubt, in whatever way you can find to do so, realizing that you have chosen well the path you travel, though it moves at this time through a deep and dark valley. It is only the shadow of death that haunts you, whether it be yours or your beloved's. There is truly no death, there is only life and the experience in this illusion has the purpose of verifying and ratifying the unity of the one Creator that can withstand even the most difficult of challenges.

You are not alone, my sister. You move not only with your beloved in your heart and in your mind but with a great company of lighted souls that rejoice at your every determination to continue and who offer support when your determination flags and seems to fail.

Is there a further query, my sister?

S: Yes, just briefly. Along this line of making decisions and things like that, I'm having trouble figuring out what criteria to follow. It seems like every decision that I make feels OK for the moment, but then comes to feel not OK, it doesn't feel right. I think this was a bad decision, this isn't working, this isn't … I don't get any good feedback from the decisions and I'm sensing that when I make a right decision I will get some sense of "Yeah, this is the right thing to do." I haven't really felt spiritually great about any decisions I've made—other than to stay on the planet, that I know is the right one—but if I make a decision and it doesn't feel right and I want to back away from the decision, I'm confusing myself, you know, and what's the best way to approach this decision-making process?

I am Q'uo, and am aware of your query, my sister. To make decisions is the great experience of this illusion, to use each opportunity to choose the light, to choose the love of that which is before you. This we know is difficult in itself, even under what you would call the best of the conditions that are to be found in this illusion. When you find yourself as you have with great sorrow and confusion, the making of decisions is even more difficult, but with this increased difficulty comes also the opportunity to reap the greater metaphysical benefit from even attempting the decisions.

As to how those difficult choices may be best made by you at this time, we can say very little for it is these very choices that will form your experience in what you call your future and will thereby provide the greatest opportunity for you to learn that which you have set before yourself to learn and to be of the greatest service to those about you.

To approach each decision from the aspect of seeking to serve and seeking to love is that suggestion which we find is most appropriate at this time. As you look to those whom you love and under whose care they are awaiting, shall we say, these choices is to place the welfare of these entities in the greatest position of responsibility. We perceive some difficulty in interpretation and shall find additional words for this concept. Those entities which are yours to care for are those whose welfare we see is of primary importance in your life, as is your own life's journey and direction. Seek at each opportunity that presents itself to choose that opportunity which is most filled with love and service. This we find you are already attempting with a whole heart and we would reiterate our previous suggestion that if it is possible for you to once again open your heart in even the smallest degree of love for the life that is yours to live, then it will be easier not only to feel the presence of the one known as R, but to feel the direction that is yours to take, for it is the symbiotic love of life relationship—your love of life and life's love for you—that will allow you to feel that your movement is guided and is appropriate.

We may suggest the taking of time in the beginning or end of your day or at any time when you can sit in an uninterrupted fashion, meditating upon the feeling within your heart and visualizing a channel of love opening there and feeling the connection with your life and the opportunities and challenges before you, opening so that you are able to move not just from the intellectual assessment of possibility, but more importantly are able to feel and move from the flowing of sensitivity of love from your heart and to your heart. If you can be regular in this meditative practice you can begin to build once again the feeling of connection to this life that has been severed by the death of the one known as R.

Is there a further query, my sister?

S: No. Thank you very much. I'll work on that.

Carla: I have one. I would like to know something about an expectation that I didn't have met. I expected if we did hear from R at all, that R would be like Don was after his suicide, that he would be laughing at how seriously he had taken everything and be in really good shape, but I felt an entity that was deeply enraged and really angry and a lot of things about having to leave S. Does that mean that he too has not been able to let go, that he is just holding on really hard? What's going on here? Is it a personality shell that's holding on like that? I'm just totally befuddled by the fact that he was experiencing a lot of negative emotions? I just wonder where is he, what form-making body, the between incarnations thing, what's going on?

I am Q'uo, and I'm aware of your query, my sister. We are having some difficulty with this instrument but shall attempt a brief response. The one known as R spoke through your instrument in a manner which he felt would be of the greatest service to the one known as S, for the one known as R is of the awareness that the one known as S has great sorrow and suffering at this time and though he is well aware of those principles of love, light and unity which both shared during his incarnation, it was his opinion that the one known as S would be more comforted to know that he also felt a great splitting and loss when it came his time to depart the incarnation, for each of these entities had plans which did not include such an early departure, shall we say.

The one known as R resides within the green-ray body this time, that body that is imbued with love and compassion and great passionate emotion. This entity is busying itself with the refining of those lessons that it was able to learn and process within its incarnation and awaits, as the entity known as Michael mentioned, the movement of the one known as S from this incarnation and awaits this rejoining with great joy, knowing that should the incarnation of the one known as S last many, many years in your measure, it will be but a brief moment as time is reckoned within the illusion now enjoyed by the one known as R. This entity has fulfilled its purpose, yet wished, as most positively-orientated entities, to do far more and to be of even greater service and sorrows that this was not possible. Yet, this entity knows that all is truly well and offers its encouragement in its own way at this time and shall continue to do so.

Is there a further query, my sister?

Carla: Just a follow-up. Is he with Don?

I am Quo, and I'm aware of your query, my sister. We find that the ones known as R and Don are members of a great grouping of entities of light that serve this planet at this time in a manner which is likened to a group consciousness, though each remains individualized in intention and ability to express love and to serve in a unique fashion.

Is there a further query, my sister.

Carla: No, thank you Q'uo.

I am Q'uo, and again we thank you, my sister, Is there a final query at this time?

(No further queries.)

I am Q'uo. It has been our great privilege to offer our selves and our opinions at this circle of seeking. We are grateful to be asked to serve in this manner and we cannot express enough the joy that such opportunity gives us. We thank you, my friends, and we hope that some of the words spoken this day may bring comfort to each heart present. We can only remind each doughty seeker that this illusion will test each fiber of your being and will refine your desire to seek and to serve. That is what this illusion is constructed to do and though it seems that it is a long and torturous journey it is in your larger span of life but an eye-blink in eternity and you shall be most grateful to have had the opportunity to experience this illusion when the opportunity has gone and you have found yourself on the other side of this illusion, shall we say, rejoicing for what you have gained, rejoicing even more for what you have given, for as the one known as R was well aware of, the love that you take with you is the love that you make.

We are those of Q'uo, and we leave you at this time in the love and in the light of the one infinite Creator. Adonai, my friends. Adonai. ♣

The Aaron/Q'uo Dialogues, Session 8
October 29, 1992

(This session was preceded by a period of tuning and meditation.)

Aaron: Greetings to you, my dear ones. I am Aaron. Q'uo and I are practicing being polite and each waiting for the other to speak first. Our hearts are full of the loving energy that you send out, full of the joy of your meeting. I wish that you could see with our eyes the radiance growing out of this room.

Barbara, K and I spoke a bit in the car about what subject matter you might wish to discuss tonight, about what direction you might wish this to go. Of course, the questions must come out of the deepest questions of your hearts, but I also want to remind you that what we share is not new. You know that we are not teaching you anything, only reminding you of that which you already know.

For those who might be drawn to read this work at a later time, I feel that the greatest value lies not in our conceptual answers to your questions, but in this shared energy itself. You are approaching a time when Earth will become fourth density, when many who are presently third-density energy will graduate from this plane. You are approaching a time when each of you will be fully telepathic to others, when there will be no holding back and no clinging to another, but just sharing that which is. At that point there still will be an emotional body. You will still feel emotions but there will be equanimity about that which arises, and thus, no need to fling it at another; total compassion toward what you feel from another, no fear or closing, no sense of being attacked by another's pain but compassion to that pain.

What is it like to be that way? Each of you is approaching that more and more in your life so that now it is possible for five humans and two spirits to just hang out together, to enjoy each other's energy. The humans have reached a level of consciousness where, when there is some reactivity, it is noticed quickly and worked with, with love. I wonder what inspiration that might give to those who walk this path and aspire to reach that point where they can share so openly with others without the heart closing, without the reactivity that may lead to pain to beings.

Thus, while the content may be of intellectual interest and also help to inspire and teach in some ways, it feels to me that our very working together is of supreme importance. To that end, to whatever degree it is natural, I would suggest as much of a moving dialogue as possible rather than long talks. When two of you converse, you understand when the other is ready to speak. You finish that immediate thought and stop. So, if the principle known as Q'uo finds this appropriate, I would like to see our working together move in that direction as much as is possible.

We tossed many topics around in the car, as I am sure you have here. I feel not only Q'uo ready to speak here, but many of you. What are your thoughts? That is all.

Q'uo: I am Q'uo. We, too, greet you in the love and in the light of the one infinite Creator.

We approach this meeting with the greatest of joy and echo the one known as Aaron's exclamation of delight at the beauty of the energies of this circle of seeking. How much of each of you is brought together in new ways each time there is a meeting, a joining of not only minds and heart, soul and spirit, but seemingly humdrum contraptions you are carried about in! The strong effect of physical nearness is its possibility for spontaneous communication, a combustion of spirits searching, sharing and encouraging each other together.

We pause for enough time to elapse that all may sense and feel the connections of harmonizing energy swirling circularly about this group. Feel the aliveness of this fresh-forged unity. We pause.

(A pause for group meditation.)

In gratitude, we of Q'uo ask for a first query.

R: Would Q'uo suggest a way of looking at turmoil in one's life that is very emotional, to find a way to balance all that seems to be negative and pressuring, happening seemingly at the same time? Is there a general principle that can be extracted from feelings unique to me that others would enjoy too?

Q'uo: I am Q'uo. The beginning of a more friendly environment is light. When one sits in darkness, one has no perspective, no reference points. The feeling of claustrophobia surrounds the timid soul. So it is with emotional and spiritual feelings that are dark. Like the body itself, the spirit feels overwhelmed by dark emotions. Yet how to lighten the darkness and the burden of concern? We move to Aaron. I am Q'uo.

Aaron: My dear ones, first you must look at the erroneous assumption that the turmoil and darkness are your enemy. When you experience turmoil, that is just turmoil. When you experience fear, that is just fear. Then there is the secondary reaction to that turmoil or fear. It is not fear that closes your heart and sends you into the darkness, but your reaction to that turmoil or fear. Can you see the difference?

It takes a great deal of practice in awareness to begin to notice the process. First is the arising of fear. With that first notice of fear, you are still in neutral about it. You are not frightened of the fear. Then you move to the stage of feeling attacked. At that point, there is a change in the chemical balance of the body and a change in the vibrational frequency of the light body. It is seen by me as a constriction in your energy field so that the light that was moving freely through you and out of you and into you suddenly becomes trapped in this physical vessel, bouncing back and forth, truly in turmoil. It looks a bit like a pinball machine with the ball going *bing, bing, bing, bing, bing!*

You are not here to get rid of anything in your life. If turmoil or fear is what is experienced—confusion, whatever—you do not need to get rid of it, but to learn how to greet it as a friend, to allow the experience of it with your heart kept as open as it can be; no judgment if it is closing a bit, but consciously making an effort to stay open. Then the aversion to the emotion does not cause closing. Then all the old-mind matters, the remembrances in this body and other bodies of this kind of fear, the projections into the future, none of that becomes part of the issue. You are just here with this moment of fear.

Are you familiar with those sticky burrs that catch on your pants' legs as you walk through the field? The pants are the material of your fear. The burrs are all the added burdens of the past and the future. As they knot together it becomes an unworkable mass, and that is what closes you into darkness. Being mindful of that pattern in yourself, you find that you can ask yourself to stay in this moment with this very workable and much lighter bit of fear or turmoil or confusion and allow the experience of it. It takes courage. It takes sharp awareness.

When you do this, you come back to your connection with the light. This is not something you have to grasp at or create in yourself. You are not, for example, naturally depressed or frightened. The lightness, the openness, the loving-kindness, the generosity and patience, the energy, the courage. Those are all qualities that are natural to you. They are small seeds within you. But if you take a small seed, put it in a pot and then put it in a dark closet, it cannot grow. It needs light.

Your mindfulness of your reactions to fear is a way of opening the closet door and inviting in light, a statement, "Fear is not who I am. I am experiencing fear at this moment, experiencing confusion, experiencing perhaps the outgrowths of fear as anger or greed, but that is not who I am." As you learn to do this, you start to see that each of those catalysts is in fact a gift offering you the chance to practice just what you most need to practice, which is how to be with a painful catalyst without pulling the closet door closed behind yourself, without needing to seek that protection; in essence, how to allow yourself to stay open and vulnerable. This is your deepest connection with the light, this deep knowing: "In essence, I am spirit. I am divine and connected with the Divine. The body may be vulnerable, but I cannot be harmed if my heart is open and loving."

This is the way of opening the door: remembering your connection. Through countless times of practice, you deepen your ability to keep your heart open no matter what comes. When you heart is open, you no longer have the illusion of being in darkness. Rather, the turmoil, the anger or greed is seen more clearly as the illusion that deepens the sense of separation.

I am not suggesting that it is easy, but it is workable. My brother/sister Q'uo wishes to speak. That is all.

Q'uo: I am Q'uo and give thanks to the one known as Aaron.

As you consider the words of excellent advice, you may wonder that you seemingly already knew that which has been addressed. The question then becomes, "Why can I not put these truths into practice?"

Consider that you have two intelligences. Your first intelligence and the one which you largely use is the intelligence which came with your physical vehicle. The second intelligence is of another order. You are one of an infinite number of stations, shall we say, that in computer language runs a metaprogram which you would call a primary distortion of the One who is all: infinite Mind or intelligent Infinity. The answers come from essences bathed in this second environment, this mind with its perfect infinity, its absolute awareness. The hitch lies in running the answer back into the first animal intelligence.

There is an excellent connection between the metamind and the individual idiosyncratic mind, which you carry just for this incarnational experience. It, however, is a connection made deep within the roots of the first mind. This lies in the domain you call the subconscious. This connection has been characterized as the still, small voice. And still it is, silent to a profound level. Small it is, if it is evaluated by intellectual standards; for the metaprogramming, shall we say, of Love that is the Logos, is that which enfolds and becomes one with the listener to this blessed, silent communion.

How often has each sat to meditate and felt no realizable touch of the great Mind. Yet stubbornly, again and again, midst self-implications for being foolish and shallow do doubting seekers such as all here go again to the table of silent heaven's fare and hold up the self like a dish, saying, "Feed me. However this works, I wish to be one with this bread of heaven that is found when least expected in the course of regular meditation." The dark feeling from judging and fearing the emotions experienced is not easily lightened by pursuing logical, data-consuming thoughts and opinions. Far more skillful is the seeker which decides to move from the incarnational program into the overarching metaprogram.

Do you see, my brother, that you already are aware of perceptions concerning fear and are stuck, shall we say, more in how to place the truth in a position which will actually affect that dark-feeling mind?

(A pause while Q'uo's question is considered.)

We gather by the silence of the one known as R that he may not precisely see our query to him. That is all right. We speak to the generality of your condition.

We also have two kinds of mind as we have incarnations also. We share in the wonderment that all our seeming knowledge does not automatically become manifested in our thoughts and actions. It is, however, the more skillful use of the concern about dark-seeming situations to do something like that which we did to begin this session of working: We all sat and felt the spontaneous circulation of harmonizing and encouraging vibrations, each offering love to each, each feeling the love of each.

In times of ghastly turmoil there is the incarnational instinct to cringe, to back away or to explode into defensive action. Remembrance of an essential moment of flowing harmony moves the mind's eye to gaze and move toward that subconscious linkage into All-Mind, the spontaneous, essential feeling rather than intellectual thought processes which yields a true moment of the joy of Love itself, being placed like the light in the closet which gives you the courage to remain quietly observant, neither running away in the mind nor grasping the problem seen with such constrictive and fearing bonds.

The one known as Aaron would say, "View the situation with neither attachment nor aversion." Do you wish to query further, my brother?

R: Yes, with my intellectual mind. I would like to thank both of you for offering your thoughts. I wish to give others in the circle a chance to ask questions first. Thank you.

Aaron: This is Aaron. I wish to return to Q'uo's clear statement that your heart understands and your brain, the human incarnation, cannot follow. It is this precisely that gives you such grief, because in the wisdom of your heart you understand your connection, that this, what Q'uo has called, metaprogram is the reality and that the brain's frantic fear is illusion. And yet, you find yourself moving to the illusion. At that point anger often arises at the self. At some level there is a knowing: "I am responding to this mindless illusion. I am like a mouse on a treadmill and I cannot get off." The only way to reconnect yourself with reality is to notice the judgment that is arising and return love to the self, to have love for this being that is running around on a fear-created treadmill so that it cannot hear the deeper wisdom, that small, still voice within.

Simply put, the light is always there. When you find yourself in darkness, you must ask, "Why is it that there is this illusion of darkness? Why have I closed myself in?" You are light. You know that you are light. Yet to fully express that in the human incarnation is a very, very difficult thing. And this is precisely the way it needs to be. If it were easy, what would you be learning? I am not suggesting that your lives need to be difficult or painful, but if you were already perfect you would not be here in the incarnation. If the heart was always open and there was no reverberation to the chords of fear, then you would not need to be here in incarnative state.

When you notice the arising of that fear, if it can become a catalyst to have compassion for this being that is feeling fear, it begins to crack open the door—just a tiny bit of compassion, just a tiny bit of light coming in. It serves as a reminder: "I am stuck in the illusion. This is reality, this tiny sliver of light. Follow it. Trust it."

As my brother/sister reminded you, you have two intelligences. Habit has dictated to you that you follow the human intelligence while in incarnation, and you become very unused to following the higher intelligence. The physical body has built up the catalysts of so many lifetimes into habitual, unskillful patterns. We talk about this fight-or-flight idea. As my brother/sister said, you cringe at it or strike back defensively. But that is not natural to you, not necessary to you. It is learned behavior. It is precisely that learned behavior that serves as the tool for learning. You cannot simply decree, "I will not run in fear. I will not fight back." Yes, you can develop a strong degree of self-control, but that does not change the harmony or lack of harmony in the experience. That does not bring in love.

Can you have some compassion for the being who has developed this mindless pattern of fleeing or fighting? Can you begin to understand that your awareness of that pattern is the beginning of the path free of it? The pattern in itself is not a problem. Yes, it leads to unwholesome karma. It leads to hurt for others. In that sense, of course, it is a problem. But when you relate to it as a problem, you relate to it as something to fight against, to get rid of: "I am not going to act this way anymore." That is just more judgment to yourself, more hatred. You are involved in the resultant fear and not attending to the causes. When instead you see this being whose fearful brain has developed this fight-or-flight mechanism and feel some kindness for the being caught in a very tight place, then you allow yourself the possibility of hearing the deeper voice within, of hearing the deeper wisdom that whispers, "You are safe. Keep the heart open."

There is something else. When we know something is good for us but we do not do it, it is logical to ask why. When I say that the fight-or-flight mechanism is not natural to you but learned behavior, it was learned so many lifetimes ago when the creature that you were sought to defend itself. To continue to survive and do what is necessary to survive is natural to you, so you learned unskillful behavior in order to allow the continuity of that particular life form. As soon as fear arose, there was a sense of separation and you lost the clarity that you were connected to every other life form. Instead it became a protection of the small ego self. This was part of the distortion of self-awareness.

You have been running with that pattern ever since, each of you. Your work here is not to get rid of anything in yourself, not to change anything in yourself, but to begin to know who you truly are and to allow that reality to penetrate so that you can more fully live it rather than living the illusion. You need the illusion. It is what helps to point out the reality. It is the practice with the illusion that strengthens the reality.

By way of example, if you never knew fear—"My needs might not be met"—a fear that leads to greed, to hoarding and clinging, then what would connection and generosity mean? If you never had the sense, "I could be hurt. My needs might not be met," then of course giving would be very easy. There would be no sense of self or other, so you would give and give and give. It would be very beautiful, but what have you learned? You are here to grow, so you are constantly handed those catalysts which you need for that growth. The illusion is the catalyst. That is why you have this "veil of forgetting" that separates you from clear seeing of your spiritual reality when you take birth. Otherwise, the incarnative state would be simply a matter of self-control: "How strong can I be in this situation? How determined?" But you are here to learn faith, not self-control; to learn love, not the expression of willpower.

I said that you have learned the behavior long, long ago that you needed that fight-or-flight mechanism to defend the self. Now, when you are in that dark closet seeing only the existence of the egocentric self—"me against them" separateness—when you are in that space, then it is very difficult to see that what you are experiencing is illusion. You stay defended.

So, first there must be the awareness: "This is defended behavior. This is casting me deeper into the illusion of separation." Then you may notice the judgment arising: "I should not do that." But, my dear one, if this were a small creature, a squirrel perhaps, and you chased after it with a stick and it turned and ran, would you say, "It should not do that. It should trust me"? If such a small creature attacked you in its fear, would you say, "It should not do that. It should trust me"? Or would your heart reach out to this small creature whose fear was so intense that it had to flee or attack? You would feel compassion for it.

Can you look at yourself with that same compassion, simply seeing the patterns of so many lifetimes and knowing that now you have reached a level of consciousness, a level of growth, where you no longer need to blindly follow those patterns? But the freedom from reactivity cannot grow out of the judgment of the self that has been reactive, only out of compassion to that self. Compassion allows the light in, allows the remembering of the deeper reality of the metaprogram of love. That is all.

Q'uo: I am Q'uo. As the teacher known as Aaron states, you are in incarnation to grow from the inside of the nearly always, somewhat dark interior of the mental and emotional closet. You may question the probability of achieving growth; however, you cannot avoid growing. The illusion works with mechanical force, call it friction, wearing away at the sensibility. All you need be concerned with in terms of growing is that you honor and respect that which is occurring, focusing more and more lucidly on the delineated structure of the present moment. You, in observing the present moment, are doing all you can with the incarnational mind. Once observed, the catalyst will grow acute. There need be no further action except to turn and bless the incarnation with all its meandering, winding destinies and unexpected occurrences. We ask you to cast a warm and loving attention on yourself in the incarnational closet of flesh and limitation of viewpoint.

Into this configuration open the inner memory to the light of companionship, the light of memories which contain joy and the use of affirmative imageries such as the light of the sun dancing upon the water. This is how the metamind thinks. It cannot be termed logical. To this mind sunshine is a song, a poem, a dance, a zephyr of cool air on a hot day. So it is that many find sunshine in the midst of confusion and self-compassion in the midst of judgment by singing, as does this instrument, reading inspired writings, gazing at visual and tactile art created out of those moments of clear visionary sunlight shining through the artist to show what love is, and more, how terribly perfectly unified all is. As the plangent tones of a truly heard piece of music pierce the incarnational mind with sweetness, so can you use these non-logical images and practices to enhance and multiply the effect of silent meditation and communion.

You are light to others. Others are light to you. Beyond all else you are loved. It takes the breath away to, for even an instant, ponder the totality of this love; and it is love of All-Self by All-Self. It merely flows through you. You need not deserve it. You cannot own it. It is your real identity.

May each smile when next each discovers the self sitting in that emotional, closeted darkness. Yes, my friends, smile and reach the finger of attention to flick on the light of non-judgment and compassion.

We are those of Q'uo, and we leave this group at this time, rejoicing in being once again able to share the teaching which teaches us so much. With the master known as Aaron, may we rejoice that each gentle being who is here, has come. How miraculous the alphabet soup of shared life! Love one another and release that terrible need to find the sunshine while holding on to the limited point of view of the incarnational mind. We leave you in love and in light. We are known to you as those of Q'uo. Thank you and farewell. Adonai.

Aaron: This is Aaron. I would like to offer a few brief, practical tools for your consideration. As my brother/sister of light said, you may picture yourself in that dark closet and have compassion for this being who is afraid of the dark. It may help to take it further, to think perhaps of a child who is afraid of a dog. You walk down the street holding the child's hand, and suddenly there is a large dog in your path and the child cowers behind you. If you push that child and say, "Now pat the dog. You must," the child may conquer his fear enough to pat the dog, but he is never going to enjoy patting the dog. He never will choose to do it if he is not pushed. Or you may say to the child, "I see how afraid you are. I think this looks like a nice dog. He is big. I am going to pat him. We have become friends." And you pat him, shake his paw perhaps. The child watches with no pressure. It may make take a dozen meetings before the child is ready to come up and pat the dog himself.

You offer patience and compassion to the child. Offer yourself that same patience and compassion. Know how many lifetimes it has taken you to build up these patterns of fear and separation. When you acknowledge your own suffering, your own fear, and greet it with compassion instead of judgment, then you offer yourself a pathway back to the light. It is something that you can practice constantly in all the small catalysts of your life, the moments when somebody says or does something that irritates or offends you, just the brief moments of impatience. You do not need to practice it with the very heavy emotions. You practice with the small things. You would not ask the child to pat an elephant or a tiger before he has learned to pat the dog.

Then, of course, there are ways of bringing more awareness of light into yourself. One that I would suggest as a useful exercise for many people is to plant a garden in your mind, to think of all of those small sprouts: generosity, patience, loving-kindness, so many, many, many more … Some of them are strong flowers in yourself already and some of them you see as small seeds. Choose one that you can watch in yourself.

Now, it is very hard to measure such a one as loving-kindness, so you might want to choose one that is more easily seen in its physical form, one such as patience or generosity. You notice how often you are impatient, how often you are frightened of giving. Do you notice how often you are patient and generous? I do not speak only of material generosity here, but generosity with your time, with your energy.

Begin to watch just one small sprout in yourself. When there is momentum to be patient or to be generous, for example, and then you hear that small voice that says, "No, I am afraid," acknowledge it. Not, "You should not be afraid," but, "I hear your fear. It is okay." Just the way you do with the small child: "I hear your fear." And then make the skillful decision, if it is at all possible: "I am going to be patient. I am going to be present with the fear that says, 'My needs will not be met here,' or, 'I could be hurt,' and I am going to ask myself to be patient or to be generous. And then I am going to watch the results."

As you move into practicing that on a daily basis, you find that you can change the old-mind patterns, that you can be present with fear and reach for the light switch, that you can keep connected to that deepest truth and beauty that is you.

Another tool that comes to mind: This is an ancient Tibetan meditation practice called *Tonglen*. It is a very simple meditation. I would ask in closing if you would join me in it. First, simply be aware of yourself sitting in a cylinder of light. Breathe in. Feel the light descending through the crown chakra and down to the heart center. Exhale and release it, just the way it came in. Inhale, light descending to the heart … exhale, release … Feel yourself expanding with that light. Open to that light. Notice if there is any resistance to letting it in and soften around that resistance.

With this light filling you, bring to your heart and mind the image of a being who is suffering. It may be someone you know or a stranger across the globe; not a whole world of suffering, just one person or one life-form of whatever sort you choose. Breathing in this time, allow that light and loving energy to move to the heart center; and then, breathing out, direct it to that being who is suffering. Breathe in light and love … direct it out to the being who is suffering. Inhale light. Exhale to where it is most needed, just allowing that light and loving energy to channel through you … allowing that being's suffering to touch your heart with the wish, "You are suffering. May you find peace. May you find an end to your suffering. May you be healed," allowing yourself to be a channel for that loving energy. Please try it for a moment on your own and then we will go on to the last step.

(A pause while the group meditates.)

That being's suffering is so heavy. You may begin to see it as a dark cloud of blackness—a heavy, sticky kind of blackness. Your good wishes are felt, but the darkness is so heavy that they can not fully penetrate. We expand the meditation now. Inhale love and light. Exhale, releasing it to that being who is suffering. Now, inhale that darkness that you see, letting that, too, run through your heart, but not holding it in you in any way. You are simply the channel for its release. Exhale and release it to God, to ground of Being, which is far more skilled and able to handle that heaviness than you are. Inhale love and light, and release it to the one who is suffering. Inhale the pain and release it to the Eternal. Inhale light. Direct it to where it is needed. Inhale that suffering in whatever form you envision it. Notice any resistance to letting it touch you, to letting it come into your heart, and soften around that and then release it.

As you practice this meditation, let it bring you back into your connection with all that is, let it remind you that you truly are a channel for love, for light, for healing, and that you are also a channel through which suffering may find its release, that those who are your brothers and sisters may not carry that weight unsupported. I am going to be quiet now for several minutes and ask you just to practice this on your own.

(A pause while the group practices.)

When you feel alone, frightened and in darkness, make the conscious choice to open the door of illusion which holds you confined in darkness, and to bring in light. I know no better way of bringing in light to yourself than to wish to share that light with others. It helps you to know who you are and to remind you of your connection with all that is. The serving of others in that way, the joyous willingness to serve, helps connect you to the light and divinity in yourself. It helps you express that joy that begins to move through you. With that increasing lightness, the clouds that surround you become more and more transparent and the storm begins to blow away.

It has been a joy to share with all of you this evening and, as always, a deep gift to share energy and thought with my brother/sister of Q'uo. I thank you all for your joyous participation in this circle and for the light and love that each of you brings to your search. My love to you all. That is all. ☙

The Aaron/Q'uo Dialogues, Session 9
October 30, 1992

(This session was preceded by a period of tuning and meditation.)

Ariel: This is Ariel. I greet you with love, my brothers and sisters of the light, and with gratitude for your willingness to allow me to join your circle. It is a grace to be here in this room from which so much light emanates. This instrument spoke last night of sensing a very old and ancient energy, one that seemed in her senses to transcend all duality. There was/is/will be, indeed, such an observer.

Please understand as I speak that it is not the spirit that speaks. The spirit would be incapable of such speech, but it must come through the mental body. When there is mental body, I am imperfect. What I express to you, then, is merely my opinion with as little distortion as I am able to give it. I humbly ask that you take whatever I say with that recognition. It is not offered as Truth with a capital T, but the clearest seeing of which this one is capable. And that is all I can give you.

I once spoke to a group in another of your cities about the origins of the Earth as I had understood them and experienced them; that there were those on the immaterial planes who were stuck in some way and in need of greater catalyst for their learning; that it was understood that this must be a plane of love; that certainly negativity would enter, but that those who saw the need were willing and eager to give of themselves to lay the foundation of love. I will not speak of this in more depth here. I believe a written transcript is available.

My dear brothers and sisters, you have learned. This experiment that we have called Earth has been successful beyond our wildest imaginings. Of course, there is negativity on this plane. There would need to be. You understand that it is part of your catalyst for learning and that there is no duality, no difference between the positive and the negative in the long run and that, at the same time, negativity must be resisted with love because of the suffering that it creates.

What has occurred on this earth plane that has seemed so wonderful is that those of you of third density who are learning these lessons of faith and love graduate with far more depth, also, into the fourth- and fifth-density lessons of compassion and wisdom. Of course, there is no time pressure, so you may well ask, "What difference does it make if we learn the lessons ahead of our grade, so to speak?" The difference is that compassion and wisdom are not finite skills. The being who moves into fourth density already with deep compassion and wisdom expands those qualities far beyond what has come to be expected on other planes of learning. Our experience, then, is that those of you who move through this earth plane, working skillfully with the catalysts of this plane, have moved into an expanded sense of compassion and wisdom by the end of seventh density, and in that way expand the Infinite.

While the compassion and wisdom of that which we might call God or the Eternal are infinite, they are also ever-learning and ever-expanding. And those of you who move into seventh and finally eighth density through this plane and return to that spirit which is your essence bring a far deeper wisdom and compassion that expands the Eternal and Infinite.

That you on Earth are capable of this as you move beyond the earth plane on your journey, of course, makes this plane a target of negative energy. You understand that there has been a quarantine, as you phrase it, against physical contact, against the visitation by negative energy. And yet, of course, we must respect the free will of all beings. There has been effort, then, among those of positive polarity to help to strengthen as many as we can and teach how to work with negative energy.

Love is a gift, but it also may become a distortion. One must learn how to balance that love with strength, with faith. I have said that the learning of wisdom and compassion on the earth plane has awed us, in a sense. And yet, great care must be taken that wisdom and compassion are not learned before faith and love, but simultaneously or after. Distorted compassion can lead to a distortion of wisdom which does not oppose negativity with love, but rather, feels need to hear it out; and in that way, negativity may play on that compassion and wisdom and manipulate the, as yet, immature faith and love.

We who profess to be guides and teachers can only share what we see with complete respect to your free will. We see a situation on Earth now whereby with your own expanding understanding, your own curiosity, you are reaching out to the universe with such as these microphones with which you hope to pick up outer space signals. You are reaching out to take your true place in the universe. We cannot protect you any more than the wise parent strives to protect the child as he moves out of the sheltered home. We can only alert you to caution, not to fear but to awareness.

Many watch this experiment we call Earth with a deep sense of hope because of the power of the light that comes from this plane. It is especially groups like this that draw the attention of both positivity and negativity. You know that. The question that many of us have is, are you ready for this move into fourth density? Are you ready to deal with the onslaught of negativity that will be experienced on Earth if there is no longer a quarantine to that energy? In essence, have you developed that faith yet?

Much of the work that your groups do is the deepening of wisdom and compassion. Do not neglect the deepening of love and faith. It is harder to talk about. You can suggest skills, as the ones who are known as Q'uo and Aaron suggested last night—strategies, in a sense—for working with the catalysts of your density. Do not forget the power of prayer, of connection to that light. I know I do not need to say this to this group, but there is nothing I have said today that you do not already know. I only hope to remind you of the importance of tempering your wisdom with faith and with love so that you do not become imbalanced and more susceptible to negative influence through the distortion of love that is not yet firmly understood.

I thank you for allowing me to share this with you today. I know that my brothers/sisters of light, those that you know as Q'uo and as Aaron, would also like to speak to you and to speak to your questions. With my joyous love to each of you, I leave this instrument at this time.

Aaron: This is Aaron. My love to you all. Barbara is still in a very deep trance. You cannot call her name to bring her out of it as she is deaf. I would ask that you direct your energy to her, simply calling her in your minds as I will also do. That is all.

Q'uo: I am Q'uo. Greetings to all in the love and in the light of the one infinite Creator. The privilege of speaking with you is appreciated; and as the one known as Ariel has said, we offer opinion only.

The difficulty of aiming for an absolute is that in your universe of relativity, one may approach but never reach the absolute. Yet still, we encourage each to comfort, protect and give support to that pilgrim within which hungers for a more nearly pure experience of being transparent to eternity and the limitless light of the Logos, which offers embodiment to eternity and infinity.

Earlier there was speech concerning the long and difficult path which demands an endurance. Each wonders, perhaps, why endurance would seem to call first for faith and then for understanding and wisdom. The archetypical feature of wisdom is its ability to regulate. This is seen in the body wherein the potentiator of physical energies is that which controls and manages rather than that which is fully open and uncontrolled. However, the need for regulation of energy cannot precede the development of a firm and persistent compassion. Compassion is a corollary of faith. Thusly, the first persistence is to working with your consciousness to exhort and encourage the self to be foolishly faithful, foolish in the eyes of a pusillanimous world.

The quarrelsome world turns to one who is attempting a persistent devotion to a life in faith and says, "You have not got the picture. You do not have a clue as to the realities of the grimy situation which you call civilization and societal interaction." However, those who do attempt the living by faith are often more nearly entwined in acceptance with those viny, dark energies which curl about your illusion than those who are so cynical and worldly-wise. You see, they attempt to regulate an unforgiven incarnation.

The seeker must first, in faith, face every encyclopedic, universal kind of being that makes up the whole Self. It is to this universal Self with as much of negativity as positivity experienced that the seeker embraces. The seeker who wishes to have faith embraces all without regulating or judging the phase or facet of the whole of nature's ways. Thusly is the incarnation redeemed and forgiven by the self. This process is only hindered by the wisdom which says, "You must flee from spite and scorn, from the dirt and discordance of negative thinking, and move instead in mental, emotional and spiritual lands of light and joy." Wisdom would divide the self against the self if that self moved to learning wisdom before it had forgiven the whole Self first. How can one forgive those precincts of personality which are capable of murder, theft and a multitude of regrettable activities, except by faith?

What is faith? Can you catch it from another? Can you learn it as at school? We might suggest that it is by far the quicker entry into a faithful life to begin accepting what is precisely at that moment. If you at that moment when you decide to commit the self to faithful living are in the midst of traffic, then your first act of faith is to experience the beauty of all that is seen in the hustling, bustling street. By faith you suddenly experience sitting more lightly in your car, touching with love and reverence the steering wheel, the gears. It simply needs to be deeply accepted by the self. Then comes the long, long pilgrimage of deepening that faith of living, ever aware that faith, not words or manifestations, offer the truer suggestions and solutions to the very complex and often troublesome living environment of the incarnation. Only when the pilgrim is solidly and firmly devoted to a life in faith so that the open heart's energies flow and flow and flow without stop or hindrance is it time to consider wisdom.

May we, that is, Aaron and we, invite a query?

Aaron: I am Aaron. My dear friends, may I invite your questions, not specifically about what has been said, but whatever question is closest to your heart this morning. That is all.

Carla: As we who have been working in the spiritual path for some time go through our days, it seems that we don't become very much more intelligent in our use of affirmations than we were in the beginning. I think that praying without ceasing is the ideal, but I seem only to be able to approach it just so far.

D: Carla, you just asked a question that's been on my mind for a week.

Carla: Q'uo, how can we get closer than that to being faithful?

Aaron: I am Aaron. There is a difference between the concept of prayer without ceasing and the experience of it. When you move into it as concept, it becomes another "should," something else to grasp at. I ask you to consider in what ways you may more deeply allow the experience of it, transcending thought and concept. That is all.

Q'uo: I am Q'uo, and we shall leave you with a few thoughts and allow the energies to flow once again through Aaron and Barbara.

We may say that in learning of faith, your greatest strength is each other. We know you value each other and we encourage each to have a light and loving but utterly persistent devotion, each to each. In any relationship, each may teach, may learn, may hurt, may heal, may do together any thing which occurs, better and more efficiently than the solitary soul. Therefore, we encourage communication by your letters when there is distance between so that when all come together there is already the full and loving interplay of energies which potentiate each and, more than that, the growing Oversoul, if we may use that term, of the group by focusing upon the being as part of this or other groups. You form and reform small beginning attempts at the life of a social memory complex. You, at this juncture in space/time, are beginning to find the company of others more helpful. This is the natural progression towards your fourth-density experience. Welcome to the beginning of the New Age.

We leave this instrument and this group, glorying in the love and in the light of the one infinite Logos. Farewell and peace. I am Q'uo.

Aaron: I am Aaron. There is only so much to be said about faith itself. I do not wish to be repetitious; rather, I wish to speak from a different perspective, one that my brother/sister Q'uo brought up last night. After I spoke about opening the heart and being compassionate to oneself, Q'uo said, "You aspire to that but find yourself blocked." You also aspire to a life of faith and find yourself blocked. Many of you have high intelligence, and at times you use that intelligence as a way of grasping at understanding because you feel frustrated. You want to feel faith, but you cannot force that, you cannot create faith in yourself. You can only gently remove the blockages to faith so its natural appearance may expand in you.

What I wish to point out is that you may grasp at understanding, and in a sense that is a grasping at control. It grows out of a place of fear. Love does not deal with concepts, but with penetrating all concepts and all appearances to get at the true nature of things. When a catalyst in your life creates pain or confusion and you strive to understand it, to deal with it in an intellectual way so that you may give yourself a program—"I could do this and that and that"—that takes you further from faith. When you can notice the fear arising in you, founded on those uncomfortable catalysts, when you can notice the desire to control that grows out of the fear, then you may move back to the open heart.

I cannot say what faith is. I can only speak about how it manifests itself, and perhaps the prime manifestation that I see is the open heart. This is what I would call the heart of surrender, the heart that knows, "I am not in control. I am not running this show. I do not really understand anything, but I will try to greet with love whatever is put before me. I will try to attend the fear with compassion and allow that fear to dissolve so I may move back into love." This is the demonstration of faith, not the thinking about faith but the living in faith.

In this way, faith precedes wisdom. You do not need to know anything, just to follow the guidance of your open heart. When you follow that guidance, let go of all need to control and are simply present with whatever catalyst is there in that moment as lovingly as you can be, then the mind ceases thinking about, grasping at, planning, controlling. Then the mind is free to penetrate beyond thought and really understand at a level to which thought cannot take you.

If surrender is a manifestation of faith, then courage, willpower, determination, energy, are all ingredients which make surrender possible. How much harder it is to face the unknown than the known fear. Surrender does not mean saying, "I give up," and ceasing to express your energy. It means expressing your energy in a direction of love with no understanding of where you are going. You cannot foresee, in your human shells, where your path is taking you. You cannot know what it is that you or another needs to learn.

I would like to use an example here, a being that Barbara has seen as a past life, one that she has agonized over and for whom she has finally found real forgiveness and great love. This being was a Native American medicine man. He taught peace and organized a peace conference of sorts at the request of many others. Beings from many tribes and other races attended. There was one tribe that had great fear, and they came in and massacred the whole group. And then white soldiers on the hillside swept down and massacred those of that tribe, even the women and children.

This being that Barbara was survived all of that attack. He sat on the hillside and asked himself, "What did I do wrong? I brought this together. Somehow I should have known it could not have worked. Look at all the death, all the devastation. Am I responsible?" He had not yet learned the lessons of faith, and so he blamed himself and punished himself in his mind with guilt and remorse, with self-hatred. He forgave the others but he could not forgive himself.

What he did not understand was that this massacre in some way was necessary for them to learn peace. Had those beings come together and formed a peace treaty and signed it, it would have been a very fragile kind of peace. There was not a tribe there that did not suffer from the outburst of fear. There was not a tribe there who could not take those experiences home and say, "If we had peace, this would not happen." There was no one to blame. Everyone's fear was involved in it. This was what they needed to learn. They had tried gentler ways of learning and not been able to learn. The peace that was created some few years later was built on that experience of loss, of pain. That loss and pain was an exclamation of the need to open their hearts and trust one another so as not to continue to destroy each other.

Now this Native American, this being, sat there; and he did not have faith. He thought he knew what they needed to learn, which was peace. And he was right. That is what they needed to learn. But he thought he knew *how* they needed to learn it. You never know. You do not know what another needs to learn. You cannot take another's lessons away from them. You can only clarify your own energy as much as you can and offer as much love as is possible in any situation and then surrender: "Truly, thy will be done. I do not know anything."[9] Can you see how your efforts to understand conceptually, to pigeonhole it all and make logical explanations, offer an escape from the far harder task of having faith?

Compassion can also be misused in this way. I have spoken very, very often with people about compassion and codependence, that it is hard to have faith in a situation and give loving energy to that other being whose energy is distorted into unskillful patterns, but to say no to those unskillful patterns, that you will not aid them. Compassion becomes distorted into, "I want to help." But as soon as you say, "I want to help," you must ask yourself, "Why do I want to help? Is their pain too uncomfortable for me so I want to fix their pain? Can I trust the whole situation, come back to faith and to love, attend the fear in my own heart, seeing how my pain reflects their pain? What do I find when I get in touch with that fear in myself? Who is it that I want to fix—them or me? Do I want to fix them so I will not have to pay attention to the distortions within myself, because the mirror will have been removed that reminds me of those inner distortions? Can I have faith that this friend or loved one is in a painful situation, that I am in a painful situation, because there is something to learn? Can I truly say, 'Thy will be done,'[10] and stop trying to make anything special happen, just be present with whatever *is* with as much love as I can?"

I said before, this does not mean no energy, no effort. But where is effort given: to fix, or to surrender and offer love? To let go of the need to control, to see the fear that it springs from and let go, is one of the hardest of human experiences. Yet it is only from that place of deep faith that undistorted wisdom and compassion can develop, wisdom that penetrates into the depths of reality rather than thinking about reality, compassion that grows out of connection to all that is rather than the concept of compassion which puts a bandage over your own pain.

How do you find that kind of faith? It takes practice. That is why you are here. Remember, each of you is, in essence, an angel in an earthsuit. This body infolds the true nature of you and allows it to move through the earth-plane situations which offer you learning. The more you can allow yourself to be aware that both are real—the spirit and the physical—that you are learning on both planes at the same time, the more you can live your life in faith. When fear grabs a hold of you, it is so easy to forget who you are. Your prayer without ceasing helps you to stay connected.

When I hear the phrase "prayer without ceasing," what I think of is awareness of that flow of brilliant light, that umbilical cord, so to speak, that connects you with the Divine so that you never lose track of who you are. And when you never lose track of who you are, you cannot lose track of who anyone else is. They are just another part of you, another part of God. So that is one tool to deepening faith, and the other is awareness.

They are part of each other: prayer and awareness. Here, awareness speaks of what blocks faith, encourages a willingness to reach out for that hand of the Divine, to take that energy into yourself; and with that opening of heart to lovingly greet each catalyst, to transcend your fear and keep your heart open so that you may truly say, "Thy will be done."[11] I am not in control here. I surrender. I offer my loving energy in whatever way it can best heal this situation, in whatever way learning may best happen.

---

[9] Reference to *Holy Bible*, Matthew 6:10; Luke 22:42.

[10] ibid.

[11] ibid.

But I do not know what that is. Instead of trying to figure it out with my brain, which is the seat of fear, I will try to understand it and listen with my heart." That is the best way I know to begin to live a life in faith.

I would ask if there are questions at this time.

(There were no questions.)

It is such joy to share the loving energy in this room. I thank you all for the opportunity to speak with you and offer my thoughts. And I offer thanks to my brother/sister of Q'uo for the opportunity to pass this back and forth, to learn and teach from and with each other.

I echo the words of the one you know as Q'uo: When your hearts are open, when you are in deep sharing and communication with one another, you are coming as close as the human can come to fourth-density group experience. While you know there is no need to practice that which will be learned in another density while in this density, yet you are all making that shift. You are beginning to understand that you can keep your hearts open to one another and how much greater is your energy when it is shared, how much easier it is to have faith when that energy is shared. Enough words. My love to each of you. That is all. ✦

L/L Research

L/L Research is a subsidiary of Rock Creek Research & Development Laboratories, Inc.

P.O. Box 5195
Louisville, KY 40255-0195

www.llresearch.org

Rock Creek is a non-profit corporation dedicated to discovering and sharing information which may aid in the spiritual evolution of humankind.

ABOUT THE CONTENTS OF THIS TRANSCRIPT: This telepathic channeling has been taken from transcriptions of the weekly study and meditation meetings of the Rock Creek Research & Development Laboratories and L/L Research. It is offered in the hope that it may be useful to you. As the Confederation entities always make a point of saying, please use your discrimination and judgment in assessing this material. If something rings true to you, fine. If something does not resonate, please leave it behind, for neither we nor those of the Confederation would wish to be a stumbling block for any.

CAVEAT: This transcript is being published by L/L Research in a not yet final form. It has, however, been edited and any obvious errors have been corrected. When it is in a final form, this caveat will be removed.

© 2009 L/L Research

Sunday Meditation
November 1, 1992

Group question: The question this afternoon deals with how we really accomplish whatever it is we accomplish in our lives. We know we have feelings that come from our heart, that direct us in certain ways, and we know that we can analyze with our minds any feeling or possibility, and we are wondering, particularly in Carla's case let us say, where she experienced what seems to be a rather miraculous healing, whether this kind of healing or growth is a product of chance, of luck, of application of the intellect, of the following of the heart, of the balancing of the intellect and the heart? How anybody in general can use the intellect to assess all of the possibilities in a situation, among them being the feeling that we have in the heart, the desire to be of service to others, and to express compassion to others at all times. What part does the intellect play, what part does the heart play, and is there a balance really possible? Or should we always go with the heart?

(Carla channeling)

I am Q'uo. Greetings in the love and in the light of the one infinite Creator. It is a privilege, as always, to share our opinions with you. Please remember, as always, that our teaching has no authority past that of the opinion.

The confusion which is the environment of your query at this opening working is considerable but completely understandable, given the position in space and time which those in third-density incarnation experience. In reality or, shall we say, in a more transparent illusion there is no distinction between the analytical and the heart-centered working upon catalyst. The two are seen from the broader viewpoint as resources belonging to an unique entity, which entity has its unique point of balance betwixt mind and heart. The healing or other changes, depending upon the individual, might be aided by a larger dose of the heart's wisdom than analysis, or exactly the opposite. Each spiritual individual is moving along a path within the infinite creation which has a three-dimensional reality. In other words, each entity has its own creation. No two internally perceived creations are alike, although many will find comfort when sensing a kinship to another's way of approaching the experiences of incarnation, both limiting and expanding in nature

Let us look at this particular instrument's situation, working toward generalization while doing so. It is commonplace among those who have chosen the manner of their incarnations that there should be more than one stopping place, shall we say call it, within the incarnation. The balance of wisdom and compassion in the mind of the entity before incarnation is automatic. It is a portion of the personality. The wanderer is likely to be wise enough in a balanced manner to offer to the incarnated manifestation of self before birth one central lesson on the personal level, and a series of attainable goals within the impersonal life in service. It is grasped by the individual before the incarnation that during the forgetting process the cold, clear logic of all the goals to be met will be greatly muddled if not obliterated from any conscious knowledge. Therefore, there are the stopping places, for it is not known before it is experienced how much of the lessons learning the spirit self may tolerate without needing healing beyond that which can be offered within incarnation.

In this particular entity's case the stopping place was offered more than once up to this point within incarnation. At the younger ages, twice, and as a more mature entity also twice. This is due to the preincarnated realization that each attainable goal or lesson of love to be brought into manifestation was adequate learning for one incarnation. Therefore, it is as though those who are spiritually hungry are like the cat with more than one life. Indeed, it is not unusual for entities eager to attack the plateful of incarnational fodder to generate the potentials for more than nine lifetimes of learning.

You see, my friends, your incarnations are so much more precious than is usually palpably felt by entities during the incarnational process. Each moment of your illusory experience has been bought, shall we say, by much, much refining and preparation on the finer planes. When incarnation occurs the clock begins running down. Like a time bomb, that clock will one day ring and set off the explosion that opens the door for the entity, now without the physical form, to move through into a larger life, the life that you would call that of the spirit self.

When an entity approaches the end of an incarnational lesson, if that entity has been exhausted by this learning it will be given the opportunity either to embrace life with all of its confusions and distresses or to embrace the dropping of the physical body and the movement into whatever healing modes the learned lesson has created the need for. When this moment occurs the choice is freely offered in silence, and the love of life of the entity, or the disdain of life, create the potential for greater health within incarnation and a new lesson to be learned, or the gentle or rough path to the passage into larger life.

Neither analysis nor the wisdom of the heart create the convincing argument or balanced thought process which generated further incarnational life or the end to the incarnation. What is more vital is the simple hunger or appetite or gusto felt for the rough and tumble of incarnational life, with all its buffeting and confusion. With enough enthusiasm the persistent seeker may go through many initiations, learnings, and then the experience of the fruit of these learnings.

When the words "wisdom" and "analysis" are set up as a dynamic it is as though there were an observer apart from the owner of the analysis and the wisdom which judges the way decisions are arrived at. What this observer self often fails to realize is that the observer self is a creation, a persona developed by the internal use of both wisdom and analysis. In the subconscious, or the roots of the mind, the two have an authentic, unique balance created by all that has accumulated throughout all incarnational previous experiences. It is difficult for the intellectual mind to grasp how little it truly has to do with the deepest choices in an incarnation. Yes, it may block the rhythmic, natural action of destiny, but in blocking that it simply stops a forward motion. If it appears that another course has been taken it may seem that analysis and/or wisdom provided a choice which changed the whole life. However, along both paths, seen at the crux lie the same lessons in variant forms.

The choices you work on making skillfully are choices in substance and quality of beingness. This beingness informs whatever choices are made. We are not in any way saying that it does not matter whether one makes choices; it truly does greatly matter. We simply wish you to grasp the thought that these choices are those which have to do with one's stance or attitude towards that which is facing it rather than having to do with one situation chosen over another. There is a saying in this instrument's mind, "You can run but you cannot hide." The destiny which you skillfully offered your future incarnational self before this experience holds sway in the amphitheater of your brief existence in this one incarnational opportunity. You need not attempt to monkey overmuch with the tendencies or basic given of your incarnation. What you are here to do is refine and refine again and again, the choice of focus, of attitude, which—we correct this instrument—with which it faces the present moment which is destined to be just so.

How can we express to you the importance of your accepting the gifts of both intellect and heart's intuition and wisdom except to suggest that if one trusts one's destiny enough and if one trusts one's basic universal nature enough the balances will be offered in ways which engage both the intellect and the heart. Therefore, we suggest to you several things. Firstly, we suggest the entity respecting both tools, the intelligences of the mind, both shallow and limited, and deeper and broader, and the wisdom of the heart. Also, we suggest the focusing upon the worshipful side of the human, shall we say, nature. How natural it is to respond to the beauty about one, to flower under the kind attentions or smiles of friends or acquaintances or strangers. The more that trust in one's destiny and one's validity as an eternal and infinite being are taken as sure, the more sure-footed the entity shall be at utilizing in a skillful and graceful manner all of the assets which it has. The mistrust of self and circumstance create very nearly all of the confusions within one's incarnation. With enough trust and faith, that which is becomes transparently joyful and vital.

We may say, to move back to this instrument's very different experience at this juncture from the experience of the past, that when an entity is repeatedly tested and has made several choices to learn more, to serve more, and to be more in the same incarnation, there comes to the process a somewhat smoother or more speedy or more apparent alteration, change, or more correctly transformation. It is as though having trusted blindly, repeatedly, the next occasion which calls for the greatest trust, though it be one degree more difficult, it is also met by a more tempered incarnate entity, and, therefore, if the entity consciously realizes that there is a choice to be made, a new lesson to be taken up, it can then affirm its appetite for the vital push and shove, confusion and disturbance of the lesson to come.

Thusly, in the more mature spirit there may be radical, seemingly quick changes in circumstance. This is due to the entity refusing to resist the change and instead deciding to back the change, to even accelerate the rate of change, to welcome the next muddle and confusion of new lessons to be learned. This may be a comfort to those who at the present time feel that transformation is all too slow in coming.

We ask you to consider the manner of being that you are. You seek to become aware of your basic nature, you seek to go beyond what can be known either by mind or heart. You are, shall we say, children of the one infinite Creator; no less than that are you. Shall a spark of fire choose the manner of its burning? See yourselves in relation to the infinite Creator, sense the back-pressure of the Creator's love of you. Can you know the Creator with either compassion or analysis, either intellectual thought or intuition? In no way shall you know the Creator. Through you the Creator knows Itself. You are precious for you are being that which the Creator experiences, you are experiencing the Creator being, both of these locutions being equally so. Sense your natures, give praise and thanks that this nature is, beyond all dynamics, unified.

Before we close this, as this instrument would say, cosmic sermonette … I am Q'uo. This instrument was correct in refusing to channel further, as there was a momentary lapse of concentration, and this instrument felt correctly that it was not channeling our thoughts but its [own] diluted opinion. We have said that which we can say without further queries. Are there further queries upon this topic?

Questioner: Not from me Q'uo, thank you.

Very well, my brothers, may we work upon any other query at this time?

Questioner: No, thank you.

I am Q'uo, and we gratefully acknowledge that we have exhausted this subject for this time and place. We ask you to look in two ways at the mind and heart. Your skill in working with this dynamic is very important in learning who you are. The seeking for ever deeper roots in the mind, the blending of …

(Tape ends.) ♣

L/L Research

L/L Research is a subsidiary of Rock Creek Research & Development Laboratories, Inc.

P.O. Box 5195
Louisville, KY 40255-0195

www.llresearch.org

Rock Creek is a non-profit corporation dedicated to discovering and sharing information which may aid in the spiritual evolution of humankind.

ABOUT THE CONTENTS OF THIS TRANSCRIPT: This telepathic channeling has been taken from transcriptions of the weekly study and meditation meetings of the Rock Creek Research & Development Laboratories and L/L Research. It is offered in the hope that it may be useful to you. As the Confederation entities always make a point of saying, please use your discrimination and judgment in assessing this material. If something rings true to you, fine. If something does not resonate, please leave it behind, for neither we nor those of the Confederation would wish to be a stumbling block for any.

CAVEAT: This transcript is being published by L/L Research in a not yet final form. It has, however, been edited and any obvious errors have been corrected. When it is in a final form, this caveat will be removed.

© 2009 L/L Research

Sunday Meditation
November 8, 1992

Group question: The question this afternoon has to deal with the relationship both between males and females and the male and female portion of our brain/mind complex. We would like to know what you could tell us about this dynamic relationship, wherein the subconscious mind—the female portion—seems to be the potentiator, the one which sets into action the male portion of the mind, and in our human relationships, the male and female come together in a relationship and seem to go through the use of catalyst whereby the female undertakes the task, shall we say, of civilizing or training the male so that there is the opportunity for the male to learn the harmonious relationship and communication and sensitivity to emotions that is provided by the female, and the female has the opportunity to learn the abilities of the male to physically accomplish tasks, to go out into the world and, shall we say, "bring home the bacon."

We are wondering how this process really works at its heart, how it helps each of us, both male and female, to become whole individuals, to add that other portion of ourselves that is exemplified either by the High Priestess, the subconscious, or the Magician, the conscious, for the male and for the female. And we would like for you to give us whatever information you feel is helpful, because most of us are engaged in relationships that provide us with a great deal of catalyst and a great deal of opportunity to learn compassion and to learn communication. These are the qualities that seem to bring us together and to keep us together in relationships. What can you tell us about them, and the male and female relationship in general?

(Carla channeling)

We greet you in the love and in the light of the one infinite Creator. We are known to you as those of Q'uo. Greetings and many blessings to this group. We are privileged to be with you and to have been called to your gracious selves. We see the determination of those who have much catalyst and much stirring and busyness, to come together as those who seek the truth. And we are grateful that you so choose to lead your incarnation that it becomes possible for us to be of service to you. Blessed are those who remember the true center of being and who continue to seek it out in the hustle and bustle of busy times. This persistence and dedication will serve you well, not only in this illusion but in all illusions to come.

This session of working is to be devoted to consideration of the nature of the so-called battle of the sexes. We would begin by considering the actions of the mind as opposed to the actions of the body complex, seen archetypically. Whereas in the archetypes of the body the potentiator is wisdom, which produces careful choices of action and inaction, within the mind complex it is the feminine principle which regulates, or potentiates action or the manner of inaction. The entity which finds itself to be male shall usually find itself to have a power within the body complex which cannot be explained simply by the size of the physical vehicle compared to the size of the feminine physical vehicle. There is a quality of the essence of power within that bodily strength which the female, biologically speaking, usually does not experience in the same way.

There is an intuition or sixth sense, if you will, which has a quality of power or of truth which the entity born biologically female usually experiences, not simply at a higher level than the male but often in a different quality of energy. The choice-maker for the physical complex can be seen to embody wisdom, whereas the power of the potentiator of the mind has as its power a kind of depth of the wisdom of the heart, or compassion. And it is this compassion, in its many subtleties, to which the mind reaches for a depth of understanding of what the path of the seeker for truth might find helpful.

There is a large portion of an incarnational experience wherein one is not living the archetype, at least not consciously. Yet these same dynamics continue to rest like the pillars holding up the tent of the illusion for both male and female entities. The converse and partnership between male and female is the way in which it is most efficient to discover, experience and learn from catalyst within third density. It is not the only way. However, when the partnership between male and female is not at the head of the organized method for dealing with the relationship central to an experience, the experience will seem quite skewed. The entity, however, who has had a primary relationship which partakes strongly of this male/female partnership may rely upon the lessons of a former partnership and thusly move very nearly as effectually through catalyst, using it wisely, if the partnerships already experienced are continually given the respect which suggest to the deep mind that the lessons learned have been accepted.

Now, let us move closer and gaze at the questions of using the dynamic balance betwixt male and female energies. One way in which it is possible to use the partnership of male and female is that both male and female remain deeply defended, shall we say, in the relationship against contamination from the dynamic other, be it male or female. In this type of dynamic there is very surely a true battle betwixt the sexes, for if the male is not interested in the strengths of the female mind and sees only the inconvenience of dealing with it, it will become more and more distant from the female energy, and less and less able to experience female energy in a positive, or fertile, way. Similarly, the more the female moves further into the intuition, and, shall we say, love for love or romance which marks the female energy, the less able the female will be to understand or experience the strengths of the archetypical male.

Thusly, the battle is joined betwixt two mountains' populations, shall we say—the mountain of maleness and the mountain of femaleness. When a society moves as a whole in this direction there becomes the coarsening or roughening of the paths of peaceful interaction, and the attempt to enslave the energies and regulate the energies which are seen to be alien and threatening become a part of the societal picture. Insofar as your nation states have as populations tended to differentiate sharply between men and women and have dedicated the judgment of worthy of respect to the archetypical qualities—either of only male or only female—so the society shall show the imbalance of this hostility which creates sexual distancing.

Within the culture which you now enjoy, for instance, the male qualities of power and wisdom are seen to be, shall we say, more than equal to the more archetypical feminine qualities, and to that extent the society is impoverished by losing the close working or partnership of societal male and female. This may be seen to reflect the archetypical choice of conquering the subconscious by strength, no matter how brutally used, rather than by courtship. In a heavily matriarchal society, however, the same imbalance would exist, but those powers of physical and emotional toughness and intellectual strengths, or logical strengths, may be seen to be forced into a prostituted roughness.

Thusly, neither the matriarchal nor the patriarchal model for societal balance is accurate. The appropriate model for third-density illusion, however, may be seen not to matter in society nearly as much as in the individual, for it is the individual which is now choosing how to express love in relationship to others. The reason this query about balance between male and female is central is that it is in wisely, compassionately using this balance that an entity, whether male or female, may wend its way more and more to the "golden mean," the middle of the path of truth wherein, by becoming more and more whole within, the path becomes more and more telling and interesting as well as more productive.

There is not the necessity so much to overbalance into the opposite sex's strengths as it is good to trend—we correct this instrument—to tend more and more towards automatic recognition of the assets and willingness to use the assets of the opposite sex's strengths. For instance, the male begins, when choosing a mate and setting out to live a jointly lived life, to be more and more the archetypical patriarch, the provider, the judge and the decision making leader. However, the decisions made by the male shall become more and more truly wise as the male learns from its partner in learning, not only to appreciate the female strengths and wisdoms but to find sympathetic resonance betwixt those strengths in the female and the deeper portions of its own female side or nature.

Thusly, men do not need to become creatures of intuition and vagaries, however, if the wooing of the physical female partner is then extended, not only to wooing the female's subconscious or Goddess-like side but also towards courting the same energy within self. Thusly, the male which is alone or the female which is alone becomes, within itself, able to seek, woo and to court the subconscious, or in the female's case, is able to place intuition and whim which has the authentic ring of true punch in it, not simply into direct practice but may lean upon that portion of the deeper self which is male and may justly and cautiously work with the male energies, the male strengths, which may seat intuition and hunch into a plan of action which is logical and which has the strengths of intellectual structure to enable this compassion and wisdom [be] a more balanced expression.

The male/female partnership of mates is intended to be central. However, the centrality of this relationship is echoed in any male/female relationship where energies are moving freely and without prejudice. Thusly, even those who live in the nunnery, for instance, may work with the male and female balancing because of the many relationships within any life between a father and children, a mother and children, various relatives, friends, teachers and all of those whom one meets in the course of life. Those who are willing to rest in the atmosphere or ambiance of the male or female energy, whichever is dynamically opposite of its own, may move ahead efficiently, although not as potentially quickly as the very powerful central male/female partnership which you often call marriage.

It may be seen that the lack of skill possessed by most at accepting a feeling of vulnerability to another or alien energy creates in both sexes a fear: the fear of the unknown, the fear of the different or alien. This fear is only intensified by the maturing of the physical bodies of male and female if the physical bodies of the entities adjoining in physical—we look for the correct word and find there is not one. We shall begin the sentence again. If female or male carry these fears into their sexual relationships these fears will become deepened and more and more fixed, for the power of sexual attraction is such that both male and female feel at risk and vulnerable at this insistent demand for nearness which the body complex has. Insofar as this nearness disturbs, the intimate experience shall be accounted a dangerous one, and its fruits, to an extent, will be squandered because of the profound fear of, shall we say, losing control, not only of the situation but of the very self.

What entity with this fear has not approached the sexual act feeling more and more, in the midst of pleasure, that it is somehow using a vital energy? This is true of both male and female. It is only in the atmosphere of shared trust that the energies which are indeed put out and lost in that way by both male and female in sexual release are taken in and used to balance both male and female. Fear stops this energy exchange, and in more subtle movements of male/female energy, the same kind of fear limits and distorts the experience and causes imbalance to progress within the entity which has fear.

Now, how can male and female, which have such complex powers over each other, find a way to be fearless in a relationship and therefore begin not only to be able to express the self in its conscious way, but also to begin a more inner balance? We might suggest above all other things any exercise between male and female in which the strengths of each are together used. The male which has been able, for instance, to express an idea in such a way that it is heard because it has listened to those with more intuition speaking about how to approach the matter in communication, has given respect to the female intuition. Likewise, and we realize these are simplistic examples, the female which is able to ask a stronger, more powerful male to aid in some situation, not needing to defend against that difference but being willing to accept it enthusiastically, awakens that portion of the self which is deeply male.

For men and women in a culture, in general, to make fun of the stylized role differences betwixt male and female is an act of fear. Those who are supportive, not in a sense of *(pause)* but in the sense of true partnership, are winning for themselves that prize which is a growing inner balance, for within your query was a sure sense of the heart of the teaching. The battle between the sexes is only dimly seen as men and women in your culture play out the roles the culture offers them or seek somehow to find roles which are comfortable and sensible for them.

The true treasure lies within each of you as you express the continuing effect of communications with the male and female strengths, each hearing each, so that eventually the male knows and respects without fearing its own deep and excellent intuition. The female in the same way is far more balanced when it has been able to find a comfortable way to express authority, a provider's way of thinking, logical and sound judgment and reasoning.

Often the true riches for inner balances are not seen by two within what seems to be the perfect match. Because, in the more extremely romantic relationships, it is quite often true that the dynamic betwixt the male and female has been so persuasive as to be seductive, turning the male ever more male, the female ever more female, and each being very archetypically splendid, yet each remaining distant from the other to the extent that the balancing strengths of the opposite polarity in sex are not loved, accepted, assimilated and used within the self.

This only begins to work with this complex of energies and does not constitute a very full coverage of this central query. However, we find this to be a beginning. May we ask if there are queries before we leave this session of working?

(Pause)

We are known to you as those of Q'uo. The mystery remains a mystery, my brothers and sister. In seeking, in questioning, the great work of incarnation is accomplished. If the solutions subtly evade in a maddeningly long stream of half-learned lessons, do not let this apparent situation discourage or cut short the querying, the questing and the desiring, for it is in knowing your own desires and seeking clearly that the lessons of love shall find full sway for the outworking of circumstance in a commendable teaching situation.

We are those of Q'uo, and thank you. We would leave you now, cautioning you that we only offer opinions. We leave you in the love and in the light of the one infinite Creator. Adonai. Adonai. ✢

Sunday Meditation
November 15, 1992

Group question: Today's question has to do with our attitude. We have various attitudes, each of us, that help us or cause us to look at situations in a certain way. We would like to know a number of things about attitude. First of all, does the attitude that we have have a direct relationship to the lessons that we wish to learn if we wish to affect our attitude in order to change the way we experience our lives on a day-to-day basis? Is this something that is worthwhile doing? If so, how can we affect our attitude in a way that is meaningful rather than in the usual judging ourselves by how much we do, what we do, or how well we do it [the accomplishment factor]?

And just in general, what part does attitude play in the way we learn our lessons and live our lives?

(Carla channeling)

We are Q'uo. Greetings to you in the love and in the light of the one infinite Creator. What a blessing it is to be with you this day, and to share in the creations of each of you, for each of you possesses and is a complete creation. That which you have within you is continuous with and equal with and not separate from all that there is, yet as long as you have a personhood, your creation has a subjective component. We salute and celebrate the subjective components of each universe here, for within your creations, the mystery of faith and faith in the mystery is central. And each of you seeks truly.

We feel so privileged to dwell in this meditative state with the energies of this group and are very happy to speak on the subject of attitudes with the disclaimer that, as always, we wish each to know that we are fallible. We can and do make mistakes. Therefore, use the discrimination within your own subjective universe, for you and you alone are responsible for that creation which is a co-creation with the one infinite Father of all that there is. You create in fine company, as do we.

We are speaking, we perceive, to those who have approached the living of the workaday life with vigor, energy and willingness to work. This basic positive attitude serves you well. Yet the attitude of those who work needs adjustment as the daily routine varies according to the individual needs of each person and the changing time allotments available for your work as the subjective river of time moves with you. Were we speaking to those who truly wished not to work, we would have to begin elsewhere, but the basic attitude which each has is productive of positive polarizing. However, this potential for the good can and does, if not watched, turn and become that which creates confusion and depolarizing effects.

However, we wish each of you to see your basic energy here. Let us pause a moment while you feel within yourself this positive enjoyment of what you would call work for the good. We see each of you lighting up, shall we say, from thoughts of enjoyable labor which is of service or bears a productive fruit which then can be used for service, be it a financial aid gained by earning money or free time which can be used like the money. This is the essential attitude for those who expect to learn positive lessons through the use of daily work. It is efficient to have this positive attitude. It is productive. And by itself, it does not have the kind of contact with the deeper roots of mind that enable this basic attitude to be more informed.

As you walk about, as you do your duties, as you spend your time, where does the attitude come from? How is it that one can move within the being in such a way to affect the attitude? Firstly, we suggest that the seeker when thinking about attitude realize firstly that the attitude on the outer level is a simple vision created by complex movements of data called up from the roots of mind. This calling up is done often subconsciously to the greater extent to the extent that a person wishes quick changes in attitude. For deep changes there will be a frustration. We feel you are hoping that we can tell you a way to change attitudes, that is, spontaneous attitudes quickly. However, this is not usually swift in its processing.

The seeker who wishes to move quickly often will seize upon the quest and attempt to change the programming, to change the thinking in the direction considered helpful or appropriate for one polarizing in a positive way. However, the opposite is true. The one who fears and worries will grow closer and closer to the difficulty that is being perceived. The person who is not fearing does not hold on to the circumstance or piece of thought or programming which is or is not causing fear. Can you see how the tendency to focus on a problem simply moves you closer and closer to a surety that there is indeed a problem? The faith and will grow smaller, and the problem or difficulty grows larger. The seeker ends up feeling helpless and discontent. The fearless entity moves along and turns the attention to each thing before it, accepting it.

Now there are many things about third-density entities that predictably will not sit well. The Catholic or universal nature of humankind promises a lifetime of introspection followed by some disgust, revulsion or horror, for all possible traits of personality are potentially there in every being within the human family. The tendency, then, is to attempt to think positively and emphasize the positive. This is taking the basic attitude of "I am living; I am glad to take action," and adding some supporting structure for the emotions, that is, in thinking positively about each task, one accepts and blesses the task.

However, an entity may go a lifetime attempting, through this method, to improve an attitude or widen its outlook and not find itself satisfied. The deepest influence upon attitude is the willingness to turn from the world picture and pay attention to the mystery, to stop time and space in the mind. And in that stopped moment, worship and adore, praise and offer thanksgiving. Then in the next moment turn to the world again.

The Creator is seemingly far away. Seemingly, this wondrous mystery has created and then left the universe in which you exist. For all any can prove, this is the case. However, when the heart and emotions form the habit of turning momentarily or for a longer time to the infinite One, to the mystery of unity, there then opens a very, very primary and deep channel within the roots of mind, and joy, hope and kindness flower upward to blossom without fanfare or ado in the forefront of the mind, offering that inner home, the sweet smell and freshness that the flowers always do. Stopping to remember the Creator is like planting a seed within the self. It flowers and bears fruit in time.

Now, there needs to be patience when attempting any spiritual work. We have said often that persistence, regularity in the habit of turning toward the Creator, is the greatest virtue, the most effective trait. That which each wishes is the experience of a loving, giving self. How can you find this attitudinal posture and find it to fit the self? We have spoken before about the way females and males *(inaudible)* each other in learning the lessons of love. Consider how those seekers who have lacks perceived, and find these lacks to make them feel isolated and alone may by the technique of moving the point of view find the answer to the question.

In other words, if an entity is unhappy, because of a lack of companionship or lack of a right work to do, the focusing upon this is the first thing not to do.

But then what can be done to ameliorate the situation while the fairly long process of attitudinal change, of praise and thanksgiving, [that] is going on can be effective? We would suggest taking the "I want" statement and gazing at it as if you were the one hearing this from another. For instance, if one says "I want a companionship," turn this around and you hear a voice saying "I want companionship." Now where are voices like this one in the surrounding neighborhood or town? What entities are alone that you may *(inaudible)* with your presence? If there is a lack of supply and the attitude is poor because one feels financially poor, turn this 180 degrees. You are listening to someone who is poor. Where are the poor people in your vicinity, and how might you help them?

We suggest this reversal when a lack or limitation is perceived. If it is simply thought, it will not be very effective. If, on the other hand, one who perceives a certain lack continuously decides to serve from a feeling of abundance of love within and finds a way to serve those who are alone or those who are very poor, the activity will be coming from a place of plenty where you have forsaken the thought of being alone, and instead asked, "How may I serve those who are alone?"

In brief, we may say to control the attitudes is a poor idea. To note them and pay attention to them is an excellent idea. When fear is part of the thought, do not hold that fear unless you need it. Whatever you can look at and accept makes your faith and will larger and the lack or limitation smaller. Then turn the self towards the Creator at every possible moment, simply allowing the momentary burst of praise and thanksgiving to rise. This refreshes in the present and has fruit in the future. And finally, when you do perceive a need, find the way to express abundance as regards that need in service to others, for that which you feel is that which all feel in some way. All are of one family. There are no true strangers. Nothing is alien to you. Allow the self to relax its boundaries of thinking and this shall sharpen the observational skills.

Lastly, we would suggest that if you keep the basic attitude toward action positive and find delight in movement, then move. Do that which feels appropriate to do without worrying overmuch. Take the rough and tumble of living the everyday life and be rough and tumble with it. Let things be incomplete, imperfect and unfinished. See and accept all the errors and mistakes of judgment or of any other kind. Just see and accept and go forward. And in the middle of it all, you will find now and then that a threshold has been reached.

We would use the example of two of this group, both of whom had found a threshold passed within the same twenty-four hour day. Each entity had decided to accept some very basic things concerning the life pattern. This bore fruit in fearlessness, for what is accepted can be forgiven. The healing of the incarnation is this process of coming to accept life as it seems at all times, not necessarily the things in the life, but always and everywhere giving thanks and praise, simply because consciousness is either consciousness of something, of nothing, or of everything. We suggest simply that praise and thanksgiving move the mind and heart out of things into the absolute of all that there is.

We have found again and again that we speak with this group on one aspect of a central subject, and that is perfecting or attempting to perfect the life experience. We can only say to you that this area of consideration will continue to deepen as the life patterns of each become fuller, not only with experience, but with the vital energy which creates the appetite for more intense or full experiencing. There is only so much space in a life experience, however, that space may be filled with different qualities of light, different qualities of understanding, of compassion, or of wisdom.

Thusly, seek not only the obvious or evident improvement of the life behaviors, thoughts, and feelings, but seek in a directionless way to be more and more able to accept a fuller and fuller space within. The light within you can transform, and as you allow this quality of light to intensify, so you become as the lighthouse. The light within is not the light of self, but that limitless light which is of the one source and ending of All. Deepen your cup to hold delight in the mystery.

We would ask if there are further queries at this time.

(Pause. Comments not transcribed.)

We thank you also. We find this instrument's weariness such that we would therefore, since there are no further queries we can address briefly, leave this instrument at this time. May we say again what a delight you are, what a delight the circle is. We circle it with you, and as you bless us with allowing our service, we bless and thank you for the energy and persistence of your seeking. We leave this instrument and you in the love and in the light of the one infinite Creator and the joy we …

(Tape ends.) ✤

Sunday Meditation
November 22, 1992

Group question: The question this afternoon has to do with the general concept of how do we deal with loss, in a conscious manner, so that we are able to get the most benefit out of the experience? How do we either exercise our will or move our will aside or find a harmonious way of using a sense of grief of loss, of separation that comes when relationship ends, a relationship that has been emotionally satisfying and nurturing for us? That is the specific question, and, in general, how do we allow the greater will to move through our lives so that our small will, that may or may not be informed, can become a part of the movement of the pattern of our incarnation that brings us eventually to the realization of the unity and acceptance?

(Carla channeling)

Greetings. We are those of Q'uo. We come to you in the love and in the light of the one infinite source and ending of All. How privileged we feel to be called to speak to your group at this occasion and to have the blessing of blending our vibrations with this circle of seeking.

Your query involves the merging of two kinds of illusion. When one is dealing with those deep emotional memories and desires that stem from the roots of the being, one is dealing with the infinite and eternal consciousness that each of you is. When one is asking about the manifestations of these desires in the present illusion one is dealing with the third-density mind of the physical vehicle which offers you the opportunity for incarnation. The first mind is often called the subconscious mind, although more accurate would be the term roots of mind. The latter mind is the—we correct this instrument—in the first mind we find the roots of mind to be the location which you may consider these thoughts and emotions to stem from. However, the higher subconscious and conscious mind are involved in all mergings of these deeper desires and emotions with the moment-by-moment transient mind of new actual experience which is being observed by the entity which you are.

Therefore, we first ask your attention be drawn to the situation whereby most of the feelings which run through the stream of consciousness are dealing with the surface of the passing experience and observations which enable you to use, to control, and to shape the passing experience in a manner which conforms to your preferences. However, like deep melodies which surface again and again, those deeper energies excited and born from the entrance into the conscious mind, of fated or destined persons or events, cause the experience being overtaken by these deep desires which then move into a position of dominance in the mind and which then color for a period of time the passing experience with the deep tapestries of emotions and desires which you have created for this incarnational experience in order to learn the lessons of love which can only be taught by moving through the catalyst of entities or events processing themselves through the day-to-day experience.

As had been discussed previous to this sitting, one of these portions of personal destiny is sometimes the relationship which seems to be over. Now, in this case the relationship is over in the framework of the conscious mind of the entity which lives and dies within the flesh and personality of this incarnation. However, the relationship is anything but over from the standpoint of learning the lessons of love, for which reason both entities within this relationship chose to meet, to exchange desires, and to part, thus only beginning and setting up the conditions under which the lesson may be learned in a way which creates a lasting bias in consciousness which will polarize the consciousness that is infinite within you towards the unity with the love and light which is the Source and Father of all that there is.

Let us look at the experience narrated within your the holy work called the Bible of the one known as Jesus the Christ. When this entity was upon the hard wood of the cross with arms outstretched to welcome its destiny there were two occasions when it is recorded that this entity dealt with relationships. In the first exchange a criminal which wished to turn from its behavior and find a deeper desire asked the teacher known as Jesus to pray for it, and the teacher spoke without hesitation. Dying though it was, it turned in compassion and acceptance and faith and said "This day thou shalt be with me in paradise." There was no confusion because the teacher was suffering, for this entity has learned hope and desire only to surrender the will to the will of its Father, as it thought of the infinite Creator.

In the second exchange the teacher viewing its own mother pointed with name to a beloved friend and in a brief sentence realigned relationship away from accidents, shall we say, of birth and adjusted this relationship for a loving and compassionate opportunity for both mother and friend, as each then might comfort the other. From the sorrow of the apparent loss in both cases there may be seen to be an absence of fear, of self-pity, and an abundance and acceptance of the way destiny moves.

Let us move back onto the *terra firma* now, and gaze at the situation of lost love. Now the lover of the past is a memory. Were it a lesson learned, the memory would not come up to disquiet or sadden one. That it haunts one is a good indication that there is a deep and destined lesson of love to learn. There are three ways one might work upon this lesson. Firstly, there is the work of forgiveness. Most seekers are far more willing to forgive the other self in a relationship than to forgive the self, whether the self feels that it could have changed destiny by an action or feels that it could have changed destiny by eschewing an action. The case is that often the lack of forgiveness of the self stems from the belief that things ended wrongly. May we offer our opinion that there are no true accidents or mistakes in the metaphysical life, only opportunities. Therefore, the greater part of the work of acceptance and forgiveness is allowing the self to feel all right, that and no more, simply all right.

The second way of working upon moving into a better framework from which to view and work with deep sorrows in a life path is to focus upon the opportunities for mulling over the treasure gained during this destiny-filled relationship. That which one did not have before one has now, a center of energy, a vortex of power absent before has now been made, allowing the merging of deep life path needs with the day-to-day manifestations of destiny and accident.

You see, the sorrows of the lost love are not a negative quality but rather a praiseworthy, hollowing out and deepening of the capacity to love without expectation of any return. The reason that the lost love haunts the everyday experience is that there is still much work to do in praising and seeing the treasure in the learning of how to love so deeply in the first place. Only in this kind of sorrow does the incarnate spirit become tempered and transparent to infinity. Only in the darkness of seemingly negative emotions of loss and limitation does the deep prayer, the soulful song of love take wing and sweep the incarnate being to a point of view where the breadth of love, once felt for one entity, may be turned at world dying and yearning for your deep love and compassion. Thusly, one does well not to turn from sorrow but to turn towards it, to merge with it, and to carry this loss as a shining ornament which honors the infinite Creator.

The third thing which is skillful to do when dealing with any seeming negativity is simply to, as this instrument would say, "Praise God from whom all blessings flow." We would change it in this case to say instead "Praise the Creator from whom all sorrows flow." The turning from the self and the concerns, whether shallow or deep, of the self to the infinite Creator in praise and thanksgiving is an orientation in intelligent infinity, that is, in the Creator, or what this instrument would call Christ consciousness. This consciousness is the essential portion of both the consciousness which is infinite and the incarnate being with the bio-computer which makes so many hasty judgments. Calling forth in the conscious mind the holy, worshipful attitude in which only the Creator exists reestablishes a center within the being which merges unconscious and conscious beings together in a useful and balanced way.

It is not in any way easy to do that which we have suggested. The more intensive the desire has been to find love the more intensive the experience of love, the more the yearning for love, the more it will seem very, very difficult to so center the mind viewpoint that all these acceptances and forgivenesses and reorientations may have their just process. Therefore, we urge each to see that this is the work of not one but many incarnational experiences to deepen the source within during the incarnation. In a star-crossed, shall we say, relationship both entities, whatever the outcome in this experience, have been working with this balance for many incarnations. But allow the normalcy of day-to-day experience to move you until the next occasion when this haunting desire for a known or an unknown person or relationship looms so largely before the conscious mind that it colors all of one's thought. Then see this occasion as the treasure it is. Let the fears fall, let the heart speak all it wishes until its well of words and threnaldy of pain is fully expressed. Honor and respect the deep emotions and give them full expression. Rather than feeling them as an ending of a real life experience and only a memory allow the feelings to become living. Birth them with your awareness of the beauty of love. You have desired truly, you have loved truly. This you have experienced. It may now be separated from the constraint of belonging to one entity and the self and become that potential for love and for acceptance and compassion which may be universalized by being aware that this love is an energy unto itself.

You are able to accelerate the process of spiritual evolution whereby you are learning from the deep expressions of personal destiny and in all you do. To offer thanks and praise in any moment is your way of moving quickly, instantaneously to the mind or consciousness of unity wherein you may see that there is no loss, there is no lack, there is no separation, even in the case of a loved one which has died or been permanently separated. This love is an entity unto itself, a vortex which may pull forth either a bitterness of a judged loss or a smooth vine of a judged treasure. It is always your choice.

Two things before we open this meeting to other queries. We are error-prone and request that each use any thought each may from that which we say and leave the rest behind. And also, to accelerate the process whereby one is more observant of that merging process between deep emotions and day-to-day experience, it is well to move into silent communion with the one infinite Creator, listening to the silent voice of love unlimited and inexpressible. To spend time wisely, spend some each day with the Creator.

May we ask if there are any additional queries at this time?

(Pause)

We find that there are no queries upon this subject in addition to that which we have said. Therefore we would now ask if there be any queries upon other subject that we may address briefly at this time?

Carla: I have one about the trumpet. I would like to know about the functioning, or how to get it to really work.

I am Q'uo, and we may speak in general upon this subject, my sister. We thank you for this opportunity. When one has opened the channel to useful work with entities of the inner planes which move into the energy web of your planet and yourself, one has basically established a way of being of service as a tuned instrument. When an instrument is played it is not the instrument alone which must be excellent. The excellence of the instrument being assured, then there is the allowing of the best possible, shall we say, contracted or focused line or channel between the two and through the instrument so that the most compelling music may be played.

In working with the energies which make the trumpet move, the voices speak, the *(sounds like "aports")* appear, and the other materialization phenomena which you are familiar with, the instrument which you are must be activated in a certain way. This is like unto the polishing of the inner surface of a reed, for instance, so that the energy moving through this reed may come forth or materialize in the manifested world with unabated vigor or energy. Any, shall we say, rough spots, any blockings, any ways in which the inner surface is not smooth will baffle and frustrate the energy or breath moving through it and add limit [to] the materialization phenomenon.

There is a kind of energy which allows the materialization phenomena to occur, and this lively energy is one with each is familiar. However, it is not this energy which moves the trumpet. This lively energy is expended in poising the self without let or hindrance, without any reserve in such a way that the spirit moving through you, as the instrument, may use that generated potential for materialization in a crystallized and finely focused way. It is as though your personal, deeply felt commitment and substantive energy given to this liveliness of will may be seen as a broad spectrum potential which the breath of spirit moving through your vortex of self may pick up more and more powerfully the less tightly you personally are holding onto this energy.

We might refer the mind to the Zen parable this instrument has within its experience of the archer who spends his entire concentration upon the focusing perfectly the visualization of the target, but does not at any point while drawing the bow and releasing it open the eyes to look at the physical target. The careful medium's focus of attention is upon this static, permanent ideal of bow, of the powerful drawing of the bow, and of the releasing of the arrow, not when the personal will suggests but when the breath of spirit creates that choice.

Thusly, we suggest the encouragement of generation of this deep desire and this lively will, and then the utter and focused surrender of this and all gifts and talents to the one infinite Creator, that the breath of spirit may move through you in such a crystallized way that the personal energies become universal. In a way, it is the same objectification of deep emotions of which we spoke in talking of relationships, honoring the ability of the self to become capable of carrying those communications or attitudes which may benefit all people, and then surrendering this to the highest and best spiritual contact which is within your energies and which comes to you from that portion of the Creator, shall we say, which embodies for you your highest service.

May we answer further, my sister?

Carla: Do you pick up that I have the ability to do that?

I am Q'uo. It is our opinion that there is within each this potential, and it may be further said that deep desires are there not by mistake. The gifts and talents one has are not false; that which you desire you can do. Yes, my sister, we feel that you have this ability.

May we answer further?

Carla: Right, you are saying everybody has that ability or that potential, but … I mean, like everybody has the potential to play music, but again, some people have the talent. Everybody can learn to do something, but some people have certain talents that they learn more quickly in their development of … like music or art, where another person would have to work a lot harder, put a lot more energy into it. I am trying to feel out more in the sense of … I mean, I realize that I have, that everybody has that potential, but I am trying to see, is this something that will happen quickly for me, or is it something that will take years to develop? I am trying to see exactly about my talents or ability in that area of spiritual development.

I am Q'uo. My sister, there is a respect which we have for your free will which inhibits us from describing to you those energies which you ask about. However, perhaps a more general statement might enable you to think further upon this. We would say that when there is, as in your case, a deep desire to serve as a channel, that this desire is true. The manner of manifestation of this desire is not fixed. Destiny does not say, "You shall do this and this," it says "You shall be put in this situation wherein you may attempt to learn of love and to be of service." We encourage you to move ahead with the learning while being extremely alert for indications from spirit as to the finer and finer choices which determine the direction of learning and service so that you may find your own unique way of serving and of loving.

Thusly, in the area of channeling, for instance, some channel as healers, some as teachers, some as prophets, some as those channeling this or that spiritual resource of an impersonal nature, some channeling from a source of a more personal or individual nature. So at each juncture be on the lookout for synchronistic occurrences, for those small signs of happenstance which may seem coincidental to others but which are subjectively interesting to you. Notice and remember these occurrences and pay them attention, for it is by these signs that you will change and change again the seeming direction of your quest to serve so that as your personality within this life matures and ripens it may be informed as to its best avenue of service.

This is for all entities a process which has the characteristic of both occurring over a long period of time and of coming to a central crux, at which moment a great deal is made clear within you subjectively as a palpable realization. Therefore, surrender to patience and a complete lack of expectation in a day-to-day search, simply doing your inner work, and when the moment comes wherein you find your true voice as an instrument you will know it with a certainty which is beyond time and space, and it shall feel right for you. When that moment has come, cleave unto it and stand upon this rock and do not look back.

May we answer you further, my sister?

Carla: No, thank you very much.

My sister, may we share our great joy in speaking with you. It is a true pleasure, and we are full of love for you and for your devotion.

Is there another query at this time?

(Pause)

We are known to you as Q'uo. Through this instrument's perceptors we feel the deepening of the evening upon your planet, the world is becoming less busy and more quiet about you as the energies of the day and the light put themselves gently to rest. It is a precious time, that time when the energies of your planet are very quiet, those of the daylight going to their rest, those of the powerful and magical night only just beginning to stir. Into this parentheses in time insert yourself, viewing the light and the darkness as one thing. Feel the unity of all that seems light and dark, sad and joyful, feel with us the perfection of the mystery-filled Creator. We know not this mystery but we rejoice in it.

We leave this instrument and you in this love and this light, this one great original Thought, for that is all that there is. Until we speak with you again, we say to you adonai. Farewell in the Creator's love and light. We are Q'uo. ☙

L/L Research

L/L Research is a subsidiary of Rock Creek Research & Development Laboratories, Inc.

P.O. Box 5195
Louisville, KY 40255-0195

www.llresearch.org

Rock Creek is a non-profit corporation dedicated to discovering and sharing information which may aid in the spiritual evolution of humankind.

ABOUT THE CONTENTS OF THIS TRANSCRIPT: This telepathic channeling has been taken from transcriptions of the weekly study and meditation meetings of the Rock Creek Research & Development Laboratories and L/L Research. It is offered in the hope that it may be useful to you. As the Confederation entities always make a point of saying, please use your discrimination and judgment in assessing this material. If something rings true to you, fine. If something does not resonate, please leave it behind, for neither we nor those of the Confederation would wish to be a stumbling block for any.

CAVEAT: This transcript is being published by L/L Research in a not yet final form. It has, however, been edited and any obvious errors have been corrected. When it is in a final form, this caveat will be removed.

© 2009 L/L Research

Sunday Meditation
November 29, 1992

Group question: The question this afternoon has to do with our expectations. It seems like we're always expecting, usually, more of ourselves than we actually accomplish and feeling poor about not having accomplished everything that we had in our expectations. We are wondering today what it is appropriate for the seeker of truth to expect both in the mundane everyday life and of the self in the spiritual life, the metaphysical world. What kind of expectations are reasonable, are helpful and are appropriate for the seeker of truth in both of these areas?

(Tape ends.)

L/L Research

Sunday Meditation
December 13, 1992

Group question: The question today has to do with the general kind or level of angst that we each find in our lives no matter what the particular experience, whether we are not being able to fulfill our creative identity and desires we know we have, or the ability to find the balance in our lives so that we are able to move through our lives without being swayed overly much either towards the sadness or the joy, the ability to find balance between being and doing. Each of us seems to have some kind of angst, some necessity for dealing with a situation that is difficult, that provides us with worries, with fears, with challenges, with work of some nature that needs to be done. We are wanting to know if there is some level of changing this angst or this way of perceiving our experience so that we are more in line of what we feel is fulfilling our abilities, of walking a balanced life, of being of service to others, and wonder what you may have to say to us in that regard.

(Carla channeling)

We are known to you as those of Q'uo. Greetings in the love and the light of the one infinite Creator whose blessing is upon us all. We feel most privileged to be sharing in this circle of seeking and thank you for giving us the opportunity to be of service to you. We ask that each seeker realize that we are not final authorities, we make mistakes, and are as you, seekers along an infinite path of learning and becoming more and more that which we seek. Therefore, we ask each to use his own discrimination to take up those thoughts which have an interest and to leave behind those which do not, for only in this way may we feel free, without infringing upon your free will, to offer our opinions.

You ask us about the pain of living. What is the necessity of it, how can it be transformed? We must begin with a larger canvas, so if you would, come with us in mind. We take you to the point at which the infinite and eternal consciousness which you are chose to come into manifestation or an incarnational experience. What were you co-creating with the infinite One when you created the opportunities and overarching destiny which you did indeed co-create? It seems logical to assume that the choice to come into manifestation in this manner was based upon an advantage to be gained from so doing. There are things which entities in incarnational, physical bodies can do which discarnate spirits cannot. Those in incarnation cannot know. Those not in manifestation cannot escape knowing that all things are one, that there is one Source, one great original Thought in which all exist and which is in everything. In the illusion of manifestation this truth is escaped, cleanly and completely. There is no way of knowing while in incarnation that you are one with anything or anybody. All things seem to have limits and seem to be separate, whether these things are people, relationships or ideas.

The darkness of the valley of the shadow of death, to quote one of your culture's holy works, is the setting of the stage for your journey through this incarnation, for are you not all born with the life sentence of inescapable death? Therefore, you live in the shadow of that known outcome throughout the incarnational experience. So you have chosen to enter into an illusion which blocks all knowledge of unity from the conscious, logical mind. Further, you have come into an illusion which is eternally mysterious; that is, nothing is known no matter whether one seeks to the limits of the microscope or the telescope. One cannot find the basic reason "why," a basic method of "how," or a good definition of "what" the essence of the experience of manifestation might be, for as telescopes grow more powerful infinity is simply seen in more depth. As microscopes grow more powerful all that may be seen is the path of energy left by your electron particle. Now, if you are fields of energy, interacting in an illusion whose trademark is mystery and shadow there must be a reason not immediately obvious for your choice of coming into this illusion.

We shall pause.

(Pause)

This illusion is the third such level, shall we say, of learning for the infinite portions of the one Creator. To experience the first being the level of the elements, the experience of being rock, sea, air. Those experiences are simple yet move deeply and slowly, and consciousness then graduates to another level of illusion. In this illusion, for those portions of consciousness which now know that they exist and begin to move in order to seek the light, the easiest example of this movement is the turning of the flower and leaf to the sun to receive light. In these two illusions there is not self-consciousness, but with graduation into the third-density illusion which you now experience, you as co-creator are in a physical vehicle which has the ability to be conscious of itself experiencing the illusion.

There is a purpose for this particular illusion, in our opinion. Just as the purpose in the first density is to experience manifestation at its basic level, and just as the second density's purpose is to experience and learn the movement, the choice towards being fed, being comforted, being warmed, finding light, so in third density the individual seekers of light become self-conscious and decide to interact. Your illusion has everything to do with learning not only who and what and why you are as you are but also in learning how to interact with those about you. Upon graduation from this density the next series of lessons starts with learning to be a complex of entities which have all memories in common. In the next density this veil of mystery and forgetting which you now experience is gradually lifted, and, once again, you know that you are all One.

Only in third density is the unity hidden. This is in order that each may make an all-important choice of how to proceed with the evolution of the spirit, for there are two paths to the one infinite Creator in general. One path is radiant, giving, loving and unifying, and is called service-to-others path or the positive path of seeking. The other path to the one infinite Creator is magnetic, attractive, charismatic, and may be called the path of service to self or the negative path. Each of these two paths is a valid path to follow and will bring the seeker to the growing awareness of the nature of the mystery of Creator and self. We are those of the positive path, as we find it to be the more efficient path, and in our opinion the more agreeable one to follow.

Therefore, as you approach the choice of which path to follow, nothing can be known for sure, for it is all important that this choice be made in faith and not because of any proof or fact, for only in faith, only in the mid-air of that leap of faith is the choice truly made to love. Once the pilgrim's soul has made the choice to learn to love by attempting the positive path of service to others then there shall be the unfolding of the destiny which you co-created. This does not mean that free will is abridged thereby; it is as though you have furnished yourself with a place to begin a journey and a place where that journey ends.

See, you begin in Louisville and go to Chicago. In the journey there you may well travel through China but you will end up in Chicago. This is what you experience as the rough and tumble of the frustrations of your days. You have a destiny at work in you. The more clearly you make and remake the choice of polarity, the more you have the emotional calmness to be aware of whatever hints and synchronicities that are around to offer you the nudges you need to choose this or that way to be, to act and to respond to the seemingly good and seemingly bad things which occur to you. So you see, rather than your angst being a suffering without a context, this angst is as the ballast, the weight in your frail barque of being.

As you sail across uncharted waters your only rudder is your basic faith that all is well, that you have not misplanned these things which are occurring. The more you begin to realize that there are no mistakes the more you can move past wondering why the suffering was necessary and, therefore, the more time you have to take to pay attention to the situation in which you experience the suffering. Is this suffering necessary? Well, my friends, we may say that the discomfort of pain is necessary.

Now, the more the discomfort is resisted the harsher the discomfort. As we are on the journey of the mind and the spirit you shall constantly be changing and transforming because of your experiences. These changes are uncomfortable and, therefore, there is pain. To the extent that you cooperate with these energies of transformation, then to this extent the discomfort may not breed fear. You can look at the suffering and say, "I must be changing pretty well," but if you need the fear, allow it. There is nothing wrong with protecting your delicate and sensitive inner self. It is possible to allow this fear and then try just a little less fear, and then a little less, and move slowly, supporting the self, not discouraging the self by railing against the lack of courage or railing against destiny for the discomfort which change brings.

Perhaps what we would leave you with in this portion of this working is the thought that if you are learning lessons of love your first lesson is to love, accept and forgive yourself. In one of your holy works it is written that there are only two laws of being, to love the infinite Creator and to love all others as you love yourself. What entities often do not realize is that they are loving others more than they are loving themselves. How hard are you on yourself, my friends. Attempt to support and refresh your own self in your pilgrimage just as you would any friend. Attempt not the courage but the lack of discouragement. When you feel discouraged, find that portion of your spirit which cradles you and comforts you, and allow that comfort to fill and calm the rough seas, the rough seas of emotional pain. Then simply open your eyes and gaze upon that manifestation which barely hides the imminent glory of the one infinite Creator.

My friends, you are loved so very much by the infinite One, you are so precious. You are unique. Your nexus of experiences and biases is irreplaceable. Feel that jewel within yourself grow and glow and allow the Creator to move through each facet of this jewel of essence, and this shall be your rudder on the uncharted sea.

We would at this time open the meeting to any questions that any might have. May we take a first query?

Questioner: Yes, Quo, in the negative polarity, do they view themselves as being of negative polarity? Do they have a concept of polarity?

I am Q'uo. My brother, there are very, very few which, having no concept of polarity, are nevertheless of the negative polarity. However, the negative polarity is far more difficult than the positive polarity to do work in consciousness using *(inaudible)*. This is due to the fact that in order to graduate, shall we say, from the third-density illusion in the positive path it is necessary for an entity to be working in service to others at least 51 percent of the time, whereas in order to achieve graduation along the negative path of polarity it is necessary to be working in service to the self 99 percent of the time at a minimum.

Therefore, those who follow the path of negative polarity are almost always quite well aware of the process whereby all energies and entities about that person are subsumed and consumed by that person in order to bring added strength and power to the self. The times of slavery, shall we say, of which negatively polarizing entities are capable is large, however all are to one extent or another conscious.

May we answer you further, my brother?

Questioner: Yes, do the negative polarity people or entities, do they view us as positive polarity and themselves as negative, or do they not use this terminology or way of thinking? Perhaps I am not asking that clearly, I am not sure.

I am Q'uo. We believe we have the gist of your query. From the standpoint of the negative path the positive path is naive and weak. From the standpoint of the negative path the negative entity feels that it must look out for itself, and shall take all opportunities to take advantage of others who are naive and weak. It further feels that if these entities which are naive and weak learn from this experience to protect the self and use others who are naive and weak, then they have been of service in teaching a previously naive "babe in the woods" the nature of "the real world."

Indeed, almost no negatively oriented entity wishes to use such prejudicial language about its path. The language is more often couched in terms of affirming the self. This is not to be confused with the process of accepting the imperfect and universal self as a heart of preparation for loving others as you love yourself. Do you see this, my brother?

Questioner: Yes, thank you.

May we answer you further?

Questioner: Yes, I'd like someone else to have a turn.

Questioner: I have a question for you, Q'uo. What is the role of comfort—physical comfort—within the illusion, on the path of learning? If you can answer that question, what is the role of comfort in the metaphysical sense?

I am Q'uo. My brother, there is no inherent virtue in discomfort. The difficulties into which one falls by wishing for comfort have to do more with an addiction to a certain expectation than with comfort itself. One may indeed be comfortable, happy, wealthy or other seemingly good things, and be quite miserable because of need, for some form of discomfort lies within the soul. The notion of comfort, further, is one which suggests that there is a place in which one is comfortable. This invariably is not so. The true comfort is in accepting and cooperating with the destiny in which one flows like the raft in the torrent of the river.

May we answer you more specifically?

Questioner: Is there then a place for wishing of discomfort, as far as, metaphysically speaking, wishing for learning? As opposed to wishing for comfort and being couched within the illusion?

My brother, the fine joke of comfort and discomfort is that at the beginning of any learning there is tremendous feeling of discomfort while there is very little seeming work being done. The wheels, shall we say, are spinning, and even the slight bit of change which is occurring is causing tremendous amounts of emotional, mental or physical discomfort. As the lesson begins to sink in, usually the fourth or fifth time the genre of experience has come around again and the seeker is getting the hang of this particular lesson of love, the strides being made towards transformation are far greater, change is occurring at a far more deeply biased level, yet the experience of discomfort is somewhat less because comfort actually lies, as we said, in accepting one's place in the flow of change.

As the end of any lesson approaches, this realization of the flowing nature of learning and destiny is clearer and clearer. Finally, one is somewhat comfortable, and then of course it is time for another lesson to begin. Thus, there is always the discomfort, the angst, but the amount of angst is not necessarily consonant with the amount of change but is rather more nearly consonant with the amount of resistance to or standing athwart of that change because of preconceived ideas about what one's path of destiny is. It is well to release all expectations beyond a certain point in order for the play of the wind of destiny to aid rather than to seem to hinder.

May we answer you further, my brother?

Questioner: No, Q'uo. I thank you for your patience with me. I appreciate the different viewpoint and will take time to think about it.

I am Q'uo, and we appreciate your patience with us, for we attempt to give answers on several levels at once in order to speak to each within the circle, and this, while perhaps helpful, at least we intend it to be, certainly does little to keep us simple.

Is there another query at this time which we may obfuscate and confuse you with our answer to?

(Pause)

I am Q'uo, and we find that our sense of humor has run away with us again. We shall put it differently. May we answer another query at this time?

Questioner: Yes, Q'uo. I do not want to monopolize the time here because I am so full of questions, but I am curious as to … We had so many reports of people having encounters with reptilian-type humanoid forms. I was wondering, this is just a thought that occurred to me, seems to make sense, if there could be a planet which would [have had] reptilian life forms, perhaps a third density or a fourth density, and their body forms made good vehicles for negative polarity entities to reside in. Does it work like that or is it somewhat different? Is that clear?

I am Q'uo, and yes, the query is clear. The physical vehicle which carries consciousness is not ever biased towards positive or negative evolution, for this is evolution of consciousness. This consciousness is infinite and eternal and uses physical vehicles in order to come into manifestation and experience the limitations which allow self-knowledge. This consciousness can use any vehicle. It is this consciousness which has the ability to choose, to learn, and to love the infinite Creator, either by loving others and serving them as the self or simply loving the self and serving the self.

The reason that both polarities are acceptable ways to move towards the infinite Creator is that the service-to-self entity is quite correct when it sees that service to self is the service to the infinite Creator. Nothing that exists is not the infinite Creator, there is nothing to be of service to except the infinite Unity. However, the consciousness can choose to separate the self from others and use others or it can choose to attempt to unify itself with all others in service as if each entity were the self.

Does this answer your query or may we answer further?

Questioner: Yes, it answers it somewhat. I guess that I am still not clear. Do you not think that there are races … perhaps I should state it this way—when you are in a negative polarity, when this is your choosing, do you form societies, do you all live together or do you intersperse among the populace of the positive polarities?

I am Q'uo. My brother, both polarities exist at this time upon your planet. Some examples of more or less negative polarities are the corporation where the credit for the work goes to the leader of a team, and those who are within the corporation attempt to use others in order to advance, and the married state in which each partner attempts to gain control over the other. You see, we are not speaking of negative races, of beings, but of negativity itself. The actual look of a predominantly negatively oriented society is handsome or beautiful, neat and tidy, the hallmark of service to self being control and order.

May we answer you further, my brother?

Questioner: No, that is all I have right now.

Is there a final query?

Questioner: I wonder if there is any query that we may answer for you, Q'uo? *(Inaudible)* joke is on me.

I am Q'uo. Your queries are to us a great blessing. They enable us to pursue our own path of learning. As we attempt to share our thoughts with you we learn a great deal from you and we are most grateful for that privilege. We would at this time rejoice in having been with you all. As you go upon your way may many blessings befall you and may you be merry with one another. We leave you in the love and in the light of the one infinite Creator. We are known to you as the principle of Q'uo. Adonai.

Year 1993

January 3, 1993 to May 29, 1993

Sunday Meditation
January 3, 1993

Group question: How much can we either consciously or subconsciously affect the way we look at the experiences in our daily round of activities and what we can do to sow seeds of a wider perspective, a lighter perspective, one that takes the broader view and gives us the opportunity to go through our lives with less turmoil, less of the up and down, or if this is even advisable, is it better for us just to work with the way we go up and down—do people really have an effect upon their attitude or is it a figment of our imagination?

(Carla channeling)

I am known to you as Q'uo. My greetings to you in the love and the light of the one infinite Creator. We feel our thoughts streaming to meld with yours in a unison of peace and praise, and we are most appreciative of the privilege of sharing the comfort of meditative awareness with this circle of seeking. You ask us this day about the effect one's attitude has upon one's life, whether it does, how it does, and so forth.

To begin to answer that query, we would turn it around and say that the experiences which constitute an incarnation affect one's attitude and are designed to do that, so one cannot begin with a blank slate in speaking of attitudes, for there are lessons to be learned, catalysts to be experienced and reacted to in the life regardless of which attitude these programs of material or lessons are received.

Let us spend a bit of thought upon this before moving forward. You are already aware of so much in the field of metaphysics, having focused upon it intensively. However, sometimes the basic fundamental of a cosmological system such as the one we offer can seem fresh and new, because the material has not been dealt with in just this application. Such is the case with the plan which you as co-creators, with the aid of your higher self, set out to experience during this particular incarnation. There was a destiny, shall we call it, of kinds of human experience—that is, experience which can be had by humans or third-density creatures—that was the helping of food on the incarnational plate. These lessons of loving were meant only for your own learning and growth. There was not in your minds as you planned these lessons a mischievous or wicked impulse, but only the ambitions of the seeker who wishes to stretch and grow within while offering service in the name of the infinite One. Consequently, you gave to your future incarnational self a potential for incarnational experience that you yourself felt was the very best possible.

Now, we all know how the eyes can be larger then the stomach, how that incarnational plate may have been loaded generously. Nevertheless, it is to be remembered that there is nothing intrinsically mischievous or wicked about the lessons that fly before you in the gale of experience as you experience it. No matter how fierce the winds and storms may seem they are as you yourself wished them to be in terms of that which was inevitability going to be dealt with as you lived through this incarnational time. When the difficulties seem overwhelming it is always easier to malign destiny than to buckle down and do the laborious work of digesting the catalyst instead. However, as a beginning to speaking of attitudes we may say that these attitudes do not address a random life plan of catalytic experiences; rather, they address the stuff of which lessons are made. The fractional broken pieces of a whole lesson come bit by bit into the net of your personal energies and are there for a blessing and for learning and growth.

This having been said, we ask that you take some of your time when reflecting simply to put your being carefully within the awareness of yourself as an infinite and eternal being who wishes both to serve and to grow in the love of the infinite One. Into this arena where free will meets destiny and chooses its reaction comes that called the attitude. An attitude, we may note, is etymologically a word meaning "the way of leaning or tending." To take an attitude in the dance, for instance, is to turn the foot and leg sideways while raising it upwards instead of raising it straight. The attitude is the slant which you may put upon the straightforward march of life events. And, yes, the attitude one takes does have a great deal to do with how rough the incarnational experience seems as you progress through it.

The attitude of those who hunger is that they wish food now. We say this to remind each that the consideration of an attitude is a luxury brought about by having a full stomach, a warm shelter, and comrades in arms, as it were. Those simply attempting survival have only the background attitude of desire for life. But most within your culture have the luxury of experimentation, with the inward turning of the mind as it meets new situations. We would say to you that that which has ripened within you will come forth as an attitude, and you may feel as if you have consciously done great things, when in fact the choice of attitude has been a small one in the present, the greater part of the work on that particular lesson being done beforehand so that you could respect and accept the incoming data as recognizable. It is the old lesson unlearned which becomes the new lesson, where the novelty of the experience catches one flatfooted, or with an old and still unlearned lesson. The boredom and distress which has accompanied past failure causes the attitude to change.

So, we would look first at new lessons and then at the true culprit which you are after. In new, or novel to you lessons of love the remembrance that you are in tune with your own destiny is often enough of an attitudinal adjustment to allow you to accept and process new material without undue difficulty. However, when you are revisiting old tangles of emotion, you are attempting to let light, air and warmth into that which is dark, cold and closed. The very process of accepting the data is painful because it is recognized that this is difficult, that is, unlearned material and there is the feeling of "Oh no, here we go again!"

Look for a moment at the fear at that turn of thought and see the dulling, freezing, darkening effect of fear. We do not encourage you to go forward as if you had no fear if your distress is considerable, but would indeed encourage you if you can do this at any crux, to recognize and accept these older and seemingly more painful lessons even though they are painful. The barriers put up by fear could seem to be an attitude barrier through which truth simply will not flow. So much of the work of having a positive attitude is clearing away the inevitable irritation that grows upon one at life itself for handing you your own failings, as seen by your self, then asking you with those failings to tackle that which is too hard for you.

The first adjustment, then, is simply to accept difficult material. You may work in another density on accepting it with total and unconditional love. In terms of the choice made in third density for the light, it is well that you focus on the basic choice, of saying "yes" to whatever the incarnation brings. Accepting difficult material is in itself difficult. Simply to accept is excellent work for you as a soul, for in accepting this difficult lesson of love as it manifests to you you are expressing faith in the nature of this material. Do you see that in order *(inaudible)* this material you would have to say to life itself, "I do not believe that there is a reason for this suffering, limitation and loss. I do not believe I am a loved child in my Father's care."

Now, in seeking the Creator we so often assume that, of course, we accept that we are children under the one great original Creator's care. However, in the day to day experience this seeming unconditional acceptance is refused and ignored by the thoughts of doubting the goodness of a destiny which would so bombard you with difficult situations and emotions. Once you have seen this portion of your attitude come into focus, that is a simple and profound faith in the system of learning lessons in your density. Then you may choose wisely how you may approach the sense impressions which make up the daily experience. If all things are good but often unknown, then it is with eager interest and positive hopes that one would take up every new thing that came forward to the sinecure of attention.

Yet this remains not so, because the nature of one who is cut off from the processes of the deep mind cannot stay consciously at all times in the deep rhythms of existence. The feeling of being lost on the sea of troubles is quite literally cut off from the sea of consciousness in which all that is separate comes into one unified stem or root, and is ultimately lost in the mystery of Godhead. So, persistently you shall, even though affirming the goodness of all experience and affirming the goodness of your lessons, come up again and again against the outrageous, unacceptable, painful experiences which, by subtle or bold means, shake your comfort apart and force you to deal not only with the situation but with your own feelings about that situation.

You see, you can know that all is well and know that everything is for you to learn, but this does not keep the unruly emotions of a deeply sensitive being which has been cut off from the resting place of eternity from feeling many, many painful things, and seemingly having to feel them in the darkness of solitude, whether it be total solitude or simply the deep loneliness of inner solitude. You cannot expect any attitude whatsoever to buffer you from feeling emotions. This, we feel, is where your query was aimed. We hope you can see that all we said before stands as the foundation upon which we can talk about having attitudes.

Yes, my friends, the practice of a particular bend of attention and way of consideration is a tremendous force in shaping your learning experiences and in performing the service which you came to offer. Part of the work of any wanderer is the living of the life itself, for when (that) which has been in a more compassionate vibration, or wiser one, has all of its forces in harmony inwardly then the breathing in and breathing out of everyday living is in itself the central portion of the service which you came to offer, that service being to enable consciousness within this planetary sphere to be lightened. Insofar as the eyes of your heart are lightened, so is the planetary vibration lightened.

Now, as you go forward you may feel that this seems very easy: "I will just take what comes with good humor." However, the incarnation will turn around and surprise you as soon as you think thusly. Again, what is important in the creation of an attitude is largely that fundamental way in [which] you as a servant of the good are ready to deal with destiny. In doing this you shall again and again find in theory that you are doing well, but what are all these unhappy and turbulent emotions, why must you suffer? This is where we came in, this is what you asked and about this we may say that building upon the foundation of faith which undergirds all of your existence you may focus upon your emotions, not upon the events causing the emotions, with good results as far as aiding yourself by attitude.

If you focus on events you are lost in meaningless detail. If you focus on your emotions, you see that when you have pain in the emotional body, you resist, tighten up and say "no" in a speechless, silent way. Now, step back from this knot of negation and see that the work of the attitude is concerned with holding, loving and forgiving that self that is in a knot of pain. The attitude is not relevant to the facts in the way you meant it. It is relevant to how you deal with the emotions which you feel as you move through this lesson. If you are angry, a good attitude cannot make you not angry. However, it can kick in like the afterburner and say, "I accept myself angry as well as calm."

In this self-acceptance lies the compassion and love which the lesson was intended to teach. The events themselves do not teach, and one's reactions to the events do not fully teach; but the way one deals with one's unredeemed and lost emotions make a great difference. The attitude can be adjusted by daily, silent meditation. This is a good foundation upon which to build each day. However, much of the day is spent in a far more active and less contemplative mode. Within this active mode there seems little time for the reseating of one's consciousness into the center of a life lived in faith. However, one small word is enough to change the attitude, whether it be "Love," or, as this instrument prays often, "Jesus," or any other short expression of truth. This is enough to feed the flame of balance within.

This, shall we say, balanced fire can pilot one emotionally. The fire is the fire of love. This engine which moves the attitude is fueled by love. And this love comes into the painful emotional reactions and accepts that painful, twisted, knotted self. It also accepts just the same the times when you are not in pain but feel wonderful, and then the acceptance is that of the fond relative which sees the children playing on the grass on a summer day and glows with the joy of it. You can be pleased with yourself, this is a good attitude. Just let yourself be equally pleased when you are having unlovable and unpretty reactions. Let your compassion flow to yourself. This is the best attitude.

There are other ways to affect the attitude besides prayer. A song upon the lips or in the mind always helps. The joking with oneself or with another is almost always helpful. The attempts made to soften another's pain, when another comes to you for aid have a profound positive effect on you. So that we encourage each to rejoice in the outworking of destiny and to attempt to allow your frame of mind to be that which it must be because of what is happening, so that you are not thrown, or dismayed, or judgmental with yourself when you stumble and fall. Let your attitude be that all is well even as you pick yourself up again and yet again, dust yourself off, as this instrument's song goes, and start all over again.

The crux of having a good attitude is in that moment of recognition and forgiveness of the self by the self. May you rejoice in your destiny and find it within yourself, faithfully and persistently, to cooperate with it, for as you attempt through having an attitude to do these things the puzzles you encounter will be simplified to the extent you have ceased judging yourself as you do your lessons.

At this time we have finished with the direct communication to this one query. Are there further queries at this time?

Questioner: *(Inaudible).*

I am Q'uo. We find this sentiment hilarious, and wish you the same. Are there any further queries?

Questioner: Thank you very much.

And we, my friends, thank you as you sit in the gently descending early darkness of winter in your pleasant domicile. We find ourselves, as always, reluctant to let go of this channel, yet we must. Please know, however, that although we have different concepts of time and space as our illusions are different, yet we are with you in your time and space in a faithful and stable way, a strength for you to call on. We are most happy that you do call upon us, for we can give one thing, and that is our unconditional love. And we do so enjoy being with those who call upon us not to share information, but just to be able to send the vibrations of love and support that are the other part of our service to you. We may speak to you of many things, but the vibratory connection between us is that carrier wave of love, and this is never away from you simply because we do not have a voice. No words are necessary. Love is experienced in love. We let you now go away from the quiet of meditation and into the world at large for some more helpings of catalytic experience. May your attitude be full of joy and compassion, and always, my friends, good humor. Be merry with each other.

We are known to you as the principle of Q'uo. We leave you in the love and in the light of the one infinite and glorious Creator. In that shining light we say adonai. Adonai. ✤

L/L Research

L/L Research is a subsidiary of Rock Creek Research & Development Laboratories, Inc.

P.O. Box 5195
Louisville, KY 40255-0195

www.llresearch.org

Rock Creek is a non-profit corporation dedicated to discovering and sharing information which may aid in the spiritual evolution of humankind.

ABOUT THE CONTENTS OF THIS TRANSCRIPT: This telepathic channeling has been taken from transcriptions of the weekly study and meditation meetings of the Rock Creek Research & Development Laboratories and L/L Research. It is offered in the hope that it may be useful to you. As the Confederation entities always make a point of saying, please use your discrimination and judgment in assessing this material. If something rings true to you, fine. If something does not resonate, please leave it behind, for neither we nor those of the Confederation would wish to be a stumbling block for any.

CAVEAT: This transcript is being published by L/L Research in a not yet final form. It has, however, been edited and any obvious errors have been corrected. When it is in a final form, this caveat will be removed.

© 2009 L/L Research

Sunday Meditation
January 10, 1993

Group question: The question this afternoon is from V in San Diego, and she would like to know a little bit about some books, a group, and a contact that she has been getting information from, and inspiration from, and would like to know what Q'uo has to say as regards the nature of the information that she's been getting from Metatron, who's been working with her on an inspirational and a channeling basis, I believe. She would also like to know about a book called *The Keys of Enoch*, and her study of this particular book has been closely linked with her work with Metatron.

She would also like to know about a book called *Love (and Love): Through the Doorway*, written by Solera. It has to do with the date that passed in 1991, I believe … January 11th … At any rate, it was a time during which a special doorway was supposedly opened into the New Age so that there would be a greater intensity and variety of spiritually awakening experiences open to people.

She'd also like to know about a group called Starborn Unlimited. This is a group that I believe concentrates on people who believe that they are from other planets and very likely other densities, what Ra calls wanderers … a group formed around that concept that shares information about those from elsewhere and the nature of their mission or work upon this planet in being those who help to lighten the vibrations and aid with the birthing of the New Age upon this planet.

And lastly she would like to know about a little book called *E. T. 101* that is published by the Intergalactic Council Publications and written by Master [Jho]. And they are supposedly related to the Council of Nine, and this also has to do with the nature of entities that are from elsewhere, and those, such as Q'uo, who have offered their services in the aid of growth of mind, body and spirit on this planet during its time of transition.

We would like to know what you have to say to V on these topics and any other comments that you would care to make.

(Carla channeling)

Greetings in the love and in the light of the one infinite Creator. We are known to you as those of the principle Q'uo. It is our privilege to share your meditation and to speak with you concerning questions having to do with the correctness or authority of various entities and written volumes. We begin by saying that we do not have any authority over you. We are prone to error. Our opinions, though offered because we feel them to be worthwhile considerations, do not constitute error-free information, but rather careful opinion of one who is on the positive, or service-to-others, path. Each individual entity, each group of entities, in the end all the unity of entities, insofar as they have the capacity to activate, evaluate and judge have no capacity for logically, rationally proving any authority from the outside in. In our opinion, neither any entity's self, higher self, nor any teacher that still speaks or thinks or considers has knowledge of the mystery of the infinite Creator.

By saying this we wish to establish a basis upon which we may build. The foundation of the right consideration of an entity's position as judge of its own creation depends firstly upon there being no authority that is final. No hand or word has the master's authority over servants of the infinite One, for the infinite One has established that in all manifested creation there be no final, provable answers. As entities discover what seem to be definitive answers, the edge or furthest limit of knowledge is pushed back, and it is discovered that beyond that new pioneering frontier of knowledge there lies still an infinite mystery.

Now, it is well for a student of any subject or field to do research, read, and gather tools and resources for coming to understand that field of inquiry. Those who seek along a spiritual path are not so different from those who seek to learn how to work one of your machines or learn a previously unknown skill. There is the studying, the processing of many facts into subjectively formed categories and organizations, and in the end there is [you] with a more enlightened point of view concerning the field of inquiry which has been studied.

We encourage those who hunger and are not yet filled by spiritual food to seek out experiences with entities visible or invisible and to read that which they consider helpful. All of the information on each page of written work, each thought from a channeling source, is to be enjoyed. However, this is not to say that all is simply to be accepted. Nor are we saying that if many things seem wrong about a source there is no good in it, for even the most inaccurate contact, dealing with the most fear-driven subjects, are attempting to serve the one infinite Creator. And those which listen to or read these perhaps wrong-headed thoughts may be offered much erroneously fearful information. Still, there is at least the gathering together for reasons of spiritual inquiry. And as this energy brings entities together to seek, so no matter how faulty the group may seem there is the effect of help from each consciousness present to each other as all form a circle of seeking.

There are several ways to consider how to form one's own opinions and value them. We might suggest that when information is being evaluated the seeker stop to reflect as to which energy center or centers are being activated by this information. For instance, information which focuses upon matters of survival is driven by the instinctual energies of the red ray, [all in] the reflection, naturally, from the yellow ray physical existence. We speak of inner rays here, rather than densities.

If information is offered concerning the moving together of some who are different from others, or simply if there is information about groupings and joining or avoiding groups it may be seen that there are many energies of the yellow ray. And if there is information concerning this or that messiah or special chosen entity, then it must be left to the entity itself to evaluate whether the attraction of this savior is resonating with the red, the orange, and/or the yellow ray.

All of this sort of information tends not to activate or enhance the healing powers of the opened heart or green ray. It is within the more abstruse and abstract regions of theoretical considerations that the inspiration of words or thoughts might be offered which open the heart or the powers and energies of communication. And it is within the student only that the indigo ray is activated by any material whatsoever.

For work to be done in consciousness, the consciousness must have its attention upon doing the work. We might take a different tack in this matter of personal discrimination. Now, we are saying simply that each spiritual seeker, having its own universe, must and shall evaluate for itself all stimulus which comes into the sensory net of awareness. From the first impressions to the end of the most involved and recondite argument all that is processed by a spiritual student is accurate to that student, and the only authority is that student, for the infinite Creator Itself, while offering constant love and support, does not wish to influence the experiences of any being. All beings are free to experience what and as each chooses. This is that which is the seeker's gift to the infinite One.

No outer authority may be considered, in our opinion, a satisfactory substitute for an individual's inwardly moved framework of opinion. So we encourage each student to think of itself as responsible in that the will of the infinite Creator is that there be love. Each is love, and each experiences love. This is that which is the truth insofar as we know it. Putting this truth into manifestation is a task whose characteristic is polarity or apparent difference. Without this, there can be no manifestation, for love experienced as love is an eternal tautology when considered as a way of knowing as opposed to the way we grasp being[ness].

So each of you is sovereign—the judge and jury of those things which come to each entity's attention. If that is accepted, then it can be seen that there is a certain desirable character, or group of characteristics, which may be attributed to a responsibly working spiritual student. The teacher known to you as Jesus the Christ spoke of this when it said to its students to be wise as serpents and innocent as doves. The serpent is a symbol for wisdom, and it is wise in apparent manifestation also. The first sense is that of the symbol. This symbol of wisdom is expressed in your cultural myth by the gift of the serpent which was making available the knowledge of good or evil. In other words, wisdom has to do with a personal ability to judge whether something is good to that person. This kind of decision is strictly personal, and cannot and should not be offered in dogmatic fashion for others.

The other way in which the serpent is wise is that when an enemy or possible enemy comes into hearing or sensory range the serpent removes itself cautiously. These both are good ways of being wise. When one considers the innocence of doves and asks how that can be applied to the judgment of information, we can only suggest that each entity knows of those individuals to whom all things are signs of disappointment, trouble and doom, while others with the same basic situation find much to make merry about and much to give thanks and praise for. The innocence, the purity, the untouched nature of the open and loving green-ray energy center—the open, loving, compassionate heart—can see beauty in almost any situation, for as it speaks to itself it hears the outer world.

We find that this is a good beginning upon this topic and invite further queries both now from this group and, in the future, from the one known as V. We hope that this transmission has been clear in why it refrains from offering opinions considering the validity of sources.

Before we leave this topic we would simply say that there is much, much of fear in any human experience. The physical vehicle is fragile, and it is known that it is mortal. Many of the fear-driven topics, which may be considered by many such as this instrument to have little effectual truth, have a truth in a larger or archetypical sense, for there is a wonderful urgency about this present moment, about this present cycle, about this present year, and so forth. These are the minutes, the last minutes, of each of your incarnations. There may be millions of these last minutes, but they can be counted. Thusly, there is a deep and natural capacity to fear, for one's worst fears, those of annihilation, stand starkly, and without evidential answer, before each seeker's life. At the end of that last minute of the incarnational experience, that consciousness that is the seeker goes through a door and it closes behind that entity, leaving those who are still experiencing the illusion of third density to remain ignorant of that which occurs thereafter.

The more compassionate way to deal with this existential fear is to realize and affirm the wonder and blessing of each present moment. If disaster or catastrophe is to be part of an entity's destiny, it shall occur, regardless of planning attempts to protect the self from such a fate. If all is to be peaceful concerning a seeker's last days in this illusion, so it shall be, although the seeker stands within a hundred which are slain. The attitude of gazing with a full and loving heart at whatever is occurring is the more compassionate and loving approach to the quandary of existence without answers. Appreciate and attempt to inhabit fully each moment, each minute and hour of each day of this experience, one at a time, and whatever the outer circumstances, the inner spiritual journey shall be as full of light and blessing as the experiencer can hold.

We would at this time ask if there be any queries? May we have a query at this time?

Questioner: Not from me, Q'uo. Thank you very much. That was very helpful.

Questioner: Not from me, either, Q'uo. Thanks for *(inaudible)*.

I am Q'uo, and we have enjoyed being with you also, my brother, and are grateful that you allow us to be of service. We always wish to linger with this good company, but it is time for us to go. And so we caress each beautiful spirit in hugs of brotherhood and offer always our love and blessing in the name of the one infinite Creator. We leave you in that Creator, in love and insofar love is manifest, in love and light. It is the season of the growing light. May each ray of the Creator's love and light that enters your heart find a happy home. We are those known to you as Q'uo. Adonai, my friends, Adonai. ✤

The Aaron/Q'uo Dialogues, Session 10
January 17, 1993

(This session was preceded by a period of tuning and meditation.)

Group question: Concerning codependency and compassion, "How do I live more lovingly for others and still live with respect for myself?" This question relates to the following statements from Aaron: "You aspire to perfect service and to prayer without ceasing. The being cannot pray without ceasing while it is moored in judgment and confusion. The heart and energy are not open. It can pray without ceasing when it notes the arising of fear and allows fear to be a catalyst to compassion and connection. Heartfelt prayer arises from that connection. Primary is the question of making friends with your own humanness and imperfections in the incarnative state."

Aaron: My greetings and love to you all. I am Aaron. I phrased this question some weeks ago because it seems to come from so many of your hearts. I wonder if it would be useful for you to offer any additional thoughts you have about this question. In the rephrasing of it as it comes from your own hearts, there is sometimes that twist that helps you see where the distortion lies. I would pause here for a moment, then, and ask if there are any additions to the question. That is all.

Carla: How can we be of service to others without dumping all over ourselves, using up our time, talent and treasure and not having anything left over for our little special projects? Others are asked to clarify or add to this question.

K: I think it is right to the point.

Aaron: I am Aaron. Let us first speak about the word "codependence." All beings are, in fact, codependent. The word has picked up bad connotations in your language, as if there were something negative about being codependent. But, in fact, it is not codependence in itself that is negative. The negativity derives from fear. When codependence is acknowledged as part of your connection with all that is, it is a wholesome state.

You breathe in the air. You are codependent with the trees that help create the atmosphere. Your bodies are largely water. At your death that water in your body moves back into the soil. In your breath there is moisture. The moisture from your body helps the trees grow. Codependence, then, is not the problem. It is simply a statement of your non-separation, your inter-being. Rather, what we need to address is codependence as separation; that is, that state of fear which leads you to acts and words and simultaneous resentment about those acts and words, or the fear that leads you to encourage others in unwholesome acts as a protection to the self.

When two beings interact and wish mutually to serve one another, certainly that is codependence.

But it is a skillful codependence where each being learns that it is part of a greater whole and honors its interactions with other beings. The right hand does not withhold comfort from the left hand. They know themselves as part of the same body. Yet within the extended earth-plane experience, you view others as separate from self. Then negative codependence arises. We define negative codependence, then, as acts and words based on an illusion of separation. Within that illusion of separation, fear has arisen and also a lack of clarity of the being's highest purpose.

Each of you has within you places of deep fear. There is some preference not to look into those places, a need to not confront that fear in yourself. When another's demands upon you allow you escape from that confrontation, a part of you says, "Oh no, incessant demands," and a part of you says, "Thank you. Thank you for the protection of your demands."

Last month I talked to a mother who wanted very much to write. That was her expressed desire. She had a baby, perhaps a four-year-old child, and that baby had a tendency to whine, to pull on her constantly for attention, which tendency I noticed as we were talking. The child's self-entertainment was that it constantly came over and interrupted. Of course, the mother has unconsciously taught it this behavior. When you use the term codependence in a negative way, it grows out of this type of relationship where the mother insists that she wants to write, wants her child to become more independent so that she has freedom for her work, and yet surreptitiously encourages that dependence because it protects her from writing. At a much deeper level, the writing terrifies her. This, then, is what we might define as unwholesome codependence.

As with everything else in your life, negative codependence is an invitation. When you see a repetitive pattern that seems to hamper you in some way, it would seem wise to ask yourself, "What does the continuation of this pattern protect me from? Is there any way that I am encouraging it?" Then you may begin to look at the fear that has led to continuation of that pattern.

At first it seems almost impossible to change it, to say no. There is self-discipline involved here. At some point, as you look at the patterns which seem discouraging to you, you need to ask yourself, "What if I just say no," and then watch very, very carefully to see what happens. Now here is another area of confusion, of distortion perhaps, because many of you do get this far and decide, "I am going to say no," but you are not really aware what it is you are saying no to. In your mind, you think you are saying no to the other and to their uncomfortable demands. That *no*, then, has arisen from a place of anger. You still do not see that what you are saying no to is your own fear.

For this mother I just described, she might say no finally to that child: "No, you must sit down and entertain yourself. Here are crayons. Here is a book. Here are blocks. I am not to be disturbed for half an hour." But it does not come out that way. Instead it comes out as, "No! You sit down and play with your toys! I have had enough!" That kind of anger pours out. Who is she really angry at? What is the anger really about?

When you are very clear in yourselves that you need to do something a certain way and that your choice is not harmful to another, it is not hard to say no. It becomes hard when there is no clarity, because you do not know whether you want to say no and end the behavior or whether you want to allow the behavior to continue. So, some of you get to the point of saying no but your no is said in anger, which escalates the tension between you, rather than speaking with love.

I have a good deal more I would like to say here. I feel Q'uo wishes to speak and will turn this over to my brother/sister. That is all.

Q'uo: We are those of Q'uo. Greetings to all in this circle of seeking in the love and ineffable light of the one infinite Creator. It is such a thrill to blend our vibrations with your own as we allow our energies to merge with your own and become a hymn of praise and thanksgiving to the one Source and Creator of all that there is.

We are most especially glad to have this opportunity to work with the one known as Aaron. This is unique in our experience of inner- and outer-plane cooperation; and perhaps you could say that Aaron and we are codependent in teaching our best for service to you, as you are codependent in sharing what we offer and using that which you find useful. We do not claim authority over you. Please use your discrimination and leave behind any information which does not meet with your needs and opinions.

We would not be a stumbling block before you. This being said, we would like to state our opinion of the portion of this large query upon which we have begun work, for there are several portions to this issue.

Firstly, there is the portion of codependency which works with the Creator, Its design and Its and your co-created agenda for this incarnational experience. Secondly, there is the portion wherein the seeker is working to find the heart of its own self. Thirdly, there is the portion dealing with relationships, not central but rather having to do with the self or the society in regards to the hook which hooks you into so-called codependent behavior. Fourthly, there is the portion devoted to the consideration of the seeker in relation to its central entities: the mate and the family; and in unusual occasions, a special or another acquaintance.

Perhaps you may see our feeling that in dealing with the central relationships of one's incarnational experience, you are dealing with the Creator's plan, your work within this incarnation and your generalized buttons, shall we say, or sensitive places wherein connections with the self or society are found to be frustrating in this codependent way. Before we can consider fully the central codependency, however, let us begin with this latter, for it shall prove to be the way we move back into this series of discussions.

Here you are: you, the seeker. And although the lifemate or family member has seemingly associated with you in an unskillful way, and you with the other, there is still a full travel of free will. What force moves within your heart that causes the exchange of hurt and emotional pain? Let us look at the force of need.

Do you see, my friends, you are entities who wish to be of service to others? Therefore, just as we, so you need others in order to be of service. This flavor of need undoubtedly played a role in your choice of this partner as a co-Creator, and again within the illusion in manifestation. This other was chosen because this other needs you. Now, this works very well in bringing together entities, both of which have planned to work upon changing fear to free joy, for did not the other entity also choose you because the other needed to be needed also? Thusly, a loving symbiosis wherein each helps the other and each happily acknowledges the need for the other becomes cramped and crushed by the seeming demands of space and time, for those who need express desire which will take up all space and time.

The need to be needed is likewise unlimited. And, my friends, each other portion of the manifested personality also makes plans upon the available time. And that which worked so perfectly as symbiosis when there was time enough and many fewer complexities of personality hits the crunch of a far more complex agenda for living. Symbiosis is turned into codependency.

The fear has several flavors. Perhaps the most acute is the fear of running out of time. There are other fears here, too: the fear of not being appreciated, the fear of abandonment, the fear of the month! These things change, but the tendency to react to your own fear does not change its flavor like the content of this month's fear, which will inevitably give way to your changing journey in consciousness.

So, we ask you to begin looking at the contexts in which you live and give and love and attempt to serve others. We move back to the one known as Aaron. We leave this instrument in love and in light. We are those of the principle of Q'uo.

Aaron: This is Aaron. Jim, I can see the thought patterns forming in your mind; but with Barbara's eyes closed, I cannot see whether those patterns find a continuity to your fingertips and to the keyboard. Thus, my question: Is this still too fast?

Jim: Yes.

Aaron: I will slow down as much as I am able. When there is a gap between the continuity of my energy, Barbara drifts in and out of the state needed to most clearly channel me. It will take some practice on her part to sit there for some moments with a blank and trust that the next thought is coming.

I appreciate Q'uo's distinction between living symbiosis and codependence. Symbiosis is alive, a flowering of the energy of each to each, where perhaps codependence has its emphasis on the fear and need of dependence. To be codependent on another there must be two. In fact, that is how you perceive yourselves. You are not your beloved friend or family member, you are not the water you drink … That is conventional reality. But in terms of a deeper reality, there is no separation.

When you care for a loved one with the sense, "When my work is done for this one, then and only then I can attend to myself," this is delusion. This is seeing through the eyes of conventional reality. When you see that your service to your loved one is truly also meeting your needs, that your needs intermesh so perfectly, then you are seeing with clarity, with wisdom. This understanding of your fundamental connection with all that is, is essential to your growth.

We speak about love and fear. If you watch yourself carefully, you can see yourself drift in and out … fear and separation … love and connection … Observe it in yourself as you tend to another's needs. Are you looking at your watch? "How much more time need I give? When will I go and do what I want to do?" My dear ones, what did you come to do? To build this or that building? To drive to the market? To tackle this or that goal? Is that the purpose for which you incarnated? Even what would seem to be the lofty purpose—to write this book, to help that friend—are they the purpose of your incarnation? Yes, the book may be a gift to many or the conversation with your friend a gift to that one. The walk through the woods may bring joy to your heart. But you incarnated for one basic reason: to deepen your experience of faith and love; to move away from delusion of a separate self; to move into such deep awareness of your true nature that your acts, words and thoughts most consistently reflect that awareness.

Do you know what you need to do in order to best practice that clarity, faith and love? In a sense, the practice of faith deepens faith. First there must be clear seeing that you do not foster dependence to avoid your own fears. Once that is established and you are able to move from a space of clarity, much of your confusion will end. You will begin to see that what you most need to do in service to others is exactly what is most needed for the learning of the self.

I would suggest that as you ask yourself to have faith in that statement and observe it carefully, you will find that much of the clamor, "I need/I want", simply dissolves. Did you really need to do that project? Would not a shorter walk do as well? Yes, you must attend to your own needs. You must care for this human body and nurture all the aspects of you. But how much of the clamor to constantly be *doing* grows out of deep self-nurturing and how much from fear?

What happens within the heart when you watch the arising of "I need"? What happens when you watch that arising and smile at that solid, separate self? What do you really need to grow beyond the delusion of this small ego self, to understand your true nature, to manifest your energy in service to all without differentiation of self and other? When you serve the divine energy, either in your divine manifestation or in human manifestation, without distinction of self and other, it is then and only then that the spirit finds true freedom. This freedom is the fruit of the practice of faith and love.

That practice takes self-discipline, but not the discipline that you perceive. And here is where you often get into trouble. Your self-discipline often takes the form, "I will do this for *him* or *her*, for *another*." Can you see, my dear ones, that resentment rises with that separation? With "I will do this for *us*," there is no resentment. As I serve you, I serve myself. As I help you to find healing, I find healing. As I help you to understand, I learn.

Some of your projects and busyness are the ego's wild attempts to escape from this ultimate reality of connection. The ego does not die easily. It screams. It kicks. With attention we learn to hear both voices. The contented baby, pain eased, falls asleep in the mother's arms; and that mother looks tenderly at her child, so glad that she was able to ease its pain. But there is still the small voice in that mother that says, "But I did not get to finish the chapter in my book," or, "I missed the end of my movie on TV." Then she squirms with guilt and discomfort.

Can we learn to smile at that voice? As she cared for her baby's voice of pain, can we offer compassion to our own voice of pain? Can we learn to hear it for what it is: ego making a last-ditch effort to assert itself? Then we may bask in the beauty of a deeper level of being, of the connection that grows out of actions and words that are clearly not for you, but for *us*. As you smile at the ego self that does not want to give up, you shift your perspective from fear to love, loving even that ego self and letting it be. Then the heart is free to connect into that deeper level of being, and the heart knows, "I have just done exactly what I needed to do."

We spoke about faith. You all know that in third density your prime lessons are of faith and love. In our last joint session with Q'uo, the one known as Ariel spoke of the impetuousness with which older third-density incarnate beings sometimes prefer to overlook the learning of faith and love and move into the pathways of deepening compassion and wisdom. If faith and love are learned simultaneously with this deepening of compassion and wisdom, it works well. But when faith and love are overlooked, there is often distortion, even physical distortion of the body where the upper chakras are open and attention is not given to the blockage of the lower chakras.

One aspect of deepening faith that is overlooked by many of you is that when you watch this shift in yourself—service to other versus service to self—as you watch yourself shift in perspective, faith grows from blind faith to a verified faith. Intuitively you know that you are moving deeper into connection. Your heart knows that you are doing the work you came to do, not getting rid of ego but allowing ego to dissolve in the light and energy of ultimate reality. That reality knows the self as unlimited, divine, connected to all that is. When you bring your attention back to this deepening of faith, you may simply remind yourself, "This is why I am here."

This is the self-discipline that is called for. It is not a voice that says, "I *must* meet his needs." It is not an intellect that says, "You *should* have compassion." It is not judgmental in that way. Rather, it is the voice of the heart. It is the voice that dissolves all boundaries, dissolves all fear, and brings you into that wondrous knowing of your own true Self, of God and of the self's true nature as part of God.

Can you allow each arising of "What about me?" to become a reminder: "Can I observe this fear? Can I smile at the ego kicking and screaming and let go? Can I really trust that if something needs to be done there will be a way for it to be done?" No, that does not mean you can lie back and let someone else take care of it. Effort is required. But what is the doing about? Is it an assertion of ego, at least in some part, or does it take you closer to connection and deeper love?

I thank you for your attention to these thoughts. I expect that we will be delving into this question and its many ramifications for several days. May I return you now to the energy of my brother/sister of Q'uo? That is all.

Q'uo: I am again with this instrument. I am Q'uo. We would leave you with one focus. The one known as Aaron asked, "Can you laugh and love the entity you are?" This query is central. In the context of relationship, we ask you to reflect upon the persistence of desire that is not analyzed or understood. For instance, if you think, "She is so angry with me," you may well be thinking, in truth, "I am so angry with her." The very need that was perceived as an occasion for service becomes an affront to the waking consciousness of third density when the service is rendered and no appreciation is offered. The greater the perceived service, the greater the unrealized need, often, for thanks and validation.

Now in truth, you truly wished and did wish to serve purely with no expectation of any return. But this is the point with which we wish to leave this session: Seldom can an entity offer itself so purely that the incessant, persistent and continuing arising of desire does not make more than pure the consciousness that has come to serve.[12] Can you love that self that continues very naturally to desire?

We shall pick this up with great glee at our next session of working. Meanwhile, we congratulate each of you and your various numb body parts and consciousness, and we perceive a level of fatigue in the group. We hope that you may wash that aftertaste of weariness away with companionship, some food for your physical vehicles and of course the praying without ceasing that you do not yet know that you are already doing. How we love you, my friends. We do look forward to our next opportunity to work with your queries. Meanwhile, we leave you in the joy of the love and light of the one infinite Creator in Whose name we come. We are known to you as those of the principle of Q'uo. Adonai, my friends. Adonai.

Aaron: This is Aaron. It seems redundant to add anything to that statement. My blessings and love to you all. ☙

---

[12] Clarification of this statement is pending.

The Aaron/Q'uo Dialogues, Session 11
January 18, 1993

(This session was preceded by a period of tuning and meditation.)

Aaron: Good morning and my love to you all. I am Aaron. In relation to this focus that Q'uo has offered, there are two areas I would like to bring to your consideration. One is as this instrument has just summarized and the other is to look practically at those places where you get stuck, to look with examples, real life examples, so that you may begin to pinpoint in each of you where distortion arises.

The arising of desire to serve another grows out of aspiration to be of loving service. There is a pureness and love to that aspiration, yet you find yourselves in a situation where others are making unskillful demands upon you. Perhaps they are releasing their anger to you or are asking you to do that which you know they could do for themselves.

Yesterday I spoke of the places where you allow their anger to be thrown on you or where you do for them rather than asking them to do for themselves, out of a place of fear in yourself. That is one segment of the confusion. A different segment grows out of the heart that truly wishes to serve but does not understand where that service lies. When you see another stumble, your instinct is to reach out and help; and that is a loving gesture. What of the one who stumbles, continually stumbles, because he does not want to walk on his own feet?

There is a desire to serve the other. If it was all one way or the other, if desire to serve was either 100% pure or 100% egotistically distorted, there would be no problem discerning which way it was. The struggle that you move into grows out of the fact that it is never 100%. It is rarely even 90%, but usually much more of a balance. You see the real workings of compassion in yourself, the Pure Heart connected to the pain of the other and wishing in some way to release that being from its pain. But, my dear ones, you cannot take the pain of another. You can help another learn to let go of its own pain. You can offer the love, the support, the kindness, that gives another the strength to face its own fear. But it must do that work by itself.

Here is where compassion becomes distorted. There is deep compassion and desire to alleviate suffering. But there is more. When you see another stumble and feel you must move to end that being's pain, to support them more than you already have, whose pain are you addressing? Look at this carefully in yourselves. What is the desire? Whether it is to barge in and fix their life for them or simply to lift and carry them a bit, where is that desire coming from? Is it too painful to you to watch their stumbling? Is it too close a reflection of your own stumbling? Then you see that reflection of yourself, you get just a glimpse of it, and you turn on yourself as if the very pure love and desire to alleviate suffering were nothing more than your own selfishness. So, you swing from one extreme to the other and find it so difficult to accept both are happening: "There is genuine compassion in me, a deep empathy for another. There is also fear in me."

Compassion, my friends, is that level of empathy where you so clearly understand the fears and pains of another's heart that there is truly nothing left to forgive, for there is no longer judgment. Each of you has the innate ability, the seeds, whether sprouted or not yet sprouted, for that kind of compassion within yourselves.

Another necessary part of compassion is clear seeing. Compassion is not maudlin. It penetrates into absolute reality. It knows fear when it sees it. It does not seek ownership of that fear. It is not *his* or *her* fear, just fear, *our* fear, the fear in the hearts of every being that our needs will not be met, that we will be hurt, that we will be lost or in pain.

Codependence, in its unwholesome aspect as we have defined it, is not a problem. You've heard me say there are no problems, only situations that need your loving attention. This definition is the clue. When you pay loving attention, it allows that natural seed of compassion in your heart to sprout and blossom. With compassion there is no self or other. Loving attention allows you to see where self is brought in, where fear arises and leads you to inappropriate and unskillful choices, perhaps trying to fix another or mis-serve another so as to alleviate your own pain.

What I have done so far is merely to present the situation in which you all often find yourselves. I have really said nothing that you do not already know. Hopefully, I have presented it in a clear enough form that we may now begin to address the questions, "What do I do with the fear that leads me into unskillful choices? How do I (as Q'uo challenged you) learn to love myself, to laugh at the fears that arise and let them go, and move back into that joyful connection?"

I would like to pass the microphone, as it were, to my brother/sister of Q'uo. That is all.

Q'uo: Greetings in the love and in the light of the one infinite Creator. We are those of Q'uo. May we briefly say how pleased we are and how privileged we feel to work with the one known as Aaron in sharing our thoughts this morning.

This being that is you, the seeker incarnate and manifest as human, finds itself awash in its human characteristics. The desire to control situations for an increase in comfort and security often prompts you into actions and reactions seemingly lacking in compassion. And when two together are so functioning, the term for what occurs is sometimes codependent behavior. We would like to focus in upon the seeker you are and begin to gaze at resources which one may find useful in dealing with the pain of that desire which is not fully grasped or well stated, which involves you so often in these feelings of fear and then anger and guilt at the beholding of the unskillful expression of humanity.

Remember that the way the seeker relates to another has its roots first in the seeker's basic incarnational biases; secondly in the seeker's more fundamental biases, which are the fruit of many incarnations; and lastly and most deeply in the relationship which the seeker has with its so-called higher self, or that infinite portion of self that is in common with the one infinite Creator. From the very beginning of consciousness, whether within the creation or within the incarnation, the seeker's first experiences of compassion are those of the nurturing attention of the Creator or parent. In the beginning of life as a cosmic entity or as an incarnational manifestation of that entity, the baseline of first experience is total attention and all needs met, although as a soul and as a human being, it is soon discovered that the needs and desires proliferate too quickly and thickly for the nurturing creation to answer each need in full. Yet still, the ideal of being treasured, cherished and fully nurtured remains a standard hoped for in the seeker's heart.

Turn and gaze at that heart. Do you have mixed feelings about this hungry heart with its incessant desires? How does the seeker move towards the learning of compassion for its heart? How can you as a learning and maturing soul bring understanding to bear upon your own greedy heart? We ask you to think of the infinite creation with its infinite and seemingly vastly wasteful expenditures of energy, each star blazing and consuming itself down to the smallest visible sight where the atoms move in a perfect frenzy of energy constantly moving, constantly attracted onward. The entire manifested creation of the Father hungers. You, yourself, are the object of the Creator's hungry heart. The Creator desires to know Itself, and you have been sent outward, given free will in order that the Creator might learn of Itself because of receiving your harvest of experiences. You are here to enlarge your experience, not to control it but to enter fully into it. It is not by taking thought that experience is deeply felt, but the opposite. It is by allowing deep experiences without so much control that learning eventually occurs. The thought is well taken by reflecting upon that which has been received. Thusly, you may see yourself as a natural portion of the Creator, whose hunger for safety, attention or comfort is not despicable but inevitable.

When this first vision of the self as being natural in its seeming imperfection is fully seated within your mind and heart, then you may begin to unravel the tangled thread of compassionate clarity that has become caught and twisted by the attempts you have made to escape your nature. Yes, each of you is quite pure, innocent and untouched within the deepest portion of that which is you. Now you may focus on how the relationship you have with the Creator, with your Higher Self and with your incarnation can inform and guide you well towards the shining source of that thread of pure compassion which you wish to knit up into the fabric of your lives and relationships. This is a journey from head to heart, from fear to love, from meekness to an acceptance of the eternal untidiness of catalyst, perception and experience.

We would move back to the one known as Aaron, as we find the basis in theory which we offer is far better followed by more concrete observations. We happily yield to the one known as Aaron. We are those of Q'uo.

Aaron: I am Aaron. My heartfelt thanks to my brother/sister energy of Q'uo for the wisdom with which it speaks. Yes, precisely, this is the journey from fear to love, from brain-oriented choice to heart-centered choice. But, my dear ones, you do not have to be perfect at it. You do not have to get it all at once. If you were already perfect, you would not be here in incarnation. You are learning. This sense that it should have already been learned is the source of so much suffering for you. You struggle and there is pain. Can you begin to see that all of the situations through which you move are part of the learning?

Have you seen a young child build with a pile of blocks? Perhaps the second block sits on the first, but with the placement of the third, the stack topples over. There is not yet understanding of balance. The child experiments on and on and finally begins to understand that the center of the weight of the third block must be over the other two; and then it adds a fourth.

Your situations are the building blocks on which your learning is based. Yes, I know that when a block is unskillfully placed and that block connects with another's heart, there is pain. And I know and you know that you are responsible for that misplaced block. Here is an area of concern for many of you who are older seekers: Deepening awareness of responsibility creates a new form of fear. You know that you are responsible, and thus you become increasingly impatient with your mistakes.

I certainly do not advocate irresponsibility, nor would I suggest that it is okay to harm another. But remember that you are learning, you are all learning; and one of the things you might practice is patience, patience combined with honesty which looks clearly at unskillful choices so that they need not be repeated. You are not a two-year-old with blocks. When the block is placed and topples, it needs topple once or twice and then the lesson is learned. There is no need for the self-chastisement into which error is often distorted, but simply for observation: "I keep repeating this mistake. I need to pay closer attention. Then I can do it more skillfully."

So, you are all embarked on this journey from fear to love, from the contracted heart to the open one. But it is an infinite path. I cannot speak about eighth density nor anything beyond that. I can only speak of those beings moving into seventh density by my own observation, so what I say here is conjecture; but my conjecture would be that perfect love is still being learned, even at those levels. It is not something you have to do today. Can you be a bit more patient and kind to yourselves? Can you simply remember: I do not have to perfect it today—not only do not have to, but cannot—only to improve it a bit, to understand it a bit more clearly, to take one more step.

My dear ones, on this journey of yours, this search, each step that brings you closer to unconditional love is a step taken in unknowingness. You are blind. When you believe you are not blind and think you are in control, you are walking in circles, you are not going anywhere. The next step to your growth always involves letting go of everything you thought you knew and moving out into the unknown. Can you begin to cherish yourselves for the courage and faith to keep letting go of that which is known, safe and controllable, and to launch yourselves into deeper exploration of the Infinite?

Let us shift course here and work with some concrete examples. I do not choose here to invade anyone's privacy by using set examples from the lives of those in this circle. Let me instead use hypothetical examples, but those with which you will be intimately familiar through the circumstances of your own lives.

You are each in intimate relationships with others, or have been. This may be your partner, a parent or a child. It may be a sibling or a dear friend. Q'uo has spoken about your being drawn to each other in part by the desire to serve one another and by recognition of the deep possibility of service. Sometimes this service seems not quite equal; and one, seeing its own fears arising, begins to resent the other. Sometimes one is less compassionate to the other. Sometimes one is more reactive to its own fear.

To make this concrete, I will use an example of partners of either sex. But please fit this into your own life in whatever situations you find yourself. One being strives to be ready to go out at an agreed time. The other being is always late. Let us call them being A and being B. I do not want to assign the lateness or promptness to one sex or the other. A understands that B is irritated when A says, "It is getting late. Why aren't you ready?" A sees B's need to go at its own pace and not be rushed. At first A feels anger about this because hosts and hostesses are a bit perturbed by the late arrival, and A feels, "I am being blamed and it is B's fault." At first A may make excuses and say, "Well, I was ready but I was waiting for B."

Finally, A begins to see through that fear. It needs no longer blame B. It continually asks itself, "Can I have compassion for B?" It sees the fear of fast motion in B. It sees the ambivalence of putting itself into social situations which leads B to be late. It speaks to B about all of this. It makes peace with the situation, readies itself on time and then sits and reads a book, simply waiting for B to be ready. At that point there is no quarrel between them.

A is acting compassionately but also allowing B to dwell in its own fear. Its responsibility extends only so far as pointing out to B, "It seems to me that this fear exists and is leading you to unskillful action which is disrespectful of others who are waiting for you. I can wait patiently, but I see that when our friends must hold dinner for half an hour, it is uncomfortable for them. Will you consider why you choose to do this? Will you consider an effort to be on time?"

"Consider" is the prime word here. If A says, "You must be," that is a violence to B. Can you see that? It is attacking B's pattern, attacking B's fear. It is trying to fix or change B. But it is responsible for A to point out what it sees to B very gently and ask it to consider what it might do, what it might learn, by changing the situation.

What happens when there is a bit of a shift in this pattern? As A has become comfortable with B's choice and able to leave B alone with its choice, B begins to be later and later. B is looking for a reaction. It wants someone to light a fire under it, to get it going; and A has refused to do that any more. So B becomes aware, "I must do something to provoke A." Perhaps B is even later. Perhaps A is fully dressed and ready to go and comes to see where B is, and B is still reading the paper and says, "Well, I will go shower now." At that point, A feels the arising of anger again. Perhaps B has a different approach and is almost ready but then picks an argument with A, for example. Perhaps A is the last one out the door; or as they are going out the driveway, A asks B, "Did you lock the door?" and B explodes, "You were ready all this time. Why did not you see the door was locked?!" In some way or another, A is attempting to provoke B.

Again, I ask you to fit this situation into more familiar ones in your own life if this does not mesh perfectly. I am trying to use a situation that is common enough that you all may have some familiarity with it. I understand that it may not be the most pressing codependent situation in your life.

Here A is pulled back into the fray by B's becoming more extreme in one way or another, by B's provocation. That provocation asks A to focus more clearly on its own reaction. A has reached the point where it is okay if B is late. Is it okay if B yells at A out of guilt for its own lateness or out of its own fear? Is it okay if B is twice as late? Where does A say no? How does A say no?

Now, obviously, if you have two cars, there is no problem. A can simply be ready on time and say, "I will be leaving at such and such a time. I will see you there," and leave B to its own resources. But let us assume that in this situation there is only one vehicle. Perhaps A is aware of the feud that would ensue if it called a cab and makes the decision, "I am not willing to provoke B in that way." What options does it have? How does it say no? Can A simply get into the car at the appointed time and drive away? Is that also a provocation to B? Where is it provocation and where is it an aid to learning?

I would suggest that the line is drawn not in the act itself but in the intention behind the act. If A gets into the car and drives away in anger, that is strong provocation. If A says to B an hour before the time needed to leave, "I understand you need a lot of time. We need to leave in an hour, which you have told me before is the time you need to get ready. At 8 o'clock I will be driving out the driveway. I hope that you are in the car with me. There is no anger in me as I say this. Here is ten dollars that I am leaving on the desk so that you can call a cab if you need to, but I feel a need to be on time."

In loving, non-violent movement with another being there must be a willingness to suffer the anger of another and ask another to consider your viewpoint. The strength of the soul speaks its truth, be it a major issue or a very small one. It does not speak it in hostility to another, but with the deepest compassion for the pain of the other. Nevertheless, it says, "This cannot continue. Your actions cause pain to other people, be it lateness, drinking, helplessness or displays of rage with cursing or throwing."

It is not the action of saying no, but the way no is said that is most important. If there is any intention to enrage the other further, to provoke or find revenge for past pain, no matter how that no is said, that seed of anger is still planted. You must look deeply into your own hearts. You must also remember that it cannot be 100% pure, but see if it is largely pure.

If you look and uncover some anger for past humiliation, for past discomfort, then you may ask yourself, "Is my real intention in saying no to seek revenge for that past by creating discomfort in the other? Or is my real intention to serve us, the other and myself, and lead us both into learning?" Having uncovered those subtle, unskillful intentions in yourself, you are far less likely to act on them. You may rest assured that there will be a greater amount of purity to your choice.

So what does A do here? It first must become aware of its own anger. B is abusing it. If it is able to release that anger sufficiently, it may point out that abuse to B. In some situations that may be enough, but rarely. If B had that need to abuse, unless B is very clear, it is going to repeat the situation of verbal abuse for not locking the door, or by being later and later and later to see when it finally provokes A. With the saying of no in the example we gave, saying, "I am leaving at this time. You have adequate time to be ready," A is making a clear statement of its intention from a place of non-fear.

Perhaps A might even have brought it up the day before in saying, "I think this is an awkward situation that we need to move past and this is what I plan to do," so as to give B warning. B may be threatened by that warning. And part of the next afternoon before the leaving, B may be hostile to A. Can A have compassion for that hostility it has provoked? This is part of that willingness to accept another's anger, to ask another to consider your viewpoint when you feel so strongly that your viewpoint is more skillful and love-based. It is the only way you can ask another to consider your viewpoint without doing violence to the other.

So A might ask itself ahead of time, "If my choice threatens B and B acts in a hostile way, am I willing to allow that hostility? To what degree am I willing to allow it?" When it becomes uncomfortable, A has the right to say, "No, I cannot allow it any further." But why is it uncomfortable? If B is calling A names and A can see the fear in B, would not A anticipate that fear? A has even catalyzed the fear. Why would A need to personalize it? Need A ask, "What if I am *this* or *that* that B is calling me?"

Is it disappointment, perhaps, which catches A? A may feel, "I really thought B could be clearer here, could be more mature. I feel saddened, I feel betrayed, because B is unable to meet my needs for a more mature partner." What is the pain about? Again, more clarity, more honesty, are called forth. It is A's learning as much as B's, because A must be aware, "In what way am I feeling attacked here? What am I saying no to?" When B understands that it cannot pull A into its issues, that A is going to act lovingly, non-judgmentally but firmly, then and only then is B forced back into itself with loving support from A, without hatred or criticism but with awareness, "I need to clean this up in myself."

For each of you that see yourself as A in this sort of situation, the questions to ask yourself are, "In what way does B's behavior threaten me? In what ways do my reactions to those threats lead me back into conflict and violence with B? How can I manifest my own energy more purely, with deeper awareness of which buttons B pushes, so to speak? How can I move to that point where I can ask B to consider my viewpoint, and accept that my request is a threat to B and that B is liable to react with fear? Am I willing to accept the ramifications of that fear as I ask this consideration of B?" In other words, "How do I get myself clear? What do I have to do?"

This brings us back to the spiritual perspective. You are not B's teacher if you are A. You are each other's teachers. You are not in this situation solely to teach B something. B is also here to teach you. You have joined together because you recognize the possibility of mutual service to one another and, of course, the loving connection between you as well. You are always precisely where you need to be. If the situation is very uncomfortable and makes you squirm, stop and ask yourself, "How did I get here? What learning might there be for me in this situation? What seeds have I planted in the past which have helped to create this jungle that surrounds me now? How can I transform this jungle by my loving choice, by my awareness, back into a fruitful garden?"

There is always learning in it for you. Please remember that distortions are not "bad" but merely uncomfortable. They also may be the catalyst for learning. You may come to love even these distortions. If you find yourself in conflict and with hatred arising, with bitterness arising, then you are not paying attention. If you find yourself with frustration and fear arising, that is fine. Fear and frustration do not need to be catalysts for hatred. They can also be catalysts for deeper compassion. Fear can be a warning signal, a red light flashing that says, "Pay attention!" And as you pay closer attention and find compassion for the places in yourself that feel threatened by these choices, then you move into deeper compassion for B and into intuitive wisdom of the open heart that knows how to say no to unwholesome demands.

As you see yourselves go through this cycle again and again and again, be aware, my friends, of where you wish to avoid the lessons of the incarnation. Ask yourself, "Can I embrace even this? Can I make space for it in my heart so that I can learn?"

I would like to pass the microphone back to my brother/sister of Q'uo. I also feel that there are some questions among this circle. I do know that Q'uo wishes to speak, and then perhaps we can attend to your questions. That is all.

Q'uo: We are those of Q'uo and are again with this instrument. Obviously, you did not enter incarnation and choose your family in order to become angry together. Your Higher Self and the Creator did not plan the emotional details of experiencing incarnation. Rather, as the incarnation was planned, the focus was upon the offering of the self as a rough-cut stone to the refining abrasion of circumstance, designed to polish and make beautiful and clear each facet of the gem that you truly are. You and your B, shall we say, planned to come together to be of service.[13]

Before incarnation and after it, it seems only vaguely humorous that all of the emotions felt are even possible. For when the veil of illusion is not in place, the differences between entities are healed with joy, and full travel is given to free will for each to harmonize with the other. In social complexes such as ours, for instance, each entity within the complex is unique, and the distinctions and dynamics are infinite. This is hailed as a great advantage for mutual support and interest, each learning from the harmonization process a bit of each other's uniqueness; thus building a larger harmonious uniqueness; thus becoming an energy and essence fully harmonized, and becoming infinite in energy by the full acceptance and multiplication of each uniqueness. So, too, you enter incarnation ready to learn. It is certainly a rude shock to awaken within manifestation and discover that the veil of illusion is opaque and harmonies are not visible.

We are working in this series to uncover ways of valuing and loving the self while harmoniously loving and living with others in a fully compassionate way. It is well to look to the intention of incarnation in general. There was no wickedness

---

[13] As did Aaron in his address above, Q'uo is using the letters A and B to describe the dynamics of relationship between two persons.

in each entity's choices of partners with whom to share learning and service. As each abrades the other by the dynamics betwixt them, it helps to lean back against the sure awareness of a kindly and efficient incarnational plan. Then each can turn to a clearer effort at communication with the Creator, the self and the other self, B; for there are many Bs in every A's incarnational experience. In the next working we would share further upon the clearing of communication by means of seating oneself within a faithful awareness of the intention of the self as it came into incarnational manifestation.

We would end our portion of this working at this moment, thanking each and leaving each in the love and in the light of the one infinite Creator. We turn the microphone back to the one known as Aaron. We are Q'uo.

Aaron: I am Aaron. It is indeed a joy to share this speaking with my brother/sister of Q'uo. I believe I speak for both of us when I offer thanks to the humans who have made the physical effort to come together for this sharing. I am aware of questions that have arisen from what we each have said, and also of some level of stiffness and fatigue. We will leave it to you. Do you wish to ask questions now or do you wish to end this session? This instrument's energy is adequate to continue.

(There were no questions at this time.)

My love, blessings and gratitude to you all for this opportunity to share with this loving circle of beings. Either Carla or that of Q'uo had wished yesterday to end the session with a releasing of energy. If they would like to do that now, I offer the microphone back to them. If not, we will conclude here. That is all.

L/L Research

L/L Research is a subsidiary of Rock Creek Research & Development Laboratories, Inc.

P.O. Box 5195
Louisville, KY 40255-0195

www.llresearch.org

Rock Creek is a non-profit corporation dedicated to discovering and sharing information which may aid in the spiritual evolution of humankind.

ABOUT THE CONTENTS OF THIS TRANSCRIPT: This telepathic channeling has been taken from transcriptions of the weekly study and meditation meetings of the Rock Creek Research & Development Laboratories and L/L Research. It is offered in the hope that it may be useful to you. As the Confederation entities always make a point of saying, please use your discrimination and judgment in assessing this material. If something rings true to you, fine. If something does not resonate, please leave it behind, for neither we nor those of the Confederation would wish to be a stumbling block for any.

CAVEAT: This transcript is being published by L/L Research in a not yet final form. It has, however, been edited and any obvious errors have been corrected. When it is in a final form, this caveat will be removed.

© 2009 L/L Research

The Aaron/Q'uo Dialogues, Session 12
January 18, 1993

(This session was preceded by a period of tuning and meditation.)

Group question: The topic continued from this morning's session, concerning the true meaning of compassion and clearing of communication by means of sealing oneself within the awareness of the intention of the self as it came into incarnation.

Q'uo: Greetings once again, my friends, in the love and in the light of the one infinite Creator. We are those of Q'uo, and wish again to express our and the one known as Aaron's joy at being called to your circle of seeking to offer our humble opinions upon the subjects of interest to you at this time and place in your journeys along what this instrument calls the king's highway.

Upon this highway you are neither old nor young, male or female, wealthy or impoverished. You are one who journeys as the prodigal son and daughter, having been flung far from your source of being. Now you move through illusion upon illusion in the twilight dream within a dream which is incarnational experience. As you sit here, each seeker has the sorrows of unfulfilled hopes, expectations and love. Each feels the pang of suffering. And yet, each is still attempting to find solutions to the suffering rather than finding space and time within to allow each portion of experience, including suffering, to have a hospitable room to dwell in while it visits you.

The illusion boldly states that you are here to find solutions to your problems and puzzles. It is our opinion that a more realistic view suggests that solutions are irrelevant to the process of journeying along the king's highway. What is much more important is that you ask better and clearer questions concerning this journey. This journey helps define your relationship with yourself by suggesting that there is a loving, nurturing home from which, at some point, you have departed in order to gain experience. The process of gaining this experience is, at its best, a messy one and one which persists in being contradictory, enigmatic and unsolvable. Your position as seeker, then, is one of remembrance of home and hope of return to this home. Between the beginning and the end of this journey, here each is.

As the moment comes for you to suffer, we can suggest that this model of beginning, middle and ending insists that there is a nurturer connected intimately with home, which accompanies you and is a deep portion of you. It does not offer surface comfort, but by its beingness within you it offers a context within which you may see your right relationship to your suffering self.

You chose carefully the incarnational destiny you now are in the process of experiencing, adding to your curriculum those courses or lessons concerning love which you and the Creator felt were appropriate. Thusly, you have created for yourself a destiny, or rather a destination or series of destinations towards which you inevitably shall move. Free will is maintained within this general destiny because you have the choice at any time as to how you shall travel. For instance, from this place you can reach Indiana across a bridge in about half an hour; or you can visit the Greek Islands, stop over in the Orient and return over the pole to Chicago, driving thence south to Indiana. Your Indianas are destined, but not the duration or complexity of your travel.

Knowing that your relationships are of one nature, whether they are with the Creator, discarnate entities, strangers, friends or your nearest and dearest ones, you may perhaps see that both within the illusion and within your own internal cosmology there exist many models for nurturing. When the moment of suffering occurs, your nurturing part can say within you, "I hold you with deepest love and rock you in the cradle of my love." The parent does not only hold and comfort the quiet or good child, but offers nurturing and comfort in difficulty as well.

Can you refrain from self-judgment when next you begin to be out of tune with yourself, and instead allow the nurturer within to cradle you in your distress? What we are suggesting is that living as you know it will always be a messy, difficult affair. And the spirit within wishes to nurture that very confused entity just as it is—spots, dabs, stains, dust and all. Its reaction to seeing you hurt is not to ask if you should be hurt. The nurturer goes for the Band-Aid and the cleansing swab. Then that nurturer gives you a pat and sends you back to play again. Beyond any solutions to interpersonal relationships, this nurturing is all-important for the seeker to have faith in and rely on. This being said, we would like to take a look at the ways in which one may maximize communication to others by communicating with the Creator and with the self on a continuing basis; for the unclear communications are frequently as much a matter of ignorance as they are a matter of actual difficulty.

At the beginning of this series of sessions the query boiled down to, "How can we serve others without extinguishing our own needs?" Let us look at those needs.

The need of the eternal being which you are is to continue to gather experience. All experiences are equal to the eternal Self. Much difficulty has been deliberately placed before each by the self. A grounding in this aids in communicating with the self, for there is that voice of the little child self which asks, "Why must I hurt? Why must I change? Why must I be disturbed?" When the self can answer, "This is your job. You have to be disturbed in order to learn something new," then the attitude with which you enter into the sometimes less than joyful experience of gaining experience may be softened.

We would at this time yield to our brother, the one known as Aaron. We are those of Q'uo.

Aaron: I am Aaron. My joyful thanks to my brother/sister Q'uo for the clarity of its teaching. At the end of its words, Q'uo has chosen to remind us that you are here to gather experience. Some of that experience is painful. Some is joyful. Some is comfortable and some distinctly uncomfortable. We have previously discussed the difference between pain and suffering. When it is painful, that is not pleasant; but there is only suffering when you become stuck in the illusion and begin to grasp at changing what is. It is not the discomfort of an arising physical or emotional sensation that causes your suffering. It is your aversion to what arises.

You are each asked to live with one foot in the illusion and one foot in ultimate reality. You straddle a threshold like actors in a play. You play a role here. And, like actors, you must play that role as if it matters. You must involve yourself in the illusion if there is to be learning, otherwise you might as well not have chosen incarnation; and yet, there still must be awareness. Just as the actor must have awareness that he plays to an audience so as not to turn his back on that audience, not to muffle his speech, so you must maintain awareness of your true Self while performing the myriad functions of the human personality.

When you are stuck in the small ego self, then connection is lost. That ego screams and kicks, as we spoke of earlier, fearing that its needs will not be met. If you dismiss that as illusion and disassociate yourself from it, there is the comfort of dwelling in the spiritual plane but there is no learning. And there is still duality because, at some level, disassociation is created by a separate self seeking to protect itself.

As you straddle this threshold, there seems to be a wall, an infinite wall, that divides day from night, fear from love, separation from connection. With practice you learn to allow this wall to dissolve and begin to transcend the duality which is the product of delusion. Then you learn to be in this discomforting situation without struggling, skillfully looking to resolve it in the ways in which that is possible, but also allowing the experience. You watch with the wisdom of your Higher Self. You find the ability to smile at this ego that keeps re-emerging. In short, you find the ability to be with the whole span of your being, not to prefer the physical and its sought-after pleasures, not to prefer the spiritual form nor to seek the bliss of merging yourself in that oneness which is the spirit's foundation. Instead, there is a coming together of the whole, an integration.

In October we ended our sessions speaking of faith and prayer without ceasing. We spoke of living in faith. As you allow yourself to move beyond the limits of the small ego self and recurrently experience, through meditation and through awareness, your connection with all that is, you stop struggling like a fish out of water with the experiences that life brings. As you relax into the incarnation, faith does deepen. Increasingly you find the ability to be more undefended when you are threatened. It is a matter of practice. Could you catch a ball the first time it was thrown to you? Sometimes a human child is afraid of a ball; and instead of reaching out its hands to catch, it simply bats it away. It moves to protect itself. Practice teaches it the skill of collecting that ball into itself.

As you relax the struggles with the incarnation and make the skillful decision to let go of some of the fear, as you allow yourself to experience this undefendedness, those seeds of deeper love and wisdom, of compassion and loving-kindness within your heart, begin to flower. So much of the frantic kicking and screaming—"What about me? Will I have time for what I want? Will attention be given to me? Will I be nurtured?"—so much of that frantic activity simply winds down. You begin to see from a higher perspective. Then, as Q'uo has suggested, you begin to embrace rather than condemn this human incarnation, this actor on the stage that is sometimes caught in the illusion.

I ask you to remember that the qualities of compassion and loving-kindness are natural to you. They are your natural state. When fear arises, it blocks the natural expression of love. It is neither useful to grasp at the love nor to attempt to get rid of the fear.

Coming back to a concrete example, suppose there is one who makes requests of you that seem, in your mind, to lead you to deny your own need. There you are with one foot on each side of the threshold, one foot in the illusion, saying, "I can't do this!" or, "Why does he or she keep demanding this of me?" Back to our A and B—it is simpler than constantly saying he/she, and I do not wish to assign any specific role to one sex or the other.[14] "B keeps asking this of me. B is so frightened. Why does not B do it itself? If I keep serving B, I will not have any time left for me." Anger arises, fear arises and, like that fish out of water, it just plops about. On the other side of the threshold is that level of clear seeing that says, "This is illusion. I am spirit. I am connected." Compassion arises for B. But there is distortion because there is no connection seen between the two perspectives. It becomes an either/or proposition to give or to receive.

When fear arises, self-discipline and courage may lead you not to act on that fear and greed. Here, awareness may dissolve this wall so that the human with its fear and greed and the spirit with its high aspiration merge, so that you see the whole range of your behavior. This clear seeing allows a level of faith: "No matter how much I dislike the situation I am in, it is just where I need to be. I am safe. I can experience this discomfort without closing in my armor, without further protecting myself." You remind yourself over and over, "I am safe. I can allow the fullness of experience." The fear of the human combines with the deep sorrow and loving aspiration of the spirit, which sees its perfection but because of its human aspect cannot manifest that perfection. What deep sorrow is there. But the more you keep your heart open to all of it, the more struggle falls away.

It is here that the heart begins to notice the prayer without ceasing. As Q'uo said yesterday, you already do that, you are just not yet aware of it. The divine aspect of yourself is always in deepest connection

---

[14] As in the previous session, Aaron is using the letters A and B to refer to two individuals in relationship.

with the Divine. How could it be otherwise? When you allow the presence of fear and discomfort, have faith that you are where you need to be and allow yourself to be open and vulnerable, to let go of security; then the heavens open and you come back in intactness of a body, mind and spirit to your connection with the Divine. Here again is the place where the question does not need to be asked, "What shall I do about B's demands?" A simply knows from the wisdom of its own heart.

I do not mean to imply that this work is simple. It is anything but simple. But, my friends, it is the work of all of your lifetimes, this steady progression from government by fear to response of love. Each small step you take on this, to use Q'uo's terminology, king's highway is wonderful. You, in your race, are only concentrating your attention on the road. If you would lift your head and look around you, you would see the cheering multitudes watching your every step, indeed, throwing rose petals on the road before you. They may not cover all the jagged rocks, but they are there. Can you open your eyes and begin to see yourselves as we see you?

I would like to transfer the discussion to my brother/sister Q'uo, with my thanks for this opportunity to share my thoughts. That is all.

Q'uo: I am with the instrument. I am Q'uo, and greet each of you in love and light.

We turn again and again to the moment of suffering in relationship, asking each to look with new eyes upon this frequently occurring center of experience both of joy and of sorrow and suffering. Each is A. Each is also B. This is helpful to remember when there is the suffering within relationship.

Clear communication can be of three kinds. Each is skillful, each is useful, according to your own judgment. The first clear communication is to sit down with your B and state each messy and confused feeling using sentences which begin with the word *I*. In this communication you are not attempting to break loose of the illusion but are expressing, with words which picture and mirror the illusion, the feelings and impressions that you have of the situation which has resulted in your choosing to suffer. This sharing ends with the request for the B to express similarly its own *I*, its own unapologized-for ego self. Egos are useful things to you. They run your physical vehicle, keep it warm, clothed and fed, and deliver you to the doorstep of each spiritually vital experience. They are to be honored and respected, both yours as A, yours as B and others whether they be your B or not.

Now if the B in your soap opera or drama is not willing to express its ego self, the next way of clear communication is of the self with the self, saying to the self all of the "I" statements. Allow all of the intense realizations of this suffering to be expressed, then respect that within yourself. This, then, can be that which you turn to your B: the face of one who suffers and is willing to abide its ego self, respected and allowed its voice. It is a lonelier form of clear communication, but it enables As which cannot speak within the illusion to Bs to stay within the illusion within a nurtured state, one buttressed and strengthened by the sympathy of the nurturer self within so that whatever the communication of a verbal nature may be, it is not liable to the desire for destruction which the unrespected ego self is prone to. This leaves B able to deal with its own ego self without feeling the pressure from A which would ask B to redeem or love A. This is helpful to both and clears the way in your future transactions for the increased possibility for verbal open communication because of the perceived lack of back-pressure.

The third way of cleared communication is that which takes place at all times and that to which you may become privy as you allow time, space and suffering to be what and as they are or seem to be. This does not mean withdrawing from experience; rather, it turns the order of things about. Instead of doing the various services of physical life and then having the time available in the remainder of your day to meditate, contemplate and pray, allow the mind and heart to be more and more aware that although the illusion is being visited, is useful, is vitally important and is interesting, your fundamental nature is at home and has never left. Communion is constant because there is identity. You are one with the infinite Creator. You are prayer without ceasing. It is not an activity; but rather, the praying without ceasing seems an activity until it is realized that praying without ceasing could well be your name. Your very nature is an unceasing hymn of love.

In the deepest sense, the key to moving from codependency to compassionate symbiosis in relationship is seeing yourself, both as a being in process and as a being beyond all time and space with nowhere to go except from love to love. In another way, this awareness allows you the luxury of placing neither great importance nor lack of respect upon the details of each moment's considerations. How can you find the way to have your needs met? The solution as usual is not present, but rather, is beyond the presence of illusion. It lies in knowing that much occurs which seems unfair; yet each unfairness passes and the attention is drawn elsewhere. Rather than attempting over and over to break a pattern, then, think of the relief of seeing as an A to a B, "Here is the pattern again. Here it is." The reaction of B then determines the next clear communication. If B wishes to learn and act upon the lessons of the incarnation, then both can sit down together, knowing that this is the work that they have come to do together among other services, and share the sorrow and pain that seem to be A and B's, but are A/B's in the reality that is known in the less deep illusion within your incarnation, which is the feeling of the heart.

Now if B is not yet ready to work together with you as mate, then there is the generosity of spirit that is the harvest of A's nurturing of B that allows B to say whatever it can without feeling the need to justify, condemn or defend. If even this degree of communication between entities is not available, then there is the relaxation of the illusion in the mind and heart and the allowing of the nurturer to place one in a cradled, loving space within which it is safe to become aware of the entity within, which is eternally prayer without ceasing.

None of these three modes of communication necessarily offer a solution, but then the solution would be momentary anyway. Experience moves on. Perhaps that which we would leave you with before we turn back to the one known as Aaron would be simply to suggest that when suffering arises, the clear communicator will turn to the one with whom it has transacted that suffering and begin a sentence with the word *I*, not allowing the suffering to sour and bleed and become the fine wine of old anger. If you can keep the utterance of the ego self current, you are giving yourself the maximum opportunities to become more and more clear.

This takes a kind of courage born only of blind faith, the faith that communication is effectual. We hope you may nurture that faith, because it is in relationships that the most accelerated pace of learning and spiritual evolution is possible within this illusion you call living. We know you wish to advance your learning. It is in the fire of the forging process of relationship that your opportunity for learning is maximized. Thusly, we hope that you not be discouraged and turn from the difficult relationship. If each can feel good about expressing the ego self's feelings as they arise, there is so much of freshness that airs out and aids in the amelioration of that suffering entity that is you. Thusly, what seems to be the display of ego is actually a generous offering of clarity within confusion to the one who is learning to give and live. Do you see how this love twines and winds about, seemingly separate but always one heartbeat from showing the true nature of union within?

We leave this instrument now and, with great appreciation for this marvelous adventure, turn the microphone over to the one known as Aaron. We leave each in love and light. We are those of Q'uo.

Aaron: I am Aaron. Q'uo has offered some very useful and concrete suggestions. As I listen to the thoughts offered by my brother/sister, I am struck with the idea that to use these suggestions you must be very aware: Here are three tools.

Is there anything within you that argues with the skillful use of these tools? Let us say that it seemed necessary to drive some nails into a block of wood. Let us further project that at some level this being that needs to drive the nails feels resentment about driving the nails. Perhaps every time a nail must be driven, this being must assume that responsibility and feels there is a lack of balance. Perhaps it simply hates the act of hammering because it dislikes the way it stresses its muscles. If you offer this being three hammers, it may well choose the best tool for the job; but because there is resistance to the work at hand, upon the first blow it is likely to smash its thumb, thus rendering it impossible to continue.

Thus, it would seem useful to ask yourself before you move into these three very useful steps, "Is there anything within me as A that hopes B will not respond? What part of me uses lack of communication as defense against knowing my own self more deeply? What fears have I tucked away and am carrying around with me as a burden, but fear drawing them out of my pack to examine them? If I come to B with Q'uo's suggested "*I* "—*I* feel hurt; *I* experience fear," whatever it may be—is there a part of me that subtly twists that communication in some small way so as to provoke rejection from B, therefore insuring that I need go no further in this communication but that I can handily blame B and say, "See, I tried; and B has shut me out"?

In step two, knowing your anger, knowing your fear, knowing your feeling, is urgent as Q'uo has suggested. But is there any desire to twist that again into blame so as to absent yourself from responsibility because of your own fear? Do this work with careful awareness, watching for the arising of the fear in yourself, for the arising of desire to protect. Can you greet that, too, with non-judgment? Can you smile at it as just part of the whole drama? Step back a step, remember who you are and then dive back in with a bit more clarity. Know that this fear is okay: "I need not be reactive to the situation. I need not be reactive to B's fear of the situation, should that occur. And I need not be afraid or reactive of my own fear." There is room for it all to float, space for it all.

If it is acceptable to the group, I would like to lead you in a brief guided meditation, asking you to move beyond the limits of the perceived self, to open yourself to the energy of the others in this loving circle and, as you become undefended with others' energy, to notice the arising of fear and touch that arising fear with compassion—just that. Is there energy and interest in pursuing this? That is all.

(Everyone agrees.)

I would ask you first to visualize yourselves sitting in a circle of light. Experience the fullness of your own energy. Draw your hands together before you, palms touching. Feel the energy pulsating from palm to palm. Slowly separate those hands, just a bit, and feel your energy radiating outward. You know that you do not end at your skin. Allow yourself to feel that.

Take in a deep breath and at the crown of that breath, just before the exhalation, expand outward.

(Pause)

Allow yourself to feel the energy body, the astral body, the light body, the Higher Self, all that moves beyond just this physical self, expanding outward … inhale … expand … and stabilize that expansion as you exhale. Inhale … expand … stabilize … Do it at your own pace for a few moments.

(Pause)

Allow yourself to feel the energy fields of the others in the room also expanding. You are light, you are energy, you are thought … expand outward and begin to feel the overlap of the energy that surrounds you.

(Pause)

Let that energy touch your own, and your own energy reach itself out.

(Pause)

As penetratingly as possible, notice any fear, any desire to retreat back into yourself and touch that fear with gentleness.

(Pause)

Know that you may retreat. That is not a failure. There is no "should" here, only a desire to stay as open as possible, to feel undefended in this very loving circle of friends. And yet in that undefendedness to know that the excesses and stray thoughts that you condemn in yourself may be felt by others. Can you trust another's compassion for you as you move deeper into your own compassion for them?

(Pause)

I am with you in this circle, my friends. We are, none of us, perfect. The fear which leads you to seek to armor yourself is not a contemptible trait, but is simply the manifestation of human conditioned mind. In a sense, it is a by-product of the incarnation which may be released with your loving practice and effort.

(Pause)

Again, I urge you to expand outward, just a bit more. It may help to turn your hands upright in your lap, palms up, to feel the others' energy. I will be quiet now for two or three minutes. Watch each arising desire to defend and touch it with gentle mercy.

(Pause)

Can you watch yourselves opening and closing, opening, closing a bit, opening again? May I leave you tonight with this bit of homework in whatever your relationships with others: Until we resume tomorrow, will you watch for this opening and closing? Watch also for any judgment of it. In this way you may begin to approach Q'uo's suggestions with more clarity about your own readiness to come to such communication undefended and thereby non-threatening to yourself or another.

I ask you here to reverse the process. Draw your energy back into yourself and allow it to settle. If your hands were palm up, turn them palm down on your lap. If there is any surplus energy, visualize it as a golden ball and, using your visualization or imagination, simply snip it with an imaginary scissors and let it float loose. Look for the stray bits of energy of you and gently draw them in. This is not armoring of the self, but skillful work with the energy within the illusion. To further draw your energy in, I would ask you to bring attention to your feet touching the ground. This is the human, its feet on the earth, one aspect of your entirety. Allow yourself to come back from the expanded spirit experience to the human that you also are.

I honor each of you for the courage, the sincerity and love that you bring to your seeking and your work. I thank you very much for inviting me to share my thoughts with you. I wish to return to Q'uo and Carla, who may wish to close this session. That is all.

Q'uo: I am Q'uo, and we greet you postscriptly in love and light. We find we do have the *one more thing to say* which is so typical of grand friendships.

We would leave you to merriment, comradeship and good food for your physical beings with the hope that each may listen to each and know that each is teacher to each. And as you rest into slumber this even, we encourage you to visit the ego self. There it is: you being laid to rest, yet not all of you. Allow that ego self to be the size it is right now. That is how much you need. As you continue to respect the process which engages ego and spirit, that balance shall continually shift. And it will happen that eventually you find a very small need for the ego self, for you have become independent within eternity. This experience awaits you. It is not now. Now it is just right that you have the ego self as you experience it now. It is you. It is not all of you. It is all you meet, yet it does not define any of you. Then say, "God bless this mess," and go to sleep, my friends, and rise to greet another day. Adonai. Adonai. We are those of Q'uo, and we leave you in the love and in the light of the one infinite Creator.

(Carla leads a meditation for giving back to the Creator the light that was felt by the group and included a group member's personal need for employment. The meditation ended with, "The image goes up and the rains fall down.") ♣

The Aaron/Q'uo Dialogues, Session 13
January 19, 1993

(This session was preceded by a period of tuning and meditation.)

Aaron: I am Aaron. I wish you could see this room as I see it. Through these three days, more and more light has radiated out. From my perspective, this room is a small sun situated here in the middle of the landscape.

When Q'uo and I speak to you as we have done these past two days, there is only so much you can process. Obviously, we could talk about this endlessly. As we have spoken, questions have arisen in each of your thoughts. For some of you there was a sense, "I have a question but perhaps I am not quite ready to ask it; I cannot phrase it clearly enough," or, "If I had been listening more carefully, I would know the answer," or even, "At some level I already do know the answer; I do not need to ask."

This is all fine. But perhaps it would be most useful to begin today not by hearing your one group question so much as hearing the extended questions or thoughts that have grown out of these past two days of work. Your questioning is a way of clarifying your thoughts, and also most clearly expresses to Q'uo and to me what it is that you most need to hear.

Some of you have some distress with what has been suggested these past two days, some vague discomfort which may be hard to articulate. I urge you to try. It is through expression of both that which is comfortable and that which is uncomfortable that the real questions may emerge. That is all.

(A period of group sharing and discussion followed.)

Aaron: I am Aaron. Would it be acceptable to you for us to focus more on compassion today than on codependence? I think we have pretty well covered codependence. How do you deepen compassion for this being that you are, who does move back into fear? Is that acceptable to you as a focus? I wonder if my brother/sister of Q'uo has anything to add to this. That is all.

Q'uo: I am Q'uo. Greetings once again in the love and the light of the one infinite Source and Ending of all that is.

Indeed, we do feel that the one known as Aaron and we have covered a good deal of material. It is more than sufficient for much consideration. Words are most helpful, yet insofar as there are words, there is the distance or lack of immediate sensation of being in union with the Creator, Whose very name is Love. This Love is a name which has created power. Its nature has descended throughout all levels of manifestation and constitutes your pith, your very core; Love which has been turned, shaped, or, if you look with jaundiced eye, twisted and bent into each portion of thought and feeling which each of you experiences.

As you listen to our words, realize that we, as you, have no way to tell or to perform the act of pure centering. Somehow the failure after failure after failure which each perceives in spiritual journeying adds up to a miracle of learning to love; and in spite of every feeling of failure, and perhaps because of it as well, you find yourselves where you were not before then: more capable, more sensitive to seeing your own vulnerability and imperfection.

As we come to the end of this session and speak of compassion, we ask each of you to stop thinking, to accept the mystery that is in front of us as well as you, and then we ask you to join us in turning to face this mystery. Gaze at it. Feel the stunning glory and majesty of the infinite Mystery. There, in that awareness, lies the protection that embraces vulnerability. There, in the shadow of the Mystery, lies the infinite wealth of love which feeds even the you that suffers most, even at the darkest hour.

The compassion comes not from the words. It simply takes many words for the Logos, the Love that is without words, to be approached by the incarnational self. So use all our words that have aided and clarified your situations, your progress, and have helped to define the process of becoming independent within the symbiosis with the one infinite Creator. But then to find the compassion, let us turn to the tabernacle of the Most High, as this instrument would say, and invite the awareness of the union that already exists.

We would pass the microphone to the one known as Aaron at this time. We are those of Q'uo.

Aaron: I am Aaron. Yesterday we defined compassion—a rather cold and clinical definition. As Q'uo has pointed out, words offer only concepts and not the experience itself. To speak of compassion, to probe it with the intellect, is not to experience compassion.

My dear ones, do you understand my meaning when I say that full compassion, full connection and undefendedness, are your true nature? Of course, you do not always experience that. You are human, and to be human is also part of your nature. But you are divine. How could it be otherwise?

I have described you as angels in earthsuits. These earthsuits are necessary to the incarnative experience just as a space traveler needs that which protects him from an otherwise alien environment, offers him safety from pressure, air to breathe or protection from temperature extremes. So these bodies of yours offer the spirit a situation in which it can move through those situations it needs in a semi-protected way. The Pure Spirit Body cannot dwell on this earth. The physical body that is home to the spirit bleeds when it is cut. The emotional body feels pain when it is attacked with hostile words.

Truly, we come back to faith here, to your faith in the experience of the incarnation, to the deepening of verified faith, "I am just where I need to be," working within the illusion with awareness that it is illusion and simultaneous awareness, "I must treat this illusion with respect." Perhaps respect is a key word. As you respect the physical, emotional and mental bodies, you become less judgmental of the retreat those bodies offer when confronted with pain.

You have heard me say repeatedly that you are here to learn love, unconditional love, which cannot be learned perfectly in human form, but to which you may move as close as is possible for the human. You, as an integrated whole, are learning; but also the Higher Self/spiritual body is learning. It is easy for the spiritual body to know its perfection. If it never sees imperfection, what opportunity does it have to practice non-judgment and unconditional love? Thus, the spiritual body moves into this house of the physical, joins together with the emotional and mental bodies that it may practice non-judgment, practice unconditional love toward that which was previously judged and found wanting.

One of the illusions in which you dwell, and which you rarely see, is that all of your reactivity against another is truly reactivity against the self. This is an unqualified statement: All of your judgment against another is judgment against those faults perceived or manifest in yourself. You may judge another's impatience while you do not portray the quality of impatience; but somewhere in your heart you feel the arising of that impatience, and so another's impatience is judged and found disturbing to you.

Is there anyone in this circle who has never felt hatred? Who has never felt greed? Can you see what a gift all of these discomforting emotions are? They are the constant catalyst which reminds you: Have mercy. This does not imply condoning unskillful and harmful acts and words which are reaction to emotion, but you can only find unconditional love and non-judgment through the repeated experience of working with the arising of that which has been judged in yourselves.

Yesterday Q'uo spoke of the value of the ego self. Its value is not only to remind you to watch for cars as you cross a street. The illusion of self is vital to your growth, as is the reality of no self. They are part of each other and there is no contradiction between them. If you would attend school, there must be a school and a being to attend and teachers. This is what your incarnation hands you.

As you enter repeatedly into those situations which lead to the arising of fear, the pulling in of the armor, the desire to defend, you do not move past that fear and those unwholesome responses by trying to get rid of them, but by reminding yourself, "Can I have compassion for this being that I am?"

There is a wonderful story about a Tibetan saint, Milarepa. He sat at the mouth of his cave meditating and, as the story goes, the demons of anger, of rage, of fear, of greed, appeared. They were hideous creatures. They exuded a foul smell. They dangled bloody knives and swords. Their bodies were made of decaying flesh and bones that rattled with a hideous sound. Milarepa took one look at them and said, "Come in. Come sit by my fire." They said, "Aren't you afraid of us?" "No," he replied. "Your hideous appearance only reminds me to be aware, to have mercy. Come, sit by my fire."

This instrument has asked the question, how can she retain this openness she is feeling? How can she stay undefended? One does not stay undefended, one simply notes the arising of defense each time it appears, the arising of fear, and says, "Oh, you again. Here is fear. Come, sit by my fire." Your relationships will continue to inspire fear and a desire to defend. You do not move away from that need to defend by denying it nor by wishing it away, not by judging it and saying, "I should not feel this. I should know better by now." You transcend that need to defend by embracing the ego self, comforting it, noticing the fear and inviting it to sit by the fire. You cannot transcend what you do not accept. To transcend ego, you must accept ego.

It is only then that the true manifestation of what you are can emerge. You are divine. The divinity strives to express itself constantly, but is often suppressed by your fear-based reactions. As you learn to look fear in the eye and that you need not be afraid of fear, you find you do not have to create that undefended stance. It simply emerges as natural to you. You do not have to search for connection. You experience your true connection because the blockages to that experience have been, I will not say removed, but laid aside. Like a throng of people that blocks the road before you, if you stamp your feet and say, "Get out of my way!" they taunt you. But perhaps when you smile at them and say, "Please, may I pass through?" they may step aside.

It is in this way that you learn, as a process, to keep your heart open. Keeping the heart open is not an event, but a process. Each time you do it, you become a bit more skilled at it, a bit more skilled at seeing where you have invited fear in and then challenged fear's right to be present and wanted only to be rid of it again. You become a bit more skilled at saying simply, "Here is fear. Sit by my fire, but I will not be reactive to you. I need not be reactive to you."

There is a vast difference between the experience of fear and the need to separate or defend, which is reactivity to fear. Watch that process in yourselves and you will learn how to experience it, invite it to sit by the fire and not need to be reactive to it. Your compassion for yourself deepens as you see this human submerged in a constant turmoil. One situation is no sooner resolved and comfortable, but a new one emerges creating new discomfort. How can you not embrace the courageous you that willingly moves into this incarnational turmoil to serve, to learn, to grow? Thus, your fear ceases to be a reminder for reactivity and defensiveness; and instead, when you see the arising of fear, through your skillful work with that arising, you create a new pattern, a new habit. Seeing the arising of fear becomes a reminder for compassion.

That compassion is the key to being undefended, allowing full connection between yourself and the people in situations of your life. As that level of compassion manifests itself in your own relationship to the self, it is easily transferred to others. Then, and only then, does the small ego self begin to dissolve. Then, another's fear is seen as no different from your own. There is nothing to protect because there is nothing that is not part of you, nothing that can really threaten you. Slowly, you learn to open your heart in that way to another: *our* fear, *our* pain, *our* compassion. At this point, the brain has stopped directing your choices, and the heart, with its deep wisdom and innate compassion, does the choosing with wisdom and with love. It is a most wonderful process, a process of which I stand in some awe.

I would like to pass the microphone here to our brother/sister of Q'uo. That is all.

Q'uo: We are with this instrument once again. We are those of Q'uo.

A visualization often makes clearer that which we would say. We would like you to imagine with us the house of your spiritual self in manifestation. You dwell in a culture which has a high regard for freedom. This is the highest worldly ethic: the respect for freedom of will. And so you begin by putting above the door to your house, "I have free will," or, "I have my rights." However, this house has a higher floor. The upper story of this house has a different legend over the doorway. It says, "The earth is the Lord's, and the fullness thereof."[15]

This upper story houses that *you* that knows it is in the infinite Creator and the infinite Creator in it. It knows that all things are the Creator's. Spend the time with this awareness. Climb the stairs to this second story and sit upon your own mercy seat, if you only enter for a moment, and open to the consciousness of all. When you climb down the stairs to your ground floor of everyday experience, you will find the sign above your front door changed to read, "I am worthy."

You, my friends, are worthy to receive all good things; yet if you do not receive a good thing you are still worthy. It is only your feelings and emotions bruised and battered by rude experience that communicate unworthiness. This is a false communication. Do not accept this communication, but rather, know your worthiness, your loveliness, and feel compassion rising naturally within the portion of you that remains in the second story.

We can only thank and bless each soul within this circle. It has been such a privilege for us. We bid each farewell in the love and in the light of the one infinite Creator, and turn the microphone back to the one known as Aaron that this wise teacher may also make his farewells. We are of the principle known to you as Q'uo. Adonai. Adonai.

Aaron: I am Aaron. May I offer you a bit of homework with which to practice until we meet again? Watch the arising of fear. See the process as clearly as you can. First, there is sense consciousness of that perceived threat. You may feel it in the physical body as tension in the belly, the throat or elsewhere. Note it as "tension, tension … " If it is a seen or heard perceived threat, know there is seeing or hearing. From that perceived threat, a sense of fear arises. Then comes need to defend. See that the need to defend is not the same as the fear itself. Watch it very carefully. The need to defend is reaction to the fear. Fear is so uncomfortable. There is the desire to get rid of fear, and out of that aversion arises either need to defend or need to fling the fear on another … anger, resentment, blame. Bring this wise teacher, Milarepa, into your heart. When you see fear arise, take his hand quite literally and say, "Fear, come in and sit by my fire." Just that. Begin to observe what difference awareness makes, that it is not fear, but *fear* of fear that leads to your defending and thereby being pulled into this unwholesome codependence. Watch it very carefully, even take notes if you wish. Do it as an experiment in consciousness.

As a second step, notice that there is sometimes reluctance to do this work; that even when you have proved to yourself that you can let go of fear and stay open, at some level, sometimes there is a desire not to do so, a part of you that feels, "I am not ready to be that responsible. While I want to love and feel connection, I am not sure I am ready to do it this time. A part of me wants to blame, wants to continue this unskillful codependency rather than moving into that living and loving symbiosis."

What voice is this that wants to continue the old, unwholesome patterns? Can you see that small ego self kicking and screaming? Can you smile at it? The more you fear the small ego self and strive to get rid of it with judgment, the more solidity you allow it to assume. When you smile at it with that same, "Oh, you again. Come and sit by my fire," then it allows you to reopen to the spirit that you are.

I suggest and hope that you will practice with this, and hope you will share your findings with me when we next come together. May I also ask you to keep in your minds the image that I offered yesterday? You are all spiritual warriors; and with every step that you take, every small step of growth upon this magnificent path, there are a great many loving

---

[15] *Holy Bible*, Psalm 24:1

beings on all planes that bow to your courage and strew flowers on your path. That is not said to inflate ego or make you feel that you, as an individual, are special. All beings are special, and there is nothing more valued in the entire universe than the increased opening into love of the individual spirit.

I thank you again for allowing me to share my thoughts with you. Please remember to take what is useful and discard the rest. My love is with you. That is all.

Sunday Meditation
February 7, 1993

Group question: The question today has to do with the balance one seeks to achieve between accepting what the universe or the life pattern of catalyst has given one in the way of experiences and people, and then balancing that with using these very same situations, the catalyst of a life experience, and manipulating them in such a way as to attempt at least to achieve the goals which we feel are important, the learning of lessons, the loving and acceptance of others and so forth. How do we balance accepting what the Creator and the life pattern has given us and using it to progress along the evolutionary path?

(Carla channeling)

We are those of Q'uo. Greetings and love to you, my brethren. It is in the mystery of the infinite One that we come to your calling. We thank you for asking us to offer our opinions and shall endeavor to make our words as wise as possible, asking each to discriminate as to those things which we say according to each entity's own light, for we are prone to error.

In speaking of the best way to enable your mind and heart to be satisfied with the balance between surrender and active change we find we need to move to a larger canvas and ask each if there is a serious question as to the wisdom or the charity inherent in the life pattern which is now being enjoyed more or less by each. This decision is critical, for if the seeker finds a faith and a trust in the overall plan and agenda, metaphysically speaking, for this particular incarnational experience, then much of the obfuscation which shadows the clear path may be taken out of the way, for if the incarnational plan or agenda is accepted as one which yields lessons in love and opportunities for service, then the outer picture from day to day has less ability to shake the basic steadfastness of attitude and temperament.

In any given situation there is always free will, and one is free to choose not only how to act but also how not to act. When there seems to be a difficult choice to make the seeker may sit with this situation asking only that light may be given. We suggest no more direction than this, for the direction of the Christ-conscious self or higher self are silent, sometimes subtle, and movement of mind and emotions does obscure the ability of the self to place inside the heart the true model of that which is occurring. During this period of waiting it is well to refrain from thought, and when thoughts occur, to allow them to go their way.

This is a description of meditation in general to some great extent. However, when an entity is looking for resources which inform concerning the will of the infinite Creator one needs to become very quiet … inside. One needs to request of the self a freedom from the timetable, for the first task of a seeker faced with a choice is to sit with the situation, to bathe in its feelings and its shapes and so move into it that the situation itself is clarified. We cannot offer a suggestion as to the time limit of waiting for clarification. However, we may say that the waiting time is often the opposite of that which is expected. That is, there may seem to be a very complex and difficult situation which the waiting and listening period clarifies all in an instant. Or there may be what seems to be a cut and dried arrangement or situation which has a fairly obvious either/or, asking only this or that, which may upon reflection be found rather to contain unsuspected complexities or layers of choice or decision-making.

When the feeling has come that this situation is characterized in the heart and mind in an accurate, subjective manner then there comes a time and space for evaluating for the self the foreseeable spiritual or metaphysical pattern or shape of the road down which each of the options shall lead. In this evaluation one is not considering the surface qualities first. One does not seek, shall we say, contentment, for the path of the seeker is the path which goes onward and is often uncomfortable. This reflective period needs to be long enough that an unbiased or as nearly unbiased as possible evaluation of each option is attained.

So, firstly, you have surrendered to the still, small voice in order to receive a clarified picture of your situation. Secondly, you have turned to the intelligence and deeper intuitional faculties of the mind and heart and have actively applied the self to envisioning the benefits of each option, spiritually or metaphysically speaking. This ends the mid-part of your work.

The third portion is to move back into the contemplative or meditational phase of mind energy and again allow this still, small voice its place. Its place is always with you, in you, and of you. You are not exterior to your situation. You offered this situation to yourself. Now you have received it. There is the often quoted phrase of which this instrument is aware, in the form of a short prayer. It is "God, grant me the ability to see the difference between that which I can change and that which I need to accept." Often, when all three portions of the decision-making process have been accomplished, it shall be very clear that one alternative will tend more towards the learning by the self of love and the opportunity to be of service to others in a way which is spiritual or metaphysical. In short, you are looking for the highest proportion of any opportunities to experience helpful catalyst and to offer these gifts and talents which are yours to offer on others' behalf.

We feel that at this point a further direction in the form of a further query would be helpful, as we are through generalizing. We would therefore ask the one known as R if there is a further query on this topic?

R: I will mention a line of thought that is coming to me, and will ask Q'uo to comment on it. When catalyst is experienced and is considered and an action or an active change in a direction comes to mind, when it stays there and seems to be harmonious, is it then appropriate to make the change within the illusion? To be more specific, how do you metaphysically know, feel or recognize the manifestation of reaching the point where there is a need to do rather than to surrender? Is that clear enough for a further comment?

I am Q'uo, and feel that sufficient amount of questioning has occurred for us to grasp your query, my brother. Perhaps in speaking to this point we may offer our opinion that either doing nothing and continuing with experience as it flows in the present moment, and making a change are viable and good options. The lessons of love which are yours to be exposed to shall be yours upon either path. Where skill can be learned is in the evaluation of the opportunities in each situation, based solely upon the feelings which come together in a moment during which the choice becomes perhaps not clear but distinct, in that whether you can explain it or not, you have found a peace, and this peace is the satisfactory validation of your end decision.

The emotions are treacherous if experienced only at face value. However, the emotions contain and can be refined so as more to contain enormous, infinite stores of wisdom. When the issue at hand has come into a place where one option makes all of the heart rest in an emotion of purified, dynamic peace, then you may feel you have done that which you needed to do. The decision is made. If there is no discovery of any peace, then the conservative suggestion would be to stay precisely as you are and continue doing that work which lies before you while awaiting that moment of inner insight which renders the whole entity—soul and body, shall we say—peaceful and relieved.

To act when the situation is not enough clarified within to bring one to peace then you simply realize that you may have chosen a more crooked and bumpy detour upon your path. This does not mean that you have lost your way, but only that you may choose the harder or rougher or more catalyst-heavy road.

The free will seems just a joke, and a cruel one at that, when one is looking at one's limits. However, when one moves within to the point of present infinity and can see the starry heavens rather then the place two inches in front of the nose, or even the city or nation state, then one has become larger within and has given the self more room in time/space in which to allow this decision to become obvious.

It is well to do nothing until some insight into the fears and other emotions concerning this choice have become part of self-knowledge that can be first gazed carefully at and then surrendered. As long as any portion of the seeker is withheld from the inner surrender there will be that proportion of things occurring with extra bumps and fits and starts. Thusly, if one were able it could be said that the best way to make decisions is to wait and continue doing that which you are doing, while opening the self regularly and repeatedly in simple offering of thanks and praise and the desire to be sent forth to allow light to shine through you. As you ask for this light to shine through, you begin to have the feeling that any road is good as long as this light is shining through you, as there is no exhaustion of spirit as long as the heart lies open and the incoming undistorted light is then able to move through the transparent personality and out into the waiting and thirsty world. You yourself are thirsty for the light, yet that thirst in itself is a beginning of the deepest service.

May we answer further, my brother?

R: I would ask for one additional comment along the line of … When this process is going on and there is apparently another entity involved, to which extent is it appropriate and helpful to communicate with the other entity of the process, of the work that you do, the work that you have to do on your own? I am looking for a comment on how this [work] affects another being. Is that clear enough for a comment?

I am Q'uo. My brother, there is not a decision you can make which holds for any other person besides the self. When decisions are made they need to be considered upon the merits of the situation for the self and for maximizing the self's opportunity to learn love and to offer love in service to others. If there seems to be another or others involved in the decision then the decision has not yet the maturity to be ready for the decision-making process. Before one may seize, shall we say, the moment and act in a spiritually wholesome way one needs to focus upon the self and gaze at those things which in freedom of will are options to one. In other words, as each seeker is responsible for the self, decisions are, shall we say, in our opinion better made focusing upon the direct and simple situation which is the harvest of removing, one by one, those things of which you as a seeker do not have control. Only those things which are yours alone to control come under the provenance of your own decision-making process.

May we speak further, my brother?

R: No, Q'uo, that is a lot of thinking to do for me, and I thank you very much for your comments. I would yield my place to other questions, if there are any at this point. Thank you.

We thank you also, my brother, and can express only encouragement and our love as you seek to become more clear and more filled with the true freedom which is wholehearted service to the infinite One. If that service and that center are maintained the result will be a calm and steadfast heart in the end.

May we take any other queries at this time?

Jim: Thank you Q'uo. I don't have any. I appreciate what you have to say.

I am Q'uo. Thank you, my brother.

It is our great pleasure and privilege to speak to you this day. We realize that choices are the essence of third density and that they do not simply disappear. Passive decisions are also decisions. However, we would ask each to reflect upon freedom, the freedom of the self, and attempt to see where this freedom comes from. If one is free in a chaotic way one will either be random or somewhat destructive, than somewhat positive. However, if a deeper singularity of self is sought, a deeper connection with unity, then many puzzled pieces which are not relevant to your decision-making can fall away and the true nature of the decision lies then uncovered in far more simplicity. The connection between freedom and the basic decision of serving the infinite One shall give your heart a strong structure and the best possible way to seek the understanding to move forward in support of your own spiritual evolution. Because this is far from obvious we simply wish to emphasize this consideration.

You have your homework now and we thank you once again for allowing us to so tease you. Although we are, as always, reluctant to leave this group it is indeed the decision which we have reached, that it is time for our service to withdraw from this instrument and subside into that passive carrier wave of love to which each may avail itself during meditation. We are with you in silent love and support when you ask, and we feel very blessed that you do ask. We leave you as we began in the love and in the light of the infinite Creator …

(Tape ends) ❧

L/L Research

L/L Research is a subsidiary of Rock Creek Research & Development Laboratories, Inc.

P.O. Box 5195
Louisville, KY 40255-0195

www.llresearch.org

Rock Creek is a non-profit corporation dedicated to discovering and sharing information which may aid in the spiritual evolution of humankind.

ABOUT THE CONTENTS OF THIS TRANSCRIPT: This telepathic channeling has been taken from transcriptions of the weekly study and meditation meetings of the Rock Creek Research & Development Laboratories and L/L Research. It is offered in the hope that it may be useful to you. As the Confederation entities always make a point of saying, please use your discrimination and judgment in assessing this material. If something rings true to you, fine. If something does not resonate, please leave it behind, for neither we nor those of the Confederation would wish to be a stumbling block for any.

CAVEAT: This transcript is being published by L/L Research in a not yet final form. It has, however, been edited and any obvious errors have been corrected. When it is in a final form, this caveat will be removed.

© 2009 L/L Research

Sunday Meditation
February 14, 1993

Group question: Well, the two issues that I have in mind are, first of all, if we can obtain a definition of life that would certainly be applicable to all creation and simple enough to be understood at our level. That is the first question that I had. And the second (it is the simpler one in the group), is why the rainbow colors are sort of upside down, with the purple on the bottom and the red on top. You and I spoke extensively yesterday and today, so you probably know better than I do what else I would like to ask.

And as an addition to the question on what the definition of life would be, in a form that we could understand here, we would also like some information on how the death and removal from this illusion of any one of us would affect the others that we have incarnated with who don't remember the pre-incarnative plan; and who especially if, say, a child dies at a young age, the loved ones that are left behind may engage in some expression of grief as a result of the death, that would have effect on their karma. How does the life that we live affect other people, as we remove ourselves from this illusion through the death process?

(Carla channeling)

I am Q'uo. Greetings in the love and in the light of the one infinite Creator. What a pleasure and a privilege it is for us to be with you in your meditation this afternoon. The mingled vibrations are such a blessing to us, and it is a privilege to join in your circle of seeking and light. As always, we are sharing our opinion, and ask that each use his discriminatory powers in listening to this or any material offered for spiritual seeking. Trust in your discrimination, take what is for you—what seems remembered instead of learned—and leave the rest behind you, for we would not be a stumbling block for any.

We speak to your query about a definition of life. My friends, the subject, like all metaphysical subjects, defies the use of your words. However, if this be understood as a necessary limiting factor, then we may proceed in good humor, tripping over the nouns and verbs of your illusion. The most comprehensive definition of life is this life, is manifestation. To put this another way, life is movement. Because we do not feel that this basic a definition is helpful, we shall go further, but it is well to remember that all that is, is alive—that all was created by a thought which was the character and nature of the infinite Creator. This thought we call Love, for there is no appropriate designation. However, this Love is as terrible as it is filled with wonder, and loves as passionately destruction as it does creation, for the love that is the nature of the Father, shall we say, is a love that embraces the creation as a whole process, so that all phases of this movement are equally lovely.

To focus more in on a definition of life that might be helpful, we would consider the way in which third-density entities come into the energy web of a physical vehicle. In terms of human existence, the human life is joined when the vibratory nexus of what you may call the soul enters into and mingles with a permanent bonding with a physical vehicle. There is a life of the body complex. This is inextricably enmeshed with the life of the spirit or soul, and the resulting harmony of vibratory patterns becomes a living being.

Similarly, when the movement of the spirit has ceased and separated itself from the energy nexus of the physical vehicle, that human being is not living. This occurs sometimes before the physical death and sometimes at the moment of physical death, and in some rare circumstances where there is a soul very tenacious of consciousness within this particular illusion, there remains the clinging of the soul to an unviable physical vehicle. This is usually described as a ghost or a haunting, and is a result of the spirit being unwilling to move forward.

Because there is the energy for more directed querying possible, we would like to open the meeting to a series of questions, if this is acceptable to each. We ask now if there is a query to be asked, or if each would prefer for us to go on with our, shall we say, sermonette, on our own. Is there a following query to guide our giving of information?

(Pause)

I am Q'uo, and we see that this circle wishes us to proceed. We shall. As each rests within this illusion, the questions of, "What is life?" and, "How fully am I living?" seem bright and obvious and pointed. The life looks to be obvious. If a person moves and thinks and expresses, this person is alive. If this person is not breathing, not thinking, and not moving, this person is not alive; however, this is not the simple truth. The truth is simpler, though still a mystery to us, and that is that all which proceeded, is proceeding, and will proceed from the one great original Thought or Logos of Love, lives, and this life moves with an ever more characteristic energy pattern as it moves through sub-densities of incarnation and experience, moving into matter or space/time coordinates with time/space coordinates within, and by your science largely unexplored.

We would if we could suggest in a specific way, that, "The key to further grasping the life that is within the illusion which you enjoy …" however, we cannot. We can only point the way for those who would consider and do investigatory work along these lines; and that is that the so-called "inner planes" are time/space coordinate areas, shall we say, in the twin illusions of time and space, which are precisely out of phase in a sequestered but complete harmony which echoes the manifested space/time life, so that there is a strong bridge, a common center, shall we say, which connects space/time catalyst and time/space beingness, in such a way that that which occurs in the incarnational experience of the living being is able to have a skillful and complete interfacing with the appropriate coordinates of time/space, that is, of the metaphysical or inner bodies and beings of the entity, or spirit, or soul which is living this incarnational experience.

This is an enormous aid to the ongoing and eternal spirit, for by this conjoining of the inner illusions and the outer illusions, material may be refined and refined, again and again and again, until the mystery begins to be seen—that mystery which is beyond all definitions of life, and yet a mystery which gives all life and absorbs all spent life within itself, with no loss of coherence or energy, so that in no way, regardless of the passing pageantry of changing existence, is there any iota of beingness lost, no way of learning and loving and giving ceasing or at an end.

The tools which humankind has to work with during an incarnational experience are those which can limit one. The tools of the intellect—or to use a more neutral term, the intelligence—the intuition, the learning by experience, are all good, sound tools which will be faithful workers for the entity which, in seeking, remembers to focus first upon the mystery which is Love, so that the incarnational experience begins to be pointed towards allowing the living to become the being, and the being the living. Or, to put it in more emotional terms, to allow the manifestations—whatever they may seem to be within the illusion of which you as a seeker are conscious of within yourself—to become the living, so that you are not living "this and that" in life, but rather, you have become the purified, refined essence of the incarnational experiences, which, by faith and persistent request, have become more and more deeply grounded within the energy nexus of both physical self and spirit self.

In this way one ceases being the questioner and becomes the question, and within that question knows that it is also the implicit answer. Thusly does the creation roll itself up until it is complete within you. Each seeker has its own infinite creation, and all of these unique creatures, in turn, are rolled up until there is no further manifestation and all has coalesced beyond that which knows or moves or manifests.

We would wish to focus briefly upon the query concerning the rainbow and why its spectrum seems backwards. This instrument wishes us to go ahead with this thought, so we apologize for the bad joke. No, we think it is too bad to tell. We shall move on. "Now, seriously, folks," as this instrument would say, consider if you will, the tree: its roots moving down gathering food, nourishment coming up into the tree, the leaves turning to the sun, pulling life from the surroundings, turning to the light … Now, consider the tree of what you may call life, for that is a technical term used in your white western magical tradition. Its roots are where it gets its nourishment. The Logos, descending through the bole or trunk of the tree, [be]comes light in all of its manifestations; and the most articulated of this light becomes conscious of itself in third density, and begins not only to turn towards the light but to turn in whatever way it might choose, gaining its light, its nourishment, leaf by leaf, not by instinct alone but by free will.

That which you know as light comes from the Logos, and is the first manifestation of love of the infinite Creator. It draws its life from the center of love and moves into all of the vibratory quanta which comprise the arrangement of the universe which you behold; thusly, its frame of reference is not yours. To the metaphysical way of thinking and expressing Truth, this which you now experience is the final fruit of love's traveling into manifestation. Thusly, as through a mirror you see a reflection, so your living, your experiencing, is by reflection; and all that you see, in a metaphysical sense, is, shall we say, upside down or backwards. You see, feel and think by reflection, not by direct perception.

Now, this is a large area and perhaps it would be well to stop before we begin another entire subject, and again ask if there be any queries at this time. We are those of Q'uo.

(Pause)

I am again with this instrument. I am Q'uo. We thank each for the energies brought to this circle this day. We have spoken of life. All is life. We have attempted to focus into the way of thinking about being a living human being. Firstly, the seven grosser aspects of life that is its basic definition, and secondly, the living of a life to the fullest, metaphysically speaking. We can share your hope that entities in the appropriate time/space shall decide to manifest within your illusion, to create instrumentation to measure those conjoining points between space/time and time/space which show to the eyes of those who can see what you call the aura, the existence of a human being as opposed to a physical vehicle whose silver cord has been severed. In a living being whose silver cord has been withdrawn, the aura lacks the motions characteristic of space/time time/space juncture—these junctures moving with emotion and thought in such a way that the resonating energy centers within the physical body are affected either by being regularized, spun more quickly, given more energy, given blockage, or given a glut of energy which creates its own interference difficulties.

These things can be seen by those who have become aware of their ability to see the inner plane bodies, most especially the electrical body as you have called it, or as we would perhaps prefer, the form-maker body, which is so often worked upon by those who work with the aura, with color and so forth, in their healing modalities. The instrumentation for this will, undoubtedly, bring great relief to those who wish to know objectively and in a stable and provable manner the estate of the soul within a physical vehicle. In the meantime, we may simply say that there truly is no incorrect choice when determining life or death in the medical sense, for so much is beyond the ken at all times. When faced with what seems to be a life and death decision, it indeed feels crucial to be right. The intention of being right is central. The accuracy of rightness is acceptable in its variability. Because this is so much upon the heart of the one known as *(name)*, we include these hopefully comfortable words. The following of the hunch, the knowing within and waiting for validation—these tools will aid. The use of what you call clairvisual entities to determine whether or not space/time and time/space nexi are still conjoined …

(Side one of tape ends.)

… that clairaudient ability, like any other ability, has its good and its not so accurate moments. Instrumentation rather than psychics, shall we say, will alone satisfy the mind of the scientist.

We would move on now to some brief consideration … This instrument laughed at us … perhaps a "not-brief" discussion, of the query concerning the karma and what patterns it assumes when a young one is removed so quickly from incarnational experience. Instead of focusing upon a mother and child, we would wish to look at the term "karma." A misperception which seems quite widespread among your peoples is that karma is a way of keeping metaphysical books, that karma is a ledger which must balance—debits and credits equaling. However, this is not our considered opinion of the concept karma. It seems to us that karma is the energy of action. An action accelerates an energy within some combination of energy centers, and creates within the incarnational experience a conjoined movement betwixt the body, mind and spirit complexes. It is for this that each came into incarnation.

You see, my friends, you are here to witness to the light and the love of the infinite One. Yes, there are more and less skillful ways to witness this love and this light. Those with a certain lack of metaphysical rhythm or harmony may well spend an entire incarnational experience off-guard, behind, and confused, and without any seeming learning taking place, but rather simply aimlessly buffeted about by catalyst. This person would be seen to be collecting much karma, for its acts towards itself and others might or might not be centered in love and compassion. However, this, as well as the wisest sage's life, is full of witness.

Now, certainly such an entity asleep within the dream of living shall awaken, and see that it has accelerated itself in a non-cohesive manner and is scattered in its energies. In the next lifetime, then, this entity shall co-create with the higher self or infinite One, an incarnation which addresses the illusion in such a way as to go over the same material again. Entities do not run out of chances to learn a given lesson of love; further, when all that has been accelerated within has been grasped, the lesson taken, and the impetus of karma ceased, yet still, there is a—we correct this instrument—an irretrievable and permanent karma or acceleration which is the movement from source to source or from the Creator to the Creator.

Mistakes appear to be numberlessly numerous, endlessly occurring, and it seems most risky to enter into the veil of illusion, to live the life and attempt to learn the lessons of love with no true knowledge or remembrance of the agenda. However, there is a keel, a rudder within which knows surely its destination; and from whatever place any seeming imbalance or karma might take this entity, from that precise place lies a straight and sure path along the lines of the lessons desired to be learned within the incarnation, so that what matters, metaphysically speaking, is not whether one chooses more correctly or skillfully one's actions; rather, what matters is the purity and genuine authenticity of the desire to express as a channel of the love and the light of the infinite One.

Begin to allow yourself to see that you are the Creator when you are in any emotional distress or state of anguish, just as much as you are when peace is a loving, living river within, and you have the uplifted knowledge that all is well. The report card, shall we say, is not dependent upon your abilities as choice-maker, but very much dependent upon your desire to love and serve the infinite One. This opportunity does not cease under any circumstance, and there is always an equal, whole opportunity in the present moment to choose life, and not the life that comes into manifestation and leaves, but the life that is One, and is infinite and eternal.

It is in that life, that love, and that light that we would leave this instrument and take leave of this group at this time. It has been a true pleasure to work with your queries, and we thank you for calling us to your group. If it is desired, we are very happy to be with you in meditation as a carrier wave, and that, too, is our pleasure. At this time we would leave so that our brothers and sisters of Hatonn may speak briefly. We are those of the principle of Q'uo. Adonai. Adonai.

(Pause)

I am Hatonn. Greetings in the love and in the light of the one infinite Creator. How beautiful your mingled vibrations are. We join you in joy and rest within each of you, for you do give us rest. The giving of service is our rest and our freedom, and we thank the one known as *(name)* for hoping that we would be with you at this time. Each of you is so radiant, so full of love. You do not know what you do as you seek and hope and love, but you are lightening the consciousness of your entire planetary sphere. We encourage each of you to consider yourselves worthy, to consider yourselves helpful, to acknowledge that you are channels of light. We do not say this to puff up the pride, but to stay the heart in trust and faith. We encourage you to make valid to yourself your nature, to know and affirm again and again that you are in the Creator and the Creator in you, and that as you breathe in and breathe out your entire creation is changed.

How delicate, how fleeting is your evanescent life within this beautiful illusion. Be of good cheer and merriment, my brothers, and share love with yourself and with each other, for that is your nature, and you simply are chipping away that which lies outside the radiant portion of your nature just as the gem is embedded in the living rock. Within the rock the gem lies whole, complete and fully functional. It simply is not seen. Then someone mines it, chips away what seems to be dross, facets the gem according to its makeup, and lo, it becomes obviously radiant. You are gems embedded in the rock of living flesh and bone, living thought and intellect of the body's brain. Graciously, gracefully, as you feel the losses and limitations of life, know surely that dross is being melted away, and the gem within will be that much closer to being visibly radiant.

Know that this process takes many lifetimes. Know that you are as you are—perfect, entire, whole and invisible—most of all to yourself. You see the rock. Breathe in, breathe out love, and though your vision shall always be clouded as you view yourself, perhaps to the world, you shall more and more by your desire become a light that truly lightens the consciousness of your beloved planet and of all creation. May you rest in the peace of that knowledge, and forgive yourself for being born into rock with the gem tucked safely within forever.

We are those of Hatonn, and we thank you for calling us to you. We make errors, so we ask, as always, that our words be taken lightly and used when they feel correct. We are those of Hatonn, and we leave you in the love and in the light of the infinite Creator. Adonai, my friends. Adonai vasu borragus. ✸

Sunday Meditation
February 28, 1993

Group question: Today our question concerns moderation. Carla is concerned as to how she can modify her physical activity to avoid the kinds of injuries that her arthritis has been bringing about through sewing, singing and crocheting and needlepoint and all these heavy physical activities when over-doing in any particular area can bring about an injury. She would like to know what moderation would be in her situation, and R is wondering more generally about moderation in the spiritual seeking, how one can continue persistently and consistently on the spiritual path without becoming overly concerned about the situation that one is in and working so hard to be this or that that is considered ideal that you start working against yourself and start getting frustrated and begin taking your spiritual temperature and judging yourself.

(Carla channeling)

We are those of the principle known to you as Q'uo. Greetings in the light and the love of the one infinite Creator. What a privilege and a pleasure to join our essence with your own in the warm and embracing circle of your meditation. We thank you for calling us to you this day, and hope that we may offer something of benefit, but as always, we wish for each seeker to choose carefully that which is taken in of what we or any may offer, for none that speak words is without error.

You asked us to speak of moderation. To set the stage, we move to your myth of the Garden of Eden. Within this garden all was of a plain and pure vibration. The mother and father of the race of humans was described as being tillers of this perfect paradise. The so-called fall of humankind came about because that described as Satan, or the Devil, suggested that the pure, innocent tillers and gardeners of this place could know of good and evil and yet still live. The choice of humankind was in this parable to know of good and evil. It is into this arena of dynamic opposites that humankind is, therefore, all born. The very foundation of third density is based upon what is described as a mistake; that is, a choice to know good and evil and, therefore, to die. All of the third-density environment is necessarily founded upon dynamic opposites and the choice for or against the radiance of living and dying as opposed to the magnetic pulling and grabbing at life and the fearful pushing away of death. It may seem that this choice to live and die, to be imperfect and to choose between imperfectly derived essences may be a foolish choice, but it is this very environment which creates the test conditions for the growth and the learning of that within each which may be called the seeker or the higher self, that is, that self which aspires to move more and more fully into the radiant energy of the one Creator.

This first pair, then, were immoderate, and the spiritual journey as well as physical, mental and emotional journeys of humankind may be seen to yield the greater fruits to those which seem immoderate. Examine, if you will, each his own story within this incarnation. The most productive of the choices made can be seen in retrospect to be immoderate, full of passion, and deeply, strongly felt. So our first point is that the essence of third density is dynamic balance between two extremes, and progress upon the seeker's path is aided by immoderate, full-hearted action moving towards choices which polarize the seeker's heart towards reaching out for the light and being a transparent conduit for that love and light that is the Creator.

This being said, we move to the examination of what virtue moderation might have. Perhaps we could define moderation as that activity within which there is expressed an awareness of the limitations which pertain to the sort of moderate activity being sought. If an entity, for instance, is very, very strong a moderate exercise might be the careful, evenly paced climb to a great height of one of your mountains. Moderation, to one physically limited, might be walking for a short length of time. The mountain climber and the ambler through a field or two have nothing in common about their rightness. Moderation, then, is a subjective thing. Similarly, moderate activity for one of extreme intelligence or creativity might completely ruin the mental abilities of one whose resources are limited, and that which would be moderate to the latter would be starvation for the former.

Perhaps you may see the same as being so of emotional and spiritual capacities. Moderation being always subjective, judged only by one entity which is in command of the knowledge of itself, its native capacities and its rate of enlargement or learning or development. Addressing the specific query of the one known as Carla, we point out that the activities which have been obviously immoderate for this entity are not, in and of themselves, immoderate. For one of perfect health, these activities would barely be noticed and would not be more than just and moderate.

When entities are self-destructively immoderate what seems lacking may be the willingness to accept and use the accurate evaluation of the limits of one's capacity. It is this inaccuracy with regard to the self which sets the stage for those discomforts which come from having done so far too much of an activity that the abilities of the self are not only stretched but broken. The result of this lack of accurate evaluation of the self, then, is a further limiting of that particular capacity, thus requiring a new accurate evaluation of capacity. Failure to be accurate in the self-estimate causes the cycle of being able to do less and less. Finally, at some point, the seeker is forced to reckon with the failure to be an accurate assessor of the limits of capacity.

Looking with these eyes at the spiritual life we may see that the seeker's goal, then, is not to press so far beyond the bounds of the present ability, but rather to move to the limit of what the instrument which has been given to the seeker in this incarnation can bear without injury. Thusly, the one who moves persistently, taking the small but frequent steps towards enlarging the spiritual capacity is that entity whose heed of moderation has allowed it to continue slowly but surely to press the envelop of personal limitation so that there is a maximal movement towards more and more discernment, compassion and transparency which allows the radiant energy of the One to flow most freely.

Now why would entities wish to abandon accurate sense perceptions? Why would entities reject their own situations? Why is there intoxication, that is, great immoderation resulting in lack of function? The reason for this, basically, is that always that which may be termed the Devil or the negative principle delights in suggesting to the seeker that one can do that which one wishes as much as one may fantasize, even if it be forbidden, for this will not kill; this will aid in greater expansion, in greater expansion of living. This temptation moves deeply within the sea of consciousness of each. It is the energy of spiritual greed. And it says to the conscious self, "Eat of this. You will not die." And so those who heed this siren call do the equivalent of getting in one of your automobiles, moving the gas pedal to the floor, and when hitting that curve or that cliff or that rock which cannot be maneuvered around, the crash does kill, and there is an overwhelming sense of loss.

We suggest that it is well, then, to heed [the] estimate of one's own abilities, neither puffing them up nor underestimating them. One last thought. There is one avenue in which moderation is not suggested. That is in the area of what you may call moral or ethical judgment. When faced with that which from within speaks to one of right and wrong, this sense within may be heeded without moderation as one searches for the choice which will polarize. In your holy work there is the admonition to let your yes be yes, your no be no. This immoderate firmness reflects not upon any subjective limitations of capacity but, rather, is the examination of the abstract principle. When this feeling of right and wrong is awakened, respect that ethical sense within and allow the yes to remain purely yes and the no to remain purely no. The importance of respecting this ethical impulse within cannot be overestimated. It is the foundation stone of the whole world of spiritual principles which simplify themselves more and more as experience is gained in trusting that sense of ethical rightness or justice.

Now, when one moves from the examination of a principle to the consideration of the application of this principle, then it may be seen that moderation again becomes a valid and central concern. Yet, even in the application of the principle there is virtue in immolating oneself because of the sense that the incarnation itself has moved to its center and martyrdom of some kind is necessary in order to witness to the spiritual principle. So even when one attempts to live a strongly felt life holding one's convictions and expressing them moderately there is virtue in having an accurate enough sense of one's destiny that one may know when immoderation to the point of loss, or martyrdom, is appropriate.

The tool most handy for use in applying the principle of moderation may be as simple as the use of the clock. To set the beginning and the end of activity of one kind or another. But any tool must be used by the self so that the self needs first and foremost to come into the accurate awareness of the capacities of the self. That this awareness is avoided is, shall we say, human, and those most immoderate by nature are often those whose capacities in some senses are extreme so that no effort seems to be immoderate. However, this sense of the self as indestructible must be avoided in favor of a more accurate gaze at the various kinds of capacity which make up the complex of activities of the self. Above all, this search for accurate perception takes the light touch. There is humor inherent in limitation. It is starkly compared with the joy of utter intoxication. One wishes to move somewhere between that intoxication and a lack of any use of an inherent capacity.

We ask again that that which we say be considered as opinion, and would ask if there are further queries before we leave this instrument?

All: No. Thank you very much.

I am Q'uo, and we too are filled with joy at being part of the give and take of spiritual seeking. We have found this instrument to be somewhat fearful about channeling concerning its own queries, its own concerns. Insofar as this has escalated to a fear of being a poor instrument this concern has been regrettable. Why is there a fear of getting it wrong? Why not the giving up of the self in complete trust? In each seeker's life there are times when the answers seem very, very important. Yet there need be no fear concerning the gathering of information about this matter, whatever it may be. Wherein this instrument, the lack of fear has worked against it in its evaluation of physical limitation, its fear has worked against it in the gathering of information about how to correct its behavior.

We ask each to embrace an attitude that does not partake of any fear, and further ask that in each spiritual seeker the moderation employed in moving toward spiritual goals not be the result of any fear but rather be the embracing of freedom. As the prudent and enthusiastic course is chosen and the choices made never decide through fear, but, using the subjective knowledge of the self, choose by means of the illumination of spiritual principle and the confident application thereof in the activities of the loving and radiant life.

We thank this group and this instrument for this opportunity to share, and may we say, reluctantly leave this vibratory nexus. We are with you in supportive silence at all times in which we are mentally called. This, too, is our abiding joy and we thank each for these opportunities to serve also and will be with each in meditation as requested. We leave you in the love and the light of the infinite One. We are those of Q'uo. Adonai. Adonai. ❧

L/L Research is a subsidiary of Rock Creek Research & Development Laboratories, Inc.

P.O. Box 5195
Louisville, KY 40255-0195

www.llresearch.org

Rock Creek is a non-profit corporation dedicated to discovering and sharing information which may aid in the spiritual evolution of humankind.

ABOUT THE CONTENTS OF THIS TRANSCRIPT: This telepathic channeling has been taken from transcriptions of the weekly study and meditation meetings of the Rock Creek Research & Development Laboratories and L/L Research. It is offered in the hope that it may be useful to you. As the Confederation entities always make a point of saying, please use your discrimination and judgment in assessing this material. If something rings true to you, fine. If something does not resonate, please leave it behind, for neither we nor those of the Confederation would wish to be a stumbling block for any.

CAVEAT: This transcript is being published by L/L Research in a not yet final form. It has, however, been edited and any obvious errors have been corrected. When it is in a final form, this caveat will be removed.

© 2009 L/L Research

Sunday Meditation
March 7, 1993

Group question: The question today comes from N, and it is as follows: Q'uo mentioned the aura as the outward manifestation of the form-making body or electronic body perceivable by those aware of their time/space capabilities while in incarnation. It was also mentioned, or at least I understand that the form-maker or electronic body belonged to the inner planes and that the inner planes were in a space/time continuum that has its corresponding realities in time/space existence. Since I believe that the aura is a product of the emanations of the energetic vortices or nexi generally known as chakras, and these organs constitute the etheric body, can I conclude that the ether—not the gas used in anesthesia)—is the synapses between reality and the illusion of the three-dimensional life?

(Carla channeling)

Greetings in the love and in the light of the one infinite Creator. We are those of Q'uo and feel most privileged to be called to this working to offer our thoughts upon the subject of the juncture betwixt the illusion which you now inhabit and that of reality. A couple of introductory comments seem appropriate. Firstly, as always, we ask all our opinions be considered with an open mind but not taken as authority. Your discrimination is your authority. Secondly, the format of querying is acceptable.

As we approach the question we note that the wording of the question moves our reply towards a vector probably not intended by the questioner, for the juncture of three-dimensional illusion with reality is within the spiritual complex only, and it is that direct linkage through the shuttle of intelligent energy to intelligent infinity. To move to intelligent infinity is to enter reality, however, it is also to cease being aware of the self or anything whatsoever. Intelligent infinity is all that there is with no variation within the infinity. Though there is unlimited intelligence, there is only the one Thought, or Logos of love. All other states whatsoever are illusory.

To move from this statement, we go to what we consider may more be the intent of this query and that is where the juncture might be betwixt the space/time, conscious awareness of third density and the time/space or inner planes [levels of awareness] which contain the light bodies which govern the physical vehicle in space/time [This non-physical awareness] is partially a creature of the illusion itself, that is, [it contains] the resources, both physical and mental, of the creature which is your physical vehicle. There is, however, an overshadowing influence upon this physical vehicle and its life which is of the infinite and eternal creature which is your consciousness. This consciousness is carried in time/space during the space/time in which it is connected to the particular physical vehicle of this incarnation by an inextricable connection which is popularly known as the silver cord. The energies of the chakras, then, are a blending of the natural health or lack of comfort of the physical and mental state of the being in incarnation with the complex additions of those resources and biases brought by the consciousness into manifestation during the incarnation, so that the aura, as seen by those with clear inner sight, displays not only the physical, mental and emotional state of the entity, but to a variable degree, shows the native density of the wanderers, and overtones, shall we say, of vibration which belong not only to one incarnation, but to the continuing pattern of this image [or] being which goes through many incarnations.

The connection is not broken except through death. It may be released at some point slightly prior to physical death or shortly thereafter. However, the nature of this connection is such that it simply withdraws from a non-viable physical vehicle.

Before we can speak further to this we shall require a further query. This concludes this discussion, however, we would open the meeting to any other queries which might have the interest in asking.

(Pause)

We see that there are no queries at this time ripe for the vibration. We therefore thank each. May we say that although sometimes the questions seem to be working upon a subject which has little inspiration in it, it is our opinion that there is no subject which cannot be viewed with a feeling of reverence and love. When those who attempt to be healers come to the study of spiritual principles of healing, they often are trained to be very accurate in a scientific manner. The ways in which your culture's medicine work are detailed and mechanically and biochemically complex. There is the concept of exactitude and a tremendous respect is given to detail. When someone working from the spiritual consideration of life or eternity then turns to the consideration of spiritual healing, such an entity moves as a poet or a dancer, expressing in generalities of grace, rhythm and aesthetic beauty. These two approaches harmonize to become synthesized as one broad holistic way of viewing health concerns.

The physical body is the child of the form-maker body, which is the creature of the infinite and eternal unique consciousness that expresses the "I Am" of one entity. This entity's disease may be approached through Iatrogenic measures—we correct this instrument—through allopathic measures, through the workings of such remedies as laughter, meditation and visualization, or by fasting and prayer. What we hope may be seen is that all disciplines can work together harmoniously and cooperatively, not one being greater than the other, but all being used as appropriate. As each approaches its own health concerns, remember that there is virtue in the whole circle of ways of affecting consciousness, but above all these things for the greatest health of all turn always towards the infinite One in praise, in prayer, in silence and in thanksgiving.

Questioner: Can I come up with a question for Q'uo before we leave?

You may, my brother.

Questioner: I just thought to ask you to comment in general on this thought, and that is how people who are in the medical profession in our illusion, be it a general internist, or a doctor specializing in a certain field, or a nurse or radiologist, when they come to try to synthesize what they are trained in with helping people on the spiritual sense, is there some line of thought or contemplation to consider that they can fruitfully use towards increasing their service to others, not only within the training they have but also merging it with their metaphysical belief?

I am Q'uo. My brother, the overriding hope of all true healers is that the infinite One may smile upon such efforts as can be made by the practitioner to the patient. Those who believe rigorously in any particular regimen, whether it be chemicals used in medicine, or visualizations of thought forms, will find that this dependence is not always rewarded. Happy is the doctor whose patient has a destiny still upon this plane. Happy is the doctor whose patient has some awareness of this destiny. The tools aiding healers the most in general besides being expert at their fields, include the glad awareness of a higher power and a recognition of the value of the patient's vital energy and will to live.

May we answer a further query, my brother?

Questioner: This is a general concept for me. Let me try to move the direction somewhere else a little bit. If you were a doctor who for the first time was coming to realize that the illusion is the illusion, would you recommend using meditation at first to clear up what kind of service he can blend with what you are already doing? Is that clear enough to comment on this? I am just trying to feel my way through a question which I feel may bring some inspiration to whoever may read what you are saying.

I am Q'uo, and we were not able to make sense of your query all together. Would you please query in another way?

Questioner: Perhaps I do [need to] think about it myself before I ask a question. There's not really anything that comes out specific … out very clearly, to ask a question that [may] not be the best way to ask it. I will decline to be more specific, and not ask a question at this point.

I am Q'uo. We are aware that the one known as N has asked the session question. It is our thought that the direction of questioning be left to this entity as it shall be moving with regard to examining some of the details of how vital forces are conjoined, inner to outer planes. We then await the next query to be well pointed in our responses. However, as we believe, my brother, that your concern was for the one known as N and other physicians to feel the inspiration, we would simply say that it is our understanding, if we may use that term, that physicians such as the one known as N are inspired to ask queries of sources such as this group because they already have an insight which gives a vision of the great potential of an universal healing center or combination of all of the various modes of healing so that entities which come with disease may through more than one kind of doctoring receive a more complete or more whole healing.

We would at this time thank each, especially this instrument whose faithfulness we have often noted. It is such a privilege to work with this group and to share love with you. We leave you in that love and in that light. We are those of the principle of Q'uo. Adonai. Adonai. ✣

Sunday Meditation
March 14, 1993

Group question: The question this afternoon concerns spiritual pride. We would like to hear some information about the kinds of spiritual pride that both groups and individual seekers could be aware of. From Q'uo's point of view it is probably easier to spot spiritual pride. We would like to know some of the pitfalls as well of spiritual pride and what a seeker or a group can do to balance the spiritual pride and regain the humility which seems to be such a great ally of the seeker.

(Carla channeling)

We are those of Q'uo. Greetings in the love and in the light of the one infinite Creator. How privileged we feel to be called to this group to share our opinions with you on the subject of spiritual pride. We have many group memories of this continuing topic and the concept is chosen well in that it is a lesson that is not learned once but, as far as we know, continually, again, again and again throughout the densities with which we are familiar.

When entities speak of pride there is usually an emotional bias to the term. Pride is considered as a synonym for arrogance. It is not considered appropriate to think too well of one's self. Yet before we speak of pitfalls of spiritual pride we would point out that a just and fair estimate of one's assets is a work of lucid observation and cannot be said to constitute a spiritual pride in and of itself. Indeed, the balanced seeker moves upon the seat of knowledge of the self and this seat serves it well as it does the toe dance or the high wire act through all of the situations which provide interesting food for thought and action in your day-to-day world. It is not spiritual pride accurately to estimate one's abilities or lack thereof in a given situation.

Now, spiritual pride is focused upon both by your eastern religious systems and your western religious systems. For instance, the one known as the Buddha is said to have found all of the various items of doing such as serving as a prince or king and loving and being loved to fill him up not with the fullness which true worship brings but with the growing observation that all of each activity and way of expressing the self within the life pattern was prideful folly. In this mythical story the Buddha at last is cast as a ferry man rowing other seekers across a river from one side to another, a man content at last with the fullness of everlasting change.

Within the western tradition or myth the one known as Jesus speaks often concerning entities which may feel that they are doing well. There is the example of the man who was extremely virtuous in observation of each and every commandment, yet when this seeker asked the teacher known as Jesus what more he could [do] to follow him the one known as Jesus suggested that this wealthy man sell all that he had and thus be free. This parable has made entities which have a comfortable living nervous ever since these words were heard and written down.

The parable is not so much about money or other kinds of wealth as it is about one's relationship to that which comes and goes. The body, for instance, is born and dies, yet it is not prideful to care for it that it may be comfortable and serve well. So with one's estate in life; it is not a crime to conserve one's wealth and to so use it that one is comfortable. Yet, if one wishes to hold onto the body by avoiding getting old or avoiding death, then there is the question of what takes precedence, the body or the soul? With the wealth of money or power this same question holds true. Is there the relationship of conserver or steward with wealth so that it be used prudently or with charity, or is there the grabbing onto or owning the wealth or influence? If there is the latter, then there are some possessions to be sold so that you may follow the mind which this instrument often calls Christ consciousness.

Spiritual pride is about ascribing ownership about absolutely anything at all to anyone except the infinite Creator. Examine what there is in the universe. There is one great original Thought. This Thought is the love of the infinite Creator. This living thought of love is the Logos which, potentiated by free will, has created and is creating all that there is. This creation is made of the first fruit of the Logos, the first manifestation, which is light. Out of light love has created, is created, and will create forever the infinite unity of all that there is. If this be so, each seeker is of love, made of love, made for love, made by love, made to love. To love is the infinity of a verb. So all entities may truly be seen not as nouns, not as persons or as objects, but as energetic words which activate and enable love to be expressed and received, from love to love for love's sake.

Indeed, the creation is made of mirrors, endlessly love reflecting love. Where, then, fits any individual expression? Each individual possesses its own subjective conscious awareness and is as that awareness gives it to be. Every gift, every talent, every seeming liability, every lucky and unlucky accident of fate that has shaped who you are is an occurrence drenched in love. Thusly, the way out of being caught in spiritual pride is not as one might think, to call upon humility, for humility is a kind of pride. If one is conscious of being humble it is because there has been a choice to tell oneself or to behave to others to tell them that you have the consciousness of humility. Rather, true humility is of the one who, without thinking either well or ill of the self has the impulse to serve under any conditions whatsoever. While another is seeking to be humble the truly humble entity has already found a way to be of service, perhaps by listening to the conversation of the one who is seeking to be humble. Humility, in its balanced state, simply moves with the occurrences which come before the vision in the passing moments of your day-to-day experience.

There is the challenge, then, to find a way off of the Ferris wheel or the merry-go-round of judging the self to be prideful or striving to be more humble. How, when one has felt one's prideful ownership of that which is the Creator's, does this seeker step off of the merry-go-round which rolls between the dynamics of pride and humility? It is a daring suggestion, but we do suggest that there is sometimes a need for the benign neglect of one's powers of inward perception. Thinking about being less prideful is merely an engraving mechanism for etching even deeper into the consciousness the concept of one's being prideful and seeking humility. Once one feels one has become humble that very statement is a prideful statement. Like all dynamic opposites of the spiritual life the way away from the dilemma is by turning from both extremes towards the infinite Creator's love, allowing the train of the mind to chug away into the far distance and be gone so that the silent inner countryside of the heart and the spirit may be full of the silence into which love comes. And from which the seeker may be transformed into that which love shines through.

This transparency to the infinite Creator is a product of one who continuously turns from too much examination and study to the mystery. In turning to the mystery seekers finally face their life as unknowable, as hidden within an unknowing which is absolute. Yes, much may be gained by the study of inspirational works, by listening to those whose spiritual seeking has produced fruits which can be communicated. Yet, no matter how many riches of knowledge and wisdom the seeker piles up, no final gain can be said to be produced in this way. Only in the silence of the listening and harnessing spirit is there the realization of the crystalline, shining, transparent self that is merely a sun-catcher, merely there to act within manifestation as a servant of love.

You ask what pitfalls there may be for individuals or groups. The first pitfall is to worry, to be overly concerned about such things as spiritual pride. This falls somewhat under the category of taking the spiritual temperature. The other pitfalls are those created by circumstance wherein there is the opportunity to communicate with others, not strictly attempting to voice thoughts of love but attempting in some way to defend or impress. The impulse to defend, when communicating, is that fear-driven impulse which is motivated by characteristics within such as pride. It is the desire to have another or even the self think well of who you are or what is being done by you. The desire to impress is a special kind of defense, an offensive defense shall we say, where one is moved to attempt to bedazzle or otherwise impress others with the qualities which you, yourself, consider impressive. Whether those qualities include humility or whether they are simply a list of degrees or achievements the impulse is the same and is prideful.

It is not ever necessary that others grasp who you are or what you are doing. It is acceptable, in our opinion, to be misunderstood, misvalued or misestimated. It is acceptable for others to think better of you than you think appropriate just as it is acceptable for others to think less. Release ownership of who you are. You cannot fly away from who you are, yet how closely you clutch and cling to this identity and attempt to torture it into ever more excellent details of behavior, appearance, conduct and thought. Yet, you are asked only to love and worship a mystery and to embrace others just as you embrace, forgive and accept yourself. Seek to put your life in the Creator's hands and the Creator's life will be in your hands. You then will be the perfect mirror, transparent to the light and the love of the infinite One so that there is no flaw in the backing of your light mirror. Seek simply to know your identity in love. Turn from any other consideration as frequently as possible and spend precious moments with the love that you are, with the love that you then may share.

We thank this instrument and would, at this time, move to the one known as Jim, and may we say we are grateful that this entity wishes to receive our contact at this time. We are those of Q'uo and we leave this instrument in love and in light.

(Jim channeling)

I am Q'uo, and great each again in love and in light through this instrument. At this time it is our privilege to offer ourselves in the attempt to speak to any further queries which those present may have for us. Is there a query at this time?

Carla: Well, maybe it will be cleared up when I read it, but in trying to listen to what you had to say I just kept thinking of how it felt this week when it occurred to me that I had acted as if I owned this virtuous prayer group and that, somehow, I had been doing this. There was a feeling there of distaste and I judge myself like that a lot. I judge myself all the time. I understand that you just turn from your wickedness and live, as it says in the liturgy. You just turn and behold the mystery, but at the same time there remains that voice within that will pop up again and again and tell me that that really is prideful. Could you speak to that?

I am Q'uo, and am aware of your query, my sister. It is, of course, the great strength of each seeker to look with the critical eye at all experience seeking to discern that which has value and that which does not. This critical eye, when turned upon the self, as it is most often for the conscious seeker, lends itself most frequently in the careful examination of the experience through which one moves, the responses, both mental and emotional, to each experience and continues this reflecting process over and over until there is a resolution that is acceptable to the seeker. When one attempts to view the inner and emotional response to perceive spiritual pride one is bringing to bear this critical process upon a topic which is frequently overlooked by many, for the feeling that one is proceeding well along the spiritual path is, in itself, a feeling which can both encourage and mislead. Thus, we advise each seeker to look carefully at that experience, to examine the details as they occur, to make the discriminations and choices that will alter one's perception and perhaps one's behavior. And then to move onward as one would in learning any discipline.

All learning requires practice. All learning requires a certain amount of what you would call failure, for it is the failing to hit the mark that teaches one where the weaknesses lie in the discipline. Then we advise further that the seeker should release concern for this area as it is well to release over-concern for any area of learning in order that the concern does not become over-exercised and cause a kind of blocking caution that would inhibit further progress. This is where the lightness of touch is recommended, the sense of perspective and humor with which one views the self and the world about one, for there is indeed much humor in each learning process: the attempt that is well intentioned and full of the vigor of fulfilling an ideal, the falling short that is inevitable with all learning, the recovery as [with] the kitten [that] has almost landed on its feet but stumbles somewhat as it regains its balance, and the assessment of the situation with the puzzled look upon the spiritual face, and the moving on to again tackle the ball of yarn, shall we say, in this great untangling process through which each of you moves.

Is there another query, my sister?

Carla: No, that was just splendid. I appreciate that answer. Thank you very much, Q'uo.

I am Q'uo. And we thank you, my sister. Is there another query?

R: I have a query, Q'uo. I wonder what you would say to the seekers who try to stay in touch with this particular group, who live far away in our environment, to participate in the meditations and who feel that they are frustrated being too far out to be in touch. How would you comment on those feelings that I think many of them have?

I am Q'uo, and am aware of your query, my brother. To those who feel there is inspiration in the words which move through this group and who feel physically removed at a distance, shall we say, and who wish to feel a community of purpose and who wish to walk more closely in spirit with this group we would say that we walk with each of these entities and are available to each upon their request as those who would aid in deepening their meditation …

(Side one of tape ends.)

(Jim channeling)

I am Q'uo, and we shall continue. We seek to aid each in the meditative state upon request and we offer ourselves there without words but in the joining of vibratory levels of beingness. We are also aware that those in this group are most happy to respond to queries and comments of those who read and hear the words of love and light that are available through this particular group. There is much of community that may be shared through the written word that communicates the spirit of comradeship and exemplifies the seeking of the many portions of the one Creator.

Is there another query?

R: Let me just restate for clarity and see if I understand correctly. When someone in silent meditation requests your help in deepening the meditation you are with that particular entity. Is that correct?

I am Q'uo, and this is correct, my brother. We gladly offer ourselves in the joining of vibrations with all who ask our presence in their meditative states.

Is there another query?

Carla: I have one more. I have a letter that I just sent off yesterday to a guy in New Orleans who wanted to know if there was a teacher of channeling in that area that I could recommend. There wasn't one that I could recommend, and I said to him, "Don't listen to people who tell you that it is perfectly safe to channel, because it is a crowded universe and there are all kinds of entities out there who wish to speak to you of various vibrations." And then I said, "If you wish only to contact your inner guide, perhaps I can help you by tape." Could you comment on both the first and second part of what I said to this person. Could I have answered better? Could I have answered more accurately?

I am Q'uo, and am aware of your query, my sister. To the first portion of your query we would heartily agree that, indeed, the universe [teems] with forms of life and at all times there are those that observe your illusion and who offer themselves in one way or another in the speaking through those who are seeking to serve as channels or instruments for love and light. Because the array of entities is so widely variant, from the negative to the positive polarities, we agree that it is greatly recommended that those who would seek to serve as instruments undergo a process of training that is rigorous in the preparation of the instrument so that it may offer itself in the highest level of desire to serve and be able to tune itself at each serving as instrument in order to receive the contact that it is able to withstand in a stable fashion and be able to offer its self that is well known as an instrument.

This is to say, the study of the self to gain the knowledge of who one is is important in order that this self be offered at each working and be offered at the beginning of each working as a kind of filter through which a contact may speak after this contact has been challenged, shall we say, by the instrument that knows itself well enough to offer the self as instrument.

As far as being able to aid other entities in contacting their guides, as they are called, we would suggest that this is a practice that also needs guidance, shall we say. It is well that you seek your own inner guidance as to the techniques by which you would instruct another in this process so that there is the flexibility to utilize the strengths of each seeker, be it in visualization, in working with dreams, in the meditative state, or in prayerful contemplation. Thus, your ability to serve another will be dependent in large part upon your ability to ascertain the qualities of the seeker and how best to guide this entity to utilize the qualities which are strong.

Is there a further query, my sister?

Carla: So, instead of moving directly to a technique that I know will open up an awareness of some form of guidance I should more skillfully find out what I need to know about that person and focus my own attention and that person's attention in developing that person's awareness of himself first. Is that what you are suggesting?

I am Q'uo, and am aware of your query, my sister. Yes, you are correct in your summary of our advice. It is well for each seeker to carefully study the self in order to ascertain the most effective avenues to travel in furthering the knowledge of the self and the Creator which is the great Self of all.

Is there a further query, my sister?

Carla: No. Thank you.

I am Q'uo, and again we thank you, my sister. Is there a final query at this time?

(No further queries.)

I am Q'uo, and we take this opportunity to thank each present for once again inviting our presence within your circle of seeking. It is a great joy and honor for us to walk with you with words and concepts which are but our opinions and that which we have distilled from our own journey of seeking. We ask that you take each word and use it as you will, leaving behind any words or thoughts which do not ring of truth to you.

At this time we shall take our leave of this instrument and this group, leaving each, as always, in the love and in the ineffable light of the one infinite Creator. We are known to you as those of Q'uo. Adonai, my friends. Adonai. ☃

L/L Research

L/L Research is a subsidiary of Rock Creek Research & Development Laboratories, Inc.

P.O. Box 5195
Louisville, KY 40255-0195

www.llresearch.org

Rock Creek is a non-profit corporation dedicated to discovering and sharing information which may aid in the spiritual evolution of humankind.

ABOUT THE CONTENTS OF THIS TRANSCRIPT: This telepathic channeling has been taken from transcriptions of the weekly study and meditation meetings of the Rock Creek Research & Development Laboratories and L/L Research. It is offered in the hope that it may be useful to you. As the Confederation entities always make a point of saying, please use your discrimination and judgment in assessing this material. If something rings true to you, fine. If something does not resonate, please leave it behind, for neither we nor those of the Confederation would wish to be a stumbling block for any.

CAVEAT: This transcript is being published by L/L Research in a not yet final form. It has, however, been edited and any obvious errors have been corrected. When it is in a final form, this caveat will be removed.

© 2009 L/L RESEARCH

The Aaron/Q'uo Dialogues, Session 14
March 21, 1993

(This session was preceded by a period of tuning and meditation.)

Group question: How do we open the heart?

Aaron: I am Aaron. My greetings and love to you all. As always, it is a great joy to feel the energy and light in this room and to feel the purity of your desire to serve and to learn. We are offered the question: How do you, living in this illusion as you do, keep your heart open through the many catalysts that your life offers you? If you will forgive the pun, may I come to the heart of this question by reminding you the heart never closes. You may build a wall around, but it never closes.

There is a real difference here, subtle but important. When you think of the heart as closing, with that closed heart you are totally separate from your deepest reality, which is that of the Divine within you. The heart is the center of that divinity. So as soon as you ask, "How do I keep my heart open?" at some level you are captured in the distortion, "How do I retain my divinity?" But the real question is, "How do I express that divinity, remembering that it is always there?"

If you think of the heart as a place of the purest light, truly reflecting that divine light, then you realize that the light always shines. When you build a wall around that light, you might think it is the same thing as closing the heart; but you have not turned off the light, you have just walled it in out of fear. If you hold that image, you will remember the light is still shining. Constant awareness of the presence of that light can be an important tool in the work to dissolve the wall.

The wall is going to be built over and over again as you feel threatened, as you experience fear. When there is such a wall, the external light cannot move into you; and thus, you feel yourself cut off from that divine light. And the conscious human cannot experience the divinity in itself, and thus feels itself hemmed in by the illusion.

Knowing that the light is there instead of focusing on the fear that prevents you from experiencing the reality of that light, you can focus on the light. By doing this, you avoid a dialogue with fear. You are no longer saying, "How do I get rid of the fear?" Rather, you are simply moving back in to focus on the light: "This is reality. This is what I am and what we all are." Can you hear the difference? "How do I open my heart? How do I deal with the fear?" which may get you into a war with the fear. Or, "Here is the light. Pay attention. It's harder to see today because there's fear. Focus on it. Let it blossom. Let it become real for me."

As you move back into the clarity that focus on that light allows, the wall dissolves by itself. There is no self taking down the wall, nobody *doing* this. There has simply been awareness: "Fear is present. It is blocking the light. I need to find that light and look a bit harder for it because of the presence of fear. As I let love in, fear naturally dissolves."

This process opens you to a very strong statement of who you are. You are not your fear, you are not your negativity, although that does reside in the human form. You are not the heavier densities of the body, although that is part of what you are. You are divine. You are angels.

What I suggest is not a matter of denial of that part of you which is fearful and negative, nor is it an unwillingness to allow the expression of that part; rather, it is a coming into wholeness that knows that the fear is just fear, and that allows the full expression of all the beauty in you: the loving-kindness, the generosity, the caring, the energy. It is the reminder of your true being.

This still leads to the question, "How do we do this?" It is fine to say that the heart is always open and that the focus is on the wall that closes out the light, to make that distinction. But what do you do with the wall? What do you do with fear? The heart opens and closes in the illusion which you are experiencing. It does not matter how you say it, what you are experiencing is the cutting off of light and moving back into light. When you are cut off from light, it feels very, very dark. What I have suggested is only one of the many tools you may use; this recollection, "The light is within me. I am an angel. Even if right at this moment I am not experiencing that angelness, I am still an angel."

I would hope that through these next days we can get into the many different tools with which you may work with fear or with whatever it is that closes you into that darkness. I wish to keep this opening talk short and allow my brother/sister Q'uo to speak. That is all.

Q'uo: I am Q'uo. Greetings in the love and in the light of the one infinite Creator. It is most blessed to mingle our vibrations with your own as you sit this afternoon in your circle of seeking. We thank each for this privilege and bless each in return.

To begin speaking of tools and resources, we would first establish that we use a certain model of patterns and centers of energy in-streaming and within the third-density expression, both manifest and unmanifest; that is, both space/time and time/space.

That model is the rainbow body with the seven centers of energy, the first being the red or base energy center. The energies there have to do with the vitality of the mind, the body and the spirit as they are working together within and manifestly.

The second energy center moves physically up the physical vehicle from the joining of the legs to a spot close to but below the navel. It is the orange-ray energy center or chakra, and energies there are expressing how the entity is dealing with relationship of self to self and self to another entity. This is a commonly blocked or partially blocked energy.

The next center can be described as being at that position within the physical vehicle where if you were punched you would bend over. This yellow-ray energy center expresses how the entity is managing and using the relationships of self to groups such as the nation state, the basketball team or the family.

Then the green-ray energy center is seen. This is the center about which this question has to do. Here is the first energy which does not require any energies instreaming but that of the one infinite Creator. This is the first energy which may be transferred to another's aid and assistance.

Beyond this heart chakra, within the physical area of the throat, is the blue-ray energy center or chakra. Its expression concerns communication, whether that be communion with the Creator and learning therefrom, any communication in words to others or the non-verbal communications of song, poetry, art and all alternative ways of sharing the self without stint.

At the brow is the indigo-ray energy center or chakra. This is the seat of energies expressing the entity's work in consciousness, as the entity works and strives to learn how to discipline the personality in order to be a true or authentic expression of that which one is. This energy center, though quite high upon the rainbow and upon the ambition or hope scale, is specifically the energy that tends to bring entities to call upon those like us which may offer some opinions or thoughts that may be helpful. This is to be noted, because working with the indigo ray, communicating through the blue ray and attempting to keep open the all-loving and all-compassionate heart is an effort which greatly suffers because the lower energies are not much liked—to the point that entities often choose to do most of their conscious work within the upper energies while choosing not to address issues which are unclear within the expression of energies in the first three energy centers.

To finish our rainbow we add the violet-ray energy center or crown chakra. This center is a reading or readout of the state of the expressing energies of the entity, and does not do work in and of itself. It functions as an up-to-the-minute report of the status of the blended energies of the entity.

Therefore, because seekers so often dream and hope and reach without being clear with themselves or the humdrum world, we would begin our discussion of how to keep the green-ray energy center spinning, vibrant and brilliantly radiating, with a look at the more common blockages lower than the heart, with an eye to instilling in the seeker a strong compassion towards the self, towards the illusion that startles and creates seeming outrageous insult to the self.

Have you been in a conversation where an entity wished to impress you with one skill or another that it had accomplished? So does the energy expression of the lower chakras wish to hog the internal conversation and speak of those things it does well, so as to eliminate or at least greatly diminish the need to communicate or focus upon those things which, if thought about, would muddy, slow and dim the energy. To have the patience and the self-acceptance to move in thought each day to the examination of where the seeker has been caught, where the seeker has been hurt, is a job which seems never-ending. Yet the more one is able to accept the humanity of the self enough to look in the picture of profoundly imperfect expression without blinking, the more the seeker will gain greatly. Yes, it is dirty work to affirm one's sexuality; to accept one's seeming lack of skill in dealing with the self and others is humbling. It seems as though one could not sink into one's own persistent imperfections of expression without becoming so discouraged that one retires from spiritual seeking. Yet if one is able to think of this humanity, this heavy incarnational illusion, as acceptable, the more one shall be able to be balanced and clear enough that the energy of the one infinite Creator may flow upward, circulating happily in the imperfect but balanced expressions of energy that you have as a seeker created by your work in forgiving the self, forgiving and forgiving again.

You may think of yourself in two ways. The first is to think of yourself as a prince or princess, delicate in feature and form, beautifully attired in royal robes and seated upon a huge, lumbering, beautifully decorated elephant. In this model you are working at the indigo-ray level while leaving unaccepted the more obviously earthbound portions of the self's energy. Or you may think of yourself as the elephant. This large, physically awkward looking animal contains, given that it is a human elephant, a subjective beauty which has nothing to do with form. The physical body, the mental complex, the spiritual complex, are in their energies of no-body, no-form; yet the form must be there within this illusion so that the spirit which is yourself may learn and serve and choose how to serve. In the second model, the prince or princess rides within the elephant and is that which truly is the accurate violet-ray readout or summation of the combined energies at any particular time. You must be of a form, of a set of limitations, in order to do the manifesting portion which brings to the unmanifest portion of the incarnated self all of its food for thought. Thusly, one tool may begin to be described as that which reckons with the outer elephant without becoming discouraged, disgusted or exhausted.

We would transfer the microphone to the ones known as Barbara and Aaron. We leave this instrument for this time period. We are those of the principle, Q'uo.

Aaron: I am Aaron. I take delight in sharing this work with Q'uo because our mental bodies are different, and we each offer the same teachings with different examples. One image speaks to one being's heart, another speaks to another because you are each unique. I enjoy Q'uo's image of the elephant and rider. If I may offer a different kind of image here …

You are what I call angels in earthsuits. Both are real. You are in a physical body. Without that physical body, without the emotional body, the angel would be deprived of the catalysts that this incarnative state so readily offers. Without the angel, the earthsuit is sterile. As Q'uo has pointed out, it is far easier to focus on the angelness and look with disdain on the earthsuit. There is a sense of wanting to move to a purer level where the earthsuit is no longer necessary; and in this way you grasp at graduating from this plane, rather than just being on this plane where you are and trusting that this is where you need to be. You are each exactly where you need to be.

Each of your bodies has its own frequency vibration, like a stringed instrument with four strings. The physical and emotional bodies have a heavier, lower vibration. And yet, a stringed instrument that is in tune plays beautifully and in harmony with itself. There is no need to rip out the lower strings because they do not play as high as the upper strings. Your entire being can express this harmony. The physical body and the emotional body are never going to be as highly pitched as the mental and spirit bodies. And that is fine.

One place where you shut out light is when you look with disdain on these emotional and physical bodies. You see the imperfections, and you strive to get rid of those imperfections rather than finding love for the being that you are.

The angel is perfect. The angel is unlimited. But the angel's wings can get a bit tarnished. The angel stands on the earth and its feet get caught in the mud. If the angel does not set foot on earth, where is it going to learn these lessons of love, of faith, of compassion? That is why you have taken incarnation. You are here to learn in human form and to serve in human form. To do that work you must begin to embrace the incarnation rather than treat it with impatience and disdain.

This is perhaps the hardest part of being human, especially for those of you who are old souls. You reach a time in your work where you see the light so clearly and the impurities in the lower bodies seem so solid, so heavy. You aspire to the heavens and your feet are in the mud. It makes you want to cut off your feet rather than bring a hose, lovingly hose the mud away and just watch for the next mud puddle.

Those beings who do not so clearly penetrate the illusion, who do not truly know their own angelness, do not have the same contempt for the emotional and physical bodies. They do step on others' toes. They allow themselves to express their physical and emotional imperfection without self-hatred. I am not suggesting that this way of being is good or bad, only saying that it is a unique problem with the being that reaches the end of third-density experience that it becomes increasingly impatient with its human manifestations, which it judges as lesser than the spirit manifestations. You increasingly ask perfection of yourselves, but it cuts you off from the sense of compassion for this human.

I would like to offer an image that may be of some help. You are actors in a play. As with any actor, you must read your lines with convincing honesty. They must be real for you. No matter how deep, how profound they are, if you come on to the stage and just say to the audience, "Well, this is just a play and I'm going to move through these lines quickly," the audience is not going to learn or grow from that reading. It will not be convincing, it will just be somebody up there tossing out words. In order for there to be growth, the audience must become captured by the illusion. It must become a reality for them. And yet, the actor cannot forget that he or she is an actor, cannot turn its back to the audience nor hold its hand over its mouth to muffle its words or the audience will again be deprived of the value of the play through being shut out of it.

In terms of your incarnative experience, you are actors and this is an illusion, but it must be treated with respect. It must be treated as real because you are also the audience. That part of you which is audience cannot learn if the actor's back is turned or if the actor treats the play as frivolous. This is where it gets so hard to find that place of balance where you put your whole heart and soul into the illusion while remembering, "I can't turn my back on the audience. I must be aware of the spirit body, of the reality of who I am, while I work within the illusion as fully as I can."

Coming back to this question, "How to keep the heart open?" or, as I would prefer to put it, "How to allow that light that is your true Self to shine through?" As Q'uo said, "How to keep the heart chakra spinning, the energy channels open, so that you do not become lost in the illusion nor caught in the spirit and disdaining the illusion?" How do you find that balance? You must constantly be aware. Remember that the physical and emotional bodies are gifts of the incarnative experience, not burdens that you have been asked to carry to make your learning difficult. When you relate to the elephant, to the physical and emotional bodies, as gift, you change your relationship with them. It is this remembering why you are here in these bodies that allows you to keep focused on that light of your angelness while simultaneously allowing the full experience of the incarnation.

I do not suggest that this is easy. The actor gets so caught in its lines that it forgets there is an audience there for awhile. It becomes totally trapped in the illusion of the play; and then it remembers, "Oh, there's an audience," and turns itself to play to that audience again to make sure that the physical and emotional experiences are offered openly to the Higher Self so that the mental and spirit bodies may grow in whatever ways they are offered to grow.

I have just offered Barbara a complex thought which was not channeled with complete clarity. I wish to explain this a bit. The spirit body is this spark of the Divine. It is perfect. It needs nothing beyond itself, and yet it is just a spark. It is capable of infinite expansion. The divine essence of it does not change, but its power changes so that you move from that small spark of God into a brilliant sun. This essence of divinity within each of you is not separate from God, nor is it in itself God, but is a part of that infinite energy, light and love.

If you had a vast ocean, an infinite sea, and you took a drop of water from a dropper and dropped it into that sea, no matter that it was already infinite, it would expand. You add that drop to it. Each of you is involved in this process of expanding and enhancing your own energy and light, which does not belong personally to you, but in eighth-density experience moves back fully into the Eternal and thereby expands the Infinite, expands the light and love in the universe.

So, the soul itself is not learning, but the soul within what we call the Higher Self is accompanied by the mental body. As soon as there is thought, there is distortion, because with thought there is self-awareness. As soon as you are aware of a self, you move into the distortion of self and other. This distortion is part of the illusion and is useful, even necessary for a certain distance on your path. But there is also the level of awareness that there is no separate self. Pure Awareness knows that this which has perceived itself as separate is truly of the essence of the Eternal.

Here is where you move into and out of illusion. The Higher Self then moves into the incarnative experience, manifesting form and taking on the heaviness of the emotional body so that it can work with the earth catalysts and clarify this energy that you are.

The ideas of love, compassion—what do these mean? If there was never any pain, it would be easy to feel love. You would never feel threatened. You would never close or build that wall. But what would this love mean? When you are offered the heavy catalysts that you are offered on this plane and can still forgive, still find compassion, still love, can you see that you are expanding that original spark? The light grows purer.

In effect, this small spark within you is fed by the fuel of earth's catalysts, and two responses are possible. One is that those catalysts feel so heavy that you shut the doors, thus enclosing that flame within and not allowing it to return itself to God. The second choice is that you watch the process of closing and opening, fear and love, and find compassion for the human who is experiencing this physical pain, this emotional pain. This growing compassion serves to add fuel to the spark so that it burns more and more brilliantly. The shadow falls away, and what is finally returned to God has become a sun in its own right.

So, you are in this illusion and yet being asked to relate to it openheartedly with balance, working with all the catalysts of the lower chakras, welcoming these catalysts, not preferring the upper-chakra energy, not preferring being angels to the experience of the earthsuit. This is your greatest challenge, because it is so painful to keep coming back to that earthsuit when the heart yearns to be free and back on that plane of light and love where there are no distortions of fear.

There must be constant awareness, a noticing of the beginnings of a dialogue with fear, a willingness not to get caught up in that fear and be reactive to it. Certainly there is so much pain that you experience that there is good reason to get caught up in the fear. All you can do is to remind yourself each time fear arises, "Trust. Trust even this fear. Can I allow myself to enter this illusion fully with as much love as I can bring to it?"

In a sense, it is not the pain of the illusion which causes you to build walls and close in the heart, but your fear that there will be pain. There is a difference here when you are afraid of the catalysts of your learning; that is, when you begin to shut out the lower-chakra experiences and grasp at the spiritual. But this is precisely where you are being offered the opportunity to practice compassion for the human, to see the human, this angel with its feet in the mud, and give it a hug instead of trying to chop off the legs and free the angel.

I know that these sessions will be continued, that we will have three more sessions in the next two days and do not need to cover this whole matter now. In essence, what Q'uo and I are doing today is laying the groundwork. I want to speak at length about how you work with fear, speaking in two directions: mindfulness of all the heavy physical and emotional experiences—working with your anger, your jealousy, all of that which tends to close you and create the illusion of separation—and also how you may nurture the angel.

This is what I started with today: the importance of recognizing that the light, that angelness or divinity, is always there, and remembering that you may keep focused on it. No matter how severe the darkness, you will still sense the inner light that lights that darkness if you will remember what you are. I pass this teaching to my brother/sister/friend Q'uo and will speak again to end with a brief guided meditation of bringing in light. That is all.

Q'uo: We are those of Q'uo and are again with this instrument. Greetings once more in love and light.

As the one known as Aaron says, the fuel for incarnational learning is that which affects one, usually by disturbing it, sometimes by seeming to do it injury or harm, even sometimes seeming irreparable damage. Life hurts. Change is painful. It seems as if the light of spirit is no more than a candle against the great elephantine darkness of living within physical incarnation. Welcome to the world which the cliché calls *the school of hard knocks*.

Spirit is not something which you can lose. It is your being and nature. It cannot be lost. Only the subjective awareness of the spiritual nature of the self is obscured and sight of it lost as one turns and flees from the frightening scene where pain or grievous insult seemed offered. Within every cell of your elephant, shall we say, there is spirit in manifestation. Yet it is difficult to communicate with the cells of the body that seem to be in pain or ill or hurt in this way or that.

To move in mid-metaphor to another metaphor, let us put the elephants back on stage. They rumble about in each act of your play. You are acting as well as an elephant can, yet you also wrote this play. You are also each character, hero, villain, the butler, the friend … All of the characters are you as is the critic sitting in the audience, just waiting for a poorly delivered line, a poorly developed plot or tasteless costuming of elephant girths. All is self. Need you then each day, each hour, dwell in the always chancy, often difficult concerns of relationship of self to self, self to other, self to all?

It is infinitely advisable to embrace this constant grounding in your own story, in your own drama, in each facet of relationship which has caught you this day. You cannot run out of spirit in doing this work. You can only multiply the time which you have available for having accepted that which you see this day, turning in thanks and in praise to that portion of the self which authored this play, which set this stage.

Before we leave, we would ask if there be any queries about material covered to this point.

(Pause)

We take your silence and R's statement to be a sign that so far we have been intelligible. O ponderous pachyderms, proceed. Lumber on. Find a laugh in your heart. Smile at your beloved elephant that gives its life that you might learn better to be.

We leave this instrument for this session, rejoicing in your beauty and all beauty. Thank you for this great honor. We share these thoughts with but one request, and that is that you toss away all thoughts of ours except those that you find useful, for we offer opinions, not authority. We leave each in the love and in the light of the infinite One. Adonai. We are those of Q'uo.

Aaron: I am Aaron. I would like to leave you with a brief exercise that you may practice. First, I would ask you to move into the heart center and therein to find that spark of the Divine, that place of infinite beauty and love within you, that place which is undefended and has no reference point of self. Visualize or feel that light shining out of you. If it is helpful, visualize the being who, for you, is the embodiment of truth, and merge your heart with that guru or master. As fully as you are able, allow yourself to rest in this space, empty of all self, and to radiate that loving-kindness which is the true essence of your being.

Now I ask you to turn your memory to some moment today when you felt a bit threatened. It does not have to be a big issue; it might be just a very minor slight, but some moment when you felt fear and the small ego self moved to protect, made the strong statement, "I am here—me, ego self." As you remember, see if you can feel how the solidifying of that small ego self moves you away from Pure Awareness, empty of self. As much as is possible, allow yourself to re-experience that move from center to what would seem to be the closing of the heart in protection.

What I hope you can experience is that the light does not fade. It is simply blocked. Each time this small ego self solidifies, it blocks the light. You are left with two choices then, both of which we will explore in depth tomorrow: how to work skillfully with that which blocks the light and how to return the focus to the light.

For now, let us leave working with the blockage, just put it aside until tomorrow. What I would like you to do now is to work within the frame of your present experience, feeling the self threatened, moving to protection, feeling the separation from God, the separation from your true being. I want you to simply remind yourself, "A cloud has come between me and the sun. It feels dark in here. The darker it gets, the more fear builds. But the sun is still shining. Instead of getting caught in the darkness, I am going to focus on that sun." A simple reminder: "I need not dialogue with fear, but may give myself permission to move back to my true Self. I am not denying the cloud, just letting it be and coming back to focus on the light."

This is a skill, a learnable skill. Most of you have created patterns whereby as soon as the cloud appears, you raise an umbrella, enclosing yourselves in further darkness. You must first notice the raising of the umbrella, that sensation of the heart's closing; and then you must remind yourself, "Every time there's a cloud, I don't need to raise an umbrella, only to look beyond the cloud and reconnect with the sunshine."

With great gentleness to yourselves, I would ask you to practice this through the evening and the early hours of tomorrow until we meet again. Each time there is closing and a wall being built, notice that it is happening. Give this small ego self that is feeling fear a hug. Let it know it is okay that fear is being experienced and consciously refocus on the light. No judgment about the arising of fear, no grasping at the light. You are not reaching for something that has fled, only allowing your focus to come back to what is always there, to this place of love, infinite wisdom and compassion and deepest connection with God.

I thank each of you for being a part of this circle and for the profound earnestness and love that you express by your presence. May all beings everywhere open into the light of their true being. May all beings transcend the illusion of fear so that they can more fully manifest their true nature of love in every expression of their energy. May the work of each of us help all beings find their way. My love to you all. That is all. ☙

L/L Research is a subsidiary of Rock Creek Research & Development Laboratories, Inc.

P.O. Box 5195
Louisville, KY 40255-0195

L/L Research

www.llresearch.org

Rock Creek is a non-profit corporation dedicated to discovering and sharing information which may aid in the spiritual evolution of humankind.

ABOUT THE CONTENTS OF THIS TRANSCRIPT: This telepathic channeling has been taken from transcriptions of the weekly study and meditation meetings of the Rock Creek Research & Development Laboratories and L/L Research. It is offered in the hope that it may be useful to you. As the Confederation entities always make a point of saying, please use your discrimination and judgment in assessing this material. If something rings true to you, fine. If something does not resonate, please leave it behind, for neither we nor those of the Confederation would wish to be a stumbling block for any.

CAVEAT: This transcript is being published by L/L Research in a not yet final form. It has, however, been edited and any obvious errors have been corrected. When it is in a final form, this caveat will be removed.

© 2009 L/L Research

The Aaron/Q'uo Dialogues, Session 15
March 22, 1993

(This session was preceded by a period of tuning and meditation.)

Group question: The group continued with the topic of how to open the heart center, with a special focus on how to work with the lower energy centers in preparation for the opening of the heart center.

Aaron: I am Aaron. Good morning and my love to you all. How have you done with your homework? Did you experience those moments of separating, window shades drawn tightly closed? It is a painful experience and not necessary to incarnation. Let us look together at the process. When you enter the illusion in which you feel the heart closed so that you are separated from that beloved source of light and that your own light does not shine, what is really happening at that moment?

When there is careful looking each time the heart is experienced as closed, you see the presence of fear. That in itself means nothing. Who is afraid? Afraid of what? There is a cycle in which you experience fear and separation. There must be the illusion of a solid self, separate, subject and object. As you experience the self as solid, the fear becomes more solid, enhancing the sense of separation and bringing you further from your true Self.

There is a poem by Rumi that Barbara encountered this morning. I would like to ask if K or C would read this. It is on the right-hand page of the page marked:

The moment I heard of his love, I thought
To find the beloved, I must search with
Body, mind and soul.
But, no. To find the beloved,
We must become the beloved.[16]

I would ask you always to remember that you need not seek God elsewhere. The Divine is within yourself. To me, this awareness carried deep within you is the key to working with the heavy energies and catalysts of the earth plane. As soon as you experience yourself as separate from the Divine, then self solidifies. Then fear increases and becomes stronger. Then the darkness closes in further and you become more and more enmeshed by your sense of separation, of vulnerability and of fear.

We spoke of this a bit earlier this morning; and I asked those who were listening to envision an expansive blue sky with a brilliant sun and here and there some small wisps of clouds. As the winds shift, the clouds are brought together and slowly form what seems to be a storm cloud that blocks the sun. You have two choices: to react as if that cloud were solid and move to protect yourself by fetching your jacket or your umbrella, or to remember the sun is

---

[16] Reference is pending.

still shining—"There's nothing solid here, just bits of that same material I've seen floating through the sky. They've simply come together."

Because you are human and must function at both levels, of course if it begins to pour, you put up an umbrella; but is the umbrella to protect you from harm or is it to keep you warm and dry? There is a difference. When you relate to the clouds in your life as threatening you personally, then fear solidifies, self solidifies, and your response to those personal clouds becomes one of fighting a war with them. You believe they must be gotten rid of at all costs so that you can return to the experience of the sun!

When you can, note the existence of those clouds without feeling personal threat, just clouds coming through; but because when clouds do come together it may rain, you note, "I could get wet and will then be uncomfortable. So I will very skillfully put up my umbrella." Here there is no fear, there is no personal threat. You always know that the sun is shining above the clouds. The energy does not contract with fear and prepare to do battle.

If your own personal cloud in some moment involves another being that is angry at you, raging at you even because of a self-perceived threat to itself, your fear leads you to strike back at that being verbally or even physically, or to move to protect yourself in a way that connotes your own anger. When instead you can see that being's fear and pain, you may still, figuratively, put up your umbrella. You may step back out of its reach. You may choose to leave the room or the vicinity of this angry being without reacting with fear.

There is that one moment where the self begins to solidify and you experience perceived threat. "I could be hurt. My needs might not be met," whatever the fear is about. There must be attention to that moment when there is suddenly self and other, and the other perceived as threatening to the self. There must be attention to the arising of anger, should it be there, against that perceived threat. With strong mindfulness, that first perception of solidified self, of fear and of any other heavy emotion becomes like a waving warning flag: *Pay attention!* Can there be compassion for this seeming self that is feeling fear? "Turn to the light within me, open up to the Divine within me, remember the sun is still shining."

This is a tremendously powerful tool. It takes much practice to learn to do it skillfully. And before you even begin the practice, it takes much honesty to look at the places in the self that want to respond with anger so as to get even with that which seems to threaten. Once you do that work and can pay attention to the arising of fear, and even pay attention to that which wants revenge and just treat that as more fear, give yourself a literal hug with the thought, "It's okay. Whatever I'm feeling is okay." As you offer that compassion to yourself, you begin to be able to offer it to the catalyst. Then self and other dissolve, not immediately but slowly. The more practiced you get at it, the faster the dissolution of separation. And it is no longer *my* fear, but *our* fear, *our* pain. In this way, the first arising of fear becomes a catalyst, not for hatred, but for compassion. A reminder: The heart is at risk of closing; keep it open; remember the light is still shining.

When we look at what leads to the sensation of the heart's closing—of separation from God, from others, from self—we see that need to protect. This is another area on which you may wish to focus, another tool: releasing of fear. If you pay close attention, you can literally feel the closing of the fearful heart, but you remember the light is still shining within it. You might envision the heart as a rose. Within its core is the most brilliant light imaginable, comparable only to the light of God. Sit in meditation and feel your connection with the Divine. Visualize the opening of this rose. It cannot be forced; but the allowing of the experience of loving connection opens those petals, and you experience the radiance flowing into the heart center and the radiance flowing out.

As you come out of your meditation and re-enter the active stages of your life, watch carefully. What happens when there is a catalyst which seems to threaten? Can you see the sun seeming to be cut off and the petals closing? If you remember, "This is illusion. Fear is illusion. It seems solid, but it is created out of my own delusion of a separate self," then you can ask yourself, "Is there a desire to get caught up in this fear?" Sometimes that is easier. It is very beautiful to feel your connection with all that is, but it takes a great deal of responsibility to live that connection constantly without giving in to your anger. You are human. I am not condoning giving in to anger, only suggesting that for the human there is a constant struggle to remember your connection and ask yourself to express that connection in your choices rather than to express separation.

So, you note the illusion of fear and how solid it seems. Come back to the heart center, that place where the light is still brilliant. If the fear is so intense that like the storm cloud it seems to have totally blocked out the sun, then for that moment you are going to have to be the source of light. You may not feel God's presence, and although your intellect tells you, "God is still present and I am only cutting off the experience of that," still you are not feeling it. So, where is the light and love to come from that opens this blossom, this rose, and allows reconnection?

It comes from your deep practice of loving-kindness and compassion with yourself. When you see this being sitting alone and afraid, can you reach out with love to it? What if you wandered down the street protected by your rain gear in a heavy storm and there was a child alone, sobbing on the curb? Would not your heart reach out to this being, to shelter it, to protect it? Can you not do the same for yourselves when you find yourselves soaked in a storm, hemmed in by heavy rain clouds so that you cannot experience the light?

Yes, the fear is illusion. Now you are recognizing "caught in illusion," but also changing your perspective to *know* that this is illusion: "The sun is still shining. I am going to keep myself open to that sun even if I cannot seem to experience it. And then I'm going to give love to this being that's caught in the storm, this being that wants to revenge itself, that wants to scream out its jealousy or its sense of betrayal or greed. I'm going to love that being." It is very hard, but it is the deepest gift you can give, not only to yourself but to God. For to love that which is easy to love is far less of a gift than to love even the angry, jealous, bitter parts of yourself and of all beings.

I want to speak more about different ramifications of this work, especially in connection with the specific questions you have raised. Before I do that, I would like to turn the microphone over to Q'uo so that this brother/sister/friend may offer you its own wisdom and thoughts about this work. That is all.

Q'uo: I am Q'uo. We greet each this morning in the love and in the light of the one infinite Creator. We keenly feel the pleasure of your company and gratefully respond to your call for information.

As the one known as Aaron says so clearly, the separation of the self's consciousness is an illusion. The physical vehicle is an organized illusion within the grand scheme of illusion that is sensory haven for all of third-density work. Each is aware that this is a dream. However, each knows, too, that this is a purposeful dream, a much-desired and desirable illusion—a delusion with which each seeker learns to cooperate, so that learning the lessons of love may become more and more harmonious and the spirit within more and more harmonized with.

It is easy to dismiss one's pain. We may use pain or fear to mean the whole range of defensive maneuvers and postures taken by the self as catalyst bursts upon the conscious awareness. We find, however, that the entire process is effectively weakened in its efficient functioning if the seeker looks down on its own suffering. This suffering is not the product of weakness. It is a product that is as strong as it is weak, as informative as it is repulsive. The emotions that are negative are described as heavy, yet this suggests that there needs to be a lightening of the weight of emotion. We suggest that it is the seeker which turns to the negative emotion and allows it to remain seemingly heavy, just keeping it company for the moment, who will more speedily and comfortably find itself able to allow this weight of energy to begin its natural movement, spiraling upwards from the momentary affliction or suffering experience.

We wish to borrow a tale this instrument has read to illustrate what we intend to mean. There was once an old sage who dwelt in one simple room, meditating and praying. So this sage lived for all of its fullness of years. In the twilight of its incarnation, a young, beautiful stranger burst into its humble room with a newborn child, naming the old sage as the child's father. The sage did not spend time and energy attempting to make it known that it was not the truth. Rather, the sage took the babe and straightway began to work as a shipyard laborer so that it could feed the child. Several years went by with the old man creaking and suffering as he worked the long hours. The babe grew to be a small child. One day this woman, the child's mother, entered again this sage's dwelling place and took the child away, saying that it was, after all, her child. Again, the sage did not argue with the woman but simply began again its interrupted life of meditation and prayer.

To resist one's pain is to intensify it. The pain is a lie, just as the mother lied about the sage being the child's father. However, when some catalyst strikes a resonance which causes the fear and pain of suffering, to spend effort and time objecting to the situation as a lie is to miss an important point. Yes, negative emotions are a dream within a dream, a lie within another larger system of lies or illusion; yet there is purpose here. As the one known as Aaron has put it, the moment of feeling that impulse to pain is a red flag saying, "Pay attention." Do not look away, but look attentively at that impulse. Allow that impulse its rightful focal position. Look with attentive caring. Enter into the darkness, the small death of negative feelings. If not at the moment, as soon as possible go down into the darkness of your own perceptions and listen to your own being. It suffers to change, to become new, to move on. A portion of that which you are expressing must die. Let this be as it is.

The verb *to communicate* is extremely important in this work. Allow heavy feeling to communicate, to become intelligible. Do not swat it away or cover it up. If time must pass before this acceptance of the self can take place, then that is well. But to most efficiently use the goodness of catalyst, the intensity and seeming reality of the nuances of this dark emotion need to be remembered and respected. This acts like a benediction. The suffering of self is thus forgiven by the self which respects these seemingly unacceptable feelings. This allows the energy in these feelings to resume the natural spiraling upward. Denial and resistance attempt to control and abate the suffering. Acceptance and attentiveness within the very darkness is a way to allow the self to be transformed naturally. You have often, perhaps, considered how the child is born into incarnation in pain. Yet the mother is, in the end, totally accepting of this pain, for it has brought about a beloved new life.

In the matter of the spirit's learning the lesson of love, you are both mother and midwife to the growing child of transformed consciousness that is your continual identity within the chances and changes of illusory incarnational life.

We would at this time turn the microphone back to the one known as Aaron. We are those of Q'uo.

Aaron: I am Aaron. I find deep joy in sharing this teaching/learning with all of you and with my brother/sister Q'uo, especially joy in the ways that we may enhance each other's thoughts. That which Q'uo has just expressed might be capsulated in a specific spiritual principle: Do not dialogue with fear. This does not mean "get rid of fear." As Q'uo has pointed out, there must be respect for the suffering. There is no *getting rid of* here, only being present with what is, with all of what is: the joy and the suffering, the separation and the connection, the illusion and the reality.

When I say, "Do not dialogue with fear," what I mean is, do not give fear permission to be in control. When you relate to those catalysts that lead you into fear and separation with more fear and a need to get rid of them in order to come back to some place of connection again, some place of love, then you are dialoguing with fear. Fear is controlling you then because there is still this part of you that wants to get rid of *this* and grasp at *that*. When you become able to simply be present with what is, then you are no longer reactive to it. There is just fear. There is just pain.

Yes, it may be terrible fear. It may be agonizing physical or emotional pain. It no longer has the capacity to shut out the light. You allow its presence. You move with compassion to the being that is experiencing that catalyst and immediately you are in the light, suffering whatever fear, pain, grief, bewilderment there may be, but still in the light. There is no *getting rid of* here and no grasping. The energy in the lower chakras becomes blocked when fear assumes such solidity that you begin to fight back. With the second chakra, for example—the spleen chakra—there may be a sense of a self and an other self, a sense that the other is in some way attacking you. Then need to defend arises. The energy becomes distorted at this second chakra and you begin to act, as I have just said, in a dialogue with your fear. At some level, you are aware of the distortion whereby the second chakra is no longer open and spinning freely, whereby energy is not moving through. Fear is intensified. The sense of self is intensified. And there is a grasping to get rid of this catalyst and to reopen one's energy.

We were asked about Q'uo's statement about the cells in the body. I will let Q'uo enlarge on that if my brother/sister wishes, but wish only to say to that, that each cell reflects the whole. When there is energy distortion that creates a sense of the second chakra being closed, that distortion is duplicated in each cell in the body. What I am saying here is not technically correct, only an attempt to provide a visual image that may help guide you. If you visualize that second chakra being blocked, the back, the abdomen, the head, the neck—all reflect that blockage.

Each cell in your body, in a sense, has all of these seven chakras within it. Each is a reflection of the whole. You know that there are many energy meridians through the body: organ meridians, junction meridians and so on. They all interrelate. Each reflects the whole. You do not cure the distortion of the back or neck or head or abdomen by grasping at the release of blockage any more than you cure that blockage itself by grasping at the release of blockage.

Each of you has a physical body and a light body. The light body is the more pure reflection of the spirit body, of the soul. Within the light body the energy is always entirely open. The physical body energy is heavier. It replicates that light body as best it can, but is moved and distorted by the play of physical sensation and emotion. When you focus on the perfection of the light body, there need not be grasping at that perfection, but a reminder: "I am this light body as well as the physical. I have compassion for the mud puddles into which the physical illusion leads me. But I also remember my perfection."

You might sit in meditation with awareness of where there may be distortion in the physical body and in the chakras of the physical body, and focus on the third eye, allowing yourself to begin to visualize there the entire light body. Focus on that as clearly as you can with no grasping, only an awareness, "These are both part of all I am." The seed of perfection is real. The physical body is very capable of healing itself of distortion, both energy distortion and the physical ramifications of that energy distortion, if it is simply bathed in love and allowed to reconnect with the perfection of the light body.

All of you who do energy work, such as *mudra* meditation or polarity therapy—many different names for different specific kinds of work—what you are really doing is allowing a reconnection of the physical body with its distortion and the light body, using your energy in one way or another to help forge and strengthen this connection. You do not heal another. You invite the situation in which the body may heal itself by reconnecting with its source.

This is a large topic. I will be glad to speak further on it if there is request to do so. I only want to skim the surface now in so far as it relates to working with the distortions of the lower chakras and to the physical distortions of the body.

Can you see the difference when your focus is, "I must correct this physical distortion?" You are grasping at that. The universe gives you that which you focus upon. This is the nature of the universe. When your focus is the seeming closedness of a specific chakra, and there is a grasping—"I need to fix this in myself; I need to change this, get rid of that, become that …"—the universe hears your fear. On an ultimate level there is no duality. To attain this and to get rid of that are heard as part of the same thing. When you shift your focus, the universe reads you differently.

Thus, instead of asking, "How can I get rid of my fear? I must become a more loving person, which means getting rid of my fear, getting rid of my anger" … Instead of that dialogue with fear, when your focus becomes, "How can I express this energy that I have in service to all beings and for the greatest good of all beings?"—that focus *allows* the experience of fear or anger or jealousy if that is what is present. There is no need to get rid of anything then. If your learning to express your energy more purely involves, at this moment in time, the experience of discomforting physical or emotional stimuli, so be it. You do not have to like that stimulus. Can you simply allow the presence of it and send love to the being that is experiencing it?

It is this refusal to get caught in a dialogue with fear that becomes the most important part of the reminder for compassion. It takes awareness because it is a trap that you so easily fall into because your habit of dialoguing with your fear has been so constant. I feel some confusion in all of you. I am going to give one very concrete example.

A being perhaps wants to learn to give its energy with generosity to others, and yet is aware that often when it is asked to give in a material or energy form, there is a contraction, a sense, "What if I need this time or energy or resource?" It may then state an affirmation, "I can be generous," and try to remind itself, even convince itself to be generous. It may even skillfully note the arising of fear and still say, "I will be generous." But at some level there is grasping to the generous and aversion to the fear. Instead of making the affirmation, "I will be generous," which strengthens this grasping and aversion, if the being's focus becomes, "I will work as lovingly as I can with whatever emotions are present in my experience," then the intention is very different: not to "fix" but to relate to with kindness.

Please note that I am not arguing over the use of skillful affirmation. One must ask, "Is this affirmation a way of keeping me grounded in the aspirations of the loving heart, or is it a way of disguising my fears or aversions?" When one knows one's fear of giving and returns gently to the center of the open, loving heart, one touches that core space of generosity. Then, through skillful affirmations, one reminds oneself that the core exists and one can dwell within it.

The seeds of generosity, of patience, of loving-kindness, of connection, of energy, of truth, of morality—all of these are within all of you. This is not something you have to go out of yourself to find. You only allow those seeds to express themselves. So to be generous to another you do not have to affirm and cling to, "I will be generous," only to attend to what blocks the natural impulse to generosity. Here you are not getting caught in conversation with your fear, only noting, "Fear is present," and offering it the love and compassion that it needs to begin to dissolve enough that the natural generosity may be expressed.

You will find the same principle is true with any emotion that you are experiencing. When fear leads you to shame or jealousy, a sense of betrayal, rage; when you can offer love to the human experiencing that emotion and let go of grasping at, "I shouldn't be raging. I shouldn't be jealous. I should be giving in this situation. I should be patient"; when you can see all of those judgments and just note, "Here's judgment again," and come back to the focus, "I wish to offer my energy, to manifest my energy as purely as possible for the good of all beings, including myself. I wish to touch each being with love. I *intend* to touch each being with love"—this process gives the universe a very different message. But it must be honest. You must really look into yourselves to see, "Is that the message I'm ready to offer? What fear is blocking my readiness to offer that message?" and attend to that fear over and over and over again; because each time you think fear is gone, it re-emerges. It is not a burden laid upon you, but a gift of the incarnation. Fear, pain, whatever you are experiencing, is precisely what you need in that moment to lead you more deeply to paying attention, to give you the opportunity to practice loving-kindness and compassion for yourself and all beings.

I know that there are some specific questions here. I also would like to give Q'uo further opportunity to speak so I will pass the microphone over to Q'uo, offering that Q'uo make the decision whether it wishes to speak itself before your questions or ask for those questions. That is all.

Q'uo: I am again with this instrument. I am Q'uo, and greet each again in love and in light.

To end our portion of this session of working, we would ask each to move with us in visualization. Each entity please choose the situation which first comes to mind wherein you have felt your senses thrum with the running of the energy of heavy negative emotion. Feel the first impulse hit your consciousness—this striking of the self, this violation of calm and serenity. Allow it to seem, as it does, a wrenching, tearing, pulling of the self in a descending gyre until the body is flattened on the dust of a barren land. Taste that acrid dust. Know this dust is made of self-condemnation. Feel the body as it is flattened by this suffering moment. Call out within yourself:

"The world is a trouble and a sorrow. The world is a trouble and a sorrow. The world is a trouble and a sorrow."[17]

Feel the intensification of that sorrow. Feel the healing enter into this celebration of sorrowing self. Take this body into your arms, self crooning to self, self comforting self. Rock with this poor, pained child. Sing the lullaby of faith, of hope:

"When I carry my title clear to mansions in the sky, I'll bid farewell to all my fear and wipe my weeping eye. I will wipe my weeping eye."[18]

Let the child stand on its own now. It hopes. It knows it is on a journey home. Homeward goes the sorrowing, healing soul.

---

[17] "The Only Bright Light is Jesus"—Negro Spiritual; passage was sung.

[18] *ibid.*

Breathe the fullness of that rising natural realization of the exact opposite of the original pain. Feel the strength build as the realization is allowed to bloom that this, too, is of the nature of the one infinite Creator. This, too, is of love. This, too, is holy. And rise in spirit singing, "Holy, holy, holy …"[19]

Are there any brief queries before we close our portion of this session?

(No further queries.)

We would then leave each, until later, in the love and in the light of the one infinite Creator. The one known as Aaron, we believe, will also speak not now but this afternoon, as you would say. So for now, Adonai. We are those of Q'uo.

---

[19] "Holy, Holy, Holy, Lord God Almighty"—Hymn by Reginald Heber 1783-1826 (lyrics) and John B. Dykes 1823-1876 (music); from *Christian Worship: A Hymnal*, Christian Board of Publication, The Bethany Press, St. Louis, Twelfth Printing, 1954, Hymn No. 107.

The Aaron/Q'uo Dialogues, Session 16
March 22, 1993

(This session was preceded by a period of tuning and meditation.)

R and C: How do we know what it is that we need to be doing with our lives and energies in the spiritual senses, and how can we accomplish what it is we are to do? In our hearts we know that we are spirit, but we want to know how the everyday self that lives the life knows what to work on and how to do it.

How do the three lower chakras, which are clear and balanced like Jesus' were, show or demonstrate themselves in this third density?

Barbara: I am aware that no matter how clearly I offer to give my energy, my ego creeps in, and I become afraid that I can't trust what I am doing because I know there is distortion. How do we work with that—the distortion that humans create?

K: While becoming aware of fearing a meeting with another, I opened my heart to that person without any defenses; and then I felt the knot of fear dissolve and energy moved up to my heart. Is there any principle of working with the lower energy centers that this exercise took advantage of? What are the most effective ways of working with the lower chakras that will allow us to open the heart chakra? How would the same experience look from each energy center's point of view?

Jim: How do we maintain our passion for pursuing the spiritual journey after many years of seeing that things seem to happen as they will, and perhaps the most that we can do is keep a good attitude for all changes that come our way?

(The foregoing questions and comments will be used as seed for continuing on with the topic of how to open the heart chakra that the two previous sessions have begun.)

Aaron: I am Aaron. I rejoice once again to be with you. As we continue these sessions, your energy level grows higher and there is great joy and aspiration in your vibrations. All of the questions that you are asking come together. While I will not speak at length here of this honest question of spiritual vocation, I do want to begin by stating a common misunderstanding and offering clarification.

When you consider the blockages of the lower chakras, what comes to your minds are the heavy emotions, the desires for power or control, anger or greed or jealousy. You wonder how you may clarify those energies in yourselves. The common distortion among earnest seekers is that you must get rid of all of those desires and fears in order for the heart to open and in order for the lower chakras to be clear. But that very desire to be rid of this or that in your experience backfires. This is what closes the chakras.

It is not the arising of fear and its attendant emotions of anger or greed or need to control that close the chakras, but your moving in one direction or the other from that first sensation of fear: either into action upon those desires or angers, or into need to get rid of them. Both are distortions. The arising of emotion in the human is not a distortion. It is not the fear nor the anger nor greed that keeps you returning to third-density experience, but your relationship with those emotions.

You are all spiritually sophisticated. Think of what you know of fourth-density experience, what you have been told of it. This is group energy experience where all beings are fully telepathic with one another. Everything is shared. The learning is so rapid because you have no need to hide your experiences from another nor to defend yourself from another's experience. There is total openness to whatever is expressed, with no judgment about it.

Where you each are presently, when there is heavy emotion you feel some shame about that. So there is some unwillingness to share that with another. When you hear of another's heavy emotion, there is some discomfort with it rather than equanimity. But it is total equanimity with emotion that denotes readiness for fourth-density experience.

You are not here in human incarnation to cease experiencing physical sensations or emotions. You understand that for the physical body. You know that if you stub your toe, it is going to hurt. When there is such pain, you do not try to deny the pain. You do not feel it is bad that there is pain. There is just pain. You may dislike the pain, but you do not judge it. There is simply aversion to it because it is uncomfortable. When you stub your emotional toe and there is anger or greed, you label it as "bad": "I should get rid of this or that and then I will be pure." The emotions that grow out of fear are uncomfortable. Part of your work is to learn to relate to those emotions with the same openheartedness with which you relate to that stubbed toe, without judgment of the self that is experiencing them and consequently without judgment to the other selves that are experiencing such emotions.

This is the foundation for the work of all beings in third density. It is through the constant judgment of what you experience that self solidifies and enhances the illusion of separation. You are here to reconfirm that there is no separate self, that the self solidifies through dwelling in delusion. The more you fight with the presence of an emotion, the more self solidifies, the more sense there is, "I must get rid of this or that to purify myself." What you have to do, then, is to change your relationship to that which arises in you.

This brings us back to the human living this life, feeling the closing lower chakras, feeling the arising of fear, anger, greed, prejudice, jealousy, whatever the emotion may be. Increasingly, you allow the perspective which finds compassion for the human tossed into emotions by the continuing catalysts of the incarnation. You become less and less reactive, more able to keep the heart open.

This brings us to K's experience whereby she found such compassion and connection with this other whom she was afraid to meet. When there is judgment against fear, it automatically enhances separation, which brings you back into the dialogue with fear that I spoke of earlier. Then there is a self feeling it should get rid of this and grasp at that. When you notice the arising of fear simply and with compassion to the human caught in that situation, self dissolves. There is no longer a *doer*. Then all these powerful energies I spoke of earlier, these beautiful seeds of loving-kindness, of patience, of generosity and ever so many more have the opportunity to flourish.

They are not seeds that can flourish in the self that grasps at them. No matter how much you attempt to be patient with a sense, "I should be patient," you cannot make that blossom grow any more than you can make a rose open by willing it to open. The warm light of love shined on it, the warm sunshine, is what allows the rose to open, is what allows generosity, patience, loving-kindness, energy, truthfulness, to express themselves through you.

At this point the lower chakras are open, not because you have willed them to open by willing a riddance of the issues concerned therein, but by creating so much space that the issues simply fall away. You find the ability to smile at this being that wants to be in control—not to laugh at it, not to mock it in any way or to take its pain less than fully seriously, but to hold it in love.

This is the work for which you incarnated. We have spoken of this before. The lessons of compassion and wisdom are valuable, and there is no reason not to start on those lessons in third density; but you are here to learn love and faith. And if there is not a firm foundation of those lessons of love and faith, then lessons of the higher densities will become distorted.

What does it mean to love unconditionally? What does it mean to have faith? That is another seed within you. How can you allow that seed of faith to blossom? By the constant reminder: Everything within this human experience, all the physical sensations, all the emotions, are acceptable.

Obviously, that does not give you free rein to be reactive to those emotions and harm others. But the reaction to the emotion and the experiencing of the emotion itself are two vastly different things. You are here not to learn never to be angry, but to find compassion for the human when anger arises, to find space for all your humanness.

We are asked about the one known as Jesus. The question assumed that this one's lower chakras were open, and asked, "How did that affect the upper chakras?" This one, of course, came into incarnation with the lower chakras entirely opened. And yet, even this one did experience human emotion. Even the Bible tells that at times he became angry. Certainly, he felt physical pain in his body and some aversion to that pain. The issue is not keeping the lower chakras open so that the heart center can open. The heart center may be opened while there is still some distortion in the lower chakras. The issue is, can one find such deep love for this human that one can see the distortion in the lower chakras without condemnation, fully embracing the human experience?

Jim has asked, how can one maintain a passion about this work? Perhaps one best facilitates the allowing of that passion to express itself by focusing on just this full embracing of the human. I would suggest that it is the judgment against the human that puts the damper on that sense of passion.

My dear ones, your earnest seeking and desire to express your energy with more and more purity, to do the work you came to do, so deeply moves those of us who have moved beyond the incarnative experience. Your work is a very real gift to us, as it deepens our compassion to watch you struggle and remember those struggles of our own. This is not only true of one such as myself that has moved through the earth plane, but is also true of those of Q'uo, of all beings that have moved through the different densities on whatever plane they have done so. This is your gift to us, and I thank you for it.

When you wonder what is your work here, what is it about, I ask only that you keep in your mind that the work you do is on so many different levels that you cannot begin to imagine the span of it. For now, you are human. Allow yourselves to be human. Work with the catalysts of this density. It is fine to acquaint yourselves with what comes next, both as inspiration for your work and to help you keep a balanced perspective. But you do not need to use this present incarnative experience doing the work that you will do in higher densities. Embrace this human experience and the human that you are. Cherish yourselves. If I could give just one piece of advice it would be that: Cherish yourselves.

A cry comes up from you, "Yes, Aaron, how? How do I cherish myself?" I will move on to that question in a while. I would like now to pass the microphone to Q'uo. That is all.

Q'uo: I am Q'uo. Greetings once again, my friends, in the love and in the light of the one infinite Creator. We join the one known as Aaron in thanks for the beauty of your seeking and the plangent cry of your call. It is indeed that which inspires such as we, and offers us the optimal opportunity for our own service and further learning.

May we now ask a question of you? As you followed the meditation with which we closed the previous session, did each feel the transformation of vibration that went from the impulse of negative emotion to its uplifting in the most sacred of healings? We suggest that this was one example of the process by which a way is found to work with one distortion at a time and communicate, with the purest voice of openheartedness, with the suffering portions of the self.

We said earlier that communication was a great key. There are many ways to communicate with one's distortions while within the distortion as an entity. They all partake in various ways of the use of those ways of communicating which go beyond words and intellectual considerations so that the spirit within the self may speak healing to the manifested self. If one attempts to bring into the heart chakra each felt distortion, one is violating the self, attempting to drag energy where it is not rising naturally. However, if one can see the heart as always open and allow the heart to be moved into communication with the lower chakra *in* the lower, then the combined vibrations, instead of the green muddied by forced portions of red, orange and yellow, remain crystalline—the green color shimmering upon the type of communication mentally or physically voiced. This, then, looks like a living stream of the most lovely light green, which shimmers and surrounds and gradually alleviates the blockage of red, orange or yellow so that the two colors gradually become equal in their radiance and power.

Prayer is one way of moving beyond words with words. If one can conceive of the prayer, "infinite Creator," as the Father/Mother which truly listens and truly cares unstintingly, then one may be moved to share one's confusions in the privacy of prayer. One may, for instance, as this instrument does, simply speak her heart: "Dear Creator, I am at sea. I feel frustrated. I do not know what to do. He hurt my feelings. I hurt." There does not have to be a lofty, beautiful, aesthetically pleasing quality to the prayer. Speaking one's truth when one is in pain is not likely to be pretty. It is obversely very likely to be the whine, the howl, the indignant, barbaric *NO* of the small, small child; for that which hurts is that which is not deeply understood.

The darkness is that of ignorance. Pain of incarnative quality, pain which blocks energy, is primitive pain no matter how sophisticated the source of that pain or the spiritual nature of its origin, which may be very far removed from basic, instinctual pain. So in prayer, communication is best when it is forthrightly honest, even and especially when that pain partakes of pettiness, foolishness, unjustified indignation and is full of errors in judgment. To howl your mistakes and the pain you feel is certainly to howl about that which is not so; for your pain, your self-judgment, all this is a dream within a dream, yet it is this exact dream which you wish to heal. Thusly, pray truth the best way you can.

There is a quality to other kinds of communication which, like prayer, use words to go beyond words: the reading aloud of those poems or passages of inspired writing which speak to one's distress focus and purify the heart's journey to the blockage below. Now each center is as the heart center, in truth, opening and functioning well; however, because the lower centers are concerning themselves with relationship there is no independence or spirit-driven movement available below the heart chakra. The green, blue and indigo rays, upon the other hand, are focused upon absolutes offered from the spirit within and do not depend upon any, shall we say, earthly relationship to be viable. Yet to spend all of the time in the higher energy centers with lower-chakra communication left undone is to invite the gradual attenuation of strength available for that work because of the unattended difficulties with relationships, the self to the self being chief among these.

At this point, the one known as Aaron may take the microphone, as we feel there is a natural shift at this point. We find this sharing of teaching most pleasant, and we thank each for allowing this combined use of these channels; for it is greatly heartening to both the one known as Aaron and us. We now transfer. We are those of Q'uo.

Aaron: I am Aaron. The relationship of the self to the self, how to learn to cherish this self so that one may fully cherish all selves—that is the gift of your incarnation. Can you begin to see, then, that the distortion that leads to not cherishing the self is part of the gift and not a barrier in the way of learning of this love? If there were not that arising of sensing the self as imperfect, of the arising of low self-esteem and all those many emotions that lead to less than treasuring of the self, with what would you practice? What if this self always appeared to be perfect? Somewhere on this journey of yours, you are bound to meet that which does not appear to be perfect. Without this practice, you would judge it and have strong aversion to it. All that which you judge within yourself is the gift for practicing non-judgment and unconditional love.

As humans, you work so strongly with habit and your habit says, "Judge! Get rid of!" You are so immersed in that pattern. First, you begin to see the pattern, to bring mindfulness to bear on the arising of judgment. What is this low self-esteem? You might ask yourself in a situation in which low self-esteem is present, "What if I really liked myself here despite whatever heavy emotions are arising in me? What if I really treasured myself?" When you ask that question, you may begin to see the ways that low self-esteem becomes an escape.

Unconditional love is very difficult. The human feels hurt and wants to fight back, feels betrayed and wants revenge. The human sometimes does not feel ready to be as responsible as some judgmental inner voice suggests that it should be. You have habitually used this pattern of moving into dislike of the self as an escape from the direct experience of the heavy emotions and the need to be responsible for them with kindness. It is uncomfortable not to like the self, but it perhaps is even more uncomfortable to recognize the true divinity of your nature and that you are capable of unconditional love. Here is the child pouting, "I want to get even!" The child wants to get in that one good kick. The child that is loved despite its pain and anger is far less likely to need to kick. When unworthiness arises, ask yourself, "If I were not feeling unworthiness, what might I be feeling?" What heavy emotions which are so terribly discomforting does the unworthiness mask? Can you see how much ego there is in unworthiness?

Look at the patterns that you have established. If what you see is a desire to be a bit irresponsible, that is okay, too. It does not mean that you need to act on that desire, just notice that it is there. "What if I can't really carry this off? What if my emotions begin to control and pull me into reactivity?" That is another fear. So, you back off and say, "Well, I won't even try." And then you move into that dislike of the self.

Watch unworthiness arise. Watch the way it closes off the lower chakras and then seems to give you permission to react, because any other choice becomes seemingly impossible with the lower chakras closed. You thereby hand permission to the child self to express itself. Your work is not to deny the existence of this child self nor to allow it to have its tantrums, but to hear the child self and offer it love. It is this continued remembering to love the self, whatever is being experienced, that provides full healing of the sense of unworthiness.

In a very real way you are each born, each come into incarnation, with this that needs to be healed. You do not need to be perfect to offer that love to yourself, but to learn to forgive your imperfections. You see this message in the life and especially in the death of the one known as Jesus. He told those who died on crosses beside him essentially that he loved them. This is that message of the Divine who said, "This is my beloved Son, in whom I am well pleased."[20] That is a message offered not only to the one known as Jesus, but to all of you. You are loved, not because you are perfect, not because you are without heavy emotions, not because you express your energy with perfect purity but simply because you are. It is that healing to which you are invited to come.

How do you begin to forgive yourselves? You cannot learn to cherish yourself until you forgive yourself for being less than perfect in this human form. You are not cherishing the perfect, but the human.

There are many practices one might use. As Q'uo suggested, prayer is very powerful. Ask for help. When you feel yourself condemning yourself, give that to the Divine and ask for help with it. "Lord, this human is fallible. I have hurt others and myself, and now I'm filled with condemnation of myself for that hurting. Help me find forgiveness and compassion for this imperfect human that I am."

Please notice that there is a difference between the sense of unworthiness itself and the relationship to it. When you experience unworthiness, you may then watch the arising of aversion to it and attend first to that aversion, asking yourself, "Can I just be present with the unworthiness and watch it? Can I be present with any emotions, voices, fears, memories within me which prompted the arising of unworthiness? Can I let the whole thing be and just watch it?" This gentleness brings in light and space. The heart opens. There may still be the remnants of the anger, jealousy or greed that prompted the unworthiness. There may still be an aversion to all of that, the unworthiness and the emotion, because they are uncomfortable. But they are attended to skillfully.

This is where Q'uo's image of bringing the heart center into the lower chakras may be seen. There is no force here, just a willingness to be present with all of the confusion without judgment, letting it all float. Then the unworthiness does not solidify, a self does not solidify to combat the unworthiness. Instead there is a gentle love offered to the self that is experiencing so much pain, including unworthiness. It allows a shift in perspective to this angel aspect of the self which is perfect and which you know is worthy. Within that shift, you begin to find wholeness. There is nothing left that needs to be gotten rid of. Just letting it be, allowing it to be present or to dissolve at its own speed while it is offered love.

What you will find is that your increasing ability to offer love begins a new pattern, a far more skillful pattern whereby, as I suggested yesterday with the arising of fear, the arising of unworthiness becomes a

---

[20] *Holy Bible*, Matthew 3:17.

catalyst, not for the offering of more disdain to the self but a catalyst for compassion. This reconnects the lower chakra centers to the heart center. It reconnects the spirit body to the physical and emotional bodies, and you come back into wholeness and into balance. It is here where even a sense of unworthiness becomes seen as a valuable gift for your learning, and you embrace it rather than wage a war with it.

I would like to close with a guided forgiveness meditation, which is another powerful tool in spiritual work. Before I do so, I would like to pass the microphone to Q'uo to see if my brother/sister has that which it would like to add; and then would ask briefly before the meditation that you simply stretch, as many of you are feeling tiredness in your body and I would like you to be able to sit for five or ten minutes to participate more fully in the meditation. That is all.

Q'uo: I am Q'uo, and am again with this instrument.

In communicating from the heart center to the suffering and unworthy self perceived by the self, the seeker is healing its own incarnation one small symptom at a time. The infection called life is incurable and mortal. The small infections called error or sin or distortion are not fatal, merely greatly uncomfortable. When attempting to function as a healer, then, the techniques of healing which are not mechanical or chemical involve necessarily the first healing, which is the healing of the instrument which the seeker is who wishes to heal.

The heart is the seat of intelligent healing energy brought down, first into the violet ray which contacts the Logos itself of intelligent Infinity, as this instrument would say, and then through the indigo ray of intelligent Energy. This indigo ray is that which is your work in consciousness.

We do not mean to be confusing, for we wish you to feel comfortable with our teaching. However, in order to teach with words, we must pretend that each voice within you, or rather each type of voice within you, is separate and can communicate to other voices or types of voices within you. Since the universe itself and all that there is, is within you, it is inevitable that the communication skills we encourage for the healing of incarnation or those whom the healer wishes to serve require a splitting of the perceived self so that communication's requirement of one to speak and one to listen be fulfilled.

Work in consciousness is largely the moving of energy which is intelligent through violet; then, by intention, from indigo into the blue ray of communication, which then opens the heart, which opened heart may go forth arrayed in the bright colors of love and purified emotion. There is the bringing down of pure light into an intelligible form of communication which carries purified emotion to the relationship which needs healing or, when the self is healer, to the entity to be healed.

Now when the self is engulfed in a difficulty, the heart is defended by thoughts like, "Not trouble again. I can't stand it. I can't stand me." One cannot storm those defenses, so one uses prayer, song, praise and thanksgiving, which, unlike the prayer of the unworthy one, are focused upon the beautiful, the more real, the more true. To say in the midst of sorrow, "Thank you, O beloved Father/Mother. Praise you, O One Who is all," may seem not only dishonest but irrelevant. But we suggest that you see that this is how the voice of the heart is reached. The direction of the thoughts is changed by the purified emotion taken on faith and expressed in the song, the praise, the thanks, the prayer. Thus, passion is restored to that great seat of purified emotion, purified emotion being the essence of wisdom as opposed to knowledge. The procedure, then, is to suffer; to become aware of the suffering; to pay attention by spending the coin of time; to move purposefully into the prayer, praise, thanksgiving and song, which awakens the heart; to allow this energy to pour into the heart; to allow this potentiated healing energy to move into the relationship which is the conscious focus of the suffering, and then to allow the healing of acceptance and forgiveness to take place.

We of Q'uo confess our own planning ahead. It is not a good time now for us to address how this turning to inspiration can be aided by faith, so we promise on the morrow this shall be addressed by us. For now, we ask you to take it on faith that when you do praise and thank and sing and pray, there is a spirit of Love itself that listens and responds endlessly, fruitfully and fully so that each symptom of the infection called distortion or error or sin may indeed be forgiven.

We would now turn the microphone back to the voice of Barbara, as this entity offers those meditational thoughts of the one known as Aaron. We thank each for this joy of speaking with you; and for now, Adonai. We are those of Q'uo.

Aaron: I am Aaron. I am very grateful to Q'uo for bringing in this topic of faith. It is of great importance and relevance to the subject, and it is my hope that we will both expand the communication on it tomorrow.

Forgiveness is not an event, but a process. You come to a cool lake on the first hot day of spring and desire to swim, to immerse yourself in that cooling water; yet, when you test the water, it is icy cold. With the process of forgiveness, you do not need to leap off the end of the dock into that coolness. You wade in to your ankles. How does it feel? If it feels good, you continue. If it is too cold and you cannot go any further, you stop and try again the next day, and the next and the next. I invite you, then, not to forgive, but to enter into the process of forgiveness.

To begin this process, I would like you to invite one for whom you feel love into your heart and mind, just holding them there before you. No matter how much love there may be between you, you have also caused pain to one another. Speaking that being's name silently and saying, "I love you, so it is hard to express my anger to you, but you have hurt me by something you did or said or even thought. Intentionally or unintentionally, you have caused me pain. When I look into your heart, I see that you have also known pain. I do not wish to put you out of my heart. I forgive you. I love you, even if there may still be some anger or hurt about that which was said or done. I wish to reconnect our hearts with these words and thoughts. I forgive you. I accept your pain out of which those words or acts arose. I love you."

I am going to be silent for a minute and ask you to continue this process silently with the one you hold before you, offering whatever words or thoughts feel most appropriate.

(Pause)

Gently now, allow that being to recede from the center of your awareness. In its place, invite in a being from whom you wish forgiveness. Speaking that being's name to yourself and saying, "I have hurt you through something I said or did or even thought. Intentionally or unintentionally, I have caused you pain and led you to put me out of your heart. It is so painful to be thus separated from you because I love you. Please forgive me. I also have known pain. I do not defend my words or acts, but ask your compassion for my pain, your understanding that the voice within me which spoke was the voice of fear. I admit my irresponsibility in allowing that voice of fear to dominate the voice of love. Forgive me for the ways that I have hurt you. Allow me back into your heart."

Again, I will be silent for a moment and allow you to work with this yourself, with whatever words feel most appropriate.

(Pause)

Feel that one's welcomed forgiveness. Feel your energies rejoin. Gently let that being go. Into the space that is left there, please invite yourself—this human that you are, whom you have so often judged so harshly, condemned and put out of your heart. It is so terribly painful to put yourself out of your heart in that way. So much anger, so much fear resides in this human who you are. The loving heart has room for it all. It is the fearful brain that judges and creates separation. The heart welcomes the self back in.

Look at yourself standing there, perched like a deer ready to flee because it expects the voice of judgment which it has heard so often. Speaking your own name to yourself and saying, "When did you last tell yourself, 'I love you'?" Can you offer that to yourself? Speaking your name and saying, "I love you. Yes, you are not perfect. Yes, you are sometimes reactive, frightened and unskillful. I do not love you because you are perfect. I love you because you are. All of that which I have judged about myself, I invite back into my heart. And I ask that judged part of myself, 'Can you forgive me the judging as I forgive you your imperfections? Let us be one again. Let us enter wholeness. For whatever ways I have hurt you, can you forgive me for the ways I have judged you? For whatever flaws you have manifest for which I have judged you, as you forgive me for the judging, I forgive you for being human and embrace your humanness.' It is so painful to feel this separation from myself. May I be whole. May I be healed. For whatever pain I have caused to myself, I offer forgiveness. I forgive you. I love you."

Again, I will be silent for a minute. Please continue to offer whatever wishes feel most appropriate.

(Pause)

Can you hold this being that you are up before you as one who is truly cherished and beloved? Look at yourself, at how beautiful you are, and offer yourself that love.

May all beings everywhere learn to cherish each other and themselves.

(Bell)

May all beings learn to forgive and experience the grace of being forgiven.

(Bell)

May all beings everywhere find their way home and attain perfect peace.

(Bell)

My deepest love and gratitude to you all. I wish you a goodnight. That is all. ✤

L/L Research

The Aaron/Q'uo Dialogues, Session 17
March 23, 1993

(This session was preceded by a period of tuning and meditation.)

Q'uo: I am Q'uo. Greetings to each of you in the love and in the light of the one infinite Creator. This instrument asks us to pause as the recording equipment is put into position.

(Pause)

I am Q'uo. We have adjusted the microphone so that more than those present may catch our hot air. The instrument says, "Written on the wind was not the idea."

We wish each to know of the depth of our gratitude that we have been able to dwell at some length upon the topic you have called us to your group to consider. Again, we ask that our thoughts be seen as offered without authority. Your discrimination shall tell you what is for you. Leave the rest behind without a second thought, for there is an abundance of guidance for those who trust their ears and their hearts each day as to the wisdom of that day.

We have been working with the way in which the seeker may find tools with which to understand the situation of the first three chakras and the pathways from intelligent infinity to the heart of each and every seeming blockage or confusion. We have been speaking as though the seeker, by its own mental processes, were responsible solely for the carrying out of the procedures of finding the attention turned to the heart, experiencing the heart moving the heart to the blocked heart energy and releasing and allowing that blockage to reconform to the upward spiraling line of light—that time/space pathway within manifestation which combines all energy fields as the whole spirit releases its bound energy to the limitless light whence all energy has come. However, although the seeker is solely responsible for the will and the desire to bring into harmony and ultimate unity all energies within the energy complexes of the self, yet still, there is strong and ever-present help for the seeker whose resources include a life in faith. Whether the tool of song is used, or prayer or praise or the giving of thanks when no thanks or praise seems to be appropriate, or whether the seeker chooses the great range of visualization techniques in order to more efficiently allow energy the pathway for movement, the process is given what one could call the carrier wave that creates a spiritual gravity or mass which enhances the tools and resources above mentioned.

Now a life in faith may seem to demand the acceptance of some culturally chosen holy or worshipped individual such as the Buddha or the one known as Jesus. This is not so in that such ones as Buddha or Jesus the Christ spoke clearly to indicate that they were speaking not of themselves but of the mystery which the one known as Jesus called Father, or more familiarly, Daddy. This Father/Mother Creator has sent each inspired and inspiring historical figure into a troubled world to bear witness to the light and the love of the infinite Creator. The one known as Jesus said, "If you hear me, you hear not me but my Father who speaks through me."

A life in faith is built not on objective or provable knowledge, nor must it be built from a conversion experience, so called, wherein one entity is seen in its human form as a personal redeemer. This instrument moves within the distortions in which the one known as Jesus the Christ is acclaimed as a personal savior. For this instrument, this is the path, this is the life, this is the personal truth. Each seeker must choose, not that which works for another, but that which works for the self.

Let us move, then, to what Jesus the Christ said when this entity determined that it was the time appointed for it to fulfill its destiny and depart the earth plane. Its students objected strenuously to this plan, but the one known as Jesus pointed out that unless he left this lifetime, the spirit that could move into all portions of the world scene could not come among men. So even if a personal savior is chosen, that very savior demands that the seeker move beyond the form of one blessed incarnation to seek that Spirit, that Comforter, that which the music heard this day has called the holy of holies and which this instrument knows as the Holy Spirit.

We would suggest the term guidance. Yes, each must be responsible for cherishing again and again the self, to learn to love the self that one may, for the first time, know how to love the neighbor as the self. But there is the Comforter which moves within each life. There is always guidance available. There is always the carrier wave that strengthens the will and desire to be and, in that beingness which is full, to so move in consciousness that the fragmented self which suffers is healed by love.

We would, at this point, turn the microphone to the one known as Aaron and the channel known as Barbara. We are those of Q'uo.

Aaron: I am Aaron. I greet you all with love and wish you a good morning. My thanks to my brother/sister Q'uo for leading us into this exploration of the role of faith in allowing the heart to remain open. You are beings of light. That is your nature. Even those amongst you on the earth plane who are of negative polarity have their source in that light and will eventually return to that light.

When the heart center is open, you experience that light. When you rest in the experience of that light, whatever work may be necessary with the lower centers, it feels workable. Whatever issues there may be, they are just issues and do not overwhelm. When the heart center feels closed so that you experience absence of light, you feel yourself cut off from your spiritual roots. And whatever personal issues there may be that are focused in the lower chakras, they feel overwhelming, enormous; and there is just you, this self, to deal with it.

You know that a plant grows in the sunshine. Even a shade-loving plant must have some light. You would not take a plant, a bulb perhaps, and put it in the best soil, offer it the fertilizer it needed, water it and then put it in a dark closet and expect it to grow. But you do this with yourselves. How do you bring yourself out of that closet?

First, one must be aware that one is in the closet. "I am living in darkness. I have shut myself off." Seeing that, you make the skillful decision, "I'm going to open the door. I need light in here." No matter how dark it appears, you may then begin to pray, to seek, to read inspired readings and poetry, to speak to a human friend whose faith is deep. This is not grasping at the light. It is simply opening the shades so that the light that is already there may come in. It does take the skillful decision to emerge from the darkness.

This brings us back to some of the unique patterns of the human. There is this small ego self that we talk about. It is illusion, but within the human experience it feels real and solid. This illusion has one purpose as far as it knows, and that is to maintain itself at all costs. Why? If you are that angel I spoke of yesterday and truly connected with God, why would you want to maintain the illusion of separation? What purpose has this illusion? When you incarnate, you agree to experience this veil of forgetting, an opacity that cuts you off from the clear seeing of your true nature. Again, why? Why agree to that?

For reasons I cannot easily explain, the primary lessons of third density are faith and love. What will teach you faith? If you incarnate with full awareness of who you are and what you are doing in this incarnation, with clear seeing of the divinity in yourself and in all beings and the clear experience of God, where is faith to be learned? But that faith is a foundation. Without that faith the later lessons of wisdom may so easily become distorted and move the being into negative polarity. So these muscles of faith must be built by practice.

You know that there are many planes of learning and that this earth experience is a somewhat new experiment insofar as the entire history of the universe. Perhaps the greatest success of this experiment has been the profundity of the way faith is learned, of the experience of faith on this plane. This is a gift, this veil of forgetting. Because of the veil you cannot take your divinity for granted, but must always move deeper into the experience of it, must always work to separate illusion from deeper reality. And yet, no matter how clearly you experience that deeper reality, as human, it still must be taken as a matter of faith. You are not given proof.

One thing that is occurring here is that you are strengthening the will to express your divinity and to be of service to all beings. If there were clear seeing with no veil, you might come into incarnation and say, "Yeah, I'd like to serve. Sure, why not?" But it would not be a strong decision from within the heart, not a deep answering to a call, just following the pattern: "This is what everybody's doing; I'll go along with it." Can you see the difference? Intention is all-important.

We emphasize that you have free will. We emphasize responsibility. In essence, this veil and the matter of faith offer you the opportunity to exercise that free will and responsibility without clearly knowing what you are doing, just trusting that light within you and the way it connects you to all that is. Through each incarnation lived in faith you grow into deeper readiness for that responsibility. You are responsible for what you know. To know, to have deeper wisdom and understanding, carries deeper responsibility. Without the deep support of faith, that responsibility would seem too great a burden.

When you see clearly who and what you are on the astral plane between your human lifetimes and after graduation from this plane, then your decisions to serve, for example, grow out of a strong place only of will. Because you know who you are and are ready for that responsibility in the upper densities, there is no problem. On the earth plane it can easily become distorted so that will twists itself into judgment and self-judgment. Rather than expressing love, one would simply express self-discipline. One would move into a sense, "I came to do this and I'm going to do it, and nothing's going to stop me!" But you are not here to learn that level of self-determination, not here to use force and judgment as guidance for your choices, but here to learn love as guidance for your choices. To express your energy with love, there must be that sense of connection that grows out of faith.

So, you open your closet door. You experience that light. One moment, please. We will continue in a moment.

(Pause)

Aaron: I am Aaron. Barbara and I were both experiencing the presence of some negative energy. We are comfortable that it is no longer making any effort to intrude and is welcome to listen if it would learn from our teaching. We ask that all present send love to anything that wishes to learn from the deep love expressed in these sessions.

When you open this door and allow light into yourselves, something very wonderful happens within these lower chakras. You no longer feel alone and helpless. You have been like a generator, a small generator, trying to light up a large house and aware that there just was not enough power to do so. Suddenly, you are plugged into the source. The generator is still working, but there is far more current coming through. It recharges the generator and draws the current necessary to bring light to every dark corner. Then you look at your issues with relationships, with need to control and fear, with desire for power, survival issues, whatever they may be and it no longer feels like a huge burden laid on your shoulders. Your relationship with it changes, not because you have willed that change, but truly because you have opened the door and allowed in the light.

There has to be a moment of decision: Do I want to linger here in darkness or do I wish to move into the light? Why am I clinging to the darkness? What safety have I found in the darkness? And there is some illusion of safety in darkness. It is a place to hide.

I spoke at the beginning of this talk of the small ego self's desire to maintain itself. You have grown into the pattern in your human form of thinking of the strength of this self as your protection from that which is thrown at you. "If the self is strong, if *I* can be in control, then *I* can control the pain in my life." But it does not work that way. These catalysts will continue to arise over and over again. You only move yourself into more negativity and fear when you allow the self to act through fear to assert self.

When you become aware of the pattern whereby self wants to be dominant in order to keep this being safe and you send love to that fear, open to the reality of that fear with no need to get rid of the fear, then you begin to rest in faith. "Even the fear is offered as part of my learning. I don't have to get rid of anything in my experience. My spiritual path is right here in this relationship, in this job, in this political issue. Each is an opportunity to draw in light, to offer service and love."

It is sometimes very difficult to keep track of this. Fear keeps closing in on you. In effect, all of these lower chakra issues—it does not matter what they are, issues of physical health, of money, of relationship, whatever they are—they are offered for one purpose: They give you an opportunity to change your relationship with fear by the very simple act of coming back to who you are, to affirming with faith, "There is that of the Divine within me. If I draw on that tremendous source of energy and love, then I have the ability to work lovingly and skillfully with this catalyst. I no longer need to wage war with this catalyst but can use it as an opportunity to practice expressing my energy more purely and lovingly." Then all of these situations in your life take on such a different perspective. Faith is strengthened each time you work in this more loving way.

Picturing that being in the dark room the first time it opens the shutters, it may not even have realized that there was light outside. The light seems so bright it feels blinded by it and must close the shutters again quickly. But it soon learns to enjoy and trust that light. It becomes a pattern. When it looks around and sees that the room is too dark, it remembers, "I can open the shutters."

This remembering is a major part of your work. This is part of the reason why I so emphasize mindfulness. Know when you are sitting in the dark. Know that you have the option to open the shutters. Know that you also have the option to remain in the dark. But if you do so, you have chosen that. Why are you choosing to sit in darkness? Why are you hiding in the darkness? What illusion of protection does the darkness offer as it strengthens the small ego self? Do you really need to continue that pattern, or are you ready to be kinder to yourself and allow yourself to experience your true being?

I know that there are questions at this point. I would like to turn the microphone over to Q'uo that it may speak as it chooses or, if it prefers, may ask directly for your questions. That is all.

Q'uo: I am Q'uo. Greetings again in love and in light.

The one known as Aaron asks if you are ready to experience your true nature. The living of a life in faith is the living of a life in which you are willing to practice the presence of your true nature. So many times you have heard us and any other spiritual counselor suggest the meditation, the sitting, on a persistent daily basis. The advantages of such a practice are physiologically persuasive, and many are those who practice this technique in one form or another with no intent other than the relaxation of the physical body and the slowing of the frantic stream of thought. However, we say to you, is any silence empty in a universe that is full of the unity of the nature of love?

The information which fills the silence of the listening heart is the wordless and unknowable nature of the mystery of all that there is in its full hallowed sanctity. Practicing this meditation, you open your self to your deeper, truer, mysterious Self, the very heart of all that there is. And because this mystery has been potentiated to communicate within illusion, each time you move into this silent presence it speaks a new mystery, a new message of life and wholeness. It does not take a specific credo to move into the pregnant, mysterious silence. It takes a desire to seek the truth which is great enough for you to choose to spend the precious coin of time in listening to the silent voice of your true nature, which guidance enunciates wordlessly to the resonating seat of mystery and holiness within you.

You choose not to have a faith; rather, those who live a life in faith choose to be faithful in their practice of the presence of truth, their practice of the presence of love. The one known as Jesus was accosted by temptations from the voice of fear known in this myth as the devil, Satan, in the wilderness. The one known as Jesus would not converse with this principle of negativity and fear, but spurned each temptation and said, "Get thee behind me." The conversation that you seek, then, (for one must converse with the mystery) is the conversation with love. As you choose daily to be faithful, you choose not this and that, but rather, you choose to believe that all is well and all will be well. You are seated and grounded in this faith by the practice of the presence of Love itself, as guidance brings it to you.

This instrument prays each day words which have meaning to it. We find the sentiments valuable in this context and so repeat this personal prayer without intending that each learn its words, but rather find the concept to be more accessible. This is the prayer:

"Come, Holy Spirit, fill the heart of your faithful and kindle in her the fire of your love. Send forth your Spirit and she shall be created; and you shall renew the face of the earth, O Creator, Who, by the light of the Holy Spirit did instruct the heart of the faithful so may she be ever wise and enjoy its consolation."[21]

She prays through the one known as Jesus, but we say to you that guidance is the Consciousness of Jesus the Christ. This Consciousness is transforming and life-giving, and we recommend to your own guidance the seed which is at the heart of this prayer; that is, that there is an Intelligence moving through all that there is which does indeed create each of you day by day, perfectly, as much as you can allow it. And that as you bear witness in a life of faith to this true nature that continually transforms perfectly all that there is, you may see the face of creation blossom and expand infinitely in love reflected in love. So, as you bring down into the life of faith the energy, the spirit of love which strengthens the heart that it may move further downward into each darkened place within, so the reflection upward begins and the heart is informed by the energies originally locked in lower centers; and the heart frees this energy that it may make its return to the alpha and the omega of all that there is. So, all things from beginning to ending of creation are implicit in this present moment, and the cycle or circle which is process and learning and growth reflects in your faithful hearts the eternal present moment in which love is the whole nature of all unified consciousness.

May you remain and abide in patient and persistent blindness, accepting and blessing each darkness, each fear, each sorrow, each suffering unto death, that the work of creation may express through you the life of the self that is love, in this moment and ever. May you through this process day by day so seat yourself in loving acceptance and faith that all is well, that Love itself may flow through you as light through the panes of the lantern, so that those about you may see this light and turn to this light within themselves. You are witnesses expressing in a world which has need of witnesses. What shall you witness? My friends, love one another and for the first time, rest. You are home.

We open the session now to queries. Are there queries at this time?

C: Q'uo has spoken several times this weekend about the flow of light, the crystalline green mixing with the lower chakra colors, and has referred to the colors and the flow again today. Could Q'uo speak a little more to this topic of opening our hearts?

Q'uo: I am Q'uo. The use of the colors in our teachings is not only a true reflection of quanta of vibration and fields of vibration. On a more literal level, this device is an organizational tool which enables us to offer information by the use of an organized system of images which can be visualized. We use the movement of these colors to delineate the way in which one field of energy, which is a portion of a complex of energy fields which is each entity, may by its hierarchical position move into a position in which it benignly and benevolently overshadows the less strong and less true energy field which is the self in one particular distortion, whether that distortion be of the body, mind or the emotions or the spirit. Working with visualizable images, such as light in its coloration, we then are able to offer ways in which each seeker may practice these movements of energy to the benefit of the whole person, which may be symbolized by the unbroken white light.

Would you please direct us further, my sister?

C: I can't at this time.

Q'uo: And we would simply say, in response to a reminder by this instrument, that this kind of visualization is that which is helpful in working at

---

[21] Reference is pending.

the cellular level with organisms and energies and essences within those energies which may not be native to those energies. Illness or disease is often that which is partially a product of the discontinuity or unnatural configurations of energy fields, or to put it more simply, a system of energy blockages which manifests as disease.

It is also common that in illness there are essences not naturally found within the energy complex of the self, but which are thoughtforms created by continually dwelling upon some fear or negative thought. This thoughtform then becomes independent of the entity and returns as an enemy of wholeness, bringing with it, if enough energy is involved, other thoughtforms which delight in suffering. To visualize the flow of light to each cell of the organism in each of its energy configurations from the lowest to the highest, from the most physical to the most metaphysical or non-physical, is an art in that each healer finds its own system of visualization, its own language, whether it be color or other ways of visualizing the movement and overshadowing nature of hierarchical energies.

This is not fundamentally different from that which we have offered concerning the healing of the incarnation of the self day by day, but may be seen to be an extension which, in those who feel the call and gift to heal, may be used and through experience refined as a way of loving.

Is there another query at this time?

(No further queries.)

Q'uo: We are those of Q'uo. As this series of workings draws to a close, we stretch out our love as arms of blessing and thanksgiving to each who has moved many everyday hindrances to one side in order to be together for this working. Our love and blessings to each, and our praise and thanks to the One Who is all that there is that we experienced this beauty together. May we all go forth to serve and to love, strengthened by this sharing. We would leave this instrument that the one known as Barbara may allow the one known as Aaron to offer benediction and a closing to these proceedings. We are those of the principle known to you as Q'uo. And rejoicing, we leave each in the love and the light of the one infinite Creator. Adonai, my friends, Adonai.

Aaron: I am Aaron.

Although it is a bit dissonant to the closing of this talk, I would like to offer one thought to C's question and Q'uo's answer about light on a cellular level. You see the chakra center of the body as a rainbow. If there is distortion, perhaps in the second chakra, the orange segment of the rainbow is muddied; the light not shining clearly, as the chakra itself is not spinning freely. You have many energy meridians through your body. Some of those are junction meridians and some lead off most specifically from one chakra or another. Thus, when I look at your bodies I see patterns of light. All the cells in your bodies reflect those patterns. If there is a cell in a part of your body physically distant from the second chakra but that is part of that meridian, the organ meridian of the spleen chakra, then the distortion in the spleen chakra is reflected in that cell. Each cell carries that same rainbow, but with a bit of difference.

If I might offer as example the idea of a color overlay of the body. First, color each chakra, just that point. Then with a transparent plastic overlay, lay over the whole pathway of the meridians of that chakra the color overlay related to that chakra. Do this everywhere in the body so that in some places there is the clear light of that particular chakra, in others there are overlaps of two or three or even more centers where the meridians join. Now take every single cell in that body and within it implant that same rainbow. Where there is the spleen-chakra meridian, the rainbow has an orange overlay. Where there is the heart-chakra meridian, there is a green overlay in the rainbow.

If the second chakra is blocked and that orange light is muddy, it will appear muddy in every single cell in the body. But the effect is doubled in those areas of orange overlay, those areas related most specifically to the spleen chakra, because you have muddy color over muddy color. The distortion from that chakra may manifest itself in any cell in the body, but is especially prone to manifest itself in those cells where there is double effect: muddy orange over muddy orange.

I share this with all of you in the hope that you may begin to understand the interconnectedness of your thoughts, emotions, physical sensations, cellular body and the state of your spiritual awareness and openness. You cannot clarify the lower chakras only by the openness of the upper chakras. However, when the upper chakras are open there is simply more light brought into the whole body. You must still be willing to move into the specific center where there is distortion and to work with great courage with that distortion, to work with the specific issues that create distortion.

But all of these centers are connected. If you work to correct that distortion while ignoring the upper centers, you are merely working on a body instead of an intactness of body, mind and spirit. The more awareness you can bring to this being that you are as a whole—as this angel in its earthsuit of divinity and humanness—with each moment, the more lovingly you can bring healing to where healing is needed.

There has been one unasked question amongst you to which I wish briefly to attend. You hear us speaking of these pathways to faith. From deep within some of you comes the memory of that pain in this or a past lifetime when the darkness seemed so all-encompassing that it felt as if prayer or song, reaching to God, were impossible. So there is this question: "When there is a glimmer of light, I can remember that the light is there and reconnect myself to that light. What, when the darkness is total? Where do I find help in these moments of my deepest fear, of my deepest immersion in the illusion of separation?"

My dear ones, I would ask you to remember in that heaviest darkness of your deepest grief or physical or emotional anguish that the night is always darkest before the dawn. This will pass. It takes only the smallest opening of the heart to reconnect and to begin to allow light to flow once again.

Most of you are familiar with that beautiful writing, *The Dark Night of the Soul*, by St. John of the Cross.[22] You must pass through this dark night. You each experience it in a different way. It is not offered as burden nor even, as some of you are wont to think, as quiz. It simply is: darkness, illusion, fear … Finding yourself in that darkness, you have been offered the fullest opportunity to practice. If it is impossible at that moment to practice faith, simply practice being.

In that moment of darkness you are wont to ask, "Why this darkness?" You have a sense that if you could but understand the darkness, you could protect yourself from it. Such thinking only further strengthens the illusion of self. Can you sit there in that darkness and simply know, "Here I sit in darkness and I will wait. I needn't fight with the darkness, needn't try to push it away. I needn't grasp even at faith."

My brother/sister Q'uo has spoken of prayer leading into the experience, not just of faith but of the truest knowing of yourself as the divine Self, of meditation leading you into that experience of the divine Consciousness within yourself. But sometimes meditation just leads to more silence. The seeker wants to reconnect with the Divine. What, when a meditation experience does not offer that and the darkness seems to close in?

Time and time again, the seeker goes to sit at the table of the Lord, knowing that sometimes a banquet will be offered and sometimes the table will remain bare. It is not the seeker's place to choose which will be, only to sit with as much love as it can give at that bare table and trust that this is the experience that is given and it will suffice. It is not the seeker's place to cling to the banquet, only to fully enjoy that experience of deepest connection when it is experienced and then let it go.

If you would cling to penetrating the illusion, allowing the experience of faith because of the beauty of the connection, then faith becomes dependent on those experiences. But faith exists independent of experience. Faith resides within your heart. It is the clearest statement I know that the Divine is within you, that you are angels. Just faith, faith expressed as the willingness to sit in darkness if darkness is what is there, without need to grasp at the light, but willingness to open the doors and allow in the light. Do you see the difference?

There is night and there is day. If you open the door and it is still dark, can you sit and wait patiently until the dawn? I know that this is, as your saying goes, far easier said than done. When you sit in this dark night filled with anguish because of some very deep pain in your personal life, it is very hard not to want to get rid of that pain, not to want to grasp at feelings of comfort and the presence of God. True faith just sits, knowing that God expresses itself through the darkness and not just through the light, and knowing that the dawn does follow the darkest night.

Yes, there is preference for the light. It is more comfortable. But when you huddle in fear and grasp at the light and then say, "If the light is not given,

---

[22] Reference is pending.

that denies faith, that denies God," then you are truly enclosing yourself in deeper darkness. Then you are closing the doors and shutters so that when the dawn begins you cannot appreciate its arrival.

I understand how hard this is for the human. I have been through the process of incarnation and have strong memory of the pain of such darkness. I can only tell you that the route out of that darkness is your willingness to be patient and trust: "There is that in this darkness which can serve and teach me. I will wait patiently with it, keeping my heart open, keeping the windows and doors open until the light reappears."

Q'uo has spoken several times this weekend of an upward spiral. I would ask you all to remember that all beings are on this upward spiral—not just positively-polarized beings, all beings. This is very hard for you to understand in this present third-density state. You see that of negativity in the world and feel that is a distortion, pulling away from the spiral and going downward. All beings are on this upward spiral. Negativity is a distortion, and yet even those beings that are most highly negatively polarized are sparks of the Divine and will eventually find their way fully into the light. The darkness that they draw around them and into which they entice others may be a sidetrack of the spiral, used for that being's particular path. But it is still a sidetrack that is spiraling upward.

Remembering this allows you to find more tolerance for the negativity that is seemingly external to you in the world, and for your own fear, anger and other heavy emotions. When you create the duality of good and evil and see the darkness as a spiraling downward, it enhances not just resistance, but a lack of compassion for that darkness. It enhances the fear that closes the heart. When you see negative distortion in illness of the physical body or the loss of a loved one, or some other great grief or pain, remember: "This is part of the spiral to the light. Can I embrace even this distortion and offer love to it? Can I just be patient with the experience of it? I don't even have to understand it, just to allow its presence without hatred. The presence of negative distortion does not need to be a catalyst for hatred in me. It can be a catalyst for remembering to offer love."

(Pause)

Aaron: I am Aaron. Remember your divinity, my dear ones, through prayer, meditation, whatever connects you. I earnestly hope that you will allow yourself the experience of that divinity on a daily basis while remembering that if you sit in prayer or meditation and experience only this human sitting in prayer or meditation, then that is what you need to experience. For that moment, that is your experience of divinity. Trust it will unfold as it needs to. You need only be present.

I believe that in some of your gambling centers you would find a sign hanging that says, "You must be present to win." You must be present to win: present to win out over fear, present to deepen faith, present with whatever this mind/body/spirit complex is experiencing in this moment, present with as much love as is possible. And then you cannot help but win, and find your way home.

I echo Q'uo in offering my deepest thanks to you for your presence with us in these three days, for sharing the deepest questions of your hearts and inviting us to speak our thoughts. I again re-echo Q'uo: What we have shared is our opinion and not authority. We offer it in loving service and ask that you take what is useful to you. My love to each of you, and I bow in deepest honor to each of you for the love and purity that you bring to your work. That is all. ❧

L/L Research

L/L Research is a subsidiary of Rock Creek Research & Development Laboratories, Inc.

P.O. Box 5195
Louisville, KY 40255-0195

www.llresearch.org

Rock Creek is a non-profit corporation dedicated to discovering and sharing information which may aid in the spiritual evolution of humankind.

ABOUT THE CONTENTS OF THIS TRANSCRIPT: This telepathic channeling has been taken from transcriptions of the weekly study and meditation meetings of the Rock Creek Research & Development Laboratories and L/L Research. It is offered in the hope that it may be useful to you. As the Confederation entities always make a point of saying, please use your discrimination and judgment in assessing this material. If something rings true to you, fine. If something does not resonate, please leave it behind, for neither we nor those of the Confederation would wish to be a stumbling block for any.

CAVEAT: This transcript is being published by L/L Research in a not yet final form. It has, however, been edited and any obvious errors have been corrected. When it is in a final form, this caveat will be removed.

© 2009 L/L Research

Sunday Meditation
March 28, 1993

Group question: The question today has to do with "If only I had done such and such in a certain situation, in my past, in a situation about which I now feel very badly, it would probably have turned out differently." We tend, as seekers, to beat ourselves up frequently and badly by this kind of thinking. What we would like today, Q'uo, is perception and perspective on what positive impulse it is in the seeker that causes him or her to say "If only I had done this" or "I should have done that." Is there some positive quality that we can accentuate, is there some negative or self-defeating quality there that we can be aware of to de-accentuate, and do seekers of truth really have too much to be concerned about in the way of psychic greetings or attacks in this area? How much of our worries of "I should have done that" or "If only I had done this" come from psychic greetings or are most of these of our own creations?

(Carla channeling)

I am Q'uo. Greetings in the light and in the love of the one infinite Creator. We are very glad to be called to your session of working this day and to join in your meditation and share the vibration of your circle. We thank you for the privilege of being asked to share our thoughts. In doing so we ask that each preserve its own free will and discriminate between those thoughts which aid and between those which do not, leaving those that do not behind.

We find that your query at heart is one which concerns that principle which is the—we correct this instrument—which is perhaps the most difficult spiritual principle for entities in third density to grasp. That principle is the charity of forgiveness. When any query comes concerning regrets of the past, the regrets themselves and the emotions and mental formations concerning these regrets circle about the third-density misunderstanding due to the heavy illusion of third density of the principle of forgiveness. It is felt that though one may be forgiven by the infinite Creator, that one is not thoroughly or completely forgiven by the self or by another for there remains the memory which, according to the distorted understanding in third density, would disappear or transform itself if the forgiveness had truly taken place. This is a misconception.

The great call of third density for objectification of forgiveness, acceptance and control of one's surroundings has been answered at various points in your third-density culture's long history by a series of those who came to forgive, redeem, accept and transform. We feel none of these was truer in its Christhood than the one known as Jesus the Christ which is the pattern or mythological structure into which each entity present was born. Each has made widely varying use of this mythological structure, however, it is real, for example, to this instrument that because it was absolved after a confession during this Lent season, it has begun a new life and is forgiven. This, however, does not stop this instrument from the repetition of regrets, thoughts of "if only," and desires that the past could be played again.

So we have the situation where forgiveness is intellectually considered as being accomplished but within the emotional portion of the mind, body and spirit the forgiveness is not believed because the self deeply rejects the forgiveness since there remains unhealed memory. You have perhaps heard us before speak of something we call "healing of the incarnation." In your third-density incarnative experience this is the heart of work in consciousness, for if the incarnation be healed the potentiated and polarized servant is then free to offer with purity the life to the infinite Creator. As each looks upon its "if onlys" we ask that each consider that these unhealed memories dim and make tenuous the pure light which is the manifestation of love, which empowers each servant of the one infinite Creator.

Let us turn and look at the workings of the mind complex, the phenomenon of remembrance of unhealed memory on a continuous basis. That is, when the same regret or kind of regret keeps recurring without being solved or dissolved you may turn to your computers to grasp the nature of the error. To the computer it is not an error. The computer gives to the view screen that which has not been cleared from the view screen. When the situation is such that an entity thinks a series of thoughts frequently enough to create a kind of program the accidental or aided entry into any portion of the program will cause the program to run itself through. If the program is not cleared after it has run it will repeat. If the program is preempted by looking at other material that is not cleared then when the other material is cleared the program immediately again appears on the screen. It has not ever left; the computation has not been completed.

So we are describing to you a situation in which the sorrowing or grieving entity creates a thought-form which can be triggered into appearing seemingly at random, whenever portions of the initial part of the program are run. If one can think further perhaps each can remember times when not only did one set up regrets [to] run but before the appetite for such a regret had been satisfied other regrets came into the program and were also run. Thus, if this program is not cleared it can gradually take precedence over all other programs and in extremity can cause the mind of an entity to become diseased. This is all due to the difficulty entities in the third density have at forgiving themselves.

Now, each has had experience with complete forgiveness of others by the self. Each has achieved forgiveness with regard to others who have seemingly caused catalyst to occur for the self which was painful. With the passage of time the words "I forgive you" become entirely and wholly true. The memory remains but it has been healed. Why then is it difficult to imagine healing one's own memories? We feel that it is largely because the self, if privy to the self's constant displays of, shall we say, humanity, not meaning to insult the creature that humankind is but indicating that it is a flawed or distorted or relativistic portion of a flawed, imperfect, or relativistic illusion, all manifestation whatsoever then are flawed.

This is difficult to accept. The thinker wishes the self not to be flawed, not to be relative, the seeker wishes to be whole, to be absolute, and so the seeker in truth is beyond the realm of the illusion. Yet each came here to pay close attention to the illusion, with all of its difficulties, and one of the points of business for each seeker in its work in consciousness is the work on achieving the healing of memories, the acceptance of the stream of incarnative experience as it has been experienced, and the forgiveness of the illusion and the manifested self for being flawed. The hardness of heart comes because there is not the instinct to move directly into the heart and open the self to the wholehearted request for forgiveness. Though the religious expression has enormous amounts to recommend it, the dependency upon religious expression to objectify the process of forgiveness to the greater Self—as an objectified and solidified other-self—numbs the inner sense of truth to the fact that this process of forgiveness is not external to the self.

The forgiveness by the one infinite Creator may be religiously expressed by another self to one, yet the effects of true forgiveness of memories are inconsequential unless it is also realized that this external expression of forgiveness reflects, and is only a reflection of, the actual process that has been transacted upon the metaphysical or time/space planes in the portion of the being in which energy is blocked and the computer is stuck.

Therefore, we ask that those with unhealed memories see this as an order of business to be addressed. The self must in some way open the heart to the self's need and ask with no reservation for forgiveness, and more than that, be prepared to accept that forgiveness and to drop that program and allow its spiritual energy to dissipate, allow the past to become the past. We recommend that this kind of work be done promptly and persistently and be given priority, for sorrows and hard-heartedness may make poor combination of guests, and though they speak much they do not make a good company. The time which is precious in each incarnation need not be spent with such guests if the work be done.

There are reasons that this work is work well done. Firstly, to allow any thought-form to have control over the screen, if you will, of the mind's eye is to release the stream of experience to flow into limited pools of stagnated, situational experience where nothing new is learned. Thought-forms take the place of acquiring new and transformative information. Third density is for making choices, not for repeating the same program over and over with no clearing or solution or moving on.

Secondly, if held in mind with enough tenacity and allowed to run within the mind's eye, such programs can cause the need for another self which then must go through the entire trail of manifested learning, every density. To send a self and a universe off into a parallel or split existence weakens the strength of existence now being experienced, removes some portion of the limitless and eternal self which had been the spark of the manifested self which you are, thus making the process of spiritual evolution more complex and more baffled, that is, less open to pure experience.

Thirdly, there is, when an "if only" has taken the mind repeatedly away, a kind of scarring which is obvious [and which] entities of either polarity from other densities can see, and if there is for some reason an entity or entities which does indeed have reason to greet an entity, such regrets are excellent targets for the temptation to become lost in them and take the rhythm and the impetus away from that polarized and potentiated action which has generated inner light to attract what this instrument calls the "loyal opposition" in the first place.

My friends, sorrow and sighing are deep within each entity just as laughter and glee are deep within your makeup. The purpose of incarnation is not to avoid either the tears or the laughter, either the sorrow or the joy; the goal rather circles around the respect and compassion which one may offer to each emotion felt without preferring one to the other, without denying any pure emotion. We ask you to love, accept and forgive yourselves and be brave and bold enough to open and allow the healing of the self, the healing of memories, the healing of the incarnation. Into such concerns does the light of love's spirit move.

One who seeks healing, who seeks loving, is never alone. There are strong forces which come in the name of love to aid, support and strengthen the attempts of the self to realize and know love. Express within the self the request for such help and you shall have, as this instrument says, a crowd of witnesses whose only hope is to deepen and strengthen this healing effort. Relax into that ambiance, feel the energy of those who truly come to serve those who seek the truth and the light and let your heart become easy.

We do not sense any queries at this time. If there are no queries we shall take our leave of you. Are there queries at this time?

(Pause)

We are those of Q'uo and thank each again. We wish you many blessings, we wish you good work within your consciousness, we encourage you and give you a hug of the heart, and leave you in love and in the infinite light of the one infinite Creator. We are those known to you as the principle of Q'uo. Adonai, adonai. ❧

L/L Research

L/L Research is a subsidiary of Rock Creek Research & Development Laboratories, Inc.

P.O. Box 5195
Louisville, KY 40255-0195

www.llresearch.org

Rock Creek is a non-profit corporation dedicated to discovering and sharing information which may aid in the spiritual evolution of humankind.

ABOUT THE CONTENTS OF THIS TRANSCRIPT: This telepathic channeling has been taken from transcriptions of the weekly study and meditation meetings of the Rock Creek Research & Development Laboratories and L/L Research. It is offered in the hope that it may be useful to you. As the Confederation entities always make a point of saying, please use your discrimination and judgment in assessing this material. If something rings true to you, fine. If something does not resonate, please leave it behind, for neither we nor those of the Confederation would wish to be a stumbling block for any.

CAVEAT: This transcript is being published by L/L Research in a not yet final form. It has, however, been edited and any obvious errors have been corrected. When it is in a final form, this caveat will be removed.

© 2009 L/L Research

Sunday Meditation
April 25, 1993

Group question: The question today concerns how we get ourselves back in balance when we feel out of sorts, both physically, emotionally and metaphysically. What techniques could we use to regain our center so that we can get a sense of purpose and direction in our lives when we feel there are difficulties, whether it is illness, or money problems, or insecurity about what the next day will bring? What can we do to regain balance, or is it possible to live in a metaphysical balance; is it necessary to be somewhat out of balance to continue making progress? If so, this "angst" as it has been called, is the driving force, but then what is the proper proportion? Is there a need to be concerned in the area, when we are out of balance, is there an action we can take to regain this metaphysical balance?

(Carla channeling)

We are those of Q'uo. Greetings in the love and in the light of the one infinite Creator. We are so delighted to be within your circle of seeking this day, and to be sharing in your fellowship and in the experiences which you have at this time of your year as the blooms fill the garden.

For us to discuss being in balance is to move first into a perception of the balance of the sphere. It is only human, shall we say, to think of balance as having the characteristic of balancing between two legs, as you do when you walk. In actuality, balance is more a characteristic of realizing the center of one's orb of beingness so that all of the happenstances of incarnational catalyst simply cause one to roll with the energies which are being manifested and expressed by the environment in the self. It is helpful for you to place that model of the self as the sphere in the mind simply in order to see that, metaphysically speaking, balance is not a matter of falling far, for the metaphysical being, when self-realized to any extent, is infinitely curved and not that with protrusions which catch one and bias one.

Perhaps one may see the stresses and harsher experiences of incarnational catalyst as being that which tends to more and more compactly press into the center all parts of the circle or orb of being. Perhaps from this beginning you may see that we do not have the opinion that to be in balance is to be static or fixed in position. Indeed, when all is well there is the feeling of process, the experience of ongoing energy flow. This feeling of beingness constantly moving and evolving in kind is the hope of one who sets out to know peace while seeking the truth. Such a nature is certainly not going to be fixed even if value is still held in the kind of peacefulness which is stationary. The desire to seek the truth quickly removes the probability of remaining in metaphysical place for long.

So we offer you the image of yourself as a spiritual being, as a sphere of energy which will always be rolling, yet whose center is more and more accurately and gracefully sensed so that as the abrasions of experiencing the illusion more and more refine the near-perfect roundness of your spirit you become more and more of the nature of the Infinite and less and less of the nature of that which is concerned with limitations.

What keeps a sphere from rolling? What would cause the seekers of truth to find themselves stuck? There are two categories of difficulties, the first being the declivities of the happenstances of your incarnational catalyst. There are small and large valleys into which this entity moves, only to find that there is no further downhill route and happenstance alone shall not aid in the process of moving onward one iota. Then it is that it is easy to fear, for in order to smooth the metaphysical self and be able to roll with the punches, as it were, work has not then been done on being disagreeable with circumstance, the impulse having been trained over and over to see what is occurring, to cooperate, to adapt to what is occurring and to act within the situation as you find it. Occasionally this excellent behavior lands one in a hollow and fear is very quickly offered a place around the campfire with you.

Not to feel fear when feeling trapped by circumstance is unlikely. Therefore, let us look at what kind of companion fear may be. If fear be seen as an enemy, then it must be fought, and there are no true winners in a fight with fear, for it feeds upon itself, and if great attention be paid to it, it grows even greater. If fear be seen to be a guest, then the trappings of civility are found to be wise as well as courteous, for fear is after all a familiar friend, one to be greeted, offered a drink, a bite to eat, a warm place by the fire. "Of course you are here, fear," you say, "Welcome to my world." Fear then flowers into a true friend and says, "Thank you. You see me and honor me. For that, thanks. In return, I communicate to you that you may stay here for a rest, for you may get ready to climb out of this hollow, and I will help you." Then brother fear can get behind that rolling self and aid in the climb out of that hollow circumstance.

(Pause)

I am Q'uo. We are having difficulty with this instrument. We ask your patience. We would appreciate a further tuning as this instrument deepens its state. We are those of Q'uo.

(A tuning song is sung by all.)

(Carla channeling)

We are those of Q'uo, and we thank you for aiding this instrument. We are again with this instrument in love and in light.

There are also those times when within the self there is the inner hollowing with inner stagnation or distress, the feeling of being stuck, this having not to do with circumstance or any outer manifestation. These are seasons of the soul and although they seem difficult and endless, they are extremely productive or potentially so. During these times, there is no true sense of balance, for the simple reason that the inner balance point, after a great deal of catalyst has been processed, is changing.

Often it puzzles those who experience these seasons of desert within, for the outer planes are halcyon and lovely, yet within all is certainly an arid waste. The negative reaction to this is often not true fear but rather a cold and *(inaudible)* discomfort, a feeling that one is truly unworthy, thirsty and unfed, in the spiritual sense. Again, it is well to make a friend of this discomfort, even to allow some focus upon the discomfort, a writing in a journal, or telling to oneself of just how this feels, for by doing so, by being attentive to these feelings of discomfort within, one helps one's own process of recentering according to one's emerging character.

We are attempting to give this instrument a vision of how the incarnational experience compact more and more beingness into the sphere of being so that the balance point does shift as entities become more polarized. We can only go so far with this imagery, and apologize for the limitations of this form of communication, but if you will picture a ball or field of energy in which there are shells of more and less density, and then see that this sphere has its cross-hatchings of energy and focuses of energy where lines cross, one may see that the learning that is done in an incarnation may compact one set of nodes of experience-gathering or another at different times, putting those portions under more pressure, and thus changing to some extent the way the sphere gets balanced.

The hope of entities who attempt to accelerate the rate of their evolution in spirit is to so live that the maximum amount of pressure is exerted upon the orb of self so that more and more and more of love may flow into or within the sphere or field of that which is your unique spiritual entity. Were you upon the path of service to self it would be important to study how to manipulate experience so that the balance point was not moved, but rather all energy would go to the perfection, or sheen, and the regularity of the sphere of being, these being attractant qualities. Because we speak to those upon the path of service to others, however, we assure each that it is not the point to attempt to look graceful or to seem centered, rather, dealing with times of feeling off-center or unbalanced the point is to make friends with this situation and involve the self in accepting and assimilating the growth, not with an eye to appearances but solely with the goal of so accepting and loving this discomfort of self that the stage is set for the process continuing.

After all, if you are scrambling out of a huge pothole in your spiritual road you cannot hope to look very graceful. Consider, you are being pushed from behind by Brother Fear, you have grown what little legs spheres might hope to wear so you may scrabble your way up to the surface of your spiritual path again. Where is it written that this posture is graceful? No, my friends, laugh and accept the sometimes grimy nature of the spiritual road with all its potholes. We mean by this to affirm that there is great use indeed in the disquieting experiences of being off balance, of being upset with the self, right up to the point where you as an entity have absorbed fully the material of the discomfort, have chewed through those issues that were part and parcel of removing you from your center. Indeed, to the spiritual seeker the straight and level road is a lovely thing but if it is endlessly peaceful and there is no perceived challenge the seeker turns and questions its path: is it learning enough? And it does well to do so for the seeker that asks, "Am I learning?" or, "Am I taking it easy?" is also moving into a potentiated desire for further catalyst, and that which is desired shall be received.

We encourage each to rejoice at the broad and pleasant landscape when the spiritual path is such. We encourage questioning this peace as means of potentiating any further learning that may be available. This is the way of accelerating the rate of spiritual learning. When difficulties strike and one is in the potholes of the spiritual path we encourage moving in a very conscious way into a closer rapport with the difficulties of that pothole, whatever they may be, and a friendly alliance with fear. See it, accept it, and it will not limit you but be your friend.

Above all, whether on the broad and beautiful sunny path or in the depth of a dry, rocky waste we encourage the consciousness that the Creator is with you, for this is the true center at all times in or out of balance. The seemingly smooth and the seemingly rough both alike are manifestation of perfect love. No matter where your curiosity and your sense of adventure move you in spiritual seeking you are the same distance from love that is no distance. All you experience is love, all with which you experience is love; you are love perceiving love. Yet within your illusion there is subject and object and the verb between. Use this illusion, use this separation and allow the verb between to be love, allow [yourself] to enter into loving relationship with good times and with bad, with positive and with negative. Become involved and active within each portion of your spiritual seeking. The more you can embrace your condition the more you shall radiate that love which is of the essence of you, of the situation, and of any and all agencies whatsoever.

And my friends, what a service this is. To be able to bear witness in good and in bad weather, to the sun which forever shines, to the warmth of love which never grows cold, this is to be a sun to those who may share your circumstances, this is to radiate through your physical, mental and emotional beings that spiritual truth that you are love and you are surrounded by love.

This instrument is asking us to finish our speaking, and we realize we must do that. We thank each for the privilege of speaking with you and encourage each in the sometimes difficult process of seeking the truth. We are with you in that search and we share love with you in each and every moment. We would close the channeling for this session through the one known as Jim. We would now leave this instrument. We are those of Q'uo.

(Jim channeling)

I am Q'uo, and greet each again in love and in light. It is our privilege to ask if there may be may any further queries to which we may speak before we take our leave of this group. Is there another query at this time?

Carla: So my feelings of pretty severe self-criticism during this time are a season where I am trying to assimilate some kind of changes, is that right? Is it important that I know what that change is?

I am Q'uo, and I am aware of your query, my sister. Eventually, within your total beingness, it is necessary that you understand each change so that the total spectrum of your experiences will have meaning and integrity. However, at this time, as you are in a midst of such change, it is not as important that you know the specific nature of the change as it is that you prepare yourself for change by opening your attitude and your heart to that which is being born within you. You welcome a new being. This kind of change is that which occurs a number of times during the seeker's life experience. The conscious seeker will be more prepared to endure the rigors of change than the entity who is as yet still seeking in an unconscious or automatic fashion. Thus, it is important at this time to simply open the self in love and acceptance of all those difficulties you face, whether they are generated from without your being or from within your being, for in truth all that you perceive you personalize in a fashion which blends perceiver and perceived.

Thus, your experiences become a part of you and as you progress in your journey of seeking you will find that this blending of experience occurs most easily when there is as little resistance and as great vulnerability to it as you can stably withstand and accept within your being. It is not easy to place oneself within the swirling waters of change, for it is easy to believe that one may drown or be washed ashore in a distant location unfamiliar to the present self. However, we can assure each of you that you have placed within your incarnational patterns these opportunities for rebirth of this child-like self that laughs with glee at all catalyst that it perceives, looking at the world as a place in which there is endless opportunity for experience and excitement.

This child-like nature is balanced and focused by the maturing sensibility of a seeker. This is the strength of experience, catalyst which has been processed and placed carefully within the personality as a secure building block is placed within any builded structure. However, this maturing and adult-like attitude can also be an inhibitor to further change, in that it wishes to maintain that which it has and that which it is, for it is difficult enough to accept oneself as one sees the self, and to be asked to accept that which is perhaps more unknown within the self is an added challenge, which again requires the attitude of the child, looking at all about it without fear and with complete acceptance.

Is there a further query, my sister?

Carla: Just when … when I am in a state like this, any good that I ever was at meditating—and I don't have the experience at meditating and I am not even sure I should call it meditation—I did notice you did not talk about meditation too much this time, you talked more about just remembering. Could you address the problem of not being able so well to meditate?

I am Q'uo, and I am aware of your query, my sister. As we spoke previously, the experience of change, especially when this experience is enhanced by a cyclical movement within the deeper being, is one which is felt to be chaotic and confusing, irritating and almost unable to be borne. Thus it is not surprising that one's meditations would also be affected by this confusing and chaotic experience, however, be assured that as you place yourself in a position to meditate and to open yourself to the experiences of love about you, that no matter what your perception of your experience of meditation might be there is work accomplished there, not just in the intention to meditate nor in the actual practice, whether perceived as well or poorly accomplished, but in those deeper portions of yourself to which contact is made during meditation, in order that these portions of your deeper self might be able to have their influence upon your perceptions in even the subtlest manner is the opportunity that is most helpful to the seeker of truth. For as you travel through the deeper portions of your mind and open yourself to any experience that you find there, you conduct an harmonizing expedition, shall we say, bringing together various resources that are uniquely yours, and applying them in a manner which is as mysterious as the heart of creation itself seems to each. Yet, in all the mystery and confusion, the intention, the practice, and the contact with the deeper portions of the self will provide you with the metaphysical food to fuel your journey further.

Is there a further query, my sister?

Carla: No, Q'uo, thank you very much.

I am Q'uo, and again we thank you, my sister. Is there another query at this time?

Questioner: I am just curious, Q'uo, if it is correct to say that when there is a great deal of change going on the inside then what seems to be happening on the outside is stagnant or calm. Also, the opposite of it, where there is stagnation on the inside that is mirrored by a great deal of catalyst happening to the outer self. Is that a correct observation or would you comment on it?

I am Q'uo, and am aware of your query, my brother. In the general sense, we would agree with your summation of the experience of change, for as you perceive change occurring within yourself this change has in many cases already seated itself within the deeper portions of your being and this change is now making itself apparent to your emotions and your senses, and you begin to analyze with your mind that which you experience. It is much like the aftereffect that you see as the change within the daily round of activities. As you experience the calmer waters in your daily activities you may also assume that there are inner preparations being made for future change as current catalyst is accreted, and as it is well or not so well processed there is the building of momentum so that at what you would call a future time there can be another shifting of perception that will allow you a clearer view of your path to love.

Is there a further query, my brother?

Questioner: I will ask your comment on this concept. When a change is occurring that is already being processed by the deeper self, and it only comes up to manifest as an aftereffect through the conscious mind, is it then to any advantage trying to use the conscious mind to process whatever comes up in it? What is the place of those concepts coming up in the conscious mind in the overall picture of experiencing and processing this catalyst?

I am Q'uo, and I am aware of your query, my brother. As in so much that you experience in this illusion, acceptance is the key in all of your growth and service. Thus, as you experience the washing about and spinning chaos that change brings to the outer self and which is perceived by the conscious mind, this conscious mind is best used which opens the self to acceptance of that which is occurring.

There is little that the conscious mind can add to the deeper changes that occur within. The conscious mind can inhibit and make more difficult the seeking of change. The conscious mind is much like the entity—we give this instrument the picture of the one who surfs the great waves of your ocean upon a small board, and which places the self at the crest of the wave when it begins, and shoots for the tunnel of the breaking wave in order to continue the experience of surfing the wave. The conscious mind, as it accepts the balance necessary to remain on the board and the board within the wave, can enhance the experience by moving with it. To fight or overexert the analysis is the equivalent of shifting the weight to inappropriate position upon the board, and to risking potential capsizing, shall we say.

Thus, it is well to be able to move with any experience, whether one feels that a valuable change is occurring or not. One does what one can and what feels right and well and balanced within the heart of the being, then one releases all responsibility for action and reaction and moves with experience as the swimmer upon the board moves with the power of the waves.

Is there another query, my brother?

Questioner: No, Q'uo, I would just add that I appreciate your tireless encouragement and kind words that bring in light, especially to me sometimes when I seem to be falling off the board all the time.

I am Q'uo, and we are extremely grateful to you as well, my brother, for the opportunity of speaking to those areas which are concerns in your path of seeking.

Is there a final query at this time?

(Pause)

I am Q'uo, and we thank each of you for inviting our presence to your circle of seeking this day. We realize that each of you is a diligent and conscientious seeker of truth, exerting every effort, applying every resource, and experiencing all that confronts you with the greatest amount of courage and honor. Yet we know that you feel, from time to time, that failure is your lot, and that you miss the mark far more frequently then you hit the mark. We would suggest to each of you that this may or may not be true, however, it is unimportant, for what is important is that you engage your experience with a whole heart and attempt to make some sense of all that occurs, knowing that all that occurs and all that exists exists within the greatest mystery one can imagine, and that there is at the heart of this mystery infinite love and support for all children of the one Creator that seek to return to their place of beginning, never knowing for sure until they have returned that they have never left.

Your experience is your glorification of the Creator and the food for your own soul that you engage your experience with a whole heart and with all of your strength is the most important quality of your illusion and is that which shall serve you well in all of your learning and serving.

At this time we shall take our leave of this instrument and this group, leaving each as always in the love and in the light of the one infinite Creator. We are known to you as those of Q'uo. Adonai my friends. Adonai.

Sunday Meditation
May 2, 1993

Group question: The question this afternoon has to do with the concept of the new mind, the unblemished, the virgin mind, the mind that exists before experience has made any mark on it. And we're wondering how this new mind could be called upon or used in our daily round of activities to help us process catalyst, make decisions, or simply be in the moment. What is the value of the new mind to each of us as we live our third-density lives?

(Carla channeling)

I am Q'uo. Greetings in the love and in the light of the one infinite Creator. How radiant all of you seem this day and how very glad we are to be called to this circle of seeking. We cannot thank you too much for allowing us to share our thoughts with you. We would ask, however, that each be fully aware that we speak only our opinions. We would ask each to choose from our offerings only those thoughts which have a personal ring of truth to you and allow the rest to fall aside, for we would not be a stumbling block because of our supposed authority, but must insist that we remain travelers upon the long and dusty road of spiritual seeking and the evolution of spirit.

We come to you to speak concerning the value of a certain attitude of mind. Let us speak first of the value of attitude. Consider if you will, how removed from innocence each of your actions and, indeed, your very thoughts have come. What a long trail of judgments and processes of perception go into your becoming aware of any single thought or bias. Consider how bland the texture of life as you experience it might be were you not to have this loss of innocence of the senses, and how each bias, each peculiarity of your particular mind-set or attitude has had to do with a realizing for you a way of experiencing which has, only to a minority extent, to do with the raw facts or unjudged data of any ideation or experience.

What gives the flavor to your menu of sense perceptions is an attitude. For so many among your peoples, the deeper attitudes, as you have been discussing this day, toward the self are attitudes of judgment. As you treat yourself you also treat others. There is all the difference in the world between experiencing the self remaining without opinion in relationship with another entity or an idea, and reacting to that person or idea. The attitude, then, is that which moves seemingly from the virgin or untried mind and toward a characteristic signature of a certain matrix or cluster of builded opinion which functions as a basic attitude towards life typical of spiritual principles. It is a paradox.

The value of new mind is that it is untested; yet to approach living the incarnational experience with this mind-set is to choose and intend to carry out living with an attitude. That which you seize upon as spiritual resource is, at the same time, your entry into polarity. The archetype of new mind is that which is as the struts and concrete and steel members of a structure, or like the skeleton of a structure. The archetype of new mind or the matrix of the mind is a solid structural member which is part of that structure which holds the potential for experiential process. Or to put that another way, it is a diagram in ideas rather than lines of drawing, of the processes of perception. The new mind is all about where perception begins and all about where perception ends, because new mind is that which begins each onset of experience.

Stop here and pay attention to your environment for a moment. We shall pause. We are those of Q'uo.

(Pause)

We are again with this instrument. We are those of Q'uo. Did your number of thoughts exceed one hundred? Perhaps. The possibilities, however, for noticing were almost endless. The hum of the busy electrical appliances, the various barely perceived scents of lilac and other flowers; of incense from earlier this day, of the newly cleaned floors, the smell of rain, the various sounds made by a circle of seated people breathing and making the small sounds; so much, just in physical sense perception. Then add to that the greedy amount of perception which is reached for by the mind, the emotions and the spirit's desire for truth. All of these things in one present moment and it is already gone, and there is another fullness to contemplate. If we are to praise attitudes—and we do indeed affirm that—then we must reconcile ourselves to defending or postulating the paradox of choiceless awareness which the phrase "new mind" denotes, and the value of choiceless awareness in making choices, which is what attitudes are about.

Let us illustrate. One entity approaches a fence. Because the entity is inwardly looking, the entity does not mind where it goes, so it turns and walks along the fence. This is not only choiceless awareness in that there is a graceful and seamless acceptance of a change of direction to cooperate with the electromagnetic fields of wood and metal. There is another entity which is determined to go towards something on the other side of the fence. This entity is choicelessly aware of the fence and nonetheless climbs over it. Depending upon an entity's attitude, however, it might be considered unfortunate to have the necessity of going along the fence line. It might be equally offensive to another to climb the fence. The more sharp the choice, the more precious the attitude of choiceless awareness. The more challenging the circumstance, the more useful is grace.

Each seeks beyond all reason due to what can be called a spiritual instinct. That instinct for a spiritual truth that endures is so strong that no system of distraction has kept each here present from attending to its demands. You by your very nature seek the source that is the key to your nature, seek to align yourselves squarely and truly with that which is most deeply true. The sum total of this, hopefully, is to create more and more awareness within the self of the abundance which your experience holds, for it is your nature, spiritually speaking, to open wider and wider as your experience deepens and accumulates, until all of creation is whole and entire within you, moment by moment.

In the concept of new mind, there is the connoted concept of the wholeness of that which comes before the processes of perception, and again is summed up as the end result of all working through of the processes of perception. In effect, then, the source and the ending of wholeness provide the basis for an attitude which then disposes the seeker to approach each present moment as if it were whole, entire and everlasting, which, by the way, each moment is. You live now in eternity, yet you are participating in a very deep and thorough-going illusion. This is not a particularly comfortable situation, of this we are fully aware. We remember this. Yet, how we regard with excitement each of your intense hopes and feelings, for without the illusion which you enjoy, with a much more light-filled and clear illusion informing us that all is well, we do not have the opportunity to live in blind faith. We have no particular value in choosing to think of ourselves as whole and not needing experiential processes to affirm our beingness, but you have the opportunity to express that blind faith that you actually are all right, that this or that destiny may befall you; nevertheless, your nature is whole. Experience merely tells you a story about this wholeness, and tells it more or less in order depending upon the amount of awareness of the process you have achieved and the amount of honesty towards the self and the self's true feelings that you have achieved.

You can look at the value of new mind also in regards to freedom. The freedom to choose, the right to have free will is basic to the entire process of choosing that which you shall desire. Unless you are truly free, the choices of what to desire mean little or nothing. It is our opinion that each entity's freedom of will is complete. Each being which is here has chosen to be here, has chosen to enter upon the challenge of an incarnational experience. As you process the occurrences that arise you make thousands of choices, most of which you make automatically, yet those choices you do make are so deeply impressed by the choice that moves beneath, around and beyond the manifested choices.

How very important, my friends, is such a choice as to accept everything that the present moment offers on faith. Yet, do not each of you do this in living a life? Does the attitude not come to you again and again? Accept … allow … assimilate … seek again … And do you not feel hope and joy springing from that affirmation made in ignorance, that, "Yes, this shall be acceptable, this shall be well. I am whole and can therefore encompass all." How can we achieve choiceless awareness? Each knows its own best ways. Meditation, contemplation, prayer, these are just words unless they be seized and vigorously applied. At any level you may see the whole or untouched cheek-by-jowl with the most amazing wilderness of conflicting opinion and conjecture.

You may choose that line of thinking, then, which suits you. But who chooses? Allow that thought to dissolve the intellect. Who chooses? If you choose, you are not choiceless. Yet the one who chooses, chooses most skillfully, most humanly, most full of polarity, when the choice is made with the new mind of entirety and wholeness. The one known as Jesus said, "I am come that you might have life, and have it more abundantly." There is in the Christ consciousness that choiceless acceptance of the Creator's will. There is for each entity the same potential for being true to and complete within the personal line of destiny that accompanies the complete freedom of choice—another paradox.

You see, when speaking of spiritual matters, it is important to speak in such a way that the intellectual mind is buffaloed into surrender and the heart within, that is a far better representation of new mind, become ascendant. Move now in thought deeper and deeper. Picture the mind as a tree and move down the trunk through the roots, deeper and deeper until the tiniest particles of root are interacting with the soil and creating more abundant life. Down, down, down, until you feel the thousands and thousands of years your species has existed within these hills, these rocks, these rivers, and these oceans. How many generations, how many lives here amid the grandeur of your experiential home for this tiny portion of infinite experience that is yours within the present illusion. Feel the strength of the roots of mind and the security with which the archetypical mind enters into the soil of eternity.

Now picture this life as light being drawn up into the archetypical mind of your selfhood. See beyond that selfhood where there is eternity meeting the racial mind and, deeper than that, the archetypical, and then see how it acquires familiarity within the particular as you move into the subconscious and then the conscious mind. Do you feel that connection now with eternity? Can you feel how sturdy is that root of mind we have called choiceless awareness this day, and how it does inform your being? For in one sense you are thousands and thousands of feelings and thoughts and processes of perception. In another sense just as true, you are one with all, you are within the Creator, the Creator is within you, and there is only unity.

We have led you a merry chase this day. Perhaps you may smile when you remember the twists and turns of this speaking. We hope that the humor of choosing choiceless awareness sinks deeply into each. For truly, spiritual evolution is, among other things, extremely full of humor. May each laugh and love the self, and that selfless One which makes all one. May each love each other and share in the processes of learning and encouraging each other.

We now would turn to the questions. For this purpose we would transfer to the one known as Jim. We thank this instrument. We are those of Q'uo, and leave this instrument at this time.

(Jim channeling)

I am Q'uo, and am again with this instrument. At this time we would ask if there may be any queries to which we may speak more briefly?

Carla: I'd like to ask if it might be said that through choiceless awareness, through choosing that choiceless awareness, we become truly creative in our third-density experience, more consciously creative?

I am Q'uo, and am aware of your query my sister. It is a feature, shall we say, of choiceless awareness that that quality of working with energy fields and ideas that you call creativity is given the greatest opportunity for expression, for this energy of thought and inspiration runs ceaselessly through each entity's life experience and is available for inspiration as the entity is able to open the self in an unguarded and vulnerable way to this energy. Whether this choice to experience awareness without choice is made in the conscious sense or in the subconscious sense, the entity is able to feel the pulse of its own being and to express this sensation in any avenue available, whether it be of the physical creation, or of the mental creation, or of the simple experience and expression of awareness internally.

Thus, in short, our answer is yes, my sister, your ability to become a co-creator is in direct proportion to your ability to open yourself to the possibilities of the moment, as you offer yourself in your beingness to each moment.

Is there a further query, my sister?

Carla: Thank you. I just wish to say that it seems that in our choiceless awareness we become—we realize that all of creation is something we do together and it inspires more honor and respect for our oneness. Thank you.

I am Q'uo. We agree with your eloquent statement, and thank you as well. Is there another query?

Carla: I would like to try. I didn't understand very much what I channeled. I had the idea that the archetype of the Matrix of the Mind, part of that image is that it's reaching out to the Potentiator of the Mind, so it seems like that there is a choice involved in the archetype. I'm a little confused. Could you speak to that at all?

I am Q'uo, and am aware of your query, my sister. There is in this first archetype the male entity, the magician standing, and as your cards show in their redesigned form, the entity holds a sphere. This sphere represents the nearness of spirit and the immanence of the archetype of the High Priestess, that is much as you would call the force which brings manifested spirit into the illusion as it potentiates thought and action in the conscious mind. The conscious mind has placed itself in this proximity with the hope, shall we say, that such potentiation shall occur. In this placing of itself in this proximity to the subconscious mind there is, indeed, a choice which has been made, much as you would make the choice for experiencing choiceless awareness. However, the choice in this case is made preincarnatively so that the Magician that is placed in proximity to the High Priestess has not of its own consciousness chosen, but has been, as are each of us, placed by the grace and creative power of the one Creator. The proximity, however, is that which presents the possibility of potentiation and the gaining of experience.

Is there a further query, my sister?

Carla: No, I'll have to read that, but thank you very much, Q'uo.

I am Q'uo, and we thank you once again, my sister. Is there another query?

(Pause)

I am Q'uo, and as we observe the depletion of queries, we shall take this opportunity to once again thank each present for inviting our company to your circle of seeking. We are greatly inspired by the dedication to seeking that each of you possesses and which each brings to this circle with such daring and creativity, shall we say. We look at each entity and see the valiant warrior walking carefully in the darkness of the illusion, examining that which surrounds and which moves within it, and offering that which is found with sincerity and a certain childlike glee. This is quite moving to each of us, for we are aware of the difficulties of your illusion and we appreciate the effort required to keep moving in the mystery and to offer the services to others without fail, each aiding each upon the journey.

At this time we shall take our leave of this group, leaving each, as always, in the love and in the light of the one infinite Creator. We are known to you as those of Q'uo. Adonai, my friends. Adonai. ✤

Special Meditation
May 6, 1993

Group question: The question this morning has to do with *(inaudible)* healing work with Carla. Her basic concern is that she not cause any difficulties for either Carla or herself. She is particularly concerned about various imbalances of a physical nature within her own body at this time; there are back pains, a growth in her vagina, and certain out of line areas in her spine, and she wants to be sure there's not any excessive flow of energy, either from her to Carla or Carla to her, and would like to know if there would be any difficulty in going ahead with the healing chelations, and would like to know if she could have more than one session with Carla or if one would be the most advisable? We would like your comments on these areas and the healing work, in general, D will be doing with Carla.

Let us pray together

(Carla channeling)

We are those of Q'uo, and we greet you in love and in light in the name of the infinite Creator. We thank you for the privilege of being called to your group during this working. Your queries concern the non-chemical body of learning—we correct this instrument—of healing techniques and see that you are concerned as to their possible damaging effect.

Perhaps the concept with which we would begin our commentary is concerning the situation when a healer attempts to offer to one which is considered diseased the catalyst which may be taken advantage of by the patient. It is well that the healer continue. No matter what the details and stories to the contrary point might be, the healer offers an opportunity. Within this opportunity there is for the one who wishes to be healed the choice that can be made to cooperate with and to affirm the healing that is being offered, thus doing the work itself, or it can feel that for some reason this opportunity is not one which is wished and then no cooperation is forthcoming.

In neither event has there been a difficulty because of a certain amount of irregularity in the various color balancings of the chakras of the healer. Neither healer nor healee must come to the eucharist of transformation already perfected. Rather, the healing ability moves through the one which has committed itself to be a healer. The healer's skill, then, is to a great extent involved in continuing to attempt to match the basic vibratory rate of the self with the vibratory rate of the one original Thought which is infinite intelligence or love.

It is well that a healer not consider its detailed picture of balanced health as perceived by the self. The more skilful attitude is to persist in whatever circumstances with the attempt to move the vibrational focus in tuning to as close to the original Logos as possible in any given circumstance.

Again, with that entity to be healed, the preparation involved is a surrender to one's own frailty as a being within incarnation, and to rejoice in the energy which is being shared, and to cultivate a willingness to experience change. None of this, however, has to do with the relative balance within. What we would like to make clear is that neither healer nor patient must need approach perfection. If the heart speaks its desire when the healer moves into readiness to heal, this energy of heart is the key empowerment which creates the open flow of the infinite love and light of the Creator.

So, healing being one more kind of channeling, you may see the same guidelines to apply: that is, purify the intention, be persistent in the practices, and refrain from judging the performance of the self or those worked upon. This is a beginning to the queries which are with this circle this day. May we ask more for more detailed queries at this time? We are those of Q'uo.

D: I think I'd just like to clarify my understanding of what you've just said, which is basically the error *(inaudible)* has been to worry unnecessarily about the preparations, and so long as my intent is solid within the heart and provided I am myself, which is maintaining the ability to align myself during the actual treatment, [that] is really all that is necessary. Is this correct?

I am Q'uo. Yes, my sister, this is correct with but one small addition. Among your peoples' food bears an important part. Much energy is given to the procuring and consumption of foodstuffs. Therefore, one way in which the deeper self is most easily notified that there are strong desires for purification or for the raising of the vibration is to institute some sort of care on a routine basis concerning the foodstuffs ingested.

The difference in the diet does not make so much of the difference up as the persistent daily taking of the care with the vitamins, perhaps, or with a certain part of the diet. This is a way to keep within the mind the desire to be a purified channel. It does not mean that one should deprive the self, but that it aids the field of intention of the healer to readily be reminding the self of the desire to be a better instrument for the Creator. This has the excellent side effect of creating within the mundane life a certain pleasing relaxation which is [dependent] upon one whose decisions regarding such things as foodstuffs are in a comfortable and at least subjective feeling of balance.

May we answer further, my sister?

D: I appreciate you discussing the feeding thing. That's been very much on my mind in the last few months, most especially with the intention of clearing this imbalance, to balance the diet. There seems to be a sabotage effort, if I may call it that, with an intense warning that goes within. I'm sure that many other healers experience this as they're attempting to find that inner balance, but it seems the more one pushes with intent to clear out and to become of a higher vibrational level in all areas including meditation and balance of diet and what not, it seems that the old habits maintain their forces at an even greater level.

Can you comment on this pushing/pulling process and is this just part of the process and it just needs to be given time, or are there, when you stir up with intent for positive, bringing more positive light into you and creating those positive things such as bringing in better foodstuffs, when you're attempting to bring that in to your lifestyle on a daily basis, what causes this great resistance and is it just a matter of time in which one will work itself out or are other factors involved within a particular healer itself that prevents this from occurring naturally?

I am Q'uo. We struggle to give a concept to this instrument. Let us begin at the middle. The service a healer does for the one to be healed comes utterly through the healer and through to one to be healed and represents a potential where, shall we say tangled light may resume its proper arising of hues. Because the healer wishes to create a channel where this light of love moves without hindrance it works upon the food and upon the attitude.

The main part, however, is involved in something which almost gets lost in the considerations of diet and meditation. That is, that the perfect channel has a life of its own to some extent. Before, however the healer opens this channel, whatever the level of work on the self beforehand, the channel then requests the most excellent flow of healing energy which it can carry in a stable manner. By requesting this privileged energy in this way, whatever the imperfections of the channel, the energy will be such as not to be too much for the channel to carry.

Could you please question further to point us in a more specific direction, my sister?

D: Just give me a moment. Then, in reference to the clearing done this morning, I was fairly on target. Can you just tell me yes or no on that, and I'll go further?

I am Q'uo. We affirm that that which you did was good work.

D: OK, there are certain directions I would like to go, I'm just not sure which are the proper directions and the proper order for directions, so I will start, I suppose, with the pendulum leading on karma, which I would like to know whether it would be more effective to do this, just prior to treatment and after treatment, and if you would be able to take me through the procedure of guiding me how to take the proper measurement as I go down through chakra centers, so that I can get the best and most accurate reading. After that I would like to follow up with some questions in reference to the chakra centers, and go from there. Is this acceptable?

I am Q'uo. We are not able to do your learning for you. We therefore do not feel it wise to share our opinions with you upon a specific set of readings from the pendulum, shall we say. We leave you high and dry there. However, when this has been done and you as a student of this technique have thought concerning your experiences and have drawn queries from them, then those queries constitute a portion of your own struggles to learn which we may respond to without interference in free will. Is this alteration acceptable, my sister?

D: I understand completely and I apologize for asking that. I'm still educating myself in reference as to how to ask the specific questions. That's perfectly acceptable with me and in which case I would like to ask, there are two things I would like to do. I would like to ask in reference to doing meditational practice on myself, because it has been done, and I am concerned with the incorrect directions I am giving myself in reference to clearing.

You have made reference quite a while ago in another session in having to do with … we are as a people basically redundant and very detail orientated, and the general idea here I'm getting is that for all of the detail carrying out that we do, those details are basically for us to work out so that we can come to a higher concept of what is really occurring, in which case some of these questions I ask in reference to my chakra clearing may be very detailed, but they also might be helpful for me to be able to come to that higher point, and I ask if that's acceptable with you?

I would also like to review, then, that work which was done on a friend of mine who is now not within this realm, and find out … I do not want to go beyond the law of free will or confusion, but I'm curious as to whether or not I can ask certain questions in reference to those chelations in order to be able to determine either errors or mistakes that might have been made, or [are there] things that I might be able to do correctly in the future for others, having done that experience, and that's my question?

We are Q'uo, and are aware of this last query which we find difficult to make into one question …

D: There are many …

May we just say that if your queries stem from experiences and those experiences already part of your healing experience bring queries to bear, we are gratified to listen to them and respond as we may, my sister.

Is there another query to follow-up?

D: Yes, in that case, may I begin with the questions that I wrote?

I am Q'uo. Proceed.

D: OK. First I would like to know whether I can [have] permission from the entity known as E to release this information to this group. He was very willing as a patient during the time that we did work on this. It was great learning for me, and I need to know if it is necessary to ask permission and is it acceptable to be given, because much of these questions are going to be directly related to work done on him.

I am Q'uo. We find that the entity released hindrance to you at the end of the time period wherein it was receiving aid, therefore you may query.

D: Great, thank you for that. In session one, there were three sessions, in session one I realized that the preparation work was quite inadequate and during [which] many mistakes were made. The first error was in skipping over the placement of the hand upon the ankles and then again I overlooked the first chakra when I went back. I then went back to try to rectify this. Does the order in which one moves make a significant difference when practicing or clearing in a generalized manner, and also when an error, and you make a mistake and move, is it best to continue moving upward, or should the healer retreat back to the area which has been overlooked, in which case, what is the proper procedure for backtracking and inserting this step?

I am Q'uo. My sister, the ways that various healers choose to enter the body field are variously efficacious. Some have a knack of finding one way for all patients and this is good. Others feel sensitive to a specific patient and alter a routine for that reason. Routines then vary greatly. To some extent it does not greatly matter. Perhaps we would say simply that it is well to work either up the chakras or down the meridians. That is, working from the bottom up, the first work would go into working with the back and the trunk of the torso first, the head coming up at the top of the chakras and then all the muscles worked.

The other most used technique is to begin with various movements and polarity work at the head and move slowly down the torso, arms and legs. To the extent that such order within the session gives to the healer a good feeling of having not left anything out, this is excellent to the healing forces within. A regular technique is also excellent because it allows the patient's emotions to remain calm as it knows where it shall be touched next.

Therefore, you are quite wise to have a technique that usually does not vary. When something is forgotten with the technique however, it is perhaps the more skillful option to fall back to that which has been forgotten, do it, and keeping the hand always in contact with the body, move gracefully and slowly and with confidence to the place where you left off, and begin again. The key here is slowness and calmness for the patient if the patient [that] is attempting to be a part of the healing process is relaxed and used to that rhythm which you have set up. Therefore, if the rhythm is broken the slow touch moving back to reclaim that portion of the healing technique and then the slow touch trailing back to where one left off keeps that patient's emotional and mental bodies open and receptive. Whereas if the hand were jerked off the physical vehicle of the patient and haste taken in running back to redo the left out portion, the harmony of the session would be broken and with that some of the potential the healing work in that session might have.

May we answer you further, my sister?

D: You answered that one perfectly, you covered everything I had running through my mind when I did that. Due to the poor conditions in which we were operating, oftentimes I found myself uncomfortable and out of proper alignment due to the fact that I could not maintain my body vertically for very long without slumping forward or backward for better comfort. What happens when a healer cannot maintain this vertical posture? Does the incoming energy reflect off the body instead of going through the body and how does it affect the healing?

Listening to you this morning I am now going to interject this into the question, I am guessing that the energy we are working with is so intelligent that, so as it knows not to do harm to either one, and because the intention is there regardless of the moving back and forth or the incorrect positioning, if the energy will still flow properly and accordingly and in which case should the healer concentrate on personal comfort and intent alone, and disregard the fact that this vertical positioning may be off?

I am Q'uo, and yes, my sister, you have penetrated that problem easily. The goal in being a servant is to offer a service. The better the posture, the better the attitude, the better the frame of mind, the better of any attribute chosen, then the better the experience for the channel or healer. As to the feelings of the patient, it does not bear any meaning whether the healer is more or less totally comfortable or erect or not erect. So most thought then may always be taken for the work and only secondary thought need be taken for a passing discomfort. Of course, if there is a strong element of discomfort present it becomes very difficult to clear the mind and heart in order to tune and be a channel for healing. So you may see that this is one judgment call a healer must responsible for making.

Is there a further query, my sister?

D: Just a confirmation then. In which case, if a healer becomes extremely uncomfortable, provided the healer moves slowly, with intent as to not to disturb the patient, the healer may, if the healer wishes to continue the treatment and not just adjust either a chair or whatever, provided the hands are kept on, or the healer goes through the drop/disconnect procedure and then moves the chair to better comfort, and then proceeds with the healing, this is perfectly acceptable provided the healer takes the care to do this slowly and so as not to disturb the patient. Can you choose to at that time discontinue the treatment, in which case, this is the second question, if that is the case and there is too much discomfort can the session be ended right there or does a clearing need to be continued through? Can you stop in the middle of treatment and will that leave the patient high and dry, or is there some procedure in which you can quickly close so as to remove yourself from the patient and allow the patient to absorb whatever energy has been given and the patient will be alright after that procedure has been cut in half?

We are Q'uo. When there is sufficient discomfort to end a session in an untimely manner [and] there is the energy which has been called for, it is appropriate to consign that energy which carries healing back to the one infinite Source. The ending without the completion of a certain series is acceptable. However, to stop, shall we say, cold is unwise. Better to take these energies, move them with hand to the last position and from this position ask these energies to move back to be released into the infinite light of the one Creator, thus sealing and blessing both the patient, the channel, and the mutual work.

Is there a further query, my sister?

D: You answered that one fine, yes. When the procedure was completed E was very anxious to get up and I neglected to offer him a glass of water which was her instructions from the sessions that I had attended with Barbara Brennan I was curious as to the anxiousness on his part, if it was strictly due to his personality or was his insistence to get up a reflection of some of the healing in part, and it was also recommended that the patients rest a while after treatment. Can you comment on the purpose for this resting, as well to explain why the water was included as a required step. Also, should this water be previously charged as well prior to treatment and the drinking of it, and how does the water interact with the energetic healing process. Also if the patient does not rest immediately after this treatment will this in any way …

(Side one of tape ends.)

(Carla channeling)

Not only is water an excellent thing to use, but oil is also excellent. Both of these substances carry electromagnetic charge, and therefore are helpful in the seating within and without of changes offered at the cellular level. When such are forgotten, it simply jolts this newly offered body memory and therefore it may not be well seated or as well seated in body memory as those things which then were given a nice space of quiet in which these energies could take hold.

May we answer you further, my sister?

D: E experienced a great deal of dizziness for days afterwards, and mentioned that his taste buds were registering foodstuffs as hot. Was this due in part to the healing or the energy activating certain things within him, or were these at this point just other symptoms of his disease?

We are Q'uo. My sister, we find that this constitutes a question for your inquiry, not ours.

D: OK, we'll move on. Did any movement whatsoever during those treatments cause injury to either E or myself. Understanding now that intent and everything that you've explained this morning, I'm just curious. At the time I did not have that complete understanding, and was concerned about backflow. I experienced afterwards dull burning headaches and what not, and again you may refer this back to me, but I am guessing that that was due to non-cleansing afterwards, in which case I'd like to move to cleansing procedures after chelations to find out what would be the best method to cleanse oneself of such energies as I found just treating oneself from the energies that it has been using. Are there other methods aside from taking a bath that a healer may use to clear oneself of the energies that have been exchanged during a session?

I am Q'uo. My sister, it is most important to your work that you do indeed form a very regular habit concerning cleanliness with laying on of hands. One such as yourself which is sensitive to the electrical body vibrations of entities, in working with the body you are working also with the finer bodies. It is the simple truth that when you work upon other being's pain you pick that up within your physical vehicle through the hands which you are laying on. Prior to a session there needs to be a moment, however long you personally feel it should be, where you protect the self and ask for angelic help for each, you and the patient. You then ask for this same white light within which no negative error may occur, to cover not only yourself but also the patient in the working itself.

After such a session again you must needs cleanse the hands at least with the soap and the water. Any cleansing technique which you personally find symbolically satisfactory is a good way of symbolizing your desire to be a perfect, clean, clear channel. The portion that is physiological in the hand washing and so forth is a far more [important] consideration after a session than before.

May we answer in any more detail, my sister?

D: If the healer is working on several patients that particular day, I'm assuming it would be wise to symbolically cleanse oneself after each patient. Would that be sufficient, and after a full day's worth of work, is there additional work the healer must do in reference to cleansing from all of the sickness and varieties of sicknesses that the healer has come in contact with, or is this basic cleansing after each patient sufficient considering that before it works on each patient it will certainly ask for the light to protect itself?

I am Q'uo. For most entities which work to any substantial degree with such do prefer the bathing after the day's work. In fact, it is not strictly necessary, however, the water does rinse some remaining accumulated, shall we say, thought form grime from the finer bodies within the energy nexus of the physical body and there does seem a feeling of lightness that showering afterwards does bring.

May we answer you further, my sister?

D: In adding particular salts to *(inaudible)* and what not, does this make a tremendous difference as opposed to just taking a regular shower, or are all of those procedures no matter what one adopts, no matter what one finds comfortable for helping the self, I'm assuming and I'm guessing that no one thing is greater than the other. It is really a personal choice one makes in reference to how one chooses to bathe and what materials one chooses to bathe in, am correct in this assumption?

I am Q'uo. Yes.

D: OK, I just need a moment here to review. I want to recover some stuff to do with that session. Is there a degree of illness so progressed that it's wise for a beginner such as myself to refrain from attempting to give energetic healing? Are there danger signs one should heed during these treatments to avoid, well, I'm going to mix that question, I'm just going to say is there a point in which a healer should refrain from attempting to give energy to another who is in either terminal illness or very, very ill and the energy levels are very, very low, or is it perfectly acceptable to give healing right up until to the point of their passing through this incarnation, strictly due to the fact that you are offering that energy to the patient and it their choice no matter what they choose to do with it, therefore there should be no harm to you. I'm trying to determine whether or not there are certain levels that are too dangerous to work with, or whether you are really buffered by the intent of what you are doing throughout the entire process no matter who you work on?

I am Q'uo.

Carla: I'm sorry. I've got Q'uo, but Q'uo's not saying anything. Just repeat the question and maybe I can …

D: I am concerned about the degree a patient may have, is there any danger to working with any patient with any degree of illness whatsoever, or does the entire procedure working with intent and understanding intelligent energy as it exists, does that buffer the healer from any negativity or darkness from the illness that may be within a patient?

(Carla channeling)

I am Q'uo, we are sorry for the pause but this instrument was too deep, and we simply had to bring her back forward. It is to be borne in mind that nothing is being done to engage the ill health of the entity, no outcome is intended when doing healing work. Let us specify, if someone comes to you with AIDS, say, and asks for a healing, [and] after the healing then continues to deteriorate, yet shows an improved spirit of charity, one may say that this entity is not cured, however it has been healed.

No healer or patient can truly judge the precise nature of an illness, nor is there any necessity to do so, rather the effort is made to create a bridge whereby a higher truth by grace and force of destiny may overshadow and thus transform some disease into a condition of ease or wellness. Therefore, no concern need be taken no matter how seemingly ill an entity is, for picking up, shall we say, severe illness from such a person. The realized or crystallized healer simply offers a catalyst with no outcome in mind and the prayer, "Not my will, but thine."

May we answer further?

D: That answer fairly summed up many, many questions, I just need a moment. I want to make sure I don't neglect anything here. Just a concern I had as a healer while working on the patient. My concentration was fairly there, I attempted during those sessions to remain as aware as I possibly could and in touch. As a healer in the state that I am at present I have much difficulty determining when to make a next move, due to the fact that I'm either not practiced enough or not sensitive enough to judge from the energy flows within my hands to know when to move on. During those chelations I relied on my guides to work with me and attempted to remain open enough to know when to move, but we're still basically in the dark, understandably. I understand that, but are there any other methods that as a healer I can incorporate while this procedure is moving along that might help aid my sensitivity to be able to understand when to move onward, or is this something that must be developed through many, many chelations and must be left up to me to determine?

I am Q'uo. Firstly, much must be left up to the student for its own good. To offer the easy shortcut is to cut you off from your own wisdom.

D: Alright …

Carla: Was there another part to that question because I seem to keep going to sleep …

D: No. Carla, don't even worry about it …

Carla: OK.

D: They're doing a great job here in being able to cut out a lot of the detail in that I needed to move through to get to the basic point. There is a point in, oh yes there is a point in which when I worked on E, and there was a dramatic release of pain when I touched his feet during the beginning of his chelations, he requested that I redo it because I guess the relief felt so great at the time. I did not feel good about doing this but went ahead due to his request anyway. And as I had finished the complete chelation treatment, went back to again place my fingers upon his feet and insert new energy. This caused immediate pain within him and I realized that this was not a correct thing to do. Under those circumstance was it best to do what I had done which was just attempt to withdraw, and can you give me any information whatsoever in reference to how going back over once treatment has been given to a patient, how this may hinder or hurt the treatment that's already been given, in the example that was given to us for clearing?

I am Q'uo. In terms of the psychological portion of such healing it is well to move with dignity to an ending and allow that ending to be just, not thereafter going back to offer an encore on one particular portion. This creates a better atmosphere for healing, whereas going back to do this or that creates the atmosphere of not enough. If it is simply the back rub then one can go back and forth depending on what needs to be rubbed, but in healing one is not simply pressing muscles and asking them to relax, one is working at the cellular level in creating opportunities for the transformation of a life-form as a whole. Therefore, it is well simply to refrain from going back over that which has already been offered, completed and blessed.

May we answer you further, my sister?

D: Just a moment here. At a certain point in the third session I requested that E's guides [work] along with mine. As my hands were placed on his second and third chakras I left them there, that if Ernie would accept it and if it were agreeable with all that his guides come in and do internal work that I was not adept at doing, which might further enable him while I was there acting as a channel, in which case because I had great difficulty determining how long to stay, or understanding, or being able to feel what was occurring, I had to use my judgment, in which case I felt inadequate in judging how much time was necessary for any particular guide to do anything without being able to communicate with those guides in some way, shape or form, sensing or feeling, emotionally knowing, I felt that I was rather blank in this area.

Also, when I retrieved some mucus from his chakras and lifted it up and gave it to the guides, again I questioned how much time was necessary to be able to give the guides the necessary time to neutralize that mucus. Are there tips or anything that I might be able to work with, knowing that I am working in the dark and I'm most concerned with not cutting off the efforts or the workings of those guides. If in the future I work on patients, how much time should I allow for these particular healings, knowing that I am completely in the dark, and having difficulty with accepting my own judgment in this area. Can you comment on this?

We are Q'uo. In dealing with the guides we suggest the practice, when there are no patients, in a form of address to the guides. Perhaps the visualization of greeting guide or guides, as you may feel them to be, giving them respect, bowing to their help and thanking them in a visioned way within. Then placing in the mind's eye so that the guides may move into this situation the condition of the patient as you find it. Then the requesting that this patient's guides move in their wise ways into the situation. Then an inner affirmation that this indeed is being done and that these essences are indeed now working to alleviate the illness. Once this has been respected, seen into the beginning of the functioning and thanked and blessed, that then need not be repeated in that same day at least, for that would indicate that there was some lack of faith that this had indeed had taken place.

Indeed, in general terms, it is important that a healer begin to accept its hunches, for no healer ever knew a bell to ring in the head when some energy work was finished, rather the healer of this kind of energy simply has a feeling that the energy has stopped, then it moves on. Over time experience brings not only the awareness of the energy flow and its surcease, but also the awareness that you were very close to being accurate before you had enough data to begin to perceive more clearly the ebb and flow of energy.

May we answer in one final query at this time?

D: Yes. In all of my closings I felt inadequate before doing procedures, I had great difficulty determining the orb field, how far that extended. I, reading in the *Hands Of Light* book, Barbara describes this process most carefully as moving with the heart towards the infinite oneness, and then this process cannot be mental. In the sessions I was working with, though, I was only able to at best create the mental picture of my interpretation of what the heart feeling might be, because I could not move into the heart and feel the emotional feeling, so I did this rather intellectually. In moving back to a session I worked on with an entity called S, when I worked on this procedure with her she did indeed remark that she saw angelic beings which was also described in the book and in which case I was also very mental at that point, or felt I was being mental.

Therefore, in comparing my intentions with those which are described in the book and attempting to do the best efforts that I can, I wish to have you comment on the difference between heartfelt rising and mental rising and perhaps you can offer me some tips in reference in being able to connect more closely to the heart and working around mental, or comment on the fact that the mental workings of my mind at the time were sufficient enough to create the closing. And that is my final query.

I am Q'uo. My sister, the closing of the door of opportunity is an event at the end of a healing which has a magical function. There are those who actually create a noise such as a clap when such magical activity has been finished. The insistence of the one known as Barbara that the healer's perceived ending move from the heart is based on the magical aspect of the heart as opposed to the intelligence. A closing which has been perceived by the self as coming from the intellect may well be that which does not contain enough resonance to properly seal the working.

Thusly, the descent into the heart, if as a whole the ending is mixed between brain and heart, then perhaps while learning is taking place the student may offer what closing he may make at that time, but before leaving the ending move deliberately into the heart and give an unspoken or spoken thought along the line of "This is done, this is finished," or blessings that this may be well, and then the hands clap together once or simply the foot quietly stomped against the floor, thus preserving the form which respects and recognizes the magical that is the unusual portion to this form of healing.

We thank the one known as D for having these interests and asking these most interesting queries. We thank each in this group for calling us and offer each our blessings and love. We leave you now in the illimitable light and love of the one infinite Creator. Adonai. Adonai. ☥

Special Meditation
May 8, 1993

Group question: Our question to start this session off with is, since it seems that we on the edge of the Milky Way galaxy have evolved in a pattern that includes very concrete and minute and complex use of the conscious mind, we are wondering if it is necessary in our continued evolution for us to utilize any of the creations of the conscious mind that we have come up with that have furthered our evolution and if it's necessary to recapitulate this journey in an orderly fashion, take back in all of the creations of our mind and of our culture as part of our continued evolution, or is there another avenue of evolution that is more effective. Is the work we have done as a result of the veil dividing the mind to the conscious and the unconscious work that is useful in our evolutionary process?

(Carla channeling)

We are those of Q'uo. Greetings in the love and in the light of the one infinite Creator. We are thankful that you have called us to this session of working this bright and lovely morning.

We feel blessed and privileged to blend our vibrations and our thoughts with your own. We shall embroider together. Your query is one which we shall attempt to take care to answer because queries along this line deal with matter which is slippery and not readily reduced to words. The query stands athwart one set of suppositions and looks at another kind of supposition. We [will] deal with each separately.

Firstly, we deal with the matter of colors. The taking back of the omega of all that was implicit in alpha in a universe of perceived motion is achieved by quanta. Thusly, although the group consciousness or individual consciousness does not have the ordering of it, the various colors, if you will, or emanations of light which are the basis of all structure follow the laws of motion, this is so.

To address the other set of suppositions involved in the query, although the methods of learning about the self and the environment within third density involve a vast array of setting down of details, this method of learning about the self is not a method of learning that endures to a significant extent beyond your fourth density. There are other ways of learning about the self to which the third density begins to be privy that are expanded in the next density of experience and that rather take the majority of consideration thereafter.

This is not to denigrate the scientific method, so-called by this instrument, or indeed to look down upon any means whatsoever which self-conscious entities use in the attempt to order and understand their environment. We do find the various earnest numberings and detailings of order counted off by your peoples in some wise humorous for facts are seen by some among your peoples to have the effect of a magical charm or protection. There is the addition of one fact upon another in a way which seems to us to be the intoning of familiar and safe and secure things, as if entities were made more and more solid and real as they enumerate details concerning the self and the environment.

There is in this detailed ordering of the environment much to recommend. We recommend the suitable dependence upon such sets of facts as your biology and other life sciences. We recommend such orderings of your culture as may be found in your social arts and in your fine arts. The scientific fact and the scientific systems of your peoples are monumental achievements of the intellect. The creations of artists are another ordering of the firmament of ideas and concepts. The latter method of ordering has one portion which is that which is the birthplace of methods of ordering which you shall develop in further densities. This being the whole self or melding style of adding detail in which details are compressed into emotion and this emotion given subjective color and form, thus creating a fused statement of essence or existence.

Thusly, it is not so that the endless ordering of fact which may be proven is that system of ordering the self and environment which will produce the path of spiritual evolution through to the last beat of this creation. However, it is not to be scorned. We find the amusement you have noted creeping into our usually augustly calm minds when facts are held before one as a shield, or when it is felt that the correct ordering of facts shall in itself bring about an evolution in spirit.

We find much to recommend in the nascent skills of artistry and intuition which each seeker has also, and we encourage each to use the visual and auditory senses inwardly in creating ways of expressing the essence of the self as artists do when they produce the picture, the song, or the spoken performance, such as the play, the poem, or the dance.

We would now ask for [any] following query. We are those of Q'uo.

D: Confirm what you just said, speaking, detailed speaking *(inaudible)* is not perhaps as directly flowing back towards oneness as the feelings and movement that we perceive, as we create *(inaudible)* in speaking of those facts as almost the shield in front of us which perhaps helps to blind us towards that feeling of going back to oneness *(inaudible)* the natural movement that generally flows through us when we do not think so much, that we just do. This is a more natural a more elevated way of moving back towards oneness, am I correct in this?

We are those of Q'uo, you are right, my sister …

D: Then we must concentrate as seekers on pulling ourselves backward from that typical tendency of the mind to categorize and chart and detail and remind ourselves on a regular basis to remove ourselves from that activity more often and it would be more advantageous to focus within meditations on the whole general feeling. This concept which you introduced yesterday alleviated immediately a lot of questions that I had put together within my mind and I noted that when you spoke I resonated with what you were saying and the detailing somewhat disappeared and I understood the whole.

The question that I and other young seekers have when so honestly seeking, we have a tendency of not accepting that general feeling that wells within us, that wholeness, and I'm assuming that if we maintain that wholeness more within us, that flow, that comes more within us, we would be able to view our surroundings and our environment and our lives in a more removed way which would allow us to feel more light as we move through this seeking.

I'm assuming that this is correct and I wanted to thank you for doing that for me because it is quite helpful to come here and remove myself from the meticulous line. So, in essence, I am thanking you and I am also asking you if this correct, a correct manner in which to move?

I am Q'uo. Yes, my sister in some the moving of the integrated self with feelings of wholeness turning always all of the self over and over again is the most efficacious way to most accurately record and memorialize in fitting tribute of emotion and manifestation the quanta of light and love that the entity moves through in the incarnational experience.

We would, however, state that there is no prejudice against the detailed study of the third-density physical environment and state further that this intellectual means of learning does constitute not only in the large sense a dead end, but in the closer sense it represents also that which furnishes the culture in which you live with those abilities to have personal leisure time which constitute the ability to spend the incarnational time working to integrate and fuse the expression of life so that these petty details needs must be honored as those learnings which produce the opportunity of the whole self to move forward metaphysically.

However, the basic sense of our answer is that yes, indeed, to work to enlarge within the self that integrated expression of one's essence in manifestation is, shall we say, the high road towards what may be called compassionate understanding and if you will but think of entities which you have thought wise you will touch upon memories of those simple and unintellectual entities whose spirits were not at all enhanced by detailed knowledge, but whose metaphysical natures expressed themselves as those of the wise and masterful spirits, not because they understood any detail, or because they were able to speak to this wisdom, but because their nature was grounded in the whole life experienced unily or in a unified manner.

We welcome a following query.

D: Before I move with any of my questions, does anybody else want to query further about that?

For the purposes of exploring some of my own perceptions here, I'm going to ask a few questions having to do with the aura and the chakra system *(inaudible)*. Within our physical mind/body/spirit complex—and I would appreciate if you feel I am moving with that shielding you just spoke of, I would like you to know that, and I also understand that if there are things that are best left for me to further study I will accept that as your answering.

The first question I have is that researcher have [divided] our aura and chakra system into seven layers for the purpose of labeling, into which resemble our concept of consciousness and light moving into physical manifestation. The chakras, then, have these seven layers which have been defined many times by many researchers. If I'm correct, the reality is that these layers, in fact, really reach out toward infinity, but in the limitation of our logos it holds us to viewing only the seven layers or concentrating on the seven layers, since our concentration within third density lies within clearing the first three layers to allow the universal light to flow from the seventh layer inwards. Is there purpose to exploring beyond the seven layers which would then prove useful in aiding in our healing techniques, or is this a diversion or unhelpful to the purposes of our third-density experience?

I am Q'uo. My sister, the subjective nature of a healer's individual method of perception create for that one healer the needs and requirements of that healer's work. One healer might find the need for the grasp of a system of visualizing which involves only seven colors in seven simple bands. Another healer might find that the seven times seven, as you mentioned, of the bodies, each color existing in a band of ever finer material, one for each chakra, to be that visualization which makes that healer feel able to heal and therefore this is necessary information.

In effect, as long as the healer has a consistent and compelling individual method of visualizing the movement of light this system of visualization is virtually and functionally accurate. We are not attempting to be obscure but are saying that almost any consistent method of visualizing the passage of energy will work for the one which has healing gifts and the desire to manifest these gifts. The healing ability is not raised by these visualizations or managed or controlled in their nature because of this system of visualization, rather the healing energy is channeled through the instrument, and what occurs as the healer does its work is that the healer discovers a way of visualizing the procession of this light in motion or this energy in such and such a way which does not interfere with the healing energy's own intelligent movement.

The goal here is for the healer to become transparent to this energy so that it is completely calm and is functioning as conscious catalyst. However, in order that the mind of the healer be stayed and comforted some method or system of visualizing the traduction of this energy is necessary. Therefore, we urge that each healer—however modest or great the healing gift, each is a healer—that each healer find that level of detail and informative embroidery which is wholly sufficient and satisfactory for the self, knowing that the purpose of this visualization structure is to so secure and quiet the instincts of reason and so sweeten and make cooperative the nature that the infinite energy of the one Creator may flow freely and intelligently to do its work.

(Pause)

We are those of Q'uo. We are those of Q'uo, and find that this instrument feels that we were not clear.

We move over, we perceive that there was in the query a concern about how subtle the levels of colorings could be. We affirm that there is possible a detailing of sub-colorations which approaches infinity. We were saying that only as much of this detail as was necessary for the healer to feel a quietude of understanding was appropriate. We welcome a following query.

D: In pertaining to the two chelations I did on Carla, in which case I experimented with them myself, in the first session, more intent, more nervousness, more of that seeking of visualizations of *(inaudible)* attempting to bring myself to more awareness, the clues or things that may help me in my system.

The first time I did the chelations on Carla and I had experienced this other time I felt an uncomfortable heat and I would visualize energy flowing, which at this point I'm not able to determine a pattern yet but I understand that that needs further working. The second time I attempted this chelation I removed myself from this attempt to find detail or find symptoms of what was occurring and I placed myself in a acceptance of what was occurring, utilizing love as more of the energies that were flowing through me and more of the essence of myself slipping through me and what I experienced was less of the censuring but still an overall feeling that the healing was somewhat complete.

I could not determine between the first and the second whether or not this new awareness and understanding without this deep searching and just channeling through acceptance, whether this might have been of a higher level of channeling due to my own acceptance of what was occurring. My question, I suppose is, is the seeking and searching and attempting to learn while I'm doing these chelations in this instance hindering my ability which is flowing from my natural essence to Carla. I felt that I could not determine which was a better healing or whether it was necessary that I determine if one was better or not. I felt good about both just because the intent was there but I was curious as to if you could comment on the quality of each of those healings?

I am Q'uo. We can comment …

(Side one of tape ends.)

(Carla channeling)

… And the qualities of alertness and exactitude in the stance of watchfulness bring about a keenness of desire felt within the self. The session of healing approached from a whole self or integrated standpoint when the energy is allowed its work …

(A noise is heard. Carla laughs.)

Carla: It's OK, I've still got her I just need to get back down …

(Carla channeling)

I am Q'uo, we remark at this instrument's sense of humor. The healing session done from the standpoint of one who accepts and allows the free flow of healing energy and which trusts and has faith in the intelligence of this energy is effective to perhaps a deeper degree than the session done from the standpoint of keen awareness, however, the keenness is especially useful in preparation for a healing session to bring the nerve within to a fine tuning so that the healer is fully awake and aware within the self. Then in the actual session this keenness rests ever so lightly on the unified ocean of serene calm in which metaphysical healing takes place. So, each attitude is effective, one more so before the session when preparations are made within the self, the other for use within the session when the energies of faith are most appropriate.

Carla: I think that they're waiting for you to ask another question …

D: I do have another query. In relating to the white light experience that I had a year and a half ago where I saw a clear band, I wonder if you are referring to when you speak of a healer attempting to become clear and transparent. Was this visualization that I saw the actual reality of that transparency and can a healer or myself be able to utilize that transparency in my practice towards becoming transparent? I also notice that as I speak to you I get a lot of light flashing as we are speaking and I'm assuming that I'm registering the communication pattern here.

I am attempting to learn how to develop the inner eye to a greater degree, and need to know whether or not what I witnessed a year and a half ago can be utilized in my attempt to become clear, transparently clear, and I should use that as a tool to aim for or whether or not this is a product which just occurs and I should not concern myself with what occurs.

For instance, yesterday when I was doing my chakra clearing with the intent to be more whole and more pure and accepting, when I got to the upper levels clearing my charkas I noticed the movement was much faster, the light was moving much faster than it had ever before and these seemed to be products of my, perhaps, more mature attempts at clearing oneself. I am trying to determine whether or not I can utilize what I visualized in a prior session as a tool for aligning myself with that transparent core which I saw, and if this would be useful in the future to being able to maintain that alignment as well as being able to use that inner eye to see further into either the patient or into the situation at hand while I'm healing?

I am Q'uo. We are aware of your query and at the same time find it impossible to answer simply. We shall attempt to be clear. The inner vision is such that were we to tell you a self-consistent system of seeing and were you to believe us you would thenceforth see innerly in the manner which it had been made possible for you to perceive. This does not mean that the visualizations of a healer are unreal but that the nature of actual consciousness is so plastic and so unaffected by the laws of motion that they can adapt to any set of expectations and can move intelligently within the sensing entity to fill in any blanks, as it were, that the system pulled to one had left out.

Therefore, were we to give a positive vote to your vision of transparency you would then feel it was a good image and a teaching or good for teaching the self-image. Were we to ask that this image not be followed then another way of sensing within would need to be found. The wiser, we feel, of the two ways of responding is to suggest that it be realized within that there is a dissolving nature to a true transparency, that as the healer seeks within for a more and more unified view of the self and a more and more generous view of the potential of the balanced self in offering as a healer, [one could] use such transparent energy as was visualized by you in your past as a reminder of that universal, penetrating, dissolving quality of transparency, so that the small roughnesses or unevennesses of personhood when viewed during preparations for a session may be then subjected by the self to that penetrating, dissolving light of transparency, so that the self [and] it's various personal rough edges and uneven bits may be seen to subdue themselves into a non-interference with the work of the service which you wish to render.

We ask that the healer not be limited by that visualization achieved already, but rather we would ask of the creative healer that he open within in each preparation for healing to any newly manifesting systems of perception or kinds of perception. If the healer feels comforted by one system of seeing energies and essences then that healer will be very effective along the lines of stress created by that structure. However, if a healer can be flexible in allowing new visualizations to occur and to allow thought to pour in on them only after such experiences are completed we feel that this latter path is the more creative and the more designed to maximize the path of service.

We welcome following questions at this point.

D: I was just a little confused in reference to some visualizations I was having and I'm going to attempt to remain aware. There are two questions, actually, I'll start with. I don't know whether you can describe this or not. When I feel the uncomfortable heat throughout my body, can you explain in the metaphysical sense what is occurring and what is this sensation that is being felt, what exactly occurs within the body? I know the energy is running through and it is causing an effect. How is this effecting the organs and the skin so that I feel this somewhat burning from inside out that makes it highly uncomfortable at times? Is there any way that you can describe what is occurring in a better fashion than I am able to perceive other than the fact that light is flowing through me and I'm feeling hot?

I am Q'uo. If you perceive this heat as of the nerves and then allow an analogue to the physical nervous system in the form of the nervous system of the electrical body then you may see this heat felt as being a measure of the amount of electrical energy which is expressing in the physical analogue as pain in the electrical body analogue which is moving into your healing apparatus, shall we say, as heat. Basically, you are feeling a measure of heat equal to the measure of physical pain.

This would, if allowed to go undealt with, create difficulties for you as a healer, for stress on this nervous system of the causal body allowed within the healer can create pain for the healer. Therefore, we strongly suggest that such heat or any other way you may have subjectively of recording stress or imbalance be visualized then as moving from within the healing apparatus, both physical and non-physical, and being shunted out along the exterior of this healing apparatus and given back to the source, this strongly visualized during and after the healing work, especially afterwards.

As before, we would again recommend the washing of the hands or other ritually done actions which seat within the emotions the fact that the connection made during healing has now been broken, and any effects picked up from the subject or patient shunted harmlessly away from the self and given back to the one infinite Creator.

We would ask for a closing query at this time.

D: My closing query is, I guess, would have to do with the color seen from my fingertips, which registered as an apple green, and I have with practice to a very small degree been able to stretch this energy outward and I know that this through intent can be stretched for long distances and what not. Again, must I rely on that intent alone to stretch that healing from the fingertips?

I also am curious about the coloring of that, because it is not the deep coloring of the primary colors, it is a very light tinted, and I'm just curious as to whether that is because it is a combination of white light that emanates in combination with the green heart color. And if you can somehow elaborate on those healings that occur, I know that from Barbara Brennan book they are able to, some healers are able to channel different colors through their fingers.

This may be a little advanced for me at this point, but I was wondering if you could comment on the procedure, basic procedure, how this actually occurs. As a healer, would I be drawing down the higher energies, and would I concentrate on a particular color coming through or is it best to leave that at this time and just concentrate on allowing the energy as it intelligently moves through to heal others. Is it best at this point just to leave that as is.

The other question I have in reference to orb fields, is in noticing in photographs and attempting to view orb fields within photographs of individuals, the movements that I visualize or see, are they the state of the entity at the time the photo was taken? I understand to a degree that you can move deeper and see beyond into, I guess, further into that orb field of the individual, but I was just curious as to what it was I was viewing in those photographs, whether I was viewing something that was taken at the time or whether I am able to visualize that orb pattern of the entity in the present as well. That maybe a slightly confused question, but if you could make any sense out of it I would appreciate it.

I am Q'uo. We shall attempt sense, my sister. Firstly, in the matter of the energy from the fingers this radiation may be affected by sharp intent. However, we would suggest a slightly different approach. We suggest that the sharp intent, the desire to stretch and to move further be applied to the self in preparation for this donning of a mantle of healing, shall we say. You—we correct this instrument—you may visualize, for instance, the self moving into a bath of white light, receiving from that bath a cleansing and purifying so that you are more and more one-pointed in service to the infinite One.

When the mantle of healing is donned and that healer becomes the self, the transparent self then may be felt to have the lid taken off and the energy of self simply allowed to move to its real strength. This relaxation of visualization in the event shall find that healer self radiating far greater a strength of field, far more penetrating a field than the field of the healer that is still attempting to control, attempting to stretch, attempting to go further. These forceful emotions point the self and hone the spirit, however, the more relaxed or more feminine of the mindsets in allowing that radiation to swell produce a much more efficacious field in the actual healing work.

Concerning the matter again of working with colors, the power of healing is limited only by an entity's considerations of how powerful healing is. We speak here not of curing or changing manifestations but of whether there is power available to heal or to make balanced that which is unbalanced. The more detailed color systems work for entities because they have built one visualization upon another and have found this system to make it possible to visualize very detailed work. We suggest that these color systems may be seen to be subjective and to represent choices made by entities which are attempting to order the bewildering universe of subjective perceptions.

Now, it is well not to be foundered and rendered helpless by one's own subjective or interior perceptions. It is nothing but the sense of self which demands that this inner wilderness be ordered and we fully accept that there is virtue in any good internally consistent method of visualizing the various fields and levels of energy using color. What keeps us from telling you that one way is more accurate than another is that in our opinion no one way is more accurate than another. For instance, there are a very complex series of color visualizations connected with the tree of life of the kabala. These color systems represent a ten chakra system which many find to be more useful than the seven chakra system which we have used. It is our feeling, however, that much can be learned by the one or by the other means.

This alarming and perhaps reckless seeming attitude on our part is due to our perception that within each possibly described color field there lies the potential color field, there lie the potentials for all colors, and the shadings of the colors then affected by everything from the energies of heavenly bodies to the interpenetration of all color fields by a succeeding system of energies which are of a higher order so that any color can be taken apart to see the sub-colorations within that density or level of energy, not to mention those energies which are subsumed under it, yet color or tint it somewhat, or those overarching energies expressing themselves as colors which color the whole because of the overarching nature of that field.

We realize this is frustrating information, however, we do wish to affirm the use of some imaging system and encourage that any individual healer choose a system such as the one given by the one known as Barbara, and work with it on a continuing basis using the color structure described therein until such time as this system is felt to be in any way lacking. In other words the working with the colors is all work in the area of the healer dealing with the healer's mind. The healer functions as a catalyst which offers healing to the patient. The energy itself is intelligent. What the visualization of the healer does more than anything else is so arrange the mind that the work of healing may go forward unimpaired.

It is not that a visualization of color through the hand does not in some way help psychic surgery as described in the query, but rather that the psychic surgery and all other manifestations are created by the intelligent energy itself and are allowed that creation by the faith or certitude which the healer has achieved with regard to the lightness and goodness of this energy. Thus, if visualizing sub-colorations will in the future serve to aid in the building up of faith and a feeling of doing precise and fastidious work, then just as we encourage this instrument to pray to the one known as Jesus the Christ, we encourage you to work with these color visualizations in the way given in one particular system …

(Tape ends.)

L/L Research

L/L Research is a subsidiary of Rock Creek Research & Development Laboratories, Inc.

P.O. Box 5195
Louisville, KY 40255-0195

www.llresearch.org

Rock Creek is a non-profit corporation dedicated to discovering and sharing information which may aid in the spiritual evolution of humankind.

ABOUT THE CONTENTS OF THIS TRANSCRIPT: This telepathic channeling has been taken from transcriptions of the weekly study and meditation meetings of the Rock Creek Research & Development Laboratories and L/L Research. It is offered in the hope that it may be useful to you. As the Confederation entities always make a point of saying, please use your discrimination and judgment in assessing this material. If something rings true to you, fine. If something does not resonate, please leave it behind, for neither we nor those of the Confederation would wish to be a stumbling block for any.

CAVEAT: This transcript is being published by L/L Research in a not yet final form. It has, however, been edited and any obvious errors have been corrected. When it is in a final form, this caveat will be removed.

© 2009 L/L Research

Sunday Meditation
May 9, 1993

Group question: We'd like to know this morning about the flow of energy that moves through the healer in a couple of different situations. Number one: when the healer is either attempting to clear his or herself and wishes the energy centers to be the most brilliant and active for the offering of the service of healing, where does the energy flow? Does it flow top down in the energy centers or from the bottom up, and when the healer is attempting to offer itself as a healer, does the energy flow in the same pattern or is it another pattern? Could you tell us how the energy flows in both situations where the healer wishes to purify itself or when the healer wishes to offer itself as a healer?

(Jim channeling)

We are those of Q'uo, and greet you in the love and in the light of the one infinite Creator. It is a pleasure to be called to this early meeting of your group and we are excited to be asked to share our thoughts on the subject of arranging the tuning or the vibration. We request, as always, that individual truth only be recognized and other statements we may offer which find no home be discarded.

The practice of cleansing one's vibrations and tuning and purifying them in preparation for spiritual work is a very simple process, yet one which lends itself to great varieties of adaptations depending on the preferences and the belief structures of the cleanser.

The basic, shall we say, technique that this instrument uses suffices as well as any, and we would suggest it is the beginning of our answer. In this practice, the entity ritually cleanses the mouth, the hands and empties the bladder, thus expressing the desire to be washed thoroughly of all wickedness. It then asks to see within the chakra colors in their configuration, beginning with the red, or lowest center, working first with the red, the orange and the yellow. These may be viewed and adjusted separately, then seen together and regulated. Then the heart chakra is called for, and the first three chakras, reanimated if necessary to form a more apt base for the actual size of the green energy center. Then the blue and the indigo centers are viewed, again spending enough time with each to achieve a visualization of all the chakras moving evenly and easily.

The heart of the tuning process is just this much, however, in order to make this procedure more beautiful in offering of the self in service to the one infinite Creator, each entity which prepares develops its own system of progress and requests for help and protection. Many create movements which touch in some ritual way the four directions about the place of working, saluting each direction and calling upon that direction's power for protection.

For instance, with this particular channel, the myth of the Christ is used and the archangels are called to their four stations, which are the four directions, and then [asked] as symbols of the heavenly host to stand as protection of the contact, the channel and the session of working when the time has come for the energies to be used.

We suggest, rather than a directional visualization of energy flow, rather, the visualization of the awareness of the whole self in every cell all ready and empty, awaiting the flow through the self. In this awaiting, there need be no feeling of urging a direction, and when the hands are used to point the energy, it may be firmly visualized, not that the flow is quick or slow, but that the appendages are lightened of every normal burden of weight or substance and are become hollow receptacles through which the infinite Creator may work.

We would welcome queries in more detail at this time, that we might be of more specific service. We are Q'uo.

Carla: R, do you have any questions? I do, but I can wait if you have some.

R: I don't have a question at this time.

Carla: Okay. When attempting to clear blockages that one is aware exists, and in doing so, not for the purpose of healing others, but for the purpose of healing self, oftentimes the energy feels stagnant in one or two chakras, and I feel difficulty in releasing or understanding what is occurring, in which case, I don't understand if the energy is unable to move through and therefore it is creating backup and does not know where to go and I can feel that pressure in the physical sense. I am quite unsure how to release this energy which has somehow gotten stuck and do not know how to do it either through thought or emotion, and I was wondering if you could give me tips in reference to either diverting the energy or helping it to move through the blockages or sending it back out to release the pressure.

I am Q'uo. My sister, we would suggest two ways of working with these experiences. Firstly, your particular inner nature is profoundly affected by visualization, therefore we would suggest that this ability to visualize be harnessed for your own good use. In cases where stagnation of a center is perceived, there needs the feeling that one may but sit and become able to separate from this blockage enough to have effect upon it. The method of doing this is in a rough way described, to move into a posture of request and mentally request the aid of your guidance and with that guidance felt some subjective way, then you with guidance might be suggested to establish a place for you both in time/space from which you together may visualize a prolonged process of clarifying, speeding up, regulating and brightening the energy center in which blockage is perceived. This way, you are able to harness the impersonal side of your own ability and use it upon the self.

Carla: That was very interesting. I'll certainly try that. The only other question I have in reference to the chosen path of self healing through the evening with asked guidance … is there anything I can do to perhaps aid, either in visualization or in chakra opening, to aid the guides as they work with me through the evening to help clear this?

I am Q'uo. My sister, your greatest aid to guidance is a repeated inward affirmation to their existence, to their power and their desire to serve the one infinite Creator on your behalf. The more firm and sure the foot of the one who stands to serve in the name of the infinite Mystery, the more sure shall be that aid, for in work with this mystery, all feet stand firm on nothing, and that nothing is called faith. Allow that faith to become more conscious, to become more part of the momentary experience. Allow the floor of faith to be under your feet along with the floors of Earth and carpet.

This establishing within the inner world of self of the holy of holies is the beginning of a life truly lived not in the world. If only Earth be touched, those not of the world must still be in it. When the fair carpet of faith is overstrewn upon the mundane ground of experience, all of the mundane experience becomes charged with potential, for what would be called by this instrument magical work, that is, work which creates changes within your own consciousness.

May we speak further, my sister?

Carla: Ha! I'd love for you to speak further always … um … running out of questions here. You are answering everything with such greatness. You've been wonderful for me these last few days, and I want to thank you for that. If there is further info, you can go into that. I think I am beginning to truly grasp what you are saying, and if there is further information, I'll take it. If not, I will leave the room open for other questions.

(Pause)

My sister, there shall always be further information as long as there is the inquisitive ear and the inquiring mind We are also feeling most privileged for having been able to spend this time with your circle of seeking. It has been a great privilege and pleasure, and perhaps you know we do not speak fulsomely, but only honestly. We lift our hearts to the one Creator and know you stand with us with all love and amaze[ment], rejoicing in this mystery that calls us forth from dust to behold we know not what, yet must we continue to be about this business, seeking always the infinite Creator and Its service. We leave you in the love and the light of the one infinite Creator, and know that this love is bestowed each to each. We encourage all attempts to love and support each other.

Carla: Q'uo, can I ask you one last question?

You may.

Carla: It's just a curiosity of mine. In the friend that passed, who I know is full well taken care of and is on another journey wherever, due to the circumstances in which he left and the great love I felt towards that entity, I've wanted to know if it is common for those within an incarnation to offer a service to those who are not incarnate, and wanted to know if it was appropriate to offer the service of asking that entity if there was anything, while I am here, that might be helpful for his peace of mind or whatever, that I might do in reference to his loved ones. I don't expect to step beyond things which are beyond me, but if there is a way to offer that service, I would like to do so and as well wish him on his journey, that it may be well and full of love and light.

We are those of Q'uo, and in our opinion the highest service for one who has moved recently into larger life is to intercede, that this entity may more easily look and see that which is hard to see until much is accepted. Prayers interceding for the orientation of the newly arrived friend are very much in order so that this entity may know where it is and be quickly moved within a comfortable set of circumstances seen subjectively.

This instrument informs us we must depart, and so we shall, leaving …

Carla: Thank you for that.

I am Quo. We are rude not to say "Thank you, my sister," however, we shall indeed take our leave of this instrument and each of you now in love and in the infinite light of the one great Mystery. Adonai. Adonai. We are those of Q'uo. ❦

L/L Research

L/L Research is a subsidiary of Rock Creek Research & Development Laboratories, Inc.

P.O. Box 5195
Louisville, KY 40255-0195

www.llresearch.org

Rock Creek is a non-profit corporation dedicated to discovering and sharing information which may aid in the spiritual evolution of humankind.

ABOUT THE CONTENTS OF THIS TRANSCRIPT: This telepathic channeling has been taken from transcriptions of the weekly study and meditation meetings of the Rock Creek Research & Development Laboratories and L/L Research. It is offered in the hope that it may be useful to you. As the Confederation entities always make a point of saying, please use your discrimination and judgment in assessing this material. If something rings true to you, fine. If something does not resonate, please leave it behind, for neither we nor those of the Confederation would wish to be a stumbling block for any.

CAVEAT: This transcript is being published by L/L Research in a not yet final form. It has, however, been edited and any obvious errors have been corrected. When it is in a final form, this caveat will be removed.

© 2009 L/L Research

Sunday Meditation
May 16, 1993

(S channeling)

I am Hatonn, and I greet you, my brothers and sisters, in the love and light of our one infinite Creator. It is a great joy to us to join you this evening, for so large a gathering of your peoples in the seeking for which you have come together is a wonderful sight for us, to blend our vibrations with yours, to become one, and to share in your oneness.

My friends, this evening we would share a few thoughts on the subject of becoming one with your brothers and sisters, with your other selves. There comes a time in each life when one will experience doubts in their seeking. One might wonder at the path that has been chosen when one struggles with the concept of seeing a brother or a sister who is not quite as one would expect, and still within the self would realize that though there are conflicts, there is still the oneness, the sameness, the reflection of the self in the entity that is causing the conflict.

My friends, this opportunity which has been made available at a certain point in many lives is indeed a great step, one which with love, with the sharing of the heart and mind and the spirit will perhaps cause some of the doubts to be allayed. The path you have chosen, my friends, as you well know, may have many bends, many curves, but the blessings which are bestowed are so beautiful. The lessons you have chosen in the preincarnative state to undergo are those that have the capability of becoming one within your self, bringing the lesson home so to speak. As the harvest becomes closer, my friends, these lessons of love and of sharing yourselves, the learning, the experience of becoming one with those that you perceived as being troublesome to your spirit, are great lessons and are ones to be thankful for.

At this time we would like to transfer this contact. I am Hatonn.

(Carla channeling)

I am Hatonn. I greet you now through this instrument once more in the love and the light of the infinite Creator. We shall continue through this instrument. Let us compare perception of other selves by consciousness as a type of mirror. The type of mirror which the illusion surrounding you provides for your use is the type which is used in your carnivals. Far from receiving an adequate reflection, each mirror is purposefully warped in order that an imperfect and distorted image is seen by the one who goes to the carnival. Some mirrors seem to reflect a jolly and harmonious image, and cause one to laugh. Other mirrors seem to reflect to us a looming and menacing shape. And so you go through the illusion, day by day perceiving and categorizing the images from the mirrors as good and as evil, as friend and stranger and enemy, as harmonious and inharmonious. And you do not realize that you are in a carnival and that, my friends, is the only reason that the carnival mirrors are in place. The more emphasis that is placed upon the distortions by the carnival-goer, the more distorted the images will become, the more complex, the more interesting. Each carnival-goer chooses the nature of his entertainment by choosing to see the image he prefers to see, by watching for it, by finding it, by naming it and calling it his own.

At some point in the carnival, either by good fortune, by inspiration, or by the cold use of intellectual gifts, it may become apparent to the carnival-goer that there is an exit from the house of mirrors. And so, the carnival-goer which has decided to seek the exit leaves the hall of mirrors. Behold, he has entered another hall of mirrors. Those you discard are discarded; those you do not recognize remain a portion of the reflecting surface of your consciousness. And so begins a new carnival, and at the new level of awareness that the seeker has found and cherishes and nurtures by imitation the carnival goes on, the flags wave, the merry-go-round plays a merry tune. And still you see a distorted image of each other self, less distorted than before in many cases.

Until one day, by good luck or inspiration or the cold use of intellect, the carnival-goer again finds the exit. There are many, many mirrors, many rooms full of them and many exits, for your seeking and your learning is a process. We cannot offer to you the instantaneous realization that will last. We can promise you that such moments will come to you. The mirrors are blown away in the wind and you see clearly, as if through glass with no lead to keep an image reflecting, and you look at yourself in every one you see and you are indeed one with all that there is and you say again and again, "There, too, am I." And this realization is wonderful and joyful. But we cannot promise to you that you will keep it, for you are within the illusion which you inhabit in order to work with mirrors.

For a great portion of your incarnation you will be dealing with the carnival. It may be possible in a life-long friendship of mate, of bosom friend, that all the mirrors be vanquished and that you may see yourselves face to face, and rejoice that you have known the Creator. It is more likely that you shall only be able to do this intermittently. But to know what you are after is the key to seeking. As long as you seek, you shall find. This promise written in your holy works is not part of any lie. We can only ask that you take care in what you seek, for you shall find it. We ask that at any time you become discouraged you stop at the first available moment and look into the one mirror that you carry with you that will give you a true image. We ask that you look into the silence, for there is a center and a hope, a joy and a love in the midst of that silence that can create a new kingdom for you, and for your family. Let your desire be turned to that which you have a proper need to attend to—your own consciousness.

My friends, when you lift up your consciousness into the great mirror of light, you offer a gift to yourself, to all those about you, and to your planet, the nature of which is indescribable. You can leave the carnival—there is a way out. And while you are gone, and have raised yourself up into a focus too fine for this illusion, you may descend once again and join the carnival and ride the horses on the merry-go-round, and eat the cotton candy and laugh and choose to find in your hall of mirrors good and kindly images. How do you choose to see yourself is your illusion; it is your choice. We do not deny any of those things which are negative, seen against the positive standard of a healthy, smiling, vibrant evolution. We do not deny hate or death or jealousy, pain or anguish or loss. We only say to you that they are a part of that which is an illusion, and that at the heart of each of these things is a transformation which is so positive that joy leaps from every tear that we may shed in the learning of these lessons.

Therefore, whatever face you see, it is your choice. Put your name to it and do not let world opinion of any type or degree sway you, for you can be a messenger of light, and you may give that message to anyone whose path intersects yours simply by seeing that other self as the Creator. We ask that you begin always by attempting to gain a true reflection of yourself, for it is only when the carnival-goer is lifted from the hall of mirrors that the mirrors become part of a manageable, reasonable and loving consciousness. This day has the carnival become a bit hectic. Do you wish more for yourself? Very well then, my friends, begin that process by utterly forgiving yourself, by loving yourself most dearly, and by lifting yourself through meditation to the light. What consolation there is in that light. What healing there is in that love.

We are aware that there are questions in this group, and therefore we would pause only to offer our vibrations to those who find that it deepens their meditative states. If you would be patient we shall pause briefly to share our blessing on each of you. I am Hatonn.

(Pause)

I am Hatonn. I leave you, my friends, through this instrument but never in the unspoken sense. We are always pleased to be with you if you so desire. We ask that you be most discriminating as you listen to us as we are imperfect and fallible, much like yourselves. Use what thoughts we have that are of help to you. Discard the rest. Our own selves, our greater selves, we greet you and bid you farewell. We are those of Hatonn. We leave you in the ineffable love and the infinite light of the one Creator. Adonai.

(Jim channeling)

I am Latwii, and I greet you, my friends, in the love and in the light of our infinite Creator. It is with great joy that we join your group this evening. Again, it is our privilege to be asked to provide our humble service of attempting to answer those queries which may be of value to you in your seeking. May we then ask for the first query?

C: Latwii, in another meditation I channeled the one called Nona, and as I channeled vocally, I began to feel my hands beginning to move and gesture, and I had not experienced anything like this before. Could you make any comment about what was happening?

I am Latwii, and am aware of your query, my brother. As various instruments take part in the process of vocalized channeling, there is frequently an abundance of the energies being transmitted that requires some outlet so that there is not an overloading of the normal means of transmission. In your particular case, this outlet was the use of the manual appendages to serve as a diversion for the excess of energy that the ones known as Nona were providing that evening. Your particular sensitivity allowed what might be viewed as a mismatch in the energy to be transmitted as compared to the receptivity or normal level of receptivity of your particular instrument. Therefore, the one known as Nona found the use of your, as you call them, hands to be most efficacious in relieving your instrument of the excess of energy.

May we answer you further, my brother?

C: No, thank you very much.

We thank you, my brother. Is there another query at this time?

K: Yes, Latwii. Are there more clairvoyants and psychics and healers now or at this point in time than there were, say, twenty years ago?

I am Latwii, and am aware of your query, my sister. You may notice an increase in not only the absolute number of such entities, but also in the percentage as a proportion of your planet's total population.

May we answer you further, my sister?

K: So the answer is yes to my question. Is that right?

I am Latwii. This is correct.

K: Thank you.

We thank you, my sister. Is there another query at this time?

Carla: Is this due to third-density, fourth-density kids being born, or to wanderers or what?

I am Latwii. There are, my sister, not only these factors to be considered but more as well. Not only have those known as wanderers incarnated with latent abilities awaiting activation in service to this planet, and not only have the children of the harvest of other third-density planets begun early incarnations on this planet which shall be, as you know, a positive fourth-density planet …

(Side one of tape ends.)

(Jim channeling)

I am Latwii. We shall continue. There are also those native to this density planet who have by what you may call seniority of vibration incarnated with hopes of achieving what you may call the harvest or the graduation into the next density of being. These entities have through many incarnations upon this planet developed certain abilities that are now available to be used in greater ease and facility than at any previous time, as you call it. You may also consider the increase in the vibratory level of the catalyst which each entity faces in the daily round of activities. This increased level or intensity of opportunities for growth allows many entities to be able to use the catalyst in a fashion which develops those abilities which may be called psychic or of a paranormal nature.

May we answer you further, my sister?

Carla: No, thank you.

I am Latwii. We thank you. Is there another query at this time?

K: Yes, just one more question along the same line. I was talking with a clairvoyant yesterday, and she said that I had a healing aura about me, and I had not really heard of such a thing before. And, well, would you comment on that, about a healing aura about anybody?

I am Latwii, and am aware of your query, my sister. To one who is sensitive to the energies which surround each entity, the perception of those energies may vary according to the, shall we say, the depth of sensitivity of the clairvoyant, as you call it, entity. One may see the ease of the melding of the mind, the body and the spirit reflected in the aura and interpret this balance of the being as a healing aura, for, indeed, such an entity, having balanced the self to a certain degree, is able to generate the feelings of peace, serenity and joy which are most soothing and quite healing in their manifestations.

Another entity of the clairvoyant nature may look at the same auric energies and note that, indeed, within the field of energies lie the specific abilities of this entity to serve as what your peoples call the healer, having incarnated with these abilities either in potentiation awaiting the activation or in partial activation.

Therefore, it is both necessary to look at the one who is perceiving the auric energies and its ability to so perceive, and to look at the one being perceived to determine if there are those specific abilities defined as the healing abilities contained within the auric field or if there is a more general configuration of mind, body and spirit which in some also provide the faculty of healing.

May we answer you further, my sister?

K: No, that's fine, thank you.

I am Latwii, and we thank you, my sister, and greet you after your absence.

K: Thank you also. We missed you.

Is there another query at this time?

K: I have one. This morning my message was to forget what I feel are earthly moral responsibilities or obligations, and to let myself go on my path freely, not to tip myself down to one area. Can you expand on that?

I am Latwii, and am aware of your query, my sister. We may speak in a general sense about the nature of such a message but cannot be specific, for when the self at its deeper levels begins the communication with what you might call the conscious waking self, there is the direction from the inner being which is being reflected as clearly as the conscious self can perceive such reflection, and the necessity in such cases is that the conscious self seek more and more to perceive more and more clearly those messages which arise from within.

The concept of allowing the self to move along the path of evolution in a free and open manner is a concept which has meaning to an entity which works with the blue-ray energy center of the throat. Such a configuration of energy is then experienced by the seeker in a manner which promotes the clear communication of the self with the self and with other selves, accepting the self and other selves, and freely expressing the self to all which surround the self. In this manner, the giving of freedom and acceptance to others springs from the giving of freedom and acceptance to the self, for you are also a mirror and reflect that which is your being to those about you.

Therefore, as you seek to move freely along your path of evolution, you shall also give that freedom to others and shall inspire such freedom to those who come in contact with you. It is therefore helpful to consider the deeper ramifications and implications of such a message as you meditate upon it that you might continually refine that journey that lies before you and which you have long traveled, making refinement upon refinement. And as you continue upon this journey, you shall find those messages arising from within your deeper self to be more and more frequent, more and more clearly perceived.

May we answer you further, my sister?

K: No, thank you, Latwii.

We thank you, my sister. Is there another query at this time?

J: This is a hard question to get into words but I want to try. A friend and I this last week or week and a half have been experiencing a sense of pressure, of tension, almost a sense of reverberation from the planet, as if the planet itself was in some kind of especial pressure or tension, just a number of symptoms. And we wonder if there is a particular reason or cause. Could you comment on that?

I am Latwii, and am aware of your query, my sister. The planet, the entity upon which you walk, is also partaking in the process of evolution, for all portions of the creation are one and move with the Creator as it becomes aware of Itself. As you know, the cycle which is now ending upon this planet is very close at hand, and its transformation has not been what you might call smooth, for many upon this planet have had difficulty in realizing the love that exists in each moment, each situation and each entity. Therefore, the seeming inharmonious expression or perception in the mirror has been experienced by many upon this planet's surface for a great portion of what you call time so that these vibrations of disharmony have entered into the planet itself. And as the planet begins its transit into that density of love, there is the momentary mismatch of vibratory frequencies. This mismatch becomes apparent to those who are sensitive in many ways, but we can assure each that the mismatch or stress suffered is but momentary, and in its way also offers a greater opportunity for each entity upon the planet and for the planet itself to find that love in the moment which has not been found previously. For love is at the heart of all creation, and no moment is without its own infinite share of that love.

Therefore, when such distressing feelings are felt, rejoice that the planet is giving birth to itself and each entity upon it, and that the birth is attended by love.

May we answer you further, my sister?

J: No, thank you. That is what I expected.

We thank you, my sister. Is there another query at this time?

K: Yes, let me go just a little bit further. These vibrations that are more intense now, that you mentioned a moment ago, are they beginning now to sift down to, well, say, the average person who has been going about his life totally unaware of what's happening?

I am Latwii, and am aware of your query, my sister. This is correct with the qualification that for many upon your planet who do not yet feel with the sensitive inner being that the vibrations' intensity are reflected in a more gross or general manner; that is, many will be found to speak of what is called the "good old days," when times were more peaceful and there was time to reflect and a feeling of ease was more apparent. You will see the return to such days in mind, in entertainment, in clothing, and in the various ways that your peoples express their inner being and feeling. Therefore, such intensity of vibrations are—we correct this instrument—such intensity of vibrations is noticed by each entity upon your planet, yet noticed in an infinite variety of ways.

May we answer you further, my sister?

K: No, that makes sense. Thank you very much.

We thank you once again. Is there another query at this time?

J: Well, just a little follow-up question on that one. When I first was asking the question, I was thinking that this is like a labor pain, but I didn't want to say that, but then you said those words. When human beings give birth, labor pains usually increase in frequency and in intensity. Is that going to be the pattern for the planet?

I am Latwii, and am aware of your query, my sister. Though the future is not known, we can look upon the direction in which your planet and its various populations are moving, and can suggest that such shall be most likely the case, for the planet has for a great portion of what you call time known its populations by their hostile expressions of power over others, and these vibrations have created an inertial residue which seeks to be balanced in the short period of time which remains. In order for the balance to be achieved it is most likely that it shall be allowed its full run, shall we say, and the intensity of catalyst shall continue to increase so that the use of catalyst in the remaining time might be most efficient.

You might consider the great learning which comes with the situation which you call traumatic. In but a brief span of time great transformations can occur when the entities involved in the situation are, shall we say, made aware of the need to call upon the great and deeply held inner reserves with which each entity enters each incarnation, but which each entity is but faintly aware exists within.

May we answer you further, my sister?

J: No, thank you, that's fine.

M: Latwii, to what extent can one person send positive vibrations to another person?

I am Latwii, and am aware of your query, my sister. Depending upon the entity's clearing and balancing of the energy centers, the degree of ability is variable and ranges from most ineffective to infinitely effective.

May we answer you further, my sister?

M: No, thank you.

I am Latwii, and we thank you, my sister. Is there another query at this time?

Carla: How's the instrument holding up?

We find the instrument somewhat weary, but able to continue for another short span of your time.

May we ask if there is another query?

Carla: Well, as long as you've got a query left, Latwii. I ran across a very unusual situation recently. I met a friend's wife who had the most unusual thing happen to her twice. She became pregnant and a heartbeat was discovered and she went quite a ways with the pregnancy, four or five months so that she was big, and then the pregnancy disappeared. You would think it were an hysterical pregnancy except for the fact that her husband's a doctor and he heard the heartbeat of the child. What type of entity needs this form of nurture, and where are these children going? Let me add that I do not doubt this woman's word or ability of her husband to use his stethoscope.

I am Latwii, and am aware of your query, my sister. In the situation of which you speak, you may see evidence of the entity which needs but a short span of time within your third-density illusion in order to accomplish the task which it has set before it. It is most common among your people's perception of the way of the incarnation that the incarnation shall begin with a, as it is called, normal pregnancy, birth, childhood, adolescence and some portion of the adult years experienced before the passing of the illusion is accomplished. Yet if one could look with unfettered eye at the experiences which are truly occurring within your illusion, one would see a great array and a variety of means of being and learning those lessons which this density has to offer.

The experience of which you have spoken is not as uncommon as one might believe. Many are the entities at this time in your planet's evolution which seek but specific and short term experiences within your illusion. The lessons which are then learned are of great value, for most usually such lessons are of the nature of completion, that is, the graduation is at hand and but one course credit remains.

May we answer you further, my sister?

Carla: Just one thing. These children were not stillborn. There was no physical evidence that they were ever there. Where did they go?

I am Latwii, and am aware of your query, my sister. These entities move into this illusion as each has moved into this illusion, and leave this illusion in the same manner, though the entities living, as you call it, within this illusion have not become totally aware of their presence.

May we answer you further, my sister?

Carla: Do you think there's any chance at all I could understand what you're saying or do you think that it's probably beyond me?

I am Latwii, and we shall attempt clarity. The concept is so simple that we apologize for assuming that the questioner was familiar with it. We suggest that all exits, shall we say, from this illusion are exits in which the third-density yellow-ray physical vehicle, whatever its degree of manifestation, is left so that the etheric or indigo-ray body may be entered, the incarnation reviewed, the lessons discerned, and the further needs for incarnation determined. Therefore, the exit is from the yellow-ray body to the indigo-ray body in each case, whether the incarnation has been what you call long in years or hardly apparent at all.

May we answer you further, my sister?

Carla: So, what you're saying then, is that in the case of this unusual woman, she is capable of absorbing the physical material used to house the child which had such a short incarnation so that it did not have to be spontaneously aborted and gotten rid of all at once, but simply absorbed into the body of the mother. Is that what you're saying?

I am Latwii, and am aware of your query, my sister. This is partially correct. The entity exiting the physical vehicle also provides some degree of assistance in the absorption of that vehicle which it exits. There are in other cases entities which may be seen as what you would call the guides or angelic presences which also provide such aid, as does the entity's higher self or oversoul, as you may call it. Each situation is unique and each situation will be provided the aid which is appropriate, that aid having been preincarnatively chosen by each entity involved.

May we answer you further, my sister?

Carla: Well, was this great service that R is performing the key to her inexplicable weight gain?

I am Latwii, and am aware of your query, my sister. We find in this instance some bar upon the distance we may travel in attempting to reveal the nature of this situation.

Carla: That's okay, I had a hunch about it anyway. Just checking. Thank you.

I am Latwii. May we ask if there is another query at this time?

J: This feels like a personal question, but I'd like to try it anyway. Latwii, are you presently embodied in a space/time location?

I am Latwii, and am aware of your query, my sister. The nature of our existence at this, what you would call, time is such that we inhabit the analog of a space/time physical vehicle within the density of light. Therefore, the vehicle which we inhabit, though it is an analog of the vehicle which you inhabit, would not be able to be perceived by the great majority of your peoples in any way because of the, shall we say, density of light contained within it, which to your physical senses is quite without substance or perceptibility. When we communicate through instruments such as this instrument, we transmit in a time/space or thought form so that our space/time physical vehicle generates a form of thought that may penetrate the interlocking densities and planes within each density to reach the instrument which opens itself to our thought form.

Therefore, to answer your query, our normal, shall we say, existence is within a space/time physical vehicle of light, but when we communicate with groups such as this one, we partake in the analog to your meditative state and transmit our thoughts in a thought form vehicle.

May we answer you further, my sister?

J: No, thank you.

I am Latwii. We thank you, my sister. May we ask for one final query at this time?

L: Thank you, Latwii. Where is it best to bring a new way of medicine into this society?

I am Latwii, and am aware of your query, my sister. We find that there is no place which does not call for the type of healing of which you speak, for the sorrow and suffering and ignorance of the truth of unity within each is great upon your planet at this time. There are many who seek wholeness, and do not know that already they are whole. There are many who seek love and acceptance, and do not know they are love, they are loved. There are many who exist within the illusion and believe that the illusion as they perceive it is all that there is, and they call in their subconscious mind for an exit to the illusion however it can be found. And yet they are unaware that to look within the self is the exit into unity.

Therefore, as one seeks to be that known as the healer in whatever form that healing may take, we may suggest that you cannot miss the mark, for all about you are those who call for that healing that you have to give. And may we humbly suggest to each that the greatest healing is that love which is at the heart of your being and may be shared at each moment of your existence with each entity you meet. There is no greater magic nor healing than the love, the forgiveness and the compassion for those who walk upon the path of evolution with you.

Therefore, give as you can, be as you are, and those gifts which are yours shall shine as beacons in the night and shall be noticed by all who call and the healing shall occur. For such is the way of the one infinite Creator that all cycles shall be completed, all the pieces of the creation shall be reassembled into one, and all who seek love shall find it all about them.

At this time we feel it appropriate to take our leave of this instrument, for we find that this instrument is somewhat weary. We thank each present for calling for our humble service, and we remind each that we are but your brothers and sisters in light, fallible and imperfect. Take that we have offered which is of value to you; leave that which is not. It is our privilege to be with you whenever you call in your private meditations or in your group meditations such as this evening. We leave you now in love and light, in the power and in the peace of the one infinite Creator. We are known to you as those of Latwii …

(Tape ends.) ☙

L/L Research

L/L Research is a subsidiary of Rock Creek Research & Development Laboratories, Inc.

P.O. Box 5195
Louisville, KY 40255-0195

www.llresearch.org

Rock Creek is a non-profit corporation dedicated to discovering and sharing information which may aid in the spiritual evolution of humankind.

ABOUT THE CONTENTS OF THIS TRANSCRIPT: This telepathic channeling has been taken from transcriptions of the weekly study and meditation meetings of the Rock Creek Research & Development Laboratories and L/L Research. It is offered in the hope that it may be useful to you. As the Confederation entities always make a point of saying, please use your discrimination and judgment in assessing this material. If something rings true to you, fine. If something does not resonate, please leave it behind, for neither we nor those of the Confederation would wish to be a stumbling block for any.

CAVEAT: This transcript is being published by L/L Research in a not yet final form. It has, however, been edited and any obvious errors have been corrected. When it is in a final form, this caveat will be removed.

© 2009 L/L Research

Sunday Meditation
May 23, 1993

Group question: The question today has to do with why entities who incarnate in this particular illusion choose one sexual orientation over the other. Is there an advantage or are there opportunities to choosing male over female or female over male in dealing with the various catalysts and learnings that are available in this third density?

(Carla channeling)

Greetings and welcome. We are known to you as those of Q'uo. We greet you in the love and in the light of the one infinite Creator. It is a privilege and a blessing to join this circle of seeking and to share our thoughts with you. We thank you for calling for this type of information, and are most honored to be here. We do request that each seeker accept our lack of authority. We are fellow travelers rather than authoritative sources, therefore, we ask each to keep those thoughts of ours which may aid, and allow any that do not seem appropriate to be forgotten, for we would not represent a stumbling block for any.

The query concerning the advantages of male or female sexuality begins with the note that sexuality itself has advantages. The advantages of being polarized are a fruitfulness which one cannot gain without polarity. This may be seen to be literally true in human sexuality, wherein male and female come together to allow the opportunity of a pregnancy to occur. In the sense of working with one's conscious awareness of the passing moments of experience, polarity is that which actively encourages the self to move into relationship. The sexual polarity creates a bias towards seeking companionship. The companionship may then move in any of a number of ways, all of which bear fruit in terms of an increased rate of catalyst, and therefore, an increased opportunity to learn from the catalyst.

Archetypically speaking, this sexuality can be seen to be that difference between the Matrix of the Mind and the Potentiator of the Mind, in that the male energy is seen as that which reaches, as does the Matrix of the Mind. The female may be seen likewise as that which awaits the reaching. In the cultural roles prevalent among your peoples, these roles are seen to hold somewhat towards true; that is, to the male of a mated pair, there is given the most affirmative training towards the bias of feeling a responsibility to provide for a family, to nurture and tend a wife and children by working and offering the fruits of that labor. The cultural feminine archetype, as opposed to the archetype of the deep mind, is considerably clouded and complex compared to the cultural role of the feminine gender, say, one hundred of your years in the past. However, there is a tendency still, and an inevitable one, towards the female's perception of the self as one which nurtures and supports by the presence, by the loving and intuitive caring, by the qualities of compassionate gentleness, and intuitive hunching or guessing.

In broad strokes, then, it may be seen that entities which wish to learn the lessons of unselfish service through labor away from the family are drawn to the male sexuality. Those wishing to work in relationships and to learn the lessons of unselfish loving and serving through presence, may well choose the feminine gender. However, at a more goal-oriented level, these goals having to do with what you may call karma, male or female gender may well be chosen regardless of the implications of any sexual bias in order to set up the appropriate relationship wherein lies the work of the incarnation.

Thusly, if one with whom you have a tie which is karmic has the need to establish the sexuality as male, then in order to come into a desired mated relationship, for instance, you would choose the female gender in order to arrange the niceties of convention so that it would be possible to choose during the incarnation to take on this relationship. Within this relationship, you, as a woman, might be needing to work in what seems to be a more masculine series of lessons of responsibility and provision. However, the sexuality would have been chosen only in order to set the stage for the work in relationship.

It is quite common to choose gender for the purpose of aiding destiny, for most work done by men and women within incarnations this late in third density are working with the balancing of relationships, so that harmony and the kind of balance required to ride the bicycle with no hands might be achieved, not for one but for both. Thusly, one will see many relationships, none of which seem to be particularly similar, one with the other. This is because the soul choosing to do this work has acquired many, many lifetimes as both sexual choices—the biological male and female—and now are refining understandings gained in previous work with these relationships.

It is to be noted that the refining process, though it takes place in a much smaller arena than the first learnings, is nonetheless as difficult—or usually more difficult—and intensive work. We find this to continue beyond your density, that is, that the work of refining the choice for service to others begins with one decision and then becomes more and more complex, decision by decision and relationship by relationship. This continues as far as we know, becoming more and more detailed and difficult or intensive, until that moment when all detail is first glimpsed clearly as irrelevant, and the face turns for the final time to gaze in infinite love at the source and ending of all that is.

Each entity has the capacity to take advantage both of male and female orientations within one lifetime of experiential catalyst. We encourage seekers to investigate and deeply consider the perceptions from the standpoint of the opposite sexual gender. For instance, it is certainly reliably interesting for a woman to encourage those qualities the culture encourages and the archetype suggests: the bearing and raising of the children, the nurturing of the loved circle of family and friends through thoughtfulness and presence, the qualities of attractiveness and charm. These are most fruitful to investigate. Often the society and culture do not insist that the male viewpoint be included in this role-playing, yet how much more aware does a female become which has actively pursued the consideration of the male within the mated relationship?

Two queries are relevant: Firstly, "Were I a male …"—that "I" being the female—"Were I a male in this situation with these necessities, what pressures, what sensibilities, what cultural expectations would I then have access to that I do not as a female?" Conversely, although it is excellent for the male to wholeheartedly enter into those biases which the culture and archetypical mind suggest, it is very catalytic to focus upon creating adequate supply for the self and the loved ones, to be the leader and the tender of the physical plant of home and assets; yet, it is also fruitful for the male to ask himself, "If I were a woman, how would my perception of my role and its requirements be altered?"

We bring to this instrument's mind the suggestion of an image from your holy work. In this scene from your Bible, there is a woman who has been unclean and very ill for many years. This woman strives merely to touch the hem of the robe worn by the teacher known as Jesus. The entity, Jesus, becomes aware that this woman has indeed touched the hem of his robe, for this entity feels the healing energy moving through him, and he asks, "Who touched me?" The woman owns her action and explains that she wished to be healed. The teacher known as Jesus then says, "Go, for your faith has made you whole." In this instance, the entity known as Jesus stands waiting as the female, and is literally reached by a biological female functioning as a male in reaching out.

We may encourage each to feel within the self the full range of male to female qualities as they arise within, for *all* aspects of polarity teach. However, it is especially helpful to move in mind to the extreme that is the antithesis of the self, and so attempt to furnish the mind and the spirit with a more and more universal perspective. This perspective is certainly reached partially by swinging between male and female. However, in each case where an entity is more markedly in the cultural stereotype of its sex, therein lies the opportunity to increase one's depth of compassion by moving firmly and regularly into the opposite perspective.

Note within the mind's conversations as well as conversations with others, instances wherein generalities are made stating that women are such-and-such or men are such-and-such. It will be seen quickly that the generalizations cover, but do not obliterate, uneasiness and even fear of some aspect of the otherness of the other sexual gender. In terms of the red ray, marked polarity is greatly beneficial betwixt the two biological sexes. In terms of orange and yellow-ray relationship potential, it is as helpful to be devoted to considering the antithetical point of view as it is to be an advocate for one's own gender.

As one gazes at the third density, one may see a movement which seems, and in many ways very deeply seems, to tend more and more towards the feminine principle, for the goals of third density are the choice of how to serve the infinite One and how to become more and more a witness to and a co-creator of love. Lessons learned revolve completely around love, not around wisdom but around love. The one known as Jesus expressed deeply feminine approaches to the challenges of hostile environment and relationships. The qualities of verbal submissiveness and reaching in love to encourage peace and great tolerance were emphasized in this incarnation. Indeed, the principle which this instrument calls "Christ consciousness" is one of unrelieved compassion, that is, compassion unrelieved by wisdom.

Thusly, females in their cultural training find themselves more cognizant of what may be called, "the Mind of Christ," and find sacrifice more tolerable and acceptable, thereby creating much energy available for potentiating love and the learning of loving. It only awaits the male's decision, however, to work with attitudes of inner peace for this to be available to males as well as females.

In the end, at this level of discussion, we come back to the benefits of having sexuality. We celebrate the fruitfulness of this polarity which brings entities together to learn, to love together, for the giving and accepting of love and all its fruits, advantages and disadvantages, is the proper business of humankind. Each knows the depth of the illusion of sexuality. Each is aware of the self at levels which do not alter because of being male or female. This Personhood is infinite, and from this standpoint, we encourage each to be aware of one final thing, that is the person within that is the self, that is one with that great Self which is love embodied and incarnate in the great original Thought or Logos. The Creator is not male. The Creator is not female. Yet, the Creator is reached by both equally within illusion. When a point of view is needed, and the biases of male and female … *(inaudible)*.

We encourage each to move through considerations as male and as female, and then to reach within the self to that level where all selves are persons equally, and stand firmly and confidently gazing from that point of view to look at the biases brought about by gender, by birth, and by relationships.

Although this instrument wishes to have had more aid to channel upon this topic, we find that sexuality is relatively shallow in terms of its ability to create unique perspective. Certainly from within the incarnation, women easily see men as generalities, and men see women as generalities and experience great differences betwixt the two. However, free will is such that these differences simply create alternate forms of the same catalyst, so that biological sexuality does not have deep reasons for being chosen. We consider the outworking of relationships to be focal and most central to learning of love. Yet, in each mated pair, both entities shall don and discard both male and female type roles depending upon the energies necessary to be expressed in order to balance the relationship.

We apologize to this instrument for disappointing it, and we thank this group that it has allowed us this opportunity to share these thoughts. At this time, we would take any questions that any might have and close the meeting. We would prefer to transfer at this time to the one known as Jim. We are those of Q'uo, and leave this instrument in love and in light.

(Jim channeling)

I am Q'uo, and greet each again in love and in light through this instrument. At this time it is our privilege to offer ourselves to any further queries which those present may have to offer to us. Is there a query at this time?

Carla: Well, I noticed that at no time did you say that there is any actual difference between the two sexes. Did you intend that, and simply mean to say that all of the differences were apparent and shallow?

I am Q'uo, and am aware of your query, my sister. Let us begin by suggesting that it was our intention to speak to the strongest qualities of each of the sexes and not to move into areas of difference at this circle of seeking. There are qualities of the archetypical mind which gravitate to each sexual orientation which provide avenues of service and opportunity for learning to each of the two sexual possibilities. This is a study which is, in our opinion, one of great depth and breadth as well, and it was our intention at this working to move more upon the general nature of each of the two sexes, swimming, shall we say, in more shallow waters than choosing to dive deeply into those qualities which are significant to one or the other sex.

Is there another query, my sister?

Carla: No, I can accept that. Thank you, Q'uo.

I am Q'uo, and again we thank you, my sister. Is there another query?

Questioner: I have a question, Q'uo. I just wonder if the reason that so many prophets or enlightened ones seem to be in a male form—the archetypical concept of wisdom and seeking being the male—or is this concept that I am raising here misguided?

I am Q'uo, and am aware of your query, my brother. There is the seeds—we correct this instrument—there are the seeds of truth in that which you have observed. However, there are also other factors to be considered, these also related to the quality of the Magician, or Matrix of the Mind, which is potentiated into the activity of seeking by the High Priestess, the Potentiator of the Mind. Thus, as this quality of seeking manifests in your illusion, especially within the more recent centuries of your illusion and its various cultures, there has been the predominance of the male influence upon most of the recorded histories of these cultures, which has had the effect of displaying the achievements of the male members of the culture, and, indeed, in making opportunities for them.

This is a more, shall we say, common or traditional way of reflecting archetypical energies and has not always been the mode of cultural expression upon your planet, but has been more recent, shall we say, in its histories of culture. Thus, the feminine quality which potentiates the seeking has been less apparent than the masculine quality, which has been potentiated by the feminine qualities of both the subconscious mind of the male and of the conscious and subconscious qualities of the female in what is generally called the supporting role.

Is there another query, my brother?

Questioner: Is it correct to say that in order to progress along the spiritual path in conscious seeking seekers must find a way how to fuse the masculine and feminine qualities inherent within each, to go on seeking?

I am Q'uo, and we find this statement to be correct, my brother. Is there another query?

Questioner: No, there is no query from me. I just wanted to say that it has been great sharing company with you again, as it is always.

I am Q'uo, and again we thank you, my brother, and may take this opportunity to express our great gratitude at sharing your presence as well as the presence of each entity in this circle. We take great joy in so doing.

Is there another query at this time?

Carla: Not from me.

I am Q'uo, and we are greatly full of the joyful feeling that comes from sharing the spiritual journey in this manner with each of you. We are especially grateful to be able to utilize each of the two instruments and to be able to have our humble opinions expressed in your words. We hope that you will remember that we are but your brothers and sisters in seeking, and we would ask that you take only those words which ring of truth into your hearts, leaving all others behind.

At this time we shall take our leave of this instrument and this group, leaving each, as always, in great joy in the love and in the light of the one infinite Creator. We are known to you as those of Q'uo. Adonai, my friends. Adonai. ❧

Intensive Meditation
May 29, 1993

Group question: The question this evening has to do with the definition and explanation of the concepts of guru, teacher and guide, the teacher and guide as are used in the terms of inner plane or spiritual and angelic presences that look out for us or have guardianship over us in some fashion. What is the difference in definition in guru, teacher and guide?

(Carla channeling)

I am Oxal. Greetings in the love and in the light of the one infinite Creator. It is our privilege to be with you this evening, and we greet gladly each in love, in light, in harmony and in seeking. We especially greet the one known as S and thank this instrument for allowing us to work once again in that grand collaboration on behalf of the infinite intelligence which bears inadequate names such as love. To attempt to harmonize together in the service of the infinite One is not only, we feel, of service to those upon your sphere who call for this kind of information but also to us, for we are here to serve yet cannot break the laws of free will and are able to speak through instruments such as this one and the one known as S.

We do not say that we only can speak through instruments but rather that we prefer the most careful and fastidious observance of the law of confusion and do not choose alternative ways which in your past we have tried and have found wanting because of breaches in free will. Therefore, each instrument bears our thanks for allowing this collaboration and harmonization of the treasures of time and memory and service.

When the student approaches the quest for truth he finds himself upon that which your song discussed, the long journey, the journey without foreseeable end, the quest for truth without final or certain results, for in that spiritual walk the truth recedes infinitely before the progress of consciousness. We are not authorities, we simply have walked, as you would say, longer along the path of spiritual evolution. Our opinions and our thoughts are precisely that. Therefore, we ask each to take from our discussion those thoughts found personally helpful and to leave without a backward glance all other thoughts, for we would not be a stumbling block before any.

We thank each for grasping the centrality of personal discrimination with regards to spiritually orientated information, and each, of course, requests helpers in the search for the truth. The student has a certain kind of character or personality and to each student the way is unique. Therefore, to some one kind of second voice may offer the best communication and dialogue; to others another different style or different level, so that each kind of spiritual counselor, teacher and guide has its appropriate place and function. In this discussion please bear in mind that we do not offer judgment as to which path is appropriate, but recommend rather the individual's increasing knowledge of itself, its personality biases, and therefore its preferred kind of teacher, counselor or guide.

We would at this time transfer this contact to the one known as S. We leave this instrument in love and light, we are those of Oxal.

(S channeling)

I am Oxal. Most humbly we speak to you in the love and in the light of the one infinite Creator. We have been some time away from this contact with this instrument who even now is about the process of adjusting its energies to ours once again. We feel it important for this group to understand the process which this instrument has just undergone and which we would like to express our gratitude to this instrument for its fastidiousness and attending to. This is the process of challenging the contact. No less than three times were we challenged by this instrument in the name of what it holds highest. Most humbly and gratefully were we able to meet this challenge, for indeed the seeker who reaches into the darkness within third density for information which may avail in a spiritual way must be most scrupulous that the information that is obtained is used for the very highest purposes and in the very clearest way that the student of spiritual evolution is able to manage.

We ourselves have been long upon this very same path and as we lean back a little in the saddle, as this instrument would care to put it, to reach a helping hand to those who request it we are most acutely aware that no two requests are alike and that each student is ultimately its own master. Oh, the little that we have to offer to you who in some sense upon this evening are our students in comparison to what each has within, for each is the bearer of a light and a love which is that of the infinite Creator. Each has worlds wrapped in worlds wrapped in worlds without end within. This glorious divinity is accessible to all and to each, so the poor pittance of information which we may have to offer is only by way of pointing haltingly towards the one light that is the life of all.

We have been asked to address the question of the nature of the student/teacher relationship. Indeed, this is a question which can hardly be avoided for the teacher/student relationship is all about you. This instrument regards as teacher the one known as Carla and the one known as Jim. In this respect we would hasten to point out this instrument to a great extent expresses its own personal biases. Now, these biases have great use for this instrument. They are in fact quite precious to the seeking which this instrument undertakes. Nevertheless, the biases work in part to obscure the natural relationship to other selves which to this instrument are equally teachers.

Brother, mother, father, friend, colleague, wife, husband, child—all of these and many more relationships involve the teaching function. Each and every experience [of] self to self is an experience of holding up the sacred mirror which can be shared in the precious experience of mutuality, which is in some way uniquely possible within the third-density working. Each self offers to one a reflection of the one self that one is. So even if it should be the case that the social and experiential nexus in which one relates to another self suggests a certain asymmetry in the relation, such that one is in the role of teacher while the other is in the role of student, even so it needs to be understood by both parties that in the very measure that one is teacher to another, one is also pupil.

We realize that this is a very difficult concept to work within a functional way within a density which is very conscious of social standing. It is nevertheless a central point and must not be neglected. The types of teaching function do vary considerably, however, and when it comes to the question of the type and the nature of the teaching which is offered it is necessary to take into account differences in the approach to the teacher/student relationship, differences which may for a time indeed involve the appearance of asymmetry.

Thus, for example, should one wish to acquire the skill of working with the machine you call the computer, one would search out another who had already acquired such skill and was willing to pass on this information. Now, to the extent that one wishes to learn the information which the skilled computer operator has to offer, one opens oneself to the teacher of the computer, and avails oneself of the wisdom which is forthcoming. Now, this is a rather easily circumscribed function even within your social complex for it is generally clear to most that there is a relatively easily circumscribed area of expertise in which the teacher of the computer works. One does not, for instance, feel compelled to use the same teacher that teaches computers for spiritual counsel or perhaps for counsel upon the athletic field. These are different areas and in this regard, a difference in the relationship teacher to pupil may well be appropriate and given the appropriate circumstances may well emerge.

Thus, the first point that we would make upon the issue of the differentiated teacher/student relations is that they are not absolute relations for the most part, but involve regions of development. This end can be—we correct this instrument. The same thing can be said in the nature of spiritual work, that is to say that there are areas of spiritual development which each may be working on differentially at a given time and depending upon the nature of the spiritual development being worked upon, it may or may not be appropriate to put oneself in an apprentice relationship to another who serves as teacher.

We come then to that more highly potentiated teacher/student relationship you have called the relationship to the guru. We have found as a result of our work with your peoples that this guru relationship is one which prevails within a particular cultural interpretation which is not primarily your own, that being the oriental tradition. This is not to say that some similar functions are not to be found within your own more immediate traditions. There is, however, a point of principle it is appropriate to address when considering the nature of the function of the guru. A guru is first of all a fellow human being and a fellow seeker. The guru secondly can well be regarded as a teacher in a special sense, that is, a teacher that has a particular kind of spiritual understanding which the student would acquire, but, thirdly, the guru offers itself as a teacher in an unique way when it takes charge, if we may put it in this way, of the spiritual development of the student.

We have found to our own experience that the question of free will is at issue when the guru too willingly takes charge of the spiritual development of the seeker. There are many different kinds of gurus and many different levels of development among gurus. Some, indeed, appreciate the value, even at the cost of a seemingly slower or more confused spiritual path, of allowing the student to find its own way. The guru all too often finds it easier to operate within a framework of belief, a framework of practice, and even a framework of faith which seems to work well enough for it, but does not necessarily translate into effective working for the student.

In fact, no matter how well matched may be student and guru there comes a time in the life of every student when the guru must detach itself and allow the student to find its own way. The guru does this without judgment, without expectation, but only in a genuine and heartfelt desire to seek and to assist in the manner which is most befitting the nature of the relationship that has uniquely evolved between that particular student and that particular guru.

Thus far we have spoken primarily to those kinds of teaching which take place within third density with both the teacher and the student being incarnate mind/body/spirit complexes functioning within third density. There are other modalities of teaching as all those within this circle must be aware. Such a modality is that which we share with you this evening, and such a modality is that which other instruments channeling other sources likewise share with you upon the occasion of the assemblage of other circles of seeking.

In order to more clearly speak to the nature of the distinction that exists amongst many of these forms of service which the discarnate teachers engage in, it is useful to note so that we may be clear about the distinction between the inner planes and the so-called outer planes of your experiential nexus. Those planes which we designate inner are planes which are part of the third density of the current incarnational cycle now completing its revolution within the Earth planetary sphere. The inner planes are planes which are occupied by many, many, many other mind/body/spirit complexes, not presently incarnate. Many of these mind/body/spirit complexes have chosen as a mode of service to assist in those small ways it is possible to assist those who are currently working in incarnation within the third density.

How might this service be availed you ask? It is as simple as listening for the chirping of a beloved bird upon a new spring day. One's inner guidance is always available to one for each here is an infinitely precious part of the one infinite creation, and each has a veritable host of loving administering spirits deeply caring about one's own personal destiny. Such spirits occupy themselves offering love, offering what gentle nudges and suggestions as may be given in silence, and let it be said that these spiritual ministers to the struggling self are infinitely patient, for well they are aware how seldom it is possible to hear the beloved chirp of a single bird in the great cacophony of sounds that fill up your density. So rare is it for any to heed and yet the administrations continue unabated and undiscouraged.

Yes, there are a great many who speak through into your density via the channel from the inner planes. Some are greatly wise, some are less so. There is great love and comfort to be availed for one who allows the inner guides to have their say, to have their sway.

Now we come to an area which is perhaps somewhat more difficult to grasp. We ask as you consider this material that you bear in mind the nature of the task at hand, not just for you individually, but for all who have begun the great quest of being an individual consciousness. All seek, and the goal of all seeking is the one Creator. It happens that within the course of the development of the creations that there have evolved patterns for this seeking to find expression. These patterns we may express by means of the concept of densities. Seeking is not complete when one has achieved such focus, such balance as permits the completion …

(Side one of tape ends.)

(S channeling)

… and we are again with this instrument. Of tasting it to the fullest and of beginning to understand the need for a sense of direction and focus within this experience of all embracing love. Even when this task which is by no means easy is achieved, there still lies before the evolving spirit still other densities.

In the fifth density wisdom is developed. We ourselves are a social memory complex which has come together from many different sources representing many and various experiential nexuses in convergence with one another at the point that we are ready to transit to the density which is the sixth. For us, those who have worked long within the wisdom density, the task, as strange as it might seem to you is to be less wise and to rediscover the sources of compassion we originally encountered so long ago. Our task is to blend this compassion with the many wisdoms we have acquired. We feel more and more the call of this task and as we are called into this task we seek the opportunity to serve. For us your calling is a great and wonderful such opportunity and thus it appears to us that you who call from within the dark faith of third density

seeking have so much you may teach us by your dedication that we who offer ourselves in service as teachers to you find that you appear to us as teachers to us.

So we find that the question of the proper relation between student and teacher is a very complicated one indeed. There is no formula for right teaching; there is no formula for the proper [way] for right teaching; there is no formula for the proper way to go about being a student. We would prefer to say that the teacher/student relationship is ephemeral and is essentially an event that is of the order of an opportunity. It is an opportunity or mutual sharing in a way that does not bias in advance the outcome of that sharing. Only teaching which is given without expectation and openly is teaching which partakes of this unique and seemingly paradoxical effect whereby the student is simultaneously teacher to the teacher.

We speak to you by the grace of the Council that sits in protective concern keeping an ever watchful eye upon the doings within this planetary influence. We have been given permission to attempt to achieve within this planetary influence at this time that unique balance of teaching and learning which shall simultaneously permit the growth, the evolution, of those mind/body/spirits incarnate within third density Earth and ourselves. We ourselves are equally at risk in the offering of this service as you are in performing the service, for us, of requesting it.

This is our understanding of the nature of the balances at work within the teacher/student relation. It is a most complex and compelling relation, this teacher/student relation. We ask that you consider well and consider deeply when broaching the subject of entering into such a relation with any other, for it is a sacred bond of mutual seeking which is thereby established, is it not?

We feel that we have said enough upon this inexhaustible topic to make a beginning. For us this will suffice for the narns. May we, however, offer ourselves in response to any queries which those present may yet have upon their minds? We are those of Oxal.

Questioner: I will pose a question for those of Oxal, and the question concerns a seeker who wishes to avail himself or herself more in the listening to the guidance from within that is sometimes called angelic presences or the inner guides or personal guides. Would you comment on ways to increase one's sensitivity, if you just desire for this communication to come through to the conscious mind and not fall, if I can call it that way, [into] common pitfalls or distractions that also lie along the way of this type of seeking. Is that query clear enough for comment?

I am Oxal. We are again with this instrument. My brother, your query is amply clear and we will comment to the best of our ability. It seems to us to be appropriate to point out at this juncture that the most important single task facing any seeker is the task of knowing the self, for if the self is a babble of voices struggling to be heard it is not likely that any clear sense of direction shall come from attending to one particular voice within the babble.

Observe, if you will, the experience of taking a stroll upon a pleasant sunny day. One is surrounded by plants in full bloom, the soft leaves of the sheltering trees rustling gently overhead, the thousand different sounds, many of them too small to be singled out, in the plant life all around; the light slanting softly through the rustling leaves forming patterns upon the ground that change like the shifting colors of the kaleidoscope. Surrounded by all this beauty the walker nevertheless takes in so very little of it, for the walker is beset by an internal dialogue, thoughts which seemingly posses the mind, going where they will besetting the attention with a continuing bombardment of concepts, associations, desires. How then does one learn to see the shimmering light, how then does one learn to hear the rustling leaves, how then does one learn to watch for or listen to the thousand subtle sights and sounds that are part of the minute kingdom all around?

One must listen past the internal dialogue. It does not help to propose another dialogue running counter to the first in the hopes of achieving victory over the first and thereby gaining access to the sights and sounds. One needs only to let go. One does not even need to let go, one needs only to listen, to watch.

A similar experience happens in relation to one's inner guides, the angelic presences and the higher sources of inspiration. They are constantly available. There may even be a word inserted edgewise into one's internal dialogue. Listening back to these voices may be likened to that reaching back after the vanishing dream upon the awaking and the reintroduction into the round of daily affairs. The more one tries often the less one succeeds in reaching back for that dream that has eluded one. The more one merely allows the dream to once again have its sway the easier it becomes to explore what has transpired within the dream.

This, we realize, speaks somewhat indirectly to your query, but we desire to observe the law of free will in responding to such a query and therefore must needs limit our response to the general principle of allowing oneself to open to one's very rich inner resources of which the voices of guides and angelic presences are some.

Have we spoken to your query, my brother?

Questioner: Yes, you have spoken well to my query and I thank you for offering more food for thought, so to speak …

I am Oxal, and we thank you, my brother. Are there further queries at this time?

(No further queries.)

We find that we have spoken rather long, it being for us a pleasure once again to be reunited with this instrument which so gladly serves. At this time we leave you growing in the love and light of the one infinite Creator. I am Oxal. Adonai, my friends. Adonai.

www.ingramcontent.com/pod-product-compliance
Lightning Source LLC
Chambersburg PA
CBHW080420230426
43662CB00015B/2156